ANTHROPOLOGY: A BRIEF INTRODUCTION

CAROL R. EMBER
Hunter College of the City University of New York

MELVIN EMBER
Human Relations Area Files

PRENTICE HALL, Englewood Cliffs, New Jersey 07632

Library of Congress Cataloging-in-Publication Data

EMBER, CAROL R.
  Anthropology : a brief introduction / CAROL R. EMBER, MELVIN
  EMBER.
    p. cm.
  An abridged version of Anthropology, 6th ed.
  Includes bibliographical references and index.
  ISBN 0-13-029901-4
    1. Anthropology. I. Ember, Melvin. II. Title.
GN25.E46   1992
301—dc20   91-20006

Acquisitions editor: *Nancy Roberts*
Editorial/production supervision
  and interior design: *Edie Riker*
Cover design: *Ben Santora*
Cover photo illustration: *Roderick Chen/SuperStock*
Prepress buyer: *Kelly Behr*
Manufacturing buyer: *Mary Ann Gloriande*

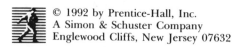

© 1992 by Prentice-Hall, Inc.
A Simon & Schuster Company
Englewood Cliffs, New Jersey 07632

Printed in the United States of America

10 9 8 7 6 5 4 3 2 1

ISBN   0-13-029901-4

Prentice-Hall International (UK) Limited, *London*
Prentice-Hall of Australia Pty. Limited, *Sydney*
Prentice-Hall Canada Inc., *Toronto*
Prentice-Hall Hispanoamericana, S.A., *Mexico*
Prentice-Hall of India Private Limited, *New Delhi*
Prentice-Hall of Japan, Inc., *Tokyo*
Simon & Schuster Asia Pte. Ltd., *Singapore*
Editora Prentice-Hall do Brasil, Ltda., *Rio de Janeiro*

Contents

iii

Preface

This text, an abridged version of *Anthropology*, Sixth Edition, is designed for instructors who teach quarter courses in general anthropology or who assign a lot of supplementary reading and therefore need a brief general text. We hope our readers will let us know how this text suits their needs.

In the preparation of this text, and in each individual chapter, we try to integrate the materials so that the sequence of presentation is ordered, rather than encyclopedic. We feel that this style of organization makes the book both more readable and more comprehensible. At the same time we try to cover many of the major problems and achievements of research in the specialized field of study to which each chapter is devoted.

Our aim is to arouse the curiosity of students about how and why human populations have come to be different or similar. We discuss theories and the arguments and evidence pertaining to them, even if there is no agreement in the field on a particular explanation. We believe it is important to convey not only what is known but also what is not known or only dimly suspected, so that students may acquire some feeling for what anthropology is and what it could be. We hope that this way of writing a textbook will arouse the interest and involvement of the student, because we hope to convey some of the excitement and problems and disappointments of researchers who are working on the frontiers of our discipline.

Features of the Book

Readability. We continue to try to minimize technical jargon, using only those terms students must know to appreciate some of the achievements of anthropology and to take advanced courses. Trying to make complicated research findings relatively easy to read about continues to be one of our major challenges. We think readability is essential not only because it may enhance the reader's understanding of what we write, but also because it should also make learning about anthropology more enjoyable! When new terms are introduced, which of course must happen sometimes, they are set off in boldface type and defined right away. A glossary at the back of the book serves as a convenient reference for the student.

References. Because we believe firmly in the importance of evidence, we think it essential to tell our readers, both professional and student, of the sources of our statements. We do this by providing complete references in footnotes. A complete bibliography is also provided at the end of the book.

Summaries.   In addition to the overview provided at the beginning of each chapter, there is a detailed summary at the end of the chapter that will help the student review the major concepts and findings discussed.

Supplements.   An Instructor's Manual with Tests is available for this edition.

Acknowledgments

We thank Delia Patricia Mathews for retrieving most of the library materials we needed. We thank the staff at Prentice Hall for various kinds of help, particularly Nancy Roberts, editor for anthropology.

We also want to thank the Project on Gender in the Curriculum. We are pleased that our text was selected for review by the Project. The extensive review written by Louise Lamphere of the University of New Mexico was very helpful.

We thank Olga Soffer-Bobyshev of the University of Illinois-Urbana for suggesting illustrations to accompany our discussion of the Upper Paleolithic.

We are grateful to many other individuals, including a few who wish to remain anonymous, who devoted a lot of time and effort to reviewing our chapters and making suggestions for the sixth edition. These reviewers include Joan B. Silk, UCLA; John G. Fleagle, SUNY—Stony Brook; Erik Trinkaus, University of New Mexico; Kim Hill, University of Michigan; Robert Wenke, University of Washington; Mahir Saul, University of Illinois—Urbana; Ronald Cohen, University of Florida; Dean Sheils, University of Wisconsin—La Crosse; and Mark Cohen, SUNY—Plattsburgh.

Reviewers for this abridged edition who offered helpful suggestions were: Andris Skreija, University of Nebraska—Omaha; Maria-Luisa Urdaneta, University of Texas—San Antonio; Joyce Lucks, University of Wisconsin Center—Washington County; Joseph Stimpfl, University of Nebraska; John Staeck, Rutgers University; Robert Townsend, College of Lake County; Eric Joost, Hillsborough Community College; Patricia Rice, West Virginia University; Michael Cothran, Jefferson State Community College; William Wedenoja, Southwest Missouri State University; Linda E. Duchin, Tacoma Community College; Keith Morton, California State University—Northridge.

We thank you all for your help.

Carol R. Ember and *Melvin Ember*

1

What Is Anthropology?

Anthropology defines itself as a discipline of infinite curiosity about human beings. But this definition—which comes from the Greek *anthropos* for "man, human" and *logos* for "study"—is not complete. Anthropologists do seek answers to an enormous variety of questions about humans. They are interested in discovering when, where, and why humans appeared on the earth, how and why they have changed since then, and how and why modern human populations vary in certain physical features. Anthropologists are also interested in how and why societies in the past and present have varied in their customary ideas and practices.

But a definition of anthropology as the study of human beings is not complete, for according to such a definition anthropology would appear to incorporate a whole catalog of disciplines: sociology, psychology, political science, economics, history, human biology, and perhaps even the humanistic disciplines of philosophy and literature. Needless to say, the many other disciplines concerned with humans would not be happy to be regarded as subbranches of anthropology. After all, most of them have been separate disciplines longer than anthropology, and each considers its own jurisdiction to be somewhat distinctive. There must, then, be something unique about anthropology—a reason for its having developed as a separate discipline and for its having retained a separate identity over the approximately 100 years since its beginning.

1

THE SCOPE OF ANTHROPOLOGY

Anthropologists are generally thought of as individuals who travel to little-known corners of the world to study exotic peoples, or who dig deep into the earth to uncover the fossil remains or the tools and pots of people who lived long ago. These views, though clearly stereotyped, do indicate how anthropology differs from other disciplines concerned with humans: anthropology is broader in scope (geographically and historically) than these other fields of study. Anthropology is concerned explicitly and directly with all varieties of people throughout the world, not only those close at hand or within a limited area. It is also interested in people of all periods. Beginning with the immediate ancestors of humans who lived a few million years ago, anthropology traces the development of humans until the present. Every part of the world that has ever contained a human population is of interest to anthropologists.

Anthropologists have not always been as broad and comprehensive in their concerns as they are today. Traditionally, they concentrated on non-Western cultures and left the study of Western civilization and similarly complex societies, with their recorded histories, to other disciplines. In recent years, however, this general division of labor among the disciplines has begun to disappear. Now anthropologists can be found at work in cities of the industrial world, as well as in remote villages of the non-Western world.

What induces the anthropologist to choose so broad a subject for study? In part, he or she is motivated by the belief that any suggested generalization about human beings, any possible explanation of some characteristic of human culture or biology, should be shown to apply to many times and places of human existence. If a generalization or explanation does not prove to apply widely, we are entitled or even obliged to be skeptical about it. The skeptical attitude, in the absence of persuasive evidence, is our best protection against accepting ideas about humans that are wrong.

For example, when American educators discovered in the 1960s that black schoolchildren rarely drank milk, they assumed that lack of money or education was the cause. But evidence from anthropology suggested a different explanation. Anthropologists had known for years that in many parts of the world where milking animals are kept, people do not drink fresh milk; rather, they sour it before they drink it, or they make it into yogurt. Why this is so is now clear. Many people lack an enzyme, lactase, that is necessary for breaking down lactose, the sugar in milk. Such people cannot digest milk properly, and drinking it will make them sick, causing bloating, cramps, stomach gas, and diarrhea. Various studies indicate that milk intolerance is found in many parts of the world.[1] The condition is common in adulthood among Orientals, southern Europeans, Arabs and Jews, West Africans, Eski-

[1] Gail G. Harrison. "Primary Adult Lactase Deficiency: A Problem in Anthropological Genetics." *American Anthropologist*, 77 (1975): 812–35.

mos, and North and South American Indians, as well as American blacks! Because anthropologists are acquainted with human life in an enormous variety of geographical and historical settings, they are often able to correct or clarify beliefs and practices generally accepted by their contemporaries.

THE HOLISTIC APPROACH

In addition to the worldwide as well as historical scope of anthropology, another distinguishing feature of the discipline is its **holistic** or multifaceted approach to the study of human beings. Anthropologists not only study all varieties of people; they also study many aspects of human experience. For example, when describing a group of people he or she has studied, an anthropologist might discuss the history of the area in which the people live, the physical environment, the organization of family life, the general features of their language, the group's settlement patterns, political and economic systems, religion, and styles of art and dress.

In the past, individual anthropologists tried to be holistic and cover all aspects of the subject. Today, as in many other disciplines, so much information has been accumulated that anthropologists tend to specialize in one topic or area. Thus, one anthropologist may investigate the physical characteristics of our prehistoric ancestors. Another may study the biological effect of the environment on a human population over time. Still another will concentrate on the customs of a particular group of people. Despite this specialization, however, the discipline of anthropology retains its holistic orientation in that its many different specialties, taken together, describe many aspects of human existence, both past and present, on all levels of complexity.

THE ANTHROPOLOGICAL CURIOSITY

Thus far we have described anthropology as being broader in scope, both historically and geographically, and more holistic in approach than other disciplines concerned with human beings. But this statement again implies that anthropology is the all-inclusive human science. How, then, is anthropology really different from these other disciplines? We suggest that anthropology's distinctiveness may lie principally in the kind of curiosity it arouses.

Anthropologists are concerned with many types of questions: Where, when, and why did people first begin living in cities? Why do some people have darker skin than others? Why do some languages contain more color terms than other languages? Why, in some societies, are men allowed to be married to several women simultaneously? Although these questions seem to deal with very different aspects of human existence, they have at least one thing in common: they all deal with *typical characteristics* of particular populations. The typical characteristic of a people might be relatively dark skin, a language having many color terms, or the practice of having several wives. In fact, it could be almost any human trait or custom. This concern with typical characteristics of populations is perhaps the most distinguishing feature of anthropology. Thus, for example, where economists might take our monetary system for granted and study how it operates, anthropologists ask why *only* some societies during the last few thousand years used money. In short, anthropologists are curious about the typical characteristics of human populations—how and why such populations and their characteristics have varied—throughout the ages.

FIELDS OF ANTHROPOLOGY

Different anthropologists may concentrate on different typical characteristics of populations. (see Figure 1) Some are concerned primarily with *biological* or *physical* characteristics of human populations; others are interested principally in what we call *cultural* characteristics. Hence, there are two broad classifications of subject matter in anthropology: **physical** (biological) **anthropology** and **cultural anthropology**. Physical anthropology is one major field of anthropology. Cultural anthropology is divided into three major subfields—archeology, linguistics, and ethnology. Ethnology, the study of recent cultures, is often referred to by the parent name, cultural anthropology.

Physical Anthropology

There are two distinct sets of questions that physical anthropology seeks to answer. The first set includes questions about the emergence of humans and their later evolution (an area of physical anthropology called **human paleontology** or **paleoanthropology**). The second set includes questions about how and why contemporary human populations vary biologically (an area referred to as **human variation**).

Characteristics of Concern			Distant Past	Recent Past and Present
	Physical		Human Evolution	Human Variation
			PHYSICAL ANTHROPOLOGY	
	Cultural	L A N G U A G E	Historical Linguistics	Descriptive or Structural Linguistics
			LINGUISTICS	
		O T H E R	Cultural History	Cultural Variation
			ARCHEOLOGY	**ETHNOLOGY** (Cultural Anthropology)

FIGURE 1-1 The four major subdisciplines of anthropology (in bold letters) may be classified according to subject matter (physical or cultural) and according to the period with which each is concerned (distant past versus recent past and present).

In order to reconstruct human evolution, human paleontologists search for and study the buried, hardened remains or impressions—known as **fossils**—of humans, prehumans, and related animals. Paleontologists working in East Africa, for instance, have excavated the fossil remains of humanlike beings who lived more than 3 million years ago. These findings have suggested the approximate dates when our ancestors began to develop two-legged walking, very flexible hands, and a larger brain.

In attempting to clarify evolutionary relationships, human paleontologists may use not only the fossil record but also geological information on the succession of climates, environments, and plant and animal populations. Moreover, when reconstructing the past of humans, paleontologists are also interested in the behavior and evolution of our closest relatives among the mammals—the prosimians, monkeys, and apes, which, like ourselves, are members of the order of **Primates**. (Those anthropologists, psychologists, and biologists who specialize in the study of primates are called *primatologists.*) Species of primates are observed in the wild and in the laboratory. One especially popular subject of study is the chimpanzee, which bears a close resemblance to humans in behavior and physical appearance, has a similar blood chemistry, and is susceptible to many of the same diseases.

From primate studies, physical anthropologists try to discover those characteristics that are distinctly human, as opposed to those that might be part of the primate heritage. With this information, they may be able to guess what our prehistoric ancestors were like. The inferences from primate studies are checked against the fossil record. The evidence from the earth, collected in bits and pieces, is correlated with scientific observations of our closest living relatives.

In short, physical anthropologists piece together bits of information obtained from a number of different sources. They construct theories that explain the changes observed in the fossil record and then attempt to evaluate these theories by checking one kind of evidence against another. Human paleontology thus overlaps a great deal with disciplines such as geology, general vertebrate (and particularly primate) paleontology, comparative anatomy, and the study of comparative primate behavior.

The second major area of physical anthropology—the study of human variation—investigates how and why contemporary human populations differ in physical or biological characteristics. All living people belong to one species, ***Homo sapiens***, for all can successfully interbreed. Yet there is much that varies among human populations. The investigators of human variation ask such questions as these: Why are some peoples taller than others? How have human populations adapted physically to their environmental conditions? Are some peoples, such as Eskimos, better equipped than other peoples to endure cold? Does darker skin pigmentation offer special protection against the tropical sun?

To better understand the biological variations observable among contemporary human populations, physical anthropologists use the principles, concepts, and techniques of three other disciplines: human genetics (the study of human traits that are inherited); population biology (the study of environmental effects on, and interaction with, population characteristics); and epidemiology (the study of how and why diseases affect different populations in different ways). Research on human variation, therefore, overlaps with research in other fields. Those who consider themselves physical anthropologists, however, are concerned most with human populations and how they vary biologically.

Cultural Anthropology

To an anthropologist, the term **culture** generally refers to the customary ways of thinking and behaving of a particular population or society. The culture of a social group, therefore, is composed of its language, general knowledge, religious beliefs, food preferences, music, work habits, taboos, and so forth. **Archeology, anthropological linguistics**, and **ethnology**, the subdisciplines we consider next, are all directly concerned with human culture. Thus, they can be grouped under the broad classification of cultural anthropology.

Archeology. The archeologist seeks not only to reconstruct the daily life and customs of peoples who lived in the past but also to trace cultural changes in their societies and to offer possible explanations of those changes. This concern is similar to that of the historian, but the archeologist reaches much farther back in time. The historian deals only with societies possessing written records and is therefore limited to the last 5000 years of human history. But human societies have existed for perhaps a million years, and almost all in the last 5000 years did not have writing. For all those past societies lacking a written record, the archeologist serves as historian. Lacking written records for study, archeologists must try to reconstruct history from the remains of human cultures. Some of these remains are as grand as the Mayan temples discovered at Chichén Itzá in Yucatán, Mexico. More often they are as ordinary as bits of broken pottery, stone tools, and even garbage heaps.

Most archeologists deal with **prehistory**, the time before written records. However, there is a specialty within archeology, called **historical archeology**, that studies the remains of recent peoples who left written records. This specialty, as its name implies, employs the methods of archeologists *and* the methods of historians to study recent societies for which we have both archeological and historical information.

In trying to understand how and why ways of life have changed through time in different parts of the world, archeologists collect materials from sites of human occupation. Usually, these sites must be unearthed. On the basis of materials they have collected and excavated, they then ask various questions: Where, when, and why did the distinctive human characteristic of toolmaking first emerge? Where, when, and why did agriculture first develop? Where, when, and why did people first begin to live in cities?

To collect the data they need in order to suggest answers to these and other questions, archeologists use techniques and findings borrowed from a number of other disciplines, as well as what they may infer from anthropological studies of recent and contemporary cultures. For example, to guess where to dig for evidence of early toolmaking, archeologists rely on geology to tell them where sites of early human occupation are likely to be found close to the existing surface of the earth. (The evidence available today indicates that the earliest toolmakers lived in East Africa.) To infer when agriculture first developed, archeologists date the relevant excavated materials by a process originally developed by chemists. And to try to understand why cities first emerged, archeologists may need information from historians, geographers, and others about how recent and contemporary cities may relate economically and politically to their hinterlands. If we can discover what recent and contemporary cities have in common, perhaps we can speculate on why cities developed originally. Archeologists can then test these speculations. Thus, archeologists use information from the present and recent past in trying to understand the distant past.

Anthropological Linguistics. A second branch of cultural anthropology is linguistics, the study of languages. As a science, the study of languages is somewhat older than anthropology. The two disciplines became closely associated in the early days of anthropological fieldwork, when anthropologists enlisted the help of linguists in studying unwritten languages. In contrast with other linguists, then, anthropological linguists are interested primarily in the history and structure of formerly unwritten languages.

Like physical anthropologists, linguists are interested both in change that have taken place over time and in contemporary variation. Some anthropological linguists are concerned with the emergence of languages and also with the divergence of languages over thousands of years. The study of how languages change over time and how they may be related is known as **historical linguistics**. Anthropological linguists are also interested in how contemporary languages differ—especially in the way they differ in construction. This area of linguistics is generally called **structural** (or **descriptive) linguistics**. The study of how language is used in actual speech is called **sociolinguistics**.

In contrast with the human paleontologist and archeologist, who have physical remains to help them reconstruct change over time, the historical linguist is dealing only with languages—and usually unwritten ones at that. (Writing is only about 5000 years old, and the vast majority of languages before and since have not been written.) Because an unwritten language must be heard in order to be studied, it does not leave any traces once its speakers have died off. Linguists interested in reconstructing the history of unwritten languages must begin in the present, with comparisons of contemporary languages. On the basis of these comparisons, they may draw inferences about the kinds of change in language that may have occurred in the past and that may account for similarities and differences observed in the present. The historical linguist typically asks such questions as these: Did two or more contemporary languages diverge from a common ancestral language? If they are related, how far back in time did they begin to differ?

Unlike the historical linguist, the descriptive (or structural) linguist is typically concerned with discovering and recording the rules that determine how sounds and words are put together in speech. For example, a structural description of a particular language might tell us that the sounds *t* and *k* are interchangeable in a word without causing a difference in meaning. In the island of American Samoa, one could say *Tutuila* or *Kukuila* as the name of the largest island and everyone, except perhaps the visiting anthropologist, would understand that the same island was being mentioned.

The sociolinguist is interested in determining how contemporary languages differ, and particularly how people speak differently in various social contexts. In English, for example, we do not address everyone we meet in the same way. "Hi, Joe" may be the customary way a person greets a friend. But the same person would probably feel uncomfortable addressing a doctor by first name; instead, he or she would probably say "Good morning, Dr. Smith." Such variations in languages, which are determined by the social status of the persons being addressed, are significant for the sociolinguist.

Ethnology. Ethnologists seek to understand how and why peoples today and in the recent past differ in their customary ways of thinking and acting. Ethnology, then, is concerned with patterns of thought and behavior, such as marriage customs, kinship organization, political and economic systems, religion, folk art, and music, and with the ways in which these patterns differ in contemporary societies. Ethnologists also study the dynamics of culture—that is, how various cultures develop and change. In addition, they are interested in the relationship between beliefs and practices within a culture. Thus, the aim of ethnologists is largely the same as that of archeologists. However, ethnologists generally use data collected through observation and interviewing of living peoples. Archeologists, on the other hand, must work with fragmentary remains of past cultures, on the basis of which they can only make guesses about the actual customs of prehistoric peoples.

One type of ethnologist, the **ethnographer**, usually spends a year or so living with, talking to, and observing the people whose customs he or she is studying. This fieldwork provides the data for a detailed description (an **ethnography**) of many aspects of the customary behavior and thought of those people. The ethnographer not only tries to describe the general patterns of their life but also may suggest answers to such questions as these: How are economic and political behavior related? How may the customs of people be adapted to environmental conditions? Is there any relationship between beliefs about the supernatural and beliefs or practices in the natural world? In other words, the ethnographer depicts the way of life of a particular group of people and may also suggest explanations for some of the customs he or she has observed.

Because so many cultures have undergone extensive change in the recent past, it is fortunate that another type of ethnologist, the **ethnohistorian**, is prepared to study how the ways of life of a particular group of people have changed over time. Ethnohistorians investigate written documents (which may or may not have been produced by anthropologists). They may spend many years going through documents, such as missionary accounts, reports by traders and explorers, and government records, to try to establish the sequence of cultural change that has occurred. Unlike ethnographers, who rely mostly on their own observations, ethnohistorians rely on the reports of others. Often, they must attempt to piece together and make sense of widely scattered, and even apparently contradictory, information. Thus, the ethnohistorian's research is very much like that of the historian, except that the ethnohistorian is usually concerned with the history of a people who did not themselves leave written records. The ethnohistorian tries to reconstruct the recent history of a people and may also suggest why certain changes in their way of life took place.

With the data collected and analyzed by the ethnographer and ethnohistorian, the work of a third type of ethnologist, the **cross-cultural researcher**, can be done. The cross-cultural researcher is interested in discovering why certain cultural characteristics may be found in some societies but not in others. Why, for example, do some societies have plural marriages (one spouse of one sex and two or more spouses of the other sex), circumcision of adolescent boys, or belief in a high god or supreme being? In testing possible answers to such questions, cross-cultural researchers use data from many cultures to try to arrive at general explanations of cultural variation.

All types of cultural anthropologists may be interested in many aspects of customary behavior and thought, from economic behavior to political behavior to styles of art, music, and religion. Thus, cultural anthropology overlaps with disciplines that concentrate on some particular aspect of human existence, such as sociology, psychology, economics, political science, art, music, and comparative religion. The distinctive feature of cultural anthropology is its interest in how all these aspects of human existence vary from society to society, in all historical periods and in all parts of the world.

THE USEFULNESS OF ANTHROPOLOGY

For many centuries, the idea of traveling to the moon was only a dream. Yet in 1969 the dream became a reality when an American Air Force officer gingerly planted his space boot in the moon dust. As the moon shot demonstrates, we know a great deal about the laws of nature in the physical world. If we did not understand so much, the technological achievements we are so proud of would not be possible.

In comparison, we know little about people, about how and why they behave as they do. When we consider the great number of social problems facing us, the importance and relevance of continuing research in cultural anthropology and the other social sciences become evident. Since social problems such as violence in the streets and wars between nations are products of human activity, we need to find out what conditions produce those problems. Once we gain such understanding, we may be able to change the conditions and so solve the problems.

That anthropology and other sciences dealing with humans began to develop only relatively recently is not in itself a sufficient reason for our knowing so little. Why, in our quest for knowledge of all kinds, did we wait so long to study ourselves? Leslie White has suggested that in the history of science those phenomena most remote from us and least significant as determinants of human behavior were the first to be studied. The reason for this, he suggests, is that humans like to think of themselves as citadels of free will, subject to no laws of nature. Hence, there is no need to see ourselves as objects to be explained.[2] Even today, society's unwillingness to accept the notion that human behavior is objectively explainable is reflected in the popularity of astrology as a determining factor in human behavior. It is highly improbable that the stars could account for human behavior when there are no known mechanisms by which they could influence people. Yet as long as such far-removed and improbable "causes" can pass for explanations, more reasonable explanations will not be sought, much less tested.

The belief that it is impossible to account for human behavior scientifically, either because our actions and beliefs are too individualistic and complex or because human beings are understandable only in otherworldly terms, is a self-fulfilling idea. We cannot discover principles explaining human behavior if we neither believe there are such principles nor bother to look for them. The result is ensured from the beginning: those who do not believe in principles of human behavior will be reinforced by their finding none. If we are to increase our understanding of human beings, we first have to believe it is possible to do so.

Anthropology is useful, then, to the degree that it contributes to our understanding of human beings. In addition, it is useful because it helps us to avoid misunderstandings between peoples. If we can understand why other groups are different from ourselves, we might have less reason to condemn them for behavior that appears strange to us. We may then come to realize that many differences among peoples are products of physical and cultural adaptations to different environments.

For example, someone not very knowledgeable about the !Kung[3] of the Kalahari Desert of southern Africa might decide that those people are savages. The !Kung wear little clothing, have few possessions, live in meager

[2] Leslie A. White. "The Expansion of the Scope of Science." In Morton Fried, ed., *Readings in Anthropology*, 2nd ed., vol. 1. New York: Thomas Y. Crowell, 1968, pp. 15–24.
[3] The exclamation point in the word !Kung signifies a clicking sound made with the tongue.

shelters, and enjoy none of our technological niceties. But let us reflect on how a typical American community might react if it awoke to find itself in an environment similar to that in which the !Kung live. The Americans would find that the arid land makes both agriculture and animal husbandry impossible, and they might have to think about adopting a nomadic existence. They might then discard many of their material possessions so that they could travel easily, in order to take advantage of changing water and wild food supplies. Because of the extreme heat and the lack of extra water for laundry, they might find it more practical to be almost naked than to wear clothes. They would undoubtedly find it impossible to build elaborate homes. For social security, they might start to share the food brought into the group. Thus, if they survived at all, they might end up looking and acting far more like the !Kung than like typical Americans.

Physical differences, too, may be seen as results of adaptations to the environment. For example, in our society we admire people who are tall and slim. However, if these same individuals were forced to live above the Arctic Circle, they might wish they could trade their tall, slim bodies for short, compact ones, since stocky physiques appear to conserve body heat more effectively and may therefore be more adaptive in cold climates.

Exposure to anthropology might help to alleviate some of the misunderstandings that arise between people of different cultural groups from subtle causes operating below the level of consciousness. For example, different cultures have different conceptions of the gestures and interpersonal distances that are appropriate under various circumstances. Arabs consider it proper to stand close enough to other people to smell them.[4] Judging from the popularity of deodorants in our culture, Americans seem to prefer to keep the olfactory dimension out of interpersonal relations. When someone comes too close, we may feel he or she is being too intimate. However, we should remember that this person may only be acting according to a culturally conditioned conception of what is proper in a given situation. If our intolerance for others results in part from a lack of understanding of why peoples vary, then the knowledge accumulated by anthropologists may help lessen that intolerance.

Knowledge of our past may also bring forth a feeling of humility and a sense of accomplishment. If we are to attempt to deal with the problems of our world, we must be aware of our vulnerability, so that we do not think the problems will solve themselves. But we also have to think enough of our accomplishments to believe we can find solutions to our problems.

It may be that much of the trouble people get themselves into is a result of their feelings of self-importance and invulnerability—in short, their lack of humility. Knowing something about our evolutionary past may help us to understand and accept our place in the biological world. Just as for any other

[4] Edward T. Hall, *The Hidden Dimension.* Garden City, N.Y.: Doubleday, 1966, pp. 144–53.

form of life, there is no guarantee that any particular human population, or even the entire human species, will perpetuate itself indefinitely. The earth changes, the environment changes, and humanity itself changes, so that what survives and flourishes in the present might not do so in the future.

Yet our vulnerability should not make us feel powerless. There are many reasons to feel confident about the future. Consider what we have accomplished so far. By means of tools and weapons fashioned from sticks and stones, we were able to hunt animals larger and more powerful than ourselves. We discovered how to make fire, and we learned to use it to keep ourselves warm and to cook our food. As we domesticated plants and animals, we gained greater control over our food supply and were able to establish more permanent settlements. We mined and smelted ores to fashion more durable tools. We built cities and irrigation systems, monuments and ships. We made it possible to travel from one continent to another in a single day. We conquered various illnesses and prolonged human life.

In short, human beings and their cultures have changed considerably over the course of time. Some human populations—though different ones at different times—have been able to adapt to changing circumstances. Let us hope that humans continue to adapt to the challenges of the present and the future.

SUMMARY

1. Anthropology is literally the *study of human beings*. It differs from other disciplines concerned with people in that it is broader in scope. It is concerned with humans in all places of the world (not simply those places close to us), and it traces human evolution and cultural development from millions of years ago to the present day.
2. Another distinguishing feature of anthropology is its holistic approach to the study of human beings. Not only do anthropologists study all varieties of people, they also study all aspects of those people's experiences.
3. Anthropologists are concerned with identifying and explaining typical characteristics of particular human populations. Such a characteristic might be any human trait or custom.
4. Physical anthropology is one of the major fields of the discipline. Physical anthropology studies the emergence of humans and their later physical evolution (an area called human paleontology). It also studies how and why contemporary human populations vary biologically (a subject area called human variation).
5. The second broad area of concern to anthropology is cultural anthropology. Its three subfields—archeology, anthropological linguistics, and ethnology—all deal with aspects of human culture—that is, with the customary ways of thinking and behaving of a particular society.
6. Archeologists seek not only to reconstruct the daily life and customs of prehistoric peoples but also to trace cultural changes and offer possible explanations of those changes. Therefore, archeologists try to reconstruct history from the remains of human cultures.
7. Anthropological linguists are concerned with the emergence of language and with the divergence of languages over time (a subject known as historical linguistics). They also study how contemporary languages differ, both in construction (structural or descriptive linguistics) and in use in actual speech (sociolinguistics).

8. The ethnologist seeks to understand how and why peoples of today and the recent past differ in their customary ways of thinking and acting. One type of ethnologist, the ethnographer, usually spends a year or so living with, talking to, and observing the customs of a particular population. Later, he or she may prepare a detailed report of the group's behavior, which is called an ethnography. Another type of ethnologist, the ethnohistorian, investigates written documents to determine how the ways of life of a particular group of people have changed over time. A third type of ethnologist—the cross-cultural researcher—studies data collected by ethnographers and ethnohistorians for a large number of societies and attempts to discover which explanations of particular customs may be generally applicable.

9. Anthropology may help people to be more tolerant. Anthropological studies can show us why other people are the way they are, both culturally and physically. Customs or actions of theirs that may appear improper or offensive to us may be adaptations to particular environmental and social conditions.

10. Anthropology is also valuable in that knowledge of our past may bring us both a feeling of humility and a sense of accomplishment. Like any other form of life, we have no guarantee that any particular human population will perpetuate itself indefinitely. Yet knowledge of our achievements in the past may give us confidence in our ability to solve the problems of the future.

2

Evolution

Astronomers estimate that the universe has been in existence for some 15 billion years. To make this awesome history more understandable, Carl Sagan has devised a calendar that condenses this span into a single year.[1] Using as a scale twenty-four days for every billion years and one second for every 475 years, Sagan moves from the "Big Bang," or beginning of the universe, on January 1 to the origin of the Milky Way on May 1. September 9 marks the beginning of our solar system and September 25 the origin of life on earth. At 10:30 in the evening of December 31, the first humans appear. Sagan's compression of history provides us with a manageable way to compare the short span of human existence with the total time span of the universe: human beings have been around for only about ninety minutes out of a twelve-month period! In this book, we are concerned with what has happened in the last few hours of the year.

Some 70 million years ago, the first primates may have appeared. They are believed to be ancestral to all living primates, including monkeys, apes, and humans. The early primates may or may not have lived in trees, but they had fingers and could grasp things. Later (about 35 million years ago) they began to be replaced by the first monkeys and apes. Some 20 million years

[1] Carl Sagan. "A Cosmic Calendar." *Natural History*, December 1975, pp. 70–73.

after the appearance of monkeys and apes, the immediate apelike ancestors of humans probably emerged. At least 50,000 years ago, "modern" humans evolved (Table 2-1).

How do we account for the biological and cultural evolution of humans? The details of the emergence of primates and the evolution of humans and

TABLE 2-1   An overview of human evolution: biological and cultural

Time (years ago)	Geologic Epoch	Fossil Record (first appearance)	Archeological Periods (Old World)	Major Cultural Developments (first appearance)
			Bronze Age	Cities and states; social inequality; full-time craft specialists
5500 (3500 B.C.)				
			Neolithic	Domesticated plants and animals; permanent villages
10,000 (8000 B.C.)				
			Mesolithic	Broad-spectrum food collecting; increasingly sedentary communities; many kinds of microliths
14,000 (12,000 B.C.)	Pleistocene	Earliest humans in New World		
			Upper Paleolithic	Cave paintings; female figurines; many kinds of blade tools
50,000		Modern humans *Homo sapiens sapiens*	Middle Paleolithic	Religious beliefs (?); burials; Mousterian tools
100,000 250,000 700,000		Neanderthal *H. sapiens* *Earliest Homo sapiens* (?)		Use of fire; Acheulian tools
1,500,000 1,800,000		*Homo erectus*	Lower Paleolithic	Hunting and/or scavenging; seasonal campsites; Oldowan tools
2,000,000 3,000,000	Pliocene	*Homo habilis* Earliest hominids *Australopithecus*		Earliest stone tools
5,000,000 12,000,000	Miocene	Diversification of apes Sivapithecines		
22,500,000		Dryopithecines Earliest apes (?)		
29,000,000 32,000,000	Oligocene	Propliopithecids, e.g., *Aegyptopithecus* Earliest anthropoids Parapithecids		
38,000,000 50,000,000 53,500,000	Eocene			
65,000,000	Paleocene	*Plesiadapis*		
70,000,000	Late Cretaceous	Earliest primates *Purgatorius*		

Geological dates from W. A. Berggren and J. A. Van Couvering, "The Late Neocene: Biostratigraphy, Geochronology and Paleo-climatology of the Last 15 Million Years in Marine and Continental Sequences." *Palaeogeography, Palaeoclimatology, Palaeoecology,* 16 (1974): 13–16, 165.

their cultures will be covered in subsequent chapters. In this chapter, we focus on how the modern theory of evolution accounts for change over time.

THE THEORY OF NATURAL SELECTION

After studying changes in plants, fossil animals, and varieties of domestic and wild pigeons, Charles Darwin (1809–1882) rejected the notion that each species was created independently. The results of his investigations pointed clearly, he thought, to the evolution of species through change. More than that, they pointed to a mechanism—**natural selection**—that might explain how evolution took place. While Darwin was completing the work necessary to support his theory, he was sent a manuscript by Alfred Russell Wallace, a naturalist who had independently reached conclusions about the evolution of species that matched his own. In 1858, the two men presented the astonishing theory of natural selection to their colleagues at a meeting of the Linnaean Society of London.[2]

In 1859, when Darwin published *The Origin of Species*, he wrote, "I am fully convinced that species are not immutable; but that those belonging to what are called the same genera are lineal descendants of some other and generally extinct species, in the same manner as the acknowledged varieties of any one species.[3] His conclusions outraged those who believed in the biblical account of creation. Evolutionary evidence was sufficiently convincing to make some people interpret the Bible metaphorically or figuratively, but the fundamentalists who worshiped the literal word of "The Book" would not compromise their beliefs. The result was years of bitter controversy.

Until 1871 (when *The Descent of Man* was published), Darwin avoided stating categorically that humans were descended from nonhuman forms, but the implications of his theory were clear. People began immediately to take sides. In June 1860, at the annual meeting of the British Association for the Advancement of Science, Bishop Wilberforce saw an opportunity to attack the Darwinists. Concluding his speech, he faced Thomas Huxley, one of the Darwinists' chief advocates, and inquired, "Was it through his grandfather or his grandmother that he claimed descent from a monkey?" Huxley responded,

> If . . . the question is put to me would I rather have a miserable ape for a grandfather than a man highly endowed by nature and possessing great means and influence and yet who employs those faculties and that influence for the mere purpose of introducing ridicule into a grave scientific discussion—I unhesitatingly affirm my preference for the ape.[4]

[2] G. Ledyard Stebbins. *Processes of Organic Evolution*, 3rd ed. Englewood Cliffs, N.J.: Prentice Hall, 1977, p. 10.
[3] Charles Darwin. "The Origin of Species." In Louise B. Young, ed., *Evolution of Man*. New York: Oxford University Press, 1970, p. 78.
[4] Quoted in Ashley Montagu's introduction to Thomas H. Huxley, "Man's Place in Nature," in Young, ed., *Evolution of Man*, pp. 183–84.

One of the most famous confrontations between evolutionists and their critics occurred at the 1927 Scopes trial in Tennessee. John Scopes, defended by the renowned lawyer Clarence Darrow, was convicted of teaching evolution. Scopes's opponents won the court decision, but the real victors were the proponents of Darwin's theory. The wide publicity given the trial and the discussion it generated greatly increased the public's awareness and understanding of evolution—if not its total acceptance. Even recently people have protested the teaching of evolution and requested equal treatment for the biblical story of creation.

Darwin was not the first person to view the creation of new species as evolutionary, but he was the first to provide a comprehensive, well-documented explanation for the way evolution had occurred. He pointed out that each species is composed of a great variety of individuals, some of which are better adapted to their environment than others. The better-adapted individuals generally produce more offspring over generations than the poorer-adapted. Thus, over time natural selection results in increasing proportions of individuals with advantageous traits.

When we say that certain traits are advantageous, we mean that they result in greater reproductive success in a particular environment. The phrase *particular environment* is very important. Even though a species may become better adapted to a particular environment over time, we cannot say that one species adapted to its environment is "better" than another species adapted to a different environment. For example, we may like to think of ourselves as better than the other animals, but humans are clearly less adapted than fish for living underwater, bats for catching flying insects, and raccoons for living on suburban garbage.

Changes in a species can be expected to occur as the environment changes or as some members of the species move into a new environment. With environmental change, different traits become adaptive. The forms of the species that possess the more adaptive traits will become more frequent, whereas those forms whose characteristics make continued existence more difficult or impossible in the modified environment will eventually become extinct. According to Wallace's theory as originally presented, environmental difficulties would mean that

> those forming the least numerous and most feebly organized variety would suffer first, and, were the pressure severe, must soon become extinct. . . . the parent species would next suffer, would gradually diminish in numbers, and with a recurrence of similar unfavorable conditions might also become extinct. The superior variety would then alone remain. . . .[5]

Consider how the theory of natural selection would explain why giraffes became long-necked. Originally, the necks of giraffes varied in length, as

[5] Alfred Russell Wallace. "On the Tendency of Varieties to Depart Indefinitely from the Original Type." *Journal of the Proceedings of the Linnaean Society*, August 1858. Reprinted in Young, ed., *Evolution of Man*, p. 75.

happens with virtually any physical characteristic in a population. During a period when food was scarce, those giraffes with longer necks who could reach higher tree leaves might be better able to survive and suckle their offspring, and thus they would leave more offspring than shorter-necked giraffes. Eventually, the shorter-necked giraffes would diminish in number and the longer-necked giraffes would increase. The resultant population of giraffes would still have variation in neck length, but on the average would be longer-necked than earlier forms.

Because some life forms reproduce rapidly, it is possible to observe some examples of natural selection operating over relatively short periods in changing environments. Within the last 100 years in England, for example, scientists have been able to observe natural selection in action. When certain areas of the country became heavily industrialized, the pale bark of trees in those regions became coated with black soot. Light-colored moths, formerly well adapted to blend with their environment, became clearly visible against the sooty background of the trees and were easy prey for birds. Darker moths, previously at a disadvantage against the light bark, were now better adapted for survival. Their dark color became an advantage, and subsequently the darker moths became the predominant variety in industrial regions.

Natural selection is also apparent in the newly acquired resistance of houseflies to the insecticide DDT. In the last thirty-five years, since DDT use became common, several new, DDT-resistant strains of houseflies have evolved. In the early DDT environment, many houseflies were killed. But the few that survived were the ones that reproduced—and their resistant characteristics became common to the housefly populations. To the chagrin of medical practitioners, similar resistances develop in bacteria. A particular antibiotic may lose its effectiveness after it comes into wide use, because new, resistant bacterial strains emerge. These new strains will become more frequent than the original ones because of natural selection.

The theory of natural selection answered many questions, but it also raised at least one whose answer eluded even Darwin. The appearance of a beneficial trait may assist the survival of an organism, but what happens when the organism reproduces by mating with members that do not possess this new variation? Will not the new adaptive trait eventually disappear if subsequent generations mate with individuals that lack this trait? Darwin knew variations were transmitted through heredity, but he could not explain the source of new variations and the mode of inheritance. Gregor Mendel's pioneering studies in the science of genetics provided the foundation for the answers, but his discoveries were not widely known until 1900.

HEREDITY

Gregor Mendel's Experiments

Mendel (1822–1884), an Austrian monk and amateur botanist, bred several varieties of pea plants and made detailed observations of their offspring. He chose as breeding partners plants that differed by only one observable trait: tall plants were crossed with short ones and yellow ones with green, for example.

When the pollen from a yellow pea plant was transferred to a green pea plant, Mendel observed a curious phenomenon: all of the first-generation offspring bore yellow peas. It seemed that the green trait had disappeared. But when seeds from this first generation were crossed, they produced both yellow and green pea plants in a ratio of three yellow to one green pea plant. Apparently, Mendel reasoned, the green trait had not been lost or altered; the yellow trait was simply **dominant** and the green trait was **recessive**. Mendel observed similar results with other traits. Tallness dominated shortness, and the factor for smooth-skinned peas dominated the factor for wrinkled ones. In each cross, the three-to-one ratio appeared in the second generation. Self-fertilization, however, produced different results. Green pea plants always yielded green pea plants, and short plants always produced short plants.

From his numerical results, Mendel concluded that some yellow pea plants were pure for that trait, whereas others also possessed a green factor. That is, although two plants might both have yellow peas, one of them might produce offspring with green peas. In such cases, the full complement of inherited traits, the **genotype**, differed from the observable appearance, or **phenotype**.

Genes: The Conveyors of Inherited Traits

Mendel's units of heredity were what we now call **genes**. He concluded that these units occurred in pairs for each trait, and that offspring inherited one unit of the pair from each parent. Today we call each member of a gene pair or group an **allele**. If the two genes, or alleles, for a trait are the same, the organism is **homozygous** for that trait; if the two genes for a characteristic differ, the organism is **heterozygous** for that trait. A pea plant that contains a pair of genes for yellow is homozygous for the trait. A yellow pea plant with a dominant gene for yellow and a recessive gene for green, although phenotypically yellow, has a heterozygous genotype. As Mendel demonstrated, the recessive green gene can reappear in subsequent generations. But Mendel knew nothing of the composition of genes or the processes that transmit them from parent to offspring. Many years of scientific research have yielded much of the missing information.

The genes of higher organisms (not including bacteria and primitive plants such as green-blue algae) are located on ropelike bodies called **chromosomes** within the nucleus of every one of the organism's cells. Chromosomes, like genes, usually occur in pairs. Each allele for a given trait is carried in the identical position on corresponding chromosomes. The two genes that determined the color of Mendel's peas, for example, were opposite each other on a pair of chromosomes.

Mitosis and Meiosis.   The body cells of every plant or animal carry chromosome pairs in a number appropriate for its species. Humans have twenty-three pairs, or a total of forty-six chromosomes, each carrying many times that number of genes. Each new body cell receives this number of chromosomes during cellular reproduction, or **mitosis**, as each pair of chromosomes duplicates itself.

But what happens when a sperm cell and an egg cell unite to form a new organism? What prevents the human baby from receiving twice the number of chromosomes characteristic of its species—twenty-three pairs from the sperm and twenty-three pairs from the egg? The process by which the reproductive cells are formed, **meiosis**, ensures that this will not happen. Each reproductive cell contains *half* the number of chromosomes appropriate for the species. Only one member of each chromosome pair is carried in every egg or sperm. At fertilization, the human embryo normally receives twenty-three separate chromosomes from its mother and the same number from its father, which add up to the twenty-three pairs.

DNA and RNA. As we have said, genes are located on chromosomes. Each gene carries a set of instructions encoded in its chemical structure. It is from this coded information carried in genes that a cell makes all the rest of its structural parts and chemical machinery. It appears that in every living organism, heredity is controlled by the same chemical substance, **DNA** (deoxyribonucleic acid). An enormous amount of recent research has been directed toward understanding DNA—what its structure is, how it duplicates itself in reproduction, and how it conveys or instructs the formation of a complete organism.

One of the most important keys to understanding human development and genetics is the structure and function of DNA. In 1951, biologist James Watson, with British chemist Francis Crick, proposed that DNA is a long, two-stranded molecule shaped like a double helix. The model they proposed for DNA also suggested how it could reduplicate itself within minutes. Subsequent research has substantiated their model of both the structure and the function of DNA.[6]

Additional research has focused on how DNA directs the making of an organism according to the instructions in its genetic code. It now appears that another nucleic acid, **RNA** (ribonucleic acid), "copies" the blueprint from DNA and "carries" the instructions to the cytoplasm of a cell. The instructions are then "translated" into the production of proteins, the basic building blocks of cells. Thus, DNA is the language of life. As George and Muriel Beadle put it,

> the deciphering of the DNA code has revealed our possession of a language much older than hieroglyphics, a language as old as life itself, a language that is the most living language of all—even if its letters are invisible and its words are buried deep in the cells of our bodies.[7]

---

[6] George Beadle and Muriel Beadle. *The Language of Life.* Garden City, N.Y.: Doubleday, 1966, pp. 173–99.
[7] Ibid., p. 216.

SOURCES OF VARIABILITY

Natural selection proceeds only when individuals within a population vary. There are two genetic sources of variation: genetic recombination and mutation.

Genetic Recombination

The distribution of traits from parents to children varies from one offspring to another. Brothers and sisters, after all, do not look exactly alike, nor does each child resemble 50 percent of the mother and 50 percent of the father. This variation occurs because when a sperm cell or an egg is formed, the single member of each chromosome pair it receives is a matter of chance. Each reproductive cell, then, carries a *random assortment* of chromosomes and their respective genes. At fertilization, the egg and sperm that unite are different from every other egg carried by the mother and every other sperm carried by the father. A *unique* offspring is thus produced by a shuffling of the parents' genes. One cause of this shuffling is the random **segregation** or sorting of chromosomes in meiosis: an individual could conceivably get any of the possible assortments of the paternal and maternal chromosomes. Another cause of the shuffling of parental genes is **crossing-over**, the exchange of sections of chromosomes between one chromosome and another.[8] Thus, after meiosis the egg and sperm do not receive just a random mixture of complete paternal and maternal chromosomes; because of crossing-over they also receive chromosomes in which some of the sections may have been replaced.

The traits displayed by each organism are not simply the result of combinations of dominant and recessive genes, as Mendel had hypothesized. In humans, most traits are influenced by the activity of many genes. Skin color, for example, is the result of several inherited characteristics. A brownish shade results from the presence of a pigment known as *melanin*; the degree of darkness in the hue depends largely on the amount of melanin present and how it is distributed in the layers of the skin. Another factor contributing to the color of all human skin is the blood that flows in blood vessels located in the outer layers of the skin. Thus, skin color is determined by genes that bear various instructions. Humans carry at least five different genes for the manufacture of melanin, and many other genes for the other components of skin hue. In fact, almost all physical characteristics in humans are the result of the concerted action of many genes. Some traits are sex-linked. The so-called X chromosome, which together with the presence or absence of a Y chromosome determines sex, may also carry the gene for hemophilia or the gene for color blindness. The expression of these two characteristics depends on the sex of the organism.

---

[8] Colin Patterson. *Evolution.* London: British Museum; Ithaca, N.Y.: Cornell University Press, 1978, pp. 41–42.

These processes of genetic recombination ensure that variety is achieved, and genetic variation within a species is essential for the operation of natural selection. Evolution and genetic variation, then, are inseparable.

At any given moment, the major source of variability in a population is genetic recombination. Ultimately, however, the major source of the variability on which natural selection proceeds is mutation. This is because mutation replenishes the supply of variability, which is constantly being reduced by the selective elimination of less-fit variants.

Mutation

A **mutation** is a change in the molecular structure or DNA code of a gene. Such a change produces an altered gene. Mutations occur randomly and are usually harmful to an individual, since any change in the intricate structure of a gene is likely to impair the delicate balance within an organism and between an organism and its environment.[9]

What causes mutations? Rates of mutation increase among organisms exposed to certain chemicals or to certain dosages of radiation such as X-rays. But the majority of mutations are thought to occur because of occasional mismating of the chemical bases that make up DNA.[10] Just as a typist will make errors in copying a manuscript, so will DNA, in duplicating itself, occasionally change its code.[11] A mutation will result from such an error.

Mutations are sometimes lethal. Tay-Sachs disease, for example, is caused by two recessive mutant genes. Its effects are blindness, severe retardation, and death by the age of three or four. An organism with both recessive mutant genes for a given harmful trait will probably die before it can reproduce—and often before it is born. But the trait can be passed on by individuals who are heterozygous for the recessive gene.

We can discuss the relative merits or disadvantages of a mutant gene *only* in terms of the physical, cultural, and genetic environment of that gene.[12] Galactosemia, for example, is caused by a recessive mutant gene and usually results in mental retardation and blindness. But it can be prevented by dietary restrictions begun at an early age. In this instance, the intervention of human culture counteracts the mutant gene and allows the afflicted individual to lead a normal life. Thus, some cultural factors can modify the effects of natural selection by helping to perpetuate a harmful mutant gene. People with the galactosemia trait who are enabled to function normally can reproduce and pass on one of the recessive genes to their children. Without cultural interference, natural selection would prevent such reproduction, for in most cases natural selection works to retain only those mutations that aid survival.

---

[9] Stebbins. *Processes of Organic Evolution*, p. 58.
[10] Ibid., pp. 62–63.
[11] Beadle and Beadle. *The Language of Life*, p. 123.
[12] Theodosius Dobzhansky. *Mankind Evolving: The Evolution of the Human Species.* New Haven: Yale University Press, 1962, pp. 138–40.

Even though mutations are not usually adaptive, those that are will multiply in a population relatively quickly, by natural selection. As Theodosius Dobzhansky has suggested:

> consistently useful mutants are like needles in a haystack of harmful ones. A needle in a haystack is hard to find, even though one may be sure it is there. But if the needle is valuable, the task of finding it is facilitated by setting the haystack on fire and looking for the needle among the ashes. The role of the fire in this parable is played in biological evolution by natural selection.[13]

THE ORIGIN OF SPECIES

One of the most controversial aspects of Darwin's theory was the suggestion that one species could, over time, evolve into another. **Speciation**, or the development of a new species, does not happen suddenly. Nor is it the result of one or two mutations in the history of a single family.

Speciation may occur if one subgroup of a species finds itself in a radically different environment. In the subgroup's adaptation to the new environment, enough genetic changes may occur to result in a new variety, or **race**. Races, however, are not separate species. They are simply slight variants of a single species that can interbreed. As Dobzhansky explains, "perhaps there is no recorded instance of intermarriage between some races, say of Eskimos with Papuans, but Eskimos as well as Papuans do interbreed with other races; channels, however tortuous, for gene exchange exist between all human races.[14]

But a species usually cannot breed successfully with a different species. Generally, the genetic makeup of separate species is so different that reproduction is impossible. If members of different species did mate, it is unlikely that the egg would be fertilized, or, if it were, that the embryo would survive. If birth did occur, the offspring would either die or be infertile. What is the explanation for this differentiation? How does one group of organisms become so unlike another group having the same ancestry that it forms a totally new species?

Speciation may occur if the populations become so separated from each other geographically that gene exchanges are no longer possible. In adapting to their separate environments, the two populations may undergo enough genetic changes to prevent them from interbreeding. Numerous factors can prevent the exchange of genes. Two species living in the same area may breed at different times of the year, or their behavior during breeding—their courtship rituals—may be distinct. The difference in body structure of closely related forms may in itself bar interbreeding. Geographic barriers may also prevent interbreeding.

[13] Ibid., p. 139.
[14] Ibid., p. 193.

Once species differentiation does occur the evolutionary process cannot
be reversed; the new species can no longer mate with other species related to
its parent population. Humans and gorillas, for example had the same distant
ancestors, but their evolutionary paths have diverged irreversibly.

NATURAL SELECTION OF BEHAVIORAL TRAITS

Until now we have discussed how natural selection might operate to change a
population's physical traits, such as the color of moths or the neck length of
giraffes. But natural selection can also operate on the behavioral characteristics of populations. Although this idea is not new, it is now receiving more
attention. The new approaches called **sociobiology**[15] and **behavioral ecology**[16]
involve the application of evolutionary principles to the behavior of animals.
(Behavioral ecology is interested in how all kinds of behavior relate to the
environment; sociobiology is particularly interested in social organization and
social behavior.) The typical behaviors of a species are assumed to be adaptive
and to have evolved by natural selection. For example, why do related species
exhibit different social behaviors even though they derive from a common
ancestral species?

Consider the lion, as compared with other cats. Although members of
the cat family are normally solitary creatures, lions live in social groups called
prides. Why? George Schaller has suggested that lion social groups may have
evolved primarily because group hunting is a more successful way to catch
large mammals in open terrain. He has observed that not only are several
lions more successful in catching prey than are solitary lions, but several lions
are more likely to catch and kill large and dangerous prey such as giraffes.
Then, too, young cubs are generally safer from predators when in a social
group than when alone with their mothers. Thus, the social behavior of lions
probably evolved primarily because it provided selective advantages in the
lions' open-country environment.[17]

The sociobiological approach has aroused controversy because it assumes that genes are important determinants of human behavior. For example, all human societies have marriage and the family, the prohibition of
incest, and a division of roles between males and females. Sociobiologists
contend that these universal behaviors may have some genetic basis in the
human species; otherwise, why would they be universal? Many anthropologists and other social scientists are critical of this idea. They say that cultural
behavior is learned, and that something cultural may be universal because it
has been learned universally.

[15] David P. Barash. *Sociobiology and Behavior*. New York: Elsevier, 1977.
[16] J. R. Krebs and N. B. Davies, eds. *Behavioural Ecology: An Evolutionary Approach*, 2nd ed.
    Sunderland, Mass.: Sinauer Associates, 1984.
[17] George B. Schaller. *The Serengeti Lion: A Study of Predator-Prey Relations*. Chicago: University of
    Chicago Press, 1972. Cited in Edward O. Wilson, *Sociobiology*, Cambridge, Mass.: Harvard
    University Press, Belknap Press, 1975, p. 504.

THE EVOLUTION OF CULTURE

Whether much or any of human cultural behavior can be explained by heredity, there is no question that culture has evolved. We became hunters and gatherers, using tools as well as muscles and teeth. We began to grow plants and animals for food. We built cities and complex political systems. Can these and other cultural change be explained by natural selection even if cultural behavior has no genetic component? To answer this question, we must remember that the operation of natural selection requires three conditions. First, natural selection requires variation upon which to operate. Second, there must be differential reproduction, that is, differences in reproductive success. And third, there must be a mechanism for duplicating adaptive traits. Do these three requirements apply to cultural behavior? How is cultural evolution like or unlike biological evolution?

In biological evolution, variability comes from genetic recombination and mutation. In cultural evolution, it comes from recombination of learned behaviors and from invention.[18] Cultures are not closed or reproductively isolated, as species are. A species cannot borrow genetic traits from another species, but a culture can borrow new things and behaviors from other cultures. The custom of growing corn, which has spread from the New World to many other areas, is an example of this phenomenon.

As for the requirement of differential reproduction, it does not matter whether the trait in question is genetic or learned or both. As Henry Nissen has emphasized, "behavioral incompetence leads to extinction as surely as does morphological disproportion or deficiency in any vital organ. Behavior is subject to selection as much as bodily size or resistance to disease.[19] Finally, although learned traits are obviously not passed to offspring through genetic inheritance, parents who exhibit adaptive behavioral traits are more likely to "reproduce" those traits in their children, who may learn them by imitation or by parental instruction. Children and adults may also copy adaptive traits they see in people outside the family. Thus, even though biological and cultural evolution are not the same, it seems reasonable to assume that natural selection may generally operate on learned cultural behavior as well as on genes.

Biological and cultural evolution in humans may not be completely separate processes. As we will discuss, some of the most important biological features of humans—such as two-legged walking and relatively large brains—may have been favored by natural selection because our ancestors made tools

[18] Donald T. Campbell. "Variation and Selective Retention in Socio-Cultural Evolution." In Herbert Barringer, George Blankstein, and Raymond Mack, eds., *Social Change in Developing Areas: A Re-Interpretation of Evolutionary Theory.* Cambridge, Mass.: Schenkman, 1965, pp. 19–49.

[19] Henry W. Nissen. "Axes of Behavioral Comparison." In Anne Roe and George Gaylord Simpson, eds., *Behavior and Evolution.* New Haven: Yale University Press, 1958, pp. 183–205.

(a cultural trait). Conversely, the cultural trait of informal and formal education may have been favored by natural selection because humans have a long period of immaturity (a biological trait).

As long as the human species continues to exist, there is no reason to suppose that natural selection of biological and cultural traits will cease. However, evolution depends on varying and often unpredictable changes in the physical and social environment. Given our imperfect understanding of human evolution, both biological and cultural, there is no way of knowing now where evolution may take us in the future.

SUMMARY

1. If we think of the history of the universe in terms of twelve months, the history of humans would take up only about one and a half hours of this period. Although the universe is some 15 billion years old, modern humans have existed for at least 50,000 years.
2. Charles Darwin and Alfred Wallace proposed the mechanism of natural selection to account for the evolution of species. Those organisms best adapted to a particular environment produce the most offspring over time.
3. In the process of natural selection, changes in species can be expected to occur as the environment changes or as some members of a species move into a new environment. Natural selection can also operate on the behavioral or social characteristics of populations.
4. Mendel's and subsequent research in genetics and our understanding of the structure and function of DNA, the "language of life," help us to understand the mechanism by which traits may be passed from one generation to the next.
5. Natural selection depends upon variation within a population. The two sources of biological variation are genetic recombination and mutation.
6. Speciation—the development of a new species—may occur if one subgroup becomes separated from other subgroups so that they can no longer interbreed. In adapting to different environments, these subpopulations may undergo enough genetic changes to prevent interbreeding, even if they reestablish contact. Once species differentiation occurs, the evolutionary process cannot be reversed.
7. Humans are a product of the interaction of biological and cultural evolution. Culturally, traits are transmitted by learning and imitation. Cultural evolution is more subject to conscious human control and change than biological evolution. Still, both types of evolution may be subject to natural selection.

3

Primate Evolution
From Early Primates to Hominoids

Humans belong to the order of *Primates*. How do primates differ from other mammals? And what distinguishes humans from the other primates? After discussing these questions, we turn to the evolution of the primates: when, where, and why did the early primates emerge, and how and why did they diverge? Our overview covers the period from about 70 million years ago to the end of the Miocene, about 5 million years ago.

The primates that survive today are divided into two suborders: the **prosimians** (literally, premonkeys) and the **anthropoids**. The prosimians include lemurs and lorises. The prosimians resemble other mammals more than the anthropoid primates do. For example, the prosimians depend much more on smell for information than do anthropoids. Also in contrast with the anthropoids, they have more mobile ears, whiskers, longer snouts, and relatively fixed facial expressions. The prosimians also exhibit many traits shared by all primates, including grasping hands, stereoscopic vision, and enlarged visual centers in the brain. The anthropoid suborder includes tarsiers, monkeys, the lesser apes (gibbons, siamangs), the great apes (orangutans, gorillas, champanzees), and humans. Most anthropoids share several traits in varying degree. They have rounded brain cases; reduced, nonmobile outer ears; and relatively small, flat faces instead of muzzles. They have highly efficient reproductive systems, including a placenta that is formed more fully than in any prosimian. They have highly dexterous hands.[1]

Common Primate Traits

All primates belong to the class Mammalia, and they share all the common features of mammals. Except for humans, their bodies are covered with hair or fur, which provides insulation. And even humans have some hair in various places, though perhaps not for insulation. Mammals are *warmblooded*; that is, they maintain a constant warm temperature. Almost all mammals give birth to live young that develop to a considerable size within the mother and are nourished by suckling from the mother's mammary glands. The young have a relatively long period of dependence on adults after birth. This period is also a time of learning, for a great deal of adult mammal behavior is learned rather than instinctive. Play is a learning technique common to mammal young and is especially important to primates.

In addition to their mammalian features, the primates have a number of physical and social traits that set them apart from other mammals.

No one of the primates' features is unique to primates; animals from other orders share one or more of the characteristics listed below. But the complex of all these traits *is* unique to primates.[2]

Many skeletal features of the primates reflect an **arboreal** (tree-living) existence. All primate hind limbs are structured principally to provide support, although they are flexible enough to allow some primates—orangutans, for instance—to suspend themselves from their hind limbs. The forelimbs are especially flexible, built to withstand both pushing and pulling forces. Each of the hind limbs and forelimbs has one bone in the upper portion and two bones in the lower portion (with the exception of the tarsier). This feature is little changed since the time of our earliest primate ancestors. It has remained in modern primates (although many other mammals have lost it) because the double bones give great mobility for rotating arms and legs. Another characteristic structure of primates is the clavicle, or collarbone. The clavicle also gives primates great freedom of movement, allowing them to move the shoulders both up and down and back and forth. Although humans obviously do not use this flexibility for arboreal activity, they do use it for other activities. Without a clavicle we could not throw a spear or a ball; no fine tools could be made, no doorknobs turned, if we did not have rotatable forearms.

Primates generally are **omnivorous**; that is, they eat all kinds of food, including insects and small animals as well as fruits, seeds, leaves, and roots.

---

[1] J. R. Napier and P. H. Napier. *A Handbook of Living Primates.* New York: Academic Press, 1967, pp. 32–33.

[2] Our discussion of common primate traits is based largely on Napier and Napier, *A Handbook of Living Primates.*

The teeth of primates reflect this omnivorous diet. The chewing teeth—the **molars** and **premolars**—are very unspecialized, particularly in comparison with those of other groups of animals, such as the grazers. The front teeth—the **incisors** and **canines**—are often quite specialized, principally in the lower primates. For example, in many prosimians the slender, tightly packed lower incisors and canines form a "dental comb" the animals use in scraping hardened gum (which is a food for them) from tree trunks.[3]

Primate hands are extremely flexible. All primates have prehensile hands, which can be wrapped around an object; this allows them to grasp with one hand. Primates have five digits on both hands and feet (in some cases, one digit may be reduced to a stub), and their nails, with few exceptions, are broad and flat, not clawlike. This structure allows them to grip objects; so do the hairless, sensitive pads on their fingers, toes, heels, and palms. Many primates have **opposable thumbs**—a feature that allows an even more precise and powerful grip.

Vision is extremely important to primate life. Compared with other mammals, primates have a relatively larger portion of the brain devoted to vision rather than smell. Primates are characterized by stereoscopic or depth vision. Their eyes are directed forward, rather than sideways as in other animals—a trait that allows them to focus on an object (insects or other food, or a distant branch) with both eyes at once. Most primates also have color vision. By and large, these tendencies are more developed in anthropoids than in prosimians.

Another important primate feature is a large brain relative to body size. That is, primates generally have larger brains than animals of similar size, perhaps because their survival depends upon an enormous amount of learning, as we discuss later. In general, animals with large brains seem to grow up slower and live longer.[4] The slower an animal grows up and the longer it lives, the more it can learn.

The primate reproductive system sets this order of animals apart from other mammals. Primate males have a pendulous penis that is not attached to the abdomen by skin (a trait shared by a few other animals, including bats and bears). Most primate females have two mammary glands, or breasts, on the chest (a few prosimians have multiple nipples). The uterus is usually constructed to hold a single fetus, not a litter as with most other animals. This reproductive system can be seen as emphasizing quality over quantity—an adaptation probably related to the selective pressures of life in the trees.[5] After all, how many babies could a tree-living mother keep safe at one time? The young primates, except for humans, are relatively well developed at birth

[3] Simon K. Bearder. "Lorises, Bushbabies, and Tarsiers: Diverse Societies in Solitary Foragers." In Barbara Smuts et al., eds. *Primate Societies.* Chicago: University of Chicago Press, 1987, p. 14.

[4] Alison F. Richard. *Primates in Nature.* New York: W. H. Freeman and Company Publishers, 1985, pp. 22ff.

[5] Robert D. Martin. "Strategies of Reproduction." *Natural History,* November 1975, p. 50.

(prosimians, monkeys, and apes generally can cling to their mothers from birth), but they all (including humans) have a long maturation period. For example, the rhesus monkey is not sexually mature until about three years of age, the chimpanzee not until about age nine.

For the most part, primates are social animals. And just as physical traits such as grasping hands and stereoscopic vision may have developed as adaptations to the environment, so may many patterns of social behavior. For most primates, particularly those that are **diurnal** (active during the day), group life may be crucial to survival.

Experiments and observation show that youth is a time for learning, and the way most primates learn reflects their social nature. The young learn from all the members of the group, not just from their mothers. According to Hans Kummer, primates live in "a type of society which through constant association of young and old and through a long life duration exploits their large brains to produce adults of great experience."[6]

The prolonged dependency of infant monkeys and apes offers an evolutionary advantage in that it allows infants more time to observe, note, and learn the complex behaviors essential to survival, while enjoying the care and protection of a mature teacher. Young primates learn manipulative and motor skills as well as social patterns. During infancy, chimpanzees learn how to move through the trees and on the ground, and they attempt the intricacies of nest preparation, taking their first shaky steps toward mastering their physical environment. The ability to manipulate objects as tools is probably innate to chimpanzees, but the actual tool-using patterns are learned, often from the mother. Jane Goodall cites an occasion when a female with diarrhea picked up a handful of leaves to wipe her bottom. Her two-year-old infant watched closely and then twice picked up leaves to wipe its own clean behind.[7]

DISTINCTIVE HUMAN TRAITS

We turn now to some of the features that distinguish us—humans—from the other primates. Although we like to think of ourselves as unique, many of the traits we discuss here are at the extreme of a continuum that can be traced from the prosimians through the apes.

Physical Traits

Of all the primates, only humans consistently walk erect on two feet. Gibbons, chimpanzees, and gorillas may stand or walk on two feet some of the time, but only for very short periods. All other primates require thick, heavy musculature to hold their heads erect; this structure is missing in humans, for our heads are better balanced on top of our spinal columns. A dish-shaped pelvis (peculiar to humans), straight lower limbs, and arched, nonprehensile feet are

---

[6] Hans Kummer. *Primate Societies: Group Techniques of Ecological Adaptation.* Chicago: Aldine-Atherton, 1971, p. 38.
[7] Jane van Lawick-Goodall. *In the Shadow of Man.* Boston: Houghton Mifflin, 1971, p. 242.

all related to human **bipedalism**. Because we are fully bipedal, we can carry objects without impairing our locomotor efficiency. (In Chapter 4 we consider the effects bipedalism may have had on such diverse traits as toolmaking, prolonged infant dependency, and the division of labor by sex.) Although many primates have opposable thumbs that enable them to grasp and examine objects, the greater length and flexibility of the human thumb allows us to handle objects with more firmness and precision.

The human brain is large and complex, particularly the **cerebral cortex**, the center of speech and other higher mental activities. The brain of the average adult human measures more than 1300 cubic centimeters, compared with 525 cubic centimeters for the gorilla, the primate with the next largest brain. The frontal areas of the human brain are also larger than those of other primates, so that humans have more prominent foreheads than monkeys or gorillas. Human teeth reflect our completely omnivorous diet and are not very specialized. Many other primates have long lower canines, which are accommodated by a space in the upper jaw; in humans, the canines both look and act very much like incisors, and there are no spaces between the teeth. The human jaw is shaped like a parabolic arch, rather than a U shape as in the apes, and is composed of relatively thin bones and light muscles. Humans have chins; other primates do not. Humans are relatively hairless; other primates are not.

One other distinctive human trait is the sexuality of human females, who are receptive to intercourse more or less continuously; most other primate females are receptive more periodically. (Female pygmy chimpanzees are receptive to intercourse nearly as often as human females.[8]) Primate (and other mammal) species that lack breeding seasons are very likely to have long dependency periods. Although this suggests that natural selection in humans would favor reproduction throughout the year, because humans have very long dependency periods, it is not clear why human females should be more or less *continuously* sexual. After all, there is the monkey and ape way to have births occur throughout the year—periodic sexual receptivity in females around the time of ovulation during the menstrual cycle. So we still have to explain why more or less continuous female sexuality may have been favored in humans.

One suggestion is that this trait became selectively advantageous only *after* male-female bonding developed.[9] (Later, in the chapter on marriage and

---

[8] Nancy Thompson-Handler, Richard K. Malenky, and Noel Badrian. "Sexual Behavior of *Pan paniscus* under Natural Conditions in the Lomako Forest, Equateur, Zaire." In Randall L. Susman, ed., *The Pygmy Chimpanzee: Evolutionary Biology and Behavior*. New York: Plenum, 1984, pp. 347–66.

[9] By male-female bonding we mean that at least one of the sexes is "faithful," i.e., typically has intercourse with just one opposite-sex partner throughout at least one estrus or menstrual cycle or breeding season. Note that the bonding may not be monogamous; an individual may be bonded to more than one individual of the opposite sex. See Melvin Ember and Carol R. Ember, "Male-Female Bonding: A Cross-Species Study of Mammals and Birds," *Behavior Science Research*, 14 (1979): 37–41.

the family, we discuss some theories suggesting why male-female bonding, which in humans we call "marriage," may have developed.) The combination of long dependency, group living, *and* male-female bonding—a combination unique to humans among the primates—may have favored a switch from the common higher-primate pattern of periodic female receptivity to the pattern of more or less continuous female receptivity.[10]

Such a switch might have been favored in humans because periodic female sexuality would probably undermine male-female bonding in multi-male/multi-female groups. Field research on nonhuman primates strongly suggests that males usually attempt to mate with sexually receptive females. If the female (or females) a male was bonded to were not receptive at certain times but other females in the group were, it seems likely that the male would try to mate with those other females. Frequent "extramarital affairs" might jeopardize the male-female bond, which would presumably reduce the reproductive success of both males and females. Hence, natural selection may have favored more or less continuous sexual receptivity in human females if humans already had the combination of long dependency, group living (and the possibility of "extramarital affairs"), and marriage. If bonded adults lived alone, as in gibbons, noncontinuous female receptivity would not threaten bonding, because "extramarital" sex would not be likely to occur.

The theory just described does not suggest that frequent sex is the glue of pair-bonding. Indeed it appears that male-female bonding is significantly more likely in species that have restricted breeding seasons.[11] Seasonal breeding would pose little threat to male-female bonds, because all females would be sexually receptive at more or less the same time. So, since the combination of long dependency, group living, and male-female bonding occurs only in humans, that combination of traits may explain why continuous female sexuality developed in humans.

Behavioral Abilities

In comparison with other primates, a much greater proportion of human behavior is learned and culturally patterned. As with many physical traits, we can trace a continuum in the learning abilities of all primates. The great apes, including orangutans, gorillas, and chimpanzees, are probably about equal in learning ability.[12] Old and New World monkeys do much less well in learning tests, and surprisingly gibbons perform more poorly than most monkeys.

Toolmaking.   The same kind of continuum is evident in inventiveness and toolmaking. There is no evidence that any nonhuman primates except great apes use tools, although several species of monkeys use "weapons"—

[10] Carol R. Ember and Melvin Ember. "The Evolution of Human Female Sexuality: A Cross-Species Perspective." *Journal of Anthropological Research*, 40 (1984): 208–9.

[11] Ember and Ember. "Male-Female Bonding," p. 43.

[12] Duane M. Rumbaugh. "Learning Skills of Anthropoids." In L. A. Rosenblum, ed., *Primate Behavior*. New York: Academic Press, 1970, 1: 52–58.

branches, stones, or fruit dropped onto predators below them on the ground. Chimpanzees both fashion and use tools in the wild. They strip leaves from sticks and then use the sticks to "fish" termites from their mound-shaped nests. They use leaves to mop up termites, to sponge up water, or to wipe themselves clean.

One example of chimpanzee tool use suggests planning. In Guinea, West Africa, observers watched a number of chimpanzees crack oil palm nuts with two stones. The "platform" stone had a hollow depression; the other stone was used for pounding. The observers assumed that the stones had been brought by the chimpanzees to the palm trees, since no stones like them were nearby and the chimps were observed to leave the pounding stone on top of or near the platform stone when they were finished.[13]

In captivity, chimpanzees have been observed to be inventive toolmakers. One mother chimpanzee was seen examining and cleaning her son's teeth, using tools she had fashioned from twigs. She even extracted a baby tooth he was about to lose.[14]

Humans have usually been considered the only toolmaking animal, but observations such as these call for modification of the definition of toolmaking. If we define toolmaking as adapting a natural object for a specific purpose, then at least some of the great apes are toolmakers. As far as we know, though, humans are unique in their ability to use one tool to make another. In the words of Goodall, "the point at which tool-using and tool-making, as such, acquire evolutionary significance is surely when an animal can adapt its ability to manipulate objects to a wide variety of purposes, and when it can use an object spontaneously to solve a brand-new problem that without the use of a tool would prove insoluble."[15]

Language. Only humans have spoken, symbolic language. But, as with toolmaking abilities, the line between human language and the communications of other primates is not as sharp as we once thought. In the wild, vervet monkeys make different alarm calls to warn of different predators. Observers playing back tape recordings of these calls found that monkeys responded to them differently, depending upon the call. If the monkeys heard an "eagle" call they looked up; if they heard a "leopard" call they ran high into the trees.[16]

Chimpanzees are especially communicative, using gestures and many vocalizations in the wild. Researchers have used this "natural talent" to teach chimpanzees symbolic language in experimental settings. Beatrice T. and R. Allen Gardner raised a female chimpanzee named Washoe and trained her to

[13] Observation by Sugiyama, cited by Allison Jolly, *The Evolution of Primate Behavior*, 2nd ed. New York: Macmillan, 1985, p. 53.
[14] "The First Dentist." *Newsweek*, March 5, 1973, p. 73.
[15] van Lawick-Goodall. *In the Shadow of Man*, p. 240.
[16] Robert M. Seyfarth, Dorothy L. Cheney, and Peter Marler. "Monkey Response to Three Different Alarm Calls: Evidence of Predator Classification and Semantic Communication." *Science*, November 14, 1980, pp. 801–3.

communicate with startling effectiveness by means of American Sign Language hand gestures.[17] After a year of training, she was able to associate gestures with specific activities. For example, if thirsty, Washoe would make the signal for "give me" followed by the one for "drink." As she learned, the instructions grew more detailed. If all she wanted was water, she would merely signal for "drink." But if she craved soda pop, as she did more and more, she prefaced the drink signal with the sweet signal—a quick touching of the tongue with her fingers. More recently, the Gardners have had even more success in training four other chimpanzees, who were taught by fluent deaf users of American Sign Language.[18]

A chimpanzee named Sarah has been taught to read and write with plastic symbols; her written vocabulary is 130 "words."[19] She can perform complex tasks such as simultaneously putting an apple in a pail and a banana in a dish on written command—a feat that requires an understanding of sentence structure as well as words. A chimpanzee named Lana became so proficient in a symbolic language called Yerkish that she scored 95 on some tests in comprehension and sentence completion after six months of training.[20]

Other Human Traits.   Although many primates are omnivores, eating insects and small reptiles in addition to plants (some even hunt small mammals), humans have long hunted very large animals. Also, humans are one of the few primates that are completely terrestrial. We do not even sleep in trees, as many other ground-living primates do. Perhaps our ancestors lost their perches when the forests receded, or cultural advances such as weapons or fire may have eliminated the need to seek nightly shelter in the trees. In addition, we have the longest dependency period of any of the primates, requiring extensive parental care for at least six years and usually partial care until we reach sexual maturity in the early teens.

Finally, humans are unlike almost all other primates in having a division of labor by sex in food-getting. Among nonhuman primates, both males and females forage for themselves after infancy. In humans, there is more sex-role specialization, perhaps because men, unencumbered by infants and small children, were freer to hunt and chase large animals. We consider the possible causes and consequences of a sexual division of labor among humans in a later chapter on sex and culture.

Having examined our so-called unique traits and the traits we share with

[17] R. Allen Gardner and Beatrice T. Gardner. "Teaching Sign Language to a Chimpanzee." *Science*, August 15, 1969, pp. 664–72.

[18] Beatrice T. Gardner and R. Allen Gardner. "Two Comparative Psychologists Look at Language Acquisition." In K. E. Nelson, ed. *Children's Language*. New York: Halsted Press, 1980, 2: 331–69.

[19] Ann James Premack and David Premack. "Teaching Language to an Ape." *Scientific American*, October 1972, pp. 92–99.

[20] Duane M. Rumbaugh, Timothy V. Gill, and E. C. von Glaserfeld. "Reading and Sentence Completion by a Chimpanzee (Pan)." *Science*, November 16, 1973, pp. 731–33.

other primates, we now turn to ask what selective forces may have favored the emergence of primates.

INTERPRETING THE FOSSIL RECORD

The story of primate evolution is still fragmentary and tentative, and it will probably always be so. Paleontologists have to make inferences or educated guesses about what happened in evolutionary history, where and when events occurred, and why they happened the way they did. These inferences make use of a number of kinds of information—fossilized bones and teeth from extinct biological forms; indicators of ancient environments and climates discovered by geologists; and comparisons of the anatomical, physiological, and behavioral characteristics of living animals. But even though paleontological inferences will always be tentative, some inferences are supported more strongly by the available evidence than others. A particular inference based on one kind of evidence can be checked against other kinds of evidence. In this way, some inferences come to be discarded and others tentatively accepted.

How can paleontologists know about what may have happened millions of years ago? There is no written record from that period from which they can draw inferences. But we do have another kind of evidence for primate evolution: fossils. And we have ways of "reading" the records left by fossils and of telling how old fossils are.

A fossil may be an impression of an insect or leaf on sediment now turned to stone. Or it may consist of the actual hardened remains of an animal's skeletal structure. It is this second type of fossil—bone turned to stone—that has given paleontologists the most information about primate evolution.

When an animal dies, the organic matter that made up its body quickly begins to deteriorate. The teeth and skeletal structure are composed largely of inorganic mineral salts, and soon they are all that remains. Under most conditions, these parts eventually deteriorate too. But once in a great while conditions are favorable for preservation—for instance, when volcanic ash, limestone, or highly mineralized ground water is present to form a high-mineral environment. Under such circumstances, the minerals in the ground become bound into the structure of the teeth or bone, hardening and thus making them less likely to deteriorate.

Paleontologists can tell a great deal about an extinct animal from its fossilized bones or teeth, but reading the fossil record is not easy. For one thing, the very formation of a fossil depends a good deal on luck; so does the discovery of that fossil eons later. Thus, the fossil record contains remains of only a small proportion of all the animals and plants that ever lived. In addition, fossils are often fragmented or distorted, and similar fossils may come from widely separate geographical areas. Although we can tell the age of a fossil with some accuracy, methods of dating are not always exact enough for the paleontologist to determine whether a fossil is older than, contemporaneous with, or more recent than other fossils. For this reason too, evolutionary lines are difficult to trace.

A further complication is an artificial one: the problem of **taxonomy**, or classification. Over the period that paleontologists have been discovering primate remains, different assumptions have guided scientists in making judgments about the taxonomic status of fossils. Even when paleontologists agree in theory, they often have honest differences of opinion about the status of a fossil. After all, we cannot conclude without doubt that two similar fossil forms belonged to the same species, because we cannot know that they interbred.

Despite all these problems, fossils do provide a wealth of information. In studying primate evolution, paleontologists ask two important questions as they examine an animal fossil: What was the animal's means of food-getting? And what was its means of locomotion? Often the answers to both questions can be determined from a few fragments of bone or teeth.

Much of the evidence for primate evolution comes from teeth, which along with jaws are the most common animal parts to be preserved as fossils. Animals vary in *dentition*, the number and kinds of teeth they have, their size, and their arrangement in the mouth. Dentition provides clues to evolutionary relationships because animals with similar evolutionary histories often have similar teeth. Dentition also suggests the relative size of an animal and often offers clues about its diet.

Paleontologists can tell much about an animal's posture and locomotion from fragments of its skeleton. They can often judge whether the animal was a brachiator and whether it walked on all fours (quadrupedalism) or upright (bipedalism). The bone structure also tells much about the soft tissues. The form and size of muscles can be estimated by marks found on the bones to which the muscles were attached. Finally, fragments of the skull or vertebrae provide clues about the proportions and structure of the brain and spinal cord. From such evidence, scientists can tell whether areas of the brain associated with vision, or smell, or memory were enlarged.

THE EMERGENCE OF PRIMATES

With a rudimentary understanding of the kinds of information fossils provide and of the methods of dating that allow scientists to tell the age of fossils, we can look at, and suggest answers to, some major questions about primate evolution. When did the earliest primates appear? What were they like, and what kind of animal did they evolve from? Where did they live? What was their environment like? And which of their traits seem to have been favored by that environment?

The Earliest Possible Primates

Finds made by two paleontologists in eastern Montana in 1964 suggest that some very early primates may have existed as far back as the Late Cretaceous period—some 70 million years ago. Molars from two species (one from the Cretaceous period, the other from the Paleocene) of the genus **Purgatorius** show some primate characteristics.[21] The earlier of these species is very old indeed. It was contemporaneous with at least six species of dinosaurs.

Both of these earliest primate finds illustrate how much of the paleontologist's work depends on inference. *Purgatorius* may have been a primate, but it is impossible to tell for sure. The Cretaceous specimen consists of only one tooth found with fauna dating from that period. Because the tooth has some characteristics like those found in the teeth of some later Paleocene primates, some paleontologists think it represents a very early primate form. Fossil finds from the middle **Paleocene** epoch (about 60 million years ago) are much more abundant; several genera have been identified. The earliest *Purgatorius* remains consist only of teeth, but we have some skeletal parts of the later primates.

Paleocene and early Eocene archaic primates have been found in both Europe and North America. The similarities between some European and North American finds are often quite striking. For example, a cat-sized primate called **Plesiadapis** was first discovered in northern France. Later, similar fossils were found in Wyoming and Colorado. The North American fossils differ very little from the French specimens. It seems that *Plesiadapis* and closely related genera flourished in both North America and Europe.[22]

How could a nonbird species be found on two different continents? The answer to this puzzle, and to many similar puzzles in fossil distributions, is provided by the **continental-drift theory**.[23] At one time, about 180 million years ago, the continents were not separated as they are today. Instead, they formed a single supercontinent; the rest of the earth was covered by sea. Continental drift has since broken up that supercontinent. But even after the primates emerged, until about 60 million years ago, North America and Europe were connected in the vicinity of Greenland. *Plesiadapis* and other early primates probably ranged from North America to Europe.[24] Only in

[21] L. Van Valen and R. E. Sloan. "The Earliest Primates." *Science*, November 5, 1965, pp. 743–45; and Frederick S. Szalay. "The Beginnings of Primates." *Evolution*, 22 (1968): 19–36.
[22] D. E. Russell. "Les Mammifères Paléocènes." *Mémoires du Muséum d'Histoire Naturelle* 13 (1964): 1–324, cited in Elwyn L. Simons, *Primate Evolution: An Introduction to Man's Place in Nature*, New York: Macmillan, 1972, pp. 110–12; and P. D. Gingerich, *Cranial Anatomy and Evolution of Early Tertiary Plesiadapidae (Mammalia, Primates)*. Papers on Paleontology, no. 15. Ann Arbor: Museum of Paleontology, University of Michigan, 1976.
[23] A. Hallam. "Alfred Wegener and the Hypothesis of Continental Drift." *Scientific American*, February 1975, pp. 88–97.
[24] Malcolm C. McKenna. "Was Europe Connected Directly to North America Prior to the Middle Eocene?" In T. Dobzhansky, M. K. Hecht, and W. C. Steere, eds., *Evolutionary Biology*. New York: Appleton-Century-Crofts, 1972, 6: 179–88.

relatively recent times (geologically speaking) have the continents moved far enough apart so that the intervening seas could block gene flow between related populations.

The Environment

During the late Cretaceous and early Paleocene, many new mammal forms began to appear—so many that this time is known as the beginning of the *age of mammals*. Larger reptiles such as dinosaurs were dying out, and at the same time many new and different mammal forms were branching out from the more primitive Cretaceous ones. Paleontologists think primates evolved from one of these *radiations,* or extensive diversifications, probably from **insectivores** (the order or major grouping of mammals, including modern shrews and moles, that is adapted to feeding on insects).

These changes in the earth's population may have been favored by environmental changes that marked the end of the Cretaceous period and the beginning of the Paleocene. Shifts in climate, vegetation, and fauna signal the beginning of every major epoch, and many important changes were taking place at this time.

The climate of the Cretaceous period was almost uniformly damp and mild. Around the beginning of the Paleocene epoch, both seasonal and geographic fluctuations in temperature began to develop. At this time the climate became much drier in many areas, and vast swamplands disappeared. With changes in climate came changes in vegetation. During the Cretaceous period, the first deciduous (not evergreen) trees, flowering plants, and grasses were emerging.

The new kinds of plant life opened up sources of food and protection for new animal forms. They created new habitats. Important to primate evolution was the Late Cretaceous forest. The new deciduous plant life provided an abundant food supply for insects. The result was that insects proliferated in both number and variety, and this led in turn to an increase in insectivores—the mammals that ate the insects. The insectivores were very adaptable, for they took advantage of many different habitats—underground, in water, on the ground, and above ground—the woody habitat of bushes, shrubs, vines, and trees.

It is this last adaptation that may have been the most important to primate evolution. The woody habitat had been exploited only partially in earlier periods. But sometime during the Late Cretaceous period, several different kinds, or *taxa,* of small animals, one of which may have been the archaic primate, began to take advantage of this habitat.

What May Have Favored the Emergence of Primates?

Why did the primates emerge? The traditional view of primate origins has come to be known as *arboreal theory.* According to this view, which has lately been criticized, the primates evolved from insectivores that took to the trees.

Different paleontologists have emphasized different possible adaptations to life in the trees. In 1912, G. Elliot Smith suggested that taking to the trees favored vision over smell. Searching for food by sniffing and feeling with the snout might suit terrestrial insectivores, but vision would be more useful in an animal that searched for food in the maze of tree branches. With smaller snouts and the declining importance of the sense of smell, the eyes of the early primates would have come to face forward. Frederic Wood Jones emphasized changes in the hand and foot. He thought that tree climbing would favor grasping hands and feet, with the hind limbs becoming more specialized for support and propulsion. In 1921, Treacher Collins suggested that the eyes of the early primates came to face forward not just because the snout got smaller. Rather, he thought that three-dimensional binocular vision would be favored because an animal jumping from branch to branch would be more likely to survive if it could accurately judge distances across open space.[25] In 1968, Frederick Szalay suggested that a shift in diet—from insects to seeds, fruits, and leaves—might have been important in the differentiation of primates from insectivores. Lower-cusped, bulbous teeth, better for chewing tough husks and fruits, are an identifying feature of the earliest primates (indeed the *only* identifying feature where no skull or bone fossils have been found).[26]

Arboreal theory still has some proponents, but in 1974 Matt Cartmill highlighted some crucial weaknesses in the theory.[27] He argued that tree living is not a good explanation for many of the primate features because there are a number of living mammals that dwell in trees but seem to do very well without primatelike characteristics. One of the best examples, he says, is the tree squirrel. Its eyes are not front-facing, its sense of smell is not reduced in comparison with other rodents, it has claws rather than nails, and it lacks an opposable thumb. Yet these squirrels are very successful in the trees: they can leap accurately from tree to tree, they can walk over or under small branches, they can go up and down vertical surfaces, and they can even hang from their hind legs to get food below them. Furthermore, other animals have some primate traits but do not live in trees or do not move around in trees as primates do. For example, carnivores such as cats, hawks, and owls have forward-facing eyes, and the chameleon (a reptile) and some Australian marsupial mammals that prey on insects in bushes and shrubs have grasping hands and feet.

Cartmill thinks, then, that some factor other than moving about in trees may account for the emergence of the primates. He proposes that the early primates may have been basically insect-eaters, and that three-dimensional vision, grasping hands and feet, and reduced claws may have been selectively

---

[25] Richard. *Primates in Nature*, p. 31; and Matt Cartmill. "Rethinking Primate Origins." *Science*, April 26, 1974, pp. 436–37.
[26] Szalay. "The Beginnings of Primates," pp. 32–33.
[27] Cartmill. "Rethinking Primate Origins," pp. 436–43.

advantageous for hunting insects on the slender vines and branches that fill the undergrowth of tropical forests. Three-dimensional vision would allow the insect hunter to gauge the prey's distance accurately. Grasping feet would allow the predator to move quietly up narrow supports to reach the prey, which could then be grabbed with the hands. Claws, Cartmill argues, would make it difficult to grasp very slender branches. And the sense of smell would have become reduced, not so much because it was no longer useful, but because the location of the eyes at the front of the face would leave less room for a snout.

Robert Sussman has recently suggested a theory that builds on Cartmill's *visual predation theory* and Szalay's idea about a dietary shift.[28] Sussman accepts Cartmill's point that the early primates were likely to eat and move about mostly on small branches. This would explain why the early primates would have had nails rather than claws (as do squirrels) and grasping hands and feet. If an animal is moving mostly on small, slender branches and hardly ever travels on large trunks and branches (as do squirrels), grasping hands and feet and reduced claws or nails would be advantageous. Sussman also accepts Szalay's point that the early primates probably ate the new types of plant food (flowers, seeds, and fruits) that were beginning to become abundant at the time as flowering trees and plants spread throughout the world. But Sussman asks an important question: If the early primates ate mostly plant foods rather than speedy insects, why did they become more reliant on vision than on smell? Sussman suggests it was because the early primates were probably nocturnal (as many prosimians still are): if they were to locate and manipulate small food items at the ends of slender branches in dim light, they would need improved vision.

We still have very little fossil evidence of the earliest primates. When additional fossils become available, we may be more able to evaluate the various explanations that have been suggested for the emergence of primates.

The Early Primates: What They Looked Like

From the clues provided by fossils, comparative anatomy, physiology, behavior, and our knowledge of the Paleocene and Eocene environments, we can put together a composite sketch of what early primates must have been like. In general, the primates of the Paleocene epoch seem to have looked a little like the mice and rats of today. Most of the Paleocene primates were quite small; the cat-sized *Plesiadapis* in France is among the largest early primates we know of.[29] Its mode of locomotion is believed to have been similar to a

---

[28] Robert W. Sussman. *The Ecology and Behavior of Free-ranging Primates.* Manuscript in preparation. Also Robert W. Sussman and Peter H. Raven, "Pollination by Lemurs and Marsupials: An Archaic Coevolutionary System," *Science*, May 19, 1978, pp. 734–35.

[29] Simons, *Primate Evolution*, p. 112.

squirrel's. It probably got around by springing and jumping, as well as walking on all fours.

Although there is debate about whether the earliest primates lived in the trees, later primates in the **Eocene** epoch (from 54 to 38 million years ago) were apparently doing so, judging from their anatomy. Eocene prosimians not only moved around the way modern prosimians do; some also looked quite a bit like living prosimians. Through the evolutionary process of natural selection, their eyes became located closer to the front of the face and their snout was reduced. Digits became longer and were specialized for grasping.

THE EMERGENCE OF ANTHROPOIDS

The anthropoids of today—monkeys, apes, and humans—are the most successful living primates and include well over 150 species. Unfortunately, the fossil record documenting the emergence of the anthropoids is extremely spotty, and there is virtually no record of the Old World forms (the catarrhines) in the two areas where they are most abundant today—the rain forests of sub-Saharan Africa and Southeast Asia.[30] Undisputed remains of early anthropoids date from the Early Oligocene, after 38 million years ago in the Fayum area southwest of Cairo, Egypt.

The Fayum today is an uninviting area of desert badlands, but during the **Oligocene** epoch (38 to 22.5 million years ago) it was a tropical rain forest quite close to the shores of the Mediterranean Sea. The area had a warm climate, and it contained many rivers and lakes. The Fayum, in fact, was far more inviting than the northern continents at this time, for the climates of both North America and Eurasia were beginning to cool during the Oligocene. The general cooling seems to have resulted in the virtual disappearance of primates from the northern areas, at least for a time.

Two main types of anthropoid have been found in the Fayum. The monkeylike **parapithecids** had three premolars, as do most prosimians and the New World monkeys. They were generally quite small, weighing under three pounds. Their relatively small eye sockets suggest that they were not nocturnal. And their teeth suggest that they ate mostly fruits and seeds. The other type of anthropoid found in the Fayum, the **propliopithecids**, had apelike teeth. For example, in contrast with the parapithecids, who had three premolars, the propliopithecids had only two premolars, just like modern apes, humans, and Old World monkeys. **Aegyptopithecus**, the best-known propliopithecid, probably moved around quadrupedally in the trees, weighed about thirteen pounds, and ate mostly fruit. Although its teeth and jaws are apelike, the rest of *Aegyptopithecus's* skeleton is similar to that of the modern

---

[30] John G. Fleagle and Richard F. Kay. "The Paleobiology of Catarrhines." In Eric Delson, ed., *Ancestors: The Hard Evidence.* New York: Alan R. Liss, 1985, p. 25.

South American howler monkey.[31] Because the propliopithecids lack the specialized characteristics of living Old World monkeys and apes (catarrhines), but share the dental formula of the catarrhines, it is thought that the propliopithecids were primitive catarrhines, ancestral to both the Old World monkeys and the **hominoids** (apes and humans).[32]

The Miocene Anthropoids: Monkeys, Apes, and Hominids(?)

During the **Miocene** epoch (22.5 to 5 million years ago), monkeys and apes clearly diverged in appearance, and numerous kinds of apes appeared in Europe, Asia, and Africa. In the Early Miocene, the temperatures were considerably warmer than the temperatures in the Oligocene. From Early to Late Miocene conditions became drier.[33] We can infer that late in the Miocene (between about 8 and 5 million years ago) the direct ancestor of humans (the first hominid) may have emerged in Africa. The inference about *where* hominids emerged is based on the fact that undisputed hominids lived in East Africa after about 5 million years ago. The inference about *when* hominids emerged is based not on fossil evidence but on comparative molecular and biochemical analyses of modern apes and humans.

Some of the anthropoids in the Early Miocene (about 22 to 15 million years ago) are very similar to modern monkeys; others are described as proto-apes. The proto-apes have been found mostly in Africa.[34] Compared with the Oligocene anthropoids, the Early Miocene proto-apes were quite diverse. They ranged in size from that of the modern gibbon (about 10 pounds) to that of the modern chimpanzee (about 100 pounds). And in contrast with the Oligocene anthropoids, who appear to have been arboreal quadrupeds, some of the Early Miocene species appear to have been terrestrial at least some of the time; others appear to have been arboreal brachiators (moving through the trees by swinging from the arms rather than by walking on all fours).

The hominoids that lived 14 to 8 million years ago have been classified as apes (rather than proto-apes), even though they did not look completely like modern apes. They ranged from gibbonlike to gorillalike in size.

Most paleontologists divide the Middle and Late Miocene apes into two groups: **Dryopithecus**, found primarily in Europe, and **Sivapithecus**, found primarily in western and southern Asia.[35] The genus *Dryopithecus* is known mostly from its teeth. Judging from the dryopithecines' teeth—which consist

---

[31] Fleagle and Kay. "The Paleobiology of Catarrhines," pp. 25, 30.
[32] John G. Fleagle. *Primate Adaptation & Evolution*. San Diego: Academic Press, 1988, p. 339. See also J. G. Fleagle and R. F. Kay, "New Interpretations of the Phyletic Position of Oligocene Hominoids," in Russell L. Ciochon and Robert S. Corruccini, eds., *New Interpretations of Ape and Human Ancestry*, New York: Plenum, 1983, p. 205.
[33] Fleagle. *Primate Adaptation & Evolution*, p. 363.
[34] Fleagle and Kay. "The Paleobiology of Catarrhines," p. 31.
[35] Fleagle. *Primate Adaptation & Evolution*, p. 382.

of small to medium incisors and relatively small molars and pre-molars with thin enamel—their owners probably ate relatively soft foods (fruits, leaves, and young plants). The dryopithecines disappear from the fossil record after about 9 million years ago, perhaps because climates became cooler and habitats less forested in the areas where they lived.[36]

Most species of *Sivapithecus* were larger than the dryopithecines that lived somewhat earlier (some were as large as a present-day male organgutan or a female gorilla).[37] Compared with the dryopithecines' teeth, the sivapithecines' molars and premolars are relatively larger (adjusting for differences in body size) and more thickly enameled, and their canines are somewhat reduced.[38] Many paleontologists think that these apes with their thickly enameled teeth were probably adapted to habitats and had diets that were different from the dryopithecines'. The thick enamel and large molars suggest that sivapithecines depended more on hard foods such as seeds. Such a diet would be possible because the sivapithecines lived in open woodlands and grasslands—habitats where seeds would be plentiful. Such habitats became more common in the world after the Early Miocene.[39]

It is still very difficult to identify the evolutionary lines leading from Miocene apes to modern apes and humans. Only the orangutans have been linked to the later Miocene ape, *Sivapithecus*.[40]

Who or what are hominids, and how do they differ from other hominoids? The hominid family comprises modern humans, their ancestors, and other extinct bipedal hominoids. The family includes at least two genera: **Homo** (including modern humans) and **Australopithecus** (a genus of hominids that lived during the Pliocene and Pleistocene epochs). In general, hominids are characterized by a number of identifying traits. (The earliest ones may not have had all of these traits, but later ones did.) They are bipeds. They have an enlarged brain. Their faces are relatively small and relatively nonprotruding. And their teeth are small and arranged on jaws that are parabolic in shape (viewed from above or below), rather than U-shaped as in the apes.

In 1966, on the basis of biochemical comparison of blood proteins in the different surviving primates, Vincent Sarich and Allan Wilson estimated that gibbons diverged from the other hominoids about 12 million years ago, orangutans 10 million years ago, and the other apes (gorillas and chimps)

---

[36] David Pilbeam. "Recent Finds and Interpretation of Miocene Hominoids." *Annual Review of Anthropology*, 8 (1979): 345–46.

[37] Fleagle. *Primate Adaptation & Evolution*, pp. 382–385.

[38] Pilbeam. "Recent Finds and Interpretation of Miocene Hominoids," pp. 346–47.

[39] M. Pickford. "Sequence and Environments of the Lower and Middle Miocene Hominoids of Western Kenya." In Ciochon and Corruccini, eds. *New Interpretations of Ape and Human Ancestry*, pp. 436–37.

[40] Fleagle. *Primate Adaptation & Evolution*, pp. 388–90.

from hominids only 4.5 million years ago. These estimates depended on the assumption that the more similar in chemistry the bloods of different primates are (for instance, chimpanzees and humans), the closer those primates are in evolutionary time. In other words, the more similar the bloods of related species, the more recently they diverged.[41]

Subsequent comparative studies of the living primates, employing a variety of techniques (including comparisons of their DNA), have confirmed the probable recency of the hominid divergence from chimpanzees and gorillas. The DNA comparisons place the split somewhat earlier than the Sarich and Wilson estimate, but not by much: the DNA comparisons suggest that the common ancestor of chimpanzees, gorillas, and hominids lived 6 to 7 million years ago.[42]

Most paleontologists are now persuaded that the hominid-ape split probably occurred in the later part of the Miocene, between 6 and 10 million years ago. A major reason they are now so persuaded is that recent fossil finds in Pakistan and Turkey (skull finds more complete than just teeth and jaws) suggest that sivapithecines were not very hominidlike.[43] As we noted above, sivapithecines are now thought to be ancestral to orangutans.

So what does the available evidence tell us about where and when hominids first emerged? Unfortunately, the answer is nothing as yet. For we still do not have any definitely hominid fossils in Africa from the Late Miocene (8 to 5 million years ago)—the presumed place and time hominids emerged.[44] And definitely hominid fossils dating from the Late Miocene have not been found anywhere else as yet. So all we know definitely now is that primates with undisputably hominid characteristics lived 3 to 4 million years ago in East Africa. We turn to these undisputed hominids in the next chapter.

SUMMARY

1. No one trait is unique to primates. However, primates do share the following features: two bones in the lower part of the leg and in the forearms, a collarbone, flexible prehensile hands that can grasp, stereoscopic vision, relatively large brains, only one (or sometimes two) offspring at a time, long maturation of the young, and a high degree of dependence on social life and learning.

[41] Vincent M. Sarich and Allan C. Wilson. "Quantitative Immunochemistry and the Evolution of the Primate Albumins: Micro-Component Fixations." *Science*, December 23, 1966, pp. 1563–66; Vincent M. Sarich. "The Origin of Hominids: An Immunological Approach." In S. L. Washburn and Phyllis C. Jay, eds., *Perspectives on Human Evolution*. New York: Holt, Rinehart & Winston, 1968, 1: 99–121; and Roger Lewin. "Is the Orangutan a Living Fossil?" *Science*, December 16, 1983, pp. 1222–23.

[42] J. E. Cronin. "Apes, Humans, and Molecular Clocks: A Reappraisal." In Ciochon and Corruccini, eds., *New Interpretations of Ape and Human Ancestry*, pp. 115–36.

[43] Lewin. "Is the Orangutan a Living Fossil?" See also Fleagle, *Primate Adaptation & Evolution*, pp. 384–85, 390–91.

[44] David Pilbeam. "The Descent of Hominoids and Hominids." *Scientific American*, March 1984, p. 88.

2. The order Primates is divided into two suborders: the prosimians and the anthro-poids. The prosimians (lemurs and lorises) are in some respects closer to other mammals than are the anthropoid primates. Prosimians depend more on smell for information. They have mobile ears, whiskers, longer snouts, and relatively fixed facial expressions. The anthropoids are subdivided into tarsiers, New World monkeys, Old World monkeys, and hominoids (apes and humans). Anthropoids have rounded brain cases; reduced, nonmobile outer ears; and relatively small, flat faces instead of muzzles. They have highly dexterous hands. The anthropoid apes consist of the lesser apes (gibbons and siamangs) and the great apes (orang-utans, gorillas, and chimpanzees).
3. The differences between humans and the other anthropoids show us what makes humans distinctive as a species. Humans are totally bipedal: they walk on two legs and do not need the arms for locomotion. The human brain is the largest and most complex, particularly the cerebral cortex. Human females are more or less continuously receptive to sexual intercourse, unlike the females of almost all other primates. Offspring have a proportionately longer dependency stage. And in comparison with other primates, more human behavior is learned and culturally patterned. Spoken, symbolic language and the use of tools to make other tools are uniquely human behavioral traits. Humans also have a marked sexual division of labor in food-getting.
4. We cannot know for sure how primates evolved. But fossils, a knowledge of ancient environments, and an understanding of comparative anatomy and behav-ior give us enough clues so that we have a tentative idea of when, where, and why primates emerged and diverged.
5. The surviving primates—prosimians, New World monkeys, Old World monkeys, apes, and humans—are thought to be descendants of small, originally terrestrial insectivores.
6. Changes in climate during the Late Cretaceous favored the extensive develop-ment of deciduous forest and their understories of bushes, shrubs, and vines. Many of the flowering trees and plants emerged during this period. The early primates probably began to exploit these forests, which provided a largely un-tapped habitat with many new food resources. The earliest primates may have emerged some 70 million years ago.
7. The traditional view of primate evolution is that arboreal (tree) life would have favored many of the common primate features, including distinctive dentition, greater reliance on vision over smell, three-dimensional binocular vision, and grasping hands and feet. A second theory proposes that some of the distinctive primate characteristics were selectively advantageous for hunting insects on the slender vines and branches that filled the undergrowth of forests. A third theory suggests that the distinctive features of primates (including reliance more on vision than on smell) were favored because the early primates were nocturnal feeders on flowers, fruits, and seeds, which they had to locate on slender branches in dim light.
8. Undisputed remains of early anthropoids unearthed in Egypt date from the Early Oligocene (after 38 million years ago). They include the monkeylike parapithecids and the propliopithecids, who had apelike teeth.
9. During the Miocene epoch, which began about 22 million years ago, monkeys and apes clearly diverged and numerous kinds of apes appeared in Europe, Asia, and Africa. The Miocene proto-apes and apes were very diverse in size, ranging from about 10 pounds to 300 pounds. Unlike the Oligocene anthropoids, who all appear to have been arboreal quadrupeds, some of the Miocene apes were at least partly terrestrial and others were arboreal brachiators. The two main groups of

apes in the Middle and Late Miocene were the dryopithecines (with thin-enameled cheek teeth) and the sivapithecines (with larger and more thickly enameled cheek teeth).

10. The fossil record does not yet tell us who the first hominid was, but biochemical and genetic analyses of modern apes and humans suggest that the hominid-ape split occurred during the Late Miocene (between about 8 and 5 million years ago). Since undisputed hominids lived in East Africa after about 5 million years ago, the first hominid probably emerged in Africa.

4

Early Hominids and Their Cultures

Undisputed bipedal hominids lived in East Africa about 4 million years ago. These hominids, and others who lived in East and South Africa until 2 million years ago, are generally classified in the genus *Australopithecus*. And some East African hominids that are nearly 2 million years old are classified in our own genus, *Homo*. In this chapter we discuss what we know or suspect about the emergence and relationship of the australopithecines and *Homo*. We also discuss the life styles or cultures of the hominids from about 4 million until about 250,000 years ago, when the first members of our own species, *Homo sapiens*, may have emerged.

TRENDS IN HOMINID EVOLUTION

Perhaps the most crucial change in early hominid evolution was the development of bipedal locomotion, or walking on two legs. We now know from the fossil record that other important physical changes—including the expansion of the brain, modification of the female pelvis to allow bigger-brained babies to be born, and reduction of the face, teeth, and jaws—did not occur until about 2 million years after the emergence of bipedalism. Other human characteristics—including an extended period of infant and child dependency and more meat-eating—may also have developed after that time.

Bipedalism

We do not know whether bipedalism developed quickly or gradually, since the fossil record is very skimpy between 8 and 4 million years ago. We do know that many of the Miocene anthropoids, judging from the skeletal anatomy, were capable of assuming an upright posture. For example, brachiation (arm swinging through the trees) puts an animal in an upright position; so does climbing up and down trees with the use of grasping hands and feet. It is also likely that the proto-hominids were capable of occasional bipedalism, just like many modern monkeys and apes.[1]

Definitely bipedal hominids apparently emerged first in Africa. The physical environment in Africa was changing from tropical forest to more open country.[2] The proto-apes flourished at the very beginning of the Miocene epoch, when lush tropical rain forests were the predominant habitat. Somewhat later in the Miocene, about 16 to 11 million years ago, a drying trend set in that continued into the Pliocene. Gradually the African rain forests, deprived of intense humidity and rainfall, gave way mostly to **savannas** (grasslands) and scattered deciduous woodlands. The tree-dwelling primates did not completely lose their customary habitats, since some forest areas remained, and natural selection continued to favor the better-adapted tree dwellers in those forest areas. But the new, more open country probably favored characteristics adapted to ground living in some primates as well as other animals. In the evolutionary line leading to humans, these adaptations included bipedalism.

So what in particular may have favored the emergence of bipedal hominids? There are several possible explanations for this development. One idea is that bipedalism was adaptive for life amid the tall grasses of the savannas because an erect posture may have made it easier to spot ground predators as well as potential prey.[3] This theory does not adequately account for the development of bipedalism, however. Baboons and some other Old World monkeys also live in savanna environments, yet although they can stand erect, and occasionally do so, they have not evolved fully bipedal locomotion.

Other theories stress the importance of freeing the hands. If some hand activity is critical while an animal is moving, selection may favor bipedalism because it frees the hands for other activities at the same time. What hand activities might have been so critical?

Gordon Hewes has suggested that carrying food in the hands was the critical activity—if it were necessary to carry food from one locale to another,

---

[1] M. D. Rose. "Food Acquisition and the Evolution of Positional Behaviour: The Case of Bipedalism." In David J. Chivers, Bernard A. Wood, and Alan Bilsborough, eds., *Food Acquisition and Processing in Primates*. New York: Plenum, 1984, pp. 509–24.

[2] John Napier. "The Antiquity of Human Walking." *Scientific American*, April 1967, pp. 56–66.

[3] Kenneth Oakley. "On Man's Use of Fire, With Comments on Tool-Making and Hunting." In S. L. Washburn, ed., *Social Life of Early Man*. Chicago: Aldine, 1964, p. 186.

moving about only on the hind limbs would have been adaptive.[4] Hewes emphasized the importance of carrying hunted or scavenged meat, but many paleontologists now question whether early hominids hunted or even scavenged.[5] However, the ability to carry any food to a place safe from predators may have been one of the more important advantages of bipedalism. C. Owen Lovejoy has suggested that food carrying might have been important for another reason. If males provisioned females and their babies by carrying food back to a home base, the females would have been able to conserve energy by not traveling around and therefore might have been able to produce and care for more babies.[6] Thus, whatever the advantages of food carrying, the more bipedal a protohominid was, the more it might reproduce.

Bipedalism might also have been favored by natural selection because the freeing of the hands would allow proto-hominids to use, and perhaps even make, tools that they could carry as they moved about. Consider how advantageous such tool use might have been. Sherwood Washburn has noted that some contemporary ground-living primates dig for roots to eat, "and if they could use a stone or a stick they might easily double their food supply."[7] David Pilbeam also suggests why tool use by the early savanna dwellers may have appreciably increased the number and amount of plant foods they could eat: in order to be eaten, many of the plant foods in the savanna probably had to be chopped, crushed, or otherwise prepared with the aid of tools.[8] In the new open-country habitat, tools my also have been used to kill and butcher animals for food. Without tools, primates in general are not well equipped physically for regular hunting. Their teeth and jaws are not sharp and strong enough, and their speed afoot is not fast enough. So the use of tools to kill and butcher game might have enlarged even further the potential supply of food available in the environment.

Finally, tools may have been used as weapons against predators, which would have been a great threat to the relatively defenseless ground-dwelling proto-hominids. As Milford Wolpoff notes, "faced with a predator, a hominid who knew how to use a club for defense but did not have one available was just as dead as one to whom the notion never occurred."[9] In Wolpoff's opinion, it was the advantage of carrying weapons *continuously* that was responsible for transforming occasional bipedalism to completely bipedal locomotion.

[4] Gordon W. Hewes. "Food Transport and the Origin of Hominid Bipedalism." *American Anthropoligist*, 63 (1961): 687–710.

[5] Pat Shipman. "Scavenging or Hunting in Early Hominids: Theoretical Framework and Tests." *American Anthropologist*, 88 (1986): 27–43; Erik Trinkaus. "Bodies, Brawn, Brains and Noses: Human Ancestors and Human Predation." In M. H. Nitecki and D. V. Nitecki, eds., *The Evolution of Human Hunting*. New York: Plenum, 1987, p. 115 (pp. 107–45).

[6] C. Owen Lovejoy. "The Origin of Man." *Science*, January 23, 1981, pp. 341–50.

[7] Sherwood Washburn. "Tools and Human Evolution." *Scientific American*, September 1960, p. 63.

[8] David Pilbeam. *The Ascent of Man*. New York: Macmillan, 1972, p. 153.

[9] Milford H. Wolpoff. "Competitive Exclusion among Lower Pleistocene Hominids: The Single Species Hypothesis." *Man*, 6 (1971): 602.

But some anthropologists question the idea that tool use and toolmaking may have favored bipedalism. They point out that our first evidence of stone tools appears at least a million years *after* the emergence of bipedalism. So how could toolmaking be responsible for bipedalism? Wolpoff suggests an answer. Even though bipedalism appears to be at least a million years older than stone tools, it is not unlikely that proto-hominids used tools made of wood and bone, neither of which would be as likely as stone to survive in the archeological record. Moreover, unmodified stone tools present in the archeological record might not be recognizable as tools.[10]

All theories about the origin of bipedalism are, of course, speculative. We do not yet have direct evidence that any of the factors we have discussed were actually responsible for bipedalism. Any or all of these factors—being able to see far, carrying food back to a home base, carrying tools that included weapons—may explain the transformation of an occasionally bipedal proto-hominid to a completely bipedal hominid.

Expansion of the Brain

The first definitely bipedal hominids, the australopithecines, had relatively small cranial capacities, ranging from about 380 to 530 cubic centimeters (cc)—not much larger than that of chimpanzees. But around 2 million years ago, half a million years after stone tools appear, some hominids classified as members of our genus, *Homo*, had cranial capacities of about 750 cc. *Homo erectus* of about 1 million years ago had a cranial capacity of less than 1000 cc. Modern humans average slightly more than 1300 cc. Figure 4-1 illustrates the expansion of the brain.

Since the australopithecines were quite small, the later increase in brain size might have been a result of later hominids' bigger bodies. When we correct for body size, however, it turns out that brain size increased not only absolutely but also relatively after 2 million years ago. Between about 4 and 2 million years ago, relative brain size remained just about the same. Only in the last 2 million years has the hominid brain doubled in relative size (and tripled in absolute size).[11]

What may have favored the increase in brain size? Many anthropologists think that the increase is linked to the emergence of stone toolmaking between 2.5 and 2 million years ago. The reasoning is that stone toolmaking was important for the survival of our ancestors, and therefore natural selection would have favored bigger-brained individuals because they had motor and conceptual skills that enabled them to be better toolmakers. According to this

---

[10] M. H. Wolpoff. "Ramapithecus and Human Origins: An Anthropologist's Perspective of Changing Interpretations." In Russell L. Ciochon and Robert S. Corruccini, eds., *New Interpretations of Ape and Human Ancestry*. New York: Plenum, 1983, p. 666.

[11] Henry M. McHenry. "The Pattern of Human Evolution: Studies on Bipedalism, Mastication, and Encephalization." *Annual Review of Anthropology*, 11 (1982): 160–61.

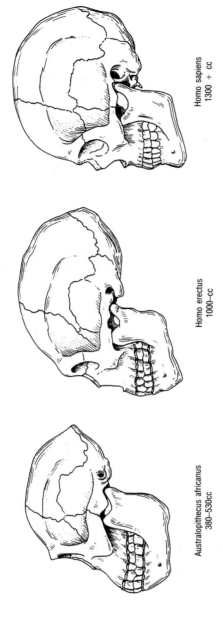

Australopithecus africanus
380–530cc

Homo erectus
1000–cc

Homo sapiens
1300 + cc

FIGURE 4-1 Comparison of the estimated cranial capacities in *Australopithecus africanus, Homo erectus,* and *Homo sapiens,* demonstrating the expansion of the brain in hominid evolution. (*Estimated cranial capacities from Ian Tattersall, Eric Delson, John Van Couvering, eds.* Encyclopedia of Human Evolution and Prehistory. *New York: Garland Publishing, 1988, pp. 80, 263, 268.*)

view, the expansion of the brain and more and more sophisticated toolmaking would have developed together. Other anthropologists think that the expansion of the brain may have been favored by other factors, such as warfare, hunting, longer life, and language.[12]

Whatever the factors selecting for bigger brains, natural selection also favored the widening of the female pelvis to allow larger-brained babies to be born. But there was probably a limit to how far the pelvis could widen and still be adapted to bipedalism. Something had to give, and that something was the degree of physical development of the human infant at birth: the human infant is born with cranial bones so plastic that they can overlap. Because birth takes place before the cranial bones have hardened, the human infant with its relatively large brain can pass through the opening in the mother's pelvis.

Reduction of the Face, Teeth, and Jaws

As in the case of the brain, substantial changes in the face, teeth, and jaws do not appear in hominid evolution until about 2 million years ago. Until then, the lower part of the face is quite protruding, the canines project beyond the other teeth (and there are spaces in the opposite jaw that the projecting canines fit into), males have much bigger canines than females, and the jaws are U-shaped (viewed from above or below) as in the apes. About 2 million years ago these traits begin to change. The australopithecines of that time have smaller canines (and no spaces in the opposite jaw for them to fit into), there is little difference between the male and female canines, and the jaws are now parobolic in shape, as in later hominids.[13]

In contrast with hominids in the genus *Homo* (the first examples of which are nearly 2 million years old), the australopithecines all have cheek teeth that are very large relative to their estimated body weight. This difference from *Homo* suggests that the australopithecines' diet may have been especially high in plant foods,[14] including small, tough objects such as seeds, roots, and tubers. The australopithecines also have relatively large faces that project forward below the eyes and thick jawbones. It is particularly in the *Homo* forms that we first see reductions in the size of the face, smaller cheek teeth, and smaller jaws.

Changes Not Firmly Dated

The fossil evidence, which we discuss shortly, suggests when (and in which hominids) changes occurred in brain size and in the face, teeth, and jaws. Other changes in the evolution of hominids cannot as yet be confidently dated

[12] Ibid., p. 162.
[13] Ibid., p. 158.
[14] David Pilbeam and Stephen Jay Gould. "Size and Scaling of Human Evolution." *Science*, December 6, 1974, p. 899.

with regard to time and particular hominid. For example, we know that modern humans are relatively hairless compared with the other surviving primates. But we do not know when hominids became relatively hairless, because fossilized bones do not tell us whether their owners were hairy. On the other hand, we suspect that most of the other characteristically human traits have developed after the brain began to increase in size (during the evolution of the genus *Homo*). These changes include the extension of the period of infant and child dependency, the scavenging and hunting of meat, the development of a division of labor by sex, and the sharing of food.

One of the possible consequences of brain expansion was the lessening of maturity at birth, as we have noted. That babies were born more immature may at least partially explain the lengthening of the period of infant and child dependency in hominids. Compared with other animals, we spend not only a longer proportion of our life span, but also the longest absolute period, in a dependent state. Prolonged infant dependency has probably been of great significance in human cultural evolution. According to Dobzhansky,

> it is this helplessness and prolonged dependence on the ministrations of the parents and other persons that favors in man the socialization and learning process on which the transmission of culture wholly depends. This may have been an overwhelming advantage of the human growth pattern in the process of evolution.[15]

Although some use of tools for digging, defense, scavenging, or hunting may have influenced the development of bipedalism, full bipedalism may have made possible more efficient toolmaking and consequently more efficient scavenging and hunting. As we shall see, there are archeological signs that early hominids may have been scavenging and/or hunting animals at least as far back as Lower Pleistocene times. We have fairly good evidence that *Homo erectus* was butchering and presumably eating big game after a million years ago. Whether or not the big game were hunted is not yet clear.

But whenever hominids began to hunt regularly, the development of hunting, combined with longer infant and child dependency, may have fostered a division of labor by sex: men doing the hunting while women tended the children and did other work closer to home. The demands of nursing might have made it difficult for women to hunt. Certainly, it would have been awkward, if not impossible, for a mother carrying a nursing child to chase animals. Alternatively, if she left the child at home, she would not have been able to travel very far to hunt. Since the men would have been free to roam farther from home, they probably became the hunters. While the men were away hunting, the women may have gathered wild plants within an area that could be covered in a few hours.

---

[15] Theodosius Dobzhansky. *Mankind Evolving: The Evolution of the Human Species.* New Haven: Yale University Press, 1962, p. 196.

The division of labor by sex may have given rise to another distinctively human characteristic: the sharing of food. If men primarily hunted and women primarily gathered plant foods, the only way each sex could obtain a complete diet would have been to share the results of their respective labors.

What is the evidence that the physical and cultural changes we have been discussing occurred during the evolution of the hominids? We shall now trace the sequence of known hominid fossils and how they are associated with the development of bipedalism, brain expansion, and reduction of the face, jaws, and teeth. We also trace the sequence of cultural changes in toolmaking, scavenging and hunting, and other aspects of cultural development.

AUSTRALOPITHECINES: THE EARLIEST DEFINITE HOMINIDS

Recent fossil finds from Hadar, in the Afar triangle of Ethiopia, and Laetoli, Tanzania, clearly show that bipedal hominids lived in East Africa between 4 and 3 million years ago. At Laetoli, more than fifty hardened humanlike footprints about 3.6 million years old give striking confirmation that the hominids there were fully bipedal. But their bipedalism does not mean that these earliest definite hominids were completely terrestrial. Recent studies of the skeletal remains at Hadar suggest that the hominids there spent part of the time in trees, possibly feeding, sleeping, and/or avoiding predators. All of the australopithecines, including the later ones, seem to have been capable of climbing and moving in trees.[16]

The hominids at Hadar and Laetoli are classified by some paleontologists as belonging to the species *Australopithecus afarensis*. Other paleontologists do not think that these hominids should be placed in a separate species, because of their resemblances to the later hominid species *Australopithecus africanus*, which lived between about 3 and 2 million years ago. And then there were the robust australopithecines who lived between 2 and 1 million years ago. Some paleontologists classify all the robust specimens, from East as well as South Africa, as *Australopithecus robustus*. But most paleontologists think that the East and South African specimens belonged to two different species; the East African species is called *Australopithecus boisei* and the South African species is called *A. robustus*. Current thinking, then, divides the genus *Australopithecus* into two, three, or four species.[17] (Figure 4-2 shows the locations of the major sites where early hominids have been found.)

[16] Randall L. Susman, Jack T. Stern, Jr., and William L. Jungers. "Locomotor Adaptations in the Hadar Hominids." In Eric Delson, ed., *Ancestors: The Hard Evidence*. New York: Alan R. Liss, 1985, pp. 184–92. See also Rose, "Food Acquisition and the Evolution of Positional Behaviour."

[17] Niles Eldredge and Ian Tattersall. *The Myths of Human Evolution*. New York: Columbia University Press, 1982, pp. 131–41.

0   600
miles

Hadar

Koobi Fora
Omo
Peninj
Olduvai
Laetoli

Makapansgat
Taung   Sterkfontein
Swartkrans and
Kromdraai

FIGURE 4-2   Locations of Major *Australopithecus* and *Homo* Sites in East and South Africa

Australopithecus afarensis

The candidates for *A. afarensis* status come from two separate excavations.[18] Remains from at least fourteen hominids were unearthed at Laetoli, Tanzania. Although the remains there consisted largely of teeth and jaws, there is no question that the Laetoli hominids were bipedal, since it was at the Laetoli site that the now famous trail of footprints was found. Two hominids walking erect and side by side left their tracks in the ground 3.6 million years ago! The remains of at least thirty-five individuals have been found at Hadar. The Hadar finds are quite remarkable for their completeness. Whereas paleontologists often find just parts of the cranium and jaws, many parts of the rest of the skeleton were also found at Hadar. For example, paleontologists found 40 percent of the skeleton of a female hominid they named Lucy after the Beatles' song "Lucy in the Sky with Diamonds."[19] An analysis of Lucy's pelvis indicates clearly that she was a bipedal walker;[20] but she probably also climbed

---

[18] Donald C. Johanson and Tim D. White. "A Systematic Assessment of Early African Hominids." *Science*, January 26, 1979, pp. 321–30; and Tim D. White, "Les Australopithèques." *La Recherche*, November 1982, pp. 1258–70.

[19] Donald C. Johanson and Maitland Edey. *Lucy: The Beginnings of Humankind.* New York: Simon & Schuster, 1981, pp. 17–18.

[20] C. Owen Lovejoy. "Evolution of Human Walking." *Scientific American*, November 1988, pp. 118–25.

a lot in the trees, judging by her leg bones and joints which are not as large proportionately as in modern humans.[21]

Those paleontologists who believe the Laetoli and Hadar hominids should be given the separate species name *A. afarensis* base their decision primarily on some features of the skull, teeth, and jaws that they believe are more apelike than those of the later hominids previously classified as *A. africanus*. For example, the incisors and canines of the Laetoli and Hadar hominids are rather large and their tooth rows are typically straight (not forming a parabolic arch). The canines of *A. afarensis* project beyond the other teeth, and there is a space in the opposite jaw that the projecting canine fits into. Furthermore, as in the apes, males have much bigger canines than females.[22]

Individuals are quite small. Lucy, for example, was about 3.5 feet tall, and the largest individuals at these sites, presumably males, were about 5 feet tall.[23] The brains of the Laetoli and Hadar hominids also tend to be small: cranial capacity is estimated at 415 cc, just slightly less than that of later australopithecines classified as *A. africanus*.[24]

Australopithecus africanus

From the remains of hundreds of finds, a fairly complete picture of *A. africanus* can be drawn. The estimated cranial capacity is between 428 and 485 cc. In contrast, modern humans have a cranial capacity of between 1000 and 2000 cc.[25] *A. africanus* was quite small: the adults were only about 3.5 to 4.5 feet tall and weighed about 45 to 90 pounds.[26] *A. africanus* retained the large chinless jaw of the ape, but its dental features were similar to those of modern humans—broad incisors, short canines, and a parabolic dental arch. Though the premolars and molars were larger than in modern humans, their form was quite similar.

The broad, bowl-shaped pelvis, which is very similar to the human pelvis in form and in areas for muscle attachments, provides evidence for bipedalism. In both *A. africanus* and modern humans, the pelvis curves back, carrying

[21] William L. Jungers, "Relative Joint Size and Hominoid Locomotor Adaptations with Implications for the Evolution of Hominid Bipedalism." *Journal of Human Evolution*, 17 (1988): 247–65.

[22] Tim D. White, Donald C. Johanson, and William H. Kimbel. *"Australopithecus africanus: Its Phyletic Position Reconsidered." South African Journal of Science*, 77 (1981): 445–70; and Johanson and White. "A Systematic Assessment of Early African Hominids."

[23] Bernard G. Campbell. *Humankind Emerging*, 4th ed. Boston: Little, Brown, 1985, p. 202.

[24] McHenry. "The Pattern of Human Evolution," p. 161.

[25] Ralph Holloway. "The Casts of Fossil Hominid Brains." *Scientific American*, July 1974, pp. 106–15.

[26] Frederick S. Szalay and Eric Delson. *Evolutionary History of the Primates*. New York: Academic Press, 1979, p. 504.

the spine and trunk erect. In contrast, the ape's pelvis does not curve back; the spine and trunk are carried forward.

The shape of the curve of the australopithecine spine also suggests that these hominids walked erect. Analysis of hip-joint and femoral-bone fossils further indicates that the australopithecines walked fully upright, and that at least the later ones walked with the same direct, striding gait observed in modern humans.[27]

Australopithecus Robustus and Boisei

Paleontologists may disagree about whether *A. afarensis* is separate from *A. africanus*. But there is little disagreement that at least one other australopithecine species—a robust species, *Australopithecus robustus*—existed between about 2 and 1 million years ago. Robust australopithecines were found first in South Africa and later in East Africa. As we noted above, the East and South African robust australopithecines are sometimes classified together as *A. robustus*; more often the later and even more robust East African finds are classified as *Australopithecus boisei*. In contrast to *A. africanus*, the robust australopithecines had larger molars and premolars, smaller incisors and canines, and well-developed cranial crests and ridges. Whereas *A. africanus* individuals are estimated to have weighed 45 to 90 pounds, *A. robustus* individuals are estimated to have weighed 80 to 120 pounds. And whereas *A. africanus* was 3.5 to 4.5 feet tall, *A. robustus* was 4.5 to 5 + feet tall. *A. robustus* was larger not only in height but also in its thicker cranial bones and more robust upper-arm and shoulder bones.[28]

It used to be thought that the *africanus* and *robustus* species might have had different dietary adaptations, *africanus* being a meat-eater and *robustus* a vegetarian. But this view is now largely rejected. There is no significant difference in tooth-wear patterns suggesting a meat-eating/vegetarian contrast. And since both *A. africanus* and *A. robustus* had relatively large cheek teeth too, it would seem that both depended mostly on a vegetable diet.[29] The robust australopithecines are not believed to be ancestral to our own genus, *Homo*.[30]

There is considerable agreement among paleontologists about these aspects of early hominid evolution: (1) there were at least two separate hominid lines between 3 and 1 million years ago; (2) the robust australopithecines were not ancestral to modern humans but became extinct after a million years ago; and (3) *Homo habilis* (and successive *Homo* species) were in the direct ancestral line to modern humans.

---

[27] C. Owen Lovejoy, Kingsbury Heiple, and Albert Bernstein. "The Gait of *Australopithecus*." *American Journal of Physical Anthropology*, 38 (1973): 757–79.

[28] Szalay and Delson. *Evolutionary History of the Primates*, p. 504.

[29] Ibid., pp. 504–8; and Pilbeam and Gould. "Size and Scaling in Human Evolution."

[30] C. Stringer. "Evolution of a Species." *Geographical Magazine*, 57 (1985): 601–7.

EARLY SPECIES OF *HOMO*

Hominids with a brain absolutely and relatively larger than that of the australopithecines appear about 2 million years ago. These hominids, classified in
our own genus, *Homo*, are generally called **Homo habilis** after the fossils
found in East Africa and named by Louis Leakey, Phillip Tobias, and John
Napier. (Less than half a million years later a larger-brained species, *Homo
erectus*, appears in East Africa.) Apparently, the robust australopithecines
were contemporaneous with both *Homo habilis* and *Homo erectus* in East
Africa.[31] Compared with the australopithecines, *Homo habilis* was slightly
larger and had a significantly larger brain (ranging from 600 to 800 cc) and
more rounded brain case.[32]

Stone tools found at a number of sites in East Africa are at least 2 million
years old.[33] Some anthropologists surmise that *Homo habilis*, rather than the
australopithecines, made those tools. After all, H. *habilis* had the greater brain
capacity. But the fact of the matter is that none of the earliest stone tools have
been found directly associated with fossils, and so it is impossible as yet to
know who made them. We turn now to those tools and what archeologists
guess about the life styles of their makers, the hominids (whoever they were)
who lived between about 2 and 1.5 million years ago.

EARLY HOMINID CULTURES

Tool Traditions

Regularly patterned tools are considered by some to be archeological signs of
culture because *culture* is conventionally defined as learned and shared patterns of behavior, thought, and feeling. Therefore, tools made according to a
standard pattern and found in different places presuppose some culture. The
earliest patterned stone tools found so far come from Hadar, Ethiopia, and
may be 2.4 million years old.[34] More securely dated stone tools have been
found in Omo, Ethiopia, from about 2 million years ago.[35] These early tools
were apparently made by striking a stone with another stone, a technique
known as **percussion flaking**. Both the sharp-edged flakes and the sharp-

[31] Noel T. Boaz. "Hominid Evolution in Eastern Africa during the Pliocene and Early Pleis-
tocene." *Annual Review of Anthropology*, 8 (1979): 73, 78.
[32] Ibid., p. 77; and N. T. Boaz. "Morphological Trends and Phylogenetic Relationships from
Middle Miocene Hominoids to Late Pliocene Hominids." In Ciochon and Corruccini, eds.,
New Interpretations of Ape and Human Ancestry, pp. 714–15.
[33] Glynn Ll. Isaac. "The Archaeology of Human Origins: Studies of the Lower Pleistocene in East
Africa, 1971–1981." In Fred Wendorf and Angela E. Close, eds., *Advances in World
Archaeology*. Orlando, Fla.: Academic Press, 1984, 3: 7–8.
[34] Roger Lewin. "Ethiopian Stone Tools Are World's Oldest." *Science*, February 20, 1981, pp.
806–7.
[35] Isaac. "The Archaeology of Human Origins," pp. 7–8.

edged cores (the pieces of stone left after flakes are removed) were used as tools. If the stone has facets removed from only one side of the cutting edge, we call it a **unifacial tool**. If the stone has facets removed from both sides, we call it a **bifacial tool**.

What were these tools used for? What do they tell us about early hominid culture? Unfortunately, little can be inferred about life styles from the earliest tool sites because little else is found with the tools. In contrast, finds of later tool assemblages at Olduvai Gorge in Tanzania have yielded a rich harvest of cultural information.

The Olduvai site was uncovered accidentally in 1911 when a German entomologist chasing a butterfly followed it into the gorge and found a number of fossil remains. Beginning in the 1930s, Louis and Mary Leakey patiently searched the gorge for clues to the evolution of early humans. Of the Olduvai site, Louis Leakey wrote,

> [It] is a fossil hunter's dream, for it shears 300 feet through stratum after stratum of earth's history as through a gigantic layer cake. Here, within reach, lie countless fossils and artifacts which but for the faulting and erosion would have remained sealed under thick layers of consolidated rock.[36]

The oldest cultural materials from Olduvai (Bed I) date from Lower Pleistocene times. The stone *artifacts* (things made by humans) include bifacial and unifacial core tools and sharp-edged flakes. Flake tools predominate. The kind of tool assemblage found in Bed I and to some extent in later (higher) layers is referred to as **Oldowan**.[37]

Life Styles

Archeologists have speculated about the possible life styles of early hominids from Olduvai and other sites. Some of these speculations come from analysis of what can be done with the tools, microscopic analysis of wear on the tools, and examination of the marks the tools make on bones; other speculations are based on what is found with the tools.

Nicholas Toth and Peter Jones have experimented with what can be done with Oldowan tools. The flakes appear to be very versatile: they can be used for slitting the hides of animals, dismembering animals, and whittling wood into sharp-pointed sticks (wooden spears or digging sticks). The larger stone tools (choppers and scrapers) can be used to hack off branches or perform rough butchery.[38] None of the early flaked stone tools can plausibly be thought of as a weapon. So, if the toolmaking hominids were hunting or defending themselves with weapons, they had to have used wooden spears,

[36] L. S. B. Leakey. "Finding the World's Earliest Man." *National Geographic*, September 1960, p. 424.
[37] Desmond Clark. *The Prehistory of Africa*. New York: Praeger, 1970, p. 68.
[38] Reported in Isaac, "The Archaeology of Human Origins," pp. 11–13.

clubs, or unmodified stones as missiles. Later Oldowan tool assemblages also include stones that were flaked and battered into a rounded shape. The unmodified stones and the shaped stones might have been lethal projectiles.[39]

Experiments may tell us what can be done with tools, but of course they do not tell us what was actually done with them. Other techniques, such as microscopic analysis of the wear on tools, are more informative. Lawrence Keeley has analyzed the kind of "polish" that develops on tools with different uses and has shown that at least some of the early tools were used for cutting meat, cutting or whittling wood, and cutting plant stems.[40]

There seems to be no question that some hominids shortly after 2 million years ago were cutting up animal carcasses for meat, But were they scavenging meat (taking meat from carcasses that other animals had killed)? Or were they themselves hunting and killing the animals? Based on her analysis of cut marks on bone from Bed I in Olduvai Gorge, Pat Shipman suggests that scavenging, not hunting, was the major meat-getting activity of the hominids living there between 2 and 1.7 million years ago. For example, cut marks made by stone tools usually (but not always) overlie teeth marks made by carnivores, which suggests that the hominids were often procuring the meat of animals killed and partially eaten by predators. However, the fact that the cut marks were sometimes made first suggests to Shipman that the hominids were also sometimes the hunters.[41] On the other hand, prior cut marks may indicate only that the hominids scavenged before the carnivores!

The artifact and animal remains from Bed I and the lower part of Bed II at Olduvai suggest a few other things about the life styles of the hominids there. First, it seems that the hominids moved around during the year; most of the sites in what is now the Olduvai Gorge appear to have been used only in the dry season, judging from an analysis of the kinds of animal bones found there.[42] Second, whether or not the early Olduvai hominids were hunters or more likely scavengers, they apparently exploited a wide range of animals. Although most of the bones are from medium-sized antelopes and wild pigs, even large animals such as elephants and giraffes seem to have been eaten.[43] It is clear that the Olduvai hominids scavenged and/or hunted for meat, but we cannot tell yet how important meat-eating was in their diet.

There is also no consensus yet about how to characterize the Olduvai

---

[39] Ibid., p. 13.
[40] Reported in ibid.
[41] Shipman. "Scavenging or Hunting in Early Hominids," pp. 27–43. For the idea that scavenging may have been an important food-getting strategy even for proto-hominids, see Frederick S. Szalay, "Hunting-Scavenging Protohominids: A Model for Hominid Origins," *Man*, 10 (1975): 420–29.
[42] John D. Speth and Dave D. Davis. "Seasonal Variability in Early Hominid Predation." *Science*, April 30, 1976, pp. 441–45.
[43] Glynn Isaac. "The Diet of Early Man: Aspects of Archaeological Evidence from Lower and Middle Pleistocene Sites in Africa." *World Archaeology*, 2 (1971): 289.

sites. In the 1970s, there was a tendency to think of these sites (which contain tools and animal bones) as home bases to which hominids (presumably male) brought meat to share with others (perhaps mostly nursing mothers and young children). In short, the scenario involved a home base, a division of labor by sex, and food sharing. But archeologists now are not so sure; the sites might just have been places where hominids ate, not stayed. (After all, we don't live in restaurants!) But the fact that mostly limb bones from food animals are found together with tools at the sites suggests that the hominids deliberately brought scavenged or hunted meat to these places.[44] So the evidence from Olduvai does not necessarily indicate a scenario of home base, division of labor by sex, and food sharing; on the other hand, it does not rule out such a scenario.

HOMO ERECTUS

Until recently, fossil finds in Java and China suggested that **Homo erectus** was not more than about 700,000 years old. But in 1975 near Lake Rudolf in Kenya, Richard Leakey's team found a *Homo erectus* cranium that was 1.6 to 1.3 million years old. Thus, the evidence now suggests that *Homo erectus* emerged in East Africa, rather than in Asia as previously thought.[45]

The Discovery in Java and Later Finds

In 1891, Eugene Dubois, a Dutch anatomist digging in Java, found what he called **Pithecanthropus erectus**, meaning "erect ape man." (We now refer to this hominid as *Homo erectus*.) The discovery was not the first humanlike fossil found—Neanderthals, which we discuss in the next chapter, were known many years earlier. But no one was certain, not even Dubois himself, whether the fossil he found in Java was an ape or a human.

The actual find consisted of a cranium and a thighbone. For many years it was thought that the fragments were not even from the same animal. The skull was too large to be that of a modern ape but was smaller than that of an average human, having a cranial capacity between the average ape's 500 cc and the average modern human's 1300+ cc. The thighbone, however, matched that of a modern human. Did the two fragments in fact belong together? The question was resolved many years later by fluorine analysis. The amount of fluorine that accumulates in bones increases the longer the bones lie in the earth. If fossils from the same deposit contain the same

---

[44] Isaac. "The Archaeology of Human Origins," pp. 31–32, 61–68.
[45] R. E. F. Leakey. "An Overview of the East Rudolf Hominidae." In Yves Coppens, F. Clark Howell, Glynn Ll. Isaac, and Richard E. F. Leakey, eds., *Earliest Man and Environments in the Lake Rudolf Basin.* Chicago: University of Chicago Press, 1976, pp. 476–83; and G. H. Curtis, R. Drake, T. E. Cerling, and J. Hampel. "Age of the KBS Tuff in the Koobi Fora Formation, East Rudolf, Kenya." *Nature*, 258 (1975): 395–98.

amount of fluorine, they are the same age; if they contain different amounts, fluorine analysis can establish their relative ages. The skull fragment and thighbone found by Dubois were tested for fluorine content and found to be the same age.

We now know from a large number of finds that *Homo erectus* was the first hominid species to be widely distributed in the Old World. Appearing first about 1.6 million years ago in East Africa and then about 1 million years ago in Asia, *Homo erectus* may also have spread to Europe. However, some anthropologists think that the finds in Europe thought to be *Homo erectus* are actually early examples of *Homo sapiens*, just like some of the finds in southern Africa and the Near East that were also previously thought to be *Homo erectus*.[46]

Physical Characteristics
of *Homo Erectus*

The *Homo erectus* skull generally was long, low, and thickly walled, with a flat frontal area and prominent brow ridges. Compared to the australopithecines, *Homo erectus* had relatively small teeth. The brain was larger than that found in any of the australopithecines but smaller than the average brain of a modern human.[47] *Homo erectus* had a prominent, projecting nose, in contrast to the australopithecines' flat, nonprojecting noses.[48] From the neck down, *Homo erectus* was practically indistinguishable from *Homo sapiens*. The size of the long bones indicates that a *Homo erectus* male was about 5.5 to 6 feet tall.

The remains from near Peking (now Beijing) are perhaps 500,000 years more recent than the remains from Java. Consistent with the general trends in hominid evolution, the Peking specimens had higher and less sloping foreheads, and their cranial capacity was about 1054 cc, compared with the 900 cc average for the Java specimens.[49] *Homo erectus* from Peking had a shorter, rounder palate than the Java forms. Thus, the Peking *erectus* face resembled more closely the modern human face, but the jaw did not have a chin. The teeth in the Peking jaw were smaller than those of the australopithecines and the Java *erectus* specimens. The smaller teeth in the Peking specimens, especially the smaller canines, may be related to the use of fire for cooking.

Homo Erectus Cultures

The archeological finds of tools and other cultural artifacts dating from 1.6 million years ago to about 300,000 to 100,000 years ago are assumed to have been produced by *Homo erectus*. But we do not usually have fossils associated

---

[46] Milford H. Wolpoff and Abel Nkini. "Early and Early Middle Pleistocene Hominids from Asia and Africa." In Delson, ed., *Ancestors*, pp. 202–5. See also G. P. Rightmire, "The Tempo of Change in the Evolution of Mid-Pleistocene *Homo*," in Delson, ed., *Ancestors*, pp. 255–64.

[47] Ian Tattersall. *Man's Ancestors*. London: John Murray, 1970, pp. 51–54.

[48] Robert G. Franciscus and Erik Trinkaus. "Nasal Morphology and the Emergence of *Homo erectus*." *American Journal of Physical Anthropology*, 75 (1988): 517–27.

[49] Wu Rukang and Lin Shenglong. "Peking Man." *Scientific American*, June 1983, p. 90.

with these materials. Therefore it is possible that some of the tools during this period were produced by hominids other than *Homo erectus*, such as australopithecines earlier and *Homo sapiens* later. Since the so-called Acheulian tool assemblages dating from 1.5 million years ago to more than a million years later are very similar to each other, and since *Homo erectus* is the only hominid that spans the entire period, it is conventionally assumed that *erectus* was responsible for most if not all of the Acheulian tool assemblages we describe below.[50]

The Use of Fire

Suggestive but not conclusive evidence of the deliberate use of fire comes from Kenya in East Africa and is over 1.4 million years old.[51] Better evidence of human control of fire comes from China and Europe after about 500,000 years ago. Some have suggested that humans spread out of Africa into areas with freezing winters only when they began to control fire.

Fire was not only important for warmth; it also made cooking possible. Thousands of splintered and charred animal bones found in the Zhoukoudian caves (near Peking) may be the remains of meals. Where or when the use of fire began is not known. The most reasonable guess is that naturally occurring fires, produced by volcanoes and lightning, may have been used by *Home erectus* to sustain and start other fires. The control of fire was a major step in increasing the energy under human control. Cooking with fire made all kinds of possible food (not just meat) more safely digestible and therefore more usable. Fires would also have kept predators away.

The Acheulian Tool Tradition

A stone toolmaking tradition known as the **Acheulian**, after the site at St. Acheul, France, where the first examples were found, is generally associated with *Homo erectus*. This tradition appears first in East Africa about 1.5 million years ago,[52] and it persists in later times when *Homo sapiens* was on the scene. Perhaps because they had begun to use fire, humans with an Acheulian culture may have been the first to move out of the tropics and subtropics and into temperate areas such as Europe and East Asia. Acheulian stone-tool assemblages are characterized by a wide variety of small and large tools, including small flakes (which may have been used for butchering) and large bifacial implements such as the so-called hand axes (which may have been used for digging or pounding).

During the Acheulian period, a technique developed that enabled the toolmaker to produce flake tools of a predetermined size instead of simply chipping flakes away from the core at random. In this **Levalloisian** method,

[50] David W. Phillipson. *African Archaeology*. Cambridge: Cambridge University Press, 1985, p. 55.
[51] Isaac. "The Archaeology of Human Origins," pp. 35–36.
[52] Phillipson. *African Archaeology*, p. 32.

the toolmaker first shaped the core and prepared a "striking platform" at one end. Flakes of predetermined and standard sizes could then be knocked off.

Big-Game Eating

Some of the Acheulian sites have produced evidence of big-game eating. F. Clark Howell, who excavated the sites at Torralba and Ambrona, Spain, found a substantial number of elephant remains and unmistakable evidence of human presence in the form of fire and tools. Howell suggests that *Homo erectus* at those sites used fire to frighten elephants into muddy bogs, from which they would be unable to escape.[53] To hunt elephants in this way, these hominids would have had to plan and work cooperatively in fairly large groups. But do these finds of bones of large and medium-size animals, in association with tools, tell us that *Homo erectus* was a big-game hunter? Some archeologists who have reanalyzed the evidence form Torralba think that the big game may have been scavenged. Because the Torralba and Ambrona sites are near ancient streams, many of the elephants could have died naturally— their bones accumulating in certain spots because of the flow of water.[54] Thus, whether *Homo erectus* hunted big game at Torralba and Ambrona is debatable, but the people there probably at least consumed big game as well as hunted smaller game.

The cultures of early hominids are traditionally classified as Lower Paleolithic or early Stone Age. In the next chapters, we discuss the emergence of *Homo sapiens* and cultural developments in the Middle and Upper Paleolithic periods.

SUMMARY

1. The drying trend in climate that began about 16 to 11 million years ago diminished the African rain forests and gave rise to grasslands. This change reduced the habitats for tree dwellers and created selective pressures for terrestrial adaptation— pressures that favored bipedalism.
2. One of the crucial changes in early hominid evolution was the development of bipedalism. There are several theories for this development: it may have increased the emerging hominid's ability to see predators and potential prey while moving through the tall grasses of the savanna; by freeing the hands for carrying it may have facilitated transferring food from one place to another; and finally, tool use, which requires free hands, may have favored two-legged walking.
3. Other important physical changes—including the expansion of the brain, modification of the female pelvis to allow bigger-brained babies to be born, and reduction of the face, teeth, and jaws—did not begin until about 2 million years after the

[53] F. Clark Howell. "Observations on the Earlier Phases of the European Lower Paleolithic." In *Recent Studies in Paleoanthropology. American Anthropologist*, special publication, April 1966, pp. 111–40.
[54] Richard G. Klein. "Reconstructing How Early People Exploited Animals: Problems and Prospects." In Nitecki and Nitecki, eds., *The Evolution of Human Hunting*, pp. 11–45; and Lewis R. Binford. "Were There Elephant Hunters at Torralba?" In Nitecki and Nitecki, eds., *The Evolution of Human Hunting*, pp. 47–105.

emergence of bipedalism. By that time (about 2 million years ago) hominids had come to depend to some extent on scavenging and possibly hunting meat.

4. Undisputed hominids dating back to between 4 and 3 million years ago have been found in East Africa. These definitely bipedal hominids are now generally classified in the genus *Australopithecus*. Some East African hominids nearly 2 million years old are classified as *Homo habilis*, an early species of our own genus, *Homo*.

5. The earliest patterned stone tools date back 2.5 to 2 million years. We do not yet know who made them. These tools were made by striking a stone with another stone to remove sharp-edged flakes. Both the flakes and the sharp-edged cores were used as tools. This early tool tradition is named Oldowan.

6. *Homo erectus*, with a larger brain capacity than *Homo habilis*, emerged about 1.6 million years ago. The earliest *erectus* finds are from East Africa. *H. erectus* specimens date back about 1 million years in Asia and are more recent in Europe. The tools and other cultural artifacts from about 1.5 million to about 300,000 years ago probably were produced by *Homo erectus*; Acheulian is the name given to the tool tradition of this period. Acheulian tools include both small flake tools and large tools (including hand axes and cleavers). Flake tools of a pre-determined size were produced during the Acheulian. There is evidence that *Homo erectus* had learned to control fire, which would have made it possible to survive freezing winters in temperate regions, and there is evidence in some sites of big-game eating and possibly hunting.

5

The Emergence of *Homo sapiens* and Their Cultures

Humans who looked very much like people living now appeared at least 50,000 years ago and possibly earlier. How do we know that they looked like modern people? Obviously only by skeletal remains. One paleontologist, Chris Stringer, characterizes the modern human as having "a domed skull, a chin, small eyebrows [brow ridges] and a rather puny skeleton."[1] Some of us might not like to be called "puny," but modern humans are definitely puny compared with *Homo erectus* (and even with earlier forms of our species, *Homo sapiens*). In this chapter we discuss the fossil evidence for the transition from *Homo erectus* to modern humans, which may have begun 500,000 years ago. We also discuss what we know archeologically about the cultures of *Homo sapiens* who lived from about 150,000 to between 14,000 and 10,000 years ago.

THE TRANSITION FROM *HOMO ERECTUS* TO *HOMO SAPIENS*

Most anthropologists agree that *Homo erectus* evolved into *Homo sapiens*. But there is disagreement about how and where the transition occurred. There is also disagreement about how to classify some fossils from 500,000 to about 200,000 years ago that have a mixture of *Homo erectus* and *Homo sapiens* traits.[2]

[1] C. Stringer. "Evolution of a Species." *Geographical Magazine*, 57 (1985): 601–7.
[2] Ibid.

A particular fossil might be called *Homo erectus* by some anthropologists and "archaic" *Homo sapiens* by others. And, as we shall see, still other anthropologists see so much continuity between *Homo erectus* and *Homo sapiens* that they think it is completely arbitrary to call them different species; according to these anthropologists, *H. erectus* and *H. sapiens* may just be earlier and later varieties of the same species.

The fossils with mixed traits have been found in Africa, Europe, and Asia. For example, a specimen from the Broken Hill mine in Zambia, central Africa, dates from about 200,000 years ago. Its mixed traits include a cranial capacity of over 1200 cc (well within the range of modern *Homo sapiens*) together with a low forehead and large brow ridges, which are characteristic of earlier *Homo erectus* specimens.[3] Other fossils with mixed traits have been found at Bodo, Hopefield, Ndutu, Elandsfontein, and Rabat in Africa; Heidelberg, Bilzingsleben, Petralona, Arago, Steinheim, and Swanscombe in Europe; and Dali and Solo in Asia.

NEANDERTALS AND OTHER DEFINITE *HOMO SAPIENS*

There may be disagreement about how to classify the mixed-trait fossils from 500,000 to 200,000 years ago, but there is hardly any disagreement about the fossils that are less than 200,000 years old. Nearly all anthropologists agree that they were definitely *Homo sapiens*. Mind you, these early definite *Homo sapiens* did not look completely like modern humans. But they were not so different from us either, not even the ones called Neandertals, after the valley in Germany where the first evidence of them was found.

Somehow, through the years Neandertals have become the victims of their cartoon image, which usually misrepresents them as burly and more ape than human. Actually, they might go unnoticed in a cross section of the world's population today.

In 1856, three years before Darwin's publication of *The Origin of Species*, a skullcap and other fossilized bones were discovered in a cave in the Neander Valley (*Tal* is the German word for valley) near Dusseldorf, Germany. The fossils in the Neander Valley were the first that scholars could tentatively consider as an early hominid. (The fossils classified as *Homo erectus* were not found until later in the nineteenth century, and the fossils belonging to the genus *Australopithecus* were not found until the twentieth century.) After Darwin's revolutionary work was published, the Neandertal find aroused considerable controversy. A few evolutionist scholars, such as Thomas Huxley, thought that the Neandertal was not that different from modern humans. Others dismissed the Neandertal as irrelevant to human evolution; they saw it as a pathological freak, a peculiar, disease-ridden individual. However, simi-

---

[3] G. Philip Rightmire. "*Homo sapiens* in Sub-Saharan Africa." In Fred H. Smith and Frank Spencer, eds., *The Origins of Modern Humans: A World Survey of the Fossil Evidence*. New York: Alan R. Liss, 1984, p. 303.

lar fossils turned up later in Belgium, Yugoslavia, France, and elsewhere in Europe, which meant that the original Neandertal find could not be dismissed as an oddity.[4]

The dominant reaction to the original and subsequent Neandertal-like finds was that the Neandertals were too "brutish" and "primitive" to have possibly been ancestral to modern humans. This view prevailed in the scholarly community until well into the 1950s. A major proponent of this view was Marcellin Boule, who claimed between 1908 and 1913 that the Neandertals would not have been capable of complete bipedalism. Since the 1950s, however, a number of studies have disputed Boule's claim, and it is now generally agreed that the skeletal traits of the Neandertals are completely consistent with bipedalism. Perhaps more important, when the much more ancient australopithecine and *Homo erectus* fossils were accepted as hominids in the 1940s and 1950s, anthropologists realized that the Neandertals did not look that different from modern humans—despite their sloping foreheads, large brow ridges, flattened braincases, large jaws, and nearly absent chins.[5] After all, they did have larger brains than modern humans on the average.[6]

It took almost 100 years to accept the idea that Neandertals were not that different from modern humans and therefore should be classified as *Homo sapiens neanderthalensis*. But, as we shall see, there is still debate over whether the Neandertals in western Europe were ancestral to modern-looking people who lived later in western Europe, after about 40,000 years ago. In any case, Neandertals lived in other places besides western Europe. A large number of fossils from central Europe (Yugoslavia, Czechoslovakia, Hungary) strongly resemble those from western Europe, although some features, such as a projecting midface, are less pronounced.[7] Neandertals have also been found in southwestern Asia (Israel, Iraq) and Central Asia (Soviet Uzbekistan). One of the largest collections of Neandertal fossils comes from Shanidar Cave in the mountains of northeastern Iraq, where Ralph Solecki unearthed the skeletons of nine individuals.[8]

The Neandertals have received a great deal of scholarly and popular attention, probably because they were the first premodern humans to be found. But we now know that other premodern *Homo sapiens*, some perhaps older than Neandertals, lived elsewhere in the Old World—in East, South, and North Africa as well as in Java and China.[9] These other premodern but definite *Homo sapiens* are sometimes considered Neandertal-like, but more

[4] Frank Spencer. "The Neandertals and Their Evolutionary Significance: A Brief Historical Survey." In Smith and Spencer, eds., *The Origins of Modern Humans*, pp. 1–50.

[5] Erik Trinkaus. "Pathology and the Posture of the La Chapelle-aux-Saints Neandertal." *American Journal of Physical Anthropology*, 67, (1985): 19–41.

[6] Spencer. "The Neandertals and Their Evolutionary Significance," p. 20.

[7] Fred H. Smith. "Fossil Hominids from the Upper Pleistocene of Central Europe and the Origin of Modern Humans." In Smith and Spencer, eds., *The Origins of Modern Humans*, p. 187.

[8] Erik Trinkaus. "Western Asia." In Smith and Spencer, eds., *The Origins of Modern Humans*, pp. 251–53.

[9] See various chapters in Smith and Spencer, eds., *The Origins of Modern Humans*.

often they are named after the places where they were found (as indeed the original Neandertal was). For example, the cranium from China called *Homo sapiens daliensis* was named after the Chinese county (Dali) in which it was found in 1978.[10]

MIDDLE PALEOLITHIC CULTURES

The period of cultural history associated with the Neandertals is traditionally called the Middle Paleolithic in Europe and the Near East and dates from about 100,000 to about 40,000 years ago. For Africa, the term *Middle Stone Age* is used instead of *Middle Paleolithic* for the period that ends around the same time but begins perhaps as early as 200,000 years ago. The tool assemblages from this period are generally referred to as *Mousterian* in Europe and the Near East, and as *post-Acheulian* in Africa.

Tool Assemblages

The Mousterian. The **Mousterian** type of tool complex is named after the tool assemblage found in a rock-shelter at Le Moustier in the Dordogne region of France. A Mousterian tool assemblage differs from an Acheulian assemblage in that the Mousterian has a higher proportion of flake tools. Neandertals seem to have improved the flaking techniques of *Homo erectus*. Earlier, the core was carefully shaped by percussion flaking (it was a *prepared core*) before the flake was struck off. In this way, the toolmaker could control the size and shape of the flake desired and thus produce different types of tools. The Mousterian technique of producing flakes is basically the same as the Acheulian in that a prepared core and percussion flaking were used. But with the Mousterian technique, instead of obtaining only two or three long, large flakes, the toolmaker flaked until the core was almost used up. The flakes were then retouched and specialized tools made.[11] Not only did this conserve the flint but, since most of the core was used, it also resulted in more cutting or working edge of tool per pound of flint.

Although the tool assemblages in particular sites may be characterized as Mousterian, one site may have more or fewer scrapers, points, and so forth, than another site. A number of archeologists have suggested possible reasons for this variation. For example, Sally and Lewis Binford suggested that different activities may have occurred in different sites: some sites may have been used for butchering and other sites may have been base-camps. Hence, the kinds of tools found in different sites should vary.[12] And Paul Fish has

[10] Wu Xinzhi and Wu Maolin. "Early *Homo sapiens* in China." In Wu Rukang and John W. Olsen, eds., *Paleoanthropology and Paleolithic Archaeology in the People's Republic of China*. Orlando, Fla.: Academic Press, 1985, pp. 91–106.
[11] Jacques Bordaz. *Tools of the Old and New Stone Age*. Garden City, N.Y.: Natural History Press, 1970, p. 39.
[12] Sally R. Binford and Lewis R. Binford. "Stone Tools and Human Behavior," *Scientific American*, 220 (April 1969): 70–84.

suggested that some sites may have more tools produced by the Levalloisian technique (discussed in the previous chapter) because larger pieces of flint were available.[13]

The Post-Acheulian in Africa.   Like Mousterian tools, many of the post-Acheulian tools in Africa during the Middle Stone Age were struck off prepared cores in the Levalloisian way. The assemblages consist mostly of various types of flake tools. A well-described sequence of such tools comes from the area around the mouth of the Klasies River on the southern coast of South Africa.

This area contains rock-shelters and small caves in which early and later *Homo sapiens* lived. The oldest cultural remains in one of the caves may date back 120,000 years.[14] These earliest tools include parallel-sided flake blades (probably used as knives), pointed flakes (possibly spearpoints), burins or gravers (chisellike tools), and scrapers. Similar tools discovered at another South African site, Border Cave, may have been used almost 200,000 years ago.[15]

Homesites

Most of the excavated Middle Paleolithic homesites in Europe and the Near East are located in caves and rock-shelters. The same is true for the excavated Middle Stone Age homesites in sub-Saharan Africa. We might conclude, therefore, that Neandertals and other early *Homo sapiens* lived mostly in caves or rock-shelters. But that conclusion could be incorrect. Caves and rock-shelters may be overrepresented in the archeological record because they are more likely to be found than sites originally in the open but now hidden by thousands of years of **sediment**. Sediment is the dust, debris, and decay that accumulates over time; when we dust the furniture and vacuum the floor, we are removing sediment.

Quite a few homesites of early *Homo sapiens* were in the open. In Africa, open-air sites were located on floodplains, at the edges of lakes, and by springs.[16] Many open-air sites have been found in Europe, particularly eastern Europe. The occupants of the well-known site at Moldova in western Russia lived in river-valley houses framed with wood and covered with animal skins. Mammoth bones arranged in patterns around the remains of hearths were apparently used to help hold the animal skins in place. Even though the winter climate near the edge of the glacier nearby was cold at that time, there

[13] Paul R. Fish. "Beyond Tools: Middle Paleolithic Debitage Analysis and Cultural Inference." *Journal of Anthropological Research,* 37 (1981): 377.

[14] Karl W. Butzer. "Geomorphology and Sediment Stratigraphy." In Ronald Singer and John Wymer, *The Middle Stone Age at Klasies River Mouth in South Africa.* Chicago: University of Chicago, 1982, p. 42.

[15] David W. Phillipson. *African Archaeology.* Cambridge: Cambridge University Press, 1985, pp. 61–62.

[16] Richard G. Klein. "The Ecology of Early Man in Southern Africa." *Science,* July 8, 1977, p. 120.

would still have been animals to hunt because the plant food for the game was not buried under deep snow.

The hunters probably moved away in the summer to higher land between the river valleys. In all likelihood, the higher ground was grazing land for the large herds of animals the Moldova hunters depended on for meat. In the winter river-valley sites, archeologists have found skeletons of wolf, arctic fox, and hare with their paws missing. These animals probably were skinned for pelts that were made into clothing.[17]

Food-Getting

How early *Homo sapiens* got their food probably varied with their environments. In Africa they lived in rain forest as well as savanna and semiarid desert. In western and eastern Europe they had to adapt to cold; during periods of increased glaciation, much of the environment was steppe grassland and tundra.

The European environment during this time was much richer in animal resources than the tundra of northern countries is today. Indeed, the European environment inhabited by Neandertals abounded in game, both big and small. The tundra and alpine animals included reindeer, bison, wild oxen, horses, mammoths, rhinoceroses, and deer, as well as bears, wolves, and foxes.[18] Some European sites have also yielded bird and fish remains. For example, people in a summer camp in northern Germany apparently hunted swans and ducks and fished for perch and pike.[19] Little, however, is known about the particular plant foods the European Neandertals may have consumed; the remains of plants are unlikely to survive thousands of years in a nonarid environment.

In Africa too, early *Homo sapiens* varied in how they got food. For example, we know that the people living at the mouth of the Klasies River in South Africa ate a great deal of shellfish, as well as meat from small grazers such as antelopes and large grazers such as eland and buffalo.[20] But archeologists disagree about how the Klasies River people got their meat when they began to occupy the caves in the area.

Richard Klein thinks they hunted large as well as small game. Klein speculates that since the remains of eland of all ages have been found in Cave 1 at this site, the people there probably hunted the eland by driving them into corrals or other traps, where animals of all ages could be killed. Klein thinks that buffalo were hunted differently. Buffalo tend to charge attackers, which would make it difficult to drive them into traps. Klein believes that since bones

[17] Richard G. Klein. "Ice-Age Hunters of the Ukraine." *Scientific American*, June 1974, pp. 96–105.

[18] Francois Bordes. "Mousterian Cultures in France." *Science*, September 22, 1961, pp. 803–10.

[19] Thomas C. Patterson, *The Evolution of Ancient Societies: A World Archaeology*. Englewood Cliffs, N.J.: Prentice-Hall, 1981.

[20] Phillipson, *African Archaeology*, p. 63.

from mostly very young and very old buffalo are found in the cave, the hunters were able to stalk and kill only the most vulnerable animals.[21]

Lewis Binford thinks the Klasies River people hunted only small grazers and scavenged eland and buffalo meat from the kills of large carnivores. He argues that sites should contain all or almost all of the bones from animals that were hunted. According to Binford, since more or less complete skeletons are found only from small animals, the Klasies River people were not at first hunting all the animals they used for food.[22]

THE EMERGENCE OF MODERN HUMANS

Cro-Magnon humans, who appear in western Europe about 35,000 years ago, were once thought to be the earliest specimens of modern humans, or *Homo sapiens sapiens*. (The Cro-Magnons are named after the rock-shelter in France where they were first found in 1868.[23]) But we now know that modern-looking humans appear earlier outside of Europe. As of now, the oldest known fossils classified as *Homo sapiens sapiens* come from Africa. Some of these fossils, discovered in one of the Klasies River Mouth caves, are well over 50,000 years old and possibly as old as 100,000 years.[24] Other modern-looking fossils of about the same age have been found in Border Cave in South Africa, and a find at Omo in Ethiopia may be an early *Homo sapiens sapiens*.[25] Remains of anatomically modern humans 40,000 to 50,000 years old have been found at two sites in Israel (Skhul and Qafzeh),[26] and there are finds in Borneo (Niah) from about 40,000 years ago and in Australia (Lake Mungo) from about 30,000 years ago.[27]

These modern-looking humans differed from the Neandertals and other early *Homo sapiens* in that they had higher, more bulging foreheads, thinner and lighter bones, smaller faces and jaws, chins (the bony protuberances that

---

[21] Richard G. Klein. "The Stone Age Prehistory of Southern Africa." *Annual Review of Anthropology*, 12 (1983): 38–39.

[22] Lewis R. Binford, *Faunal Remains from Klasies River Mouth*. Orlando, Fla.: Academic Press, 1984, pp. 195–97. To explain the lack of complete skeletons of large animals, Klein (see previous footnote) suggests that the hunters butchered the large animals elsewhere and could carry home only small sections of them.

[23] C. B. Stringer, J. J. Hublin, and B. Vandermeersch. "The Origin of Anatomically Modern Humans in Western Europe." In Smith and Spencer, eds., *The Origins of Modern Humans*, p. 107.

[24] Ronald Singer and John Wymer. *The Middle Stone Age at Klasies River Mouth in South Africa*. Chicago: University of Chicago Press, 1982, p. 149.

[25] Günter Bräuer. "A Craniological Approach to the Origin of Anatomically Modern *Homo sapiens* in Africa and Implications for the Appearance of Modern Europeans." In Smith and Spencer, eds., *The Origins of Modern Humans*, pp. 387–89, 394; and Rightmire. "*Homo sapiens* in Sub-Saharan Africa," p. 320.

[26] Trinkaus. "Western Asia," p. 286; and Stringer, Hublin, and Vandermeersch. "The Origin of Anatomically Modern Humans in Western Europe," p. 123.

[27] Stringer, Hublin, and Vandermeersch, "The Origin of Anatomically Modern Humans in Western Europe," p. 121.

remain after projecting faces recede), and slight bone ridges (or no ridges at all) over the eyes and at the back of the head.

Theories about the Origins of Modern Humans

Two theories about the origins of modern humans continue to be debated among anthropologists. One, which can be called the *single-origin* theory, suggests that modern humans emerged in just one part of the Old World and then spread to other parts superseding Neandertals and other premodern *Homo sapiens*. The second theory, which can be called the *continuous-evolution* theory, suggests that modern humans emerged gradually in various parts of the Old World, becoming the varieties of humans we see today.[28]

According to the single-origin theory, most of the Neandertals and other premodern *Homo sapiens* did not evolve into modern humans. Rather, according to this view, most Neandertals became extinct after 35,000 years ago because they were replaced by modern humans. The presumed place of origin of the first modern humans has varied over the years as new fossils have been discovered. In the 1950s the source population was presumed to be the Neandertals in the Near East, who were referred to as "generalized" or "progressive" Neandertals. Later, when earlier *Homo sapiens sapiens* were found in Africa, some anthropologists postulated that modern humans emerged first in Africa and then moved to the Near East and from there to Europe and Asia.

According to the continuous-evolution theory, *Homo erectus* populations in various parts of the Old World gradually evolved into anatomically modern-looking humans. To the theorists espousing this view, the "transitional" or "archaic" *Homo sapiens* and the Neandertals and other definite *Homo sapiens* represent phases in the gradual development of more "modern" anatomical features. Indeed, as we have noted, some of these theorists see so much continuity between *Homo erectus* and modern humans that they classify *Homo erectus* as *Homo sapiens erectus*.

To explain why human evolution would proceed gradually and in the same direction in the various parts of the Old World, many continuous-evolution theorists postulate that cultural improvements in cutting-tool and cooking technology occurred all over the Old World. According to these theorists, these cultural improvements relaxed the prior natural selection for heavy bones and musculature in the skull. The argument is that unless many plant and animal foods were cut into small pieces and thoroughly cooked (in hearths or pits that were more efficient thermally), they would be hard to

---

[28] For arguments supporting the "single-origin" theory, see the chapters by Günter Bräuer, F. Clark Howell, and C. B. Stringer et al., in Smith and Spencer, eds., *The Origins of Modern Humans*. For arguments supporting the "continuous-evolution" theory, see the chapters by C. L. Brace et al., David W. Frayer, Fred H. Smith, and Milford W. Wolpoff et al., in the same volume.

chew and digest. Thus people previously needed robust jaws and thick skull bones to support the large muscles that enabled them to cut and chew their food. But robust bone and muscle were no longer needed after people began to cut and cook more effectively.[29]

The single-origin and continuous-evolution theories are not the only possible interpretations of the available fossil record. There is also the intermediate interpretation that there may have been some replacement of one population by another, some local continuous evolution, and in addition some substantial interbreeding between early modern humans who spread out of Africa and some of the populations they encountered in North Africa, Europe, and Asia.[30] As we discuss in the chapter on human variation, although modern humans are all *Homo sapiens sapiens*, human populations vary in physical features perhaps mostly because natural selection favors different features in different environments.

UPPER PALEOLITHIC CULTURES

The period of cultural history in Europe, the Near East, and Asia known as the Upper Paleolithic dates from about 40,000 years ago to the period known as the Mesolithic (about 14,000 to about 10,000 years ago, depending on the area). In Africa, the cultural period comparable to the Upper Paleolithic is known as the Later Stone Age and begins around the same time. (To simplify terminology, we use the term *Upper Paleolithic* in referring to cultural developments in all areas of the Old World during this period.)

In many respects, life styles during the Upper Paleolithic were similar to life styles before. People were still mainly hunters and gatherers and fishers who probably lived in highly mobile bands. They made their camps out in the open (in skin-covered huts) and in caves and rock-shelters. And they continued to produce smaller and smaller stone tools.

But the Upper Paleolithic is also characterized by a variety of new developments. One of the most striking is the emergence of art—painting on cave walls and stone slabs and the carving of decorative objects and personal ornaments out of bone, antler, shell, and stone. (Perhaps for this as well as other purposes, people began to obtain materials from distant sources.) Since more archeological sites date from the Upper Paleolithic than from any previous period, and since some Upper Paleolithic sites seem larger than any before, many archeologists think that the human population increased considerably during the Upper Paleolithic.[31] And new inventions, such as the bow and arrow, the spear-thrower, and tiny replaceable blades that could be fitted into handles, appear for the first time.[32]

[29] Erik Trinkaus: "The Neandertals and Modern Human Origins." *Annual Review of Anthropology*, 15 (1986): 198 (193–218).
[30] Ibid., p. 210.
[31] Randall White. "Rethinking the Middle/Upper Paleolithic Transition." *Current Anthropology*, 23 (1982): 169–75.
[32] Lawrence Guy Straus. Comment on ibid. *Current Anthropology*, 23 (1982): 185–86.

Homesites

As was the case in the known Middle Paleolithic sites, most of the Upper Paleolithic remains that have been excavated were situated in caves and rock-shelters. In southwestern France, some groups seem to have paved parts of the floor of the shelter with stones. Tentlike structures were built in some caves, apparently to keep out the cold.[33] Some open-air sites have also been excavated. (For a generalized reconstruction, see Figure 5-1.) The site at Dolni Vestonice in Czechoslovakia, dated to around 25,000 years ago, is one of the first for which there is an entire settlement plan.[34]

The settlement seems to have consisted of four tentlike huts, probably made from animal skins, with a great open hearth in the center. Around the outside were mammoth bones, some rammed into the ground, which suggests that the huts were surrounded by a wall. All told, there were bone heaps from about 100 mammoths. Each hut probably housed a group of related families—about 20 to 25 people. (One hut was approximately twenty-seven by forty-five feet and had five hearths distributed inside it, presumably one for each family.) With 20 to 25 people per hut, and assuming that all four huts were occupied at the same time, the population of the settlement would have been 100 to 125. Up a hill from the settlement was a fifth and different kind of hut. It was dug into the ground and contained a bake oven and more than 2300 small, fired fragments of animal figurines. There were also some hollow bones that may have been musical instruments. Another interesting feature of the settlement was a burial find, of a woman with a disfigured face. She may have been a particularly important personage, since her face was found engraved on an ivory plaque near the settlement's central hearth.

Tools: The Blade Technique

Upper Paleolithic toolmaking appears to have its roots in the Mousterian and post-Acheulian traditions, since flake tools are found in many Upper Paleolithic sites. Numerous blade tools have also been uncovered. Blades were found in Middle Paleolithic assemblages as well, but they were not widely used until the Upper Paleolithic. In the **blade** technique of toolmaking, a core is prepared by shaping a piece of flint with a hammerstone into a pyramidal or cylindrical form. Then a series of blades, more than twice as long as they are wide, are struck off.

The Upper Paleolithic period is also noted for the production of large numbers of bone and antler tools. The manufacture of these implements may have been made easier by the development of many varieties of burins. **Burins**, or gravers, are chisellike stone tools used for carving; bone and antler

[33] Patterson. *The Evolution of Ancient Societies.*
[34] Bohuslav Klima. "The First Ground-Plan of an Upper Paleolithic Loess Settlement in Middle Europe and Its Meaning." In Robert J. Braidwood and Gordon R. Willey, eds., *Courses toward Urban Life: Archaeological Consideration of Some Cultural Alternatives.* Viking Fund Publications in Anthropology, no. 32. Chicago: Aldine, 1962, pp. 193–210.

FIGURE 5-1 Here we see the type of mammoth-bone shelters constructed about 15,000 years ago on the East European Plain. Often mammoth skulls formed part of the foundation for the tusk, long bone, and wooden frame, covered with hide. As many as 95 mammoth mandibles were arranged around the outside in a herringbone pattern. Ten men and women could have constructed this elaborate shelter of 258 square feet in six days, using 46,000 pounds of bone. (Source: *National Geographic, October 1988, used with permission.*)

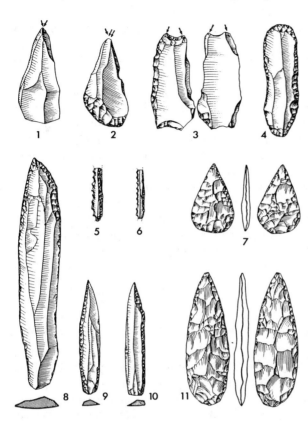

FIGURE 5-2   Upper Paleolithic tool kit from Hungary and Czechoslovakia.
Burin (1), burin-scraper (2), multiple burin (3), end-scraper on retouched blade (4), denticulated backed bladelets (5,6), pointed retouched blade (8), gravette points (9,10), bifacial points (7,11). *(Source: Francois Bordes,* The Old Stone Age, *trans. J. E. Anderson. New York: World University Library, 1968.)*

needles, awls, and projectile points could be produced with them.[35] Burins have been found in Middle and Lower Paleolithic sites but are present in great number and variety only in the Upper Paleolithic (see Figure 5-2). **Pressure flaking** also appeared during the Upper Paleolithic. In the traditional percussion method, used since Oldowan choppers were first made at least 2 million years before, the core was struck with a hammerstone to knock off the flake. In pressure flaking, small flakes were struck off by pressing against the core with a bone, wood, or antler tool. Pressure flaking gave the toolmaker greater control in the shaping of the tool.

As time went on, all over the Old World smaller and smaller blade tools were produced. The very tiny ones, called **microliths**, were often hafted or fitted into handles, one blade at a time or several blades together, to serve as spears, adzes, knives, and sickles. The hafting required the inventing of a way to trim the blade's back edge so that it would be blunt rather than sharp. In this way the blades would not split the handles into which they might be

---

[35] Bordaz. *Tools of the Old and New Stone Age,* p. 68.

inserted; the blunting would also prevent the users of an unhafted blade from cutting themselves.[36]

Some archeologists think that the blade technique was adopted because it made for more economical use of flint. André Leroi-Gourhan of the Musée de l'Homme in Paris has calculated that with the old Acheulian technique, a two-pound lump of flint yielded sixteen inches of working edge and produced only two hand axes. If the more advanced Mousterian technique were used, a lump of equal size would yield two yards of working edge. The Upper Paleolithic blade technique, however, yielded twenty-five yards of working edge.[37] With the same amount of material, a significantly greater number of tools could be produced. Getting the most out of a valuable resource may have been particularly important in areas lacking large flint deposits.

Jacques Bordaz believes that the evolution of toolmaking techniques, which continually increased the amount of usable edge that could be gotten out of a lump of flint, was significant because people could then spend more time in regions where flint was unavailable:

> Hunters and gatherers can only carry a limited amount of material with them during their seasonal migrations and hunting expeditions. With more efficient methods of knapping flint, their range could be extended farther and for longer periods of time into areas where flint was locally unavailable, of poorer quality, or difficult in access.[38]

Another reason for adopting the blade toolmaking technique may have been that it made for easy repair of tools. For example, the cutting edge of a tool might consist of a line of razorlike microliths set into a piece of wood. The tool would not be usable if just one of the cutting edge's microliths broke off or was chipped. But if the user carried a small prepared core of flint from which an identical-sized microlith could be struck off, the tool could be repaired easily by replacing the lost or broken microlith. A spear whose point was lost could be repaired similarly. Thus, the main purpose of the blade toolmaking technique may not have been to make more economical use of flint, but rather to allow easy replacement of damaged blades.[39]

How Were the Tools Used?   Ideally, the study of tools should reveal not only how the implements were made but also how they were used. One way of suggesting what a particular tool was used for in the past is to observe the manner in which similar tools are used by members of contemporary societies, preferably societies with subsistence activities and environments

---

[36] Phillipson. *African Archaeology*, p. 58.
[37] Bordaz. *Tools of the Old and New Stone Age*, p. 68.
[38] Ibid., p. 57.
[39] We thank Robert L. Kelly (personal communication) for bringing this possibility to our attention. See also J. Desmond Clark, "Interpretations of Prehistoric Technology from Ancient Egyptian and Other Sources. Part II: Prehistoric Arrow Forms in Africa as Shown by Surviving Examples of the Traditional Arrows of the San Bushmen," *Paleorient*, 3 (1977): 136.

similar to those of the ancient toolmakers. This method of study is called **ethnographic analogy**. The problem with reasoning from ethnographic analogy, however, is obvious: we cannot be sure that the original use of a tool has not changed. For example, just because we use an implement called a toothbrush on our teeth does not mean that a much later society will also use it on teeth. When selecting contemporary cultures that may provide the most informative and accurate comparisons, we should try to choose those that derive from the ancient culture we are interested in. If the cultures being compared are historically related—prehistoric and contemporary Pueblo cultures in the southwestern United States, for example—there is a greater likelihood that both groups used a particular kind of tool in similar ways and for similar purposes.

Another way of suggesting what a particular kind of tool was used for in the past is to compare the visible and microscopic wear marks on the prehistoric tools with the wear marks on similar tools made and experimentally used by contemporary researchers. The idea behind this approach is that different uses leave different wear marks. A pioneer in this research was S. A. Semenov, who re-created prehistoric stone tools and used them in a variety of ways to find out which uses left which kinds of wear marks. For example, by cutting into meat with his re-created stone knives, he produced a polish on the edges that was like the polish found on blades from a prehistoric site in Siberia. This finding led Semenov to infer that the Siberian blades were probably also used to cut meat.[40]

Inventions for Killing.   During the Upper Paleolithic, and probably for the first time, spears were shot from a spear-thrower rather than thrown with the arm. We know this because bone and antler **atlatls** (the Aztec word for "spear-thrower") have been found in some sites. A spear propelled off a grooved board could be sent through the air with increased force, causing it to travel farther and hit harder, and with less effort by the thrower. The bow and arrow was used in various places during the Upper Paleolithic. Harpoons, used for fishing and perhaps for reindeer hunting, were also invented at this time.

Art

The earliest discovered traces of art are beads and carvings, and somewhat later paintings, from Upper Paleolithic sites. We might expect that early artistic efforts were crude, but the cave paintings of Spain and southern France show a marked degree of skill. So do the naturalistic paintings on slabs of stone excavated in southern Africa. Some of those slabs appear to have

---

[40] S. A. Semenov. *Prehistoric Technology*, trans. M. W. Thompson. Bath, England: Adams & Dart, 1970, p. 103. For a more recent discussion of research following this strategy, see Lawrence H. Keeley, *Experimental Determination of Stone Tool Uses: A Microwear Analysis*, Chicago: University of Chicago Press, 1980.

been painted as much as 28,000 years ago, which suggests that painting in Africa is as old as painting in Europe.[41]

Peter J. Ucko and Andrée Rosenfeld have identified three principal locations of paintings in the caves of western Europe: (1) in obviously inhabited rock-shelters and cave entrances—art as decoration or "art for art's sake"; (2) in "galleries" immediately off the inhabited areas of caves; and (3) in the inner reaches of caves, whose difficulty of access has been interpreted by some as a sign that magical-religious activities were performed there.[42]

The subjects of the paintings are mostly animals. The paintings rest on bare walls, with no backdrops or environmental trappings. Perhaps, like many contemporary peoples, Upper Paleolithic men and women believed that the drawing of a human image could cause death or injury. If that were indeed their belief, it might explain why human figures are rarely depicted in cave art. Another explanation for the focus on animals might be that these people sought to improve their luck at hunting. This theory is suggested by evidence of chips in the painted figures, perhaps made by spears thrown at the drawings. But if hunting magic was the chief motivation for the paintings, it is difficult to explain why only a few show signs of being speared. Perhaps the paintings were inspired by the need to increase the supply of animals. Cave art seems to have reached a peak toward the end of the Upper Paleolithic period, when herds of game were decreasing.

Another interpretation of Upper Paleolithic cave art has been suggested by Leroi-Gourhan. On the basis of a statistical analysis of the types of paintings and their locations within each of sixty-six caves, he concluded that choice of subject and placement of the paintings were not haphazard or arbitrary but probably had some symbolic significance. For example, female animals were usually located in the central chambers of the caves and were associated with what may be considered female signs—enclosed circles. Male animals, located at the entrances and back portions of the caves, were associated with presumably male signs—dots and barbed symbols.[43]

The particular symbolic significance of the cave paintings in southwestern France is more explicitly revealed, perhaps, by the results of a more recent, quite sophisticated statistical study.[44] The data suggest that the animals portrayed in the cave paintings were mostly the ones that the painters preferred for meat and for materials such as hides. For example, wild cattle (bovines) and horses are portrayed more often than we would expect by chance, probably because they were larger and heavier (meatier) than the

[41] Phillipson. *African Archaeology*, p. 73.
[42] Peter J. Ucko and Andrée Rosenfeld. *Paleolithic Cave Art*. New York: McGraw-Hill, 1967.
[43] André Leroi-Gourhan. "The Evolution of Paleolithic Art." *Scientific American*, February 1968, pp. 58–70.
[44] Patricia C. Rice and Ann L. Paterson. "Cave Art and Bones: Exploring the Interrelationships." *American Anthropologist*, 87 (1985): 94–100. For similar results of a study of cave art in Spain, see Patricia C. Rice and Ann L. Paterson, "Validating the Cave Art—Archeofaunal Relationship in Cantabrian Spain," *American Anthropologist*, 88 (1986): 658–67.

other animals in the environment. In addition, the paintings mostly portray animals that the painters may have feared the most because of their size, speed, natural weapons such as tusks and horns, and unpredictability of behavior. That is, mammoths, bovines, and horses are portrayed more often than deer and reindeer. Thus, the data seem consistent with the idea that "the art is related to the importance of hunting in the economy of Upper Paleolithic people."[45] Also consistent with this idea, the investigators point out, is the fact that the art of the cultural period following the Upper Paleolithic seems again to reflect how people got their food. But in that period, when food-getting no longer depended on the hunting of large game (because they were becoming extinct), the art no longer focused on portrayals of animals.

Upper Paleolithic art was not confined to cave paintings. Many shafts of spears and similar objects were decorated with figures of animals. Alexander Marshack has an interesting interpretation of some of the engravings made during the Upper Paleolithic. He believes that as far back as 30,000 B.C., hunters may have used a system of notation, engraved on bone and stone, to mark the phases of the moon. If this is true, it would mean that Upper Paleolithic people were capable of complex thought and had sophisticated knowledge of their environment.[46] In addition, figurines representing the human female in exaggerated form have been found at Upper Paleolithic sites. Called *Venuses*, these women are portrayed with broad hips and large breasts and abdomens. It has been suggested that the figurines may have been an ideal type, or an expression of a desire for fertility.

What the Venus figurines symbolized is still controversial. As is usually the case in current scholarly controversies, there is little or no evidence available now that might allow us to accept or reject a particular interpretation. But not all controversies in anthropology continue because of lack of evidence. Sometimes a controversy continues because there is some (usually disputed) evidence on all sides! This is the case with the controversy to which we now turn—whether there were people in the Americas prior to 12,000 years ago.

THE EARLIEST HUMANS AND THEIR CULTURES IN THE NEW WORLD

So far in this chapter we have dealt only with the Old World—Africa, Europe, and Asia. What about the New World—North and South America? How long have humans lived there, and what were their earliest cultures like?

Because only *Homo sapiens* fossils have been found in North and South America, migrations of humans to the New World had to have taken place sometime after the emergence of *Homo sapiens*. But exactly when these migrations occurred is subject to debate. On the one hand, some anthropologists think there are indications of humans in the Americas as far back as 20,000 to

---

[45] Rice and Paterson. "Cave Art and Bones," p. 98.
[46] Alexander Marshack. *The Roots of Civilization.* New York: McGraw-Hill, 1972.

50,000 years ago. On the other hand, there are anthropologists who see no good evidence of a human presence in the Americas until after 12,000 years ago. Obviously, the opposing positions in this debate cannot both be correct.

The anthropologists who think that humans were present in the Americas before 12,000 years ago point to a number of presumably older finds—including human skeletal remains and bone and stone "tools"—at a large number of sites all over the New World. But the dating of these finds is not accepted by many archeologists. So, for example, the supposedly old skeletal remains may not be very old, and some of the tools may be intrusions from more recent periods. In addition, some of the things thought to be tools may not have been made by humans; rather, these scattered, usually single pieces of stone and bone may have been fractured by natural fires and geological processes. Perhaps the most telling criticism of the idea of an ancient occupation of the Americas is that archeologists have not yet found any tool kits (assemblages of different tools) that are undisputably more than 12,000 years old. (In contrast, we know that Australia was occupied more than 30,000 years ago, because anthropologists have found tool kits there that are definitely that old.) As of now, then, the evidence available does not unquestionably confirm a human presence in the New World prior to 12,000 years ago.[47]

If there is disagreement about when people entered the New World, there is almost unanimous consensus on where and how they did. They probably came into North America from Siberia, walking across the land that bridged what is now the Bering Strait between Siberia and Alaska. This "land bridge" existed because the ice sheets that partly covered the high latitudes of the world contained so much of the world's water (they were thousands of feet thick in some places) that the Bering Strait was dry land. Since then the glaciers have mostly melted, and the Bering "bridge" has been covered by a higher sea level.

According to comparative linguists Morris Swadesh and Joseph Greenberg, there were three waves of migration into the New World.[48] First came the speakers of a language that diverged over time into most of the languages found in the New World; the speakers of these related languages came to occupy all of South and Central America as well as most of North America. Next came the ancestors of the people who speak languages belonging to the Nadené family, which today includes Navaho and Apache in the southwestern United States as well as the several Athapaskan languages of northern California, coastal Oregon, northwestern Canada, and Alaska. Finally, perhaps 4,000 years ago, came the ancestors of the Eskimo and Aleut (the latter came to occupy the islands southwest of Alaska and the adjacent mainland.)

[47] Roger C. Owen. "The Americas: The Case against an Ice-Age Human Population." In Smith and Spencer, eds., *The Origins of Modern Humans*, pp. 517–63. See also Dena F. Dincauze, "An Archaeo-Logical Evaluation of the Case for Pre-Clovis Occupations," in Fred Wendorf and Angela E. Close, eds., *Advances in World Archaeology*, Orlando, Fla.: Academic Press, 1984, 3: 275–323.

[48] Cited in Owen, "The Americas," pp. 524–25.

The tool assemblages from the earliest definite sites of human occupation are quite similar to one another. Most of the sites investigated by archeologists are *kill sites*, where game had been slaughtered and then butchered. Most occur along ancient lakes or creeks, where the animals probably came to drink, or at the bases of cliffs, over which herds were probably stampeded.

Archeological remains of these apparently earliest New World hunters have been found in a number of places in the United States, Mexico, and Canada. One of these places was just south of the furthest reaches of the last glaciation, the area east of the Rockies known as the High Plains. This area abounded with mammoths (huge elephants, now extinct), bison, wild camels, and wild horses. The mammoth was one of the principal game animals beginning about 12,000 years ago. The tools found with mammoth kills are known as the *Clovis complex*, which includes the Clovis projectile point as well as stone scrapers and knives and bone tools. The Clovis projectile point is large and leaf-shaped, flaked on both sides. It has a broad groove in the middle, presumably so that the point could be attached to a wooden spear shaft.[49]

The mammoth disappeared about 10,000 years ago (for possible reasons, see Chapter 7), and the major game animal became the now extinct large, straight-horned bison. The hunters of that bison used a projectile point called the Folsom point, which was somewhat smaller than the Clovis point. Since tools are also found with many other kinds of animal remains, including wolf, turtle, rabbit, horse, fox, deer, and camel, the bison hunters obviously depended on other animals as well.[50] In the Rio Grande valley, the Folsom toolmakers characteristically established a base camp on low dune ridges overlooking both a large pond and broad, open grazing areas. If we assume that the pond provided water for the grazing herds, the people in the camp would have been in an excellent position to watch the herds.[51]

As the climate of the American Southwest became drier, the animals and the cultural adaptations changed somewhat. About 9000 years ago the smaller modern bison replaced the earlier straight-horned variety.[52] Base camps began to be located farther from ponds and grazing areas and closer to streams. If the ponds were no longer reliable sources of water during these drier times, the animals probably no longer frequented them—which would explain why the hunters had to change the sites of their base camps. Not that much is known about the plant foods these people may have exploited, but on the desert fringes plant gathering may have been vital. In Nevada and Utah, archeologists have found milling stones and other artifacts for processing plant food.[53]

---

[49] Joe B. Wheat. "A Paleo-Indian Bison Kill." *Scientific American,* January 1967, pp. 44–47.
[50] J. D. Jennings, *Prehistory of North America.* New York: McGraw-Hill, 1968, pp. 72–88.
[51] W. James Judge and Jerry Dawson. "Paleo-Indian Settlement Technology in New Mexico." *Science,* June 16, 1972, pp. 1210–16.
[52] Wheat. "A Paleo-Indian Bison Kill."
[53] Brian M. Fagan, *People of the Earth: An Introduction to World Prehistory,* 6th ed. Glenview, Ill.: Scott, Foresman and Company, 1989, p. 221.

The Olsen-Chubbuck site, a kill site excavated in Colorado, shows the organization that may have been involved in the hunting of bison.[54] In a dry gulch dated to 6500 B.C. were the remains of 200 bison. At the bottom were complete skeletons and at the top, completely butchered animals. This clearly suggests that hunters deliberately stampeded the animals into a natural trap— an arroyo, or steep-sided dry gully. The animals in front were probably pushed by the ones behind into the arroyo. Joe Wheat estimates that the hunters may have obtained 55,000 pounds of meat from this one kill! Judging from recent Plains Indians, for whom bison meat lasted approximately one month, and estimating that each person would have eaten a pound a day, the kill at the Olsen-Chubbuck site may have fed a band of over 150 people for a month. The hunters must have been highly organized not only for the stampede itself but also for butchering. It seems that the enormous carcasses had to be carried to flat ground for that job. In addition, the 55,000 pounds of meat and hides had to be carried back to camp.[55]

Although big game may have been most important on the High Plains, other areas show different adaptations. For example, people in woodland regions of the United States seem to have depended more heavily on plant food and smaller game. In some woodland areas, fish and shellfish may have been a vital part of the diet.[56] And in some areas, the lower Illinois River valley being one example, people who depended on game and wild vegetable foods managed to get enough such food to live in permanent villages of perhaps 100 to 150 people.[57]

In recent and modern times too, the peoples of the world have varied culturally. In the next chapter we discuss how they vary physically.

SUMMARY

1. Most anthropologists agree that *Homo erectus* began to evolve into *Homo sapiens* after about 500,000 years ago. But there is disagreement about how and where the transition occurred. The mixed traits of the transitional fossils include large cranial capacities (well within the range of modern humans) together with low foreheads and large brow ridges (which are characteristic of *Homo erectus* specimens). The earliest definite *Homo sapiens*, who did not look completely like modern humans, appeared after about 200,000 years ago.
2. Premodern *Homo sapiens* have been found in many parts of the Old World—in Africa and Asia as well as in Europe. Some of these *Homo sapiens* may have lived earlier than the Neandertals of Europe, who were the first premodern humans to be found. There is still debate over whether the Neandertals in western Europe became extinct, or survived and were ancestral to the modern-looking people who lived in western Europe after about 40,000 years ago.
3. The period of cultural history associated with the Neandertals is traditionally called the Middle Paleolithic in Europe and the Near East and dates from about

[54] Wheat. "A Paleo-Indian Bison Kill."
[55] Ibid.
[56] Fagan. *People of the Earth*, p. 227.
[57] Ibid.

100,000 to about 40,000 years ago. For Africa, the term *Middle Stone Age* is used to refer to the period that ends around the same time but begins perhaps as early as 200,000 years ago. The assemblages of flake tools from this period are generally referred to as *Mousterian* in Europe and the Near East, and as *post-Acheulian* in Africa.

4. How early *Homo sapiens* got their food probably varied with their environments. Small animals and birds were hunted, large animals were hunted and/or scavenged, and in some places the people seem also to have fished. Little is known about the plant foods that may have been collected, because the remains of plants are unlikely to survive over thousands of years.

5. Fossil remains of fully modern-looking humans have been found in Africa, the Near East, Asia, and Australia, as well as in Europe. The oldest of these fossils have been found in South Africa.

6. Two theories about the origins of modern humans continue to be debated among anthropologists. One, which can be called the *single-origin* theory, suggests that modern humans emerged in just one part of the Old World (the Near East and, more recently, Africa have been the postulated places of origin) and spread to other parts of the Old World, superseding Neandertals and other premodern *Homo sapiens*. The second theory, which can be called the *continuous-evolution* theory, suggests that modern humans emerged gradually in various parts of the Old World, becoming the varieties of humans we see today.

7. The period of cultural history known as the Upper Paleolithic (in Europe, the Near East, and Asia) or the Later Stone Age (in Africa) dates from about 40,000 years ago to about 14,000 to 10,000 years ago. In many respects, life styles were similar to life styles before. People were still mainly hunters and gatherers and fishers who probably lived in highly mobile bands. They made their camps out in the open and in caves and rock-shelters. And they produced smaller and smaller stone tools.

8. The Upper Paleolithic is also characterized by a variety of new developments: the emergence of art, population growth, and new inventions such as the bow and arrow, the spear-thrower, and microliths—tiny replaceable stone blades that could be fitted into handles. Some archeologists think that the blade technique (and pressure rather than percussion flaking) was adopted because it yielded more working edge per pound of flint than the earlier methods of toolmaking. Other archeologists think that the blade technique was adopted because it made for easy repair of tools: if one of a cutting edge's microliths broke off or was chipped, it could be easily replaced.

9. Investigators attempt to determine the functions of ancient tools by observing modern cultures with similar technologies and by making and using the tools themselves.

10. Only *Homo sapiens* remains have been found in the New World. The prevailing opinion is that humans migrated to the New World over a land bridge between Siberia and Alaska in the area of what is now the Bering Strait. But when this occurred is subject to debate. The evidence now available does not unquestionably confirm a human presence in the Americas prior to about 12,000 years ago.

6

Human Variation

In the preceding chapter, we discussed the emergence of people like our-selves, *Homo sapiens sapiens*. Just as the cultures of those human beings dif-fered in some respects, so do the cultures of peoples in recent times, as we will see in the chapters that follow. But anthropologists are also concerned with how recent human populations vary physically—how they resemble or differ from each other, and why.

Human populations vary in their frequencies of biological traits, both visible and invisible. External or visible characteristics (such as skin color, height, and body build) are, of course, the most obvious variations. Popula-tions also vary in internal, invisible biological traits such as susceptibility to disease. How can we explain all these variations? It appears that many, if not most, of them may represent adaptations to different environments.

FACTORS PRODUCING HUMAN VARIATION

Biological variation in human populations is the result of genetic and environ-mental variation. We will give examples later in the chapter of how environ-ment may affect biological characteristics; here we focus on how genetic variation may be produced by one or more of the following processes: muta-tion and natural selection, genetic drift, and gene flow.

Mutation and Natural Selection

Mutations, or changes in the chemistry of a gene, are the ultimate source of all genetic variation. Mutations can be lethal or sublethal, reducing the reproductive rates of their carriers. They can also be beneficial, enhancing the potential for survival in a particular environment. Although most mutations are harmful, beneficial ones occur occasionally. Because natural selection favors them, the traits produced by the beneficial mutations become characteristics of the population. For example, in Chapter 2 we discussed the advantage dark moths had over light moths when certain areas of England became industrialized. Predators could not easily see the darker moths against the soot-covered trees, and these moths soon outnumbered the lighter variety. Since human populations live in a great variety of environments, we would expect natural selection to favor somewhat different traits in those different environments. Variation in skin color and body build are among the many features that may be explained by natural selection.

But certain traits found among human populations, such as red (versus blond or black) hair color or thick (versus thin) lips, may not make any difference in survival, no matter where the carriers of these traits live. So far as we know now, they are neutral traits, yet they are distributed unevenly among the world's populations. Natural selection does not seem to account for their distribution, as neutral traits do not seem to confer any advantages on their carriers. The sometimes different and sometimes similar frequencies of neutral traits in human populations may result, then, from genetic drift or gene flow.

Genetic Drift

The term **genetic drift** is now used to refer to various random processes that affect gene frequencies in small, relatively isolated populations. Genetic drift is also known as the *Sewall Wright effect*, after the geneticist who first directed attention to this evolutionary process.[1]

One variety of genetic drift occurs when a small population recently derived from a larger one expands in relative isolation.[2] Called the **founder effect**, this process might occur, for example, if a family with ten children—all of whom exhibit a particular rare, but neutral, trait—moved to a tiny country hamlet. If all members of the family remained in the hamlet, married, and produced children who also stayed there and produced more children, and if

---

[1] Laura Newell Morros. "The Small Population." In Laura Newell Morris, ed., *Human Populations, Genetic Variation, and Evolution.* San Francisco: Chandler, 1971, p. 302. See also W. F. Bodmer and L. L. Cavalli-Sforza, *Genetics, Evolution, and Man,* San Francisco: W. H. Freeman & Company Publishers, 1976, pp. 381ff.

[2] Morris. "The Small Population," p. 309. See also Bodmer and Cavalli-Sforza, *Genetics, Evolution, and Man,* pp. 383–85.

the hamlet remained isolated from the outside world, the trait might become relatively common among residents of the area in a few generations.[3]

Gene Flow

A **gene pool** consists of all the genes possessed by the members of a given population. **Gene flow** is the process whereby genes pass from the gene pool of one population to the gene pool of another population through mating and reproduction. Unlike the other three evolutionary processes (mutation, natural selection, and genetic drift), which act generally to differentiate populations, gene flow tends to work in the opposite direction: it makes differing populations more similar over time as genes are exchanged between them. For example, if a group of blue-eyed Scandinavians interbreeds with a population of dark-eyed Italians, the proportion of genes for blue eyes in the Italian population will increase. Hence, gene flow may make some populations look similar even though they were originally different.

Although gene flow is often made possible by the movement of people (to trade, to raid, to settle), gene flow does not necessarily occur as a result. A group may move to a new place but refuse to interbreed with the natives of that area. In the United States, for example, the Amish of Pennsylvania have tried to remain isolated. Nevertheless, some marriages have occurred between Amish and non-Amish people, and reproduction has introduced new genes into the Amish gene pool.[4]

BIOLOGICAL VARIATION IN HUMAN POPULATIONS

The most noticeable biological variations among populations are those that are on the surface—skin color, body build, stature, and facial features. There are also many biological variations we do not see, such as variation in susceptibility to different diseases. Certain of these variations may be explainable as adaptations to differing physical or social environments or as consequences of other physical or cultural changes. However, there are many biological variations among human populations for which we do not yet have explanations.

Body Build and Facial Construction

Scientists have suggested that the body build of many birds and mammals may vary according to the temperature of the environment in which they live. For example, Julian Huxley, in a series of studies on the puffin (a short-necked sea bird), found that puffins in cold northern regions were considerably larger or more robust than those living in warmer southern areas.[5] **Berg-**

---

[3] H. Bentley Glass. "The Genetics of the Dunkers." *Scientific American*, August 1953, pp. 76–81.
[4] Laura Newell Morris. "Gene Flow." In Morris, ed., *Human Populations*, pp. 409–10. See also Bonder and Cavalli-Sforza, *Genetics, Evolution, and Man*, pp. 403–6.
[5] Julian Huxley. *Evolution in Action*. New York: Mentor Books, 1957, pp. 43–44.

mann's rule describes what seems to be a general relationship: the slenderer populations of a species inhabit the warmer parts of its geographical range, and the more robust populations inhabit the cooler areas.

The studies by D. F. Roberts of variations in the mean body weights of people living in regions with widely differing temperatures have provided support for Bergmann's rule.[6] Roberts discovered that the lowest body weights were found among residents of areas with the highest mean annual temperatures, and vice versa. For example, where the mean annual temperatures are 70° to 82° F., people weigh, on the average, only 110 to 120 pounds. Populations with average weights over 140 pounds live where the temperature averages 40° F.

Allen's rule describes another probable variation in body build: protruding body parts (particularly arms and legs) are relatively shorter in the cooler areas of a species' range than in the warmer areas.

The rationale behind these theories is that the long-limbed, lean body type often found in tropical regions provides more surface area in relation to body mass and thus facilitates the dissipation of body heat. In contrast, the chunkier, shorter-limbed body type found among the residents of cold regions promotes retention of body heat because the amount of surface area relative to body mass is lessened. The build of the Eskimos appears to exemplify Bergmann's and Allen's rules. Their relatively large bodies and short legs may be adapted to the cold temperatures in which they live.

Is is not clear, however, whether differences in body build between populations are due solely to natural selection of different genes under different conditions of cold or heat. Some of the variation may be induced during the life span of individuals.[7] Alphonse Riesenfeld has provided some experimental evidence that extreme cold affects body proportions during growth and development. Rats raised under conditions of extreme cold generally show changes that resemble characteristics of humans in cold environments. These cold-related changes include long-bone shortening consistent with Allen's rule.[8]

Like body build, facial structure may be affected by environment. Riesenfeld found that the facial width of rats increased in cold temperatures and their nasal openings grew smaller.[9] Because the rats raised in cold environments are genetically similar to those raised in warmer environments, we can confidently conclude that environment, not genes, brought about these

---

[6] D. F. Roberts. "Body Weight, Race, and Climate." *American Journal of Physical Anthropology*, 2 (1953): 553–58. Cited in Stanley M. Garn, *Human Races*, 3rd ed., Springfield, Ill.: Charles C. Thomas, 1971, p. 73. See also D. F. Roberts, *Climate and Human Variability*, 2nd ed., Menlo Park, Calif.: Cummings, 1978.

[7] Marshall T. Newman. "The Application of Ecological Rules to the Racial Anthropology of the Aboriginal New World." *American Anthropologist*, 55 (1953): 311–27.

[8] Alphonse Riesenfeld. "The Effect of Extreme Temperatures and Starvation on the Body Proportions of the Rat." *American Journal of Physical Anthropology*, 39 (1973): 427–59.

[9] Ibid., pp. 452–53.

changes in rats. How much the environment directly affects variation in the human face is not yet clear. We do know that variation in climate is associated with facial variation. For example, people living in the humid tropics tend to have broad, short, flat noses, whereas people living in climates with low humidity (with cold or hot temperatures) tend to have long, thin noses. A relatively narrow nose may be a more efficient humidifier of drier air than a broad nose.[10]

Height

Human populations vary in average height. Why? Although adaptation to heat and cold may have some effect on the varying height of human populations, as implied by Allen's rule, such variation may also be produced by other, nongenetic conditions such as nutrition, medical care, and physical or psychological stress. After all, if stature can increase dramatically in a generation as in Japan after 1945 or children of migrants to the United States, genetic influences are not likely to be so important.[11]

What does research suggest about the effects of nutrition on height? Studies of humans and other animals suggest that nutrition exerts a major effect on rate of growth, but not necessarily on the ultimate height of an individual. Undernutrition in infancy, childhood, and adolescence results in slow skeletal growth and a delay in sexual maturation, but a longer period of growth.[12] So malnourished individuals may be short early in life, but they can end up as tall as well nourished individuals because they grow for a longer time.[13] But malnutrition might still produce differences in average height between populations because shorter people (who need less food) may be more likely than taller people to survive and reproduce. A Peruvian study has shown that poor small parents have more surviving children than poor large parents.[14] Also, data from eighteenth- and nineteenth-century England, France, and Germany show that stature decreased during times of famine in those countries.[15] So small body size may have a selective advantage if people are poorly nourished.

Some researchers have found evidence linking variation in ultimate height to stress in infancy. For example, Thomas Landauer and John Whiting

[10] J. S. Weiner. "Nose Shape and Climate." *Journal of Physical Anthropology,* 4 (1954): 615–18; A. T. Steegman, Jr. "Human Adaptation to Cold." In Albert Damon, ed., *Physiological Anthropology.* New York: Oxford University Press, 1975, pp. 130–66.

[11] Stanley M. Garn, Meinhard Robinow, and Stephen M. Bailey. "Genetic and Nutritional Interactions." In Derrick B. Jelliffe and E. F. Patrice Jelliffe, eds., *Nutrition and Growth,* New York: Plenum, 1979, pp. 34–35.

[12] Felix P. Heald. "The Adolescent." In Jelliffe and Jelliffe, eds., *Nutrition and Growth,* p. 241.

[13] Napoleon Wolanski. "The Adult." In Jelliffe and Jelliffe, eds., *Nutrition and Growth,* p. 257.

[14] A. R. Frisancho, J. Sanchez, D. Pallardel, and L. Yanez. "Adaptive Significance of Small Body Size under Poor Socioeconomic Conditions in Southern Peru." *American Journal of Physical Anthropology,* 39 (1973): 255–62. Cited in Theresa Overfield, *Biologic Variation in Health and Illness: Race, Age, and Sex Differences,* Menlo Park, Calif.: Addison-Wesley, 1985, p. 36.

[15] William A. Stini. *Ecology and Human Adaptation.* Dubuque, Iowa: Wm. C. Brown, 1975, pp. 3–4.

examined the relationship between certain infant-care practices judged to be stressful and the stature of adult males in eighty societies.[16] The impetus for this study came from research suggesting that rats stressed in infancy (that is, subjected to apparently stressful treatment such as handling, electric shock, vibration, and temperature extremes) developed longer skeletons and longer tails and were also somewhat heavier than nonstressed rats.

Landauer and Whiting collected and correlated data about infant-care procedures and adult-male stature in humans. In some societies, children are subjected to stressful practices from birth to the age of two. These practices include circumcision; branding of the skin with sharp objects; the piercing of the nose, ears, or lips for the insertion of ornaments; the molding and stretching of the head and limbs for cosmetic purposes; and vaccination. In these societies, male adults are more than two inches taller on average than males raised in societies without such customs.

Another kind of stress that may influence adult stature is early mother-infant separation. In a cross-cultural study of sixty-nine societies, Gunders and Whiting found that males are taller in societies that practice early mother-infant separation than in societies where such customs are lacking or are minimally practiced.[17]

Might nutritional differences explain the cross-cultural results relating height to stress? The answer apparently is no, although the presence of milk in the diet seems also to predict greater height. In two separate cross-cultural studies, more plentiful food and larger amounts of protein in the diet did not predict greater height. But the presence of animal milk in the diet did.[18] However, Landauer and Whiting found that stress predicted two inches of greater height in societies without milking animals as well as in societies with milking animals.[19]

Perhaps the most persuasive evidence of the effect of stress on height comes from an experimental study conducted by Landauer and Whiting in Kenya.[20] A child health clinic was set up and parents were invited to bring their children in for checkups. Although most adults and older children had been vaccinated against smallpox and other diseases, many children had not been vaccinated. The researchers arranged for a randomly selected sample of children to be vaccinated before they were two years old. (The other unvacci-

[16] Thomas K. Landauer and John W. M. Whiting. "Infantile Stimulation and Adult Stature of Human Males." *American Anthropologist*, 66 (1964): 1008.

[17] S. Gunders and J. W. M. Whiting. "Mother-Infant Separation and Physical Growth." *Ethnology*, 7 (1968): 196–206.

[18] Gunders and Whiting. "Mother-Infant Separation and Physical Growth," pp. 201–2; and J. Patrick Gray and Linda D. Wolfe. "Height and Sexual Dimorphism of Stature among Human Societies." *American Journal of Physical Anthropology*, 53 (1980): 446–52.

[19] Thomas K. Landauer and John W. M. Whiting. "Correlates and Consequences of Stress in Infancy." In Ruth H. Munroe, Robert L. Munroe, and Beatrice B. Whiting, eds., *Handbook of Cross-Cultural Human Development*. New York: Garland, 1981, pp. 361–65.

[20] Ibid., pp. 369–70.

nated children were vaccinated after they were two.) At seven years of age the two groups of children were compared on height. Consistent with the cross-cultural evidence on the possible effect of stress on height, the children vaccinated before the age of two were significantly taller than the children vaccinated at a later age. Since the children vaccinated before the age of two were selected randomly for early vaccination, it is unlikely that nutritional or other differences between the two groups account for the difference between them in height.

In several areas of the world, people have recently been getting taller. For example, between World Wars I and II, the average height of males in the United States increased by two inches.[21] As mentioned earlier, Japan since World War II shows the same trend.

What accounts for this recent trend toward greater height? Several factors may be involved. One may be new stresses early in life. Births in hospitals, which have become more common in recent times, usually involve the separation of newborns from mothers. As we have noted, mother-infant separation after birth may be stressful for the infant. And vaccinations in infancy have also become more common.[22]

The trend toward greater stature might be caused by improvements in nutrition. Another possible explanation is **heterosis (hybrid vigor)**. These latter terms refer to the possibility that matings between individuals with different genetic characteristics produce healthier and more numerous off-spring.[23] As a result of increased social and geographic mobility, matings between different kinds of people across cultures and continents are fairly common nowadays. Increased height in the offspring of these matings may be partially a consequence of the hybrid vigor so produced. For example, the increased stature in Japan noted above could be due partly to the numerous matings between U. S. citizens and Japanese after World War II.

Any or all of the genetic and environmental factors just discussed may affect human size. Further research will probably help determine which of these factors are the most important.

Skin Color

Human populations obviously differ in average skin color. Many people consider skin color the most important indicator of racial distinction and sometimes treat others differently solely on this basis. But anthropologists, in addition to being critical of racial discrimination (for reasons we discuss later in this chapter), also note that skin color is not a good indicator of race. For example, extremely dark skin is found most commonly in Africa. However, there are natives of southern India whose skin is as dark as, or darken than,

---

[21] Stini. *Ecology and Human Adaptation*, p. 3.

[22] Thomas K. Landauer. "Infantile Vaccination and the Secular Trend in Stature." *Ethos*, 1 (1973): 499–503.

[23] Albert Damon. "Stature Increase among Italian-Americans: Environmental, Genetic, or Both?" *American Journal of Physical Anthropology*, 23 (1965): 401–8.

that of many Africans. Yet these people are not closely related to Africans, either genetically or historically.

How can we explain the wide range of skin colors among the peoples of the world? The answer appears to be extremely complex. Scientists do not yet fully understand why some people have very light skin whereas others have very dark, reddish, or yellowish skin. But we do have some theories that may partially account for variation in skin color.

We know that skin color is influenced by the brownish black pigment called **melanin.** The more melanin in the skin, the darker the skin will be. Furthermore, the amount of melanin in the skin seems to be related to the climate in which a person lives. **Gloger's rule** states that populations of birds and mammals living in warm, humid climates have more melanin (and therefore darker skin, fur, or feathers) than do populations of the same species living in cooler, drier areas. On the whole, this association with climate holds true for people as well as for birds and other mammals.

The populations of darker-skinned humans do live mostly in warm climates (although all residents of warm climates do not have dark skins). Dark pigmentation seems to have at least one specific advantage in tropical climates. Melanin protects the sensitive inner layers of the skin from the sun's damaging ultraviolet rays; therefore, dark-skinned people living in sunny areas are safer from sunburn and skin cancers than light-skinned people. Dark skin may also confer a number of other important biological advantages in tropical environments, such as greater resistance to tropical diseases.[24]

What, then, might be the advantages of light-colored skin? Presumably, there must be some benefits; otherwise, through the process of natural selection, human populations would all tend to have relatively dark skin. Although light-skinned people are more susceptible to sunburn and skin cancers, the ultraviolet radiation that light skin absorbs also facilitates the body's production of vitamin D. Vitamin D helps the body incorporate calcium and thus is necessary for the proper growth and maintenance of bones. Too much vitamin D, however, can cause illness. Thus, the light-colored skin of people in temperate latitudes maximizes ultraviolet penetration, perhaps ensuring production of sufficient amounts of vitamin D for good health, whereas the dark skin of people in tropical latitudes minimizes ultraviolet penetration, perhaps thereby preventing illness from too much vitamin D.[25] Light skin may also confer another advantage in colder environments: it is less likely to be damaged by frostbite.[26]

---

[24] Anthony P. Polednak. "Connective Tissue Responses in Negroes in Relation to Disease." *American Journal of Physical Anthropology*, 41 (1974): 49–57. See also Richard F. Branda and John W. Eaton, "Skin Color and Nutrient Photoylsis: An Evolutionary Hypothesis," *Science*, August 18, 1978, pp. 625–26.

[25] W. Farnsworth Loomis. "Skin-Pigment Regulation of Vitamin-D Biosynthesis in Man." *Science*, August 4, 1967, pp. 501–6.

[26] Peter W. Post, Farrington Daniels Jr., and Robert T. Binford, Jr. "Cold Injury and the Evolution of 'White' Skin." *Human Biology*, 47 (1975): 65–80.

Susceptibility to Infectious Diseases

Certain populations seem to have developed inherited resistances to certain infectious diseases. That is, populations repeatedly decimated by certain diseases in the past now have a high frequency of genetic characteristics that minimize the effects of these diseases. As Arno Motulsky has pointed out, if there are genes that protect people from dying when they are infected by one of the diseases prevalent in their area, these genes will tend to become more common in succeeding generations.[27]

A field study of the infectious disease myxomatosis in rabbits supports this theory. When the virus responsible for the disease was first introduced into the Australian rabbit population, more than 95 percent of the infected animals died. But among the offspring of animals exposed to successive epidemics of myxomatosis, the percentage of animals that died from the disease decreased from year to year. The more epidemics the animals' ancestors had lived through, the smaller the percentage of current animals that died of the disease. Thus, the data suggested that the rabbits had developed a genetic resistance to myxomatosis.[28]

Infectious diseases seem to follow a similar pattern among human populations. When tuberculosis first strikes a population that has had no previous contact with it, the disease is commonly fatal. But some populations seem to have inherited a resistance to death from tuberculosis. For example, the Ashkenazi Jews in America (those whose ancestors came from central and eastern Europe) are one of several populations whose ancestors survived many years of exposure to tuberculosis in the crowded European ghettos where they had previously lived. Although the rate of tuberculosis infection is identical among American Jews and non-Jews, the rate of tuberculosis mortality is significantly lower among Jews than among non-Jews in this country.[29] After reviewing other data on this subject, Motulsky thinks it likely "that the present relatively high resistance of Western populations to tuberculosis is genetically conditioned through natural selection during long contact with the disease.[30]

We tend to think of measles as a childhood disease that kills virtually no one. Indeed, it is rapidly becoming a childhood disease that almost no one gets anymore, because we now have a vaccine against it. But when first introduced into populations, the measles virus can kill large numbers of people. In 1949, the Tupari Indians of Brazil numbered about 200 people. By 1955, two-thirds of the Tupari had died of measles introduced into the tribe by rubber gatherers in the area.[31] Large numbers of people died of measles in

---

[27] Arno Motulsky. "Metabolic Polymorphisms and the Role of Infectious Diseases in Human Evolution." In Morris, ed., *Human Populations, Genetic Variation, and Evolution*, p. 223.
[28] Ibid., p. 226.
[29] Ibid., p. 229.
[30] Ibid., p. 230.
[31] Ibid., p. 233.

epidemics in the Faroe Islands in 1846, in Hawaii in 1848, in the Fiji Islands in 1874, and among the Canadian Eskimos quite recently. It is possible that where mortality rates from measles are low, populations have acquired a genetic resistance to death from this disease.[32]

Some researchers suggest that nongenetic factors may be more important than genetic factors in differential resistance to infectious disease. For example, cultural practices more than genetic susceptibility may explain the epidemics of measles among the Yanomamö Indians of Venezuela and Brazil. The Yanomamö frequently visit other villages. That together with the non-isolation of sick individuals promoted a very rapid spread of the disease. Many individuals were sick at the same time, so there were not enough healthy people to feed and care for the sick; mothers down with measles could not even nurse their babies. Thus, cultural factors may increase exposure to a disease and worsen its effect on a population.[33]

Sickle-Cell Anemia

Another biological variation, the causes of which we are beginning to understand, is an abnormality of the red blood cells known as **sickle-cell anemia**, or **sicklemia**. This is a condition in which the red blood cells assume a crescent (sickle) shape when deprived of oxygen, instead of the normal (disk) shape. The sickle-shaped red blood cells tend to rupture, thereby causing severe anemia. The abnormally shaped cells also tend to form clumps that clog smaller blood vessels. This impairs circulation and causes pain in the abdomen, back, head, and extremities. The heart may become enlarged and brain cells may atrophy.

The sickle-cell trait is an inherited condition for which people can be either homozygous or heterozgous. A person who is homozygous for the trait has received a sickling gene from each parent and will therefore have sickle-cell anemia. Offspring who are heterozygous for the trait have received the sickle-cell gene from one parent only. These children generally will not develop sicklemia. (In some cases, a heterozygous individual may have a mild case of anemia.) However, a heterozygous person can pass on the trait. And if such a person mates with a person who is also heterozygous for sicklemia, the statistical probability is that 25 percent of their children will have the homozygous form of this condition.

Without medical care, individuals homozygous for sicklemia usually die before reaching maturity.[34] Since this would tend to decrease the number of sickle-cell genes in a population's gene pool, why has sicklemia not disap-

[32] Ibid.

[33] James V. Neel et al. "Notes on the Effect of Measles and Measles Vaccine in a Virgin-Soil Population of South American Indians." *American Journal of Epidemiology,* 91 (1970): 418–29.

[34] Motulsky. "Metabolic Polymorphisms and the Role of Infectious Diseases in Human Evolution," p. 237.

peared? At the very least, we would expect the condition to have become extremely rare, assuming that natural selection should have continuously weeded out this potentially lethal trait.

And yet sickle-cell anemia is still very common—particularly in equatorial Africa, where up to 40 percent of the population carry the trait. Nine percent of American blacks also carry the sickle-cell trait.[35] For this reason, the sickle-cell trait was once thought to be a specifically "Negroid" characteristic. But research has shown that this is not quite the case. The sickle-cell trait crosses "racial" lines: it is widespread in Greece, Turkey, and India. Why does the trait occur so frequently?

Studies indicate that the heterozygous carrier of the sickle-cell trait may be protected against a kind of malaria that kills many people in the regions where sicklemia is most prevalent. Malaria is carried principally by the *Anopheles gambiae* mosquito, common in tropical areas. Motulsky points out that the sickling trait does not necessarily keep people from contracting malaria, but it greatly decreases the rate of mortality from malaria—and in evolutionary terms, the overall effect is the same.[36] Heterozygous carriers have also been reported to have higher fertility in malarial areas.[37]

The point is that since persons homozygous for sicklemia rarely reproduce, and since many "normal" persons (those lacking the sickle-cell gene) die early or reproduce less because of malaria, individuals who are heterozygous for sicklemia may be favored by natural selection in malarial regions. Hence, the sickling trait is likely to persist among certain populations until the threat of malaria disappears. When that happens, the sickle-cell trait will no longer confer any advantage on its carriers.[38]

Lactase Deficiency

When American educators discovered that black schoolchildren very often did not drink milk, they assumed that lack of money or of education was the reason. These assumptions provided the impetus for establishing the school milk programs prevalent around the country.

However, it now appears that after infancy many people lack an enzyme, lactase, that is necessary for breaking down lactose, the sugar in milk.[39] A person without lactase cannot digest milk properly, and drinking it will cause bloating, cramps, stomach gas, and diarrhea. A study conducted in Baltimore among 321 black and 221 white children in grades 1 through 6 in two elementary schools indicated that 85 percent of the black children *and* 17 percent of the white children were milk-intolerant.[40]

[35] Anthony C. Allison. "Sickle Cells and Evolution." *Scientific American*, August 1956, p. 87.
[36] Motulsky. "Metabolic Polymorphisms and the Role of Infectious Diseases in Human Evolution," p. 238.
[37] Research reported in Frank B. Livingston, "Malaria and Human Polymorphisms" *Annual Review of Genetics*, 5 (1971): 33–64, esp. 45–46.
[38] Allison. "Sickle Cells and Evolution," p. 87.
[39] Overfield. *Biologic Variation in Health and Illness*, p. 52.
[40] Jane E. Brodey. "Effects of Milk on Blacks Noted." *New York Times*, October 15, 1971, p. 15.

More recent studies indicate that milk intolerance is frequent in many parts of the world.[41] The condition is common in adults among Orientals, southern Europeans, Mediterranean peoples (Arabs and Jews), West Africans, North American blacks, Eskimos, and North and South American Indians.

What accounts for this widespread adult intolerance of milk? One hypothesis is that milk tolerance is a physiological adaptation resulting from continuous milk consumption over the life span. Another possible explanation is that a regulatory gene is involved—although the function of regulatory genes is not yet fully understood.[42] Robert McCracken suggests that perhaps all human populations were once lactase-deficient.[43] With the advent of dairy farming and the common use of milk as a basic food by some populations, natural selection might have favored those individuals with the genetic ability to produce lactase in adulthood.

But people in some dairying societies do not produce lactase in adulthood. Rather, they seem to have developed a cultural solution to the problem of lactase deficiency: they transform their milk into cheese, yogurt, sour cream, and other milk products that are low in lactose. To make these low-lactose products, people separate the lactose-rich whey from the curds or treat the milk with a bacterium *(Latobacillus)* that breaks down the lactose, thus making the milk product digestible by a lactase-deficient person.

So why in some dairy societies did natural selection favor a biological solution (the production in adulthood of the enzyme lactase) rather than the cultural solution? William Durham has collected evidence that natural selection may favor the biological solution in dairying societies further from the equator. The theory is that lactose behaves biochemically like vitamin D, facilitating the absorption of calcium—but only in people who produce lactase so that they can absorb the lactose. Because people in more temperate latitudes are not exposed to that much sunlight, particularly in winter, and therefore make less vitamin D in their skin, natural selection may have favored the lactase way of absorbing dietary calcium.[44] In other words, natural selection may favor lactase production in adulthood, as well as lighter skin, in higher latitudes.

THE CONCEPT OF RACE

Fortunately, internal variations such as lactase deficiency have never caused tensions among peoples—perhaps because such differences are not imme-

---

[41] Gail G. Harrison. "Primary Adult Lactase Deficiency: A Problem in Anthropological Genetics." *American Anthropologist*, 77 (1975): 812–35.

[42] Ibid., pp. 826, 829.

[43] Robert D. McCracken. "Lactase Deficiency: An Example of Dietary Evolution." *Current Anthropology*, 12 (1971): 479–500.

[44] First reported in an unsigned article, "Biology and Culture Meet in Milk," *Science*, January 2, 1981, p. 40. See also William H. Durham, *Coevolution: Genes, Culture, and Human Diversity*, Stanford, Calif.: Stanford University Press, 1991.

diately obvious. Unfortunately, the same cannot be said for some of the more obvious external human differences.

Race and Racism

For as long as any of us can remember, countless aggressive actions—from fist fights to large-scale riots and countrywide civil wars—have stemmed from tension and misunderstandings among various "races." "The race problem" has become such a common phrase that most of us take the concept of race for granted, not bothering to consider what it does, and does not, mean.

The word **race** is used in a variety of ways. Consider, for example, what we mean when we refer to the "human race." Obviously, that phrase is supposed to include *all* people and does not have anything to do with the usual meaning of race. The "Aryan race" was supposed to be the group of blond-haired, blue-eyed, white-skinned people whom Hitler wanted to dominate the world, to which end he attempted to destroy as many members of the "Jewish race" as he could. But who are the Aryans? Technically, Aryans are any people, including the German-speaking Jews in Hitler's Germany, who speak one of the Indo-European languages. The Indo-European languages include such disparate modern tongues as Greek, Hindi, Polish, Icelandic, German, Gaelic, and English, and many Aryans speaking these languages have neither blond hair nor blue eyes. Similarly, the Jewish race does not exist in anthropological terms, since all kinds of people may be Jews, whether or not they descend from the ancient Near Eastern population that spoke the Hebrew language. There are light-skinned Danish Jews and dark Jewish Arabs. One of the most orthodox Jewish groups in the United States is based in New York City and is composed entirely of black people.

Nevertheless, most people in this country do identify themselves with a "racial" group, most often one of the three races most popularly recognized: the Caucasoid (white), Negroid (black), and Mongoloid (yellow and red). Many people think that certain biological traits are characteristic of each race. Another popular belief is that although the races have become "adulterated" through miscegenation (marriage and breeding between different races), some individuals still exist who typify the "pure" Caucasoid, Negroid, and Mongoloid types. The inaccuracy of such a classification should be obvious. Although many Caucasoids have straight hair and light skin, some have curly or quite frizzy hair and rather dark skin. Not all Negroids have wide noses or thick lips. And many people do not easily fit into any of the three major racial types at all.

But racial stereotypes persist—largely because of the ease with which such obvious traits as skin color can be recognized and used to classify people. In itself, this tendency to attribute certain biological factors to all members of a supposed race, while inaccurate, is not disturbing. What is disturbing is the frequent association of the race concept with racism.

Race concepts have often been, and still are, used by certain groups to justify their exploitation of other groups. A blatant example of how racism is linked to inaccurate concepts of race is the treatment accorded American blacks. Most of the people who tried to justify the virtual elimination of black civil rights did so because of a belief in blacks' inherent (genetic) inferiority to whites. In fact, no such inferiority has been demonstrated. This racist outlook may be a remnant of slavery days, when white slaveholders assumed that their servants were inferior—and tried to convince the slaves that they were—in order to perpetuate the system.

The Arbitrariness of the Concept of Race

The major difficulty with the race concept is its arbitrariness. The number of races into which the world's population can be divided depends on who is doing the classifying, because each classifier may use different traits as the basis for the classification. Any variable traits—such as skin color, blood type, and hair, nose, and lip shape—could be considered when developing a racial classification. But unfortunately for the classifiers, many of these traits do not vary together. Even the supposedly distinguishing features of a Mongoloid person—the so-called **Mongoloid spot**, a dark patch of skin at the base of the spine that disappears as the person grows older; shovel-shaped incisor teeth; and the **epicanthic fold**, a bit of skin overlapping the eyelid—are not limited to people traditionally classified as Mongoloid. Southern Africa's Bushmen have epicanthic folds, for example, and Caucasoids can have Mongoloid spots.

Thus, since the number of races in each classification of peoples depends on the traits used in the classification, and since many anthropologists base their classifications on different traits, there is no right or wrong number of races. William Boyd says there are five races, Carleton Coon recognizes nine, and Joseph Birdsell counts thirty-two.[45]

Racial taxonomies in anthropology typically involve the identification of both geographical races and local races. A **geographical race** is a set of at least once-neighboring populations that has certain distinctive trait frequencies. Thus, the traditional trio of races (Negroid, Mongoloid, Caucasoid) would be considered geographical. Stanley Garn identifies a total of nine geographical races: European-Caucasoid and Western Asiatic; Northern Mongoloid and Eastern Asiatic; African-Negroid; Indian; Micronesian; Melanesian; Polynesian; American; and Australian.[46] A **local race** is like a **Mendelian population**: it is a breeding population, or local group, whose members usually interbreed. Garn identifies approximately thirty-two local races.[47]

Anthropologists not only disagree on the number of races into which people can be classified; many would argue that the concept of race is not

---

[45] Theodosius Dobzhansky. *Mankind Evolving: The Evolution of the Human Species*. New Haven: Yale University Press, 1962, p. 266.

[46] Garn. *Human Races*, pp. 152–67.

[47] Ibid., pp.169–79.

particularly useful scientifically. Racial categories hardly ever correspond to the variations in human biology we want to explain. For example, populations classified as belonging to the same "race" may differ considerably in height, skin color, and body build. In addition, "racial" differences explain only a small percentage of the known genetic differences among humans. R. C. Lewontin estimates that only about 6 percent of genetic diversity can be explained by "racial" differences.[48] Racial taxonomies, then, may hinder rather than facilitate the study of human variation.

Racial and Cultural Variation: Is There a Relationship?

In the past, biological variation was believed to be related not only to the geographical location of a particular group of people, but also to their cultural characteristics. Even today, many persons hold the racist viewpoint that the biological inferiority of certain races is reflected in the supposedly primitive quality of their cultures. Racists refuse to recognize that the facts of history very often contradict their theories.

Race and Civilization.   Many of today's so-called underdeveloped nations—primarily in Asia, Africa, and South America—had developed complex and sophisticated civilizations long before Europe reached beyond a simple level of technology or tribal organization. The advanced societies of the Shang dynasty in China, the Mayans in Mesoamerica, and the African empires of Ghana, Mali, and Songhay were all founded and developed by nonwhites.

Between 1523 and 1028 B.C., China had a complex form of government, armies, metal tools and weapons, and production and storage facilities for large quantities of grain. The early Chinese civilization also had a form of writing and elaborate religious rituals.[49] From A.D. 300 to 900, the Mayans were a large population with a thriving economy. They built many large and beautiful cities, in which were centered great pyramids and luxurious palaces.[50] According to legend, the West African civilization of Ghana was founded during the second century A.D. By A.D. 770 (the time of the Sonniki rulers), Ghana had developed two capital cities—one Moslem and the other non-Moslem—each with its own ruler and both supported largely by Ghana's lucrative gold market.[51]

Considering how recently northern Europeans developed civilizations, it seems odd that some whites should label Africans, South American Indians, and other societies backward in terms of historical achievement, or biologically inferior in terms of capacity for civilization. But racists, both white and

---

[48] R. C. Lewontin. "The Apportionment of Human Diversity." In Theodosius Dobzhansky, ed., *Evolutionary Biology*. New York: Plenum, 1972, pp. 381–98.

[49] L. Carrington Goodrich. *A Short History of the Chinese People*, 3rd ed. New York: Harper & Row, 1959, pp. 7–15.

[50] Michael D. Coe. *The Maya*. New York: Praeger, 1966, pp. 74–76.

[51] Elizabeth Barlett Thompson. *Africa, Past and Present*. Boston: Houghton Mifflin, 1966, p. 89.

nonwhite, choose to ignore the fact that many populations have achieved remarkable advances in civilization. Most significant, racists refuse to believe that they can acknowledge the achievements of another group without in any way downgrading the achievements of their own.

Race, Culture, and Infectious Disease. Although biological variations cannot set fixed limits on the development of a particular culture, they may strongly influence it. Earlier, we discussed how continued exposure to epidemics of infectious diseases, such as tuberculosis and measles, can cause succeeding generations to acquire a genetic resistance to death from such diseases. But on a short-term basis, differential susceptibility to disease may have affected the outcome of contact between different societies.[52] A possible example of this is the rapid defeat of the Aztecs of Mexico by Cortez and his conquistadors. In 1520, a member of Cortez's army unwittingly transmitted smallpox to the Indians. The disease spread rapidly through the population, killing at least half of the Indians, who were thus at a considerable disadvantage in their battle with the Spanish.[53]

Outbreaks of smallpox repeatedly decimated many American Indian populations in North America a century or two later. In the early nineteenth century, the Massachusetts and Narragansett Indians, with populations of 30,000 and 9000, respectively, were reduced by smallpox to a few hundred members. Extremely high mortality rates were also noted among the Crow, the Blackfoot, and other Indian groups during the nineteenth century. The germ theory alone cannot explain these epidemics. Once the European settlers realized how susceptible the Indians were to smallpox, they purposely distributed infected blankets to them. Motulsky calls the spread of smallpox "one of the first examples of biological warfare."[54]

Race and Intelligence. Perhaps the most controversial aspect of the racial distinctions made among people is the relationship, if any, between race and intelligence.

In the nineteenth century, European white supremacists attempted to find scientific justification for what they felt was the genetically inherited mental inferiority of blacks. They did this by measuring skulls. It was believed that the larger the skull, the greater the cranial capacity and the bigger (hence, also better) the brain.

Interest in skull measurement was first aroused by a number of separate researchers in different parts of Europe who tried to determine the relative intelligence of round-headed versus narrow-headed individuals. Not surprisingly, their results were generally either inconclusive or contradictory. Paul Broca held that round-headed Frenchmen were superior in intelligence to narrow-headed Frenchmen, while Otto Ammon concluded that Baden's

[52] William H. McNeill. *Plagues and Peoples.* Garden City, N. Y.: Doubleday Anchor, 1976.
[53] Motulsky. "Metabolic Polymorphisms and the Role of Infectious Diseases in Human Evolution," p. 232.
[54] Ibid.

more intelligent residents had narrow heads. The Italian Livi concluded that southern Italians with round heads were of superior intelligence.

Although the skull-measuring mania quickly disappeared and is no longer upheld as evidence of racial superiority, the actions of these men paved the way for other attempts to justify racism. Other, more insidious, and often more powerful, "facts" are used today to demonstrate the presumed intellectual superiority of white people—namely, statistics from intelligence tests.

The first large-scale intelligence testing in this country began with our entry into World War I. Thousands of draftees were given the so-called Alpha and Beta IQ tests to determine military assignments. Later, psychologists arranged the test results according to race and found what they had expected—blacks scored consistently lower than whites. This was viewed as scientific proof of the innate intellectual inferiority of blacks and was used to justify further discrimination against blacks, both in and out of the army.[55]

Otto Klineberg's subsequent statistical analyses of IQ-test results demonstrated that blacks from northern states scored higher than blacks from the South. Although dedicated racists explained that this was due to the northward migration of innately intelligent blacks, most academics attributed the result to the influence of superior education and more stimulating environments in the North. When further studies showed that northern blacks scored higher than southern whites, the better-education-in-the-North theory gained support—but again racists insisted such results were due to northward migration by all innately intelligent whites.

As a further test of his conclusions, Klineberg gave IQ tests to black schoolgirls born and partly raised in the South who had spent varying lengths of time in New York City. He found that the longer the girls had been in the North, the higher their average IQ. In addition to providing support for the belief that blacks are not inherently inferior to whites, these findings suggested that cultural factors can and do influence IQ scores, and that IQ is not a fixed quantity but can be raised by contact with an improved environment.

The controversy about race and intelligence was fueled in 1969 by Arthur Jensen. He showed that although the IQ scores of American blacks overlapped considerably with the IQ scores of whites, the average score for blacks was 15 points lower than the average for whites. Jensen also presented evidence of a considerable genetic component in IQ scores; he estimated that approximately 80 percent of a person's IQ score is genetically determined. His evidence came from comparisons of the IQ scores of identical twins with those of other pairs of biological relatives (parent and child, first cousins, and so forth). For example, identical twins (with presumably the same genes) have

---

[55] Otto Klineberg. *Negro Intelligence and Selective Migration.* New York: Columbia University Press, 1935; and Otto Klineberg, ed. *Characteristics of the American Negro.* New York: Harper & Brothers, 1944.

more similar IQ scores even when reared apart than do nonidentical twins and siblings reared together.[56] The problem is not with Jensen's findings, but with how we are to interpret them. Since IQ scores presumably have a large genetic component, the lower average score for blacks implies to some that blacks are genetically inferior to whites. But others contend that the evidence presented by Jensen implies no such thing.

The critics of the genetic interpretation point to at least two problems. First, there is the issue of exactly what IQ tests measure. There is widespread recognition now that IQ tests are probably not accurate measures of "intelligence" because they are probably biased in favor of the subculture of the test constructors. That is, many of the questions on the test refer to things what white, middle-class children are more familiar with, thus giving such children an advantage.[57] So far, no one has come up with a "culture-fair" test. There is more agreement that although the IQ test may not measure "intelligence' well, it may predict scholastic success or how well a child will do in the primarily white-oriented school system.[58]

A second major problem with a purely genetic interpretation of the Jensen results is that many studies also show that IQ scores can be influenced by environment. Economically deprived children, whether black or white, will generally score lower than affluent white or black children. And training of children with low IQ scores clearly improves their test scores.[59] So, the critics argue, the average difference between blacks and whites in IQ cannot be attributed to presumed genetic differences. For all we know, the 15-point average difference may be due completely to differences in environment or to test bias.

Theodosius Dobzhansky emphasizes that conclusions about the causes of different levels of achievement on IQ tests cannot be drawn until both black and white people have equal opportunities to develop their potentials. He stresses the need for an open society existing under the democratic ideal—where every person is given an equal opportunity to develop whatever gifts or aptitudes he or she possesses and chooses to develop.[60]

THE FUTURE OF HUMAN VARIATION

Laboratory fertilization, subsequent transplantation of the embryo, and successful birth have been accomplished with humans and nonhumans.

---

[56] Arthur Jensen. "How Much Can We Boost IQ and Scholastic Achievement?" *Harvard Educational Review,* 29 (1969): 1–123.

[57] M. W. Smith. "Alfred Binet's Remarkable Questions: A Cross-National and Cross-Temporal Analysis of the Cultural Biases Built Into the Stanford-Binet Intelligence Scale and Other Binet Tests." *Genetic Psychology Monographs,* 89 (1974): 307–34.

[58] Theodosius Dobzhansky. *Genetic Diversity and Human Equality.* New York: Basic Books, 1973, p. 11.

[59] Ibid., pp. 14–15.

[60] Dobzhansky. *Mankind Evolving,* p. 243.

Cloning—the exact reproduction of an individual from cellular tissue—has been achieved with frogs. And genetic engineering—the substitution of some genes for others—is increasingly practiced in nonhuman organisms. Indeed, genetic engineering may soon be used in humans to eliminate certain disorders that are produced by defective genes.

What are the implications of such practices for the genetic future of humans? Will it really be possible someday to control the genetic makeup of our species? If so, will the effects be positive or negative?

It is interesting to speculate on the development of a "perfect human." Aside from the serious ethical question of who would decide what the perfect human should be like, there is the serious biological question of whether such a development might in the long run be detrimental to the human species, for what is perfectly suited to one physical or social environment may be totally unsuited to another. And the collection of physical, emotional, and intellectual attributes that might be "perfect" in the twentieth century might be inappropriate in the twenty-first.[61] Even defects such as the sickle-cell trait may confer advantages under certain conditions, as we have seen.

In the long run, the perpetuation of genetic variability is probably more advantageous than the creation of a "perfect" and invariable human being. In the event of dramatic changes in the world environment, absolute uniformity in the human species might be an evolutionary dead end. Such uniformity might lead to the extinction of the human species if new conditions favored genetic or cultural variations that were no longer present in the species. Perhaps our best hope for maximizing our chances of survival is to tolerate, and even encourage, the persistence of many aspects of human variation, both biological and cultural.[62]

SUMMARY

1. Genetic variation in humans, as well as in other species, is the result of one or more of the following processes: mutation and natural selection, genetic drift, and gene flow. Biological variation in human populations results from both genetic and environmental variation.
2. Human biological variation can be both external (such as skin color, body build, stature, and facial features) or internal (such as susceptibility to disease). Certain of these variations may be explained as adaptations to differing physical or social environments or as consequences of other physical or cultural changes. However, there are many biological variations among human populations for which we still have no explanations.
3. The major problem with the concept of race is its arbitrariness. The number of races into which the world's population can be divided depends on who is doing the classifying, because each classifier may use different traits as the basis for classifica-

[61] J. B. S. Haldane. "Human Evolution: Past and Future." In Glenn L. Jepsen, Ernst Mayr, and George Gaylord Simpson, eds., *Genetics, Paleontology, and Evolution.* New York: Atheneum, 1963, pp. 405–18.
[62] George Gaylord Simpson. *The Meaning of Evolution.* New York: Bantam, 1971, pp. 297–308.

tion. Racial classifiers identify both geographical and local races. A geographical race is a set of at least once-neighboring populations that has certain distinctive trait frequencies. A local race is a breeding population—that is, a local group whose members usually interbreed. Race concepts have often been, and still are, used by some groups to justify their exploitation of other groups.

4. Perhaps the most controversial aspect of racial discrimination is the relationship, if any, between race and intelligence. Attempts have been made to show, by IQ tests and other means, the innate intellectual superiority of one race to another. But there is doubt that IQ tests measure intelligence fairly. Since there is evidence that IQ scores are influenced by both genes and environment, conclusions about the causes of differences on IQ tests cannot be drawn until the people being compared have equal opportunities to develop their potentials.

7

The Emergence of Food Production and the Rise of States

Toward the end of the period known as the Upper Paleolithic, which we know best archeologically for Europe, people seem to have gotten most of their food from hunting the available migratory herds of large animals, such as wild cattle, antelope, bison, and mammoths. These hunter-gatherers were probably highly mobile in order to follow the migrations of the animals. Beginning about 14,000 years ago, people in some regions began to depend less on big-game hunting and more on relatively stationary food resources such as fish, shellfish, small game, and wild plants. Salt- and freshwater food supplies may have become more abundant in many areas after the glaciers withdrew. As the ice melted, the level of the oceans rose and formed inlets and bays where crabs, clams, and sea mammals could be found. In some areas, particularly Europe and the Near East, the exploitation of local and relatively permanent resources may have accounted for an increasingly settled way of life. The cultural period in Europe and the Near East during which these developments took place is called the **Mesolithic,** or the Middle Stone Age.[1]

[1] Lewis R. Binford. "Post-Pleistocene Adaptations." In Stuart Struever, ed., *Prehistoric Agriculture.* Garden City, N. Y.: Natural History Press, 1971, p. 27. Originally published in Sally R. Binford and Lewis R. Binford, eds., *New Perspectives in Archaeology*, Chicago: Aldine, 1968.

Other areas of the world show a similar switch to what is called *broad-spectrum* food collecting, but they do not always show an increasingly settled life style.

We see the first evidence of a changeover to food production—the cultivation and domestication of plants and animals—in the Near East about 8000 B.C. This shift has been called the "Neolithic revolution," and it occurred, probably independently, in a number of other areas as well. There is evidence of cultivation some time after 6800 B.C. in the lowland plains of Southeast Asia (what is now Malaysia, Thailand, Cambodia, and Vietnam) and in sub-Saharan Africa after 3000 B.C. In the New World, there appear to have been a number of places of original cultivation and domestication. The highlands of Mesoamerica (after about 5000 B.C.) and the central Andes around Peru (by about 5600 B.C.) were probably the most important in terms of food plants still used today.

In this chapter, we discuss what is believed about the origins of food production and settled life (**sedentarism**)—how and why people in different places may have come to cultivate and domesticate plants and animals and to live in permanent villages. Agriculture and a sedentary life did not necessarily go together. In some regions of the world, people began to live in permanent villages before they cultivated and domesticated plants and animals, whereas in other places people planted crops without settling down permanently. Much of our discussion focuses on the Near East and Europe, the areas we know best archeologically for the developments leading to food production and settled life. As much as we can, however, we try to indicate how data from other areas appear to suggest patterns different from, or similar to, those in Europe and the Near East.

Then we turn to the rise of the earliest cities and states. Beginning about 3500 B.C., cities and states arose in different parts of the world, first apparently in the Near East, and somewhat later around the eastern Mediterranean, in the Indus Valley of northwest India, in northern China, and in Mexico and Peru.

PREAGRICULTURAL DEVELOPMENTS

Europe

After about 10,000 years ago in Europe, the glaciers began to disappear. With their disappearance came other environmental changes: the oceans rose and the waters inundated some of the richest fodder-producing coastal plains. Other areas, particularly in Scandinavia, were opened up for human occupation as the glaciers retreated and the temperatures rose.[2] The cold, treeless plains (**tundras**) and grasslands eventually gave way to dense mixed forests,

---

[2] Desmond Collins. "Later Hunters in Europe." In Desmond Collins, ed., *The Origins of Europe.* New York: Thomas Y. Crowell, 1976, pp. 88–125.

mostly birch, oak, and pine, and the mammoths became extinct. During this time, too, the melting of the glaciers created islands, inlets, and bays and moved the sea inland. The warming waterways began to abound with fish and other aquatic resources.[3]

Archeologists believe these environmental changes induced some European groups to alter their food-getting strategies. The disappearance of the tundras and grasslands meant that hunters could no longer obtain large quantities of meat simply by remaining close to large migratory herds of animals, as they did during Upper Paleolithic times. Even though there were deer and other game around, the density of animals per square mile had decreased, and it had become difficult to stalk and kill animals sheltered in the thick woods. Thus, in many areas of Mesolithic Europe people seemed to have turned from a reliance on big-game hunting to the intensive collecting of wild grains, mollusks, fish, and small game to make up for the extinction of the mammoths and the northward migration of the reindeer.

The Near East

Cultural developments in the Near East seem to have paralleled those in Europe.[4] Here too there seems to have been a shift from mobile big-game hunting to the utilization of a broad spectrum of natural resources. There is evidence that people subsisted on a variety of resources, including fish, mollusks, and other water life; wild deer, sheep, and goats; and wild grains, nuts, and legumes.[5] The increased utilization of such stationary food sources as wild grain may partially explain why some people in the Near East began to lead more sedentary lives during the Mesolithic.

Even today, a traveler passing through the Anatolian highlands of Turkey and other mountainous regions in the Near East may see thick stands of wild wheat and barley growing as densely as if they had been cultivated. Wielding flint sickles, Mesolithic people could easily have harvested a bountiful crop from such wild stands. Just how productive this type of resource can be was demonstrated in a field experiment duplicating prehistoric conditions. Using the kind of flint-blade sickle a Mesolithic worker would have used, researchers were able to harvest a little over two pounds of wild grain in an hour. A Mesolithic family of four, working only during the few weeks of the harvest season, probably could have reaped more wheat and barley than they needed for the entire year.[6]

The amount of wild wheat harvested in the experiment prompted Kent Flannery to conclude, "Such a harvest would almost necessitate some degree of sedentism—after all, where could they go with an estimated metric ton of

---

[3] Chester S. Chard. *Man in Prehistory.* New York: McGraw-Hill, 1969, p. 171.
[4] Binford. "Post-Pleistocene Adaptations," pp. 45–49.
[5] Kent V. Flannery. "The Origins of Agriculture." *Annual Review of Anthropology,* 2 (1973): 274.
[6] Jack R. Harlan. "A Wild Wheat Harvest in Turkey." *Archaeology,* 20, no. 3 (June 1967): 197–201.

clean wheat?"[7] Moreover, the stone equipment used for grinding would have been a clumsy burden to carry. Part of the harvest would probably have been set aside for immediate consumption, ground, and then cooked either by roasting or boiling. The rest of the harvest would have been stored to supply food for the remainder of the year. A grain diet, then, could have been the impetus for the construction of roasters, grinders, and storage pits by some Mesolithic people, as well as for the construction of solid, fairly permanent housing. Once a village was built, people may have been reluctant to abandon it. We can visualize the earliest preagricultural settlements clustered around such naturally rich regions, as archeological evidence indeed suggests they were.

Other Areas

People in other areas in the world also shifted from hunting big game to collecting many types of food before they apparently began to practice agriculture. The still-sparse archeological record suggests that such a change occurred in Southeast Asia, which may have been one of the important centers of original plant and animal domestication. The faunal remains in inland sites there indicate that many different sources of food were being exploited from the same base camps. For example, at these base camps we find the remains of animals from high mountain ridges as well as lowland river valleys; birds and primates from nearby forests; bats from caves; and fish from streams. The few coastal sites indicate that many kinds of fish and shellfish were collected, and that animals such as deer, wild cattle, and rhinoceros were hunted.[8] As in Europe, the preagricultural developments in Southeast Asia probably were responses to changes in the climate and environment, including a warming trend, more moisture, and a higher sea level.[9]

In Africa too the preagricultural period was marked by a warmer, wetter environment (after about 5500 B.C.). The now-numerous lakes, rivers, and other bodies of water provided fish, shellfish, and other resources that apparently allowed people to settle more permanently than they had before. For example, there were lakes in what is now the southern and central Sahara desert, where people hunted hippopotamuses and crocodiles and fished. This pattern of broad-spectrum food collecting seems also to have been characteristic of the areas both south and north of the Sahara.[10]

At about the same time in the Americas, people were beginning to

[7] Kent V. Flannery. "The Origins and Ecological Effects of Early Domestication in Iran and the Near East." In Struever, ed., *Prehistoric Agriculture*, p. 59. Originally published in Peter J. Ucko and G. W. Dimbleby, eds., *The Domestication and Exploitation of Plants and Animals*, Chicago: Aldine, 1969.

[8] Chester Gorman. "The Hoabinhian and After: Subsistence Patterns in Southeast Asia during the Late Pleistocene and Early Recent Periods." *World Archaeology*, 2 (1970): 315–16.

[9] Kwang-Chih Chang. "The Beginnings of Agriculture in the Far East." *Antiquity*, 44, no. 175 (September 1970): 176. See also Gorman, "The Hoabinhian and After," pp. 300–19.

[10] J. Desmond Clark. *The Prehistory of Africa*. New York: Praeger, 1970, pp. 171–72.

exploit a wide variety of wild food resources, just as they were in Europe, Asia, and Africa. For example, evidence from Alabama and Kentucky shows that by about 5000 B.C., people had begun to collect freshwater mussels as well as wild plants and small game. In the Great Basin of what is now the United States, people were beginning to spend a longer and longer period each year collecting the wild resources around and in the rivers and glacial lakes.[11]

Why Did Broad-Spectrum Collecting Develop?

It is apparent that the preagricultural switch to broad-spectrum collecting was fairly common throughout the world. Climate change may have been partly responsible for increasing the supply of certain sources of food. For example, the worldwide rise in sea level may have increased the availability of fish and shellfish. Changes in climate may have also been partly responsible for the decline in the availability of big game, particularly the large herd animals. It has been suggested that another possible cause of that decline was human activity, specifically overkilling of some of these animals. The evidence suggesting overkill is that the extinction in the New World of many of the large Pleistocene animals, such as the mammoth, may have coincided with the movement of humans from the Bering Strait region to the southern tip of South America.[12] But the overkill hypothesis has been questioned on the basis of bird as well as mammal extinctions in the New World. An enormous number of bird species also became extinct during the last few thousand years of the North American Pleistocene, and it is difficult to argue that human hunters caused those extinctions. Since the bird extinctions occurred simultaneously with the mammal extinctions, it is likely that most or nearly all the extinctions were due to climatic and other environmental changes.[13]

The decreasing availability of big game may have stimulated people to exploit new food resources. But they may have turned to a broader spectrum of resources for another reason—population growth. As Mark Cohen has noted, hunter-gatherers were "filling up" the world, and they may have had to seek new and possibly less desirable sources of food.[14] (We might think of shellfish as more desirable than mammoths, but only because we don't have to do the work to get such food. An awful lot of shellfish have to be collected, shelled, and cooked to produce the animal protein obtainable from one large

---

[11] Thomas C. Patterson. *America's Past: A New World Archaeology.* Glenview, Ill.: Scott, Foresman, 1973, p. 42.

[12] Paul S. Martin. "The Discovery of America." *Science*, March 9, 1973, pp. 969–74.

[13] Donald K. Grayson. "Pleistocene Avifaunas and the Overkill Hypothesis." *Science*, February 18, 1977, pp. 691–92. See also three articles in Paul S. Martin and Richard G. Klein, eds., *Quaternary Extinctions: A Prehistoric Revolution,* Tucson: University of Arizona Press, 1984. Larry G. Marshall, "Who Killed Cock Robin?: An Investigation of the Extinction Controversy" (pp. 785–806); Donald K. Grayson, "Explaining Pleistocene Extinctions: Thoughts on the Structure of a Debate" (pp. 807–23); and R. Dale Guthrie, "Mosaics, Allelochemics and Nutrients: An Ecological Theory of Late Pleistocene Megafaunal Extinctions" (pp. 259–98).

[14] Mark Nathan Cohen. *The Food Crisis in Prehistory: Overpopulation and the Origins of Agriculture.* New Haven: Yale University Press, 1977, pp. 12, 85.

animal.) Consistent with the idea that the world was filling up around this time is that not until after 30,000 years ago did hunter-gatherers begin to move into deserts, polar regions, and tropical forests.[15] Since those would not be habitats of choice, they would not be exploited until the rest of the world was filled up.

Sedentarism and Population Growth

Although some population growth undoubtedly occurred throughout the hunting and gathering phase of world history, some anthropologists have suggested that populations would have increased dramatically when people began to settle down. The evidence for this suggestion comes largely from a comparison of recent nomadic and sedentary !Kung populations.

The settling down of a previously nomadic group may reduce the spacing between births.[16] Nomadic !Kung have children spaced four years apart on the average; in contrast, recently sedentarized !Kung have children about three years apart. Why might birth spacing change with settling down? One possibility is that people decide to alter their birth-spacing behavior. The spacing of children far apart can be accomplished in a number of ways. One way, given the cultural absence of contraceptives, is prolonged sexual abstinence after the birth of a child, which is common in recent human societies. Another possible way is infanticide.[17] Nomadic groups may be motivated to have children farther apart because of the problem of carrying small children. Carrying one small child is difficult enough; carrying two might be too burdensome. Sedentary populations presumably could have their children spaced more closely because carrying children would not always be necessary.

Although some nomadic groups may have deliberately spaced births by abstinence or infanticide, there is no evidence that such practices explain why four years separate births among the nomadic !Kung. There may be another explanation, involving an unintended effect of how babies are fed. Nancy Howell and Richard Lee have suggested that the presence of baby foods other than mother's milk may be responsible for the decreased birth spacing in sedentary agricultural !Kung groups.[18] It is now well established that the longer a mother nurses her baby without supplementary foods, the longer the

---

[15] Ibid., p. 85; and Fekri A. Hassan. *Demographic Archaeology*. New York: Academic Press, 1981, p. 207.

[16] Robert Sussman. "Child Transport, Family Size, and the Increase in Human Population Size during the Neolithic." *Current Anthropology*, 13 (April 1972): 258–67; and Richard B. Lee. "Population Growth and the Beginnings of Sedentary Life among the !Kung Bushmen." In Brian Spooner, ed., *Population Growth: Anthropological Implications*. Cambridge, Mass.: M.I.T. Press, 1972, pp. 329–42.

[17] For some examples of societies that have practiced infanticide, see David R. Harris, "Settling Down: An Evolutionary Model for the Transformation of Mobile Bands into Sedentary Communities," in J. Friedman and M. J. Rowlands, eds., *The Evolution of Social Systems*, London: Duckworth, 1977, pp. 401–17.

[18] Nancy Howell. *Demography of the Dobe !Kung*. New York: Academic Press, 1979; and Richard B. Lee. *The !Kung San: Men, Women, and Work in a Foraging Society*. Cambridge: Cambridge University Press, 1979.

mother is unlikely to start ovulating again. Nomadic !Kung women have little to give their babies in the way of soft digestible food, and the babies depend largely on mother's milk for two to three years. But sedentary !Kung mothers can give their babies soft foods such as cereal (from cultivated grain) and milk from domesticated animals. Such changes in feeding practices may shorten birth spacing by shortening the interval between birth and the resumption of ovulation. In preagricultural sedentary communities, it is possible that baby foods made from wild grains might have had the same effect. For this reason alone, therefore, populations may have grown even before people started to farm or herd.

Another reason sedentary !Kung women may have more babies than nomadic !Kung women has to do with the ratio of body fat to body weight. It is suspected by some investigators that a critical minimum of fat in the body may be necessary for ovulation. A sedentary !Kung woman may have more fatty tissue than a nomadic !Kung woman, who walks many miles daily to gather wild plant foods and who may be carrying a child around with her. Thus, sedentary !Kung women might resume ovulating sooner after the birth of a baby and so may be likely to have more closely spaced children. If some critical amount of fat is necessary for ovulation, that would explain why in our own society women athletes (such as long-distance runners and gymnasts) and ballet dancers, who have little body fat, do not ovulate regularly.[19]

Mesolithic Technology

Technologically, Mesolithic cultures did not differ radically from Upper Paleolithic cultures. (*Mesolithic*, like the term *Upper Paleolithic*, properly applies only to cultural developments in the Old World. However, we use the term *Mesolithic* here for some general preagricultural trends.) The trend toward smaller and lighter tools continued. *Microliths*, small blades half an inch to two inches long, which were made in late Upper Paleolithic times, were now used in quantity. In place of the one-piece flint implement, Mesolithic peoples in Europe, Asia, and Africa equipped themselves with composite tools—that is, tools made of more than one material.

Microliths could be fitted into grooves in bone or wood to form arrows, harpoons, daggers, and sickles. A sickle, for example, was made by inserting several microliths into a groove in a wooden or bone handle. The blades were held in place by resin. A broken microlith could be replaced like a blade in a razor. Besides being adaptable for many uses, microliths could be made from many varieties of available stone; Mesolithic people were no longer limited to flint. Since they did not need the large flint nodules to make large core and flake tools, they could use small pebbles of flint to make the small blades.[20]

[19] Rose E. Frisch. "Fatness, Puberty, and Fertility." *Natural History*, October 1980, pp. 16–27; and Howell. *Demography of the Dobe !Kung*.
[20] S. A. Semenov. *Prehistoric Technology*, trans. M. W. Thompson. Bath, England: Adams & Dart, 1970, pp. 63, 203–4.

THE DOMESTICATION OF PLANTS AND ANIMALS

Neolithic means *"of the new stone age"*; the term originally signified the cultural stage in which humans invented ground-stone tools and pottery. However, we now know that both characteristics were present in earlier times, so we cannot define a Neolithic state of culture on the basis of these two criteria. At present, Western archeologists define the Neolithic in terms of the presence of domesticated plants and animals. In this type of culture, people began to produce food rather than merely collect it.

The line between food collecting and food producing occurs when people begin to plant crops and to keep and breed animals. How do we know when this transition occurred? In fact, archeologically we do not see the beginning of food production. We can see signs of it only after plants and animals show differences from their wild varieties. When people plant crops, we refer to the process as *cultivation*. It is only when the crops cultivated and the animals raised are different from wild varieties that we speak of plant and animal **domestication**.

How do we know, in a particular site, that domestication occurred? Domesticated plants have characteristics different from those of wild plants of the same types. For example, wild grains of barley and wheat have a fragile **rachis** (the seed-bearing part of the stem), which shatters easily, releasing the seeds. Domesticated grains have a tough rachis, which does not shatter easily.

How did the domesticated plants get to be different from the wild varieties? Artificial or human selection, deliberate or accidental, obviously was required. Consider why the rachis of wheat and barley may have changed. As we said, when wild grain ripens in the field, the seed-bearing part, or rachis, shatters easily, scattering the seed. This is selectively advantageous under wild conditions, since it is nature's method of propagating the species. Plants with a tough rachis, therefore, have only a slight chance of reproducing themselves under natural conditions, but are more desirable for planting. When humans arrived with sickles and flails to collect the wild strands of grain, the seeds harvested probably contained a higher proportion of tough-rachis mutants, since these could best withstand the rough treatment of harvest processing. If planted, the harvested seeds would be more likely to produce tough-rachis plants. If in each successive harvest seeds from tough-rachis plants would less likely be lost, tough-rachis plants would come to predominate.[21]

Domesticated species of animals also differ from the wild varieties. For example, the horns of wild goats in the Near East are shaped differently from those of domesticated goats.[22] But differences in physical characteristics may

---

[21] Daniel Zohary. "The Progenitors of Wheat and Barley in Relation to Domestication and Agricultural Dispersal in the Old World." In Ucko and Dimbleby, eds., *The Domestication and Exploitation of Plants and Animals*, pp. 47–66.

[22] Kent V. Flannery. "The Ecology of Early Food Production in Mesopotamia." *Science*, March 12, 1965, p. 1252.

not be the only indicators of domestication. Some archeologists believe that imbalances in the sex and age ratios of animal remains at sites suggest that domestication had occurred. For example, at Zawi Chemi Shanidar in Iraq, the proportion of young to mature sheep remains was much higher than the ratio of young to mature sheep in wild herds. One possible inference to be drawn from this evidence is that the animals were domesticated, the adult sheep being saved for breeding purposes while the young were eaten. (If mostly young animals were eaten, and only a few animals were allowed to grow old, most of the bones found in a site would be from the young animals that were killed regularly for food.)[23]

Domestication in the Near East

For some time most archeologists have thought that the Fertile Crescent (see Figure 7-1), the arc of land stretching from the western slopes of the Zagros Mountains in Iran through southern Turkey and southward to Israel and the Jordan Valley, was one of the earliest centers of plant and animal domestication. We know that several varieties of domesticated wheat were being grown there after about 8000 B.C., as were barley, lentils, and peas. And there is evidence that goats, sheep, pigs, cattle, and dogs were being raised at about the same time. Let us turn to an early Neolithic site in the Near East to see what life there may have been like after people began to depend on domesticated plants and animals for food.

Ali Kosh.   At the stratified site of Ali Kosh in what is now southwestern Iran, we see the remains of a community that starts out about 7500 B.C. living mostly on wild plants and animals. Over the next two thousand years, until about 5500 B.C., we see agriculture and herding becoming increasingly important. And after 5500 B.C. we see the appearance of two innovations—irrigation and the use of domesticated cattle—that seem to stimulate a minor population explosion during the following millennium.

From 7500 to 6750 B.C., the people at Ali Kosh cut little slabs of raw clay out of the ground to build very small multiroom structures. The rooms excavated by archeologists are seldom more than seven by ten feet, and there is no evidence that the structures were definitely houses where people actually spent time or slept. Instead they may have been storage rooms. On the other hand, house rooms of even smaller size are known in other areas of the world, so it is possible that the people at Ali Kosh in its earliest phase were actually living in those tiny unbaked "brick" houses.

We have a lot of evidence about what the people at Ali Kosh ate. They got some of their food from cultivated emmer wheat and a kind of barley, and a considerable amount from domesticated goats. We know the goats were

---

[23] Ibid., p. 1253. For the view that a high proportion of immature animals does not necessarily indicate domestication, see Stephen Collier and J. Peter White, "Get Them Young? Age and Sex Inferences on Animal Domestication in Archaeology," *American Antiquity,* 41 (1976): 96–102.

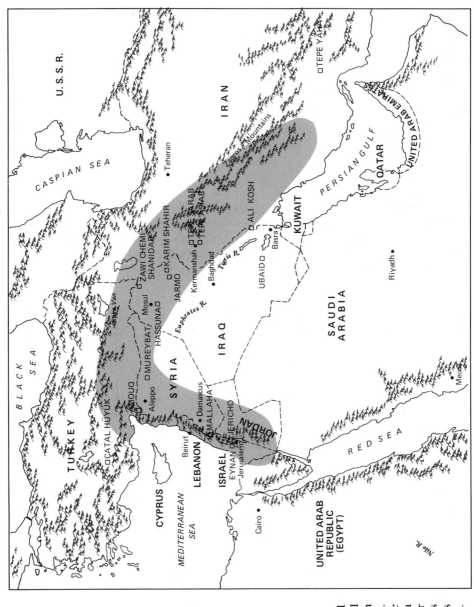

FIGURE 7–1
Early agricultural
settlements in
the Near East.
Modern cities are
represented by a
dot. The darker
color indicates
the area known as
the Fertile Crescent.

domesticated because wild goats do not seem to have lived in the area. Also, virtually no bones from elderly goats were found in the site, which suggests that the goats were domesticated and herded, rather than hunted. Moreover, it would seem from the horn cores found in the site that mostly young male goats were eaten, which suggests that the females were kept for breeding and milking. But with all these signs of deliberate food production, there is an enormous amount of evidence (literally tens of thousands of seeds and bone fragments) that the people at the beginning of Ali Kosh depended mostly on wild plants (legumes and grasses) and wild animals (including gazelles, wild oxen, and wild pigs). They also collected fish, such as carp and catfish, and shellfish, such as mussels, as well as waterfowl that visited the area during part of the year.

The flint tools used during this earliest phase at Ali Kosh were varied and abundant. They include tens of thousands of tiny flint blades, some only a few millimeters wide. About 1 percent of the chipped stone found by archeologists was **obsidian**, or volcanic glass, which came from what is now eastern Turkey, several hundred miles away. Thus, the people at Ali Kosh during its earliest phase definitely had some kind of contact with people elsewhere. This contact is also suggested by the fact that the emmer wheat they cultivated did not have a wild relative in the area.

From 6750 to 6000 B.C., the people increased their consumption of cultivated food plants: 40 percent of the seed remains in the hearths and refuse areas are now from emmer wheat and barley. The proportion of the diet coming from wild plants is much reduced, probably because the cultivated plants have the same growing season and grow in the same kind of soil as the wild plants. Grazing by the goats and sheep that were kept may also have contributed to the reduction of wild plant foods in the area and in the diet. The village may or may not have gotten larger, but the multiroom houses definitely had. The rooms are now larger than ten by ten feet. The walls are much thicker, and the clay-slab bricks are now held together by a mud mortar. Also, the walls now often have a coat of smooth mud plaster on both sides. The stamped-mud house floors were apparently covered with rush or reed mats. There were courtyards with domed brick ovens and brick-lined roasting pits. Understandably, considering the summer heat in the area, none of the ovens found by archeologists was inside a house.

Even though the village probably contained no more than 100 individuals, it participated in an extensive trading network. Seashells were probably obtained from the Persian Gulf, which is some distance to the south; copper may have come from what is now central Iran; obsidian was still coming from eastern Turkey; and turquoise somehow made its way from what is now the border between Iran and Afghanistan. Some of these materials were used as ornaments worn by both sexes—or so it seems from burials found under the floors of the houses.

After about 5500 B.C., the area around Ali Kosh begins to show signs of a much larger population, apparently made possible by a more complex agriculture employing irrigation and plows drawn by domesticated cattle. In the next thousand years, by 4500 B.C., the population of the area probably tripled. This population growth was apparently part of the cultural developments that culminated in the rise of urban civilization in the Near East.[24]

Population growth may have occurred in the area around Ali Kosh but did not continue in all areas of the Near East after domestication. For example, one of the largest early villages in the Near East, 'Ain Ghazal (on the outskirts of what is now Amman, Jordan), suffered a decline in population and standard of living over time, perhaps because the environment around 'Ain Ghazal could not permanently support a large village.[25]

Domestication in Southeast Asia, China, and Africa

A number of areas in the world other than the Near East appear to have been early centers of independent plant and animal domestication. One such area, which may have been a center of domestication almost as early as the Near East, was mainland Southeast Asia. The dates of the earliest cultivation there are not clear. Some plants found in Spirit Cave in northwest Thailand date from about 6800 B.C., but these specimens are not clearly distinguishable from wild varieties. They may have been wild, or they may have been cultivated but not yet changed in appearance.

Most of the early cultivation in mainland Southeast Asia seems to have occurred in the plains and low terraces around rivers, although the main subsistence foods of early cultivators were probably the fish and shellfish in nearby waters. The first plants to be domesticated were probably not cereal grains, as in the Near East. Indeed, some early cultivated crops may not have been used for food. Bamboo and a variety of bottle gourd, for example, were probably grown for use as containers. However, other plants were probably grown to be eaten: herbs, roots, tubers such as taro and yams, fruits, beans, and water chestnuts.[26]

The earliest evidence of cereal cultivation outside the Near East dates from China. Late in the sixth millenium B.C. in North China there were sites where foxtail millet was cultivated. Storage pits, storage pots, and large numbers of grinding stones suggest that millet was an important item in the diet. Judging from the wild-animal bones and the hunting and fishing tools that have been found, people still depended on hunting and fishing somewhat, even though domesticated pigs (as well as dogs) were present. In South

[24] Frank Hole, Kent V. Flannery, and James A. Neely. *Prehistory and Human Ecology of the Deh Luran Plain*. Memoirs of the Museum of Anthropology, no. 1. Ann Arbor: University of Michigan, 1969.

[25] See Alan H. Simmons, Ilse Köhler-Rollefson, Gary O. Rollefson, Rolfe Mandel, and Zeidan Kafafi. " 'Ain Ghazal: A Major Neolithic Settlement in Central Jordan." *Science*, April 1, 1988, pp. 35–39.

[26] Chang. "The Beginnings of Agriculture in the Far East," pp. 175–85.

China archeologists have found, dating from about the same time, a village by the edge of a small lake where people cultivated rice, bottle gourds, water chestnuts, and the datelike fruit called jujube. The people in South China also raised water buffalo, pigs, and dogs. And, as in the north China sites, they got some of their food from hunting and fishing.[27]

Some plants and animals were domesticated first in Africa, but there probably was not only one center of domestication. Most of the early domestications probably occurred in the wide and broad belt of woodland-savanna country south of the Sahara and north of the equator.[28] Among the cereal grains, sorghum was probably first domesticated in the central or eastern part of this belt, bulrush millet and a kind of rice (different from Asian rice) in the western part, and finger millet in the east. In what we now call West Africa, groundnuts (peanuts) and yams were domesticated.[29] Some of these domestications are estimated to have occurred after about 3000 B.C.[30] In addition to these domesticated plants, the ass, cat, and guinea fowl may also have been first domesticated in Africa.[31]

Domestication in the New World

In the New World, evidence of independent domestication of plants comes from at least three areas: Mexico, South America, and the eastern United States. Possibly the first plants to be domesticated in the New World were members of the cucurbit family; they included a variety of the bottle gourd, summer squash, and pumpkins. Although probably not an important source of food anywhere, the woody bottle gourd could have been used as a water jug or cut into bowls. People may also have made musical instruments and art objects out of the bottle gourd. It is difficult to establish exactly when and where the New World variety of bottle gourd was first domesticated. Some suspect it is native to Africa and floated to the New World like a runaway buoy.[32] Fragments and seeds of bottle gourd do date from as far back as 7400 B.C. in Oaxaca, Mexico. Summer squash was probably domesticated in Mexico between 7400 and 6700 B.C.[33]

[27] K. C. Chang. "In Search of China's Beginnings: New Light on an Old Civilization." *American Scientist,* 69 (1981): 148–60.

[28] Jack R. Harlan. J. M. J. De Wet, and Ann Stemler. "Plant Domestication and Indigenous African Agriculture." In Jack R. Harlan, Jan M. J. De Wet, and Ann B. L. Stemler, eds., *Origins of African Plant Domestication.* The Hague: Mouton, 1976, p. 13.

[29] J. W. Purseglove. "The Origins and Migrations of Crops in Tropical Africa." In Harlan, De Wet, and Stemler, eds., *Origins of African Plant Domestication,* pp. 291–309; Jack R. Harlan and Ann Stemler. "The Races of Sorghum in Africa." In Harlan, De Wet, and Stemler, eds., *Origins of African Plant Domestication,* p. 472.

[30] J. Desmond Clark. "Prehistoric Populations and Pressures Favoring Plant Domestication in Africa." In Harlan, De Wet, and Stemler, eds., *Origins of African Plant Domestication,* p. 87.

[31] Clark. *The Prehistory of Africa,* pp. 202–6.

[32] Charles B. Heiser, Jr. *Of Plants and People.* Norman: University of Oklahoma Press, 1985, p. 21.

[33] Kent V. Flannery. "The Research Problem." In Kent V. Flannery, ed., *Guila Naquitz: Archaic Foraging and Early Agriculture in Oaxaca, Mexico.* Orlando, Fla.: Academic Press, 1986, pp. 6–8.

Although the origins of maize (corn) are controversial, an early domesticated form dating from about 5000 B.C. has been found in Tehuacán, Mexico. Until 1970, the most widely accepted view was that maize was cultivated from a now-extinct "wild maize" that had tiny cobs topped by small tassels. Now other views are considered: that maize was domesticated from teosinte, a tall, wild grass that still grows widely in Mexico, or that it resulted from a cross between a perennial variety of teosinte and wild corn.[34]

People who lived in Mesoamerica (Mexico and Central America) are often credited with the invention of planting maize, beans, and squash together in the same field. This planting strategy provides a number of important advantages. Maize takes nitrogen from the soil; beans, like all legumes, put nitrogen back into the soil. The maize stalk provides a natural pole for the bean plant to twine around, and the low-growing squash can grow around the base of the tall maize plant. Beans supply people with the amino acid, lysine, that is missing in maize. Thus, maize and beans together provide all the proteins humans need. Whether teosinte was or was not the ancestor of maize, it may have provided the model for this unique combination since wild runner beans and wild squash occur naturally where teosinte grows.[35]

There are hints that plant cultivation began in South America almost as early as in Mexico. The first crops cultivated on the Peruvian coast were gourds, squash, lima beans, and possibly cotton. Around 4500 years ago, chili peppers, achira (a starchy root crop), jack beans, and guava were added. The root crops manioc and sweet potato may have been first domesticated in South America, or less likely in Mexico.[36]

Many of the plants grown in North America—such as corn, beans, and squash—were apparently introduced from Mesoamerica. However, at least two plants were probably domesticated independently in North America—sunflowers and a non-extinct variety of sumpweed. Both plants, members of the same biological family, contain seeds that are highly nutritious: they have a high fat and protein content. Sumpweed is an unusually good source of calcium, rivaled only by greens, mussels, and bones, it would also have been a very good source of iron (better than beef liver) and thiamine. Both plants may have been cultivated in the area of Kentucky, Tennessee, and southern Illinois beginning around 1500 B.C., prior to the introduction of maize.[37]

[34] Ibid.

[35] Ibid., pp. 8–9.

[36] Barbara Pickersgill and Charles B. Heiser, Jr. "Origins and Distribution of Plants Domesticated in the New World Tropics." In Charles A. Reed, ed., *Origins of Agriculture*. The Hague: Mouton, 1977, pp. 825–27.

[37] Richard A. Yarnell. "Domestication of Sunflower and Sumpweed in Eastern North America." In Richard I. Ford, ed., *The Nature and Status of Enthnobotany*. Anthropological Papers, Museum of Anthropology, no. 67. Ann Arbor: University of Michigan, 1978, pp. 289–300. See also Nancy B. Asch and David L. Asch, "The Economic Potential of *Iva annua* and Its Prehistoric Importance in the Lower Illinois Valley," in Ford, ed., *The Nature and Status of Enthnobotany*, pp. 301–42.

On the whole, domestic animals were less important economically in the New World than they were in many parts of the Old World. The animals domesticated in the New World included dogs, muscovy ducks, turkeys, guinea pigs, alpacas, and llamas. But the central Andes was the only area where animals were a significant part of the economy.[38] Guinea pigs, ducks, and turkeys were raised for food, alpacas mainly for their fur, and llamas for transporting goods. Animal domestication in the New World differed from that in the Old World because different wild species were found in the two hemispheres. The Old World plains and forests were the homes for the wild ancestors of the cattle, sheep, goats, pigs, and horses we know today. In the New World, the Pleistocene herds of horses, mastodons, mammoths, and other large animals were long extinct, allowing few opportunities for domestication of large animals.

Although there is evidence from Mexico and other parts of the Americas that cultivation was under way between the fifth and third millennia B.C., permanent villages were probably not established in Peru until about 2500 B.C. and in areas of Mesoamerica until about 1500 B.C.[39] Archeologists once thought that settled village life followed as a matter of course as soon as people had learned to domesticate plants. But evidence from the arid highlands of Mesoamerica contradicts this, and the reason may be that in highland Mesoamerica resources were widely distributed and relatively scarce in the dry season. Richard MacNeish suggests, for example, that the early cultivators depended mostly on hunting during the winter and on seed collecting and podpicking in the spring. In addition to their food-collecting activities, in the summer they planted and harvested crops such as squash, and in the fall they collected fruit and harvested the avocados they had planted. These varied activities seem to have required people to spend most of the year in small groups, gathering into larger groups only in the summer and only in moister areas.[40]

WHY DID FOOD PRODUCTION DEVELOP?

We know that an economic transformation occurred in widely separate areas of the world beginning after about 10,000 years ago, as people began to

[38] Robert J. Wenke. *Patterns in Prehistory: Humankind's First Three Million Years*, 2nd ed. New York: Oxford University Press, 1984, pp. 350, 397–98.

[39] Kent V. Flannery. "The Origins of the Village as a Settlement Type in Mesoamerica and the Near East: A Comparative Study." In Ruth Tringham, ed., *Territoriality and Proxemics*. Andover, Mass.: Warner Modular Publications, 1973, R1, p.1. However, there is evidence that there could have been permanent communities as far back as 6000 B.C. in central Mexico, near what is now Mexico City; see Christine Niederberger, "Early Sedentary Economy in the Basin of Mexico," *Science*, January 12, 1979, pp. 131–42.

[40] Richard S. MacNeish. "The Evaluation of Community Patterns in the Tehuacán Valley of Mexico and Speculations about the Cultural Processes." In Ruth Tringham, ed., *Ecology and Agricultural Settlements*. Andover, Mass.: Warner Modular Publications, 1973, R2, 1–27. Originally published in Peter J. Ucko, Ruth Tringham, and G. W. Dimbleby, eds., *Man, Settlement and Urbanism*, London: Duckworth; Cambridge, Mass.: Schenkman, 1972.

domesticate plants and animals. But why did domestication occur? And why did it occur independently in a number of different places within a period of a few thousand years? (Considering that people depended only on wild plants and animals for millions of years, the differences in exactly when domestication first occurred in different parts of the world seem small.) There are many theories of why food production developed; most have tried to explain the origin of domestication in the area of the Fertile Crescent.

Gordon Childe's theory, popular in the 1950s, was that a drastic change in climate caused domestication in the Near East.[41] According to Childe, who was relying on the climate reconstruction of others, the postglacial period was marked by a decline in summer rainfall in the Near East and North Africa. As the rains supposedly decreased, people were forced to retreat into shrinking pockets, or *oases,* of food resources surrounded by desert. The lessened availability of wild resources provided an incentive for people to cultivate grains and domesticate animals, according to Childe.

Robert Braidwood criticized Childe's theory for two reasons. First, the climate changes were nowhere near as dramatic as Childe had assumed, and therefore the "oasis incentive" probably never existed. Second, the climatic changes that occurred in the Near East after the retreat of the last glaciers had probably occurred at earlier interglacial periods too, but there had never been a similar food-producing revolution before. Hence, according to Braidwood, there must be more to the explanation of why people began to produce food than simply changes in climate.[42]

Braidwood's archeological excavations in the Near East indicated to him that domestication began in regions where local plants and animals were species that could be domesticated. Wild sheep, goats, and grains were found in areas with the oldest farming villages. Braidwood and Gordon Willey claimed that in addition, people did not undertake domestication until they had learned a great deal about their environment and until their culture had evolved far enough for them to handle such undertaking: "Why did incipient food production not come earlier? Our only answer at the moment is that culture was not ready to achieve it."[43] As Braidwood had written earlier,

> there is no need to complicate the story with extraneous "causes." . . . Around 8,000 B.C. the inhabitants of the hills around the fertile crescent had come to know their habitat so well that they were beginning to domesticate the plants and animals they had been collecting and hunting. . . . From these "nuclear" zones cultural diffusion spread the new way of life to the rest of the world.[44]

[41] Cited in Gary A. Wright, "Origins of Food Production in Southwestern Asia: A Survey of Ideas," *Current Anthropology,* 12 (1971): 453–54.

[42] Robert J. Braidwood. "The Agricultural Revolution." *Scientific American,* September 1960, p. 130.

[43] Robert J. Braidwood and Gordon R. Willey. "Conclusions and Afterthoughts." In Robert J. Braidwood and Gordon R. Willey, eds., *Courses toward Urban Life: Archaeological Considerations of Some Cultural Alternatives.* Vicking Fund Publications in Anthropology, no. 32. Chicago: Aldine, 1962, p. 342.

[44] Braidwood. "The Agricultural Revolution," p. 134.

But most archeologists now think we should try to explain why people were not "ready" earlier to achieve domestication. Both Lewis Binford and Kent Flannery have suggested that *some change* in external circumstances, not necessarily environmental, must have induced or favored the changeover to food production.[45] As Flannery points out, there is no evidence of a great economic incentive for hunter-gatherers to become food producers. In fact, as we shall see in the chapter on food-getting, some contemporary hunter-gathers may actually obtain adequate nutrition with far *less* work than many agriculturists. So what might push food collectors to become food producers?

Binford and Flannery thought that the incentive to domesticate animals and plants may have been a desire to reproduce what was wildly abundant in the most bountiful or optimum hunting and gathering areas. Because of population growth in the optimum areas, people might have moved to surrounding areas containing fewer wild resources. It would have been in those marginal areas that people turned to food production in order to reproduce what they used to have.

The Binford-Flannery model seems to fit the archeological record in the Levant (the southwestern part of the Fertile Crescent), where population increases did precede the first signs of domestication.[46] But as Flannery admits, in some regions, such as southwestern Iran, the optimum hunting-gathering areas do not show a population increase before the emergence of domestication.[47]

The Binford-Flannery model focuses on population pressure in a small area as the incentive to turn to food production. Mark Cohen theorizes it was population pressure on a global scale that explains why so many of the world's peoples adopted agriculture within the span of a few thousand years.[48] He argues that hunter-gatherers all over the world gradually increased in population so that by about 10,000 years ago the world was more or less filled with food collectors. Thus, people could no longer relieve population pressure by moving to uninhabited areas. To support their increasing populations, they would have had to exploit a broader range of less desirable wild foods; that is, they would have had to switch to broad-spectrum collecting, or they would have had to increase the yields of the most desirable wild plants by weeding, protecting them from animal pests, and perhaps deliberately planting the most productive among them. Cohen thinks that people might have tried a variety of these strategies to support themselves but would generally have ended up depending on cultivation because that would have been the most efficient way to allow more people to live in one place.

Another possible incentive to turn to food production may have been

[45] Binford. "Post-Pleistocene Adaptations," pp. 22–49; and Flannery. "The Origins and Ecological Effects of Early Domestication in Iran and the Near East," pp. 50–70.
[46] Wright. "Origins of Food Production in Southwestern Asia," p. 470.
[47] Flannery. "The Research Problem," pp. 10–11.
[48] Mark N. Cohen. "Population Pressure and the Origins of Agriculture." In Reed, ed., *Origins of Agriculture*, pp. 138–41. See also Cohen, *The Food Crisis in Prehistory*, p. 279.

the postglacial emergence of greater seasonal variation in rainfall.[49] In the dry seasons certain nutrients would have been less available. For example, grazing animals get lean when grasses are not plentiful, and so meat from hunting would have been in short supply in the dry seasons. Although it may seem surprising, some recent hunter-gatherers have starved when they had to rely on lean meat. If they could have somehow increased their carbohydrate or fat intake, they might have been more likely to get through the periods of lean game.[50] So, it is possible that some wild-food collectors in the past thought of planting crops to get them through the dry seasons when hunting, fishing, and gathering did not provide enough carbohydrates and fat for them to avoid starvation.

CONSEQUENCES OF THE RISE OF FOOD PRODUCTION

We do not know for sure that population pressure was responsible (at least partially) for plant and animal domestication. But we do know that population growth accelerated after the rise of food production. There were other consequences too. Paradoxically, perhaps, health seems to have declined.

Accelerated Population Growth

As we have seen, settling down (even before the rise of food production) may have increased the rate of human population growth. But population growth seems to have accelerated after the emergence of farming and herding, possibly because the spacing between births was reduced further and therefore fertility (the number of births per mother) increased. One reason for the increased fertility may have been the greater value of children in farming and herding economies. There is evidence from recent population studies that fertility rates are higher where children contribute more to the economy.[51] Not only may parents desire more children to help with chores, but the increased workload of mothers may inadvertently decrease birth spacing. The busier a mother is, the less frequently she may nurse and the more likely her baby will be given supplementary food by babysitters such as older siblings.[52] Less frequent nursing[53] and greater reliance on food other than mother's milk may result in an earlier resumption of ovulation after the birth of a baby.

---

[49] Guthrie. "Mosaics, Allelochemics, and Nutrients," p. 291; and Flannery. "The Research Problem," p. 14.

[50] John D. Speth and Katherine A. Spielmann. "Energy Source, Protein Metabolism, and Hunter-Gatherer Subsistence Strategies." *Journal of Anthropological Archaeology*, 2 (1983): 1–31.

[51] Benjamin White. "Demand for Labor and Population Growth in Colonial Java." *Human Ecology*, 1, no. 3 (March 1973): 217–36. See also John D. Kasarda, "Economic Structure and Fertility: A Comparative Analysis," *Demography*, 8, no. 3 (August 1971): 307–18.

[52] Carol R. Ember. "The Relative Decline in Women's Contribution to Agriculture with Intensification." *American Anthropologist*, 85 (1983): 285–304.

[53] Melvin Konner and Carol Worthman. "Nursing Frequency, Gonadal Function, and Birth Spacing among !Kung Hunter-Gatherers." *Science*, February 15, 1980, pp. 788–91.

(Farmers and herders are likely to have animal milk to feed to babies and also cereals that have been transformed by cooking into soft, mushy porridges.) Therefore the spacing between births may have decreased (and the number of births per mother may have increased) when mothers got busier after the rise of food production.

Declining Health

Although the rise of food production may have led to increased fertility, this does not mean that health generally improved. In fact, it appears that health may often have declined with the transition to food production. Although the two trends may seem paradoxical, rapid population growth can occur if each mother gives birth to a large number of babies, even if many of them die early because of disease or poor nutrition.

The evidence that health may have declined after the rise of food production comes from studies of the bone and teeth of some prehistoric populations, before and after the emergence of food production. Nutritional and disease problems are indicated by such features as incomplete formation of tooth enamel, nonaccidental bone lesions (incompletely filled in bone), reduction in stature, and decreased life expectancy. Many of the studied prehistoric populations that relied heavily on agriculture seem to show less adequate nutrition and higher infection rates than populations living in the same areas prior to agriculture. Some of the agricultural populations are shorter and had lower life expectancies.[54]

The reasons for a decline in health in those populations are not yet clear. Greater malnutrition can result from an overdependence on a few dietary staples that lack some necessary nutrients. Overdependence on a few sources of food may also increase the risk of famine because the fewer the staple crops, the greater the danger to the food supply posed by a weather-caused crop failure. But some or most nutritional problems may be the result of unequal access, between and within communities, to food and other resources.[55]

As we will see, social stratification or socioeconomic inequality seems to develop frequently after the rise of food production. The effects of stratification and political dominance on the general level of health seem to be illustrated in the skeletal remains of prehistoric native Americans who died in

[54] Anna Curtenius Roosevelt. "Population, Health, and the Evolution of Subsistence: Conclusions from the Conference." In Mark Nathan Cohen and George J. Armelagos, eds., *Paleopathology at the Origins of Agriculture.* Orlando, Fla.: Academic Press 1984, pp. 559–84. See also Mark Nathan Cohen and George J. Armelagos, "Paleopathology at the Origins of Agriculture: Editors' Summation," in the same volume, pp. 585–602; and Mark N. Cohen, "The Significance of Long Term Changes in Human Diet and Food Economy," in Marvin Harris and Eric B. Ross, eds., *Food and Evolution: Toward a Theory of Human Food Habits,* Philadelphia: Temple University Press, 1987 p. 269–273.
[55] Roosevelt. "Population, Health, and the Evolution of Subsistence"; and Cohen and Armelagos. "Paleopathology at the Origins of Agriculture."

what is now Illinois between A.D. 950 and 1300 (the period spanning the changeover in that region from hunting and gathering to agriculture). The agricultural people living in the area of Dickson's Mounds (burial sites named after the doctor who first excavated them) were apparently in much worse health than their hunter-gatherer ancestors. But curiously, archeological evidence suggests they were still also hunting and fishing. A balanced diet was apparently available, but who was getting it? Possibly it was the elite at Cahokia (110 miles away, where perhaps 30,000 people lived) who were getting most of the meat and fish. The individuals near Dickson's Mounds who collected the meat and fish may have gotten luxury items such as shell necklaces from the Cahokia elite, but many of the people buried at Dickson's Mounds were clearly not benefiting nutritionally from the relationship with Cahokia.[56]

ORIGINS OF CITIES AND STATES

From the time agriculture first developed until about 6000 B.C., people in the Near East lived in fairly small villages. There were few differences in wealth and status from household to household, and there was apparently no governmental authority beyond the village. There is no evidence that these villages had any public buildings or craft specialists, or that one community was very different in size from its neighbors. In short, these settlements had none of the characteristics we commonly associate with "civilization."

But sometime around 6000 B.C. in parts of the Near East—and at later times in other places—a great transformation in the quality and scale of human life seems to have begun. For the first time, we can see evidence of differences in wealth and status among households. Communities began to differ in size and to specialize in certain crafts. There are signs that some political officials had acquired authority over several communities. By about 3500 B.C. we can see many, if not all, the conventional characteristics of **civilization**: large cities; many kinds of full-time craft specialists; monumental architecture; great differences in wealth and status; and the kind of strong, centralized political system we call the state.

This type of transformation has occurred many times and in many places in human history. The most ancient civilizations arose in the Near East around 3500 B.C., in northwestern India after 2500 B.C., in northern China around 1650 B.C., and in the New World (in Mexico and Peru) a few hundred years before the time of Christ.[57] At least some of these civilizations evolved

---

[56] Alan H. Goodman and George J. Armelagos. "Disease and Death at Dr. Dickson's Mounds." *Natural History*, September 1985, p. 18. See also Alan H. Goodman, John Lallo, George J. Armelagos, and Jerome C. Rose, "Health Changes at Dickson Mounds, Illinois (A.D. 950–1300)," in Cohen and Armelagos, *Paleopathology at the Origins of Agriculture*, p. 300.

[57] Robert J. Wenke. *Patterns in Prehistory: Humankind's First Three Million Years*, 3rd ed. New York: Oxford University Press, 1990. See also Elman R. Service, *Origins of the State and Civilization: The Process of Cultural Evolution*, New York: W. W. Norton & Co., Inc., 1975, p. 5.

independently of the others—for example, those in the New World and those in the Old World. Why did they do so? What conditions favored the emergence of centralized, statelike political systems? What conditions favored the establishment of cities? (We ask this last question separately, because archeologists are not yet certain that all the ancient state societies had cities when they first developed centralized government.) Here we discuss some of the things archeologists have learned or suspect about the growth of ancient civilizations. Our discussion focuses primarily on the Near East and Mexico because archeologists know the most about the sequence of cultural development in these two areas. (See Figure 7-2 for the locations of the earliest civilizations.)

Archeological Inferences about Civilization

The most ancient civilizations have been studied by archeologists rather than historians because those civilizations evolved before the advent of writing. How do archeologists infer that a particular people in the preliterate past had social classes, cities, or centralized government?

It appears that the earliest Neolithic societies were *egalitarian:* people did not differ much in wealth, prestige, or power. Some later societies show signs of social inequality. One kind of evidence of inequality in an ancient society is provided by burial finds. Archeologists generally assume that inequality in death reflects inequality in life, at least in status and perhaps also in wealth and power. Thus, we can be fairly sure that a society had differences in status if only some people were buried with special objects, such as jewelry or pots filled with food. And we can be fairly sure that high status was assigned at birth rather than achieved in later life if we find noticeable differences in children's tombs. For example, some (but not all) child burials from as early as 5500 to 5000 B.C. at Tell es-Sawwan in Iraq, and from about 800 B.C. at La Venta in Mexico, are filled with statues and ornaments suggesting that some children had high status from birth.[58] But burials indicating differences in status do not necessarily mean a society had significant differences in wealth. It is only when archeologists find other substantial differences, as in house size and furnishings, that we can be sure the society had different socioeconomic classes of people.

Some archeologists think that states first evolved around 3500 B.C. in Greater Mesopotamia, the area now shared by southern Iraq and southwestern Iran. Archeologists do not always agree on how a state should be defined, but most seem to agree that centralized decision making affecting a substantial population is the key criterion. Other characteristics are usually, but not always, found in these first states. Such states usually have cities with a substantial proportion of the population not involved directly in the collection or production of food (which means that people in cities are heavily depen-

---

[58] Kent V. Flannery. "The Cultural Evolution of Civilizations." *Annual Review of Ecology and Systematics*, 3 (1972): 399–425.

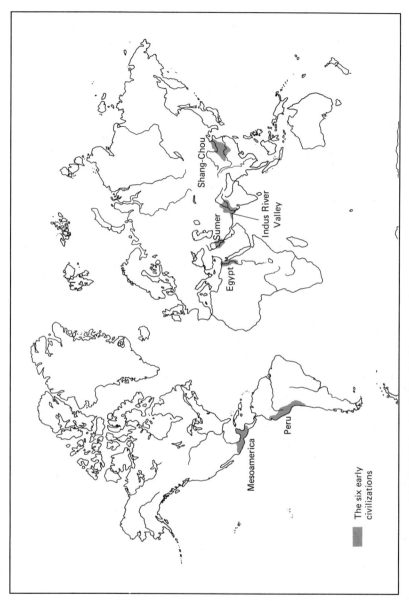

FIGURE 7-2 Six Early Civilizations
(*Adapted from* Origins of the State and Civilization: The Process of Cultural Evolution, *by Elman R. Service. By permission of W. W. Norton & Company, Inc. Copyright © 1975 by W. W. Norton & Company, Inc.*)

Shang-Chou

Sumer

Indus River Valley

Egypt

Mesoamerica

Peru

The six early civilizations

dent on people elsewhere); full-time religious and craft specialists; public buildings; and often an official art style. There is a hierarchical social structure topped by an elite class from which the leaders are drawn. The government tries to claim a monopoly on the use of force. (Our own state society says that citizens do not have the right "to take the law into their own hands.") The state uses its force or threat of force to tax its population and to draft people for work or war.[59]

How can archeologists tell, from the information provided by material remains, whether a society was a state or not? This depends in part on what is used as the criterion for a state. For example, Henry Wright and Gregory Johnson define a state as a centralized political hierarchy with at least three levels of administration.[60] But how might archeologists infer that such a hierarchy existed in some area? Wright and Johnson suggest that the way settlement sites differ in size is one indication of how many levels of administration there were in an area.

During the early Uruk period (just before 3500 B.C.) in what is now southwestern Iran, there were some fifty settlements that seem to fall into three groups in terms of size.[61] There were about forty-five small villages; three or four "towns"; and one large center, Susa. These three types of settlements seem to have been part of a three-level administration hierarchy, since many small villages could not trade with Susa without passing through a settlement intermediate in size. Because a three-level hierarchy is Wright and Johnson's criterion of a state, they think a state had emerged in the area by early Uruk times.

Let us turn now to the major features of the cultural sequences leading to the first states in southern Iraq.

Cities and States in Southern Iraq

Farming communities have not been found in the arid lowland plains of southern Iraq—the area known as Sumer, where some of the earliest cities and states developed. Perhaps silt from the Tigris and Euphrates rivers has covered them. Or, as has been suggested, Sumer may not have been settled by agriculturalists until people learned how to drain and irrigate river-valley soils otherwise too wet or too dry for cultivation. At any rate, small communities depending partially on agriculture had emerged in the hilly areas north and east of Sumer early in the Neolithic. Later, by about 6000 B.C., a mixed herding-farming economy developed in those areas.

---

[59] Ibid. See also Charles L. Redman, *The Rise of Civilization: From Early Farmers to Urban Society in the Ancient Near East,* San Francisco: W. H. Freeman and Company Publishers, 1978, pp. 215–16.

[60] Henry T. Wright and Gregory A. Johnson. "Population, Exchange, and Early State Formation in Southwestern Iran." *American Anthropologist,* 77 (1975): 267.

[61] The discussion in the remainder of this section draws from ibid., pp. 269–74.

The Formative Era.   Elman Service calls the period from about 5000 to 3500 B.C. the *formative era,* for it saw the coming together of many changes that seem to have played a part in the development of cities and states. Service suggests that with the development of small-scale irrigation, lowland river areas began to attract settlers. The rivers provided not only water for irrigation but also mollusks, fish, and water birds for food. And they provided routes by which to import needed raw materials, such as hardwood and stone, that were lacking in the region of Sumer.

We see a number of changes during this period that suggest an increasingly complex social and political life. We see differences in status reflected in the burial of statues and ornaments with children. We see different villages specializing in the production of different goods—pottery in some, copper and stone tools in others.[62] We see the building of temples in certain places that may have been centers of political as well as religious authority for several communities.[63] Some anthropologists think that chiefdoms, each having authority over a number of villages, had developed by this time.[64]

Sumerian Civilization.   By about 3500 B.C., there were a number of cities in the area of Sumer. Most were enclosed in a fortress wall and surrounded by an agricultural area. Shortly after the first forms of writing appeared—about 3000 B.C.—all of Sumer was unified under a single government. After that time, Sumer became an empire. It had great urban centers. Imposing temples, commonly set on artificial mounds, dominated the cities. (In the city of Warka the temple mound was about 150 feet high.) The empire was very complex. It included an elaborate system for the administration of justice, codified laws, specialized government officials, a professional standing army, and even sewer systems in the cities. Among the many specialized crafts were brickmaking, pottery, carpentry, jewelry making, leatherworking, metallurgy, basketmaking, stonecutting, and sculpture. Sumerians learned to construct and use wheeled wagons, sailboats, horse-drawn chariots, and spears, swords, and armor of bronze.[65]

As economic specialization developed, social stratification became more elaborate. Sumerian documents describe a system of social classes: nobles, priests, merchants, craftworkers, bureaucrats, soldiers, farmers, free citizens, and slaves all had their special place. Slaves were common in Sumer; they were often captives, brought back as the spoils of war. Metallurgists belonged to the working-class aristocracy because they possessed closely guarded trade secrets. Like nuclear physicists in our society, metallurgists were respected both for their somewhat mysterious knowledge and because their profession was strategically important for the society.

[62] Flannery. "The Cultural Evolution of Civilizations."
[63] Service. *Origins of the State and Civilization,* p. 207.
[64] Ibid.; and Flannery. "The Cultural Evolution of Civilizations."
[65] This description of Sumerian civilization is based on Samuel Noel Kramer, *The Sumerians: Their History, Culture, and Character,* Chicago: University of Chicago Press, 1963.

We see the first evidence of writing around 3000 B.C. The earliest Sumerian writings were in the form of ledgers containing inventories of items stored in the temples and records of livestock or other items owned or managed by the temples. Sumerian writing was wedge-shaped, or **cuneiform**, formed by pressing a stylus against a damp clay tablet. For contracts and other important documents, the tablet was fired to create a virtually permanent record. (Egyptian writing, or **hieroglyphics**, appeared about the same time. Hieroglyphics were written on rolls woven from papyrus reeds, from which our word *paper* derives.)

Cities and States in Middle America

Cities and states emerged in Mesoamerica later than they did in the Near East. The later appearance of civilization in Mesoamerica may be linked to the later emergence of agriculture in the New World, as we saw earlier. We will focus primarily on the developments that led to the rise of the city-state of Teotihuacán, which reached its height shortly after the time of Christ. Teotihuacán is located in a valley of the same name, which in turn is the northeastern part of the larger Valley of Mexico.

The Formative Period. The formative period in the area around Teotihuacán (1000–300 B.C.) was characterized initially by small, scattered farming villages on the hilly slopes just south of the Teotihuacán Valley. There were probably a few hundred people in each hamlet, and each of these scattered groups was probably politically autonomous. After about 500 B.C., there seems to have been a population shift to settlements on the valley floor, probably in association with the use of irrigation. Between about 300 and 200 B.C. we see the emergence of small "elite" centers in the valley, each of which had an earth or stone raised platform. Residences or small temples of poles and thatch originally stood on these platforms. That some individuals, particularly those in the elite centers, were buried in special tombs supplied with ornaments, headdresses, carved bowls, and a good deal of food indicates the presence of some social inequality.[66] The elite centers may indicate the presence of a number of chiefdoms.

The City and State of Teotihuacán. About 150 years before the time of Christ, no more than about 3000 people lived in scattered villages in the Teotihuacán Valley. In A.D. 100 there was a city of 80,000. By A.D. 500, well over 100,000 people, or approximately 90 percent of the entire valley population, seem to have been drawn or coerced into Teotihuacán.[67]

The layout of the city of Teotihuacán shows a tremendous amount of planning. This suggests that from its beginning, the valley may have been

[66] Mary W. Helms. *Middle America.* Englewood Cliffs, N.J.: Prentice-Hall, 1975, pp. 34–36, 54–55. See also William T. Sanders, Jeffrey R. Parsons, and Robert S. Santley, *The Basin of Mexico: Ecological Processes in the Evolution of a Civilization,* New York: Academic Press, 1979.
[67] Wenke, *Patterns in Prehistory,* 2nd ed., p. 368; and René Millon. "Teotihuacán." *Scientific American,* June 1967, pp. 38–48.

politically unified under a centralized state. Mapping has revealed that the streets and most of the buildings are laid out in a grid pattern. The grid follows a basic modular unit of fifty-seven square meters. Residential structures are often squares of this size, and many streets are spaced according to multiples of the basic unit. Even the river that ran through the center of the city was channeled to conform to the grid pattern. Perhaps the most outstanding feature of the city is the colossal scale of its architecture. Two pyramids dominate the metropolis, the so-called Pyramid of the Moon and the Pyramid of the Sun. At its base the latter is as big as the great Pyramid of Cheops in Egypt. At the height of its power, the metropolis of Teotihuacán encompassed a larger area than imperial Rome.[68]

The thousands of residential structures built after A.D. 300 follow a standard pattern. Narrow streets separate the one-story buildings, each of which has high, windowless walls. Patios and shafts provide interior light. The layout of rooms suggests that each building consisted of several apartments; more than 100 people may have lived in one of these apartment compounds. There is variation from compound to compound in the size of rooms and the elaborateness of interior decoration, suggesting considerable variation in wealth.[69]

At the height of its power (A.D. 200–500), much of Mesoamerica seems to have been influenced by Teotihuacán. Archeologically, this is suggested by the extensive spread of Teotihuacán-style pottery and architectural elements. Undoubtedly, large numbers of people in Teotihuacán were engaged in production for, and the conduct of, long-distance trade. Perhaps 25 percent of the city's population worked at various specialized crafts, mostly the manufacture of projectile points and cutting and scraping tools from volcanic obsidian. The Teotihuacán Valley had major deposits of obsidian, which was apparently in great demand over much of Mesoamerica. Judging from materials found in graves, there was an enormous flow of foreign goods into the city, including precious stones, feathers from colorful birds in the tropical lowlands, and cotton.[70]

The City of Monte Albán.   Teotihuacán was probably not the earliest city-state in Mesoamerica: there is evidence of political unification somewhat earlier, about 500 B.C., in the Valley of Oaxaca in southern Mexico, with the city of Monte Albán at its center. Monte Albán presents an interesting contrast to Teotihuacán. Whereas Teotihuacán seems to completely dominate its valley, containing almost all of its inhabitants and craftspeople, Monte Albán did not. The various villages in the Valley of Oaxaca seem to have specialized in different crafts, and Monte Albán did not monopolize craft production. After

[68] Millon. "Teotihuacán," pp. 38–44.
[69] René Millon. "Social Relations in Ancient Teotihuacán." In Eric R. Wolf, ed., *The Valley of Mexico: Studies in Pre-Hispanic Ecology and Society.* Albuquerque: University of New Mexico Press, 1976, pp. 215–20.
[70] Helms. *Middle America,* pp. 61–63.

the political unification of the valley, cities and towns other than Monte Albán remained important: the population of Monte Albán grew only to 30,000 or so. Unlike Teotihuacán, Monte Albán was not an important commercial or market center, it was not laid out in a grid pattern, and its architecture was not that different from other settlements in the valley in which it was located.[71]

Monte Albán did not have the kinds of resources that Teotihuacán had. It was located on top of a mountain in the center of the valley, far from either good soil or permanent water supplies that could have been used for irrigation. (Even finding drinking water must have been difficult.) No natural resources for trade were nearby, nor is there much evidence that Monte Albán was used as a ceremonial center. Because the city was at the top of a steep mountain, it is unlikely that it could have been a central marketplace for valleywide trade.

Why, then, did Monte Albán rise to become one of the early centers of Mesoamerican civilization? Richard Blanton suggests it may have originally been founded in the late formative period (500–400 B.C.) as a neutral place where representatives of the different political units in the valley could reside to coordinate activities affecting the whole valley. Thus, Monte Albán may have been like the cities of Brasília, Washington, D.C., and Athens, all of which were originally founded in "neutral," nonproductive areas. Such a center, lacking obvious resources, would not, at least initially, threaten the various political units around it. Later it might become a metropolis dominating a more politically unified region, as Monte Albán came to do in the Valley of Oaxaca.[72]

Other Centers of Mesoamerican Civilization.   In addition to Teotihuacán and Oaxaca, there were other Mesoamerican state societies, which developed somewhat later. For example, there are a number of centers with monumental architecture, presumably built by speakers of Mayan languages, in the highlands and lowlands of modern-day Guatemala and the Yucatán Peninsula of modern-day Mexico. Judging from surface appearances, the Mayan centers do not appear to have been as densely populated or as urbanized as Teotihuacán or Monte Albán. But recent evidence suggests that the Mayan centers were more densely populated and more dependent on intensive agriculture than was once thought.[73] And recent translations of Mayan

[71] Richard E. Blanton. "The Rise of Cities." In Jeremy A. Sabloff, ed., *Supplement to the Handbook of Middle American Indians.* Austin: University of Texas Press, 1981, 1:397. See also Joyce Marcus, "On the Nature of the Mesoamerican City," in Evon Z. Vogt and Richard M. Leventhal, eds., *Prehistoric Settlement Patterns: Essays in Honor of Gordon R. Willey,* Albuquerque: University of New Mexico Press, 1983, pp. 195–242.

[72] Richard Blanton. "The Origins of Monte Albán." In C. Cleland, ed., *Cultural Continuity and Change.* New York: Academic Press, 1976, pp. 223–32; and Richard Blanton. *Monte Albán: Settlement Patterns at the Ancient Zapotec Capital.* New York: Academic Press, 1978.

[73] B. L. Turner. "Population Density in the Classic Maya Lowlands: New Evidence for Old Approaches." *Geographical Review,* 66, no. 1 (January 1970); 72–82. See also Peter D. Harrison and B. L. Turner II, eds., *Pre-Hispanic Maya Agriculture,* Albuquerque: University of New Mexico Press, 1978.

picture writing indicate a much more developed form of writing than previously thought.[74] It is apparent now that Mayan urbanization and cultural complexity were underestimated because of the dense tropical forest that now covers much of the area of Mayan civilization.

The First Cities and States in Other Areas

So far we have discussed the emergence of cities and states in southern Iraq and Mesoamerica whose development is best, if only imperfectly, known archeologically. But other state societies probably arose more or less independently in many other areas of the world as well. We say "independently" because such states seem to have emerged without colonization or conquest by other states.

Almost at the same time as the Sumerian Empire, the great dynastic age was beginning in the Nile Valley in Egypt. The Old Kingdom, or early dynastic period, began about 3100 B.C. with a capital at Memphis. The archeological evidence from the early centuries is limited, but most of the population appears to have lived in largely self-sufficient villages. Many of the great pyramids and palaces were built around 2500 B.C.[75]

In the Indus Valley of northwestern India, a large state society had developed by 2300 B.C. This Harappan civilization did not have much in the way of monumental architecture, such as pyramids and palaces, and it was also unusual in other respects. The state apparently controlled an enormous territory—over a million square kilometers. There was not just one major city but many, each built according to a similar pattern and with a municipal water and sewage system.[76]

The Shang dynasty in northern China (1750 B.C.) has long been mentioned as the earliest state society in the Far East. But recent research suggests an earlier one, the Xia dynasty, may have emerged in the same general area by 2200 B.C.[77] In any case, the Shang dynasty had all the earmarks of statehood: a stratified, specialized society; religious, economic, and administrative unification; and a distinctive art style.[78]

In South America, state societies may have emerged after 200 B.C. in the area of modern-day Peru.[79] In sub-Saharan Africa by A.D. 800, the western Sudan had a succession of city-states. One of them was called Ghana, and it became a major source of gold for the Mediterranean world.[80] And in North

---

[74] Stephen D. Houston. "The Phonetic Decipherment of Mayan Glyphs." *Antiquity*, 62 (1988): 126–35.

[75] Wenke. *Patterns in Prehistory*, 2nd ed., p. 289.

[76] Ibid., pp. 305–20.

[77] Chang. "In Search of China's Beginnings," pp. 148–60.

[78] Kwang-Chih Chang. *The Archaeology of Ancient China*. New Haven: Yale University Press, 1968, pp. 235–55.

[79] Wenke. *Patterns in Prehistory*, 2nd ed., p. 404.

[80] Brian M. Fagan. *People of the Earth: An Introduction to World Prehistory*, 6th ed. Glenview, Ill.: Scott, Foresman and Company, 1989, pp. 428–30.

America there is some evidence that a state-level society possibly existed in the area around St. Louis by A.D. 1050. Huge mounds of earth 100 feet high mark the site there called Cahokia.[81]

Theories about the Origin of the State

We have seen that states developed in many parts of the world. Why did they evolve when and where they did? A number of theories have been proposed. We will consider the ones that have frequently been discussed by archeologists.[82]

Irrigation.   Irrigation seems to have been important in many of the areas in which early state societies developed. Irrigation made the land habitable or productive in parts of Mesoamerica, southern Iraq, the Nile Valley, and other areas. It has been suggested that the labor and management needed for the upkeep of an irrigation system leads to the formation of a political elite (the overseers of the system), who eventually become the governors of the society.[83] Proponents of this view believe that both the city and civilization were outgrowths of the administrative requirements of an irrigation system.

Critics note that this theory does not seem to apply to all areas where cities and states may have emerged independently. For example, in southern Iraq, the irrigation systems serving the early cities were generally small in scale and probably did not require extensive labor and management. Large-scale irrigation works were not constructed until after cities had been fully established.[84] Thus, irrigation could not have been the main stimulus for the development of cities and states in Sumer. Even in China, for which the irrigation theory was first formulated, there is no evidence of large-scale irrigation as early as Shang times.[85]

Although large-scale irrigation may not always have preceded the emergence of the first cities and states, even small-scale irrigation systems could have resulted in unequal access to productive land and so may have contributed to the development of a stratified society.[86] In addition, irrigation systems may have given rise to border and other disputes between adjacent groups, thereby prompting people to concentrate in cities for defense and stimulating the development of military and political controls.[87] Finally, as Robert Adams

---

[81] Melvin L. Fowler. "A Pre-Columbian Urban Center on the Mississippi." *Scientific American*, August 1975, pp. 92–101.

[82] For a more complete review of the available theories, see various chapters in Ronald Cohen and Elman R. Service, eds., *Origins of the State: The Anthropology of Political Evolution*, Philadelphia: Institute for the Study of Human Issues, 1978.

[83] Karl Wittfogel. *Oriental Despotism: A Comparative Study of Total Power.* New Haven: Yale University Press, 1957.

[84] Robert M. Adams. "The Origin of Cities." *Scientific American*, September 1960, p. 153.

[85] Paul Wheatley. *The Pivot of the Four Quarters.* Chicago: Aldine, 1971, p. 291.

[86] Adams. "The Origin of Cities," p. 153.

[87] Robert McC. Adams. *Heartland of Cities: Surveys of Ancient Settlement and Land Use on the Central Floodplain of the Euphrates.* Chicago: University of Chicago Press, 1981, p. 244.

and Elman Service both suggest, the main significance of irrigation—either large- or small-scale—may have been its intensification of production, a development that in turn may have indirectly stimulated craft specialization, trade, and administrative bureaucracy.[88]

Population Growth, Circumscription, and War.   Robert Carneiro suggests that states may emerge because of population growth in an area that is physically or socially limited. Competition and warfare in such a situation may lead to the subordination of defeated groups, who are obliged to pay tribute and to submit to the control of a more powerful group.[89] Carneiro illustrates his theory by describing how states may have emerged on the northern coast of Peru.

After the people of that area first settled into an agricultural village life, population grew at a slow, steady rate. Initially, new villages were formed as population grew. But in the narrow coastal valleys—blocked by high mountains, fronted by the sea, and surrounded by desert—this splintering-off process could not continue indefinitely. The result, Carneiro suggests, was increasing land shortage and warfare between villages as they competed for land. Since the high mountains, the sea, and the desert blocked any escape for losers, the defeated villagers had no choice but to submit to political domination. In this way, chiefdoms may have become kingdoms as the most powerful villages grew to control entire valleys. As chiefs' power expanded over several valleys, states and empires may have been born.

Carneiro notes that physical or environmental circumscription may not be the only kind of barrier that gives rise to a state. Social circumscription may be just as important. People living at the center of a high-density area may find that their migration is blocked by surrounding settlements just as effectively as it could be by mountains, sea, and desert.

Marvin Harris suggests a somewhat different form of circumscription. He argues that the first states with their coercive authority could emerge only in areas that permitted intensive grain agriculture (and the possibility of high food production) and were surrounded by areas that could *not* support intensive grain agriculture. So people in such areas might put up with the coercive authority of a state because they would suffer a sharp drop in living standards if they moved away.[90]

Carneiro suggests that his theory applies to many areas besides the northern coast of Peru, including southern Iraq and the Indus and Nile valleys. While there were no geographical barriers in areas such as northern China or the Mayan lowlands on the Yucatán Peninsula, the development of

[88] Ibid., p. 243; and Service. *Origins of the State and Civilization*, pp. 274–75.
[89] Robert L. Carneiro. "A Theory of the Origin of the State." *Science*, August 21, 1970, pp. 733–38. See also William T. Sanders and Barbara J. Price, *Mesoamerica*, New York: Random House, 1968, pp. 230–32.
[90] Marvin Harris. *Cultural Materialism: The Struggle for a Science of Culture.* New York: Random House, 1979, pp. 101–2. See also Wenke, *Patterns in Prehistory*, 3rd ed.

states in those areas may have been the result of social circumscription. Carneiro's theory seems to be supported for southern Iraq, where there is archeological evidence of population growth, circumscription, and warfare.[91] And there is evidence of population growth prior to the emergence of the state in the Teotihuacán Valley.[92]

But population growth does not necessarily mean population pressure. For example, the populations in the Teotihuacán Valley and the Oaxaca Valley apparently did increase prior to state development, but there is no evidence that they had even begun to approach the limits of their resources. More people could have lived in both places.[93] Nor is population growth always associated with state formation. Data from southwestern Iran, for example, indicate that there was population growth long before states emerged, but that just prior to their emergence the population apparently declined.[94]

In addition, Carneiro's circumscription theory leaves an important logical question unanswered: Why would the victors in war let the defeated populations remain and pay tribute? If the victors wanted the land so much in the first place, why wouldn't they drive the defeated out?

Local and Long-Distance Trade.   It has been suggested that trade was a factor in the emergence of the earliest states.[95] Wright and Johnson have theorized that the organizational requirements of producing items for export, redistributing the items imported, and defending trading parties would foster state formation.[96]

Does the archeological evidence support the theory that trade played a crucial role in the formation of the earliest states? In southern Iraq and the Mayan lowlands, long-distance trade routes may indeed have stimulated bureaucratic growth. In the lowlands of southern Iraq, as we have seen, people

[91] T. Cuyler Young, Jr. "Population Densities and Early Mesopotamian Urbanism." In P. J. Ucko, R. Tringham, and G. W. Dimbleby, eds., *Man, Settlement and Urbanism.* Cambridge, Mass.: Schenkman, 1972, pp. 827–42.

[92] Sanders and Price. *Mesoamerica,* p. 141.

[93] Richard E. Blanton, Stephen A. Kowalewski, Gary Feinman, and Jill Appel. *Ancient Mesoamerica: A Comparison of Change in Three Regions.* New York: Cambridge University Press, 1981, p. 224. For the apparent absence of population pressure in the Teotihuacán Valley, see Elizabeth Brumfiel, "Regional Growth in the Eastern Valley of Mexico: A Test of the 'Population Pressure' Hypothesis," in Kent V. Flannery, ed., *The Early Mesoamerican Village,* New York: Academic Press, 1976, pp. 234–50. For the Oaxaca Valley, see Gary M. Feinman, Stephen A. Kowalewski, Laura Finsten, Richard E. Blanton, and Linda Nicholas, "Long-Term Demographic Change: A Perspective from the Valley of Oaxaca, Mexico," *Journal of Field Archaeology,* 12 (1985): 333–62.

[94] Wright and Johnson. "Population, Exchange, and Early State Formation in Southwestern Iran," p. 276.

[95] Karl Polanyi, C. M. Arensberg, and Harry Pearson, eds., *Trade and Market in the Early Empires.* New York: Free Press. 1957, pp. 257–62; and William T. Sanders. "Hydraulic Agriculture, Economic Symbiosis, and the Evolution of States in Central Mexico." In Betty J. Meggers, ed., *Anthropological Archaeology in the Americas.* Washington, D. C.: Anthropological Society of Washington, 1968, p. 105.

[96] Wright and Johnson. "Population, Exchange, and Early State Formation in Southwestern Iran," p. 277.

needed wood and stone for building, and they traded with highland people for these items. In the Mayan lowlands, the development of civilization seems to have been preceded by long-distance trade: farmers in the lowland regions traded with faraway places in order to obtain salt, obsidian for cutting blades, and hard stone for grinding tools.[97] In southwestern Iran, long-distance trade did not become very important until after Susa became the center of a state society, but short-distance trade may have played the same kind of role in the formation of states. The situation in other areas is not yet known.

The Various Theories: An Evaluation.   Why do states form? As of now, no one theory seems to fit all the known situations. The reason may be that different conditions in different places may have favored the emergence of centralized government. After all, the state, by definition, implies an ability to organize large populations for a collective purpose. In some areas, this purpose may have been the need to organize trade with local or far-off regions. In other cases, the state may have emerged as a way to control defeated populations in circumscribed areas. In still other instances, a combination of factors may have fostered the development of the state type of political system.[98] It is still not clear what specific conditions led to the emergence of the state in each of the early centers. But since the question of why states formed is a lively focus of research today, more satisfactory answers may come out of ongoing and future investigations.

SUMMARY

1. In the period prior to the emergence of plant and animal domestication (which in regard to Europe and the Near East is called the Mesolithic period), there seems to have been a shift in many areas of the world to less dependence on big-game hunting and greater dependence on what is called broad-spectrum collecting. The broad spectrum of available resources frequently included aquatic resources such as fish and shellfish, a variety of wild plants, and a wide variety of smaller game. Climatic changes may have been partially responsible for the change to broad-spectrum collecting.

2. In some sites in Europe, the Near East, Africa, and Peru, the switch to broad-spectrum collecting seems to be associated with the development of more permanent communities. In other areas, such as the semiarid highlands of Mesoamerica, the switch was not associated with the development of more permanent villages. In that area, permanent settlements may have emerged only after the domestication of plants and animals.

3. The shift to the cultivation and domestication of plants and animals has been referred to as the Neolithic revolution, and it occurred, probably independently, in a number of areas. To date the earliest evidence of domestication comes from the Near East about 8000 B.C. Other centers of domestication in the Old World include North and South China bout 6000 B.C., Thailand after about 6800 B.C.,

[97] William L. Rathje. "The Origin and Development of Lowland Classic Maya Civilization." *American Antiquity,* 36 (1971): 275–85.

[98] For a discussion of how political dynamics may play an important role in state formation, see Elizabeth M. Brumfiel, "Aztec State Making: Ecology, Structure, and the Origin of the State," *American Anthropologist,* 85 (1983): 261–84.

and sub-Saharan Africa after 3000 B.C. In the New World, evidence for independent domestication comes from the highlands of Mexico (about 7000 B.C.), Peru almost as early as in Mexico, and the American Midwest about 1500 B.C.

4. Theories about why food production originated are still quite controversial, but most archeologists think that certain conditions must have pushed people to switch from collecting to producing food. Some possible causal factors include (1) population growth in regions of bountiful wild resources (which may have pushed people to move to marginal areas where they tried to reproduce their former abundance); (2) global population growth (which filled most of the world's habitable regions and may have forced people to utilize a broader spectrum of wild resources and to domesticate plants and animals); and (3) the emergence of greater seasonal variation in rainfall (which may have forced people to plant crops and raise animals to get themselves through the dry seasons).

5. Regardless of why food production originated, it seems to have had important consequences for human life. Populations generally increased substantially *after* plant and animal domestication. Even though the early cultivators were not all sedentary, sedentarism did increase with greater reliance on agriculture. Somewhat surprisingly, some prehistoric populations that relied heavily on agriculture seem to have been less healthy than prior populations that relied on hunting and gathering.

6. Archeologists do not always agree on how a state should be defined, but most seem to agree that centralized decision making affecting a substantial population is the key criterion. Most states have cities with public buildings, full-time craft and religious specialists, an official art style, and a hierarchical social structure topped by an elite class from which the leaders are drawn. Most states maintain power with a monopoly on the use of force. Force or the threat of force is used by the state to tax its population and to draft people for work or war.

7. Early state societies arose within the Near East in what is now southern Iraq and southwestern Iran. Southern Iraq, or Sumer, was unified under a single government just after 3000 B.C. It had large urban centers, imposing temples, codified laws, a standing army, wide trade networks, a complex irrigation system, and a high degree of craft specialization.

8. Probably the earliest city-state in Mesoamerica developed around 500 B.C. in the Valley of Oaxaca, with a capital at Monte Albán. Somewhat later, in the northeastern section of the Valley of Mexico, Teotihuacán developed. At the height of its power (A.D. 200–500), the city-state of Teotihuacán appears to have influenced much of Mesoamerica.

9. City-states arose early in other parts of the New World: in Guatemala, the Yucatán Peninsula of Mexico, Peru, and possibly near St. Louis. In the Old World, early states developed in Egypt, the Indus Valley of India, northern China, and West Africa.

10. There are several theories of why states arose. The irrigation theory suggests that the administrative needs of maintaining extensive irrigation systems may have been the impetus for state formation. The circumscription theory suggests that states emerge when competition and warfare in circumscribed areas lead to the subordination of defeated groups, who are obliged to submit to the control of the most powerful group. Theories involving trade suggest that the organizational requirements of producing exportable items, redistributing imported items, and defending trading parties would foster state formation. Which is correct? At this point, no one theory is able to explain the formation of every state. Perhaps different organizational requirements in different areas all favored centralized government.

8

The Concept
of Culture

We all consider ourselves to be unique individuals with a set of personal opinions, preferences, habits, and quirks. Indeed, all of us *are* unique individuals, and yet most of us share the feeling that it is wrong to eat dogs, the belief that bacteria or viruses cause illness, the habit of sleeping on a bed. There are many such feelings, beliefs, and habits that we share with most of the people who live in our society. We hardly ever think about the ideas and customs we share, but they constitute what anthropologist refer to as American "culture."

We tend not to think about our culture because it is so much a part of us that we take it for granted. If and when we become aware that other people have different feelings from ours, different beliefs, and different habits, we being to think of how we share certain ideas and customs. We would never even think of the possibility of eating dog meat if we were not aware that people in some other societies commonly do so. We would not realize that our belief in germs was cultural if we were not aware that people in some societies think that illness is caused by witchcraft or evil spirits. We could not become aware that it is our custom to sleep on beds if we were not aware that people in many societies sleep on the floor or ground. It is only when we compare ourselves with people in other societies that we become aware of cultural differences and similarities. This is, in fact, the way that anthropology as a profession began; when Europeans began to explore and move to faraway places, they were forced to confront the sometimes striking facts of cultural variation.

ATTITUDES THAT HINDER THE STUDY OF CULTURES

Many of the Europeans who first came to those faraway places were revolted or shocked by customs they observed. Such reactions are not surprising. People commonly feel that their own customary behaviors and attitudes are the correct ones, that people who do not share those patterns are immoral or inferior. But our own customs and ideas may appear bizarre or barbaric to an observer from another society. Hindus in India, for example, would consider our custom of eating beef both primitive and disgusting. In their culture, the cow is a sacred animal and may not be slaughtered for food. Even our most ordinary customs—the daily rituals we take for granted—might seem thoroughly absurd when viewed from the perspective of a foreign culture. A visitor to our society might justifiably take notes on certain strange behaviors that seem quite ordinary to us, as the following extract shows:

> The daily body ritual performed by everyone includes a mouth-rite. Despite the fact that these people are so punctilious about the care of the mouth, this rite involves a practice which strikes the uninitiated stranger as revolting. It was reported to me that the ritual consists of inserting a small bundle of hog hairs into the mouth, along with certain magical powders, and then moving the bundle in a highly formalized series of gestures. In addition to the private mouth-rite, the people seek out a holy-mouth man once or twice a year. These practitioners have an impressive set of paraphernalia, consisting of a variety of augers, awls, probes, and prods. The use of these objects in the exorcism of the evils of the mouth involves almost unbelievable ritual torture of the client. The holy-mouth man opens the client's mouth and, using the above mentioned tools, enlarges any holes which decay may have created in teeth. Magical materials are put into these holes. If there are no naturally occurring holes in the teeth, large sections of one or more teeth are gouged out so that the supernatural substance can be applied. In the client's view, the purpose of these ministrations is to arrest decay and to draw friends. The extremely sacred and traditional character of the rite is evident in the fact that the natives return to the holy-mouth man year after year, despite the fact that their teeth continue to decay.[1]

We are likely to protest that to understand the behaviors of a particular society—in this case our own—the observer must try to find out more about why the people in that society say they do things. For example, the observer might find out that periodic visits to the "holy-mouth man" are for medical, not magical, purposes. Indeed, the observer, after some questioning, might discover that the "mouth-rite" has no sacred or religious connotations whatsoever. The anthropological attitude that a society's customs and ideas should be described objectively and understood in the context of that society's problems and opportunities is called **cultural relativism**. Because this attitude

---

[1] Horace Miner. "Body Rituals among the Nacirema." *American Anthropologist*, 58 (1956): 504–5. Reproduced by permission of the American Anthropological Association from the *American Anthropologist*, 58: 504–5, 1956.

fosters empathy and understanding, it is humanistic; because it requires impartial observation and involves an attempt to test possible explanations of customs, the attitude of cultural relativism is also scientific.

In general, cultural relativism is impeded by two different but commonly held attitudes. The first is the tendency toward negative evaluation, which usually results from ethnocentrism; the second is the tendency toward positive evaluation, which often takes the form of a naive yearning for the simple life of the "noble savage."

Ethnocentrism

The person whose vision is limited strictly to his or her own needs and desires is generally ineffective in dealing with other people. We call such an individual egocentric, and we would be sorry to have such a person for a psychiatrist. The person who judges other cultures solely in terms of his or her own culture is **ethnocentric**. (This attitude is called **ethnocentrism**.) Not only are such people ill equipped to do anthropological work, but they may be unable to recognize and deal with social problems in their own society.

For example, an ethnocentric American would view as barbaric the ceremonies that initiate adolescent boys into manhood in many societies. These ceremonies often involve hazing, difficult tests of courage and endurance, and painful circumcision. The ethnocentric American would be unable to understand why anyone would willingly endure such hardships merely to be publicly accepted as an adult. However, the same type of ethnocentric thinking would make it difficult for such a person to question the American custom of confining young children to little cages called cribs and playpens, a practice that observers from another society might consider cruel. Ethnocentrism, then, hinders our understanding of the customs of other people and, at the same time, keeps us from understanding our own customs. If we think that everything we do is best, we are not likely to ask why we do what we do or why "they" do what "they" do.

The "Noble Savage"

Whenever we are weary of the complexities of civilization, we may long for a way of life that is "closer to nature" or "simpler" than our own. For instance, a young American whose parent is holding two or three jobs just to provide his or her family with bare necessities might briefly be attracted to the life style of the !Kung of the Kalahari Desert. The !Kung share their food and therefore are often free to engage in leisure activities during the greater part of the day. They obtain all their food by hunting animals and gathering wild plants. Since they have no facilities for refrigeration, sharing a freshly killed animal is clearly more sensible than hoarding rotten meat. Moreover, as it turns out, the sharing provides a kind of social-security system for the !Kung. If a hunter is unable to catch an animal on a certain day, he can obtain food for himself and his family from someone else in his band. Conversely, at some later date the game he catches will provide food for the family of some other unsuccessful hunter. This system of sharing also ensures that persons too young or too old to help with the collecting of food will still be fed.

However, the food-sharing system of the !Kung is a solution to the problems posed by their special environment and is not necessarily a practical solution to problems in our own society. Moreover, other aspects of !Kung life would not appeal to many Americans. For example, when the nomadic !Kung decide to move their camps, the women must carry all the family possessions, substantial amounts of food and water, and all young children below age four or five. This is a sizable burden to carry for any distance. And since the !Kung travel about 1500 miles in a single year,[2] it is unlikely that most American women would find the !Kung way of life enviable in all respects.

The point is not that we should avoid comparing our culture with others, but that we should not romanticize other cultures. Most of the customs of other societies probably are, or were, appropriate to their environments, just as most of our customs probably are, or were, appropriate to our own environment. Cultural relativism asks that all customs of a society be viewed objectively, not ethnocentrically or romantically.

Does cultural relativism mean that the actions of another society, or of our own, should not be judged? Does our insistence on objectivity mean that anthropologists should not make moral judgments about the cultural phenomena they observe and try to explain? Not really. Anthropologists do make judgments, and some try to change behavior they think is harmful. But judgments need not and should not preclude objectivity. Our goal in research is to strive for accurate description and explanation in spite of any judgments we might have.

We have tried so far in this chapter to convey intuitively what culture is, and we have discussed attitudes that hinder or bias the study of cultures. Now let us turn to what seem to be the defining features of culture for most anthropologists.

DEFINING FEATURES OF CULTURE

In everyday usage, the word *culture* refers to a desirable quality we can acquire by attending a sufficient number of plays and concerts and trudging through several miles of art galleries. The anthropologist, however, has a different definition, as Ralph Linton explains:

> [Culture] refers to the total way of life of any society, not simply to those parts of this way which the society regards as higher or more desirable. Thus culture,

---

[2] Richard B. Lee. "Population Growth and the Beginnings of Sedentary Life among the !Kung Bushmen." In Brian Spooner, ed., *Population Growth: Anthropological Implications.* Cambridge, Mass.: M.I.T. Press, 1972, pp. 329–42.

when applied to our own way of life, has nothing to do with playing the piano or reading Browning. For the social scientist such activities are simply elements within the totality of our culture. This totality also includes such mundane activities as washing dishes or driving an automobile, and for the purposes of cultural studies these stand quite on a par with "the finer things of life." It follows that for the social scientist there are no uncultured societies or even individuals. Every society has a culture, no matter how simple this culture may be, and every human being is cultured, in the sense of participating in some culture or other.[3]

Culture, then, refers to innumerable aspects of life. To most anthropologists, **culture** encompasses the learned behaviors, beliefs, attitudes, values, and ideals that are characteristic of a particular society or population. We are each born into a complex culture that will strongly influence how we live and behave for the remainder of our lives.

Culture Is Commonly Shared

If only one person thinks or does a certain thing, that thought or action represents a personal habit, not a pattern of culture. For a thought or action to be considered cultural, it must be commonly shared by some population or group of individuals. Even if some behavior is not commonly practiced, it is cultural if most people think it is appropriate. The idea that marriage should involve only one man and only one woman is cultural in our society. Most Americans share this idea and act accordingly when they marry. The role of president of the United States is not widely shared—after all, there is only one such person at a time—but the role is cultural because most Americans agree that it should exist, and its occupant is generally expected to exhibit certain behaviors. We usually share many values, beliefs, and behaviors with our families and friends (although anthropologists are not particularly concerned with this type of cultural group). We commonly share cultural characteristics with segments of our population whose ethnic or regional origins, religious affiliations, and occupations are the same as or similar to our own. We have certain practices, beliefs, and feelings in common with most Americans. And we share certain characteristics with people beyond our national borders who have similar interests (such as rules for international sporting events) or similar roots (as do the various English-speaking nations).

When we talk about the commonly shared customs of a society, which constitute the central concern of cultural anthropology, we are referring to a *culture*. When we talk about the commonly shared customs of a group within a society, which are a central concern of sociology, we are referring to a **subculture**. And when we study the commonly shared customs of some group that transcends national boundaries, we are talking about a phenomenon for

---

[3] Ralph Linton. *The Cultural Background of Personality.* New York: Appleton-Century-Crofts, 1945, p. 30.

which we do not have a single word (only compound phrases including the word *culture*). So, for example, we refer to *Western culture* (the cultural characteristics of societies in or derived from western Europe) and the *culture of poverty* (the presumed cultural characteristics of poor people the world over).

We must remember that even when anthropologists refer to something as cultural, there is always individual variation, which means that not everyone in a society shares a particular cultural characteristic of the society. For example, it is cultural in the United States for adults to live apart from parents. But this does not mean that all adults do so, nor that all adults wish to do so. The custom of living apart from parents is considered cultural because most adults practice that custom. As Edward Sapir noted fifty years ago, in every society studied by anthropologists—in the simplest as well as the most complex—individuals do not *all* think and act the same.[4] As we discuss below, individual variation is the source of new culture.[5]

Culture Is Learned

Not all things shared generally by a population are cultural. The typical hair color of a population is not cultural. Nor is eating. For something to be considered cultural, it must be learned as well as shared. A typical hair color (unless dyed) is not cultural because it is genetically determined. Humans eat because they must, but what and when and how they eat is learned and varies from culture to culture. Americans do not think dogs are edible, and indeed the idea of eating dogs horrifies us. But in China, as in some other societies, dog meat is considered delicious. In our society, many people consider a baked ham to be a holiday dish. However, in several societies of the Middle East, including those of Egypt and Israel, eating the meat of a pig is forbidden by sacred writings.

To some extent, all animals exhibit learned behaviors, some of which may be shared by most individuals in a population and may therefore be considered cultural. However, different animal species vary in the degree to which their shared behaviors are learned or are instinctive. The sociable ants, for instance, despite all their patterned social behavior, do not appear to have much, if any, culture. They divide their labors, construct their nests, form their raiding columns, and carry off their dead, all without having been taught to do so and without imitating the behavior of other ants. In contrast, much of the behavior of humans appears to be culturally patterned.

We are increasingly discovering that our closest biological relatives—the monkeys and the apes—also exhibit a good deal of cultural behavior. For

[4] Edward Sapir. "Why Cultural Anthropology Needs the Psychiatrist." *Psychiatry*, 1 (1938): 7–12. Cited by Pertti J. Pelto and Gretel H. Pelto. "Intra-Cultural Diversity: Some Theoretical Issues," *American Ethnologist*, 2 (1975): 1.
[5] Pelto and Pelto. "Intra-Cultural Diversity," pp. 14–15.

example, in 1953 scientists at the Japan Monkey Center observed how a particular behavioral innovation spread from monkey to monkey and eventually became part of a group's culture. The scientists left some sweet potatoes on a beach near the place where a group of Japanese monkeys lived. Attracted by the food, a young female began to wash the sand off the potatoes by plunging them into a nearby brook. Previously, the monkeys had rubbed their food clean, but this washing behavior spread throughout the group and eventually replaced the former habit of rubbing off the sand. After a number of years, 80 to 90 percent of the monkeys were washing sweet potatoes. This learned habit had become a part of the monkeys' culture.[6]

Experimenters have shown that apes and monkeys learn a wide variety of behaviors. Some of their learned responses are as basic as those involved in maternal care; others are as frivolous as the taste for candy. The proportion of an animal's life span occupied by childhood seems to reflect the degree to which the animal depends upon learned behavior for survival. Monkeys and apes have relatively long childhoods compared with other animals. Humans have by far the longest childhood of any animal, reflecting our great dependence on learned behavior. Although humans acquire much learned behavior by imitation, as do monkeys and apes, most human learned behavior is probably acquired with the aid of a unique mechanism—language.

Language. All people known to anthropologists, regardless of their kind of society, have had a highly complex system of spoken, symbolic communication that we call *language*. Language is *symbolic* in that a word or phrase can represent what it stands for *whether or not that thing is present.*

This symbolic quality of language has tremendous implications for the transmission of culture. It means that a human parent can tell a child that a snake, for example, is dangerous and should be avoided. The parent can then describe the snake in great detail—its length, diameter, color, texture, shape, and means of locomotion. The parent can also predict the kinds of places where the child is likely to encounter snakes and explain how the child can avoid them. Should the child encounter a snake, then, he or she will probably recall the symbolic word for the animal, remember as well the related information, and so avoid danger. If symbolic language did not exist, the parent would have to wait until the child actually saw a snake and then, through example, show the child that such a creature is to be avoided. Without language we could not transmit or receive information symbolically, and thus would not be heir to so rich and varied a culture.

To sum up, we may say that something is cultural if it is a learned behavior, belief, attitude, value, or ideal generally shared by the members of a group. Traditionally, anthropologists have usually been concerned with the cultural characteristics of a **society**, by which they mean a group of people

---

[6] Jun'ichiro Itani. "The Society of Japanese Monkeys." *Japan Quarterly*, 8 (1961): 421–30.

who occupy a particular territory and speak a common language not generally understood by neighboring peoples.[7] Hence, when an anthropologists speaks about *a* culture, he or she is usually referring to that set of learned and shared beliefs, values, and behaviors generally characteristic of a particular society. But now that we have defined what is cultural, we must ask a further question: How does an anthropologist go about deciding which particular behaviors, values, and beliefs of individuals are cultural?

DESCRIBING A CULTURE

Individual Variation

Describing a particular culture might seem relatively uncomplicated at first: you simply observe what the people in that society do and then record their behavior. But consider the substantial difficulties you might encounter in doing this. How would you decide which people to observe? And what would you conclude if each of the first dozen people you observed or talked to behaved quite differently in the same situation? Admittedly, you would be unlikely to encounter such extreme divergence of behaviors. Yet there would tend to be significant individual variation in the actual behaviors observed, even when individuals were responding to the same generalized situation and conforming to cultural expectations.

For example, an anthropologist interested in describing courtship and marriage in the United States would initially encounter a variety of behaviors. The anthropologist may note that one couple prefers to go to a concert on a first date, whereas another couple chooses to go bowling; some couples have very long engagements and others never become engaged at all; some couples emphasize religious rituals in the marriage ceremony but others are married by civil authorities; and so on. Despite this variability, the anthropologist, after further observation and interviewing, might begin to detect certain regularities in courting practices. Although couples may do many different things on their first and subsequent dates, they nearly always arrange the dates by themselves, they try to avoid their parents when on dates, they often manage to find themselves alone at the end of a date, they put their lips together frequently, and so forth. After a series or more and more closely spaced encounters, a man and woman may decide to declare themselves publicly as a couple, either by announcing that they are engaged or by revealing that they are living together or

---

[7] Note that by this definition, societies do not necessarily correspond to nations. There are many nations, particularly the "new" ones, that have within their boundaries different peoples speaking mutually unintelligible languages. By our definition of society, such nations are composed of many different societies and cultures. Also, by our definition of society, some societies may even include more than one nation. For example, we would have to say that Canadians and Americans form a single society because both groups generally speak English, live next to each other, and share many common beliefs, values, and practices. Not everyone would agree with such a statement; some would prefer to consider the United States and Canada two different societies because they are separate political entities.

intend to do so. Finally, if the two of them decide to marry, they must in some way have their union recorded by the civil authorities.

In our society a person who wishes to marry cannot completely disregard the customary patterns of courtship. If a man saw a woman on the street and decided he wanted to marry her, he could conceivably choose a quicker and more direct form of action than the usual dating procedure. He could get on a horse, ride to the woman's home, snatch her up in his arms, and gallop away with her. In Sicily, until recently such a couple would have been considered legally married, even if the woman had never met the man before or had no intention of marrying. But in the United States, any man who acted in such a fashion would be arrested and jailed for kidnapping and would probably have his sanity challenged. Such behavior would not be acceptable in our society. Although individual behaviors may vary, most social behavior falls within culturally acceptable limits.

Cultural Constraints

A primary limit on the range of the individual behavior variations is the culture itself. The noted French sociologist Émile Durkheim stressed that culture is something *outside* us exerting a strong coercive power on us. We do not always feel the constraints of our culture because we generally conform to the types of conduct and thought it requires. Yet when we do try to oppose cultural constraints, their strength becomes apparent.

Cultural constraints are of two basic types, *direct* and *indirect*. Naturally, the direct constraints are the more obvious. For example, if you wear clothing that is atypical of our culture, you will probably be subject to ridicule and a certain amount of social isolation. But if you choose to wear only a scanty loincloth, you will receive a stronger, more direct cultural constraint—arrest for indecent exposure.

Although indirect forms of cultural constraint are less obvious than direct ones, they are no less effective. Durkheim illustrated this point when he wrote, "I am not obliged to speak French with my fellow-countrymen, nor to use the legal currency, but I cannot possibly do otherwise. If I tried to escape this necessity, my attempt would fail miserably."[8] In other words, if Durkheim had decided he would rather speak Serbo-Croatian than French, nobody would have tried to stop him. But no one would have understood him either. And although he would not have been put into prison for trying to buy groceries with Icelandic money, he would have had difficulty convincing the local merchants to sell him food.

In a series of experiments on conformity, Solomon Asch revealed how strong cultural constraints can be. Asch coached the majority of a group of

---

[8] Emile Durkheim. *The Rules of Sociological Method*, 8th ed., trans. Sarah A. Soloway and John H. Mueller, ed. George E. Catlin. New York: Free Press, 1938, p. 3. Originally published in 1895.

college students to give deliberately incorrect answers to questions involving visual stimuli. A "critical subject," the one student in the room who was not so coached, had no idea that the other participants would purposely misinterpret the evidence presented to them. Asch found that in one-third of the experiments, the critical subject *consistently* allowed his own correct perceptions to be distorted by the obviously incorrect statements of the others. And in another 40 percent of the experiments, the critical subject yielded to the opinion of the group some of the time.[9]

The existence of social or cultural constraints, however, is not necessarily incompatible with individuality. Cultural constraints are usually exercised most forcefully around the limits of acceptable behavior. Thus, there is often a broad range of behavior within which individuals can exercise their uniqueness. And individuals do not always give in to the wishes of the majority. In the Asch experiments, many individuals (one-fourth of the critical subjects) consistently retained their independent opinions in the face of complete disagreement with the majority.

How to Discover Cultural Patterns

There are two basic ways in which an anthropologist can discover cultural patterns. When dealing with customs that are overt or highly visible within a society—for example, our custom of having a nationally elected public official known as a president—the investigator can determine the existence of such practices and study them with the aid of a few knowledgeable persons. When dealing with a particular sphere of behavior that encompasses many individual variations, or when the people studied are unaware of their pattern of behavior, the anthropologist should collect information from a sample of individuals to arrive at the cultural pattern.

One example of a cultural pattern that most people in a society are not aware of is how far apart people stand when they are having a conversation. Yet there is considerable reason to believe that unconscious cultural rules govern such behavior. These rules become obvious when we interact with people who have different rules. We may experience considerable discomfort when another person stands too close (indicating too much intimacy) or too far (indicating unfriendliness). Edward Hall reports that Arabs customarily stand quite close to others—close enough, in fact, to be able to smell the other person. In interactions between Arabs and Americans, then, the Arabs will move closer at the same time the Americans back away.[10]

If we wanted to arrive at the cultural rule for conversational distance between casual acquaintances, let us say, we could study a sample of individuals from a society and determine the *modal response,* or *mode.* The mode is a statistical term that refers to the most frequently encountered response in a

[9] Solomon Asch. "Studies of Independence and Conformity: A Minority of One against a Unanimous Majority." *Psychological Monographs,* 70 (1956): 1–70.
[10] Edward T. Hall. *The Hidden Dimension.* Garden City, N.Y.: Doubleday, 1966, pp. 159–60.

given series of responses. So, for the American pattern of casual conversational distance, we would plot the actual distance for a number of observed pairs of people. Some pairs may be 2 feet apart, some 2.5, and some 4 feet apart. If the observer counts the number of times every particular distance is observed, these counts provide what we call a *frequency distribution*. The distance with the highest frequency is the modal pattern. Very often the frequency distribution takes the form of a *bell-shaped curve*. There the characteristic measured is plotted on the horizontal axis (in this case, the distance between conversational pairs) and the number of times each distance is observed (its frequency) is plotted on the vertical axis. If we plot how a sample of American casual conversational pairs is distributed, we would probably get a bell-shaped curve that peaks at around 3 feet.[11] Is it any wonder, then, that we sometimes speak of keeping others "at arm's length"?

Frequency distributions may be calculated on the basis of behaviors exhibited or responses given by all the members of a particular population. However, to save time, the anthropologist can rely on data obtained from a representative sample of persons, called a **random sample**. The members of this sample would be selected randomly from the society or community—that is, all individuals would have an equal chance of being chosen. If a sample is random, it will probably include examples of all frequent variations of behavior exhibited within the society or community in roughly the proportions in which they occur.

Since it is relatively easy to make generalizations about public aspects of a culture, such as how football players behave during a game, random sampling is often not necessary. But in dealing with aspects of culture that are private or unconscious, such as how far people stand from each other when talking, the investigator may have to observe or interview a random sample of people if he or she is to generalize correctly about cultural patterns. The reason is that most people are not aware of others' private behavior and thoughts, nor are they aware of unconscious cultural patterns.

Although we may be able to discover by interviews and observation that a behavior, thought, or feeling is widely shared within a society, how do we establish that something commonly shared is learned, so that we can call it cultural? Establishing that something is or is not learned may be difficult. Since children are not reared apart from adult caretakers, the behaviors they exhibit as part of their genetic inheritance are not clearly separated from those they learn from others around them. We assume that particular behaviors and ideas are learned if they vary from society to society. And we suspect purely genetic determinism when particular behaviors or ideas are found in all societies. For example, as we will see in the chapter on language, children the world over seem to acquire language at about the same time, and the structure of their early utterances seems to be similar. These facts suggest that

[11] Ibid., p. 120.

human children are born with an innate grammar. However, although early-childhood language seems similar the world over, the particular languages spoken by adults in different societies show considerable variability. This variability suggests that particular languages have to be learned. Similarly, if the courtship patterns of one society differ markedly from those of another, we can be fairly certain that those courtship patterns are learned and therefore cultural. Of course, anthropologists may sometimes err in their presumption that a particular behavior, thought, or feeling is cultural.

SOME ASSUMPTIONS ABOUT CULTURE

Culture Is Generally Adaptive

There are some cultural behaviors that, if carried to an extreme, would decrease the chances of survival of a particular society. For example, certain tribes in New Guinea view women as essentially unclean and dangerous individuals with whom physical contact should be as limited as possible. Suppose the men in one such tribe decided to avoid sex with women completely. Clearly, we would not expect such a society to survive for long. Although this example may appear extreme, it indicates that customs that diminish the survival chances of a society are not likely to persist. Either the people clinging to those customs will become extinct, taking the customs with them, or the customs will be replaced, thereby possibly helping the people to survive. By either process, *maladaptive* customs (those that diminish the chances of survival and reproduction) are likely to disappear. Those customs of a society that enhance survival and reproductive chances are *adaptive* and are likely to persist. Hence, we assume that if a society has survived to be described in the annals of anthropology (the "ethnographic record"), much if not most of its cultural repertoire is adaptive, or was at one time.

When we say that a custom is adaptive, however, we mean it is adaptive only with respect to a specific physical and social environment. What may be adaptive in one environment may not be adaptive in another. Therefore, when we ask why a society may have a particular custom, we are really asking if that custom makes sense as an adaptation to that society's particular environmental conditions.

Many cultural behaviors that would otherwise appear incomprehensible to us may be understandable as a society's response to its environment. For example, we might express surprise at certain societies' postpartum sex taboos that prohibit women from engaging in sexual intercourse until their two-year-olds are ready to be weaned. But in the tropical areas where such taboos exist, they may represent a people's means of adjusting to their physical environment. If there were no such taboo and a mother had another baby soon, she could no longer continue to nurse the older baby. Without its mother's milk, the older child might succumb to **kwashiorkor**, a severe protein-deficiency disease that is common in those tropical areas. The taboo, then, may serve to give infants a better chance to survive.[12] Thus, a long postpartum sex taboo may be an adaptive custom in certain tropical countries. In nontropical areas where kwashiorkor is not a problem, the same taboo may not be advantageous.

Just as culture represents an adjustment to the physical environment and to biological demands, it may also represent an adjustment to the social environment—that is, to neighboring peoples. For example, we do not know for sure why the Hopi Indians began building their settlements on the tops of mesas. They must have had strong reasons for doing so, because there were many difficulties in building on such sites—the problem of hauling water long distances to the settlements, for instance. It is possible that the Hopi chose to locate their villages on mesa tops for defensive reasons when Athapaskan-speaking groups of Indians (the Navaho and Apache) moved into the Hopi area. In other words, the Hopi may have adjusted their living habits in accordance with social pressure.

A given custom represents one society's adaptation to its environment; it does not represent all possible adaptations. Different societies may choose different means of adjusting to the same situation. Thus, in areas of South America where people's diets are low in protein, there is no long postpartum sex taboo, but induced abortion is reported to be a common practice. This practice may serve the same function of spacing out live births and thereby preventing too early weaning of children. The Hopi Indians, when suddenly confronted by the Navaho and Apache, clearly had to take some action to protect themselves. But instead of deciding to build their settlements on easily defended mesa tops, they could conceivably have developed a standing army.

Why a society develops a particular response to a problem, rather than some other possible response, always requires explanation. The choice may depend largely on whether a particular response is possible, given the existing cultural repertoire. For example, in the Hopi case a standing army would not have been a likely response to the problem of invaders because the Hopi economy probably could not have supported any large group of full-time specialists such as soldiers. As we shall see later in the chapter on food-getting, full-time specialists have to be fed by the regular production of more food than the people involved in food production generally need, and such a level of food production was not found among the Hopi. The strategy of moving their villages to easily defended mesa tops may have been the easiest option, given the Hopi economy.

Although we may assume that societies surviving long enough to be described have generally had adaptive culture traits, this does not mean that *all* culture traits are adaptive. Some traits—such as clothing styles and rules of etiquette—may be neutral in terms of adaptation. That is, they may have no

[12] John W. M. Whiting. "Effects of Climate on Certain Cultural Practices." In Ward H. Good-enough, ed., *Explorations in Cultural Anthropology.* New York: McGraw-Hill, 1964, pp. 511–44.

direct relationship to biological needs or environmental conditions at the present time. Consider, for example, the buttons and incompletely closed seam at the end of a man's suit-jacket sleeve. This style does not appear to have any adaptive value now. In the past, when there was no central heating in buildings, the style may have been quite adaptive, enabling the wearer to close the sleeves tightly about the wrist. Neutral traits may once have had adaptive consequences, or they may never have had any.

We must remember that a society is not forced to adapt its culture to changing environmental circumstances. First, even in the face of changed circumstances, people may choose not to change their customs. For example, the Tapirapé of central Brazil did not alter their customs limiting the number of births, even though they suffered severe population losses after contact with Europeans and their diseases. The Tapirapé population fell to fewer than 100 people from over 1000. Clearly they were on the way to extinction, yet they continued to value small families. Not only did they believe a woman should have no more than three children, but they took specific steps to achieve this limitation. They practiced infanticide if twins were born, if the third child was of the same sex as the first two children, and if the possible fathers broke certain taboos during pregnancy or in the child's infancy.[13]

Of course, it is also possible that a people will behave maladaptively even if they try to alter their behavior. After all, although people may alter their behavior according to what they perceive will be helpful to them, what they perceive to be helpful may not prove to be adaptive.

Culture Is Mostly Integrated

When we hear of an unfamiliar cultural pattern, our natural response is to try to imagine how that pattern would work in our own society. We might wonder, for example, what would happen if American women adopted a long postpartum sex taboo—say, two years of abstinence after the birth of a baby. Such a question is purely whimsical, for the customs of one culture cannot easily be grafted onto another culture. A long postpartum sex taboo presupposes a lack of effective birth-control methods, but our society already has many such methods. Moreover, a long postpartum sex taboo could conceivably affect a number of important aspects of our culture, such as the idea that a happy marriage is a sexy one. The point is that with such a taboo imposed on it, our culture would no longer be the same. Too many aspects of the culture would have to be changed to accommodate the new behavior. This is so because our culture is mostly integrated.

In saying that a culture is mostly *integrated,* we mean that the elements or traits that make up that culture are not just a random assortment of customs but are mostly adjusted to or consistent with one another. One reason anthropologists believe that culture tends to be integrated is that culture is generally

---

[13] Charles Wagley. "Cultural Influences on Population: A Comparison of Two Tupi Tribes." In Patricia J. Lyon, ed., *Native South Americans: Ethnology of the Least Known Continent.* Boston: Little, Brown, 1974, pp. 377–84.

adaptive. If certain customs are more adaptive in particular settings, then those "bundles" of traits will generally be found associated under similar conditions. For example, the !Kung, as we have mentioned, subsist by hunting wild animals and gathering wild plants. They are also nomadic, have very small communities, have low population densities, share food within their bands, and have few material possessions. As we will see later, these cultural traits usually occur together when people depend on hunting and gathering for their food.

A culture may also tend to be integrated for psychological reasons. The traits of a culture—attitudes, values, ideals, and rules for behavior—are stored, after all, in the brains of individuals. Research in social psychology has suggested that people tend to modify beliefs or behaviors that are not cognitively or conceptually consistent with other information.[14] We do not expect cultures to be completely integrated, just like we do not expect individuals to be completely consistent. But if a tendency toward cognitive consistency is generally found in humans, we might expect that at least some aspects of a culture would tend to be integrated for this reason.

How this pressure for consistency works is not hard to imagine. Children, for example, seem to be very good at remembering *all* the things their parents said. If they ask for something and the parents say no, they may say, "But you said I could yesterday." This pressure for consistency may even make parents change their minds! Of course, not everything one wants to do is consistent with the rest of one's desires, but there surely is pressure from within and without to make it so.

Humans are also capable of rational decision making: they can often, if not usually, figure out that certain things are not easy to do because of other things they do. For example, if society has a long postpartum sex taboo, we might expect that most people in the society could figure out that it would be easier to observe the taboo if husband and wife did not sleep in the same bed. Or, if people drive on the left side of the road (as in England), it is easier and less dangerous to drive a car whose steering wheel is on the right, because that placement allows you to judge more accurately how close you are to cars coming at you from the opposite direction.

Consistency or integration of culture traits may also be produced by less conscious psychological processes. We know that people may generalize (transfer) their experience from one realm of life to another. For example, where children are taught it is wrong to express anger toward family and friends, it turns out that folktales parallel the child rearing: anger and aggression in the folktales tend to be directed only toward strangers, not toward family and friends. It seems as if the expression of anger is too frightening (or maladaptive) to be expressed close to home, even in folktales.

The tendency for a culture to be integrated, then, may be cognitively and emotionally, as well as adaptively, induced.

[14] Roger Brown. *Social Psychology.* New York: Free Press, 1965, pp. 549–609.

Culture Is Always Changing

When you examine the history of a society, it is obvious that its culture has changed over time. Some of the shared behaviors, beliefs, and values that were common at one time are modified or replaced at another time. In American society, we only have to consider our attitudes toward sex and marriage to realize that a lot of our culture has changed recently. The impetus for change may come from within the society or from without. From within, the unconscious or conscious pressure for consistency will produce culture change if enough people adjust old behavior and thinking to new. Change can also occur if people try to invent better ways of doing things. Michael Chibnik suggests that people who confront a new problem conduct mental or small "experiments" to decide how to behave. These experiments may give rise to new cultural traits.[15]

A good deal of culture change may be stimulated by changes in the external environment. For example, if people move into an arid area, they will have to either give up farming or develop a system of irrigation. In the modern world, changes in the social environment are probably more frequent stimuli for culture change than changes in the physical environment. Many Americans, for example, started to think seriously about conserving energy, and about using sources of energy other than oil, only after oil supplies from the Near East were curtailed in 1973 and 1974. Different societies have often affected each other, and a significant amount of culture change that has occurred in the last few hundred years has been due to the colonial expansion of Western societies into other areas of the world. North American Indians, for instance, were forced to alter their life styles drastically when they were driven off their lands and confined to reservations.

If we assume that cultures are more than random collections of behaviors, beliefs, and values—that they tend to be adaptive, integrated, and changing—then the similarities and differences between them should be understandable. That is, we can expect that similar circumstances within or outside the culture will give rise to, or favor, similar cultural responses. Although we may assume that cultural variation is understandable, the task of discovering which particular circumstances favor which particular patterns is a large and difficult one. In the chapters that follow, we hope to convey the main points of what anthropologists think they know about aspects of cultural variation, and what they do not know. We frequently describe particular cultures to illustrate aspects of cultural variation. When we do so, the reader should understand that the culture described is probably not the same now, since the sources of our material always refer to some previous time.[16]

---

[15] Michael Chibnik. "The Evolution of Cultural Rules." *Journal of Anthropological Research,* 37 (1981): 256–68.

[16] Indeed, some of the cultures we refer to may have been quite different before as well as after the time referred to. For example, the !Kung hunter-gatherers of southern Africa probably were not only hunter-gatherers in the past. There is evidence that the !Kung of the

SUMMARY

1. Despite very strong individual differences, the members of a particular society closely agree in their responses to certain phenomena because they share common beliefs, attitudes, values, ideals, and behaviors, which constitute their culture.
2. The anthropological attitude that a society's customs and ideas should be studied objectively and understood in the context of that society's culture is called cultural relativism. In general, cultural relativism is impeded by two different but commonly held attitudes: first, the tendency toward negative evaluation, or ethnocentrism; second, the tendency toward positive evaluation, which often takes the form of a native yearning for the simple life of the "noble savage."
3. Culture may be defined as the learned behaviors, beliefs, attitudes, values, and ideals generally shared by the members of a group.
4. The size of the group within which cultural traits are shared can vary from a particular society or a segment of that society to a group that transcends national boundaries. When anthropologists refer to a culture, they are usually referring to the cultural patterns of a particular society—that is, a particular territorial population speaking a language not generally understood by neighboring territorial populations.
5. A defining feature of culture is that it is learned. Although other animals exhibit some cultural behavior, humans are unusual in the number and complexity of the learned patterns they transmit to their young. And they have a unique way of transmitting their culture: through language.
6. Anthropologists seek to discover the customs and ranges of acceptable behavior that constitute the culture of a society under study. In doing so, they focus on general or shared patterns of behavior rather than on individual variations. When dealing with practices that are highly visible, or with beliefs that are almost unanimous, the investigator can rely on observation or on a few knowledgeable persons. With less obvious behaviors or attitudes, the anthropologist must collect information from a sample of individuals. The mode of a frequency distribution can then be used to express the cultural pattern.
7. Every society develops a series of ideal cultural patterns that represent what most members of the society believe to be the correct behavior in particular situations. A society's ideal cultural patterns, however, do not always agree with its actual cultural patterns.
8. One important factor that limits the range of individual variation is the culture itself, which acts directly or indirectly as a constraint on behavior. The existence of cultural constraints, however, is not necessarily incompatible with individuality.
9. Several assumptions are frequently made about culture. First, culture is generally adaptive to the particular conditions of its physical and social environment. What may be adaptive in one environment may not be adaptive in another. Some cultural traits may be neutral in terms of adaptation, some may merely have been adaptive in the past, and still others may be maladaptive. Second, culture is mostly integrated, in that the elements or traits that make up the culture are mostly adjusted to or consistent with one another. Third, culture is always changing.

Kalahari Desert have switched from hunting and gathering to herding animals, and back again, many times in the past. See Carmel Schrire, "An Inquiry Into the Evolutionary Status and Apparent Identity of San Hunter-Gatherers," *Human Ecology*, 8 (1980): 9–32.

9

Language
and Culture

Few of us can remember the moment when we first became aware that words signified something. Yet that moment was a milestone for us, not just in the acquisition of language but in becoming acquainted with all the complex, elaborate behavior that constitutes our culture. Without language, the transmission of complex traditions would be virtually impossible, and each person would be trapped within his or her own world of private sensations.

To recapture that instant when language became meaningful, we must rely on individuals such as Helen Keller who came to language late. Miss Keller, left deaf and blind by illness at the age of nineteen months, gives a moving account of the afternoon she first established contact with another human being through words.

> [My teacher] brought me my hat, and I knew I was going out into the warm sunshine. This thought, if a wordless sensation may be called a thought, made me hop and skip with pleasure.
>
> We walked down the path to the well house, attracted by the fragrance of the honeysuckle with which it was covered. Someone was drawing water and my teacher placed my hand under the spout. As the cool stream gushed over one hand she spelled into the other the word *water,* first slowly, then rapidly. Suddenly I felt a misty consciousness as of something forgotten—a thrill of returning thought; and somehow the mystery of language was revealed to me. I knew then that w-a-t-e-r meant the wonderful cool something that was flowing over my

hand. That living word awakened my soul, gave it light, hope, joy, set it free! There were barriers still, it is true, barriers that could in time be swept away.

I left the well house eager to learn. Everything had a name, and each name gave birth to a new thought. As we returned to the house every object which I touched seemed to quiver with life. That was because I saw everything with the strange, new sight that had come to me.[1]

COMMUNICATION

Against all odds, Helen Keller had come to understand the essential function language plays in all societies—namely, that of communication. The word *communication* comes from the Latin verb *communicare*, "to share," "to impart that which is *common*." We communicate by agreeing, consciously or unconsciously, to call an object, a movement, or an abstract concept by a common name. For example, speakers of English have agreed to call the color of grass green, even though we have no way of comparing precisely how two persons actually experience this color. What we share is the agreement to call this sensation *green*. Any system of language consists of publicly accepted symbols by which individuals try to share private experiences.

Our communication obviously is not limited to spoken language. We communicate directly through body stance, gesture, and tone of voice; indirectly through systems of signs and symbols, such as writing, algebraic equations, musical scores, painting, code flags, and road signs. But despite all the competing systems of communication available to us, we must recognize the overriding importance of spoken language. It is probably the major transmitter of culture, allowing us to share and pass on our complex configuration of attitudes, beliefs, and patterns of behavior.

Animal Communication

Systems of communication are not unique to human beings. Other animal species communicate in a variety of ways. One way is by sound: a bird may communicate by a call that a territory is his and should not be encroached upon; a squirrel may utter a cry that leads other squirrels to flee from danger. Another means of animal communication is odor. An ant releases a chemical when it dies, and its fellows then carry it away to the compost heap. Apparently the communication is highly effective; a healthy ant painted with the death chemical will be dragged to the funeral heap again and again.

Another means of communication, body movement, is used by bees to convey the location of food sources. Karl von Frisch discovered that the black Austrian honeybee—by choosing a round dance, a wagging dance, or a short, straight run—could communicate not only the precise direction of the source of food, but also its distance from the hive.[2]

---

[1] Helen Keller. *The Story of My Life.* New York: Dell, 1974, p. 34. Originally published in 1902.
[2] K. von Frisch. "Dialects in the Language of the Bees." *Scientific American*, August 1962, pp. 78–87.

Although primates use all three methods of communication—sound, odor, and body movement—sound is the method that most concerns us in this chapter because spoken language is our own major means of communication. Nonhuman primates communicate vocally too, making various kinds of calls (but not very many of them). In the past only human communication was thought to be symbolic. Recent research suggests that some monkey and ape calls in the wild are also symbolic.

When we say that a communication (call, word, sentence) is *symbolic,* we mean at least two things. First, the communication has meaning even when its referent (whatever is referred to) is not present. Second, the meaning is arbitrary: the receiver of the message could not guess its meaning just from the sound(s) and does not know the meaning instinctively. In other words, symbols have to be learned. There is no compelling or "natural" reason that the word *dog* in English should refer to a smallish four-legged carnivore that is the bane of letter carriers.

Scientists who have observed vervet monkeys in the wild consider at least three of their alarm calls to be symbolic because each of them *means* (refers to) a different kind of predator—eagles, pythons, leopards—and monkeys react differently to each call. Experimentally, in the absence of the referent, investigators have been able to evoke the normal reaction to a call by playing it back electronically. Another indication that the vervet alarm calls are symbolic is that infant vervets appear to need some time to learn the referent for each. When they are very young, infants apply a particular call to more animals than adult vervets apply the call to. So, for example, infant vervets will often make the "eagle" warning call when they see any flying bird. The infants learn the appropriate referent apparently through adult vervets' repetition of infants' "correct" calls; in any case, the infants gradually learn to restrict the call to eagles. This process is probably not too different from the way an American infant first applies the "word" *dada* to all adult males and gradually learns to restrict it to one person.[3]

It is widely believed that the calls of nonhuman primates mostly communicate affect (feeling), as in the chimpanzee's grunt when it finds a preferred food.[4] But Peter Marler suggests that the difference between "affective" and "symbolic" calls in nonhuman primates may be more a matter of degree than of kind. Researchers seem to consider a call affective when a large class of things is referred to. For example, one vervet call seems to be triggered by seeing any of a number of possible predators, and the call may therefore be

[3] Robert M. Seyfarth and Dorothy L. Cheney. "How Monkeys See the World: A Review of Recent Research on East African Vervet Monkeys." In Charles T. Snowdon, Charles H. Brown, and Michael R. Petersen, eds., *Primate Communication.* New York: Cambridge University Press, 1982, pp. 242, 246.

[4] Peter Marler. "Primate Vocalization: Affective or Symbolic?" In Thomas A. Sebeok and Jean Umiker-Sebeok, eds., *Speaking of Apes: A Critical Anthology of Two-Way Communication with Man.* New York: Plenum, 1980, pp. 221–22.

translated as "Be alert!" But a call tends to be labeled symbolic when a smaller set of referents (for example, eagles) is referred to.[5]

All of the nonhuman vocalizations we have described so far enable individual animals to convey messages. The sender gives a signal that is received and "decoded" by the receiver, who usually responds with a specific action or reply. How is human vocalization different? Since monkeys and apes appear to use symbols at least some of the time, it is not appropriate to emphasize symbolism as the distinctive feature of human language. However, there is a significant quantitative difference between human language and other primates' systems of vocal communication—all human languages employ a much larger set of symbols. Another and perhaps more important difference is that the other primates' vocal systems tend to be *closed:* different calls are not often combined to produce new, meaningful utterances. In contrast, as we shall see, human languages are *open* systems, governed by complex rules about how sounds and sequences of sounds can be combined to produce an infinite variety of new meanings.

The idea that humans can transmit many more complex messages than any other animal does not begin to convey how different human language is from other communication systems. No chimp could say the equivalent of "I'm going to the ball game next Wednesday with my friend Jim if it's not raining." Not only can humans talk (and think) with language about things completely out of context; they can also be deliberately or unconsciously ambiguous in their messages. If a person asks you for help, you could say, "Sure, I'll do it when I have time," leaving the other person uncertain about whether your help is ever going to materialize. We can even convey a meaning that is opposite what we actually say, as when we say "What a great day!" after looking out the window and seeing a street full of slush.

Primates in the wild do not exhibit anything close to human language. But recent attempts to teach apes human-created languages have led some scholars to question the traditional assumption that the gap between human and other animal communication is enormous. If chimpanzees and gorillas have the capacity to *use* language, then the difference between humans and nonhumans may not be as great as people used to think.

Several people have attempted to teach chimpanzees human speech. One couple, who adopted a baby chimpanzee to raise with their own newborn son, abandoned the project a year later when it became obvious that the human child was imitating the ape, not the ape the child. Keith and Cathy Hayes were able to elicit only four recognizable words from their chimp after years of effort.[6]

But chimpanzees also are able to communicate with their hands. In

[5] Ibid., pp. 223, 229.
[6] Emily Hahn. "Chimpanzees and Language." *New Yorker*, April 24, 1971, p. 54. See also Keith J. Hayes and Catherine H. Hayes, "The Intellectual Development of a Home-Raised Chimpanzee," *Proceedings of the American Philosophical Society*, 95 (1951): 105–9.

1967, Adriaan Kortlandt reported that chimpanzees in the wild used hand gestures that he interpreted to mean "Come with me." "May I pass?" "You are welcome." "Stop!" and "Be off!" among others.[7] Allen and Beatrice Gardner succeeded in teaching American Sign Language (ASL) to a chimpanzee named Washoe. The amazing extent of Washoe's ability to use the 150 signs she had learned was recorded when she was with other chimpanzees on an island and noticed that the humans across the water were drinking iced tea.

> She kept signing, "Roger ride come gimme sweet eat please hurry hurry you come please gimme sweet you hurry you come ride Roger come give Washoe fruit drink hurry hurry fruit drink please." . . . A plane flew over just then, and Washoe mentioned that, too. She signed, "You me ride in plane."[8]

Subsequent work with two chimpanzees named Sarah and Lana suggests that chimpanzees can use other kinds of nonverbal symbols besides ASL gestures to form sentences and communicate their needs. Sarah was taught to use differently shaped and colored pieces of plastic, each representing a word (she had a vocabulary of about 130 words).[9] Lana was taught to use computer-controlled equipment, by pressing keys on a console to make sentences; she even showed when those sentences were complete by pressing a key that meant *period*.[10]

Are these apes really using language? The answer to this question is still quite controversial.[11] Even though ASL is accepted by many as a genuine language, meaning that its "speakers" can express anything a spoken language can, the apes have mastered only a small portion of ASL vocabulary.[12] And although it is clear that Washoe and the other apes can string a series of signs together, critics question whether the apes are combining the signs in the kind of rule-governed way humans create sentences.

There is a lot more agreement among investigators that nonhuman primates have the ability to "symbol"—to refer to something (or a class of things) with an arbitrary "label" (gesture or sequence of sounds).[13] For example, a female gorilla named Koko (with a repertoire of about 375 signs) extended the sign for *drinking straw* to plastic tubing, hoses, cigarettes, and radio antennae. Washoe originally learned the sign *dirty* to refer to feces and other soil, and then began to use it insultingly, as in "dirty Roger," when her

[7] Reported in Hahn, "Chimpanzees and Language," p. 54.

[8] Ibid., p. 98. For a more complete description of the Washoe project, see R. Allen Gardner and Beatrice B. Gardner, "Comparative Psychology and Language Acquisition," in Sebeok and Umiker-Sebeok, eds., *Speaking of Apes*, pp. 287–330.

[9] Ann James Premack and David Premack. "Teaching Language to an Ape," *Scientific American*, October 1972, pp. 92–99.

[10] Duane M. Rumbaugh, Timothy V. Gill, and E. C. von Glasersfeld. "Reading and Sentence Completion by a Chimpanzee (Pan)." *Science*, November 16, 1973, pp. 731–33.

[11] For much of the controversy on this issue, see various chapters in Sebeok and Umiker-Sebeok, eds., *Speaking of Apes*.

[12] Jane H. Hill. "Apes and Language." *Annual Review of Anthropology*, 7 (1978): 94.

[13] Ibid., p. 98.

trainer Roger Fouts refused to give her things she wanted. Even the mistakes made by the apes suggest that they are using signs symbolically, just as words are used in spoken language. For example, the sign *cat* may be used for dog if the animal has learned *cat* first (just as our daughter Katherine said "dog" to all pictures of four-footed animals, including elephants, when she was eighteen months old).

Thus, the symbolic capacity of apes may be very much like that of young humans. How large a language capacity apes can acquire is still an open question, subject to the outcome of continuing research. But as Jane Hill notes, the results of the research thus far strongly refute the traditional claim that language is an all-or-none thing confined to humans.[14]

The Origins of Language

How long humans have had spoken language is not known. Recently, Philip Lieberman and Jeffrey Laitman have argued that language as we know it developed only after about 40,000 years ago with the emergence of modern-looking humans who had the mouth and throat anatomy we have.[15] According to Lieberman and Laitman, premodern humans did not have the vocal anatomy required for language. Their argument is based on controversial reconstructions of the mouths and throats of earlier humans, and so their conclusions are not widely accepted.[16]

Most speculation about the origins of language has centered in the question of how natural selection may have favored the open quality of language. All known human languages are open in the sense that utterances can be combined in various ways to produce new meanings.[17] Somehow a call system of communication was eventually changed to a system based on small units of sound that could be put together in many different ways to form meaningful utterances. For example, an American can combine *care* and *full* (*careful*) to mean one thing, then use each of the two elements in other combinations to mean different things. *Care* can be used to make *carefree, careless,* or *caretaker; full* can be used to make *powerful* or *wonderful.*

Can we learn anything about the origins of language by studying the languages of simpler societies? The answer is no, because such languages are not simpler or less developed than ours. Intuitively, we might suppose that languages of nonliterate peoples or peoples without writing would be much less developed than languages spoken by technologically advanced, literate societies. But this is in no sense true. The sound systems, vocabularies, and

---

[14] Ibid., p. 105.

[15] Philip Lieberman. *The Biology and Evolution of Language.* Cambridge, Mass.: Harvard University Press, 1984; and Jeffrey Laitman, "The Anatomy of Human Speech." *Natural History.* August 1984, pp. 20–27.

[16] Ronald Carlisle and Michael I. Siegel. "Additional Comments on Problems in the Interpretation of Neanderthal Speech Capabilities." *American Anthropologist,* 80 (1978): 367–72.

[17] C. F. Hockett and R. Ascher. "The Human Revolution." *Current Anthropology,* 5 (1964): 135–68.

grammars of technologically simpler peoples are in no way inferior to those of more complex societies.[18]

Of course, Australian aborigines will not be able to name the sophisticated machines used in our society. Their language, however, has the potential for doing so. As we will see later in this chapter, all languages possess the amount of vocabulary their speakers need, and languages expand in response to cultural changes. Moreover, the language of a technologically simple people, though lacking terminology for some of our conveniences, may have a rich vocabulary for events or natural phenomena that are of particular importance to that society.

If there are no primitive languages, and if the earliest languages have left no traces that would allow us to reconstruct them, does that mean we cannot investigate the origins of language? Some linguists think we can. Some say that if we can understand how children acquire language, we will learn something about the genetic basis of language. Recently, other linguists have suggested that an understanding of how *creole languages* develop will also tell us something about the origins of language. (We will discuss such languages shortly.)

The movement from calls to language, which may have taken millennia in the evolution of humans, takes but a few years for children. So, the acquisition of language by children may offer insights into the origins of speech. Although a specific language, like other cultural patterns, is learned and shared, the process by which a child acquires the structure, or grammar, of language seems to be inborn and therefore precultural. Apparently a child is equipped from birth with the capacity to reproduce all the sounds used by the world's languages and to learn any system of grammar. The language the child learns is the one spoken by his or her parents. Since this language is a system of shared symbols, it can be reformed into an infinite variety of expressions and be understood by all who share these symbols. In this way, for example, T. S. Eliot could form a sentence never before formed, "In the room the women come and go talking of Michelangelo,"[19] and the sense of his sentence, though not necessarily his private meaning, could be understood by all speakers of English.

The child's acquisition of the structure and meaning of language has been called the most difficult intellectual achievement in life. If that is so, it is pleasing to note that he or she accomplishes it with relative ease and vast enjoyment. This "difficult intellectual achievement" may in reality be a natural response to the capacity for language that is one of humans' genetic

[18] Franklin C. Southworth and Chandler J. Daswani. *Foundations of Linguistics.* New York: Free Press, 1974, p. 312. See also Franz Boas, "On Grammatical Categories," in Dell Hymes, ed., *Language in Culture and Society: A Reader in Linguistics and Anthropology,* New York: Harper & Row, Pub., 1964, pp. 121–23. Originally published in 1911.
[19] T. S. Eliot. "The Love Song of J. Alfred Prufrock." In *Collected Poems, 1909–1962.* New York: Harcourt, Brace & World, 1963.

characteristics. All over the world children begin to learn language at about the same age—and in no culture do children wait until they are seven or ten years old. By twelve or thirteen months children are able to name a few objects and actions. In addition, they seem able to grasp the underlying structure. They are able to make one key word stand for a whole sentence: "Out!" for "Take me out for a walk right now"; "Bottle!" for "I want my bottle now."

Children the world over tend to progress to two-word sentences at the age of about eighteen months. In those sentences they express themselves in "telegraph" form—using nouns, verbs, and adjectives but leaving out "little" words such as "the." So a sentence comes out "Book table" rather than "The book is on the table."[20] They do not utter their two words in random order, sometimes saying "book" first, other times saying "table" first. Rather they seem to select an order that fits the conventions of adult language. So they are likely to say "Daddy eat," not "Eat Daddy." In other words, they tend to put the subject first, as adults do. And they tend to say "Mommy coat" rather than "Coat Mommy" to indicate "Mommy's coat."[21] Since parents do not utter sentences such as "Daddy eat," children seem to know a lot about how to put words together with little or no direct teaching from their parents. Consider the five-year-old who, confronted with the unfamiliar "Gloria in Excelsis," sang quite happily, "Gloria eats eggshells." To make the words fit the structure of English grammar was more important than to make the words fit the meaning of the Christmas pageant.

Psycholinguists (psychologists who study linguistic behavior) have become aware of the inadequacy of the usual learning methods—imitation, practice, reinforcement—to explain the child's early acquisition and creative use of grammatical structure. One set of theoreticians of grammar suggest that there may be a *language-acquisition device* in the brain, as innate to humans as call systems are to the other animals.[22] As the forebrain evolved, this device may have become part of our biological inheritance. Whether the device in fact exists is not yet clear. But we do know that the actual development of individual language is not completely biologically determined; if it were, all human beings would speak the same brain-generated language. Instead, about 4000 to 5000 mutually unintelligible languages have been identified. More than 2000 of them are still spoken today, most by peoples who do not have a system of writing.

Some of these languages have developed quite recently in various places around the world where European colonial powers established commercial

[20] Roger Brown. "The First Sentence of Child and Chimpanzee." In Sebeok and Umiker-Sebeok, eds., *Speaking of Apes*, pp. 93–94.

[21] Peter A. de Villiers and Jill G. de Villiers. *Early Language*. Cambridge, Mass.: Harvard University Press, 1979, p. 48. See also Eric Wanner and Lila R. Gleitman, eds., *Language Acquisition: The State of the Art*, Cambridge: Cambridge University Press, 1982.

[22] See Noam Chomsky, *Reflections on Language*. New York: Pantheon, 1975.

enterprises that relied on imported labor, generally slaves. The laborers in one place often came from several different societies, and in the beginning would speak with their masters and with each other in some kind of *pidgin* (simplified) version of the masters' language. Pidgin languages lack many of the building blocks found in the languages of whole societies, building blocks such as prepositions (*to, on* and so forth) and auxiliary verbs (designating future and other tenses). Many pidgin languages developed into and were replaced by so-called creole languages, which incorporate much of the vocabulary of the masters' language but also have a grammar that differs from it and from the grammars of the laborers' native languages.[23]

That creole languages all over the world have striking similarities in grammar is consistent with the idea that there is a universal grammar inherited by all humans. Creoles therefore may resemble early human languages. All creoles use intonation (changing the pitch of the voice) instead of a change in word order to ask a question: "You can fix this?" in contrast with "Can you fix this?" They all express the future and the past in the same grammatical way, by the use of particles (short unchanging parts of speech such as the English *shall*) between subject and verb, and they all employ double negatives, as in the Guyana English creole "Nobody no like me."[24]

If there is a basic grammar imprinted in the human mind, we should not be surprised that children's early and later speech patterns seem to be similar across languages. We might also expect children's later speech to be similar to the structure of creole languages. And it is, according to Derek Bickerton.[25] The "errors" children make in speaking are consistent with the grammar of creoles. For example, English-speaking children three to four years old tend to ask questions by intonation alone, and they tend to use double negatives such as "I don't see no dog," even though the grown-ups around them do not speak that way and consider the children's speech "wrong."

Future research on children's acquisition of language and on the structure of creole languages may bring us closer to understanding the origins of human language. But even if there is a universal grammar, we still need to understand how and why the thousands of languages in the world vary—which brings us to the conceptual tools linguists have had to invent in order to study languages.

STRUCTURAL LINGUISTICS

In every society children do not need to be taught "grammar" to learn how to speak. They begin to grasp the essential structure of their language at a very early age, without direct instruction. If you show English-speaking children a picture of one "gork" and then a picture of two of these creatures, they will

[23] Derek Bickerton. "Creole Languages." *Scientific American,* July 1983, pp. 116–22.
[24] Ibid., p. 122.
[25] Ibid.

say there are two "gorks." They somehow know that adding an *s* to a noun means more than one. But they do not know this consciously, and grown-ups may not either. One of the most surprising features of human language is that meaningful sounds and sound sequences are combined according to rules that are often not consciously known by the speakers.

These rules should not be equated with the "rules of grammar" you may have been taught in school (so that you would speak "correctly"). Rather, when linguists talk about rules they are referring to the patterns of speaking that are discoverable in actual speech. Needless to say, there is some overlap between the actual rules of speaking and the "rules" taught in school. But there are rules that children never hear about in school, because their teachers are not linguists and are not aware of them. So when linguists use the term *grammar,* they are *not* referring to the prescriptive rules that people are supposed to follow in speaking. Rather, *grammar* to the linguist consists of the actual, often unconscious principles that predict how most people talk. As we have noted, young children may speak two-word sentences that conform to a linguistic rule, but their speech is hardly considered "correct"!

Discovering the mostly unconscious rules operating in a language is a very difficult task. Linguists have had to invent special concepts and methods of transcription (writing) to permit them to describe: (1) what the rules or principles are that predict how sounds are made and how they are used (often, slightly varying sounds are used interchangeably in words without creating a difference in meaning); (2) how sound sequences (and sometimes even individual sounds) convey meaning and how meaningful sound sequences are strung together to form words; and (3) how words are strung together to form phrases and sentences. Thus, **structural** (or **descriptive) linguistics** tries to discover the rules of **phonology** (the patterning of sounds, **morphology** (the patterning of sound sequences and words), and **syntax** (the patterning of phrases and sentences) that predict how most speakers of a language talk.

Phonology

Most of us have had the experience of trying to learn another language and finding out that some sounds are exceedingly difficult to make. One reason is that we may have never made them before and so we literally lack the necessary lip, tongue, and other muscular habits. Although the human vocal tract can theoretically make a very large number of different sounds (**phones** to linguists), each language uses only some of them. It is not that we cannot make the sounds that are strange to us; we just have not acquired the habits of making those sounds. And until the sounds become habitual for us, they continue to be difficult to make.

Finding it difficult to make certain sounds is only one of the reasons we have trouble learning a "foreign" language. Another problem is that we may not be used to combining certain sounds or making a certain sound in a particular position in a word. So English speakers find it difficult to combine z and d, as Russian speakers often do (because we never do so in English), or to pronounce words in Samoan (a South Pacific language) that begin with the sound English speakers write as *ng*, even though we have no trouble putting that sound at the end of words, as in the English *sing* and *hitting*.

In order to study the patterning of sounds, linguists who are interested in phonology have to write down speech utterances as sequences of sound. This would be almost impossible if linguists were restricted to using their own alphabet (say the one we use to write English), because other languages use sounds that are difficult to represent with the English alphabet or because the alphabet we use in English can represent a particular sound in different ways. (English writing represents the sound *f* by "f" as in "food," but also as "gh" in "tough" and "ph" in "phone.") To overcome these difficulties in writing sounds with the "letters" of existing writing systems, linguists have developed systems of transcription in which each "letter" or sound symbol is meant to represent one particular sound.

Once linguists have identified the sounds or phones used in a language, they try to identify how these sounds are classified unconsciously (by the speakers of the language) into **phonemes.** A phoneme is a set of varying sounds that do not make any difference in meaning. In other words, when one phone of a phoneme class is substituted for another phone of the same class, speakers will still say that the utterance is the same.

The ways in which sounds are grouped together into phonemes vary from language to language. In English the sound of *l* in "lake" is considered quite different from the sound of *r* in "rake"; the two sounds belong to different phonemes because they make a difference in meaning to English speakers. But in Samoan, *l* and *r* can be used interchangeably in a word without making a difference in meaning; in Samoan, these two sounds belong to the same phoneme. So, Samoan speakers may say "Leupena" sometimes and "Reupena" at other times when they are referring to someone who in English would be called "Reuben." English speakers may joke about languages that confuse *l* and *r*, but they are not usually aware that we do the same thing with other pairs of sounds. For example, consider how we pronounce the word we spell as "butter." Some people say this word with a *t* in the middle; others say it with a *d*. We recognize "butter" and "budder" as the same word; the interchangeability of *t* and *d* does not make a difference in meaning. Speakers of some other languages would hear "butter" and "budder" as different words and make fun of us for confusing *t* and *d*!

After discovering which sounds are grouped into phonemes (that is, which sounds can be substituted for each other without making a difference in meaning), linguists can begin to discover the sound sequences that are allowed in a language and the usually unconscious rules that predict those sequences. For example, words in English rarely start with three consonants. But when they do, the first consonant is always an *s*, as in "strike" and "scratch."[26] Linguists' descriptions of the patterning of sounds (phonology) in different languages may allow them to investigate why languages vary in their sound rules. For example, why are two or more consonants strung together in some languages, whereas in other languages vowels are always put between consonants? The Samoan language now has a word for "Christmas" borrowed from English. But the borrowed word has been changed to fit the rules of Samoan. In the English word two consonants come first (*k* and *r*, which we spell as "ch" and "r"). The Samoan word is *Kerisimasi:* a vowel has been inserted between each pair of consonants and the word ends with a vowel, which is exactly how all Samoan words are constructed.

Morphology

Morphology is the study of a variety of questions about words, particularly what words are and how they are formed. We take our words so much for granted that we do not realize how complicated it is to say what words are. People do not usually pause between words when they speak; if we did not know our language, a sentence would seem like a continuous stream of sounds. This is how we first hear a foreign language. It is only when we understand the language and write down what we say that we separate (by spaces) what we call *words*. But a word is really only an arbitrary sequence of sounds that has a meaning; we would not "hear" words as separate units if we did not understand the language to which they belong.

Because anthropological linguists traditionally investigated unwritten languages, sometimes without the aid of interpreters, they had to figure out which sequences of sounds conveyed meaning. And because words in many languages can often be broken down into smaller meaningful units, linguists had to invent special words to refer to those units. The smallest unit of language that has a meaning is a **morph**. One or more morphs with the same meaning make up a **morpheme**. For example, the prefix *in-*, as in *indefinite*, and the prefix *un-*, as in *unclear*, are morphs that belong to the morpheme meaning *not*. A morph or morpheme should not be confused with a word. Although some words are single morphs or morphemes (for example, *for* and *giraffe* in English), many words are built on a combination of morphs, generally prefixes, roots, and suffixes. Thus, *cow* is one word, but the word *cows* contains two meaningful units—a root (*cow*) and a suffix (pronounced like *z*) meaning more than one. The **lexicon** of a language, which a dictionary approximates, consists of words and morphs and their meanings.

It seems likely that the intuitive grasp children have of the structure of their language includes a recognition of morphology, the patterning of sound sequences and words. Once they learn that the morph/-z/ added to a noun-type word indicates more than one, they plow ahead with *mans*, and *childs;*

---

[26] Adrian Akmajian, Richard A. Demers, and Robert M. Harnish. *Linguistics: An Introduction to Language and Communication*, 2nd ed. Cambridge, Mass.: M.I.T. Press, 1984, p. 136.

once they grasp that the morpheme class pronounced /t/ or /d/ or /ed/ added to the end of a verb indicates that the action took place in the past, they apply this concept generally and invent *runned, drinked, costed.* They see a ball roll near*er* and near*er,* and they transfer this to a kite, which goes upp*er* and upp*er.* From their mistakes as well as their successes, we can see that they understand the regular uses of morphemes. By the age of seven, they have mastered many of the irregular forms as well—that is, they learn which morphs of a morpheme are used when.

The child's intuitive grasp of the dependence of some morphemes on others corresponds to the linguist's recognition of free morphemes and bound morphemes. A *free* morpheme has meaning standing alone—that is, it can be a separate word. A *bound* morpheme displays its meaning only when attached to another morpheme. The morph pronounced /-t/ of the bound morpheme meaning *past tense* is attached to the root *walk* to produce *walked;* but the /-t/ cannot stand alone or have meaning by itself.

In English, the meaning of an utterance (containing a subject, verb, object, and so forth) usually depends on the order of the words. "The dog bit the child" is different in meaning from "The child bit the dog." But in many other languages, the grammatical meaning of an utterance does not depend much, if at all, on the order of the words. Rather, meaning may be determined by how the morphs in a word are ordered. For example, in Luo (a language of East Africa) the same bound morpheme may mean the subject or object of an action. If the morpheme is the prefix to a verb, it means the subject; if it is the suffix to a verb, it means the object. Another way that grammatical meaning may be conveyed is by altering or adding a bound morpheme to a word to indicate what part of speech it is. For example, in Russian, the word for "mail" when it is the subject of a sentence is pronounced something like "pawchtah." When "mail" is used as the object of a verb, as in "I gave her the mail," the ending of the word changes to "pawchtoo." And if I say "What was in the mail?" the word becomes "pawchtyeh."

Some languages have so many bound morphemes that they might express as a complex but single word what is considered a sentence in English. For example, the English sentence "He will give it to you" can be expressed in Wishram, a Chinookan dialect that was spoken along the Columbia River in the Pacific Northwest, as *acimluda* (a-c-i-m-l-ud-a, literally "will-he-him-thee-to-give-will"). Note that the pronoun *it* in English is gender-neutral; Wishram requires that *it* be given a gender, in this case "him."[27]

Syntax

Because language is an open system, we can make up meaningful utterances that we have never heard before. We are constantly creating new phrases and

---

[27] E. Sapir and M. Swadesh. "American Indian Grammatical Categories." In Hymes, ed., *Language in Culture and Society,* p. 103.

sentences. Just as with morphology, the speakers of a language seem to have an intuitive grasp of syntax—the rules that predict how phrases and sentences are generally formed. These "rules" may be partly learned in school, but children know many of them even before they get to school. In adulthood, our understanding of morphology and syntax is so intuitive that we can even understand a nonsense sentence, such as the following famous one from Lewis Carroll's *Through the Looking-Glass:*

> 'Twas brillig, and the slithy toves
> Did gyre and gimble in the wabe

Simply from the ordering of the words in the sentence, we can surmise which part of speech a word is, as well as its function in the sentence. *Brillig* is an adjective; *slithy* an adjective; *toves* a noun and the subject of the sentence; *gyre* and *gimble* verbs; and *wabe* a noun and the object of a prepositional phrase. Of course, an understanding of morphology helps too. The *-y* ending in *slithy* is an indication that the latter is an adjective, and the *-s* ending in *toves* tells us that we most probably have more than one of these creatures.

Besides producing and understanding an infinite variety of sentences, speakers of a language can tell when a sentence is not "correct" without consulting grammar books. For example, an English-speaker can tell that "Child the dog the hit" is not an acceptable sentence, but "The child hit the dog" is fine. There must then be a set of rules underlying how phrases and sentences are constructed in a language.[28] Speakers of a language know these implicit rules of syntax, but are not usually consciously aware of them. The linguist's description of the syntax of a language tries to make these rules explicit.

Noam Chomsky's theory about syntax, known as **transformational/ generative theory**, suggests that a language has a *surface structure* and a *deep structure*. For example, the sentences "John killed Mary" and "Mary was killed by John" have very different surface structures (John is the subject of the first sentence; Mary is the subject of the second). But the sentences mean the same thing to English-speakers, so the deep structure is the same in both sentences. A transformational description of a language would not only provide the rules that describe how the basic sentences of a language are formed; it would also stipulate how those basic sentences can be transformed into more complex sentences.[29]

HISTORICAL LINGUISTICS

The field of **historical linguistics** focuses on how languages change over time. Written works provide the best data for establishing such changes. For example, the following passage from Chaucer's *Canterbury Tales*, written in the

---

[28] Akmajian, Demers, and Harnish. *Linguistics*, pp. 164–66.
[29] Southworth and Daswani. *Foundations of Linguistics*, pp. 154–57.

English of the fourteenth century, has recognizable elements but is different enough from modern English to require a translation.

A Frere ther was, a wantowne and a merye,
A lymytour, a ful solempne man.
In alle the ordres foure is noon that kan
So muche of daliaunce and fair language.
He hadde maad ful many a mariage
Of yonge wommen at his owene cost.
Unto his ordre he was a noble post.
Ful wel biloued and famulier was he
With frankeleyns ouer al in his contree,
And with worthy wommen of the toun;
For he hadde power of confessioun,
As seyde hymself, moore than a curat,
For of his ordre he was licenciat.

A Friar there was, wanton and merry,
A limiter [a friar limited to certain districts], a full solemn
[very important] man.
In all the orders four there is none that knows
So much of dalliance [flirting] and fair [engaging] language.
He had made [arranged] many a marriage
Of young women at his own cost.
Unto his order he was a noble post [pillar].
Full well beloved and familiar was he
With franklins [wealthy landowners] all over his country
And also with worthy women of the town;
For he had power of confession,
As he said himself, more than a curate,
For of his order, he was a licentiate [licensed by the Pope].[30]

From this comparison we can recognize a number of changes. A great many words are spelled differently today. In some cases, meaning has changed: *full*, for example, would be translated today as *very*. What is less evident is that changes in pronunciation have occurred. For example, the *g* in *mariage* (marriage) was pronounced *zh*, as in the French from which it was borrowed, whereas now it is pronounced like the second *g* in *George*.

Since languages spoken in the past leave no traces unless they were written, and since most of the languages known to anthropology were not written by their speakers, you might guess that historical linguists can study linguistic change only by studying written languages such as English. But that is not the case. Linguists can reconstruct changes that have occurred by comparing contemporary languages that are very similar. Such languages show phonological, morphological, and syntactic similarities because they usually derive from a common ancestral language. For example, Romanian, Italian, French, Spanish, and Portuguese have many similarities. On the basis

[30] Chaucer. *The Prologue to the Canterbury Tales, the Knightes Tale, the Nonnes Prestes Tale.* ed. Mark H. Liddell, New York: The Macmillan Company, 1926, p. 8. Modern English translation by the authors on the basis of the glossary in ibid.

of these similarities, linguists can reconstruct what the ancestral language was like and how it changed into what we call the "Romance" languages. Of course, these reconstructions can be easily tested and confirmed because we know from many surviving writings what the ancestral language (Latin) was like; and we know from documents how Latin diversified as the Roman Empire expanded. Thus, common ancestry is frequently the reason why neighboring (and sometimes even separated) languages show patterns of similarity.

But languages can be similar for other reasons too. One reason is contact between speech communities, which leads one language to borrow from the other. For example, English borrowed a lot of vocabulary from French after England was conquered by the French-speaking Normans in A.D. 1066. Languages may also show similarities even though they do not derive from a common ancestral language and even though there has been no contact or borrowing between them; such similarities may reflect common or universal features of human cultures and/or human brains. (As we noted earlier in this chapter, the grammatical similarities exhibited by creole languages may possibly reflect how the human brain is "wired.") Finally, even unrelated and separated languages may show some similarities because of the phenomenon of convergence; similarities can develop because some processes of linguistic change may have only a few possible outcomes.

Language Families and Culture History

Latin is the ancestral language of the Romance languages. We know this from documentary (written) records. But if the ancestral language of a set of similar languages is not known from written records, linguists can still reconstruct many features of that language by comparing the derived languages. (Such a reconstructed language is called a **protolanguage**.) That is, by comparing presumably related languages, linguists can become aware of the features that many of them have in common, features that were probably found in the common ancestral language. The languages that derive from the same proto-language are called a *language family*. Most languages spoken in the world today can be grouped into fewer than thirty families. The language family English belongs to is called *Indo-European*, because it includes most of the languages of Europe and some of the languages of India. About 50 percent of the world's more than 4 billion people speak Indo-European languages.[31] Another very large language family, now spoken by more than a billion people, is Sino-Tibetan, which includes the languages of northern and southern China as well as those of Tibet and Burma.

The field of historical linguistics got its start in 1786 when a British colonial judge in India, Sir William Jones, noticed similarities between Sanskrit (the language spoken and written in ancient India) and classical Greek,

---

[31] Akmajian, Demers, and Harnish. *Linguistics*, p. 356.

Latin, and more recent European languages.[32] In 1822, Jacob Grimm, one of the brothers Grimm of fairy-tale fame, formulated rules to describe the sound shifts that had occurred when the various Indo-European languages diverged from each other. So, for example, in English and the other languages in the Germanic branch of the Indo-European family, *d* regularly shifted to *t* (compare the English *two* and *ten* with the Latin *duo* and *decem*) and *p* regularly shifted to *f* (English *father* and *foot*, Latin *pater* and *pes*). Scholars generally agree that the Indo-European languages derive from a language spoken 5000 to 6000 years ago.[33] The ancestral Indo-European language, many of whose features have now been reconstructed, is called *proto-Indo-European*, or *PIE* for short.

Where did the people who spoke PIE live? Some linguists believe that the approximate location of a protolanguage is suggested by the words for plants and animals in the derived languages. More specifically, among these different languages, those words that are **cognates** (that are similar in sound and meaning) presumably refer to plants and animals that were present in the original homeland. So if we know where those animals and plants were located 5000 to 6000 years ago, we can guess where the speakers of PIE lived. Among all the cognates for trees in the Indo-European languages, Paul Friedrich has identified eighteen that he believes were present in the Eastern Ukraine in 3000 B.C.; on this basis he suggests that the eastern Ukraine was the PIE homeland.[34] Also consistent with this hypothesis is the fact that the Slavic subfamily of Indo-European (which includes most of the languages in and around the Soviet Union) has the most tree names (compared with other subfamilies) that are similar to the reconstructed words in proto-Indo-European.[35]

Marija Gimbutas thinks we can even identify the proto-Indo-Europeans archeologically. She believes that the PIE speakers were probably the people associated with what is known as the Kurgan culture (5000–2000 B.C.),which spread out of the Ukraine around 3000 B.C. The Kurgan people were herders, keeping and raising horses, cattle, sheep, and pigs. They also relied on hunting and grain cultivation. Burials suggest differences in wealth and special status for men.[36] Why the Kurgan people were able to expand to many places in Europe and the Near East is not yet clear (some have suggested that horses and horse-drawn wagons provided important military advantages). In

---

[32] Philip Baldi. *An Introduction to the Indo-European Languages*. Carbondale: Southern Illinois University Press, 1983, p. 3.

[33] Ibid., p. 12.

[34] Paul Friedrich. *Proto-Indo-European Trees: The Arboreal System of a Prehistoric People*. Chicago: University of Chicago Press, 1970, p. 168.

[35] Ibid., p. 166.

[36] Marija Gimbutas. "An Archaeologist's View of PIE" in 1975. *Journal of Indo European Studies*, 2 (1974): 293–95. For a recent overview of these problems, see Susan N. Skomal and Edgar C. Polomé, eds., *Proto-Indo-European: The Archaeology of a Linguistic Problem*. Washington, D.C.: Washington Institute for the Study of Man, 1987.

any case, it *is* clear that many Kurgan cultural elements were distributed after 3000 B.C. over a wide area of the Old World.

Comparison of the Indo-European languages and reconstruction of proto-Indo-European have suggested where the PIE speakers may have lived originally and how (as suggested by archeological evidence) they may have spread. Similarly, historical linguists and archeologists have suggested culture histories for other language families. For example, the Bantu languages in Africa (spoken by perhaps 80 million people) form a subfamily of the larger Niger-Congo family of languages. Bantu speakers currently live in a wide band across the center of the African continent and down the eastern and western sides of southern Africa. All of the Bantu languages presumably derive from people who spoke proto-Bantu. But where was their homeland?

As in the case of proto-Indo-European, different theories have been proposed about the homeland of the Bantu. But most historical linguists now agree with Joseph Greenberg's suggestion that the proto-Bantu may have lived in what is now the Middle Benue area of eastern Nigeria. This suggestion is based on two assumptions. First, the point of origin of a language is presumably where there is the greatest diversity of related languages and **dialects** (varying forms of a language); it is assumed that the original homeland has had the most time for linguistic diversity to develop, compared with an area only recently occupied by a related language. For example, England (the homeland of English) has more dialect diversity than New Zealand or Australia. The second assumption about how to locate the homeland of a group of languages is that the related languages now spoken in or near the homeland should show the most similarity to the other (in this case non-Bantu) languages spoken in that area; it is assumed that such similarity betrays a common origin even further back in time. Both of the assumptions just outlined generate the conclusion that the proto-Bantu probably lived in the Middle Benue area of eastern Nigeria.[37]

Why were the Bantu able to spread so widely over the last few thousand years? Anthropologists have only begun to guess.[38] Initially, the Bantu probably kept goats and practiced some form of agriculture, which may have allowed them to spread at the expense of hunter-gatherers. Later, as the Bantu-speakers expanded, they began to cultivate certain cereal crops and herd sheep and cattle. Around this time, after 1000 B.C., they began to use and make iron tools, which may also have given them significant advantages. In any case, by 1500 to 2000 years ago Bantu-speakers had spread throughout central Africa and into the northern reaches of southern Africa. But speakers of non-Bantu languages still live in eastern, southern, and southwestern Africa.

---

[37] Joseph H. Greenberg. "Linguistic Evidence Regarding Bantu Origins." *Journal of African History*, 13 (1972): 189–216. See also D. W. Phillipson, "Archaeology and Bantu Linguistics," *World Archaeology*, 8 (1976): 71.

[38] Phillipson. "Archaeology and Bantu Linguistics," p. 79.

The Processes of Linguistic Divergence

The historical or comparative linguist hopes to do more than record and date linguistic divergence. Just as the physical anthropologist may attempt to develop explanations for human variation, so the linguist investigates the possible causes of linguistic variation. When groups of people speaking the same language lose communication with one another because they become separated either physically or socially, they begin to accumulate small changes in phonology, morphology, and syntax (which occur continuously in any language). Eventually, if the separation continues, the former dialects of the same language will become separate languages; that is, they will become mutually unintelligible, as German and English now are.

Geographical barriers such as large bodies of water, deserts, and mountains may separate speakers of what was once the same language, but distance by itself can also produce divergence. For example, if we compare dialects of English in the British Isles, it is clear that those regions farthest away from each other are the most different linguistically (compare the northeast of Scotland and London).[39] In northern India, hundreds of semiisolated villages and regions developed hundreds of local dialects. Today, the inhabitants of each village understand the dialects of the surrounding villages, and with a little more difficulty, the dialects of the next circle of villages. But slight dialect shifts accumulate village by village, and it seems as if different languages are being spoken at the opposite ends of the region, which are separated by over a thousand miles.[40]

Even where there is little geographic separation there may still be a great deal of dialect differentiation because of social distance. So, for example, the spread of a linguistic feature may be halted by racial, religious, or social-class differences that inhibit communication.[41] In the village of Khalapur in North India, John Gumperz found substantial differences in speech between the "untouchable" groups and other groups. Members of the untouchable groups have work contacts with others, but no friendships.[42] Without friendships and the easy communication between friends, dialect differentiation can readily develop.

Whereas isolation brings divergence between speech communities, contact results in greater resemblance. This is particularly evident when contact between mutually unintelligible languages introduces *borrowed* words, which usually name some new item borrowed from the other culture—*tomato, canoe,*

---

[39] Peter Trudgill. *Sociolinguistics: An Introduction to Language and Society*, rev. ed. New York: Penguin, 1983, p. 34.

[40] John J. Gumperz. "Speech Variation and the Study of Indian Civilization." *American Anthropologist*, 63 (1961): 976–88.

[41] Trudgill, *Sociolinguistics*, p. 35.

[42] John J. Gumperz. "Dialect Differences and Social Stratification in a North Indian Village." In *Language in Social Groups: Essays by John J. Gumperz*, selected and introduced by Anwar S. Dil. Stanford, Calif.: Stanford University Press, 1971, p. 45.

sputnik, and so on. Bilingual groups within a culture may also introduce foreign words, especially when the mainstream language has no real equivalent. Thus, *siesta* has come into English, and *le weekend* into French.

Conquest and colonization often result in extensive borrowing. The Norman conquest of England introduced French as the language of the new aristocracy. It was 300 years before the educated classes began to write in English. During this time the English borrowed words from French and Latin, and the two languages—English, and French—became more alike than they would otherwise have been. About 50 percent of the English general vocabulary has been borrowed from French. As this example suggests, different social classes may borrow differentially. For example, English aristocrats eventually called their meat "pork" and "beef" (derived from the French words), but the people who raised the animals and prepared them for eating continued (at least for a while) to refer to the meat as "pig" and "bull," the original Anglo-Saxon words.

In those 300 years of extensive borrowing, the grammar of English remained relatively stable. English lost most of its inflections or case endings, but it adopted little of the French grammar. Generally, the borrowing of words (particularly free morphemes[43]) is much more common than the borrowing of grammar. As we might expect, borrowing by one language from another can make the borrowing language more different from its **sibling languages** (those derived from a common ancestral language) than it would otherwise be. Partly as a result of the French influence, the English vocabulary looks quite different from the languages to which it is actually most similar in terms of phonology and grammar—German, Dutch, and the Scandinavian languages.

RELATIONSHIPS BETWEEN LANGUAGE AND CULTURE

Some attempts to explain the diversity of languages have focused on the possible interactions between language and other aspects of culture. On the one hand, if it can be shown that a culture may affect the structure and content of its language, then it would follow that linguistic diversity derives at least in part from cultural diversity. On the other hand, the direction of influence between culture and language might work in reverse: the linguistic structures might affect other aspects of the culture.

Cultural Influences on Language

One way a society's language may reflect its corresponding culture is in **lexical content**, or vocabulary. Which experiences, events, or objects are singled out and given words may be a result of cultural characteristics.

Basic Words for Colors, Plants, and Animals. Early in this century many linguists pointed to the lexical domain (vocabulary) of color words to

[43] Uriel Weinreich. *Languages in Contact.* The Hague: Mouton, 1968, p. 31.

illustrate the supposed truth that languages vary arbitrarily or without apparent reason. Not only did different languages have different numbers of basic or fundamental color words (from two to twelve or so—for example, the words *red, green,* and *blue* in English); it was also thought that there was no consistency in the way different languages classified or divided the colors of the spectrum. But findings from a comparative (or cross-linguistic) study published in 1969 contradicted these traditional presumptions about variation in the number and meaning of basic color words. Based upon their study of at first 20 and later over 100 different languages, Brent Berlin and Paul Kay found that languages did not encode color in completely arbitrary ways.[44]

Although different languages do have different numbers of basic color words, most speakers of any language are very likely to point to the same color chips as the best representatives of particular colors. (For example, people the world over mean more or less the same color when they are asked to select the *best* "red.") Moreover, there appears to be a more or less universal sequence by which basic color words are added to a language.[45] If a language has just two basic color words, they will always refer to "black" (or dark) hues and "white" (or light) hues. If a language has three basic color words, the third word will nearly always be "red." The next category to appear is either "yellow" or "grue" (green/blue); then different words for green and blue; and so on. To be sure, we usually do not see the process by which basic color words are added to a language. But we can infer the usual sequence because, for example, if a language has a word for "yellow" it will almost always have a word for "red," whereas having a word for "red" does not mean that the language will have a word for "yellow."

Why do different societies (languages) vary in number of basic color terms? Berlin and Kay suggest that the number of basic color terms in a language increases with cultural complexity,[46] and subsequent research has supported this idea.[47] More complex societies may require a larger number of basic color terms because they have more decorated objects that can be effectively distinguished by color, or a more complex technology of dyes and paints.[48] Cross-linguistic variation in number of basic color terms does not mean that some languages make more color distinctions than others. Every language could make a particular distinction by combining words (for example, "fresh leaf" for green); a language need not have a separate basic term for that color.

A relatively large number of basic color terms is related not only to

[44] Brent Berlin and Paul Kay. *Basic Color Terms: Their Universality and Evolution.* Berkeley: University of California Press, 1969.
[45] Ibid.
[46] Ibid., p. 104.
[47] Stanley R. Witkowski and Cecil H. Brown. "Lexical Universals." *Annual Review of Anthropology,* 7 (1978): 427–51.
[48] Berlin and Kay. *Basic Color Terms.* See also Witkowski and Brown, "Lexical Universals," p. 198.

greater cultural complexity; a biological factor may also be involved.[49] Peoples with darker (more pigmented) eyes seem to have more trouble distinguishing colors at the dark (blue-green) end of the spectrum. It might be expected, then, that peoples who live nearer the equator (who tend to have darker eyes, presumably for protection against damaging ultraviolet radiation) would tend to have fewer basic color terms. And they do.[50] Moreover, it seems that the cultural and biological factors are both required to account for cross-linguistic variation in the number of basic color terms. Societies tend to have six or more such terms (with separate terms for blue and green) only when they are relatively far from the equator and only when their cultures are more complex.[51]

Echoing Berlin and Kay's finding that basic color terms seem to be added in a more or less universal sequence, other researchers have found what seem to be developmental sequences in other lexical domains. Two such domains are general, or *life-form*, terms for plants and for animals. Life-form terms are higher-order classifications. All languages have lower-order terms for specific plants and animals. For example, English has words such as *oak* and *pine*, *sparrow* and *salmon*. English speakers make finer distinctions too—*pin oak* and *white pine*, *white-throated sparrow* and *red salmon*. But why in some languages do people have a larger number of general terms such as *tree*, *bird*, and *fish*? It seems that these general terms show a universal developmental sequence too. That is, terms seem to be added in a more or less consistent order. After "plant" comes a term for "tree"; then one for "grerb" (small, green, leafy, nonwoody plant); then "bush" (for plants between tree and grerb in size); then "grass"; then "vine."[52] The life-form terms for animals seem also to be added in sequence; after "animal" comes a term for "fish"; then "bird"; then "snake"; then "wug" (for small creatures other than fish, birds, and snakes—for example, worms and bugs); then "mammal."[53]

Thus, more complex societies tend to have a larger number of general or life-form terms for plants and animals, just as they tend to have a larger number of basic color terms. Why? And do all realms or domains of vocabulary increase in size as cultural complexity increases? If we look at the total vocabulary of a language (as can be counted in a dictionary), more complex societies do have larger vocabularies.[54] But we have to remember that complex societies have many kinds of specialists, and dictionaries will include the terms

[49] Marc H. Bornstein. "The Psychophysiological Component of Cultural Difference in Color Naming and Illusion Susceptibility." *Behavior Science Notes*, 8 (1973): 41–101.

[50] Melvin Ember. "Size of Color Lexicon: Interaction of Cultural and Biological Factors." *American Anthropologist*, 80 (1978): 364–67.

[51] Ibid.

[52] Cecil H. Brown. "Folk Botanical Life-Forms: Their Universality and Growth." *American Anthropologist*, 79 (1977): 317–42.

[53] Cecil H. Brown. "Folk Zoological Life-Forms: Their Universality and Growth." *American Anthropologist*, 81 (1979): 791–817.

[54] Stanley R. Witkowski and Harold W. Burris. "Societal Complexity and Lexical Growth." *Behavior Science Research*, 16 (1981): 143–59.

used by such specialists. If we look instead at the **core** (nonspecialist) **vocabulary** of languages, it seems that all languages have a core vocabulary of more or less the same size.[55] Indeed, although some domains increase in size with cultural complexity, some remain the same and still others decrease. An example of a smaller vocabulary domain in complex societies is that of specific names for plants. Urban Americans may know general terms for plants, but they know relatively few names for specific plants. The typical individual in an uncomplex or small-scale society can commonly name 400 to 800 different plant species; a typical member of a modern urban society may be able to name only 40 to 80.[56] It seems as if life-form terms become more numerous only when ordinary people have less and less to do with plants and animals.[57]

Focal Areas.   The evidence now available strongly supports the idea that the vocabulary of a language reflects the everyday distinctions that are important in the society. Those aspects of environment or culture that are of special importance will receive greater attention in language. Even within a single society speaking the same language there is often variation in vocabulary from one region or subculture to another that reflects different concerns. An adult farmer in the American Midwest may know three simple words for boat—*boat, ship, canoe*—and a few compound variations, such as *rowboat, sailboat, motorboat, steamship.* Yet a six-year-old who lives on Long Island Sound, where sailing is a major pastime, may be able to distinguish many kinds of sailboats, such as *catboat, ketch, yawl, sloop,* and *schooner,* as well as subclasses of each, such as *bluejay, sunfish,* and *weekender.*

There are many interesting examples of *focal areas* in different cultures being reflected in their respective vocabularies. Franz Boas showed that the geographical terms of the Kwakiutl, a coastal Indian tribe of the Pacific Northwest, reflect their awareness of the importance of hunting, fishing, and other food-gathering activities essential to their survival. Locations on land are given names such as *having-blueberries* and *having-hunter's lodge*; areas of coastal waters are described as *having-difficult-currents* and *having-spring-salmon.*[58] In comparison, river crossings were important to the early English. Consider their Ox-ford and Cam-bridge—names that in modern times have lost their original meanings.

Grammar.   Most of the examples we could accumulate would show that a culture influences the names of things visible in its environment. Evidence for cultural influence on the grammatical structure of a language is less extensive. Harry Hoijer draws attention to the verb categories in the

---

[55] Ibid.

[56] Cecil H. Brown and Stanley Witkowski. "Language Universals." Appendix B in David Levinson and Martin J. Malone, eds., *Toward Explaining Human Culture: A Critical Review of the Findings of Worldwide Cross-Cultural Research.* New Haven: HRAF Press, 1980, p. 379.

[57] Cecil H. Brown. "World View and Lexical Uniformities." *Reviews in Anthropology,* 11 (1984): 106.

[58] Franz Boas. *Geographical Names of the Kwakiutl Indians.* New York: Columbia University Press, 1934.

language of the Navaho, a traditionally nomadic people. These categories center mainly in the reporting of events, or *eventings*, as he calls them. Hoijer concludes that the emphasis on events reflects the Navaho's own nomadic experience over the centuries, an experience also reflected in their myths and folklore.[59]

A linguistic emphasis on events may or may not be generally characteristic of nomadic peoples. No one has as yet investigated the matter cross-culturally or comparatively. But there are indications that systematic comparative research might turn up a number of other grammatical features that are related to cultural characteristics. For example, many languages lack the possessive transitive verb we write as "have," as in "I have." Instead, the language may say something like "it is to me." A cross-cultural study has suggested that a language may develop the verb "have" after the speakers of that language have developed a system of private property, or personal ownership of resources.[60] As we shall see later in the chapter on economics, private property is generally characteristic of more complex societies, in contrast to simpler societies which generally have some kind of communal ownership (by kin groups or communities). How people talk about owning seems to reflect how they own: where private property is absent, the verb "have" is also absent.

Linguistic Influences on Culture:
The Sapir-Whorf Hypothesis

There is general agreement among **ethnolinguists**—those anthropologists interested in the relationships between language and culture—that culture influences language. But there is less agreement about the opposite possibility—that language influences (other aspects of) culture. Edward Sapir and his student Benjamin Lee Whorf suggested that language is a force in its own right—that it affects how individuals in a society perceive and conceive reality. This suggestion is known as the Sapir-Whorf hypothesis.[61] As intriguing as this idea is, the relevant evidence is mixed. Linguists today do not generally accept the view that language coerces thought, but some suspect that particular features of language may facilitate certain patterns of

---

[59] Harry Hoijer. "Cultural Implications of Some Navaho Linguistic Categories." In Hymes, ed., *Language in Culture and Society*, p. 146. Originally published in *Language*, 27 (1951): 111–20.

[60] Karen E. Webb. "An Evolutionary Aspect of Social Structure and a Verb 'Have.'" *American Anthropologist*, 79 (1977): 42–49. See also Floyd Webster Rudmin, "Dominance, Social Control, and Ownership: A History and a Cross-Cultural Study of Motivations for Private Property," *Behavior Science Research*, 22 (1988): 130–60.

[61] Edward Sapir. "Conceptual Categories in Primitive Languages." Paper presented at the autumn meeting of the National Academy of Sciences, New Haven, 1931. Published in *Science*, 74 (1931): 578. See also John B. Carroll, ed., *Language, Thought, and Reality: Selected Writings of Benjamin Lee Whorf*, New York: John Wiley, 1956, pp. 65–86.

thought.[62] The influences may be clearest in poetry and metaphors (words and phrases applied to other than their ordinary subjects, as in "all the world's a stage").[63]

One of the serious problems in testing the Sapir-Whorf hypothesis is that researchers need to figure out how to separate the effects of other aspects of culture from the effects of language. For example, many women have argued in recent years that English perpetuates the stereotype of male dominance. For example, English does not have a neutral third-person pronoun for humans (although a baby is sometimes referred to as *it*). Consider the following sentences: "If a student is ill and cannot come to the final exam, he should contact the professor immediately." "My professor gave a pretty good lecture." "Yeah? What's his name?" We could try to avoid the third-person pronoun and repeat "the student" in the second half of the first sentence, but that would probably be considered clumsy writing. Or we could say "he or she." (Why does the "he" first sound better?) In the third sentence we could say "What's the professor's name?" Or we could say "What's his or her name?" If we are really daring, we might even say "she" or "her" instead of "he" or "his." The point of these examples is that English doesn't make it easy to refer to females *and* males in the third-person singular when the person might be of *either* sex. Custom dictates that English speakers use "he" instead of "she" unless we are talking about certain roles thought to be clearly female roles, such as housewives, nurses, and secretaries. Does our language make us think that men are more important, or do we say "he" or "his" merely because men have traditionally been more important than women in our society?

One approach that may reveal the direction of influence between language and culture is to study how children in different cultures (speaking different languages) develop concepts about themselves. Do children learn to recognize themselves as boys or girls earlier when their language emphasizes gender? Alexander Guiora and his colleagues have studied children growing up in Hebrew-speaking homes (Israel), English-speaking homes (the United States), and Finnish-speaking homes (Finland). Hebrew has the most gender emphasis of the three languages; nouns are either masculine or feminine and even second-person and plural pronouns are differentiated by gender. English emphasizes gender less, differentiating by gender only in the third-person singular, as just noted. Finnish emphasizes gender the least; although some words, such as "man" and "woman," convey gender, differentiation by gender is otherwise lacking in the language. Consistent with the idea that language may influence thought, Hebrew-speaking children acquire the concept of gender identity the earliest on the average, Finnish-speaking children the latest.[64]

[62] J. Peter Denny. "The 'Extendedness' Variable in Classifier Semantics: Universal Features and Cultural Variation." In Madeleine Mathiot, ed., *Ethnolinguistics: Boas, Sapir and Whorf Revisited*. The Hague: Mouton, 1979, p. 97.

[63] Paul Friedrich. *The Language Parallax*. Austin: University of Texas Press, 1986.

[64] Alexander Z. Guiora, Benjamin Beit-Hallahmi, Risto Fried, and Cecelia Yoder. "Language Environment and Gender Identity Attainment." *Language Learning*, 32 (1982): 289–304.

THE ETHNOGRAPHY OF SPEAKING

Traditionally, linguists concentrated on trying to understand the structure of a language, the usually unconscious rules that predict how the people of a given society typically speak. Recently, however, many linguists have begun to study how people in a society vary in how they speak. This type of linguistic study, sociolinguistics, is concerned with the *ethnography of speaking*—that is, with cultural and subcultural patterns of speech variation in different social contexts.[65]

The sociolinguist may ask, for example, what kinds of things one talks about in casual conversation with a stranger. A foreigner may know English vocabulary and grammar well but may not know that one typically chats with a stranger about the weather, or where one comes from, and not about what one ate that day or how much money one earns. A foreigner may be familiar with much of the culture of an American city, but if that person divulges the real state of his or her health and feelings to the first person who says "How are you?" he or she has much to learn about American small talk.

Social Status and Speech

That a foreign speaker of a language may know little about the "small talk" of that language is but one example of the sociolinguistic principle that what we say and how we say it are not wholly predictable by the rules of our language. Who we are socially may have a big effect on what we say and how we say it. For example, English-speaking Athabaskan Indians in Canada seem to think that conversation with a white Canadian should be avoided except when they think they know the point of view of the white (who is generally more powerful politically). On the other hand, white English speakers think they should use conversation to get to know others (as at a cocktail party). So they pause a certain amount of time to let the other person talk, but they pause a much shorter time than Indian English speakers would. If the other person doesn't respond, the white English speaker, feeling awkward, will say something else. By the time an Indian is ready to talk, the white is already talking and the Indian considers it impolite to interrupt. It is easy to see how whites and Indians can misunderstand each other. Indians think white English speakers talk too much and don't let them express their views, and whites think Indians do not want to talk or get to know them.[66]

The way in which people address each other is also of interest to sociolinguists. In English, forms of address are relatively simple. One is called either by a first name or by a title (such as *Mister, Doctor,* or *Professor*) followed by a last name. A study by Roger Brown and Marguerite Ford indicates that terms of address vary with the nature of the relationship between the speak-

[65] Dell Hymes. *Foundations in Sociolinguistics: An Ethnographic Approach.* Philadelphia: University of Pennsylvania Press, 1974, pp. 83–117.

[66] Ron Scollon and Suzanne B. K. Scollon. *Narrative, Literacy and Face in Interethnic Communication.* Norwood, N.J.: ABLEX Publishing Corporation, 1981, pp. 11–36.

ers.[67] The reciprocal use of first names generally signifies an informal or intimate relationship between two persons. A title and last name used reciprocally usually indicates a more formal or businesslike relationship between individuals who are roughly equal in status. Nonreciprocal use of first names and titles in English is reserved for speakers who recognize a marked difference in status between themselves. This difference can be a function of age (as when a child refers to her mother's friend as Mrs. Miller and is in turn addressed as Sally), or it can be drawn along occupational lines (as when a person refers to his boss by title and last name and is in turn addressed as John). In some cases, generally between boys and between men, the use of the last name alone represents a middle ground between the intimate and the formal usages.

Sex Differences in Speech

In many societies the speech of men differs from the speech of women. The variation can be slight, as in our own society and in England, or more extreme, as with the Carib Indians (in the Lesser Antilles of the West Indies), among whom women and men use different words for the same concepts. In some societies it appears that the female variety of speech is older than the male variety.[68] For example, in the American Indian language of Koasati (which used to be spoken in Louisiana), males and females used different endings in certain verbs. The differences seemed to be disappearing in the 1930s, when research on Koasati was done: young girls used the male forms and only older women used the female forms. Koasati men said that the women's speech was a better form of speech, and an interesting parallel comes from comparisons of male and female speech in Britain and the United States. Although the sex differences are hardly noticeable to most people, researchers have found that, controlling for social class, age, and ethnic differences, women usually use pronunciation and grammatical forms that are closer to standard English.[69]

The field of sociolinguistics is a relatively new specialty in linguistics. At present, sociolinguists seem to be interested primarily in describing variation in the use of language. Eventually, however, sociolinguistic research may enable us to understand why such variation exists. Why, for example, do some societies use many different status terms in address? Why do some societies use modes of speaking that vary with the sex of the speaker? An understanding of why language use varies in different contexts might suggest why structural aspects of language change over time. For as social contexts in a society change, the structure of the language might also tend to change.

---

[67] Roger Brown and Marguerite Ford. "Address in American English." *Journal of Abnormal and Social Psychology*, 62 (1961) 375–85.

[68] Trudgill. *Sociolinguistics*, pp. 79–84. See also Mary R. Haas, "Men's and Women's Speech in Koasati," *Language*, 20 (1944) 142–49.

[69] Trudgill. *Sociolinguistics*, pp. 84–85.

SUMMARY

1. The essential function language plays in all societies is that of communication. Although human communication is not limited to spoken language, such language is of overriding importance because it is the primary vehicle through which culture is shared and transmitted.

2. Systems of communication are not unique to humans. Other animal species communicate in a variety of ways—by sound, odor, body movement, and so forth. The ability of chimpanzees and gorillas to learn and use sign language suggests that symbolic communication is not unique to humans. Still, human language is distinctive as a communication system in that its spoken and symbolic nature permits an infinite number of combinations and recombinations of meaning.

3. Structural (or descriptive) linguists try to discover the rules of phonology (the patterning of sounds), morphology (the patterning of sound sequences and words), and syntax (the patterning of phrases and sentences) that predict how most speakers of a language talk. From the wide variety of possible human sounds, each language has selected some sounds, or phones, and ignored others. How sounds are grouped into sets called phonemes differs from language to language. The smallest unit of meaning is a morph; one or more morphs with the same meaning make up a morpheme. Children have an intuitive grasp of phonology, morphology, and syntax long before they learn "rules of grammar" in school.

4. By comparative analysis of cognates and grammar, historical linguists test the notion that certain languages derive from a common ancestral language, or protolanguage. The goals are to reconstruct the features of the protolanguage, to hypothesize how the offspring languages separated from the protolanguage or from each other, and to establish the approximate dates of such separations.

5. When two groups of people speaking the same language lose communication with each other because they become separated either physically or socially, they begin to accumulate small changes in phonology, morphology, and syntax. If the separation continues, the two former dialects of the same language will eventually become separate languages—that is, they will become mutually unintelligible.

6. Whereas isolation brings about divergence between speech communities, contact results in greater resemblance. This is particularly evident when contact between mutually unintelligible languages introduces borrowed words, most of which name some new item borrowed from the other culture.

7. Some attempts to explain the diversity of languages have focused on the possible interaction between language and other aspects of culture. On the one hand, if it can be shown that a culture may affect the structure and content of its language, then it would follow that linguistic diversity derives at least in part from cultural diversity. On the other hand, the direction of influence between culture and language might work in reverse: the linguistic structures might affect other aspects of the culture.

8. Recently, some linguists have begun to study variations in how people actually use language when speaking. This type of linguistic study, called sociolinguistics, is concerned with the ethnography of speaking—that is, with cultural and subcultural patterns of speaking in different social contexts.

10

Food-Getting

For most people in our society, getting food consists of a trip to the supermarket. Within the space of an hour, we can gather enough food from the shelves to last us a week. Seasons don't daunt us. Week after week, we know food will be there. But we do not think of what would happen if the food were not delivered to the supermarket. We wouldn't be able to eat—and without eating for a while, we would die. Despite the old adage "Man [or woman] does not live by bread alone," without bread or the equivalent we could not live at all. Food-getting activities, then, take precedence over other activities important to survival. Reproduction, social control (the maintenance of peace and order within a group), defense against external threat, and the transmission of knowledge and skills to future generations—none could take place without energy derived from food. Food-getting activities are also important because, as we will see in this and other chapters, the way a society gets its food may have profound effects on other aspects of its culture.

In contrast with our society, most societies have not had food-getting specialists. Rather, almost all able-bodied adults were engaged in getting food. During the 2 to 5 million years that humans have been on earth, 99 percent of the time they have obtained food by gathering wild plants, hunting wild animals, and fishing. Agriculture is a relatively recent phenomenon, dating back only about 10,000 years. And industrial or mechanized agriculture is less than a century old!

In this chapter we look first at examples of the different ways in which societies get food. Then we discuss some of the general features associated with the different patterns of food-getting. And finally we discuss the possible determinants of variation in food-getting.

FOOD COLLECTION

Food collection may be generally defined as all forms of **subsistence technology** in which food-getting is dependent on naturally occurring resources—that is, wild plants and animals. Although it was the predominant method of getting food for most of human history, today the few remaining food collectors (conventionally referred to as hunter-gatherers) generally live in what have been called the *marginal* areas of the earth—deserts, the Arctic, and dense tropical forests, habitats that do not allow easy exploitation by modern agricultural technologies.

Anthropologists are very interested in studying the relatively few food-collecting societies still available for observation. These groups may help us understand some aspects of human life in the past, when all people were hunter-gatherers. But we must be cautious in drawing inferences about the past from our observations of contemporary food-collectors for three reasons. First, earlier hunter-gatherers lived in almost all types of environments, including some very bountiful ones. Therefore, what we observe among recent and contemporary hunter-gatherers, who generally live in marginal environments, may not be comparable to what would have been observable in more favorable environments in the past.[1] Second, contemporary hunter-gatherers are not relics of the past: like all contemporary societies, they have evolved and are still evolving. This means that the adaptations we observe in contemporary groups may be different from the adaptations made by hunter-gatherers years ago. (For example, few if any contemporary hunters use stone arrowheads.) Third, recent and contemporary hunter-gatherers have been interacting with kinds of societies that did not exist until after 10,000 years ago—agriculturalists, pastoralists, and intrusive powerful state societies.[2] Let us now examine an example of a recent food-collecting society.

Australian Aborigines.   The Ngatatjara aborigines live in the Gibson Desert of western Australia.[3] When they were studied by Richard Gould in the 1960s, they still lived by gathering wild plants and hunting wild animals.

[1] Carol R. Ember. "Myths about Hunter-Gatherers." *Ethnology*, 17 (1978): 439–48.
[2] Carmel Schrire, ed. *Past and Present in Hunter Gatherer Studies.* Orlando, Fla.: Academic Press, 1984; Fred R. Myers. "Critical Trends in the Study of Hunter-Gatherers." *Annual Review of Anthropology*, 17 (1988): 261–82.
[3] The discussion of the Australian aborigines is based upon Richard A. Gould, *Yiwara: Foragers of the Australian Desert*, New York: Scribner's, 1969.

Their desert environment averages less than eight inches of rain per year, and the temperature in summer may rise to 118° F. The few permanent water holes are separated by hundreds of square miles of sand, scrub, and rock. Even before Europeans arrived in Australia, the area was sparsely populated—fewer than one person per thirty-five to forty square miles. Now there are even fewer people.

On a typical day, the camp begins to stir just before sunrise, while it is still dark. Children are sent to fetch water, and the people breakfast on water and food left over from the night before. In the cool of the early morning, the adults talk and make plans for the day. The talking goes on for a while. Where should they go for food—to places they have been to recently, or to new places? Sometimes there are other considerations. For example, one woman may want to search for plants whose bark she needs to make new sandals. When the women decide which plants are most likely to be found, they take up their digging sticks and set out with large wooden bowls of drinking water on their heads. Their children ride on their hips or walk alongside. Meanwhile, the men may have decided to hunt emus, six-foot-tall ostrichlike birds that do not fly. The men go to a creek bed where they will wait to ambush any game that may come along. They lie patiently behind a screen of brush they have set up, hoping for a chance to throw a spear at an emu or even a kangaroo. They can throw only once, because if they miss, the game will run away.

By noon the men and women are usually back at camp, the women with their wooden bowls each filled with up to fifteen pounds of fruit or other plant foods, the men more often than not with only some small game such as lizards and rabbits. Since the men's food-getting is less certain of success than the women's, most of the aborigine's diet is plant food. The daily cooked meal is eaten toward evening, after an afternoon spent resting, gossiping, and making or repairing tools.

The aborigines are a nomadic people—that is, they move their campsites frequently. The campsites may be isolated and inhabited by only a small number of people, or they may be clusters of groups including as many as eighty persons. The aborigines never establish a campsite right next to a place with water. If they should be too close, their presence would frighten game away and might cause tension with neighboring bands, who also wait for game to come to the scarce watering spots.

General Features of Food Collectors. Despite the differences in terrain and climate under which they live and the different food-collecting technologies they use. Australian aborigines and most other recent hunter-gatherers seem to have certain cultural patterns in common. Most live in small communities in sparsely populated territories and follow a nomadic life style, forming no permanent settlements. As a rule, they do not recognize individual land rights. Their communities do not generally have different classes of people and tend to have no specialized or full-time political officials. Division of labor is based principally on age and sex.[4] Men exclusively hunt large marine and land animals and usually do the fishing; women usually gather wild plant foods.[5]

Is there a typical pattern of food-getting among hunter-gatherers? Recently some anthropologists have suggested that hunter-gatherers typically get their food more from gathering than from hunting, and that women contribute more than men to subsistence (because women generally do the gathering).[6] Although gathering is the most important food-getting activity for some food collectors (for example, the Ngatatjara aborigines and the !Kung of southern Africa), this is not true for most recent food-collecting societies. A survey of 180 such societies indicates that there is a lot of variation in which food-getting activity is most important to a society: gathering is the most important activity for 30 percent of the surveyed societies, hunting for 25 percent, and fishing for 38 percent. (Perhaps, then, we should call most recent food collectors *fisher-gatherer-hunters!*) In any case, because men generally do the fishing as well as the hunting, it is the men who usually contribute more to subsistence than the women among recent food collectors.[7]

Since food collectors move their camps often and walk great distances, it may seem that the food-collecting way of life is difficult. Although we do not have enough quantitative studies to tell us what is typical of most food collectors, studies of two Australian aborigine groups[8] and of one !Kung group[9] indicate that those food collectors do not spend many hours getting food. For example, !Kung adults spend an average of about 17 hours per week collecting food. Even when you add the time spent making tools (about 6 hours a week) and doing housework (about 19 hours a week), the !Kung seem to have more leisure time than agriculturalists, as we will discuss later.

FOOD PRODUCTION

Beginning about 10,000 years ago, certain peoples in widely separated geographic locations made the revolutionary change to **food production**. That is, they began to cultivate and then domesticate plants and animals. With domes-

[4] Data from Robert B. Textor, comp., *A Cross-Cultural Summary*, New Haven: HRAF Press, 1967; and Elman R. Service, *The Hunters*, 2nd ed., Englewood Cliffs, N. J.: Prentice-Hall, 1979.

[5] George P. Murdock and Caterina Provost. "Factors in the Division of Labor by Sex: A Cross-Cultural Analysis." *Ethnology*, 12 (1973): 207.

[6] Richard B. Lee. "What Hunters Do for a Living, or, How to Make Out on Scarce Resources." In Lee and DeVore, eds., *Man the Hunter*. Chicago: Aldine, 1968, pp. 30–48; and Irven DeVore and Melvin J. Konner. "Infancy in Hunter-Gatherer Life: An Ethnological Perspective." In N. F. White, ed., *Ethology and Psychiatry*. Toronto: Ontario Mental Health Foundation and University of Toronto Press, 1974, pp. 113–41.

[7] Carol R. Ember. "Myths about Hunter-Gatherers."

[8] Frederick D. McCarthy and Margaret McArthur. "The Food Quest and the Time Factor in Aboriginal Economic Life." In C. P. Mountford, ed., *Records of the Australian-American Scientific Expedition to Amhem Land, Volume 2: Anthropology and Nutrition*. Melbourne: Melbourne University Press, 1960.

[9] Richard Borshay Lee. *The !Kung San: Men, Women, and Work in a Foraging Society*. Cambridge: Cambridge University Press, 1979, pp. 256–58, 278–80.

tication of these food sources, people acquired control over certain natural processes, such as animal breeding and seeding. Today, most peoples in the world depend for their food on some combination of domesticated plants and animals.

Anthropologists generally distinguish three major types of food-production systems—horticulture, intensive agriculture, and pastoralism.

Horticulture

The word **horticulture** may conjure up visions of people with "green thumbs" growing orchids and other flowers in greenhouses. But to anthropologists, the word means the growing of crops of *all* kinds with relatively simple tools and methods, in the absence of permanently cultivated fields. The tools are usually hand tools, such as the digging stick or hoe, not plows or other equipment pulled by animals or tractors. And the methods used do not include fertilization, irrigation, or other ways to restore soil fertility after a growing season.

There are two kinds of horticulture. The more common one involves a dependence on **extensive** or **shifting cultivation**. The land is worked for short periods and then left idle for some years. During the years when the land is not cultivated, wild plants and brush grow up; when the fields are later cleared by **slash-and-burn** (cutting and burning of trees and underbrush), nutrients are returned to the soil. The other kind of horticulture involves a dependence on long-growing tree crops. The two kinds of horticulture may be practiced in the same society, but in neither case is there permanent cultivation of field crops.

Most horticultural societies do not rely on crops alone for food. Many also hunt or fish; a few are nomadic for part of the year. For example, the northern Kayapo of the Brazilian Amazon leave their villages for as long as three months at a time to trek through the forest in search of game. The entire village participates in a trek, carrying large quantities of garden produce and moving their camp every day.[10] Other horticulturists raise domestic animals, but these are usually not large animals such as cattle and camels.[11] More often than not, the animals raised by horticulturists are smaller ones such as pigs, chickens, goats, and sheep. Let us look now at one horticultural society, the Samoans of the South Pacific.

The Samoans. The Samoans numbered about 56,000 persons in 1839, soon after European missionaries arrived.[12] The islands of Samoa, which are about 2300 miles south of the Hawaiian Islands, are volcanic in origin, with central ridges and peaks as high as 4000 feet. Though the land is generally steep, the islands have a lush plant cover watered by up to 200

---

[10] Dennis Werner. "Trekking in the Amazon Forest." *Natural History*, November 1978, pp. 42–54.
[11] Data from Textor, comp., *A Cross-Cultural Summary.*
[12] This section is based mostly on Melvin Ember's fieldwork on the islands of American Samoa in 1955–56.

inches of rain a year (about five times the amount of rain that falls on New York in a year). All that rain does not interfere much with outdoor activity, since the torrential showers do not last long and the water disappears quickly into the porous volcanic soil. The temperature is relatively constant, rarely falling below 70° or rising above 88°F. Strong cooling trade winds blow most of the year, generally from the east or southeast, and on the coasts one constantly hears the low rumble of huge Pacific swells breaking upon the coral reefs.

Samoan horticulture involves mostly three tree crops that require little work except in harvesting. Once planted, and requiring hardly more than a few years of waiting, the breadfruit tree continues to produce about two crops a year for up to half a century. Coconut trees may continue to produce for a hundred years. And banana trees make new stalks of fruit, each weighing more than fifty pounds, for many years; merely cutting down one stalk induces the plant to grow another. Young men do most of the harvesting of tree crops. Women do the occasional weeding.

The Samoans also practice shifting cultivation; men periodically clear small patches of land for a staple root crop called *taro*. The taro patches can produce a few crops before they must be allowed to revert to bush so that soil fertility can be restored. But even taro cultivation does not require much work; planting requires nothing more than slightly burying the top sliced off a root just harvested. (Young men do most of the planting and harvesting.) The taro patches are weeded infrequently, mostly by women. This kind of casual farming behavior prompted Captain Bligh, of *Mutiny on the Bounty* fame, to describe the Tahitians as lazy.[13] Captain Bligh's attitude was ethnocentric. South Pacific islanders such as the Samoans and Tahitians cannot weed as often as European farmers without risking the erosion of their soil, because in contrast with European farmlands, which are generally flat or only slightly sloping, the land of Samoa and Tahiti is mostly steep. The Samoan and Tahitian practice of not weeding crops and growing them in glorious and messy confusion means that the deep and shallow root structures of the various plants growing together can prevent the loose volcanic soil from being washed away by the torrential showers.

The Samoans keep chickens and pigs, but they are eaten only occasionally. The major source of animal protein in the Samoan diet is fish, which are caught inside and outside the reef. Younger men may swim in the deep sea outside the reef and use a sling to spear fish; older men will more likely try to catch fish by standing on the reef and throwing a four-pointed spear at fish swimming inside the reef. For many years, people in the villages of Samoa have sold copra (the sun-dried meat of the ripe coconut) to the world market

---

[13] Douglas L. Oliver. *Ancient Tahitian Society, Volume 1: Ethnography*. Honolulu: University of Hawaii Press, 1974, pp. 252–53.

for coconut oil. Men generally cut the copra from the shells after the ripe coconuts fall by themselves to the ground. With the cash earned from the sale of copra, people buy imported things such as machetes and kerosene. But people in most villages still produce most of the goods they eat.

General Features of Horticulturalists.   In most horticultural societies, simple farming techniques have tended to yield more food from a given area than is generally available to food collectors. Consequently, horticulture is generally able to support larger, more densely populated communities. The way of life of horticulturalists is generally more sedentary than that of food collectors, although communities may move after a number of years to farm a new series of plots. (Some horticulturalists have permanent villages because they depend mostly on food from trees that keep producing for a long time.) In contrast with most recent hunter-gatherer groups, horticultural societies exhibit the beginnings of social differentiation. For example, some individuals may be part-time craftworkers or part-time political officials, and certain members of a kin group may have more status than other individuals in the society.

Intensive Agriculture

People engaged in **intensive agriculture** employ a variety of techniques that enable them to cultivate fields permanently. Essential nutrients may be put back through the use of fertilizers, which may be organic material, most commonly dung from humans or other animals, or inorganic (chemical) fertilizers. But there are other ways to restore nutrients. The Luo of western Kenya plant beans around corn plants. Bacteria growing around the roots of the bean plant replace lost nitrogen, and the corn plant conveniently provides a pole for the bean plant to wind around as it grows. Some intensive agriculturalists use irrigation from streams and rivers to ensure an adequate supply of water-borne nutrients.

In general, the technology of intensive agriculturalists is more complex than that of horticulturalists. Plows rather than digging sticks are generally employed. But there is enormous variation in the degree to which intensive agriculturalists rely on mechanization rather than hand labor: in some societies the most complex machine is an animal-drawn plow; in the corn and wheat belts of the United States, huge tractors till, seed, and fertilize twelve rows at a time.[14]

Let's look now at the intensive agriculturalists of the Mekong Delta in Vietnam.

Rural Vietnam: The Mekong Delta.   The village of Khanh Hau, situated along the flat Mekong Delta, comprised about 600 families in the late

[14] Seth S. King. "Some Farm Machinery Seems Less Than Human." *New York Times*, April 8, 1979, p. E9.

1950s.[15] (After this period, village life was disrupted by the Vietnam War.) The delta area has a tropical climate, with a rainy season that lasts from May to November. As a whole, the area has been made habitable only by extensive drainage.

Wet rice cultivation is the principal agricultural activity of Khanh Hau. It is part of a complex, specialized arrangement that involves three interacting components: (1) a complex system of irrigation and water control; (2) a variety of specialized equipment, including plows, water wheels, threshing sledges, and winnowing machines; and (3) a clearly defined set of socio-economic roles—from those of landlord, tenant, and laborer to those of rice miller and rice merchant.

In the dry season, the farmer decides what sort of rice crop to plant—whether of long (120 days) or short (90 days) maturation. The choice depends on the capital at his disposal, the current cost of fertilizer, and the anticipated demand for rice. The seedbeds are prepared as soon as the rains have softened the ground in May. The soil is turned over and broken up as many as six separate times, with two-day intervals for "airing" between each operation. While the soil is being plowed and harrowed in this way, the rice seeds are soaked in water for two days to stimulate sprouting. Before the seedlings are planted, the paddy is plowed once more and harrowed twice in two directions at right angles.

Planting is a delicate, specialized operation that must usually be done quickly and is performed generally by hired male labor. But efficient planting is not enough to guarantee a good crop. Proper fertilizer and irrigation are equally important. In the irrigating, steps must be taken to ensure that the water level remains at exactly the proper depth over the entire paddy. Water is distributed by means of scoops, wheels, and mechanical pumps. Successive crops of rice ripen from late September to May; all members of the family may be called upon to help with the harvest. After each crop is harvested, it is threshed, winnowed, and dried. Normally, the rice is sorted into three portions: one is set aside for use by the household in the following year; one is for payment of hired labor and other services (such as loans from agricultural banks); and one is for cash sale on the market. Aside from the harvesting, women generally do little work in the fields; they spend most of their time on household chores. However, in families with little land, young daughters help in the fields and older daughters may hire themselves out to other farmers.

The villagers also cultivate vegetables, raise pigs, chickens, and the like, and frequently engage in fishing. The village economy usually supports three or four implement makers and a much larger number of carpenters.

General Features of Intensive-Agricultural Societies.   In contrast with horticultural groups, societies with intensive agriculture are more likely

---

[15] This discussion is based on Gerald Cannon Hickey, *Village in Vietnam*, New Haven: Yale University Press, 1964, pp. 135–65.

to have towns and cities, a high degree of craft specialization, more complex political organization, and large differences in wealth and power.

A number of studies suggest that intensive agriculturalists typically work longer hours than simpler agriculturalists.[16] For example, men engaged in intensive agriculture average nine hours of work a day, seven days a week, while women average almost eleven hours of work per day. Most of the work for women in intensive-agriculture societies involves food processing and work in and around the home, but they also spend a lot of time working in the fields. We discuss some of the implications of the work patterns for women in the chapter on sex and culture.

Intensive-agricultural societies are more likely than horticultural societies to face food shortages, even though intensive agriculture is generally more productive than horticulture.[17] Why, if more food can be produced per acre, is there more risk of shortage among intensive agriculturalists? Social scientists do not know for sure. One possibility is that intensive agriculturalists may rely more often on single crops, and such crops may fail because of fluctuations in weather, plant diseases, or insect pests. Intensive agriculturalists may also be more likely to face food shortages because they are often producing crops for a market. If the market demand drops, they may not have enough cash to buy all the other food they need.

The Commercialization of Agriculture.   Some intensive agriculturalists produce very little for sale; most of what they produce is for their own use. But there is a worldwide trend for intensive agriculturalists to produce more and more for a market. (This is called **commercialization**, which may occur in any area of life and which involves increasing dependence on buying and selling, with money usually as the medium of exchange.) The increasing commercialization of agriculture is associated with several other trends. One is that farm work is becoming more and more mechanized as hand labor becomes scarce (because of migration to industrial and service jobs in towns and cities) or too expensive. A second trend is the emergence and spread of *agribusiness,* large corporation-owned farms that may be operated by hired (as opposed to "family") labor. A third trend associated with the commercialization of agriculture (including animal raising) is a reduction in the proportion of the population engaged in food production. In the United States, for example, less than 2 percent of the total population is still on the farm.[18]

Pastoralism

Most agriculturalists raise some animals, but a small number of societies depend directly or indirectly on domesticated herds of animals for their living. We call such a system **pastoralism**. Although we might assume that

---

[16] Carol R. Ember. "The Relative Decline in Women's Contribution to Agriculture with Intensification." *American Anthropologist,* 85 (1983):289.

[17] Data from Textor, comp., *A Cross-Cultural Summary.*

[18] Dwindling Numbers on the Farm." *Nation's Business,* April 1988, p. 16.

pastoralists breed animals largely to eat their meat, this is generally not the case. Pastoralists more often get their animal protein from live animals in the form of milk; some pastoralists also regularly take blood, which is also rich in protein, from their animals to mix with other foods. The herds also indirectly provide food because pastoralists typically trade animal products for plant foods and other necessities. In fact, a large proportion of their food may actually come from trade with agricultural groups.[19] For example, some pastoral groups in the Middle East derive a good deal of their livelihood from the sale of what we call oriental rugs, which are made on handlooms from the wool of their sheep.

General Features of Pastoralism. In recent times, pastoralism has been practiced mainly in grassland and other semiarid habitats that are not especially suitable for cultivation without some significant technological input such as irrigation. Pastoralists are generally nomadic, moving with their herds to new pastures as necessary. In some areas, however, pastoralists spend much of the year in one place, usually because that place provides grazing and water for much of the year. Pastoral communities are generally small, usually consisting of a group of related families.[20] Individuals or families may own their own animals, but decisions about when and where to move the herds are generally community decisions. As we have noted, there is a great deal of interdependence between pastoral and agricultural groups. That is, trade is usually necessary for pastoral groups to survive.

Table 10-1 summarizes the general features of the various types of food-getting.

CAUSES OF DIVERSITY IN FOOD-GETTING

Of great interest to anthropologists is why different societies have different methods of getting food. Archaeological evidence suggests that major changes in food-getting—such as the domestication of plants and animals—have been independently invented in at least several areas of the world. Yet, despite these comparable inventions and their subsequent spread by migration, there is still wide diversity in the means by which people obtain food. How is this to be explained?

Cross-cultural evidence indicates that neither food collection or production is significantly associated with any particular type of habitat.[21] Certain general patterns are suggested, however, in comparisons between specific means of food production and specific types of habitat. Approximately 80 percent of all societies that practice horticulture or simple agriculture are in the tropics, whereas 75 percent of all societies that practice intensive agricul-

[19] Susan H. Lees and Daniel G. Bates. "The Origins of Specialized Nomadic Pastoralism: A Systemic Model." *American Antiquity*, 39 (1974): 187–93.
[20] Data from Textor, comp., *A Cross-Cultural Summary.*
[21] Data from Textor, comp., *A Cross-Cultural Summary.*

TABLE 10-1   Variation in food-getting: A summary of general features of recent societies

| | FOOD COLLECTORS | FOOD PRODUCERS | | |
	Hunter-Gatherers	Horticulturalists	Pastoralists	Intensive Agriculturalists
Population density	Lowest	Low-moderate	Low	Highest
Maximum community size	Small	Small-moderate	Small	Large (towns and cities)
Nomadism/ permanence of settle- ments	Generally nomadic or seminomadic	More sedentary: communities may move after several years	Generally nomadic or seminomadic	Permanent communities
Food shortages	Infrequent	Infrequent	Frequent	Frequent
Trade	Minimal	Minimal	Very important	Very important
Full-time craft specialists	None	None or few	Some	Many (high degree of craft special- ization)
Individual differences in wealth	Generally none	Generally minimal	Moderate	Considerable
Political leadership	Informal	Some part-time political officials	Part- and full- time political officials	Many full-time political officials

ture are *not* in tropical-forest environments.[22] The reason for the predominance of simple agriculture in tropical regions may be that the soil-depleting effects of high rainfall in these areas or the difficulties of weeding where vegetation grows so quickly—or both together—hinder the development of intensive agriculture.[23] There is also a problem of pest control in the tropics, as we have mentioned. Pastoralism is not usually found in tropical-forest regions.[24] This is not surprising, since a dense jungle is hardly a likely spot to herd animals.

From the information available, anthropologists have generally concluded that the physical environment by itself has a limiting, rather than a strictly determining, effect on the major types of subsistence. In other words, some environments may not permit certain types of food-getting, while allowing a number of others. The type of food-getting that can be practiced in a particular environment depends on the inhabitants' level of technological development, as is dramatically illustrated by the history of the Imperial Valley in California. The complex systems of irrigation now used in that dry-land area have made it one of the most productive regions in the world. Yet about 400

[22] Ibid.
[23] For an argument supporting the "weeding" explanation, see Robert L. Carneiro, "Slash-and-Burn Cultivation among the Kuikuru and Its Implications for Settlement Patterns," in Yehudi Cohen, ed., *Man in Adaptation: The Cultural Present*, Chicago: Aldine, 1968; and Daniel H. Janzen, "Tropical Agroecosystems," *Science*, December 21, 1972, pp. 1212–18.
[24] Data from Textor, comp., *A Cross-Cultural Summary*.

years ago, this same valley could support only hunting and gathering groups who subsisted on wild plants and animals.

THE SPREAD OF FOOD PRODUCTION

In the chapter on the emergence of food production and the rise of states, we examined a number of theories that suggested why people started to produce food even though doing so may have involved more work and more risk of famine. All the theories currently considered suggest that people made the changeover because they were *pushed* into it. Whatever the reasons for the switch to food production, we still need to explain why food production has generally supplanted food collection as the primary mode of subsistence. We cannot assume that collectors would automatically adopt production as a superior way of life once they understood the process of domestication. After all, as we have noted, domestication may entail more work and provide less security than the food-collecting way of life.

The spread of agriculture may be linked to the need for territorial expansion. As a sedentary, food-producing population grew, it may have been forced to expand into new territory. Some of this territory may have been vacant, but much of it was probably already occupied by food collectors. Although food production is not necessarily easier than collection, it is generally more productive per unit of land. Greater productivity means that more people can be supported in a given territory. In the competition for land between the faster-expanding food producers and the food collectors, the food producers may have had a significant advantage: they had more people in a given area. Thus, the hunter-gatherer groups may have been more likely to lose out in the competition for land. Some groups may have adopted cultivation, abandoning the hunter-gatherer way of life in order to survive. Other groups, continuing as food collectors, may have been forced to retreat into areas not desired by the cultivators. Today, as we have seen, the small number of remaining food collectors inhabit areas not particularly suitable for cultivation—dry lands, dense tropical forests, and polar regions.

Just as prior population growth might account for the origins of domestication, so at later periods further population growth and ensuing pressure on resources might at least partially explain the transformation of horticultural systems into intensive-agricultural systems. Ester Boserup has suggested that intensification of agriculture, with a consequent increase in yield per acre, is not likely to develop naturally out of horticulture because intensification requires much more work.[25] She argues that people will be willing to intensify their labor only if they have to. Where emigration is not feasible, the prime mover behind intensification may generally be prior population growth. The need to pay taxes or tribute to a political authority may also stimulate intensification.

---

[25] Ester Boserup. *The Conditions of Agricultural Growth: The Economics of Agrarian Change under Population Pressure.* Chicago: Aldine, 1965.

Intensive agriculture has not yet spread to every part of the world. Horticulture continues to be practiced in certain tropical regions, and there are still some pastoralists and food collectors. As we have noted, some environments may make it difficult to adopt certain subsistence practices. For example, intensive agriculture cannot supplant horticulture in some tropical environments without tremendous investments in chemical fertilizers and pesticides, not to mention the additional labor required.[26] And enormous amounts of water may be required to make agriculturalists out of hunter-gatherers and pastoralists who now exploit semiarid environments. Hence, the different kinds of food-getting practices we observe today throughout the world are likely to be with us for some time to come.

SUMMARY

1. Food collection—hunting, gathering, and fishing—depends upon wild plants and animals and is the oldest human food-getting technology. Today, however, only a small number of societies practice it, and they tend to inhabit marginal environments.

2. Food collectors can be found in a number of different physical habitats, but recent food collectors tend to live in marginal environments. Food collectors are generally nomadic and population density is low. The small bands generally consist of related families, with the division of labor usually along age and sex lines only. Personal possessions are limited, individual land rights are usually not recognized, and different classes of people are generally unknown.

3. Beginning about 10,000 years ago, certain peoples in widely separated geographical locations began to make the revolutionary changeover to food production—the cultivation and raising of plants and animals. Over the centuries, food production began to supplant food collection as the predominant mode of subsistence.

4. Horticulturalists farm with relatively simple tools and methods and do not cultivate fields permanently. Their food supply is generally sufficient to support larger, more densely populated communities than can be fed by food collection. Their way of life is generally sedentary, although communities may move after a number of years to farm a new series of plots.

5. Intensive agriculture is characterized by techniques such as fertilization and irrigation that allow fields to be cultivated permanently. In contrast with horticultural societies, intensive agriculturalists are more likely to have towns and cities, a high degree of craft specialization, large differences in wealth and power, and more complex political organization. They are also more likely to face food shortages. In the modern world, intensive agriculture is geared increasingly to production for a market.

6. Pastoralism is a subsistence technology involving principally the raising of large herds of animals. It is generally found in low-rainfall areas. Pastoralists tend to be nomadic, to have small communities consisting of related families, and to depend significantly on trade.

7. Anthropologists generally agree that the physical environment exercises a limiting rather than determining influence on the major types of food-getting. Food producers can generally support more people in a given territory than food collectors can. Therefore, food producers may have had a competitive advantage in confrontations with food collectors.

[26] Janzen. "Tropical Agroecosystems."

11

Economics
and
Social Stratification

When we think of economics, we think of things and activities involving money. We think of the costs of goods and services such as food, rent, haircuts, and movie tickets. We may also think of factories, farms, and other enterprises that produce the goods and services we need or think we need. In our society, workers may stand before a moving belt for eight hours, tightening identical bolts that glide by. For this task they are given bits of paper that may be exchanged for food, shelter, and other goods or services. But many societies (indeed, most that are known to anthropology) did not have money or the equivalent of the factory worker. Still, all societies have economic systems, whether or not these involve the use of money. All societies have customs specifying how people gain access to natural resources; customary ways of transforming or converting those resources, through labor, into necessities and other desired goods and services; and customs for distributing (and perhaps exchanging) goods and services. When certain families or groups have more access to economic resources, we say that the society is socially stratified.

THE ALLOCATION OF RESOURCES

Natural Resources: Land

Every society has access to natural resources—land, water, plants, animals, minerals. Every society has cultural rules for determining who has access to particular resources and what can be done with them. In societies like our own, where land and many other things may be bought and sold, land is divided into precisely measurable units, the borders of which are sometimes invisible. Relatively small plots of land and the resources on them are usually "owned" by individuals. Large plots of land are generally owned collectively. The owner may be a government agency, such as the National Parks Service, which owns land on behalf of the entire population of the United States. Or the owner may be what we call a corporation—a private collective of shareholders. In the United States, property ownership entails a more or less exclusive right to use land resources in whatever way the owner wishes, including the right to sell, give away, or destroy those resources.

Our system of land allocation is alien to most food collectors and most horticulturalists for two reasons. First, in their societies, individual ownership of land, or ownership by a group of unrelated shareholders, is generally unknown. If there is collective ownership, it is always by groups of related people (kinship groups) or by territorial groups (bands or villages). Second, even if there is collective ownership, such ownership is different from ours in that land is generally not bought and sold.

Thus, it is society, and not the individual, that specifies what is considered property and what are the rights and duties associated with that property.[1] These specifications are social in nature, for they may be changed over time. For example, France declared all its beaches to be public, thereby stating, in effect, that the ocean shore is not a resource that can be owned by an individual. As a result, all the hotels and individuals who had fenced off portions of the best beaches for their exclusive use had to remove the fences.

In our country, people are beginning to ask whether abuse of the rights of ownership is a factor in the growing pollution of our air and water. Hence, federal, state, and local governments are becoming more active in regulating exactly what people (and even public agencies) can do with the land they own. Such regulation may be new, but our society has always limited the rights of ownership. For example, land may be taken by the government for use in the construction of a highway; we may be paid compensation, but usually we cannot prevent confiscation. Similarly, we are not allowed to burn our houses, nor can we use them as brothels or munitions arsenals. In short, even under our individualistic system of ownership, property is not entirely private.

How societies differ in their rules for access to land and other natural

[1] E. Adamson Hoebel. *The Law of Primitive Man.* New York: Atheneum, 1968, pp. 46–63. Originally published in 1954.

resources seems in part to be related to how they differ in food-getting. Let us now examine how food collectors, horticulturalists, pastoralists, and intensive agriculturalists structure rights to land in different ways.

Food Collectors. As we have noted, members of food-collecting societies generally do not own land individually. The reason is probably that land itself has no intrinsic value for food collectors; what is of value is the presence of game and wild plant life on the land. If game moves away or food resources become less plentiful, the land is less valuable. Therefore, the greater the possibility that the wild food supply in a particular locale will fluctuate, the less desirable it is to parcel out small areas of land to individuals, and the more advantageous it is to make land ownership communal. The Hadza of Tanzania, for example, do not believe that they have exclusive rights over the land on which they hunt. Any member of the group can hunt, gather, or draw water where he or she likes.[2] But the Hadza are somewhat unusual—it is more common in food-collecting societies for a group of individuals (usually kin) to "own" land. To be sure, such ownership is not usually exclusive; typically some degree of access is provided to members of neighboring bands.[3] For example, the !Kung honor the right of hot pursuit, whereby one band is allowed to follow its game into the territory of its neighbors. The sharing of water is perhaps most characteristic of the !Kung's attitude toward the allocation of natural resources. Members of one band, as a matter of courtesy, must ask permission of a neighboring band to use a water hole in the other's territory. As a matter of tradition, the headman of a !Kung band cannot refuse.[4] The reasoning seems clear: if one band helps its neighbors when they need help, then that band can ask for help when it needs assistance.

At the other extreme, local groups in some hunter-gatherer societies try to maintain exclusive rights to particular territories. The Owens Valley Paiute in the California part of the Great Basin lived all year in permanent villages along streams. A group of villages claimed and defended a particular territory against intruders, who may or may not have been other Owens Valley Paiute. Why have some hunter-gatherers been more "territorial" than others? One suggestion is that when the plants and animals collected are predictably located and abundant, groups are more likely to be sedentary and to try to maintain exclusive control over territories. In contrast, when plant and animal resources are unpredictable in location or amount, territoriality will tend to be minimal.[5] After all, why should people defend land that does not reliably provide the resources they need?

[2] James Woodburn. "An Introduction to Hadza Ecology." In Richard B. Lee and Irven DeVore, eds., *Man the Hunter*. Chicago: Aldine, 1968, pp. 49–55.

[3] Eleanor Leacock and Richard Lee. "Introduction." In Eleanor Leacock and Richard Lee, eds., *Politics and History in Band Societies*. Cambridge: Cambridge University Press, 1982, p. 8.

[4] Lorna Marshall. "The !Kung Bushmen of the Kalahari Desert." In James L. Gibbs Jr., ed., *Peoples of Africa*. New York: Holt, Rinehart & Winston, 1965, p. 251.

[5] Rada Dyson-Hudson and Eric Alden Smith. "Human Territoriality: An Ecological Reassessment." *American Anthropologist*, 80 (1978): 21–41.

Horticulturalists. Like food collectors, most horticulturalists do not have individual or family ownership of land. This may be because rapid depletion of the soil necessitates either letting some of the land lie fallow for a period of years or abandoning an area after a few years and moving to a new location. There is no point in individuals or families claiming permanent access to land that, given their technology, is not usable permanently. But unlike food collectors, horticulturalists do allocate particular plots of land to individuals or families for their use, although these individuals or families do not own the land in our sense of potentially permanent ownership.

On Truk, a group of islands in the Pacific, people do not think of land as a unitary thing, but rather as territory and soil. Unused territory may be owned, but if the land has been cleared and improved the soil can be owned separately. Furthermore, things such as trees that are on the land may be owned separately from the land itself. A group of kin (those who descend from the same ancestress) usually holds title to various plots of soil. Members of the group receive provisional rights to cultivate soil owned by the group (children belong to the group their mother belongs to). But the kin group may take back the soil from an individual who fails to maintain it or fails to share the produce from it with others. The group may sell the soil, but only with the unanimous consent of its members; and an individual can sell his or her provisional use rights, but only with the consent of the kin group.[6]

Pastoralist. The territory of pastoral nomads far exceeds that of most horticultural societies. Since their wealth ultimately depends upon two elements—mobile herds and fixed pasturage and water—pastoralists must combine the adaptive potential of both food collectors and horticulturalists. Like food collectors, they must know the potential of their territory—which can extend as much as 1000 miles—so that they are assured a constant supply of grass and water. And like horticulturalists, after their herds graze an area clean they must move on and let that land lie fallow until the grass renews itself. Also like horticulturalists, they depend for subsistence on human manipulation of a natural resource—animals, as opposed to the horticulturalists' land. Although grazing land tends to be communally held, it is customary among pastoralists for animals to be owned by individuals.[7]

Intensive Agriculturalists. Individual ownership of land resources—including the right to use the resources and the right to sell or otherwise dispose of them—is common among intensive agriculturalists. The development of such ownership is partly a result of the possibility of using land season after season, which gives the land more or less permanent value. But the concept of individual ownership is also partly a political and social matter. So, for example, the occupation and cultivation of frontier land in the United

[6] Ward H. Goodenough. *Property, Kin, and Community on Truk.* New Haven: Yale University Press, 1951.

[7] John H. Dowling. "Property Relations and Productive Strategies in Pastoral Societies." *American Ethnologist,* 2 (1975): 422.

States was transformed by law into individual ownership. Under the Homestead Act of 1862, if a person cleared a 160-acre piece of land and farmed it for five years, the federal government would consider that person the owner of the land. This practice is similar to the custom in some societies by which a kin group, a chief, or a community is obligated to assign a parcel of land to anyone who wishes to farm it. The difference is that once the American homesteader had become the owner of the land, the laws of this country gave the homesteader the right to dispose of it at will by selling or giving it away. Once individual ownership of land has become established, property owners may use their economic, and hence political, power to pass laws that favor themselves. In the early years of the United States, only property owners could vote.

In the United States and other industrial societies, it may appear that private property owners have nearly absolute control over the use and disposal of their property. But the nearly absolute control is offset by the real absoluteness with which the owner can lose that property. In our society, this can happen through government action as the penalty for inability to pay taxes or to satisfy a debt. Or it can occur because the government decides to take the property for some public purpose (usually with some compensation to the owner) under the right of eminent domain. A family that has farmed its land for a century can lose it in one year. This often happens as a result of events over which the family has no control—a national economic depression, a drought that causes a bad crop year, a change in climate such as the one that created the Oklahoma dust bowl in the 1930s, or a period of economic stagnation such as the one that followed the Civil War. In addition, where individual ownership is the custom, it is nearly always the case that some individuals do not own any land.

Technology

In order to convert resources to food and other goods, every society makes use of a technology which includes tools, constructions (such as fish traps) and required skills (such as how to set up a fish trap). Societies vary considerably in their technologies and in the way access to technology is allocated. For example, food collectors and pastoralists typically have fairly small tool kits; they must limit their tools (and their material possessions in general) to what they can comfortably carry with them. As for access to technology, food collectors and horticulturalists generally allow equal opportunity. In the absence of specialization, most individuals have the skills to make what they need. But in an industrial society like our own, the opportunity to acquire or use a particular technology (which may be enormously expensive as well as complex) is hardly available to all. Most of us may be able to buy a drill or a hammer, but few of us can buy the factory that makes it.

Among food collectors, tools are generally considered to belong to the person who made them. There is no way of gaining superiority over others through possession of tools, because whatever resources for toolmaking are available to one are available to all. In addition, the custom of sharing applies to tools as well as to food. If a member of the band asks to borrow a spear another person is not using, that person is obligated to lend it. However, the spear is considered the personal property of its maker, and the man who kills an animal with it may be obligated to share the kill with the owner.

Pastoralists, like food collectors, are somewhat limited in their possessions, for they too are nomadic. But pastoralists can use their animals to carry some possessions. Each family owns its own tools, clothes, and perhaps a tent, as well as its own livestock. The livestock are the source of other needed articles, for the pastoralists often trade their herd products for the products of the townspeople: "Of the totality of objects contained in a nomad's home—be he a Kurd of West Iran or a Gujar in North Pakistan—only a small fraction have been produced by himself or his fellow nomads; and of the food such a family consumes in a year only a small fraction is pastoral products."[8]

Horticulturalists, on the other hand, are generally more self-sufficient than pastoralists. The knife for slashing and the hoe or stick for digging are their principal farming tools. What a person makes is considered his or her own, yet everyone is often obligated to lend tools to others. In Truk society, a man has first use of his canoe and of his farming implements. Yet if a close kinsman needs the canoe and finds it unused, he may take it without permission. A distant kinsman or neighbor must ask permission if he wishes to borrow any tools, but the owner may not refuse him. If he were to refuse, the owner would risk being scorned and refused if he were to need tools later.

Societies with intensive agriculture and industrialized societies are likely to have tools made by specialists—which means that tools must be acquired by trade or purchase. Probably because complex tools cost a considerable amount of money, they are less likely to be shared except by those who contributed to the purchase price. For example, a diesel-powered combine requires a large amount of capital for its purchase and upkeep. The person who has supplied the capital is likely to regard the machine as individual private property and to regulate its use and disposal. Farmers may not have the capital to purchase the machine they need, so they may have to borrow from a bank. The owner must then use the machine to produce enough surplus to pay for its cost and upkeep, as well as for its replacement. The owner may rent the machine to neighboring farmers during slack periods to obtain a maximum return on his or her investment.

However, expensive equipment is not always individually owned in societies with intensive agriculture or industrialized economies. Even in cap-

---

[8] Fredrik Barth. "Nomadism in the Mountain and Plateau Areas of South West Asia." In *The Problems of the Arid Zone*. Paris: UNESCO, 1960, p. 345.

italist countries, there may be cooperative ownership of machines by "cooper-atives" or co-owning with neighbors.[9]

Some equipment and facilities are too expensive for even a cooperative to afford. Governments may than allocate tax money collected from all for constructions or facilities that benefit some productive group (as well as the public): airports that benefit airlines, roads that benefit trucking firms, dams that benefit power companies. Such resources are owned collectively by the whole society, but they are subject to strict rules for their use, including additional payment. Other productive resources in industrial societies, such as factories, may be owned jointly by shareholders, who purchase a portion of a corporation's assets in return for a proportionate share of its earnings. The proportion of technology and facilities owned by various levels of government reflect the type of political/economic system: Socialist and Communist coun-tries have more public ownership than capitalist countries.

THE CONVERSION OF RESOURCES

In all societies, resources have to be transformed or converted through labor into foods, tools, and other goods. (These activities constitute what economists call *production.*) In this section, we examine what may motivate people to work, how societies may divide up the work to be done, and decision making about work. As we shall see, some aspects of the conversion of natural resources are culturally universal, but there is also an enormous amount of cultural variation.

Incentives for Labor

Why do people work? Probably all of us have asked ourselves this question at least once in a while. Our concern may not be with why other people are working, but why *we* have to work. Clearly, part of the answer is that work is necessary for survival. Although there are always some able-bodied adults who do not work as much as they should and rely on the work of others, no society would survive if most able-bodied adults were like that. In fact, most societies probably succeed in motivating most people to want to do (and even enjoy) what they have to do. But are the incentives for labor the same in all societies? Anthropologists think the answer is yes and no. One reason people may work is because they must. But why is it that people in some societies apparently work *more* than they must? Our knowledge of motivational differ-ences is highly tentative and speculative, but we can be fairly certain that a particular and often-cited motive—the profit motive, or the desire to ex-change something for more than it costs—is not universal.

[9] B. Lisa Gröger. "Of Men and Machines: Cooperation among French Family Farmers." *Ethnol-ogy*, 20 (1981): 163–75.

There can be no profit motive in people who produce food and other goods primarily for their own consumption, as do most food collectors, many if not most horticulturalists, and even some intensive agriculturalists. Such societies have what we call a *subsistence economy*, not a money or commercial economy. Anthropologists have noticed that people in subsistence economies often work less than people in commercial economies. Food collectors appear to have a considerable amount of leisure time, as do many horticulturalists. It has been estimated, for example, that the men of the horticultural Kuikuru tribe in central Brazil spend about three and a half hours a day on subsistence. It appears that the Kuikuru could produce a substantial surplus of manioc, their staple food, by working thirty minutes more a day.[10] Yet they and many other people do not produce more than they need. But why should they? They cannot store a surplus for long because it would rot; they cannot sell it because there is no market nearby; and they do not have a political authority that might collect it for some purpose. Although we often think "more is better," a food-getting strategy with such a goal might even been disastrous. This may be especially true for hunter-gatherers. The killing of more animals than a group could eat might seriously jeopardize the food supply in the future, because overhunting could reduce reproduction among the hunted animals.[11] Horticulturalists might do well to plant a little extra, just in case part of the crop failed, but a great deal extra would be a tremendous waste of time and effort.

It has been suggested that when resources are converted primarily for household consumption, people will work harder if they have more consumers in the household. That is, when there are few able-bodied workers and a proportionately large number of consumers (perhaps because there are many young children and old people), the workers have to work harder. But when there are proportionately more workers, they can work less. This idea is called *Chayanov's rule*.[12] Alexander Chayanov found this relationship in data on Russian peasants prior to the Communist revolution.[13] Michael Chibnik found support for Chayanov's rule when he compared data from twelve communities in five areas of the world (the communities ranged in complexity from New Guinea horticulturalists to commercial Swiss farmers). Although Chayanov restricted his theory to farmers that sell some of their output and do

[10] Robert L. Carneiro. "Slash-and-Burn Cultivation among the Kuikuru and Its Implications for Settlement Patterns." In Yehudi Cohen, ed., *Man in Adaptation: The Cultural Present.* Chicago: Aldine, 1968. Cited by Marshall Sahlins. *Stone Age Economics,* Chicago: Aldine, 1972, p. 68.

[11] Marvin Harris. *Cows, Pigs, Wars and Witches: The Riddles of Culture.* New York: Random House, Vintage, 1975, pp. 127–28.

[12] Sahlins, in *Stone Age Economics,* p. 87, introduced American anthropology to Chayanov and coined the phrase "Chayanov's rule."

[13] Alexander V. Chayanov. *The Theory of Peasant Economy,* ed. D. Thorner, B. Kerblay, and R. E. F. Smith. Homewood, Ill.: Richard D. Irwin, 1966, p. 78.

not hire labor, Chibnik's analysis suggests that Chayanov's rule applies even where crops are rarely sold and even where labor is often hired.[14]

But there appear to be many societies, even with subsistence economies, in which some people work harder than they need to just for their own families' subsistence. What motivates them to work harder? It turns out that many subsistence economies are not oriented just to household consumption. Rather, sharing and other transfers of food and goods often go well beyond the household, sometimes including the whole community or even groups of communities. In such societies, social rewards come to those who are generous, who give things away. Thus, people who work harder than they have to for subsistence may be motivated to do so because they gain respect or esteem thereby.[15]

In commercial economies such as our own—where foods, other goods, and services are sold and bought—people seem to be much more motivated to keep any extra income for themselves and their families. Extra income is converted into bigger dwellings, more expensive furnishings and food, and other elements of a "higher" standard of living. But the desire to improve one's standard of living is probably not the only motive operating. Some people may work partly to satisfy a need for achievement,[16] or because they find their work enjoyable. In addition, just as in precommercial societies, some people may work partly to gain respect or influence by giving some of their income away. Not only do we respect philanthropists and movie stars for giving to charities; our society encourages such giving by making it an allowable tax deduction! Still, the emphasis on giving in commercial societies is clearly less than that in subsistence economies. We consider charity by the rich appropriate and even admirable, but we would think it foolish or crazy for anyone to give so much away that he or she became poverty-stricken.

Forced Labor

The work we have discussed thus far has all been *voluntary labor*—voluntary in the sense that no formal organization within the society compels people to work and punishes them for not working. Social training and social pressure are generally powerful enough to persuade an individual to perform some useful task. In both food-collecting and horticultural societies, individuals who can stand being the butt of jokes about laziness will still be fed. At most, they will be ignored by the other members of the group. There is no reason to punish them and no way to coerce them to do the work expected of them.

[14] Michael Chibnik. "The Economic Effects of Household Demography: A Cross-Cultural Assessment of Chayanov's Theory." In Morgan D. Maclachlan, ed., *Household Economies and Their Transformations*. Monographs in Economic Anthropology, No. 3. Lanham, Md.: University Press of America, 1987, pp. 74–106.

[15] Sahlins. *Stone Age Economics*, pp. 101–48.

[16] David C. McClelland. *The Achieving Society*. New York: Van Nostrand, 1961.

More complex societies have ways of forcing people to work for the authorities—whether those authorities be kings or presidents. An indirect form of forced labor is taxation. The average Amercian's total tax (local, state, and federal) is about a third of his or her income, which means that the average person works four months out of the year for the government. If a person decided not to pay the tax, the money will be forcibly taken or the person can be put in prison.

Money is the customary form of tax payment in a commercial society. In a politically complex but nonmonetary society, persons may pay their taxes in other ways—by performing a certain number of hours of labor or by giving a certain percentage of what they produce. The **corvée,** a system of required labor, existed in the Inca empire in the central Andes prior to the Spanish conquest. Each commoner was assigned three plots of land to work: a temple plot, a state plot, and his own plot. The enormous stores of food that went into state warehouses were used to supply the nobles, the army, the artisans, and all other state employees. Men were subject to military service, to duty as personal servants for the nobility, and to public-service work.[17]

The draft or compulsory military service is a form of corvée in that failure to serve can be punished by a prison term or voluntary exile. To defend their territory, emperors of China had the Great Wall built along the northern borders of the empire. The wall extends over 1500 miles, and thousands of laborers were drafted to work on it.

Slavery is the most extreme form of forced work, in that slaves have little control over their labor. Because slaves constitute a category or class of persons in many societies, we discuss slavery more fully later in this chapter.

Division of Labor

All societies have some division of labor—some customary assignment of different kinds of work to different kinds of people. Universally, males and females and adults and children do not do the same kinds of work. In a sense, then, division of labor by sex and age is a kind of universal specialization of labor. Many societies known to anthropology divide labor only by sex and age. Other societies, as we will see, have more complex specialization.

By Sex and Age. All societies make use of sex differences to some extent in their customary assignment of labor. In the next chapter, we discuss the division of labor by sex in detail.

Age is also a universal basis for division of labor. Clearly, children cannot do work that requires a great deal of strength. But in many societies girls and boys contribute a great deal more in labor than do children in our own society. For example, they help in animal tending, weeding, and harvesting, and they do a variety of domestic chores such as child care, fetching water and fire-

---

[17] Julian H. Steward and Louis C. Faron. *Native Peoples of South America.* New York: McGraw-Hill, 1959, pp. 122–25.

wood, and cooking and cleaning. Indeed, in some societies a child six years old is considered old enough to be responsible for a younger sibling for a good part of the day.[18] Animal tending is often important work for children. Children in some societies spend more time at this task than adults.[19]

Why do children do so much work in some societies? If adults (particularly mothers) have heavy workloads, and children are physically and mentally able to do the work, a good part of the work is likely to be assigned to children.[20] As we have seen, food producers probably have more work than food collectors, so we would expect that children would be likely to work more where there is herding and farming. Consistent with this expectation, Patricia Draper and Elizabeth Cashdan have found differences in children's work between nomadic and settled !Kung. Even though recently settled !Kung have not switched completely from food collection to food production, children's (as well as adults') activities have changed considerably. The children living in nomadic camps had virtually no work at all—adults did all the gathering and hunting. But the settled children were given lots of chores ranging from helping with animals to helping with the harvest and food processing.[21] When children in a society do a great deal of work, parents may value them more and may consciously want to have more children.[22] This may be one of the reasons birth rates are higher in intensive agricultural societies.[23]

In some societies, work groups are formally organized on the basis of age. Among the Nyakyusa of southeastern Africa, for example, cattle are the principal form of wealth, and boys who are six to eleven herd the cattle for their parents' village. The boys join together in herding groups to tend the cattle of their fathers and of any neighboring families that do not have a son of herding age.[24]

Beyond Sex and Age.   In societies with relatively simple technologies, there is little specialization of labor beyond that of sex and age. But as a society's technology becomes more complex and it is able to produce large quantities of food, more and more of its people are freed from subsistence work to become specialists in some other tasks—canoe builders, weavers, priests, potters, artists, and the like.

[18] Beatrice B. Whiting and Carolyn P. Edwards. *Children of Different Worlds: The Formation of Social Behavior*. Cambridge, Mass.: Harvard University Press, 1988, p. 164.
[19] Moni Nag, Benjamin N. F. White, and R. Creighton Peet. "An Anthropological Approach to the Study of the Economic Value of Children in Java and Nepal." *Current Anthropology*, 19 (1978): 295–96 (293–301).
[20] Whiting and Edwards. *Children of Different Worlds*, pp. 97–107.
[21] Patricia Draper and Elizabeth Cashdan. "Technological Change and Child Behavior among the !Kung." *Ethnology*, 27 (1988): 348 (339–65).
[22] Nag, White, and Peet. "An Anthropological Approach to the Study of the Economic Value of Children in Java and Nepal," p. 293. See also Candice Bradley, "The Sexual Division of Labor and the Value of Children," *Behavior Science Research*, 19 (1984–1985): 160–64.
[23] Carol R. Ember. "The Relative Decline in Women's Contribution to Agriculture with Intensification." *American Anthropologist*, 85 (1983): 291–97.
[24] Monica Wilson. *Good Company: A Study of Nyakyusa Age Villages*. Boston: Beacon Press, 1963. Originally published in 1951.

A day in the life of a food collector, for instance, would be quite varied and involve a large number of skills. A man must know how to make his own traps and weapons as well as how to use them to catch a variety of animals and fish. A woman must be an amateur biologist, able to identify and gather edible food. Both know how to cook, dance, and sing.

In contrast with food collectors, horticultural societies may have some part-time specialists. Some people may devote special effort to perfecting a particular skill or craft—pottery making, weaving, housebuilding, doctoring—and in return for their products or services be given food or other gifts. Among some horticultural groups, the entire village may partially specialize in making a particular product, which can then be traded to neighboring people.

With the development of intensive agriculture, full-time specialists—potters, weavers, blacksmiths—begin to appear. The trend toward greater specialization reaches its peak in industrialized societies, where workers develop skills in one small area of the economic system. The meaninglessness of much of industrialized work was depicted by Charlie Chaplin in the film *Modern Times*; when he left the factory after repeatedly tightening the same kind of bolt all day long, he could not stop his arms from moving, as if they were still tightening bolts.

Decision Making about Work

Food collectors generally ignore many of the plant and animal species in their environment, choosing to go after only some. Why? The people may say that some animals are taboo while others are delicious. But where do such customary beliefs come from? Are they adaptive? And if there are no customary preferences for certain plants and animals, how can we explain why a food collector will go after certain foods and ignore others on a particular day? Food producers also make choices constantly. For example, a farmer has to decide when to plant, what to plant, how much to plant, when to harvest, how much to store, how much to give away or sell. Researchers have recently tried to explain why certain economic decisions become customary and why individuals make certain economic choices in their everyday lives.

A frequent source of ideas about choices is **optimal foraging theory**, which was developed originally by students of animal behavior and which has been applied to decision making by food collectors. Optimal foraging theory assumes that individuals seek to maximize the returns (in calories and nutrients) on their labor in deciding which animals and plants they will go after. Natural selection should favor optimal foraging because such decisions should increase the chances of survival and reproduction. Research in a number of different food collecting societies generally supports the optimal foraging model.[25] For example, the Aché of eastern Paraguay consistently

---

[25] Eric Alden Smith. "Anthropological Applications of Optimal Foraging Theory: A Critical Review." *Current Anthropology*, 24 (1983): 626.

prefer to hunt peccaries (wild piglike mammals) rather than armadillos. Although peccaries take much longer to find and are harder to kill than armadillos, a day spent hunting peccaries yields more than 4600 calories per hour of work, whereas hunting armadillos yields only about 1800 calories an hour.[26]

How does a farmer decide whether to plant a particular crop and how much land and labor to devote to it? A number of researchers have tried to model decision making by farmers. Christina Gladwin and others suggest that farmers make decisions in steps, with each choice point involving a yes or no answer. For example, in the high altitude region of Guatemala, farmers could choose to plant about eight possible crops (or combinations of them, such as corn and beans which grow together well). A farmer will quickly exclude some choices because of the answers to certain questions: Can I afford the seed and fertilizer? Can this crop be watered adequately? Is the altitude appropriate? And so on. If any of the answers are "no," the crop is not planted. By a further series of yes-or-no decisions, farmers presumably decide which of the remaining possibilities will be planted.[27]

Individuals may not always be able to state their decision rules for decision making clearly, nor do they always have complete knowledge about the various possibilities, particularly when some of the possibilities are new. That does not mean, however, that economic choices cannot be predicted or explained by researchers. For example, Michael Chibnik found that men in two villages in Belize (in Central America) were not able to say why they devoted more or less time to working for wages versus growing crops. But their behavior was still predictable. For example, older men grew crops more, because wage labor was more physically demanding; and in the village with a higher cost of living the men were more likely to work for wages.[28]

THE DISTRIBUTION OF GOODS AND SERVICES

Goods and services are distributed in all societies by systems that, however varied, can be classified under three general types: reciprocity, redistribution, and market or commercial exchange.[29] The three systems often coexist in a society, but one system usually predominates. The predominant system seems to be associated with the society's food-getting technology and, more specifically, its level of economic development.

[26] Kim Hill, Hillard Kaplan, Kristen Hawkes, and A. Magdalena Hurtado. "Foraging Decisions among Aché Hunter-Gatherers: New Data and Implications for Optimal Foraging Models." *Ethology and Sociobiology*, 8 (1987): 17–18.

[27] Christina H. Gladwin. "A Theory of Real-Life Choice: Applications to Agricultural Decisions." In Peggy F. Barlett, ed., *Agricultural Decision-Making: Anthropological Contributions to Rural Development*. New York: Academic Press, 1980, pp. 45–85.

[28] Michael Chibnik. "The Statistical Behavior Approach: The Choice between Wage Labor and Cash Cropping in Rural Belize." In Barlett, ed., *Agricultural Decision-Making*, pp. 87–114.

[29] Karl Polanyi. "The Economy as Instituted Process." In Karl Polanyi, Conrad Arensberg, and Harry W. Pearson, eds., *Trade and Market in the Early Empires*. New York: Free Press, 1957, pp. 243–70.

Reciprocity

Reciprocity consists of giving and taking without the use of money; it ranges from pure gift giving to equal exchanges to cheating. Technically, then, reciprocity may take three forms: **generalized reciprocity, balanced reciprocity,** and **negative reciprocity.**[30]

Generalized Reciprocity. This is gift giving without any immediate or planned return. Generalized reciprocity sustains the family in all societies. Parents give food to children because they want to, not because the child may reciprocate years later. Of course, usually someone—often a grown child—feeds the parents when they are too old to make their own living. In this sense, all societies have some kind of generalized reciprocity. But some societies depend upon it almost entirely to distribute goods and services.

The !Kung call "far-hearted" anyone who does not give gifts or who does not eventually reciprocate when given gifts. The practice of giving is not evidence of altruism, but is entrenched in their awareness of social interdependence. The !Kung remember quite well the gift-giving activities of everyone else in their own and other bands, and they express approval or disapproval openly. The necessity to reduce tensions, to avoid envy and anger, and to keep all social relations peaceful, not only within their own band but among all !Kung bands, creates continuing crosscurrents of obligation within friendship. These are maintained, renewed, or established through the generalized reciprocity of gift giving. The following two examples suggest how generalized reciprocity evens things out among the !Kung.

Lorna Marshall recounts how the !Kung divided an eland brought to a site where five bands and several visitors were camping together—over 100 people in all. The owner of the arrow that had first penetrated the eland was, by custom, the owner of the meat. He first distributed the forequarters to the two hunters who had aided him in the kill. After that, the distribution was dependent generally on kinship: each hunter shared with his wives' parents, wives, children, parents, and siblings, and they in turn shared with their kin. Sixty-three gifts of raw meat were recorded, after which further sharing of raw and cooked meat was begun. Since each large animal is distributed in the same way, over the years such generalized reciprocity results in an evening out of what people receive.

Among the !Kung, the possession of something valuable is undesirable, for it may lead to envy or even conflict. For example, when Marshall left the band that had sponsored her in 1951, she gave each woman in the band a present of enough cowrie shells to make a necklace—one large shell and twenty small ones. When she returned in 1952, there were no cowrie-shell necklaces and hardly a single shell among the people in the band. Instead, the

---

[30] Sahlins. *Stone Age Economics*, pp. 188–96.

shells appeared by ones and twos in the ornaments of the people of neighboring bands.[31]

Sharing may be most likely when people are not sure they can get the food and water they need. In other words, sharing may be most likely if resources are unpredictable. So a !Kung band may share its water with other bands because they may have water now but not in the future. But one Bushman group in the Kalahari, the Gana, has been observed to share less than other groups. It turns out that the resources available to the Gana are more predictable, because the Gana supplement their hunting and gathering with plant cultivation and goat herding. Cultivated melons (which store water) appear to buffer the Gana against water shortages, and goats appear to buffer them against shortages of game. Thus, while the !Kung distribute the meat right after a kill, the Gana dry it and then store it in their houses.[32]

The idea that unpredictability may favor sharing may also explain why some foods are more often shared than others. Wild game, for example, is usually unpredictable; when hunters go out to hunt, they cannot be sure that they will come back with meat. Wild plants, on the other hand, are more predictable; gatherers can be sure when they go out that they will come back with a least some plant foods. In any case, it does appear that game tends to be shared by food collectors much more than wild plant foods.[33]

Unpredictability is one thing; actual scarcity is another. What happens to a system of generalized reciprocity when resources are actually scarce because of a drought or other disaster? Does the ethic of giving break down? Evidence from a few societies suggests that the degree of sharing may actually *increase* during the period of actual food shortage.[34] For example, in describing the Netsilik Eskimos, Asen Balikci says, "Whenever game was abundant, sharing among non-relatives was avoided, since every family was supposedly capable of obtaining the necessary catch. In situations of scarcity, however, caribou meat was more evenly distributed throughout camp."[35] Sharing may increase during *mild* scarcity because people can minimize their deprivation. But generalized reciprocity may be strained by extreme scarcity. Ethnographic evidence from a few societies suggests that during famine, when individuals are actually dying from hunger, sharing may be limited to the household.[36]

Balanced Reciprocity. This system is more explicit and short-term in its expectations of return than generalized reciprocity. In fact, it involves a

[31] Lorna Marshall. "Sharing, Talking and Giving: Relief of Social Tensions among !Kung Bushmen." *Africa*, 31 (1961): 239–41.

[32] Elizabeth A. Cashdan. "Egalitarianism among Hunters and Gatherers." *American Anthropologist*, 82 (1980): 116–20.

[33] Hillard Kaplan and Kim Hill. "Food Sharing among Aché Foragers: Tests of Explanatory Hypotheses." *Current Anthropology*, 26 (1985): 223–46.

[34] Kathleen A. Mooney. "The Effects of Rank and Wealth on Exchange among the Coast Salish." *Ethnology*, 17 (1978): 391–406.

[35] Asen Balikci. *The Netsilik Eskimo.* Garden City, N. Y.: Natural History Press, 1970. Quoted in Mooney. "The Effects of Rank and Wealth on Exchange among the Coast Salish," p. 392.

[36] Mooney. "The Effects of Rank and Wealth on Exchange among the Coast Salish," p. 392.

straightforward immediate or limited-time trade. In balanced reciprocity, the exchange is usually motivated by the desire or need for certain objects.

The !Kung, for instance, trade with the Tswana Bantu: a gemsbok hide for a pile of tobacco; five strings of beads made from ostrich eggshell for a spear; three small skins for a good-sized knife.[37] The Semang, food collectors in the Malay Peninsula, engage in "silent trade" with the settled Malay agriculturalists. Believing it is better not to establish personal contact with foreigners, the Semang leave their surplus jungle products at an agreed-upon place near a village and return later to take whatever has been left by the villagers—usually, salt, beads, or a metal tool.[38]

Through trade, a society can dispose of goods it has in abundance and obtain goods scarce in its own territory. Since trade transactions between neighboring peoples may be crucial to their survival, it is important to maintain good relations. Various societies have developed methods of peaceful exchange that do not involve money.

The Kula Ring.   The horticultural Trobriand Islanders, who live off the eastern coast of New Guinea, have worked out an elaborate scheme for trading food and other items with the people of neighboring islands. Such trade is essential, for some of the islands are small and rocky and cannot produce enough food to sustain their inhabitants, who specialize instead in canoe building, pottery making, and other crafts. Other islands produce far more yams, taro, and pigs than they need. Yet the trade of such necessary items is carefully hidden beneath the panoply of the **kula ring**, a ceremonial exchange of valued shell ornaments.[39]

Two kinds of ornaments are involved in the ceremony of exchanges— white shell armbands *(mwali),* which travel around the circle of islands in a counterclockwise direction, and red shell necklaces *(soulava),* which travel in a clockwise direction. The possession of one or more of these ornaments allows a man to organize an expedition to the home of one of his trading partners on another island. The high point of an expedition is the ceremonial giving of the valued *kula* ornaments. Each member of the expedition receives a shell ornament from his trading partner and then remains on the island for two or three days as the guest of that person. During the visit the real trading goes on. Some of the exchange takes the form of gift giving between trading partners. There is also exchange or barter between expedition members and others on the island. By the time the visitors leave, they have accomplished a year's trading without seeming to do so. (A somewhat similar occurrence was the American and Chinese ceremonial exchange of musk oxen and pandas during the Nixon presidency. These animals are valued because they are rare,

---

[37] Marshall. "Sharing, Talking and Giving," p. 242.
[38] Service. *The Hunters,* p. 95.
[39] J. P. Singh Uberoi. *The Politics of the Kula Ring: An Analysis of the Findings of Bronislaw Malinowski.* Manchester, England: University of Manchester Press, 1962.

yet they are practically useless. Immediately after the exchanging of the gifts, the real trading of goods between the two countries began.

Whatever the reasons for the origin of the *kula* ring, which may date back nearly 2000 years, it is still an important institution in the modern nation of Papua New Guinea. For example, active participation in the *kula* ring seems to have helped candidates in the 1960s and the 1970s to be elected to the national parliament.[40]

Negative Reciprocity. This is an attempt to take advantage of another, to get something for nothing or for less than its worth. A mild form is deceitful bargaining; an extreme form is theft and other varieties of seizure. In other words, negative reciprocity ranges from "various degrees of cunning, guile, stealth, and violence to the finesse of a well-conducted horse-raid."[41]

Kinskip Distance and Type of Reciprocity. Most food-collecting and horticultural societies depend on some form of reciprocity for the distribution of goods and labor. Sahlins suggests that whether the reciprocity is generalized, balanced, or negative depends largely on the kinship distance between persons. Generalized reciprocity may be the rule for family members and close kinsmen. Balanced reciprocity may be generally practiced among equals who are not closely related. A tribesman who would consider it demeaning to trade with his own family will trade with neighboring tribes. The desire to satisfy both parties represents the desire to maintain peaceful relations between two groups. Negative reciprocity may be practiced against strangers and enemies.[42] In general, the importance of reciprocity declines with economic development.[43] In societies with intensive agriculture, and even more so in societies that are industrialized, reciprocity distributes only a small proportion of all goods and services.

Reciprocity as a Leveling Device. Reciprocal gift giving may do more than equalize the distribution of goods within a community, as in the !Kung's sharing. It may also tend to equalize the distribution of goods between communities.

Many Melanesian societies in and near New Guinea have the custom of holding pig feasts in which 50, 100, or even 2000 pigs are slaughtered. Andrew Vayda, Anthony Leeds, and David Smith have suggested that these enormous feasts, though apparently wasteful, are just one of the outcomes of a complex of cultural practices that are highly advantageous. The people of these societies cannot accurately predict how much food they will produce during the year. Some years there will be bumper crops, other years very poor crops, because of fluctuations in the weather. So it might be wise to overplant

[40] Jerry W. Leach. "Introduction." In Jerry W. Leach and Edmund Leach, eds., *The Kula: New Perspectives on Massim Exchange*. Cambridge: Cambridge University Press, 1983, pp. 12, 16.

[41] Sahlins. *Stone Age Economics*, p. 195.

[42] Ibid., pp. 196–204.

[43] Frederic L. Pryor. *The Origins of the Economy: A Comparative Study of Distribution in Primitive and Peasant Economies*. New York: Academic Press, 1977, pp. 204, 276.

just in case the yield is poor. Yet overplanting results in overproduction during average and exceptionally good years. What can be done with this extra food? Since root crops such as yams and taro do not keep well over long periods, any surplus is fed to pigs, which become, in effect, food-storing repositories. Pigs are then available for needed food during lean times. But if there are several years of surpluses, pigs can become too much of a good thing. Pigs wanting food can destroy yam and taro patches. When the pig population grows to menacing proportions, a village may invite other villages to a gigantic feast that results in a sharp reduction of the pig population and keeps the fields from being overrun. Over the years the pig feasts serve to equalize the food consumption, and especially the protein consumption, of all the villages that participate in the feasts.[44] Thus, the custom of pig feasts may be a way for villages to "bank" surplus food by storing up "social credit" with other villages, which will return that credit in subsequent feasts.

In some Melanesian societies, the pig feasts foster an element of competition among the men who give them. "Big men" may try to bolster their status and prestige by the size of their feasts. But competition is enhanced not by keeping wealth but by giving it away. A similar situation existed among many American Indian groups of the Northwest Coast, where a chief might attempt to enhance his status by holding a **potlatch**. At a potlatch, a chief and his group would give away blankets, pieces of copper, canoes, large quantities of food, and other items to their guests. The host chief and his group would later be invited to other potlatches.

The competitive element in the potlatch appears to have intensified after contact with whites. Because of the fur trade, the number of trade goods increased, and so more items could be given away. Possibly more important, the population decline among the Indians caused by diseases (such as smallpox) introduced by European traders meant that some chiefs had no direct heirs to their titles. Distant relatives might compete for the positions, each attempting to give away more than the others.[45] Chiefs may also have attempted to attract men to their half-empty villages by spectacular giveaways.[46] Although the potlatch system seems wasteful in that goods were often destroyed in the competition, the system probably also served to equalize the distribution of goods among competing groups.

On one level of analysis, the Melanesian pig feasts and the Northwest Coast potlatches were reciprocal exchanges between communities or villages. But these exchanges were not just intercommunity versions of reciprocal gift giving between individuals. Because these feasts were organized by people

[44] Andrew P. Vayda, Anthony Leeds, and David B. Smith. "The Place of Pigs in Melanesian Subsistence." In Viola E. Garfield, ed., *Symposium: Patterns of Land Utilization, and Other Papers.* Proceedings of the Annual Spring Meeting of the American Ethnological Society, 1961. Seattle: University of Washington Press, 1962, pp. 69–74.

[45] Philip Drucker. "The Potlatch." In George Dalton, ed., *Tribal and Peasant Economies: Readings in Economic Anthropology.* Garden City, N. Y.: Natural History Press, 1967, pp. 481–93.

[46] Harris. *Cows, Pigs, Wars and Witches*, p. 120.

who collected goods, they also involved another mode of distribution, which anthropologists call redistribution.

Redistribution

Redistribution is the accumulation of goods (or labor) by a particular person, or in a particular place, for the purpose of subsequent distribution. Although redistribution is found in all societies, it becomes an important mechanism only in societies that have political hierarchies—that is, chiefs or other specialized officials and agencies. In all societies, there is some redistribution, at least within the family. Members of the family pool their labor or products or income for the common good. But in many societies, there is little or no redistribution beyond the family. It seems that redistribution on a territorial basis emerges when there is a political apparatus to coordinate centralized collection and distribution of goods or to mobilize labor for some public purpose.

Redistribution systems vary from relative equality for all members of a community to gross inequality. At one extreme, illustrated by the Buin of Melanesia, "the chief is housed, dressed, and fed exactly like his bondsman."[47] Even though the chief owns most of the pigs, everyone shares equally in the consumption of the wealth. At the other extreme, a wealthy Indian landowner may live in luxury while the lower castes, dependent upon him for redistribution, live in poverty. Generally, where redistribution is an important form of distribution (in societies with higher levels of productivity), the wealthy are more likely than the poor to benefit from the redistributions.[48]

Why do redistribution systems develop? Elman Service has suggested that they may develop in agricultural societies that contain subregions suited to different kinds of crops or natural resources. Food collectors can take advantage of environmental variation by moving to different areas. With agriculture, the task is more difficult; it might be easier to move different products across different regions.[49] If the demand for different resources or products becomes too great, reciprocity between individuals might become too awkward. So it might be more efficient to have someone—a chief, perhaps—coordinate the exchanges.

Marvin Harris also feels that redistribution becomes more likely with agriculture, but for a somewhat different reason. He argues that competitive feasting, as in New Guinea, is adaptive because it encourages people to work harder to produce somewhat more than they need. Why would this be

[47] R. C. Thurnwald. "Pigs and Currency in Buin: Observations about Primitive Standards of Value and Economics." *Oceania*, 5 (1934): 125.
[48] Pryor. *The Origins of the Economy*, pp. 284–86.
[49] Elman R. Service. *Primitive Social Organization: An Evolutionary Perspective*. New York: Random House, 1962, pp. 145–46.

adaptive? Harris argues that with agriculture, people really have to produce more than they need so that they can protect themselves against crises such as crop failure. The groups that make feasts may be indirectly ensuring themselves against crises by storing up social credit with other villages, who will reciprocate by making feasts for them in the future. On the other hand, inducements to collect more than they need may not be advantageous to food-collecting groups, who might lose in the long run by overcollecting.[50]

Market or Commercial Exchange

When we think of markets we usually think of bustling colorful places in other parts of the world where goods are bought and sold. (In our own society we seldom use the word "market," although we have "supermarkets" and the "stock market" and other places for buying and selling we call "shops," "stores," and "malls.") In referring to **market** or **commercial exchange**, economists and economic anthropologists are referring to exchanges or transactions in which the "prices" are subject to supply and demand, whether or not the transactions occur in a marketplace.[51] "Market exchange" does not only involve the exchange, or buying and selling, of goods; it also involves transactions of labor, land, rentals, and credit.

On the surface, many market exchanges resemble balanced reciprocity. One person gives something and receives something in return. How then does market exchange differ from balanced reciprocity? It is easy to distinguish market exchange from balanced reciprocity when money is involved, since reciprocity is defined as not involving money. But market exchange need not always involve money.[52] For example, a landowner grants a tenant farmer the right to use the land in exchange for a portion of the crop. So to call a transaction "market exchange," we have to ask whether supply and demand determine the "price." If a tenant farmer gives only a token gift to the landowner, we would not call it market exchange, just like a Christmas gift to a teacher is not payment for teaching. However, if tenants are charged a large portion of their crops when the supply of land is short, or if landowners lower their demands when few people want to tenant-farm, then we would call the transactions "market or commercial exchange."

Although market exchange need not involve money, most commercial transactions, particularly nowadays, do involve what we call "money."

Money. Some anthropologists define money according to the functions and characteristics of the general-purpose money used in our own and other complex societies, for which nearly all goods, resources, and services can be

---

[50] Harris. *Cows, Pigs, Wars and Witches*, pp. 118–21.
[51] Stuart Plattner. "Introduction." In Stuart Plattner, ed., *Markets and Marketing.* Monographs in Economic Anthropology, No. 4. Lanham, Md.: University Press of America, 1985, p. viii.
[52] Pryor. *The Origins of the Economy*, pp. 31–33.

exchanged. According to this definition, *money* performs the basic functions of serving as a medium of exchange, a standard of value, and a store of wealth. Also, money is nonperishable, transportable, and divisible, so that transactions can be made when the goods being purchased differ in value. General-purpose money provides a way of condensing wealth: paper money is easier to carry around than bushels of wheat; a checkbook is handier than a herd of sheep and goats. In addition, general-purpose money acts as a store of wealth.

Degrees of Commercialization.
Most societies were not commercialized at all, or only barely so, when first described in the ethnographic record. That is, most did not rely on market or commercial exchange to distribute goods and services. But commercial exchange has become the dominant form of distribution in the modern world. Few modern nations depend mostly on reciprocity or redistribution to distribute goods and services. Many of the separate societies of the ethnographic past are now incorporated into larger nation-states. For example, the Trobriand Islands and other language groups in Melanesia are parts of the nation of Papua New Guinea. So there are probably no societies now that are not at least somewhat commercialized. Selling nowadays goes far beyond the nation-state; the world is now a multinational market.[53]

But there is considerable variation in the degree to which societies today depend on market or commercial exchange. Many societies still allocate land without purchase and distribute food and other goods primarily by reciprocity and redistribution, participating only peripherally in market exchange. These are societies in transition: their traditional subsistence economies are gradually becoming commercialized. Among the Luo of Kenya, for example, most families still have land that was allocated to them by their kin groups. The food they eat they mostly produce themselves. But nowadays many men also work for wages—some nearby, others far away in towns and cities (where they spend a year or two). These wages are used to pay government taxes, to pay for children's schooling, and to buy commercially produced items such as clothes, kerosene lamps, radios, fish from Lake Nyanza, tea, sugar, and coffee. Occasionally, families sell agricultural surpluses or craft items such as reed mats. Economies such as that of the Luo are not fully commercialized, but they may become so in the future.

What anthropologists call *peasant economies* are somewhat more commercialized than transitional subsistence economies such as that of the Luo. Although peasants also produce food largely for their own consumption, they *regularly* sell part of their surplus (food, other goods, or labor) to others, and land is one of the commodities they buy, rent, and sell. But although their production is somewhat commercialized, peasants still are not like the fully commercialized farmers in industrialized societies, who rely upon the market

[53] Plattner. "Introduction," p. xii.

to exchange *all* or *almost all* their crops for *all* or *almost all* the goods and services they need.

In fully commercialized societies such as our own, market or commercial exchange dominates the economy; prices and wages are regulated, or at least significantly affected, by the forces of supply and demand. A modern industrial economy may involve international as well as national markets, in which everything has a price, stated in the same money terms—natural resources, labor, goods, services, prestige items, religious and ceremonial items. Reciprocity is reserved for family members and friends or remains behind the scene in business transactions. Redistribution, however, is an important mechanism. It is practiced in the form of taxation and the use of public revenue for transfer payments and other benefits to low-income families—welfare, social security, health care, and so on. But commercial exchange is the major way goods and services are distributed.

Why Do Money and Market Exchange Develop?
Most economists think that money is invented in a society (or borrowed from another society) when trade increases and barter becomes increasingly inefficient. The more important trade is, the more difficult it is to find a person who can give something you want and wants something you have to give. Money is a valuable that can be exchanged for anything and so is an efficient medium of exchange when trade becomes important. In contrast, many anthropologists do not link the origins of money or market exchange to the necessities of trade. Instead they link the origins of money to various noncommercial "payments" such as the *kula* valuables and the taxes that have to be paid to a political authority. All of the available explanations of money suggest that money will be found mostly in societies at higher levels of economic development; and indeed this is the case. And if some simpler societies have money, dominant and more complex societies have usually introduced it.[54]

Most theories about the development of money and market exchange assume that producers have regular surpluses they want to exchange. But why do people produce surpluses in the first place? Perhaps they are motivated to produce a lot extra only when they want to obtain goods from a distance, and the suppliers of such goods are not well known to them, making reciprocity less likely as a way to obtain these goods. Some suggest that market exchange begins with external (intersocietal) trade; since kin would not likely be involved, transactions would involve bargaining (and therefore market exchange, by definition). Finally, some argue that as societies become more complex and more densely populated, social bonds between individuals become less kinlike and friendly and therefore reciprocity becomes less important.[55] Perhaps this is why traders in developing areas are often foreigners or recent immigrants.[56]

[54] Pryor. *The Origins of the Economy*, pp. 153–83.
[55] Ibid., pp. 109–11.
[56] Brian L. Foster. "Ethnicity and Commerce." *American Ethnologist*, 1 (1974): 437–47.

In any case, the result of Frederic Pryor's cross-cultural research support the notion that all types of market exchange—of goods, labor, land and credit—are more likely with higher levels of economic productivity. Pryor also finds that market exchange of goods appears at lower levels of economic development than market exchange of labor and credit; market exchange of land, probably because it is associated with private property (individual ownership), appears mostly at the highest levels of productivity. Perhaps surprisingly, smaller societies tend to have more market exchange of goods involving other societies. Larger societies can presumably get more of what they need from inside the society; for example, China has had relatively little foreign trade throughout much of its history.[57]

Possible Leveling Devices in Commercial Economies.   As we will see below, societies that depend substantially on market or commercial exchange tend to have marked differences in wealth among people. Nonetheless, there may be mechanisms that lessen the inequality, that act at least partially as leveling devices.

Some anthropologists have suggested that the *fiesta complex* in highland Indian communities of Latin America may be a mechanism that tends to equalize income.[58] In these peasant villages, a number of fiestas are held each year to celebrate important village saints. The outstanding feature of this system is the extraordinary amount of money and labor a sponsoring family must contribute. Sponsors must hire ritual specialists, pay for church services, musicians, and costumes for dancers, and cover the complete cost of food and drink for all members of the community. The costs incurred can very easily amount to a year's wages.[59]

Other anthropologists have suggested that although the richer Indians who sponsor fiestas are clearly distributing a good deal of wealth to the poorer members of their own and other communities, the fiestas do not really level wealth at all. First, true economic leveling would entail the redistribution of important productive resources such as land or animals; the fiesta only temporarily increases the general level of consumption. Second, the resources expended by the sponsors are usually extra resources that have been accumulated specifically for the fiesta—that is why the sponsors are always appointed in advance. Third, and perhaps most important, the fiestas do not seem to have reduced long-term wealth distinctions within the villages.[60]

In nations such as ours, can the income tax and the social-assistance programs it pays for (such as welfare and social security) be thought of as

[57] Pryor. *The Origins of the Economy*, pp. 125–48.

[58] See, for example, Eric Wolf, "Types of Latin American Peasantry: A Preliminary Discussion," *American Anthropologist*, 57 (1955): 452–71; and Pedro Carrasco, "The Civil-Religious Hierarchy in Mesoamerican Communities: Pre-Spanish Background and Colonial Development," *American Anthropologist*, 63 (1961):483–97.

[59] Waldemar R. Smith. *The Fiesta System and Economic Change*. New York: Columbia University Press, 1977; and Marvin Harris. *Patterns of Race in the Americas*. New York: Walker, 1964.

[60] Smith. *The Fiesta System and Economic Change;* and Harris. *Patterns of Race in the Americas.*

leveling devices? Theoretically, our tax system is supposed to work that way by taxing higher incomes at higher rates. But we know that in fact it doesn't. Those in higher income brackets can often deduct an appreciable amount from their taxable incomes and therefore pay taxes at a relatively low rate. Our tax system may help some to escape extreme poverty, but like the fiesta system, it has not eliminated marked distinctions in wealth.

SOCIAL STRATIFICATION

A long-enduring value in American society is the belief that "all men are created equal." These famous words from our Declaration of Independence do not mean that all people are equal in wealth or status, but rather that all are supposed to be equal before the law. In fact, modern industrial societies such as our own are socially stratified—that is, they contain social groups having unequal access to important advantages, such as economic resources, power, and prestige.

In even the simplest societies there are some differences in advantages based on age or sex or ability. For example, everywhere adults have more status than children, men usually more than women, and the skilled more than the unskilled. But there are some societies in which all *social groups* (for example, families) have more or less the same access or right to advantages. We call such societies *egalitarian.*

Societies vary then in the extent to which social groups (as well as individuals) have unequal access to advantages. There may be differential or unequal access to three types of advantages: wealth or economic resources, power, and prestige. As we saw earlier in this chapter, resources may range from hunting or fishing grounds to farmland to money; the different social groups in a society may or may not have unequal access to these resources. Power is a second but related advantage. It is the ability to make others do what they do not want to do; power is influence based on the threat of force. As we shall see below, when groups in a society have rules or customs that give them unequal access to wealth or resources, they generally also have unequal access to power. Finally, there is the advantage of prestige. When we speak of prestige, we mean that someone or some group is accorded particular respect or honor. But if there is always unequal access by individuals to prestige (because of differences in age, sex, or ability), there are some societies in the ethnographic record that have no social groups with unequal access to prestige.

Thus, anthropologists conventionally distinguish three types of societies in terms of the degree to which different social groups have unequal access to advantages; the three types are called *egalitarian, rank,* and *class* societies. Some societies in the ethnographic record do not fit easily into any of these three types; as with any classification scheme, some cases seem to straddle the

TABLE 11-1 Stratification in three types of societies

Type of Society	SOME SOCIAL GROUPS HAVE GREATER ACCESS TO:		
	Economic Resources	Power	Prestige
Egalitarian	No	No	No
Rank	No	No	Yes
Class/Caste	Yes	Yes	Yes

line between adjacent types.[61] But most societies are conventionally classified as belonging to just one of the three types summarized in Table 11-1. **Egalitarian societies** contain no special groups having greater access to economic resources, power, or prestige. **Rank societies** do not have unequal access to economic resources or to power, but they do contain social groups having unequal access to prestige. Rank societies, then, are partially stratified. **Class societies** have unequal access to all three advantages—economic resources, power, and prestige.

Egalitarian Societies

Egalitarian societies can be found not only among hunter-gatherers but among horticulturalists and pastoralists as well. An important point to keep in mind is that *egalitarian* does not mean that all people within such societies are the *same*. There will always be differences among individuals in age and sex and in such abilities or traits as hunting skill, perception, health, creativity, physical prowess, attractiveness, and intelligence. According to Morton Field, *egalitarian* means that within a given society "there are as many positions of prestige in any given age-sex grade as there are persons capable of filling them."[62] For instance, if a person can achieve **status** (a position of prestige) by fashioning fine spears, and if every person in the society fashions such spears, then every person acquires status as a spear maker. If status is also acquired by carving bones into artifacts, and if only three people are considered expert carvers of bones, then only those three achieve status as carvers. But the next generation might produce eight spear makers and twenty carvers. In an egalitarian society, the number of prestigious positions is adjusted to fit the number of qualified candidates. We would say, therefore, that such a society is not socially stratified.

There are, of course, differences in status and prestige arising out of differences in ability. Even in an egalitarian society, differential prestige

---

[61] In an analysis of many Indian societies in the New World, Gary Feinman and Jill Neitzel argue that rank and class societies are not systematically distinguishable. See their "Too Many Types: An Overview of Sedentary Prestate Societies in the Americas," in Michael B. Schiffer, ed., *Advances in Archaeological Method and Theory*, Orlando, Fla.: Academic Press, 1984, 7: 57.

[62] Morton H. Fried. *The Evolution of Political Society: An Essay in Political Anthropology.* New York: Random House, 1967, p. 33.

exists. But although some persons may be better hunters or more skilled artists than others, there is still equal *access* to status positions for people of the same ability. Any prestige gained by achievement of status as a great hunter, for instance, is neither transferable nor inheritable. Because a man is a great hunter, it is not assumed that his sons are also great hunters. An egalitarian society keeps inequality at a minimal level.

Just as egalitarian societies do not have social groups with unequal access to economic resources, they also do not have social groups with unequal access to power. As we will see later in the chapter on political organization, unequal access to power by social groups seems to occur only in state societies, which have full-time political officials and marked differences in wealth.

The Mbuti Pygmies of central Africa provide an example of a society almost totally equal: "Neither in ritual, hunting, kinship nor band relations do they exhibit any discernible inequalities of rank or advantage."[63] Their hunting bands have no leaders; recognition of the achievement of one person is not accompanied by privilege of any sort. Economic resources such as food are communally shared, and even tools and weapons are frequently passed from person to person. Only within the family are rights and privileges differentiated.

Rank Societies

Societies with social *ranking* generally practice agriculture or herding, but not all agricultural or pastoral societies are ranked. Ranking is characterized by social groups having unequal access to prestige or status, but *not* significantly unequal access to economic resources or power. Unequal access to prestige is often reflected in the position of chief, a rank to which only some members of a specified group in the society can succeed.

In rank societies, the position of chief is at least partially hereditary. The criterion of superior rank in some Polynesian societies, for example, was genealogical. Usually the eldest son succeeded to the position of chief, and different kinship groups were differentially ranked according to their genealogical distance from the chiefly line.

In rank societies, chiefs are often treated with deference by people of lower rank. For example, among the Trobriand Islanders of Melanesia, people of lower rank must keep their heads lower than a person of higher rank. So, when a chief is standing, commoners must bend low. When commoners have to walk past a chief who happens to be sitting, he may rise and they will bend. If the chief chooses to remain seated, they must crawl.[64]

Chiefs may sometimes look as if they are substantially richer, for they may receive many gifts and have larger storehouses. In some instances, the

[63] Michael G. Smith. "Pre-Industrial Stratification Systems."In Neil J. Smelser and Seymour Martin Lipset, eds., *Social Structure and Mobility in Economic Development*. Chicago: Aldine, 1966, p. 152.

[64] Elman R. Service. *Profiles in Ethnology*, 3rd ed. New York: Harper & Row, Pub., 1978, p. 249.

chief may be called the "owner" of the land, but other people have the right to use the land. The chief may have bigger storehouses, but his stores may be only temporary accumulations for feasts or other redistributions. The chief in a rank society cannot usually make people give him gifts or work on communal projects. Often the chief can encourage production only by working furiously on his own cultivation.[65]

Unusual among rank societies are the nineteenth-century Northwest Coast Indian tribes. They are unusual because their economy was based on food-collecting. But huge catches of salmon—which were preserved for year-round consumption—enabled them to support fairly large and permanent communities. In many ways, the Northwest Coast societies were similar to food-producing societies, even in their development of social ranking. Still, the principal means of proving one's status among the Northwest Coast Indians was to give wealth away. The tribal chiefs celebrated solemn rites by grand feasts (potlatches), at which they gave gifts to every guest.[66]

Class Societies

In class societies, as in rank societies, there is unequal access to prestige. But unlike rank societies, class societies are characterized by unequal access to economic resources and power. That is, not every person of the same sex or age has the same chance to obtain land, animals, money, or other economic benefits, or the same opportunity to exercise power.

But however social stratification came into existence (a topic we will discuss later in the chapter), it has become predominant in the world only in the last few hundred years. Fully stratified societies range from somewhat open to more or less closed class or *caste* systems.

Open Class Systems. A **class** is a category of persons who have about the same opportunity to obtain economic resources, power, and prestige. During the last sixty years, study after study has been made of classes in American towns. Sociologists have produced profiles of typical American communities, known variously as Yankee City, Middletown, Jonesville, and Old City, all of which support the premise that the United States has distinguishable, though somewhat open, social classes. Both Lloyd Warner and Paul Lunt's Yankee City study [67] and Robert and Helen Lynd's Middletown study[68] concluded that the social status or prestige of a family generally correlated with the occupation and wealth of the head of the family.

The determinants of a person's class status have changed over time in

---

[65] Marshall Sahlins. *Social Stratification in Polynesia*. Seattle: University of Washington Press, 1958, pp. 80–81.

[66] Philip Drucker. *Cultures of the North Pacific Coast*. San Francisco: Chandler, 1965, pp. 56–64.

[67] W. Lloyd Warner and Paul S. Lunt. *The Social Life of a Modern Community*. New Haven: Yale University Press, 1941.

[68] Robert S. Lynd and Helen Merrell Lynd. *Middletown*. New York: Harcourt, Brace, 1929; and Robert S. Lynd and Helen Merrell Lynd. *Middletown in Transition*. New York: Harcourt, Brace, 1937.

the United States. In 1776, for example, the middle class consisted of the families of self-employed craftspeople, shopkeepers, and farmers. By 1985, only about 8 percent of Americans were self-employed, but many more people think of themselves as belonging to the middle class. Self-employment is now a less important determinant of middle-class status than working with one's mind and having authority over others on the job.[69]

On the whole, American society is a somewhat *open* society; that is, it is possible, through effort, to move from one class to another. A university education has been a major aid in moving upward.[70] Lower-class persons may become "resocialized" at the university, which separates them from their parents and enables them to gradually learn the skills, speech, attitudes, and manners characteristic of the higher class they wish to join. So successful is this process that students from a lower class who move into a higher class may find themselves ashamed to take their new friends to their parents' homes.

Our identification with a social class begins quite early in life. The residence area chosen by our parents and our religious affiliation, school, school curriculum, clubs, sports, college (or lack of college), marriage partner, and occupation are all influential in socializing us into a particular class.

Although in America social class is not fully determined by birth, there is a high probability that most people will stay more or less within the class into which they were born and will marry within that class. That is, even if we do not inherit money from our parents, our chances of being successful are strongly influenced by our class background. The daughter of a wealthy businessman, for example, is likely to attend schools with good reputations. She will learn to speak with an accent that is more "elite." She will be likely to learn to ride horses, play tennis, and the piano, and to acquire the etiquette appropriate for attending concerts, parties, and teas. If she wishes to have a career, she has a very good chance to get into a college or graduate school of her choice, and she has social connections that can help her to get a good starting job. If she gets married, she has a very good chance of marrying a man of similar background, tastes, and likelihood of success.

Class boundaries, though vague, have been established by custom and tradition; sometimes they have been reinforced by the enactment of laws. Many of our laws serve to protect property and thus tend to favor the upper and upper-middle classes. The poor, in contrast, seem to be perennial losers in our legal system. The crimes the poor are most likely to commit are dealt with quite harshly in our judicial system, and poor people rarely have the money to secure effective legal counsel.

Classes also tend to perpetuate themselves through the bequeathing of wealth. John Brittain has suggested that in the United States, the transfer of

[69] Reeve Vanneman and Lynn Weber Cannon. *The American Perception of Class.* Philadelphia: Temple University Press, 1987, pp. 53–91.
[70] David L. Featherman and Robert M. Hauser. *Opportunity and Change.* New York: Academic Press, 1978, pp. 4, 481.

money through bequests accounts for much of the wealth of the next generation. He estimates that in 1972 approximately 65 to 85 percent of the wealth of the wealthiest 2 percent of married women in this country came from inheritance (primarily from parents, not husbands). About half of the wealth of the wealthiest 2 percent of married men in this country may have come from inheritance. The importance of inheritance seems to increase with greater wealth. That is, the wealth of richer people comes more from inheritance than the wealth of not-so-rich people.[71]

Although some class societies have more open class systems than others, the greatest likelihood is that people will remain in the class of their birth. For example, the Japanese class system has become more open in the last hundred years. A 1960 study of the upper-class business elite showed that 8 percent came from lower-class and 31 percent from middle-class backgrounds.[72] This social mobility was achieved chiefly by successful passage through the highly competitive university system. The Japanese class system is not completely open, however, for 61 percent of the business elite came from the relatively small upper class. The tendency to retain high class status even through changing times is clear.

Caste Systems

Some societies with classes have also had groups called castes. A **caste** is a ranked group, often associated with a certain occupation, in which membership is determined at birth and marriage is restricted to members of one's own caste. In India, for example, there are several thousand castes. Those members of a low caste who can get wage-paying jobs (chiefly those in urban areas) may improve their social standing in the same ways available to people in other class societies, but they generally cannot marry someone in a higher caste. Thus, a caste is a *closed* class.

Since World War II, the economic basis of the caste system in India has been undermined somewhat by the growing practice of giving cash payment for services. For instance, the son of a barber may be a teacher during the week, earning a cash salary, and confine his haircutting to weekends. But he still remains in the barber caste (Nai) and must marry within that caste.

Although few areas of the world have developed a caste system like that of India, there are castelike features in some other societies. For example, blacks in the United States have a castelike status which is determined partially by the inherited characteristic of skin color. Until recently, some states had laws prohibiting a black from marrying a white. Even when interracial marriage does occur, children of the union are often regarded as having lower

[71] John A. Brittain. *Inheritance and the Inequality of Material Wealth.* Washington, D. C.: Brookings Institution, 1978.
[72] Edward Norbeck. "Continuities in Japanese Social Stratification." In Leonard Plotnicov and Arthur Tuden, eds., *Essays in Comparative Social Stratification.* Pittsburgh: University of Pittsburgh Press, 1970.

status, even though they may have blonde hair and light skin. In the South, where treatment of blacks as a caste was most apparent, whites traditionally refused to eat with blacks, or, until recently, to sit next to them at lunch counters, on buses, and in schools. Separate drinking fountains and toilets for blacks and whites reinforced the idea of ritual uncleanness. The economic advantages and gains in prestige enjoyed by whites are well documented.[73]

Another example of a caste group in class society is the Eta of Japan.[74] Unlike blacks in America, members of the Eta caste are physically indistinguishable from other Japanese. They are a hereditary, endogamous (in-marrying) group numbering now about 3 million people, comparable to India's untouchables. Their occupations are traditionally those of farm laborer, leatherworker, and basket weaver; their standard of living is very low.

Slavery. **Slaves** are persons who do not own their own labor, and as such they represent a class. Slavery has existed in various forms in many times and places, regardless of race and culture. Sometimes it has been a closed class, or caste system, sometimes a relatively open class system. In different slave-owning societies, slaves have had different, but always some, legal rights.[75]

In ancient Greece, slaves were often conquered enemies. Since city-states were constantly conquering one another or rebelling against former conquerors, slavery was a threat to everyone. Following the Trojan War, the transition of Hecuba from queen to slave was marked by her cry "Count no mortal fortunate, no matter how favored, until he is dead."[76] Nevertheless, Greek slaves were considered human beings, and they could even acquire some status along with freedom. Andromache, the daughter-in-law of Hecuba, was taken as slave and concubine by one of the Greek heroes. When his legal wife produced no children, Andromache's slave son became heir to his father's throne. Although slaves had no rights under law, once they were freed, either by the will of their master or by purchase, they and their descendants could become assimilated into the dominant group. In other words, slavery in Greece was not seen as the justified position of inferior people. It was regarded, rather, as an act of fate—"the luck of the draw"—that relegated a victim to the lowest class in society.

Among the Nupe, a society in central Nigeria, slavery was of quite another type.[77] The methods of obtaining slaves—as part of the booty of

---

[73] Gerald D. Berreman. "Caste in India and the United States." *American Journal of Sociology*, 66 (1960); 120–27.

[74] For more information about caste in Japan and elsewhere, see Gerald D. Berreman, "Caste in the Modern World," Morristown, N. J.: General Learning Press, 1973; and Gerald D. Berreman, "Race, Caste and Other Invidious Distinctions in Social Stratification," *Race*, 13 (1972): 403–14.

[75] Pryor. *The Origins of the Economy*, p. 219.

[76] Euripides. *The Trojan Women*.

[77] S.F. Nadel. *A Black Byzantium: The Kingdom of Nupe in Nigeria*. London: Oxford University Press, 1942. The Nupe abolished slavery at the beginning of this century.

warfare, and later by purchase—were similar to those of Europeans, but the position of the slaves was very different. Mistreatment was rare. Male slaves were given the same opportunities to earn money as other dependent males in the household—younger brothers, sons, or other relatives. A slave might be given a garden plot of his own to cultivate, or he might be given a commission if his master were a craftsman or a tradesman. Slaves could acquire property, wealth, and even slaves of their own. However, all of a slave's belongings went to the master at the slave's death.

Manumission, the granting of freedom, was built into the Nupe system. If a male slave could afford the marriage payment for a free woman, the children of the resulting marriage were free; the man himself, however, remained a slave. Marriage or concubinage were the easiest ways out of bondage for a slave woman. Once she had produced a child by her master, both she and the child had free status. The woman, however, was only figuratively free: if a concubine, she had to remain in that role. As might be expected, the family trees of the nobility and the wealthy were liberally grafted with branches descended from slave concubines.

In the United States, slavery originated as a means of obtaining cheap labor, but the slaves soon came to be regarded as deserving of their low status because of their alleged inherent inferiority. Since the slaves were black, some whites justified slavery and belief in black people's inferiority by quoting Scripture out of context ("they shall be hewers of wood and drawers of water"). Slaves could not marry or make any other contracts, nor could they own property. In addition, their children were also slaves, and the master had sexual rights over the female slaves. Because the status of slavery was determined by birth in the United States, slaves constituted a caste. During the days of slavery, the United States had both a caste and a class system. And even after the abolition of slavery, as we have noted, some castelike elements remained.

As for why slavery may have developed in the first place, the cross-cultural evidence is as yet inconclusive. We do know, however, that slavery is not an inevitable stage in economic development, contrary to what some have assumed. In other words, slavery is *not* found mainly in certain economies, such as those dependent on intensive agriculture. (Unlike the United States until the Civil War, many societies with intensive agriculture did not develop any variety of slavery.) Also, the hypothesis that slavery develops where available resources are plentiful but labor is scarce is not supported by the cross-cultural evidence. All we can say definitely is that slavery does not occur in developed or industrial economies: either it disappears or it was never present in them.[78]

---

[78] Pryor. *The Origins of the Economy*, pp. 217–47.

THE EMERGENCE OF STRATIFICATION

Anthropologists are not certain why social stratification developed. Nevertheless, they are reasonably sure that higher levels of stratification emerged
relatively recently in human history. Archaeological sites until about 7500
years ago do not show any evidence of inequality. Houses do not appear to
vary much in size and content, and burials seem to be more or less the same,
suggesting that their occupants were treated more or less the same in life and
death. That stratification is a relatively recent development is also suggested
by the fact that certain cultural features associated with stratification also
developed relatively recently. For example, most societies that depend primarily upon agriculture or herding have social classes.[79] Since agriculture and
herding developed within the past 10,000 years, we may assume that most
hunter-gatherers in the distant past lacked social classes. Other recently developed cultural features associated with class stratification include fixed
settlements, political integration beyond the community level, the use of
money as a medium of exchange, and the presence of at least some full-time
specialization.[80]

Gerhard Lenski suggests that the 10,000-year-old trend toward increasing inequality has recently been reversed. He argues that inequalities of
power and privilege in industrial societies—measured in terms of the concen-
tration of political power and the distribution of income—are less pronounced than inequalities in complex preindustrial societies. Technology in
industrialized societies is so complex, he argues, that those in power are
compelled to delegate some authority to subordinates if the system is to work.
In addition, a decline in the birth rate in industrialized societies, coupled with
the need for skilled labor, has pushed the average wage of workers far above
the subsistence level, resulting in greater equality in the distribution of income. Finally, Lenski suggests that the spread of the democratic ideology, and
particularly its acceptance by elites, has significantly broadened the political
power of the lower classes.[81] A study by Phillips Cutright has tested and
supported Lenski's hypothesis that inequality has decreased with industrialization. Nations that are highly industrialized exhibit a lower level of inequality
than nations that are only somewhat industrialized.[82]

But why did social stratification develop in the first place? On the basis of
his study of Polynesian societies, Marshall Sahlins has suggested that an
increase in agricultural productivity results in social stratification.[83] According
to Sahlins, the degree of stratification is directly related to the production of a

[79] Data from Robert B. Textor, comp., *A Cross-Cultural Summary*, New Haven: HRAF Press, 1967.
[80] Ibid.
[81] Gerhard Lenski. *Power and Privilege: A Theory of Social Stratification*. Chapel Hill: University of
North Carolina Press, 1984, pp. 308–18. First published in 1966.
[82] Phillips Cutright. "Inequality: A Cross-National Analysis." *American Sociological Review*, 32
(1967): 564.
[83] Sahlins. *Social Stratification in Polynesia*.

surplus, which is made possible by greater technological efficiency. The higher the level of productivity and the larger the agricultural surplus, the greater the scope and complexity of the distribution system. This in turn enhances the status of the chief, who serves as redistributing agent. Sahlins argues that the differentiation between distributor and producer inevitably gives rise to differentiation in other aspects of life:

> First, there would be a tendency for the regulator of distribution to exert some authority over production itself—especially over productive activities which necessitate subsidization, such as communal labor or specialist labor. A degree of control of production implies a degree of control over the utilization of resources, or, in other words, some preeminent property rights. In turn, regulation of these economic processes necessitates the exercise of authority in interpersonal affairs: differences in social power emerge.[84]

Lenski's theory of the causes of stratification is similar to that of Sahlins. Lenski, too, argues that production of a surplus is the stimulus in the development of stratification, but he focuses primarily on the conflict that arises over control of that surplus. Lenski concludes that the distribution of the surplus will be determined on the basis of power. Thus, inequalities in power promote unequal access to economic resources and simultaneously give rise to inequalities in privilege and prestige.[85]

The theories of Sahlins and Lenski do not really address the question of why the redistributors will want, or be able, to acquire greater control over resources. After all, the redistributors in many rank societies do not have greater wealth than others. It has been suggested that access to economic resources becomes unequal only when there is population pressure on resources in rank or chiefdom societies.[86] Such pressure may be what induces redistributors to try to keep more land and other resources for themselves and their families.

C. K. Meek offered an example of how population pressure in northern Nigeria may have led to economic stratification. At one time, a tribal member could obtain the right to use land by asking permission of the chief and presenting him with a token gift in recognition of his status. But by 1921, the reduction in the amount of available land had led to a system under which applicants offered the chief large payments for scarce land. As a result of these payments, farms came to be regarded as private property, and differential access to such property became institutionalized.[87]

Clearly there are a number of questions about social stratification that require additional research, particularly the kinds of research that system-

[84] Ibid., p. 4.
[85] Lenski. *Power and Privilege.*
[86] See Fried, *The Evolution of Political Society*, pp. 201–2; and Michael J. Harner, "Scarcity, the Factors of Production, and Social Evolution," in Steven Polgar, ed., *Population, Ecology, and Social Evolution*, The Hague: Mouton, 1975, pp. 123–38.
[87] C. K. Meek. *Land Law and Custom in the Colonies.* London: Oxford University Press, 1940, pp. 149–50.

atically test alternative answers. Why private property develops and why classes develop are questions to which we have no answers that are based firmly on empirical research. We also do not know whether class societies generally develop out of rank societies. Although many anthropologists take for granted the sequence of egalitarian to rank to class society, we have no evidence that such a sequence has occurred generally or even in particular places. It is possible that rank societies were formerly class societies that lost unequal access by groups to economic resources and power, leaving only unequal access to prestige.

SUMMARY

1. All societies have economic systems, whether or not these involve the use of money. All societies have customs specifying access to natural resources; customary ways of transforming or converting those resources, through labor, into necessities and other desired goods and services; and customs for distributing (and perhaps exchanging) goods and services.
2. Regulation of access to natural resources is a basic factor in all economic systems. The concept of individual ownership of land—including the right to use its resources and the right to sell or otherwise dispose of them—is common among intensive agriculturalists. In contrast, food collectors, horticulturalists, and pastoralists generally lack individual ownership of land. Among pastoral nomads, however, animals are considered family property and are not usually shared.
3. Every society makes use of a technology, which includes tools, constructions, and required skills. Even though food collectors and horticulturalists tend to think of tools as "owned" by the individuals who made them, the sharing of tools is so extensive that individual ownership does not have much meaning. Among intensive agriculturalists, toolmaking tends to be a specialized activity. Tools tend not to be shared, except mainly by those who have purchased them together
4. Incentives for labor vary cross-culturally. Many societies produce just for household consumption: if there are more consumers, producers work harder. In some subsistence economies, people may work harder to obtain the social rewards that come from giving to others. Forced labor generally occurs only in complex societies.
5. Division of labor by sex and age is universal. Generally, the more technically advanced a society is, the more surplus food it produces and the more some of its members engage in specialized work.
6. Goods and services are distributed in all societies by systems that can be classified under three types: reciprocity, redistribution, and market or commercial exchange. Reciprocity is giving and taking without the use of money and may assume three forms: generalized reciprocity, balanced reciprocity, and negative reciprocity. Generalized reciprocity is gift giving without any immediate or planned return. In balanced reciprocity, individuals exchange goods and services immediately or in the short term. Negative reciprocity is generally practiced with strangers or enemies: one individual attempts to steal from another or to cheat in trading.
7. Redistribution is the accumulation of goods or labor by a particular person, or in a particular place, for the purpose of subsequent distribution. It becomes an important mechanism of distribution only in societies with political hierarchies.
8. Market or commercial exchange, where "prices" depend on supply and demand, tends to occur with increasing levels of economic productivity. Especially nowa-

days, market exchange usually involves an all-purpose medium of exchange (money). Most societies today are at least partly commercialized; the world is becoming a single market system.

9. The presence or absence of customs or rules that give certain groups unequal access to economic resources, power, and prestige can be used to distinguish three types of societies. Egalitarian societies have no unequal access to economic resources, power, or prestige—they are unstratified. Rank societies do not have unequal access to economic resources or power, but they do have unequal access to prestige. Rank societies, then, are partially stratified. Class societies have unequal access to economic resources, power, and prestige. They are more completely stratified.

10. However social stratification came into existence, it has come to dominate the globe. Stratified societies range from somewhat open class systems to caste systems, which are extremely rigid, since caste membership is fixed permanently at birth. Sometimes slavery is a rigid and closed, or caste, system; sometimes it is a relatively open class system.

11. Social stratification appears to have emerged relatively recently in human history. This conclusion is based on archaeological evidence and on the fact that a number of other cultural features associated with stratification developed relatively recently.

12. Some theories suggest that social stratification developed as productivity increased and surpluses were produced. Others suggest that stratification emerges only when there is population pressure on resources in rank societies.

12

Sex and Culture

We all know that humans come in two major varieties—female and male. The contrast is one of the facts of life we share with most animal species. But the fact that males and females always have different organs of reproduction does not explain why males and females may also differ in other physical ways. After all, there are many animal species—such as pigeons, gulls, and laboratory rats—in which the two sexes hardly differ in appearance.[1] Thus, the fact that we are a species with two sexes does not really explain why human males and females typically look different. Also, the fact that humans reproduce sexually does not explain why human males and females should differ in behavior, or be treated differently by society. Yet no society we know of treats females and males in exactly the same way. (This is why in the last chapter we were careful to say that even in egalitarian societies men usually have more advantages than women.) In this chapter we discuss how and why sex differences and sexual behavior, and attitudes about them, vary from culture to culture.

---

[1] Lila Leibowitz. *Females, Males, Families: A Biosocial Approach*. North Scituate, Mass.: Duxbury, 1978, pp. 43–44.

SEX DIFFERENCES

Physique and Physiology

As we noted at the outset, in many animal species males and females cannot readily be distinguished. Although they differ in chromosome makeup and in their external and internal organs of reproduction, they do not differ otherwise. In contrast, humans are **sexually dimorphic**—that is, the males and females of our species exhibit fairly marked differences in size and appearance. Males typically are taller and have heavier skeletons than females. Females have proportionately wider pelvises. Males have a larger proportion of body weight in muscle; females have a larger proportion in fat. Males typically have greater grip strength, proportionately larger hearts and lungs, and greater **aerobic work capacity** (greater maximum uptake of oxygen during exercise). Why these physical differences exist is still an open question. Whether or not most of them turn out to be genetically determined, we still have to understand why natural selection may have favored them.

Social Roles

Productive and Domestic Activities. In the chapter on economic systems, we noted that all societies have some sex differences in the way they assign or divide labor. What is of particular interest here about the division of labor by sex is not so much that every society has different work for males and females, but rather that so many societies divide up work in similar ways. The question, then, is why there are universal or near-universal patterns in the division of labor by sex.

Table 12-1 summarizes the worldwide patterns. We note which activities are performed by one of the sexes in all or almost all societies, which activities are usually performed by one sex, and which activities are commonly assigned to either sex or both. Does the distribution of activities in the table suggest why males and females generally do different things?

One possible explanation may be labeled the *strength theory*. The greater strength of males, and their superior capacity to mobilize strength in quick bursts of energy (because of their greater aerobic work capacity), has commonly been cited as the reason for the universal or near-universal patterns in the division of labor by sex. Certainly, activities that require lifting heavy objects (hunting large animals, butchering, clearing land, working with stone, metal, or lumber), throwing weapons, and running with great speed (as in hunting) may be best performed by males. And none of the activities females usually perform, with the possible exception of collecting firewood, seems to require the same degree of physical strength or quick bursts of energy. But the strength theory is not completely convincing, if only because it cannot readily explain all the observed patterns. For example, it is not clear that the

TABLE 12-1 Worldwide patterns in the division of labor, by sex

	Males Almost Always	Males Usually	Either Sex or Both	Females Usually	Females Almost Always
Basic subsistence activities	Hunt • large land animals • large sea animals • game birds Trap small animals	Fish Herd large animals Collect wild honey Clear land Prepare soil for planting	Collect shellfish Care for small animals Plant crops Tend crops Harvest crops Milk animals	Gather wild plants	
Food preparation and household activities		Butcher animals	Preserve meat or fish	Care for children* Cook Prepare • vegetable food • drinks • dairy products Launder Fetch water Collect fuel	
Other	Work with wood • cut trees and prepare wood • make boats • make musical instruments Work with minerals and stone • mine and quarry stone • smelt ore Work with bone, horn, shell Engage in warfare* Exercise political leadership*	Build houses Make nets Make rope	Prepare skins Make • leather products • baskets • mats • clothing • pottery	Spin yarn	

With the exception of the asterisked (*) items, the information in this table is adapted from George P. Murdock and Caterina Provost, "Factors in the Division of Labor by Sex: A Cross-Cultural Analysis," *Ethnology*, 12 (1973):203–25. The information on political leadership and warfare comes from Martin K. Whyte, "Cross-Cultural Codes Dealing with the Relative Status of Women," *Ethnology*, 17 (1978): 217; and the information on child care comes from Thomas S. Weisner and Ronald Gallimore, "My Brother's Keeper: Child and Sibling Caretaking," *Current Anthropology*, 18 (1977): 169–80.

male activities of trapping small animals, collecting wild honey, or making musical instruments require that much physical strength.

Another possible explanation of the worldwide patterns in division of labor can be called the *compatibility-with-child-care theory*. The argument here is that women's tasks tend to be those that are more compatible with child care. (We should remember that in most societies, women breast-feed their children for two years on the average). Women's tasks may be those that do not take them far from home for long periods, that do not place children in potential danger if they are taken along, and that can be stopped and resumed if child-care duties interrupt.[2] The compatibility theory may explain why *no* activities are listed in the right-hand column of Table 12-1. That is, it may be that there are no universal or near-universal women's activities because women universally must spend part of their time caring for children. The compatibility theory may also explain why men usually do tasks such as hunting, trapping, fishing, collecting honey, lumbering, and mining. These tasks are dangerous and not easily interrupted.[3] Finally, the compatibility theory may also explain why men seem to take over certain crafts in societies with full-time specialization. Producing large quantities for sale probably demands an absence of interruptions. Although we have not noted this in Table 12-1, crafts such as making baskets, mats, and pottery are women's activities in noncommercial societies but tend to be men's activities in societies with full-time craft specialists. Cooking is a good example in our own society. In the home women do most of the cooking, but chefs and bakers tend to be male.[4]

But the compatibility theory does not explain why men usually prepare soil for planting, make boats, houses, and musical instruments, or work bone, horn, and shell. None of these tasks is particularly dangerous or uninterruptable. Why, then, do males tend to do them? Additional considerations, such as *economy of effort*, may help explain patterns that cannot readily be explained by the strength and compatibility theories. For example, it may be more advantageous for men to make musical instruments, because men generally collect the hard materials involved.[5] And because they collect those materials, men may be more knowledgeable about their physical properties and so more likely to know how to work with them. The economy-of-effort interpretation

---

[2] Judith K Brown. "A Note on the Division of Labor by Sex." *American Anthropologist*, 72 (1970), 1074.

[3] Among the Aché hunter-gatherers of Paraguay, women collect the type of honey produced by stingless bees (men collect other honey), which is consistent with the compatibility theory. See Ana Magdalena Hurtado, Kristen Hawkes, Kim Hill, and Hillard Kaplan, "Female Subsistence Strategies among the Aché Hunter-Gatherers of Eastern Paraguay," *Human Ecology*, 13 (1985): 23.

[4] George P. Murdock and Caterina Provost. "Factors in the Division of Labor by Sex: A Cross-Cultural Analysis." *Ethnology*, 12 (1973): 213.

[5] Douglas R. White, Michael L. Burton, and Lilyan A. Brudner. "Entailment Theory and Method: A Cross-Cultural Analysis of the Sexual Division of Labor." *Behavior Science Research*, 12 (1977): 1–24.

also suggests it would be advantageous for one sex to perform tasks that are located near each other. Thus, if women have to be near home to take care of young children, it would be economical for them to do other household chores that are located in or near the home.

Finally, there is an explanation of division of labor that can be called the *expendability theory*. This theory suggests that men, rather than women, will tend to do the dangerous work in a society because men are more expendable, because the loss of men is less disadvantageous than the loss of women. If some men lose their lives in hunting, deep-water fishing, mining, quarrying, lumbering, and the like, reproduction need not suffer so long as most fertile women have sexual access to men, as for example if the society permits two or more women to be married to the same man.[6] In order to motivate men to do the dangerous work, societies may have to consider such work especially prestigious. After all, why would anybody do something dangerous without some special reward?

Although the various theories, singly or in combination, seem to explain much of the division of labor by sex, there are some unresolved problems. Critics of the strength theory have pointed out that in some societies women engage in very heavy labor.[7] This suggests that males generally acquire superior physical strength at least partly because they are trained for certain roles, rather than being assigned their roles on the basis of their genetically superior strength. The compatibility theory also has some problems. It suggests that labor is divided to conform to the requirements of child care. But sometimes it seems the other way around. For example, when women spend a good deal of time in agricultural work outside the home, they often ask others to watch their infants and feed them "baby food" while the mothers are unavailable to nurse.[8] So it appears that child care may conform to the division of labor.

Consider too the mountain areas of Nepal, where agricultural work is quite incompatible with child care; heavy loads must be carried up and down steep slopes, fields are far apart, and labor takes up most of the day. Yet women do this work anyway and leave their infants with others for long stretches of time.[9] And what about hunting, one of the activities most incompatible with child care and generally not done by women? Yet women do hunt in some societies. For example, many Agta women of the Philippines regu-

[6] Carol C. Mukhopadhyay and Patricia J. Higgins. "Anthropological Studies of Women's Status Revisited: 1977–1987." *Annual Review of Anthropology*, 17 (1988): 473.

[7] Brown. "A Note on the Division of Labor by Sex," pp. 1073–78; and White, Burton, and Brudner. "Entailment Theory and Method." pp. 1–24.

[8] Sara B. Nerlove. "Women's Workload and Infant Feeding Practices: A Relationship with Demographic Implications." *Ethnology*, 13 (1974): 201–14.

[9] Nancy E. Levine. "Women's Work and Infant Feeding: A Case from Rural Nepal," *Ethnology*, 27 (1988): 231–51.

larly hunt wild pig and deer.[10] In fact, women alone or in groups get almost 30 percent of the large game animals. The women's hunting does not seem to be incompatible with child care. Women take nursing babies on hunting trips, and the women who hunt do not have lower reproductive rates than the women who choose not to hunt. Of course, Agta women may find it easier to hunt because the hunting grounds are only about half an hour from the camp, dogs are used in hunting and they assist and protect the women, and the women generally go out to hunt in groups, which may make it more possible to bring nursing babies along.

As the cases just described suggest, we need to know a lot more about labor requirements. More precisely we need to know exactly how much strength is required in particular tasks, and exactly how interruptible or dangerous they are. So far, we have mostly guesses. When there is more systematically collected evidence on such aspects of particular tasks, we will be in a better position to evaluate the theories we have discussed. In any case, it should be noted that none of the theories imply that the worldwide division-of-labor patterns will persist. As we know from our own and other industrial societies, when machines replace human strength, when women have fewer children, and when women can assign child care to others, a strict division of labor by sex begins to disappear.

Relative Contributions to Subsistence.   In our society, the stereotype of the husband is that he is the breadwinner in the family; the wife is the manager of the house and children. As we know, the stereotype is becoming more myth than reality, since more than 50 percent of all married women in the United States now work outside the home. Although the stereotypic pattern no longer fits our society very well, it used to—and it does fit many of the societies known to anthropology. Take the Toda of India, for example, as they were described early in the twentieth century. They depended for subsistence almost entirely on the dairy products of their water buffalo, either by using the products directly or by selling them for grain. But women were not allowed to have anything to do with dairy work; only men tended the buffalo and prepared the dairy products. Women's work was very limited. Women prepared the purchased grain for cooking, cleaned house, and decorated clothing.[11] At the other extreme, among the Tchambuli of New Guinea the women contributed almost everything to the economy. They did all the fishing—going out early in the morning by canoe to their fish traps and returning when the sun was hot. Some of the fish caught was traded for sago

---

[10] Madeleine J. Goodman, P. Bion Griffin, Agnes A. Estioko-Griffin, and John S. Grove. "The Compatibility of Hunting and Mothering among the Agta Hunter-Gatherers of the Philippines." *Sex Roles*, 12 (1985): 1199–209.

[11] W. H. R. Rivers. *The Todas*. Oosterhout, N. B., The Netherlands: Anthropological Publications, 1967, p. 567. Originally published in 1906.

(a starch) and sugarcane, and it was the women who went on the long canoe trips to do the trading.[12]

A survey of a wide variety of societies has revealed that both men and women typically contribute to primary food-getting activities—but men usually contribute more.[13] Since women are almost always occupied with child-care responsibilities, it is not surprising that men usually do most of the primary food-getting work, which generally has to be done away from the home. Thus, what needs to be explained is why in some societies the women do more of this work than the men. Obviously, since hunting, fishing, and herding are male activities, in societies that depend on these types of food-getting men contribute more than women. And since gathering is primarily women's work, women contribute more than men in food-collecting societies that depend largely on gathering. But the vast majority of societies known to anthropology depend on agriculture or horticulture, and with the exception of clearing land and preparing the soil (which are usually men's tasks), the work of cultivation is by and large men's or women's work (see the *Either sex or both* column in Table 12-1). So we need some explanation of why women do most of the work in the fields in some societies and men in others. Different patterns predominate in different areas of the world. In Africa south of the Sahara, women generally do more than half the work in the fields. But in much of Asia men do more.[14]

One apparent explanatory factor is the kind of work done. Many writers have pointed out that intensive agriculture, particularly plow agriculture, is associated with a high level of male participation. In horticultural societies, in contrast, women contribute a good deal. According to Ester Boserup, when population increases and there is pressure to make more intensive use of the land, cultivators begin to use the plow and irrigation, and males start to do more.[15] But it is not quite clear why.

Why should women not continue to contribute a lot just because plows are used? One possibility is that plow agriculture involves a lot more labor input and therefore more male input. Men usually clear land anyway, but clearing is a more time-consuming process if intensive agriculture is practiced. It has been estimated that in one district in Nigeria, 100 days of work are required to clear one acre of virgin land for plowing by tractor; only 20 days are required to prepare the land for shifting cultivation. Furthermore, it has been suggested that less weeding is required in land that has been cleared and plowed. (Weeding is a highly interruptible task, and perhaps for that reason it may have been performed by women previously.)[16] But this suggestion does

[12] Margaret Mead. *Sex and Temperament in Three Primitive Societies.* New York: Mentor, 1950, pp. 180–82. Originally published in 1935.

[13] See Table 1 in Melvin Ember and Carol R. Ember, "The Conditions Favoring Matrilocal versus Patrilocal Residence," *American Anthropologist,* 73 (1971): 573.

[14] Ester Boserup. *Woman's Role in Economic Development.* New York: St. Martin's Press, 1970, pp. 22–25.

[16] Ibid., pp. 31–34.

not explain why women do relatively less of all agricultural tasks, including weeding, in societies that have the plow.[17]

Another explanation for why women contribute less than men to intensive agriculture is that household chores increase with intensive agriculture and thus limit the time women can spend in the fields. Intensive agriculturists rely more heavily on grain crops, which take much more work to make edible. Cereal grains (corn, wheat, oats) are usually dried before storing. They therefore take a long time to cook if they are left whole. More cooking requires more time to collect water and firewood (usually women's work) and more time to clean pots and utensils. A variety of techniques can reduce cooking time (such as soaking, grinding, or pounding), but the process that speeds up cooking the most—grinding—is very time-consuming (unless done by machine). Finally, household work may increase substantially with intensive agriculture because women in such societies have more children than women in horticultural societies. If household work increases in these ways, it is easy to understand why women cannot contribute more than, or as much as, men to intensive agriculture. But although women contribute relatively less than men to intensive agriculture, their contribution is nonetheless quite substantial: they seem to work outside the home four and a half hours a day, seven days a week, on the average.[18]

But we still have not explained why women contribute so much to horticulture in the first place. They may not have as much household work as intensive-agricultural women, but neither do the men. Why, then, don't men do relatively more in horticulture also? One possibility is that in horiticultural societies men are often drawn away from cultivation into other types of activities. There is evidence that if males are engaged in warfare when subsistence work has to be done, then it is the women who must take care of that work.[19] Men may also be withdrawn from subsistence work if they have to work in distant towns and cities for wages or if they periodically go on long-distance trading trips.[20]

When women contribute a lot to primary food-getting activities, we might expect their behavior and attitudes concerning children to be affected. Several cross-cultural studies suggest this expectation is correct. In societies with a high female contribution to food-getting, infants are fed solid foods earlier (which enables others besides mothers to feed them),[21] and girls are

[17] Carol R. Ember. "The Relative Decline in Women's Contribution to Agriculture with Intensification." *American Anthropologist*, 85 (1983): 286–87. Data from Murdock and Provost, "Factors in the Division of Labor by Sex," p. 212.

[18] Ember. "The Relative Decline in Women's Contribution to Agriculture with Intensification," pp. 287–93.

[19] Ember and Ember, "The Conditions Favoring Matrilocal versus Patrilocal Residence," pp. 579–80.

[20] Ibid. See also Peggy R. Sanday, "Toward a Theory of the Status of Women," *American Anthropologist*, 75 (1973): 1684.

[21] Nerlove. "Women's Workload and Infant Feeding Practices," pp. 207–14.

likely to be trained to be industrious (probably to help their mothers out).[22] Finally, girl babies are more valued in societies where women contribute a lot to food-getting.[23]

Political Leadership and Warfare.   In almost every society we know about, men rather than women are the leaders in the political arena. One cross-cultural society indicates that in approximately 85 percent of the surveyed societies, only men were leaders. In the societies in which some women occupied leadership positions, the women were either outnumbered by or less powerful than the men leaders.[24] In the arena of war, we find an almost universal dominance of males. In 88 percent of the world's societies, women never participate actively in war.[25]

Even in *matrilineal* societies, which seem to be oriented around women (see the chapter on marital residence and kinship), men usually occupy political positions. For example, among the Iroquois Indians of what is now New York State, women had control over resources and a great deal of influence. But men held political office, not women. The highest political body among the League of the Iroquois (which comprised five different tribal groups) was a council of fifty male chiefs. Although women could not serve on the council, they could nominate, elect, and impeach their male representatives. Women also could decide between life or death for prisoners of war, they could forbid the men of their households to go to war, and they could intervene to bring about peace.[26]

Why have men (at least so far) almost always dominated the political sphere of life? Some have suggested that men's role in warfare gives them the edge in all kinds of political leadership, particularly because they control weapons—an important resource.[27] But there is little evidence that force is usually used to obtain leadership positions.[28] Still, warfare may be related to political power for another reason. Since warfare clearly affects survival and since it occurs regularly in most of the societies we know about, decision making about war may be among the most important kinds of politics in most societies. If this is so, it may be advantageous to have those who know the most about warfare making decisions about it. As for why males and not females

[22] Alice Shlegel and Herbert Barry III. "The Cultural Consequences of Female Contribution to Subsistence." *American Anthropologist*, 88 (1986): 142–50.

[23] Ibid.

[24] Martin K. Whyte. "Cross-Cultural Codes Dealing with the Relative Status of Women." *Ethnology*, 17 (1978): 217.

[25] Ibid.

[26] Judith K. Brown. "Economic Organization and the Position of Women among the Iroquois." *Ethnohistory*, 17 (1970): 151–67.

[27] Peggy R. Sanday, "Female Status in the Public Domain." In Michelle Z. Rosaldo and Louise Lamphere, eds., *Woman, Culture, and Society*. Stanford, Calif.: Stanford University Press, 1974, pp. 189–206; and William T. Divale and Marvin Harris. "Population, Warfare, and the Male Supremacist Complex." *American Anthropologist*, 78 (1976): 521–38.

[28] Naomi Quinn. "Anthropological Studies on Women's Status" *Annual Review of Anthropology*, 6 (1977): 189–90.

usually engage in fighting, we may refer to three of the possible explanations of the worldwide patterns in the division of labor by sex. Warfare, like hunting, probably requires strength (for throwing weapons) and quick bursts of energy (for running). And certainly combat is one of the most dangerous and uninterruptible activities imaginable, hardly compatible with child care. Also, even if they do not at the moment have children, women may generally be kept out of combat because their potential fertility is more important to a population's reproduction and survival than their potential usefulness as warriors.[29] So, the strength theory, the compatibility theory, and the expendability theory might all explain the predominance of men in warfare.

Two other factors may be involved in male predominance in politics. One is the generally greater height of men. Why height should be a factor in leadership is unclear, but a number of studies suggest that taller persons are more likely to be leaders.[30] Finally, there is the possibility that men dominate politics because they get around more than women in the outside world. Male activities typically take them farther from home; women tend to work more around the home. If societies choose leaders at least in part because they know more about the larger world, then males will generally have some advantage. In support of this reasoning, Patricia Draper has found that in recently settled-down !Kung bands, where women no longer engaged in long-distance gathering, women seem to have lost much of their former influence in making decisions.[31] Involvement in child care may also detract from such influence. In a study of village leadership among the Kayapo of Brazil, Dennis Werner found that women with heavy child-care burdens are less influential, perhaps because they have fewer friends and miss many details of what is going on in the village.[32]

These various explanations suggest why men generally dominate politics, but we still need to explain why women participate in politics more in some societies than in others. Marc Ross has investigated this question in a cross-cultural survey of ninety societies. In that sample, the degree of female participation in politics varies considerably. For example, among the Mende of Sierra Leone women regularly hold high office, but among the Azande of Zaire women take no part in public life. Ross suggests that female political participation is lower where communities are organized around groups of

[29] Susan Brandt Graham. "Biology and Human Social Behavior: A Response to van den Berghe and Barash." *American Anthropologist*, 81 (1979): 357–60.

[30] Dennis Werner. "Chiefs and Presidents: A Comparison of Leadership Traits in the United States and among the Mekranoti-Kayapo of Central Brazil." *Ethos* 10 (1982): 136–48; and Ralph M. Stogdill. *Handbook of Leadership. A Survey of Theory and Research.* New York: Macmillan, 1974, cited in ibid. See also W. Penn Handwerker and Paul V. Crosbie, "Sex and Dominance," *American Anthropologist*, 84 (1982): 97–104.

[31] Patricia Draper. "!Kung Women: Contrasts in Sexual Egalitarianism in Foraging and Sedentary Contexts." In Rayna R. Reiter, ed., *Toward an Anthropology of Women.* New York: Monthly Review Press, 1975, p. 103.

[32] Dennis Werner. "Child Care and Influence among the Mekranoti of Central Brazil." *Sex Roles* 10 (1984): 395–404.

male kin, and higher in societies that bring up children with affection and nurturance. This last finding is consistent with the view that societies will emphasize more "female" values if both fathers and mothers are warm rather than punishing with their children; females in such societies should be more active in public life.[33]

The Relative Status of Women.   There are probably as many definitions of status as there are researchers interested in the topic. To some, the relative status of the sexes means how much importance society confers on males versus females. To others, it means how much power and authority men or women have relative to each other. And to still others, it means what kinds of rights men and women possess to do what they want to do. In any case, many social scientists are asking why the status of women appears to vary from one society to another. Why do women have few rights and little influence in some societies?

In the small Iraqi town of Daghara, for example, men and women live very separate lives. [34] In many respects, women appear to have very little status. In common with much of the Islamic world, women are in **purdah**. This means that they stay mostly in their houses and interior courtyards. If women must go out, which they can do only with male approval, they must shroud their faces and bodies in long, black cloaks. These cloaks must be worn in mixed company, even at home. In the larger social system, women are essentially excluded from political activities. Legally, they are considered to be under the authority of their fathers and husbands. Even the sexuality of women is controlled. There is strict emphasis on virginity prior to marriage. Since women are not permitted even casual conversations with strange men, the possibilities for extramarital or even premarital relationships are very slight. In contrast, hardly any sexual restrictions are imposed on men.

There are many theories about why women have relatively high or low status. One of the most common is that women's status will be high when they make substantial contributions to the subsistence economy. According to this theory, then, women should have very little status when food-getting depends largely on hunting, herding, or intensive agriculture. A second theory suggests that where warfare is especially important, men rather than women will be more valued and esteemed. A third theory suggests that where there are centralized political hierarchies, men will have higher status. The reasoning in the last theory is essentially the same as in the warfare theory—since men usually play the dominant role in political behavior, men's status should be higher wherever political behavior is more important or frequent. Finally,

[33]Marc H. Ross. "Female Political Participation: A Cross-Cultural Explanation." *American Anthropologist*, 88 (1986): 843–58.

[34]This description is based on the fieldwork of Elizabeth and Robert Fearnea (1956–1958), as reported in M. Kay Martin and Barbara Voorhies, *Female of the Species*. New York: Columbia University Press, 1975, pp. 304–31.

there is the theory that women will have higher status where kin groups and couples' place of residence after marriage are organized around women.

One of the problems in evaluating these theories is that decisions have to be made about what status means. Does it mean value? rights? influence? And do all these aspects of status vary together? Cross-cultural research by Martin Whyte suggests that they do not. For each sample society in his study, Whyte rated fifty-two different items that might be used to define the relative status of the sexes. These items include things such as which sex can inherit property, who has final authority over disciplining unmarried children, and whether the gods in the society are male, female, or both. The results of the study indicate that very few of these items are related. Therefore, Whyte concludes, we cannot talk about status as a single concept. Rather, it seems more appropriate to talk about the relative status of women in different spheres of life.[35]

Even though Whyte found no necessary connection between one aspect of status and another, he decided to ask whether some of the theories just mentioned correctly predict why some societies have many (as opposed to few) areas in which the status of women is high. The idea that generally high status derives from a greater contribution to subsistence is not supported at all.[36] As expected, women in intensive-agricultural societies (who contribute little to subsistence) tend to have lower status in many areas of life, just as in the Iraqi case described above. But in hunting societies (where women also do little of the work), women seem to have higher status—which contradicts the theoretical expectation. Similarly, there is no consistent evidence that a high frequency of warfare generally lowers women's status in different spheres of life.[37]

What does predict higher status for women in many areas of life? Although the results are not that strong, there is some support in Whyte's study for the theory that where kin groups and marital residence are organized around women, women have somewhat higher status (we discuss these features of society more fully in the chapter on marital residence and kinship). The Iroquois Indians are a good example. Even though Iroquois women could not hold political office, they had considerable authority within and beyond the household. Related women lived together in longhouses with husbands who belonged to other kin groups. In the longhouse, the women's authority was clear and they could ask objectionable men to leave. The women controlled the allocation of the food they produced. Allocation could influence the timing of war parties, since men could not undertake a raid without provisions. Women were involved in the selection of religious leaders, half of whom were women. Even in politics, where women could not speak or serve

---

[35] Martin K. Whyte. *The Status of Women in Preindustrial Societies*. Princeton, N.J.: Princeton University Press, 1978, pp. 95–120. For a similar view, see Quinn, "Anthropological Studies on Women's Status."

[36] Whyte. *The Status of Women in Preindustrial Societies*, pp. 124–29, 145. See also Sanday, "Toward a Theory of the Status of Women."

[37] Whyte. *The Status of Women in Preindustrial Societies*, pp. 124–30.

on the council, they largely controlled the selection of councilmen and could institute impeachment proceedings against those to whom they objected.[38]

Lower status for women in many areas of life appears to be associated with a number of indicators of general cultural complexity, and not just political hierarchies. Societies with social stratification, plow and irrigation agriculture, larger settlements, private property, and craft specialization also tend to have generally lower status for women. (One type of influence for women increases with cultural complexity—informal influence. But as Whyte points out, informal influence may simply reflect a lack of *real* influence.[39]) Why cultural complexity is associated with women having less authority in the home, less control over property, and more restricted sexual lives is not yet understood.

Western colonialism also appears to have been generally detrimental to women's status, perhaps because Westerners have been accustomed to dealing with men. There are plenty of examples of Europeans restructuring land ownership around men and teaching men modern farming techniques, even though women are usually the farmers. In addition, men more often than women could earn cash through wage labor or through sales of goods (such as furs) to Europeans.[40] Although the relative status of men and women may not have been equal before the Europeans arrived, colonial influences seem generally to have undermined the position of women.

We know some of the conditions that may enhance or decrease certain aspects of women's status, but we are still a long way from understanding cultural variation in the relative status of the sexes. Perhaps when researchers reorient their thinking and try to explain specific aspects of status (as opposed to status in general), the determining conditions may become clearer.

Personality

Reporting on three tribes in New Guinea, Margaret Mead said that "many, if not all, of the personality traits we have called masculine or feminine are as lightly linked to sex as are the clothing, the manners, and the form of head-dress that a society at a given period assigns to either sex.[41] In other words, she suggested that there were *no* universal or near-universal personality differences between the sexes. Rather, societies were free to create any such differences. She described the Arapesh males and females as essentially alike: both sexes were gentle, cooperative, and maternal. She also described the Mundugumor males and females as similar, but in this case both sexes exhibited violence and competitiveness. Finally, she described the Tchambuli as having

---

[38] Brown. "Economic Organization and the Position of Women among the Iroquois."
[39] Whyte. *The Status of Women*, p. 135.
[40] Quinn. "Anthropological Studies on Women's Status," p. 85. See also Mona Etienne and Eleanor Leacock, eds., *Women and Colonization: Anthropological Perspectives*, New York: Praeger, 1980, pp. 19–20.
[41] Mead. *Sex and Temperament in Three Primitive Societies*, p. 206.

substantial male-female differences in temperament, but opposite to what we might expect. The women were domineering, practical, and impersonal and were the chief economic providers; the men were sensitive and delicate and devoted their time to their appearance and to artistic pursuits.

But research conducted in recent years does not support Mead's view that there are no consistent sex differences in temperament. On the contrary, some sex differences in behavior occur consistently and in quite diverse societies. Which sex differences in personality are suggested by these more recent studies? Most of them have observed children in different cultural settings. The most consistent difference is in the area of aggression: boys try to hurt others more frequently then girls do. In an extensive comparative study of children's behavior—the Six Cultures project—this sex difference shows up as early as three to six years of age.[42] Research done in the United States agrees with the cross-cultural findings.[43] In a large number of observational and experimental studies, boys exhibited more aggression than girls.

Other sex differences have turned up with considerable consistency, but we have to be more cautious in accepting them, either because they have not been documented as well or because there are more exceptions. There seems to be a tendency for girls to exhibit more responsible behavior, including nurturance (trying to help others). Girls seem more likely to conform to adult wishes and commands. Boys try more often to exert dominance over others in order to get their own way. In play, boys and girls show a preference for their own sex. Boys seem to play in larger groups, girls in smaller ones. And boys seem to maintain more distance between each other, girls less.[44]

Assuming that these differences are consistent across cultures, how are they to be explained? Many writers and researchers believe that because certain sex differences are so consistent, they are probably rooted in the biological differences between the two sexes. Aggression is one of the traits talked about most often in this connection, particularly because this sex difference appears so early in life.[45] But an alternative argument can be made that because societies almost universally require adult males and females to perform different types of roles, they bring up boys and girls differently. And if they are brought up or socialized differently, presumably they will behave differently. Since most societies expect adult males to be warriors or to be

---

[42] Beatrice B. Whiting and Carolyn P. Edwards. "A Cross-Cultural Analysis of Sex Differences in the Behavior of Children Aged Three through Eleven." *Journal of Social Psychology*, 91 (1973): 171–88.

[43] Eleanor E. Maccoby and Carol N. Jacklin. *The Psychology of Sex Differences*. Stanford, Calif.: Stanford University Press, 1974.

[44] For a more extensive discussion of behavior differences and possible explanations of them, see Carol R. Ember, "A Cross-Cultural Perspective on Sex Differences," in Ruth H. Munroe, Robert L. Munroe, and Beatrice B. Whiting, eds., *Handbook of Cross-Cultural Human Development*, New York: Garland Press, 1981, pp. 531–80.

[45] Whiting and Edwards. "A Cross-Cultural Analysis of Sex Differences in the Behavior of Children Aged Three through Eleven."

prepared to be warriors, shouldn't we expect most societies to emphasize or idealize aggression in males? And since females are almost always the care-takers of infants, shouldn't we also expect societies generally to emphasize nurturant behaviors in females? Researchers tend to adopt either the biolog-ical or the socialization view, but it is quite possible that both kinds of causes are important in the development of sex differences. For example, parents might turn a slight genetic difference into a large sex difference by maximiz-ing that difference in the way they socialize boys versus girls.

It is difficult for researchers to distinguish the influence of genes (or other biological conditions) from the influence of socialization. We now have research indicating that as early as birth parents may treat boy and girl infants differently.[46] Moreover, in spite of the fact that objective observers can see no major "personality" differences between girl and boy infants, parents often claim to.[47] This means that parents may unconsciously want to see differences and may therefore produce them in socialization. So even early differences could be learned rather than genetic. Remember too that researchers cannot do experiments with people—for example, parents' behavior cannot be ma-nipulated to find out what would happen if boys and girls were treated in exactly the same way.

However, there is some experimental research on aggression in nonhu-man animals. These experiments suggest that the male hormone androgen may be partly responsible for higher levels of aggression. Females injected with androgen around the time the sexual organs develop behave more aggressively when they are older.[48] But even these results are not conclusive, because females who get more androgen show generally disturbed metabolic systems, and general metabolic disturbance may itself increase aggressiveness. Furthermore, androgen-injected females look more like males because they develop male genitals; therefore, they may be treated like males.

Is there any evidence that socialization differences may account for differences in aggression? Although a cross-cultural survey of ethnographers' reports on 101 societies does show that more societies encourage aggression in boys than in girls, *most* societies show no difference in aggression training.[49] The few societies that show differences in aggression training can hardly account for the widespread sex differences in actual aggressiveness. However, the survey does not necessarily mean that there are no consistent differences in aggression training for boys and girls. All it shows is that there are no

[46] For references to this research, see Ember, "A Cross-Cultural Perspective on Sex Differences," p. 559
[47] J. Z. Rubin, F. J. Provenzano, and R. F. Haskett. "The Eye of the Beholder: Parents' Views on the Sex of New Borns." *American Journal of Orthopsychiatry*, 44 (1974): 512–19.
[48] Lee Ellis. "Evidence of Neuroandrogenic Etiology of Sex Roles from a Combined Analysis of Human, Nonhuman Primate and Nonprimate Mammalian Studies." *Personality and Individual Differences*, 7 (1986): 525–27.
[49] Ronald P. Rohner. "Sex Differences in Aggression: Phylogenetic and Enculturation Perspectives." *Ethos*, 4 (1976): 57–72.

obvious differences. For all we know, the learning of aggression and other "masculine" traits by boys could be produced by subtle types of socialization.

One possible type of subtle socialization that could create sex differences in behavior is the type of chores children are assigned. It is possible that little boys and girls learn to behave differently because their parents ask them to different kinds of work. Beatrice and John Whiting report from the Six Cultures project that in societies where children were asked to do a great deal of work, they generally show more responsible and nurturant behavior. Since girls are almost always asked to do more work than boys, they may be more responsible and nurturant for this reason alone.[50] If this reasoning is correct, we should find that if boys are asked to do girls' work, they may learn to behave more like girls.

A study of Luo children in Kenya supports this view.[51] Girls were usually asked to babysit, cook, clean house, and fetch water and firewood. Boys were usually asked to do very little because boys' traditional work was herding cattle—and most families in the community studied had few cattle. But for some reason more boys than girls had been born, and many mothers without girls at home asked their sons to do girls' chores. Much of the behavior of the boys who did the girls' work was intermediary between the behavior of other boys and the behavior of girls. The boys who did the girls' work were more like girls in that they were less aggressive, less domineering, and more responsible than other boys, even when they weren't working. So it is possible that task assignment has an important influence on how boys and girls learn to behave. These and other subtle forms of socialization need to be investigated more thoroughly; research may help us to understand better the origins of sex differences in behavior.

Myths about Differences in Behavior.   Before we leave the subject of behavior differences, we should note some widespread beliefs about them that turn out to be unsupported. Some of these mistaken beliefs are that girls are more dependent than boys, that girls are more sociable, and that girls are more passive. The results obtained by the Six Cultures project cast doubt on all these notions.[52] First, if we think of dependency as seeking help and emotional support from others, girls are generally no more likely to behave this way than boys. To be sure, the results do indicate that boys and girls have somewhat different styles of dependency. Girls more often seek help and

---

[50] Beatrice B. Whiting and John W. M. Whiting (in collaboration with Richard Longabaugh). *Children of Six Cultures: A Psycho-Cultural Analysis.* Cambridge, Mass.: Harvard University Press, 1975. See also Beatrice B. Whiting and Carolyn P. Edwards, *Children of Different Worlds: The Formation of Social Behavior*, Cambridge, Mass.: Harvard University Press, 1988, p. 273.

[51] Carol R. Ember. "Feminine Task Assignment and the Social Behavior of Boys." *Ethos*, 1 (1973): 424–39.

[52] Whiting and Edwards. "A Cross-Cultural Analysis of Sex Differences in the Behavior of Children Aged Three through Eleven," pp. 175–79. See also Maccoby and Jacklin, *The Psychology of Sex Differences.*

contact; boys more often seek attention and approval. As for sociability, which means seeking and offering friendship, the Six Cultures results show no reliable differences between the sexes. Of course, boys and girls may be sociable in different ways because boys generally play in larger groups than girls. As for the supposed passivity of girls, the evidence is also not particularly convincing. Girls in the Six Cultures project do not consistently withdraw from aggressive attacks or comply with unreasonable demands. The only thing that emerges as a sex difference is that older girls are less likely than boys to respond to aggression with aggression. But this finding may not reflect passivity as much as the fact that girls are less aggressive than boys—which we already know.

So, some of our common ideas about sex differences are unfounded. Others, such as those dealing with aggression and responsibility, cannot be readily dismissed and should be investigated further.

SEXUALITY

In view of the way the human species reproduces, it is not surprising that sexuality is part of our nature. But no society we know of leaves sexuality to nature; all have at least some rules governing "proper" conduct. There is much variation from one society to another in the degree of sexual activity permitted or encouraged before marriage, outside marriage, and even within marriage. And societies vary markedly in their tolerance of nonheterosexual sexuality.

Cultural Regulation of Sexuality: Permissiveness versus Restrictiveness

All societies seek to regulate sexual activity to some degree, and there is a lot of variation cross-culturally. Some societies allow premarital sex, others forbid it. The same is true for extramarital sex. In addition, a society's degree of restrictiveness is not always consistent through the life span or for all aspects of sex. For example, quite a number of societies ease sexual restrictions somewhat in adolescence while many become more restrictive in adulthood.[53] Then, too, societies change over time. Our own society has traditionally been rather restrictive, but until recently (before the emergence of the AIDS epidemic) more permissive attitudes were gaining acceptance. A national survey of sexual behavior and attitudes conducted in the 1970s suggested that since Kinsey's surveys in the 1940s the acceptance of and actual frequency of premarital sex increased markedly. Somewhat surprisingly, attitudes toward extramarital sex did not change much: the vast majority of Americans surveyed in the 1970s still objected to it.[54] However, we must remember that

---

[53] David R. Heise. "Cultural Patterning of Sexual Socialization." *American Sociological Review*, 32 (1967): 726–39.

[54] Morton Hunt, *Sexual Behavior in the 1970s.* Chicago: Playboy Press, 1974, pp. 254–57.

Americans do not readily talk about sex, so we cannot be sure that behavior had really changed; perhaps people were only more willing to discuss their sexuality. In any case, attitudes toward sexuality may be less permissive now because of the fear of AIDS.

Premarital Sex. The degree to which sex before marriage is approved or disapproved of varies greatly from society to society. The Trobriand Islanders, for example, approve of and encourage premarital sex, seeing it as an important preparation for later marriage roles. Both boys and girls are given complete instruction in all forms of sexual expression at the onset of puberty and are allowed plenty of opportunity for intimacy. Some societies not only allow premarital sex on a casual basis, but specifically encourage trial marriages between adolescents.[55]

On the other hand, in many societies premarital sex is discouraged. For example, among the Tepoztlan Indians of Mexico, a girl's life becomes "crabbed, cribbed, confined" from the time of her first menstruation. A girl is not to speak to or encourage boys in the least way. To do so would be to court disgrace, to show herself to be crazy.[56]

Extramarital Sex. A Hopi, speaking to an ethnographer, reported,

> Next to the dance days with singing, feasting, and clown work, love-making with private wives was the greatest pleasure of my life. And for us who toil in the desert, these light affairs make life more pleasant. Even married men prefer a private wife now and then. At any rate there are times when a wife is not interested, and then a man must find someone else or live a worried life.[57]

The Hopi are not unusual. Extramarital sex is not uncommon in many societies. In about 69 percent of the world's societies men have extramarital sex more than occasionally, and in about 57 percent so do women. The frequency of such sex is higher than we might expect, given that only a slight majority of societies (54 percent) say they allow extramarital sex for men, and only a small number (11 percent) say they allow it for women.[58]

In several societies, then, there is quite a difference between the restrictive code and actual practice. The Navaho of fifty years ago were said to forbid adultery, but young married men under thirty were said to have 27 percent of their heterosexual contacts with women other than their wives.[59] And although Americans almost overwhelmingly reject extramarital sex, 41 percent of married men and about 18 percent of married women have had extramarital sex.[60] These findings fit the cross-cultural finding that most

[55] Clellan S. Ford and Frank A. Beach. *Patterns of Sexual Behavior.* New York: Harper, 1951, p. 191.

[56] Oscar Lewis. *Life in a Mexican Village: Tepoztlan Revisited.* Urbana: University of Illinois Press, 1951, p. 397.

[57] Leo W. Simmons. *Sun Chief.* New Haven: Yale University Press, 1942, p. 281.

[58] Gwen J. Broude and Sarah H. Greene. "Cross-Cultural Codes on Twenty Sexual Attitudes and Practices." *Ethnology,* 15 (1976): 409–29.

[59] Clyde Kluckhohn. "As an Anthropologist Views It." In A. Deutsch, ed., *Sex Habits of American Men.* Englewood Cliffs, N.J.: Prentice-Hall, 1948, p. 101.

[60] Hunt. *Sexual Behavior in the 1970s.*

societies have a double standard with regard to men and women: restrictions are considerably greater for the latter.[61] A substantial number of societies openly accept extramarital relationships. Among the Toda of India there was no censure of adultery. Indeed, "immorality attaches to the man who begrudges his wife to another."[62] The Chukchee of Siberia, who often traveled long distances, allowed a married man to engage in sex with his host's wife, with the understanding that he would offer the same hospitality when the host visited him.[63]

Sex within Marriage.   There is as much variety in the way coitus is performed as there is in sexual attitudes generally. Privacy is a nearly universal requirement. But whereas an American will usually find this in the bedroom, many other peoples are obliged to go out into the bush. The Siriono of Bolivia seem to have no option, for there may be as many as fifty hammocks ten feet apart in their small huts.[64] In some cultures coitus often occurs in the presence of others, who may be sleeping or simply looking the other way.

Time and frequency of coitus are also variable. Night is generally preferred, but some peoples, such as the Rucuyen of Brazil and the Yapese of the Pacific Caroline Islands, specifically opt for day. The Chenchu of India believe that a child conceived at night may be born blind. People in most societies abstain from intercourse during menstruation, during at least part of pregnancy, and for a period after childbirth. The Lesu, a people of New Ireland, an island off New Guinea, prohibit all members of the community from engaging in sex between the death of any member and burial.[65] Some societies prohibit sexual relations before various activities, such as hunting, fighting, planting, brewing, and iron smelting. Our own society is among the most lenient regarding restrictions on coitus within marriage, imposing only rather loose restraints during mourning, menstruation, and pregnancy.

Homosexuality.   The range in permissiveness or restrictiveness toward homosexual relations is as great as that for any other kind of sex. Among the Lepcha of the Himalayas, a man is believed to become homosexual if he eats the flesh of an uncastrated pig. But the Lepcha say that homosexual behavior is practically unheard of, and they view it with disgust.[66] Perhaps because many societies deny that homosexuality exists, little is known about homosexual practices in the restrictive societies. Among the permissive ones, there is variation in the pervasiveness of homosexuality. In some societies homosexuality is accepted, but limited to certain times and certain individuals. For example, among the Papago of the American Southwest

[61] Gwen J. Broude. "Extramarital Sex Norms in Cross-Cultural Perspective." *Behavior Science Research*, 15 (1980): 184.

[62] Ford and Beach. *Patterns of Sexual Behavior*, p. 113.

[63] Ibid., p. 114.

[64] Ibid., P. 69.

[65] Ibid., p. 76.

[66] John Morris. *Living with Lepchas: A Book about the Sikkim Himalayas*. London: Heinemann, 1938, p. 191.

there were "nights of saturnalia," in which homosexual tendencies could be expressed. The Papago also had many male transvestites, who wore women's clothing, did women's chores, and, if not married, could be visited by men.[67] Women did not have quite the same freedom of expression. They could participate in the saturnalia feasts only with their husband's permission, and female transvestites were nonexistent.

Homosexuality occurs even more widely in other societies. The Siwans of North Africa expect all males to engage in homosexual relations. In fact, fathers make arrangements for their unmarried sons to be given to an older man in a homosexual arrangement. Siwan custom limits a man to one boy. Fear of the government has made this a secret matter, but before 1909 such arrangements were made openly. Almost all men were reported to have engaged in a homosexual relationship as boys; later, when they were between sixteen and twenty, they married girls.[68] Among the most extremely pro-homosexual societies are the Etoro of New Guinea, who prefer homosexuality to heterosexuality. Heterosexuality is prohibited as many as 260 days a year and is forbidden in or near the house and gardens. Homosexuality, on the other hand, is not prohibited at any time and is believed to make crops flourish and boys become strong.[69]

Reasons for Restrictiveness

Before we deal with the question of why some societies may be more restrictive than others, we must first ask whether all forms of restrictiveness go together. The research to date suggests that societies that are restrictive with regard to one aspect of heterosexual sex tend to be restrictive with regard to other aspects. Thus, societies that frown on sexual expression by young children also punish premarital and extramarital sex.[70] Furthermore, such societies tend to insist on modesty in clothing and are constrained in their talk about sex.[71] But societies that are generally restrictive about heterosexuality are not necessarily restrictive about homosexuality. Societies restrictive about premarital sex are neither more nor less likely to restrict homosexuality. In the case of extramarital sex, the situation is somewhat different. Societies that have a considerable amount of male homosexuality tend to disapprove of males having extramarital heterosexual relationships.[72] If we are going to

[67] Ruth M. Underhill. *Social Organization of the Papago Indians.* New York: Columbia University Press, 1938, pp. 117, 186.

[68] Mahmud M. 'Abd Allah. "Siwan Customs." *Harvard African Studies,* 1 (1917): 7, 20.

[69] Raymond C. Kelly. "Witchcraft and Sexual Relations: An Exploration in the Social and Semantic Implications of the Structure of Belief." Paper presented at the annual meeting of the American Anthropological Association, Mexico City, 1974.

[70] Data from Robert B. Textor, comp., *A Cross-Cultural Summary,* New Haven: HRAF Press, 1967.

[71] William N. Stephens. "A Cross-Cultural Study of Modesty." *Behavior Science Research,* 7 (1972): 1–28.

[72] Gwen J. Broude. "Cross-Cultural Patterning of Some Sexual Attitudes and Practices." *Behavior Science Research,* 11 (1976): 243.

explain restrictiveness, then, it appears we have to consider heterosexual and homosexual restrictiveness separately.

Let us consider homosexual restrictiveness first. The ethnographic material indicates an extremely broad range of societal reactions to homosexual relationships. Why? Why do homosexual relationships occur more frequently in some societies, and why are some societies intolerant of such relationships? There are many psychological interpretations of why some people become interested in homosexual relationships, and many of these interpretations relate the phenomenon to early parent-child relationships. But so far the research has not yielded any clear-cut predictions, although a number of cross-cultural predictors about male homosexuality are intriguing.

One such finding is that societies forbidding abortion and infanticide for married women (most societies permit these practices for illegitimate births) are likely to be intolerant of male homosexuality. This and other findings are consistent with the point of view that homosexuality may be less tolerated when the society would like to increase its population. Such societies may be intolerant of all kinds of behaviors that minimize population growth. Homosexuality would have this effect, assuming that a higher frequency of homosexual relations is associated with a lower frequency of heterosexual relations. The less frequently heterosexual relations occur, the lower the number of conceptions there might be. Another indication that intolerance may be related to a desire for population growth is that societies with famines and severe food shortages are more likely to allow homosexuality. Famines and food shortages suggest population pressure on resources; under these conditions homosexuality and other practices that minimize population growth may be tolerated or even encouraged.[73]

Population pressure may also explain why our own society has become somewhat more tolerant of homosexuality recently. In the past our country could tolerate additional labor (including immigrants from other countries), and welcomed it. But now that our economy's growth has slowed, we may be increasingly aware that our population growth needs to be limited. Homosexuality (and the delay of marriage) might become more frequent. Of course, population pressure does not explain why certain individuals become homosexual, or why most individuals in some societies engage in such behavior, but it might explain why some societies view such behavior more or less permissively.

Turning now to heterosexual behavior, what kinds of societies are more permissive than others? Although we do not as yet understand the reasons, we do know that greater restrictiveness toward premarital sex tends to occur in

[73] Dennis Werner. "A Cross-Cultural Perspective on Theory and Research on Male Homosexuality," *Journal of Homosexuality*, 4 (1979): 345–62. See also Dennis Werner, "On the Societal Acceptance or Rejection of Male Homosexuality," M. A. thesis, Hunter College of the City University of New York, 1975, p. 36.

more complex societies—societies that have hierarchies of political officials, part-time or full-time craft specialists, cities and towns, and class stratification.[74] It may be that as social inequality increases and various groups come to have differential wealth, parents become more concerned with preventing their children from marrying "beneath them." Permissiveness toward premarital sexual relationships might lead a person to become attached to someone who would not be considered a desirable marriage partner. Even worse (from the family's point of view), such "unsuitable" sexual liaisons might result in a pregnancy that could make it impossible for a girl to marry "well." Controlling mating, then, may be a way of trying to control property.

As is apparent from our review in this chapter, the biological fact that humans depend on sexual reproduction does not by itself help us explain why the sexes differ in so many ways across cultures, or why societies vary in the way they handle male and female roles. We are only beginning to investigate these questions. When we eventually understand more about how and why the sexes are different or the same in roles, personality, and sexuality, we may be better able to decide how much we want the biology of sex to shape our lives.

SUMMARY

1. That humans reproduce sexually does not explain why males and females tend to differ in appearance and behavior, and to be treated differently, in all societies.
2. All or nearly all societies assign certain activities to males and other activities to females. These worldwide division-of-labor patterns may be explained mostly by sex differences in strength and/or by differences in compatibility of tasks with child care.
3. Perhaps because women almost always have child-care responsibilities, men in most societies do most of the primary subsistence work. But women contribute substantially to primary subsistence in societies that depend heavily on gathering and horticulture and where warfare occurs while subsistence work has to be done. In almost all societies men are the leaders in the political arena, and warfare is almost exclusively a male activity.
4. The relative status of women (compared to men) seems to vary from one area of life to another: whether women have relatively high status in one area does not necessarily indicate that they will have high status in another. However, less complex societies seem to approach more equal status for males and females in a variety of areas of life.
5. Recent field studies have suggested some consistent sex differences in personality: boys tend to be more aggressive than girls, and girls seem generally to be more responsible and helpful than boys.
6. Although all societies regulate sexual activity to some extent, societies vary considerably in the degree to which various kinds of sexuality are permitted. Some societies allow premarital sex; others do not. Some allow extramarital sex in certain situations; others forbid it generally.
7. Societies that are restrictive toward one aspect of heterosexual sex tend to be

[74] Data from Textor, comp., *A Cross-Cultural Summary.*

restrictive with regard to other aspects. And more complex societies tend to be more restrictive toward premarital heterosexual sex than less complex societies.

8. Societal attitudes toward homosexuality are not completely consistent with attitudes toward sexual relationships between the sexes. Societal tolerance of homosexuality is associated with tolerance of abortion and infanticide, and also with famines and food shortages.

13

Marriage
and Family

Whatever a society's attitudes toward male-female relationships, one such relationship is found in all societies—marriage. Why marriage is customary in every society we know of is a classic and perplexing question—and one we attempt to deal with in this chapter.

The universality of marriage does not mean that everyone in every society gets married. It means only that most (usually nearly all) people in every society get married at least once in their lifetimes. In addition, when we say that marriage is universal, we do not mean that marriage and family customs are the same in all societies. On the contrary, there is much variation from society to society in how one marries, whom one marries, and how many persons one marries. The only cultural universal about marriage is that no society permits people to marry parents, brothers, or sisters. Who belongs to the family also varies. The family often includes more individuals than parents and their immature offspring; it may include two or more related married couples and their children.

MARRIAGE

When anthropologists speak of marriage, they do not mean to imply that couples everywhere must get marriage certificates or have wedding ceremonies, as in our own society. **Marriage** merely means a socially approved sexual and economic union between a woman and a man. It is presumed, both by the couple and by others, to be more or less permanent, and it subsumes reciprocal rights and obligations between the two spouses and between spouses and their future children.[1]

It is a socially approved sexual union in that a married couple does not have to hide the sexual nature of their relationship. A woman might say "I want you to meet my husband," but she could not say "I want you to meet my lover" without causing some embarrassment in most societies. Although the union may ultimately be dissolved by divorce, couples in all societies begin marriage with some idea of permanence in mind. Implicit too in marriage are reciprocal rights and obligations. These may be more or less specific and formalized regarding matters of property, finances, and child rearing.

Marriage entails both a sexual and an economic relationship:

> Sexual unions without economic co-operation are common, and there are relationships between men and women involving a division of labor without sexual gratification, e.g., between brother and sister, master and maidservant, or employer and secretary, but marriage exists only when the economic and the sexual are united in one relationship, and this combination occurs only in marriage.[2]

Why Is Marriage Universal?

Since all societies practice male-female marriage as we have defined it, we can assume the custom is generally adaptive. But saying that does not specify exactly how it may be adaptive. Several interpretations have traditionally been offered to explain why all human societies have the custom of marriage. Each suggests that marriage solves a problem found in all societies—how to share the products of a division of labor by sex; how to care for infants, who are dependent for a long time; and how to minimize sexual competition. To evaluate the plausibility of these interpretations, we must ask whether marriage provides the best or the only reasonable solution to each problem. After all, we are trying to explain a custom that is presumably a universal solution. The comparative study of other animals, some of which have something like marriage, may help us to evaluate these explanations, as we will see.

Division of Labor by Sex.   We noted in the last chapter that every society known to anthropology had had a division of labor by sex. Males and females in every society perform different economic activities. This division of labor by sex has often been cited as a reason for marriage.[3] As long as a division of labor by sex exists, society has to have some mechanism by which men and women share the products of their labor. Marriage would be one way to solve this problem. But is marriage the only possible solution? This seems unlikely, since the hunter-gatherer rule of sharing could be extended

---

[1] William N. Stephens. *The Family in Cross-Cultural Perspective.* New York: Holt, Rinehart & Winston, 1963, p. 5.

[2] George P. Murdock. *Social Structure.* New York: Macmillan, 1949, p. 8.

[3] Murdock. *Social Structure*, pp. 7–8.

to include all the products brought in by both men and women. Or a small group of men and women (such as brothers and sisters) might be pledged to cooperate economically. Thus, although marriage may solve the problem of sharing the fruits of division of labor, it is clearly not the only possible solution.

Prolonged Infant Dependency.   Humans exhibit the longest period of infant dependency of any primate. The child's prolonged dependence generally places the greatest burden on the mother, who is the main child tender in most societies. As we saw in the previous chapter, the burden of prolonged child care by human females may limit the kinds of work they can do. They may need the help of a man to do certain types of work, such as hunting, that are incompatible with child care. Because of this prolonged dependency, it has been suggested, marriage is necessary.[4] But here the argument becomes essentially the same as the division-of-labor argument, and it has the same logical weakness. It is not clear why a group of men and women, like a hunter-gatherer band, could not cooperate in providing for dependent children without marriage.

Sexual Competition.   Unlike most other female primates, the human female is more or less continuously receptive to sexual activity. Some scholars have suggested that continuous female sexuality may have created a serious problem—considerable sexual competition between males for females. It is argued that society had to prevent such competition in order to survive—that it had to develop some way of minimizing the rivalry between males for females in order to reduce the chance of lethal and destructive conflict.[5]

There are several problems with this argument. First, why should continuous female receptivity make for more sexual competition in the first place? One might argue the other way around: there might be more competition over the scarcer resources that would be available if females were less frequently receptive. Second, in many animal species, even some that have relatively frequent female receptivity (like many of our close primate relatives), males do not show much aggression over females. Third, why couldn't sexual competition, even if it existed, be regulated by cultural rules other than marriage? For instance, society might have adopted a rule whereby men and women circulated among all the opposite-sex members of the group, each person staying a specified length of time with each partner. Such a system presumably would solve the problem of sexual competition. On the other hand, such a system might not work particularly well if individuals came to prefer certain other individuals. Jealousies attending these attachments might give rise to even more competition.

Other Mammals and Birds: Postpartum Requirements.   None of the theories we have discussed explain convincingly why marriage is the only

---

[4] Ibid., pp. 9–10.
[5] See, for example, Ralph Linton, *The Study of Man,* New York: Appleton-Century-Crofts, 1936, pp. 135–36.

or the best solution to a particular problem. Also, we now have some comparative evidence on mammals and birds that casts doubt on these interpretations.[6] How can evidence from other animals help us evaluate theories about human marriage? If we look at those animals that (like humans) have some sort of stable male-female mating, as compared with those that are completely promiscuous, we can perhaps see what sorts of factors may predict male-female bonding in the warm-blooded animal species. (Most birds, wolves, and beavers are among the other species that have "marriage.") Among forty mammal and bird species, none of the three factors discussed above—division of labor, prolonged infant dependency, or greater female sexuality—predicts or correlates strongly with male-female bonding. With respect to division of labor by sex, most other animals have nothing comparable to a humanlike division of labor, but many have stable male-female matings anyway. The two other supposed factors—prolonged infant dependency and female sexuality—predict just the opposite of what we might expect from these theories. Mammals and birds that have longer dependency periods or greater female sexuality are less likely to have stable matings.

Does anything predict male-female bonding? One factor does among mammals and birds, and it may also help explain human marriage. Animal species in which females can simultaneously feed themselves and their babies after birth (*postpartum*) tend not to have stable matings; those species where postpartum mothers cannot feed themselves and their babies at the same time tend to have more stable matings. Among the typical bird species, a mother would have difficulty feeding herself and her babies simultaneously. Since the young cannot fly for a while and must be protected in a nest, the mother risks losing them to other animals if she goes off to obtain food. But if she has a male attached to her (as the vast majority of bird species do), he can bring back food or take a turn watching the nest. Among animal species that have no postpartum feeding problem, babies almost immediately after birth are able to travel with the mother as she moves about to eat (as do grazers such as horses), or the mother can transport the babies as she moves about to eat (as do baboons and kangaroos). We think the human female has a postpartum feeding problem. When humans lost most of their body hair, babies could not readily travel with the mother by clinging to her fur. And when humans began to depend on certain kinds of food-getting that could be dangerous (such as hunting), mothers could not engage in such work with their infants along.

Even if we assume that human mothers have a postpartum feeding problem, we still have to ask if marriage is the best solution to the problem. We think so, because other conceivable solutions probably would not work as well. For example, if a mother took turns babysitting with another mother, neither might be able to collect enough food for both mothers and the two sets

[6] Melvin Ember and Carol R. Ember. "Male-Female Bonding: A Cross-Species Study of Mammals and Birds." *Behavior Science Research*, 14 (1979): 37–56.

of children dependent on them. But a mother and father share the *same* set of children, and therefore it would be easier for them to feed themselves and their children adequately. Another possible solution is no pair bonding at all, just a promiscuous group of males and females. But in that kind of arrangement, we think, a particular mother probably would not always be able to count on some male to watch her baby when she had to go out for food, or to bring her food when she had to watch her baby. Thus, it seems to us that the problem of postpartum feeding may by itself help explain why some animals (including humans) have more or less stable male-female bonds. Of course, there is still the question of whether the results of research on other animals can be applied to human beings. We think so, but not everybody will agree.

How Does One Marry?

All societies have social ways of marking the onset of marriage, but these vary considerably. Some cultures mark marriages by elaborate ceremonies; others have no ceremonies at all. In addition, many societies have various economic transactions.

Marking the Onset of Marriage. Many societies have ceremonies marking the beginning of marriage. But others use different social signals to indicate that a marriage has taken place.

Among the Taramiut Inuit (Eskimo), the betrothal is considered extremely important and is arranged between the parents at or before the time their children reach puberty. Later, when the youth is ready, he moves in with his betrothed's family for a trial period. If all goes well—that is, if the girl gives birth to a baby within a year or so—the couple are considered married. At this time, the wife goes with her husband to his camp.[7]

In keeping with the general openness of their society's attitudes toward sexual matters, a South Pacific Trobriand couple advertise their desire to marry "by sleeping together regularly, by showing themselves together in public, and by remaining with each other for long periods at a time."[8] When a girl accepts a small gift from a boy, she demonstrates that her parents favor the match. Before long, she moves to the boy's house, takes her meals there, and accompanies her husband all day. Then the word goes around that the couple are married.[9]

Among those societies that have ceremonies marking the onset of marriage, feasting is a common element. It expresses publicly the importance of two families being united by marriage. The Reindeer Tungus of Siberia set a wedding date after protracted negotiations between the two families and their larger kin groups. Go-betweens assume most of the responsibility for the negotiating. The wedding day opens with the two kin groups, probably

[7] Nelson H. Graburn. *Eskimos Without Igloos.* Boston: Little, Brown, 1969, pp. 188–200.
[8] Bronislaw Malinowski. *The Sexual Life of Savages in Northwestern Melanesia.* New York: Halcyon House, 1932, p. 77.
[9] Ibid., p. 88.

numbering as many as 150 people, pitching their lodges in separate areas and offering a great feast. After the groom's gifts have been presented, the bride's dowry is loaded onto reindeer and carried to the groom's lodge. There the climax of the ceremony takes place. The bride takes the wife's place—that is, at the right side of the entrance of the lodge—and members of both families sit in a circle. The groom enters and follows the bride around the circle, greeting each guest, while the guests, in their turn, kiss the bride on the mouth and hands. Finally, the go-betweens spit three times on the bride's hands, and the couple are formally husband and wife. More feasting and revelry bring the day to a close.[10]

In many cultures, marriage includes ceremonial expressions of hostility. Mock fights are staged in many societies, as among the Gusii of Kenya:

> Five young clansmen of the groom come to take the bride and two immediately find the girl and post themselves at her side to prevent her escape, while the others receive the final permission of her parents. When it has been granted the bride holds onto the house posts and must be dragged outside by the young men. Finally she goes along with them, crying and with her hands on her head.[11]

Such expressions of hostility usually occur in societies where the two sets of kin are actual or potential rivals or enemies. In many societies, it is common to marry women from "enemy" villages.

Economic Aspects of Marriage. "It's not man that marries maid, but field marries field, vineyard marries vineyard, cattle marry cattle." In its down-to-earth way, this German peasant saying indicates that in many societies marriage involves economic considerations. In our culture, economic considerations may not be explicit. However, a person (and his or her family) may consider how the intended spouse will benefit economically. In many other societies, one or more explicit economic transactions take place before or after the marriage. The economic transaction may take several forms, among them the following.

Bride Price. **Bride price** (or **bride wealth**) is a gift of money or goods given to the bride's kin by the groom or his kin. The gift usually grants the groom the right to marry the girl and the right to her children. In 47 percent of the societies in Murdock's *World Ethnographic Sample*, the groom's kin customarily pay a bride price; in almost all of those societies, a "substantial" bride price is paid.[12] Payment can be made in a number of different currencies; livestock and food are two of the more common.

Despite the connotations that the custom of paying a bride price may have for us, the practice does not reduce a woman to the position of slave (although it is associated, as we shall see, with relatively low status for women).

[10] Elman R. Service. *Profiles in Ethnology.* New York: Harper & Row, Pub., 1963, p. 104.

[11] Robert A. LeVine and Barbara B. LeVine. "Nyansongo: A Gusii Community in Kenya." In Beatrice B. Whiting, ed., *Six Cultures.* New York: John Wiley, 1963, p. 65.

[12] Data tabulated in Allan D. Coult and Robert W. Habenstein. *Cross Tabulations of Murdock's World Ethnographic Sample.* Columbia: University of Missouri Press, 1965.

The bride price may give considerable prestige to the woman and her family. Indeed, the fee paid can serve as a security. If the marriage fails through no fault of hers and the wife returns to her kin, the bride price might not be returned to the groom. On the other hand, the wife's kin may pressure her to remain with her husband, even though she does not wish to, because they do not want to return the bride price or are unable to do so.

What kinds of societies are likely to have the custom of bride price? As George P. Murdock indicated many years ago, bride price is likely where a newly married couple lives with or near the husband's parents.[13] This pattern of postmarital residence, which we discuss more fully in the next chapter, removes the bride from her kin. Bride price is also likely where women work harder than men (counting all kinds of work), and where men make most of the decisions in the household.[14] This last finding is consistent with the theory, discussed in the chapter on sex and culture, that women have relatively low status where kin groups and marital residence are organized around men (bride price is common in such societies).

Bride Service.   About 14 percent of the 565 societies in the *World Ethnographic Sample* have the custom of **bride service**. Bride service requires the groom to work for his bride's family, sometimes before the marriage begins, sometimes after. Bride service varies in duration. In some societies it lasts for only a few months; in others it lasts as long as several years.

Exchange of Females.   Only nineteen societies (about 3 percent of those listed) in the *World Ethnographic Sample* have the custom whereby a sister or female relative of the groom is exchanged for the bride.

Gift Exchange.   This marriage custom is reported for twelve societies (about 2 percent) in Murdock's sample. It involves the exchange of gifts of about equal value by the two kin groups about to be linked by marriage.

Dowry.   A **dowry** is a substantial transfer of goods or money from the bride's family to the bride, the groom, or the groom's family. Most often the gifts go to the bride.[15] Only 4 percent of the societies in Murdock's sample offer dowries. Yet the custom is still practiced in parts of eastern Europe and in sections of southern Italy and France, where land is often the major item provided by the bride's family. Parts of India also practice the dowry.

Dowry is likely when the society has a higher level of economic development, herds animals, and does not allow a man to be married simultaneously to more than one woman.[16] Dowry is almost always found in relatively complex, but not industrialized, societies.

---

[13] Murdock. *Social Science*, p. 20.

[14] Frederic L. Pryor. *The Origins of the Economy: A Comparative Study of Distribution in Primitive and Peasant Economies.* New York: Academic Press, 1977, pp. 363–64.

[15] Jack Goody and S. J. Tambiah. *Bridewealth and Dowry.* Cambridge: Cambridge University Press, 1973, p. 2.

[16] Pryor. *The Origins of the Economy.* pp. 363–65.

Restrictions on Marriage:
The Universal Incest Taboo

Hollywood and its press agents notwithstanding, marriage is not always based solely on mutual love, independently discovered and expressed by the two life partners-to-be. Nor is it based on sex alone. But even where love and sex are contributing factors, regulations specify whom one may or may not marry. Perhaps the most rigid regulation, found in *all* cultures, is the incest taboo.

The **incest taboo** is the prohibition of sexual intercourse or marriage between mother and son, father and daughter, and brother and sister. No society we know of has generally permitted either sexual intercourse or marriage between those pairs. However, there have been a few societies in which incest was permitted within the royal family (though generally forbidden to the rest of the population). The Incan and Hawaiian royal families were two such exceptions, but probably the most famous example was provided by Cleopatra of Egypt.

It seems clear that the Egyptian aristocracy and royalty indulged in father-daughter and brother-sister marriages. (Cleopatra was married to two of her younger brothers at different times.)[17] The reasons seem to have been partly religious—a member of the family of Pharaoh, who was a god, could not marry any "ordinary" human—and partly economic, for marriage within the family kept the royal property undivided.

Why is the incest taboo universal? A number of explanations have been suggested.

Childhood-Familiarity Theory. This explanation, suggested by Edward Westermarck, was given a wide hearing in the early 1920s. Westermarck argued that people who have been closely associated with each other since earliest childhood, such as siblings, are not sexually attracted to each other.[18] This theory was initially rejected because there was evidence that some children *were* sexually interested in their parents and siblings. However, some studies have suggested that there may be something to Westermarck's theory.

Yonina Talmon investigated marriage patterns among the second generation of three well-established collective communities (*kibbutzim*) in Israel. In these collectives, children live with many members of their peer group in quarters separate from their families. They are in constant interaction with their peers, from birth to maturity. The study revealed that among 125 couples, there was "not one instance in which both mates were reared from birth in the same peer group,"[19] despite parental encouragement of marriage within the peer group. Children reared in common not only avoided marriage, they also avoided any sexual relations among themselves.

---

[17] Russell Middleton. "Brother-Sister and Father-Daughter Marriage in Ancient Egypt." *American Sociological Review*, 27 (1962): 606.

[18] Edward Westermarck. *The History of Human Marriage.* London: Macmillan, 1894.

[19] Yonina Talmon. "Mate Selection in Collective Settlements." *American Sociological Review.* 29 (1964): 492.

Talmon tells us that the people reared together firmly believe that overfamiliarity breeds sexual disinterest. As one of them told her, "We are like an open book to each other. We have read the story in the book over and over again and know all about it."[20] Talmon's evidence reveals not only the onset of disinterest and even sexual antipathy among children reared together, but a correspondingly heightened fascination with newcomers or outsiders, particularly for their "mystery."

Arthur Wolf's study of the Chinese in northern Taiwan also supports the idea that something about being reared together produces sexual disinterest. Wolf focused on a community still practicing the Chinese custom of *t'ung-yang-hsi,* or "daughter-in-law raised from childhood."

> When a girl is born in a poor family . . . she is often given away or sold when but a few weeks or months old, or one or two years old, to be the future wife of a son in the family of a friend or relative which has a little son not betrothed in marriage. . . . The girl is called a "little bride" and taken home and brought up in the family together with her future husband.[21]

Wolf's evidence indicates that this arrangement is associated with sexual difficulties when the childhood "couple" later marry. Informants implied that familiarity results in disinterest and lack of stimulation. As an indication of their disinterest, these couples produce fewer offspring than spouses not raised together, they are more likely to seek extramarital sexual relationships, and they are more likely to get divorced.[22]

The Talmon and Wolf studies suggest, then, that children raised together are not likely to be sexually interested in each other when they grow up. Such disinterest is consistent with Westermarck's notion that the incest taboo may be more an avoidance of certain matings than a prohibition of them. There is one other piece of evidence consistent with his explanation of the incest taboo. Hilda and Seymour Parker recently compared two samples of fathers: those who had sexually abused their daughters and those who supposedly had not.[23] (To maximize their similarities otherwise, the Parkers selected both samples of fathers from the same prisons and psychiatric facilities.) The Parkers found that the fathers who had committed incest with their daughters were much more likely than the other sample of fathers to have had little to do with bringing up their daughters, because they were not at home or hardly at home during the daughters' first three years of life. In other words, the fathers who avoided incest had been more closely associated with their daughters in childhood, which again is consistent with Wester-

[20] Ibid., p. 504.
[21] Arthur Wolf. "Adopt a Daughter-in-Law, Marry a Sister: A Chinese Solution to the Problem of the Incest Taboo." *American Anthropologist,* 70 (1968): 864.
[22] Arthur P. Wolf and Chieh-shan Huang. *Marriage and Adoption in China,* 1845–1945. Stanford, Calif.: Stanford University Press, 1980, pp. 159, 170, 185.
[23] Hilda Parker and Seymour Parker. "Father-Daughter Sexual Abuse: An Emerging Perspective." *American Journal of Orthopsychiatry,* 56 (1986): 531–49.

marck's suggestion that the incest taboo may be result of familiarity in child-hood.

Even if there is something about familiarity in childhood that normally leads to sexual disinterest,[24] we are still left with the question of why societies generally prohibit incest. If disinterest as a result of childhood familiarity were the only factor involved, why should societies generally have to prohibit parent-child and brother-sister marriages?

Freud's Psychoanalytic Theory.   Sigmund Freud proposed that the incest taboo is a reaction against unconscious, unacceptable desires.[25] He suggested that the son is attracted to his mother (as the daughter is to her father), and as a result feels jealousy and hostility toward his father. But the son knows these feelings cannot continue, for they might lead the father to retaliate against him; therefore, they must be renounced or repressed. Usu-ally the feelings are repressed and retreat into the unconscious. But the desire to possess the mother continues to exist in the unconscious, and according to Freud, the horror of incest is a reaction to, or a defense against, the forbidden unconscious impulse. Although Freud's theory may account for the aversion felt toward incest, or at least the aversion toward parent-child incest, it does not explain why society needs an explicit taboo. Nor does it account for why parents should not be interested in committing incest with their children

Family-Disruption Theory.   This theory, often associated with Bron-islaw Malinowski,[26] can best be summed up as follows: sexual competition among family members would create so much rivalry and tension that the family could not function as an effective unit. Since the family must function effectively for society to survive, society has to curtail competition within the family. The incest taboo is thus imposed to keep the family intact.

But there are inconsistencies in this approach. Society could have shaped other rules about the sexual access of one member of the family to another that would also eliminate potentially disruptive competition. Also, why would brother-sister incest be so disruptive? As we noted, such marriages did exist in ancient Egypt. Brother-sister incest would not disrupt the authority of the parents if the children were allowed to marry when mature. The family-disruption theory, then, does not seem to explain the origin of the incest taboo.

Cooperation Theory.   This theory was proposed by the early anthro-pologist Edward B. Tylor and was elaborated by Leslie A. White and Claude Lévi-Strauss. It emphasizes the value of the incest taboo in promoting cooper-

---

[24] For a discussion of mechanisms that might lead to sexual aversion, see Seymour Parker, "The Precultural Basis of the Incest Taboo: Toward a Biosocial Theory," *American Anthropologist,* 78 (1976): 285–305. Also see Seymour Parker, "Cultural Rules, Rituals, and Behavior Regulation," *American Anthropologist,* 86 (1984): 584–600.

[25] Sigmund Freud. *A General Introduction to Psychoanalysis.* Garden City, N.Y.: Garden City Publish-ing Co., 1943. Originally published in German in 1917.

[26] Bronislaw Malinowski. *Sex and Repression in Savage Society.* London: Kegan Paul, Trench, Trubner & Co., 1927.

ation among family groups and thus helping communities to survive. As Tylor sees it, certain operations necessary for the welfare of the community can be accomplished only by large numbers of people working together. In order to break down suspicion and hostility between family groups and make such cooperation possible, early humans developed the incest taboo to ensure that individuals would marry members of other families. The ties created by intermarriage would serve to hold the community together. Thus, Tylor explains the incest taboo as an answer to the choice "between marrying out and being killed out."[27]

Although there may well be advantages to marriage outside the family, is the incest taboo necessary to promote cooperation with outside groups? For example, couldn't families have required some of their members to marry outside the family if they thought it necessary to survival, but permitted incestuous marriages when such alliances were not needed? Thus, although the incest taboo might enhance cooperation between families, the need for cooperation does not adequately explain the existence of the incest taboo in all societies, since other customs might also promote alliances. Furthermore, the cooperation theory does not explain the sexual aspect of the incest taboo. Societies could conceivably allow incestuous sex and still insist that children marry outside the family.

Inbreeding Theory.   This theory focuses on the potentially damaging consequences of inbreeding, or marrying within the family. People within the same family are likely to carry the same harmful recessive genes. Inbreeding, then, will tend to produce offspring who are more likely to die early of genetic disorders than the offspring of unrelated spouses. For many years this theory was rejected because it was thought that inbreeding need not be harmful. After all, it seems not to have produced defective offspring among the Hawaiian, Incan, and Egyptian royal lineages, if Cleopatra can be taken as an example. However, we now have a good deal of evidence, from humans as well as animals, that inbreeding is generally harmful.[28]

Genes that arise by mutation are usually harmful and recessive, and therefore the offspring of close relatives may inherit a double, and possibly lethal, dose of a recessive gene. A group of behavioral scientists has suggested that for species with widely spaced births and few offspring, natural selection would favor a mechanism that prevents inbreeding. Inbreeding is probably particularly harmful among animals (such as humans) that produce few offspring at a time, since such species can ill afford many unnecessary deaths. (Animal breeders sometimes obtain beneficial effects with inbreeding, but they usually do not care about the death rate or high risk of defective offspring.)

---

[27] Quoted in Leslie A. White, *The Science of Culture: A Study of Man and Civilization,* New York: Farrar, Straus, & Cudahy, 1949, p. 313.
[28] Curt Stern. *Principles of Human Genetics,* 3rd ed. San Francisco: W. H. Freeman & Company Publishers, 1973, pp. 494–95.

In humans, therefore, natural selection may have favored groups with the incest taboo—a cultural prohibition—since they would have had higher reproductive rates than groups without the taboo.[29] Whether or not people actually recognized the harmfulness of inbreeding, the demographic consequences of the incest taboo may account for its universality, since reproductive and hence competitive advantages probably accrued to groups practicing the taboo. Thus, although cultural solutions other than the incest taboo might provide the desired effect assumed by the family-disruption theory and the cooperation theory, the incest taboo is the only possible solution to the problem of inbreeding.[30]

Whom Should One Marry?

Probably every child in our society knows the story of Cinderella—the poor, downtrodden, but lovely girl who accidentally meets, falls in love with, and eventually marries a prince. It is a charming tale, but as a guide to mate choice in our society it is quite misleading. The majority of marriages simply do not occur in so free and coincidental a way in any society. Aside from the incest taboo, societies often have rules restricting marriage with other persons, as well as preferences about which other persons are the most desirable mates.

Even in a modern, urbanized society such as ours, where mate choice is theoretically free, people tend to marry within their own geographical area and class. For example, American studies consistently indicate that a person is likely to marry someone who lives close.[31] Since neighborhoods are frequently made up of people from similar class backgrounds, it is unlikely that many of these alliances were Cinderella stories.

Arranged Marriages.   In an appreciable number of societies, marriages are arranged: negotiations are handled by the immediate families or by go-betweens. Sometimes betrothals are completed while the future partners are still children. This was formerly the custom in much of Hindu India, China, Japan, and eastern and southern Europe. Implicit in the arranged marriage is the conviction that the joining together of two kin groups to form new social and economic ties is too important to be left to free choice and romantic love.

Exogamy and Endogamy.   Marriage partners often must be chosen from *outside* one's own kin group or community; this is known as a rule of **exogamy**. Exogamy can take many forms. It may mean marrying outside a

---

[29] David F. Aberle et al. "The Incest Taboo and the Mating Patterns of Animals." *American Anthropologist,* 65 (1963): 253–65.

[30] A mathematical model of early mating systems suggests that people may have noticed the harmful effects of inbreeding, once populations began to expand as a result of agriculture; people may therefore have deliberately adopted the incest taboo to solve the problem of inbreeding. See Melvin Ember, "On the Origin and Extension of the Incest Taboo," *Behavior Science Research,* 10 (1975): 249–81.

[31] William J. Goode. *The Family,* 2nd ed. Englewood Cliffs, N.J.: Prentice-Hall, 1982, pp. 61–62.

particular group of kin or outside a particular village or group of villages. Often, then, spouses come from quite a distance.

A rule of **endogamy** obliges a person to marry *within* a group or community. The caste groups of India have traditionally been endogamous. The higher castes believed that marriage with lower castes would "pollute" them, and such unions were forbidden.

Cousin Marriages. Our kinship terminology does not differentiate between types of cousins. In other societies such distinctions are of great significance, particularly with regard to first cousins, because they indicate which cousins are suitable marriage partners (or, in some cases, which cousins are preferred mates) and which are not. Some societies allow, or even prefer, marriage with a cross-cousin but prohibit marriage with a parallel cousin. Moslem societies usually prefer marriage with a parallel cousin and allow marriage with a cross-cousin. Most societies, however, prohibit marriage with all types of first cousins.[32]

Cross-cousins are children of siblings of the opposite sex; that is, a person's cross-cousins are father's sisters' children and mothers' brothers' children. **Parallel cousins** are children of siblings of the same sex; a person's parallel cousins, then, are father's brothers' children and mother's sisters' children. The Chippewa Indians used to practice cross-cousin marriage, as well as cross-cousin joking. With his female cross-cousins, a Chippewa man was expected to exchange broad, risqué jokes, but he would not do so with his parallel cousins, with whom severe propriety was the rule. Generally, in any society in which cross-cousin marriage is allowed but parallel-cousin is not, there is a joking relationship between a man and his female cross-cousins. This attitude contrasts with the formal and very respectful relationship the man maintains with female parallel cousins. Apparently, the joking relationship signifies the possibility of marriage, whereas the respectful relationship signifies the extension of the incest taboo to parallel cousins.

What kinds of societies allow or prefer first-cousin marriage? One cross-cultural study has presented evidence that cousin marriages are more apt to be permitted in relatively densely populated societies. Perhaps this is because the likelihood of such marriages, and therefore the risks of inbreeding, are minimal in those societies. However, many small, sparsely populated societies permit or even sometimes prefer cousin marriage. How can these cases be explained? They seem to cast doubt on the interpretation that cousin marriage should generally be prohibited in sparsely populated societies, where marriages between close relatives are more likely just by chance and where the risks of inbreeding should be greatest. It turns out that most of the small societies permitting cousin marriage have recently lost a lot of people to epidemics. Many peoples around the world, particularly in the Pacific and in North and South America, suffered severe depopulation in the first genera-

---

[32] See Table 3 in Ember, "On the Origin and Extension of the Incest Taboo," p. 262.

tion or two after contact with Europeans because they had no genetic resistance to diseases such as measles, pneumonia, and smallpox. It may be that such societies had to permit cousin marriage in order to provide enough mating possibilities among the reduced population of eligible mates.[33]

Levirate and Sororate. In many societies, cultural rules oblige individuals to marry the spouse of deceased relatives. **Levirate** is a custom whereby a man is obliged to marry his brother's widow. **Sororate** obliges a woman to marry her deceased sister's husband. Both customs are exceedingly common, being the obligatory form of second marriage in a majority of societies.[34]

Among the Chukchee of Siberia, levirate obliges the next oldest brother to become the successor husband. He cares for the widow and children, assumes the sexual privileges of the husband, and unites the deceased's reindeer herd with his own, keeping it in the name of his brother's children. If there are no brothers, the widow is married to a cousin of her first husband. Generally, the Chukchee regard the custom more as a duty than as a right. The nearest relative is obliged to care for a woman left with children and a herd.[35]

How Many Does One Marry?

We are accustomed to thinking of marriage as involving just one man and one woman at a time (**monogamy**), but most societies in the world allow a man to be married to more than one woman at the same time (**polygyny**). Polygyny's mirror image—one woman being married to more than one man at the same time (**polyandry**)—is practiced in very few societies. Polygyny and polyandry are the two types of **polygamy**, or plural marriage. **Group marriage**, in which more than one man is married to more than one woman at the same time, sometimes occurs but is not generally customary in any known society.

Monogamy. There was a time when Westerners seriously believed monogamy was the end product of civilization. Polygyny was considered base and uncivilized. However, monogamy is not necessarily a hallmark of civilization, nor is polygyny a sign of barbarism.

Only about one quarter of the 565 societies in Murdock's *World Ethnographic Sample* are strictly monogamous in the sense of permitting no other form of marriage. At any given moment, however, the majority of adults in societies permitting polygyny are married monogamously. Few or no societies have enough women to permit most men to have at least two wives.

Polygyny. Although it is not permitted in Western and other highly industrialized societies, polygyny is found in many societies throughout the world. Murdock's *World Ethnographic Sample* reports that over 70 percent of societies allow it, and there is ample evidence for its existence in our own

[33] Ibid., pp. 260–69.
[34] Murdock. *Social Structure*, p. 29.
[35] Waldemar Bogoras. "The Chukchee," pt. 3. *Memoirs of the American Museum of Natural History*, 2 (1909). Cited in Stephens, *The Family in Cross-Cultural Perspective, p. 195.*

TABLE 13-1 Four possible forms of marriage

Form of Marriage		Males	Females
Monogamy		△	= ○
Polygyny ⎫ Polygamy		△	= ○ + ○ + ...
Polyandry ⎭		△ + △ + ...	= ○
Group marriage		△ + △ + ...	= ○ + ○ + ...

△, represents male; ○, female; and =, marriage.

cultural background. The Old Testament has many references to it: King David and King Solomon are just two examples of men polygynously married.

In many societies polygyny is a mark of a man's great wealth or high status. In such societies only the very wealthy can, and are expected to, support a number of wives. Some Islamic societies, especially Arabic-speaking ones, still view polygyny in this light. However, in groups where women are important contributors to the economy, greater wealth may be obtained by having more than one wife.

Although jealousy among co-wives is generally a problem in polygynous societies, it seems to be lessened if one man is married to two or more sisters (**sororal polygyny**). It seems that sisters, having grown up together, are more likely to get along and cooperate as co-wives than are co-wives who are not also sisters (**nonsororal polygyny**). Polygynous societies often have the following customs or rules, which presumably lessen jealousy among co-wives:

1. Co-wives who are not sisters tend to have separate living quarters; sororal co-wives almost always live together.
2. Co-wives have clearly defined equal rights in matters of sex, economics, and personal possessions.
3. Senior wives often have special prestige. Although this rule might seem to enhance the jealousy of the secondary wives, later wives are usually favored somewhat because they tend to be younger and more attractive. By this custom, then, the first wife may be compensated for her loss of physical attractiveness by increased prestige.[36]

A potential for discord and jealousy exists not only among a man's wives but among his children as well. Not surprisingly, the emotional ties between child and mother are deeper than those between child and father, and the resentment of a co-wife toward her younger counterpart may also be felt by her children. If the children of one wife seem to be receiving favored treatment from their father, rivalry may develop among the other siblings.

In view of the problems that seem to accompany polygyny, how can we account for the fact that it is allowed in most of the societies known to

[36] The discussion of these customs is based on Stephens, *The Family in Cross-Cultural Perspective*, pp. 63–67.

anthropology? Linton suggested that polygyny derives from the general primate urge to collect females.[37] But if that were so, then why wouldn't all societies allow polygyny? A number of other explanations of polygyny have been suggested. We restrict our discussion here to those that statistically predict polygyny in worldwide samples of societies.

One theory is that polygyny will be permitted in societies that have a long **postpartum sex taboo.**[38] In these societies, a couple must abstain from intercourse until their child is at least a year old. John Whiting suggests that couples may abstain from sexual intercourse for a long time after birth for health reasons. A Hausa woman reported that

> a mother should not go to her husband while she has a child she is suckling. If she does, the child gets thin; he dries up, he won't be strong, he won't be healthy. If she goes after two years it is nothing, he is already strong before that, it does not matter if she conceives again after two years.[39]

The baby's illness in the first case seems to be *kwashiorkor*. Common in tropical areas, kwashiorkor is a protein-deficiency disease that seems to occur particularly in children suffering from intestinal parasites or diarrhea. By observing a long postpartum sex taboo, and thereby being sure her children are widely spaced, a woman can nurse each child longer. If a child gets protein from mother's milk during its first few years, the likelihood of contracting kwashiorkor may be greatly reduced. Consistent with Whiting's interpretation is the fact that societies with low-protein staples (those whose principal foods are root and tree crops such as taro, sweet potatoes, bananas, and breadfruit) tend to have a long postpartum sex taboo. Societies with long postpartum sex taboos also tend to be polygynous. Perhaps, then, a man's having more than one wife is a cultural adjustment to the taboo. As a Yoruba woman said,

> When we abstain from having sexual intercourse with our husband for the 2 years we nurse our babies, we know he will seek some other woman. We would rather have her under our control as a co-wife so he is not spending money outside the family.[40]

Although men might seek other sexual relationships during the period of a long postpartum sex taboo, it is not clear why polygyny is the only way to do so. After all, it is conceivable that all a man's wives might be subject to the postpartum sex taboo at the same time. Furthermore, there may be sexual outlets outside marriage.

Another explanation of polygyny is that it may be a response to an excess of women over men. Such an imbalanced sex ratio may occur because of the

[37] Linton. *The Study of Man*, p. 183.
[38] J. W. M. Whiting. "Effects of Climate on Certain Cultural Practices." In Ward H. Goodenough, ed., *Explorations in Cultural Anthropology*. New York: McGraw-Hill, 1964, pp. 511–44.
[39] Quoted in ibid., p. 518.
[40] Quoted in ibid., pp. 516–17.

prevalence of warfare in a society. Since men and not women are generally the warriors, warfare almost always takes a greater toll of men's lives. Given that almost all adults are married in noncommercial societies, polygyny may be a way of providing spouses for surplus women. Indeed, there is some evidence that societies with imbalanced sex ratios in favor of women tend to have both polygyny and high male mortality in warfare. Conversely, societies with balanced sex ratios tend to have both monogamy and low male mortality in warfare.[41]

A third explanation is that a society will allow polygyny when men marry at an older age than women. The argument is similar to the sex ratio interpretation. Delaying the age of marriage for men would produce an artificial, though not an actual, excess of marriageable women. Why marriage for men is delayed is not clear, but the delay does predict polygyny.[42]

Is one of these explanations better than the others, or are all three factors (long postpartum sex taboo, an imbalanced sex ratio in favor of women, and delayed age of marriage for men) important in explaining polygyny? One way of trying to decide among alternative explanations is to do what is called a statistical-control analysis, which allows us to see if a particular factor still predicts when the effects of other possible factors are removed. In this case, when the possible effect of sex ratio is removed, a long postpartum sex taboo no longer predicts polygyny and hence is probably not a cause of polygyny.[43] But both an actual excess of women and a late age of marriage for men seem to be strong predictors of polygyny. Added together, these two factors predict even more strongly.[44]

Polyandry. Murdock's *World Ethnographic Sample* includes only four societies (less than 1 percent of the total) where polyandry, or the marriage of several men to one woman, is practiced. Polyandry can be **fraternal** (when the husbands are brothers) or **nonfraternal**.

Some Tibetans, the Toda of India, and the Sinhalese of Sri Lanka have practiced fraternal polyandry. Marriage arrangements are quite unambiguous: the wife of one brother is accepted as the wife of all the brothers in a family, even a brother who is born after the wedding itself. For the Toda, paternity does not reside with the biological father (whom anthropologists refer to by the Latin term ***genitor***) but with the socially recognized father

[41] Melvin Ember. "Warfare, Sex Ratio, and Polygyny." *Ethnology*, 13 (1974): 197–206.
[42] Melvin Ember. "Alternative Predictors of Polygyny." *Behavior Science Research*, 19 (1984–1985): 1–23. The statistical relationship between late age of marriage for men and polygyny was first reported by Stanley R. Witkowski, "Polygyny, Age of Marriage, and Female Status," paper presented at the annual meeting of the American Anthropological Association, San Francisco, 1975.
[43] Ember. "Warfare, Sex Ratio, and Polygyny," pp. 202–5.
[44] Ember. "Alternative Predictors of Polygyny," For other predictors of polygyny, see Douglas R. White and Michael L. Burton, "Causes of Polygyny: Ecology, Economy, Kinship, and Warfare," *American Anthropologist*, 90 (1988): 871–87.

(Latin, **pater**), whose status is confirmed with a ceremony in the seventh month of the wife's pregnancy. Generally, the family lives in the same dwelling, but in Tibet each husband has his own room if the household is sufficiently wealthy. The men decide when their wife will visit each of them.

One possible explanation for polyandry is a shortage of women. The Toda and Tibetans practiced female infanticide;[45] the Sinhalese had a shortage of women but denied the practice of female infanticide.[46] If this explanation is correct, it would account for why polyandry is so rare, since an excess of men is exceedingly rare cross-culturally.

Another explanation, specific to Tibet, suggests that polyandry was a response to political and economic conditions among a certain class of serfs. These serfs were allocated a fixed amount of agricultural land by their lords, and the land could be passed on to their sons. It has been suggested that these serfs practiced polyandry as a way of preventing partition of a family's corporate lands. Rather than divide a small parcel of land between them, brothers married one woman and kept the land and household undivided. Those Tibetan groups with more land (the lords) and those with noninheritable land or no land did not practice polyandry.[47]

THE FAMILY

Although family form varies from one society to another and even within societies, all societies have families. A **family** is a social and economic unit consisting minimally of one or more parents and their children. Members of a family always have certain reciprocal rights and obligations toward each other, particularly economic ones. Family members usually live in one household, but common residence is not a defining feature of families. In our society, children may live away while they go to college. Some members of a family may deliberately set up separate households in order to work in different places.[48] In simpler societies, the family and the household tend to be indistinguishable; it is only in more complex societies, and in societies becoming dependent on commercial exchange, that some members of a family may live elsewhere.[49]

---

[45] Stephens. *The Family in Cross-Cultural Perspective*, p. 45.

[46] L. R. Hiatt. "Polyandry in Sri Lanka: A Test Case for Parental Investment Theory." *Man*, 15 (1980): 583–98.

[47] Melvyn C. Goldstein. "Stratification, Polyandry, and Family Structure in Central Tibet." *Southwestern Journal of Anthropology*, 27 (1971): 65–74.

[48] For example, see Myron Cohen, "Variations in Complexity among Chinese Family Groups: The Impact of Modernization," *Transactions of the New York Academy of Sciences*, 29 (1967): 638–44; and Myron Cohen, "Developmental Process in the Chinese Domestic Group," in Maurice Freedman, ed., *Family and Kinship in Chinese Society*, Stanford, Calif.: Stanford University Press, 1970.

[49] Burton Pasternak, *Introduction to Kinship and Social Organization*, Englewood Cliffs, N.J.: Prentice-Hall, 1976, p. 96.

Variation in Family Form

There are variations in the form of the family from society to society, and within societies. Most societies have families that are larger than the single-parent family (the parent is usually the mother, in which case the unit is called the **matrifocal family**), the monogamous (single-couple) family (called the **nuclear family**), or the polygamous (usually polygynous) family. The **extended family** is the prevailing form of family in more than half the societies known to anthropology.[50] It consists of two or more single-parent, monogamous, polygynous, or polyandrous families linked by a blood tie. The extended family consists most commonly of a married couple and one or more of the married children, all living in the same house or household. The constituent nuclear families are linked through the parent-child tie. However, an extended family is sometimes composed of families linked through a sibling tie. Such a family might consist of two married brothers, their wives, and their children. Extended families may be quite large, containing many nuclear families and including three generations.

Extended-Family Households. In a society composed of extended-family households, marriage does not bring as pronounced a change in life style as it does in our culture, where the couple typically move to a new residence and form a new, and basically independent, family unit. In extended families, the newlyweds are assimilated into an existing family unit. Margaret Mead describes such a situation in Samoa:

> In most marriages there is no sense of setting up a new and separate establishment. The change is felt in the change of residence for either husband or wife and in the reciprocal relations which spring up between the two families. But the young couple live in the main household, simply receiving a bamboo pillow, a mosquito net and a pile of mats for their bed. . . . The wife works with all the women of the household and waits on all the men. The husband shares the enterprises of the other men and boys. Neither in personal service given or received are the two marked off as a unit.[51]

The extended family is more likely than the independent nuclear family to perpetuate itself as a social unit. In contrast with the independent nuclear family, which by definition disintegrates with the death of the senior members (the parents), the extended family is always adding junior families (monogamous and/or polygamous), whose members eventually become the senior members when their elders die.

Possible Reasons for Extended-Family Households. Why do most societies known to anthropology commonly have extended-family households, whereas other societies typically do not? Since extended-family house-

[50] Coult and Habenstein. *Cross Tabulations of Murdock's World Ethnographic Sample.*
[51] Margaret Mead. *Coming of Age in Samoa.* New York: Morrow, 1928. Quoted in Stephens, *The Family in Cross-Cultural Perspective*, pp. 134–35.

holds are found more frequently in societies with sedentary agricultural economies, economic factors may play a role in determining household type. Nimkoff and Middleton have pointed out some features of agricultural life, as opposed to hunting-gathering life, that may help explain the prevalence of extended families among agriculturalists. The extended family may be a social mechanism that prevents the economically ruinous division of family property in societies where property such as cultivated land is important. Conversely, the need for mobility in hunter-gatherer societies may make extended-family households less likely in such economies. During certain seasons, the hunter-gatherers may be obliged to divide into nuclear families that scatter into other areas.[52]

But agriculture is only a weak predictor of extended-family households. Many agriculturalists lack them, and many nonagricultural societies have them. A different theory is that extended-family households come to prevail in societies that have incompatible activity requirements—that is, requirements that cannot be met by a mother or a father in a one-family household. In other words, the suggestion is that extended-family households are generally favored when the work a mother has to do outside the home (cultivating fields or gathering foods far away) makes it difficult for her to also care for her children and do other household tasks, or when the required outside activities of a father (warfare, trading trips, or wage labor far away) make it difficult for him to do his subsistence work. There is cross-cultural evidence that societies with such incompatible activity requirements are more likely to have extended-family households than societies with compatible activity requirements, regardless of whether the society is agricultural. However, even though they have incompatible activity requirements, societies with commercial or monetary exchange may not have extended family households. In commercial societies, a family may be able to obtain the necessary help by "buying" the required service.[53]

Of course, even in societies with money economies, not everyone can buy required services. Those who are poor may need to live in extended families, and extended-family living may become more common even in the middle class when the economy is depressed. As a 1983 article in a popular magazine noted,

> Whatever happened to the all-American nuclear family—Mom, Pop, two kids and a cuddly dog, nestled under one cozy, mortgaged roof? What happened was an economic squeeze: layoffs, fewer jobs for young people, more working mothers, a shortage of affordable housing and a high cost of living. Those factors, along with a rising divorce rate, a trend toward later marriages and an

---

[52] M. F. Nimkoff and Russell Middleton. "Types of Family and Types of Economy." *American Journal of Sociology,* 66 (1960): 215–25.

[53] Burton Pasternak, Carol R. Ember, and Melvin Ember. "On the Conditions Favoring Extended Family Households." *Journal of Anthropological Research,* 32 (1976): 109–23.

increase in the over sixty-five population, all hitting at once, are forcing thousands of Americans into living in multigenerational families.[54]

In many societies there are kin groups even larger than extended families. The next chapter discusses the varieties of such groupings.

SUMMARY

1. All societies known today have the custom of marriage. Marriage is a socially approved sexual and economic union between a man and a woman that is presumed to be more or less permanent, and that subsumes reciprocal rights and obligations between the two spouses and between the spouses and their children.
2. The way marriage is socially recognized varies greatly: it may involve an elaborate ceremony or none at all. Variations include childhood betrothals, trial-marriage periods, feasting, and the birth of a baby.
3. Marriage arrangements often include an economic element. The most common form is the bride price, in which the groom or his family gives an agreed-upon amount of money or goods to the bride's family. Bride service exists when the groom works for the bride's family for a specified period. In some societies, a female from the groom's family is exchanged for the bride; in others, gifts are exchanged between the two families. A dowry is a payment of goods or money by the bride's family to the bride, the groom, or the groom's family.
4. No society generally allows sex or marriage between brothers and sisters, mothers and sons, or fathers and daughters.
5. Every society tells people whom they cannot marry, whom they can marry, and sometimes even whom they should marry. In quite a few societies, marriages are arranged by the couple's kin groups. Implicit in arranged marriages is the conviction that the joining of two kin groups to form new social and economic ties is too important to be left to free choice and romantic love. Some societies have rules of exogamy, which require marriage outside one's own kin group or community; others have rules of endogamy, requiring marriage within one's group. Although most societies prohibit all first-cousin marriages, some permit or prefer marriage with cross-cousins (children of siblings of the opposite sex) and parallel cousins (children of siblings of the same sex). Many societies have customs providing for the remarriage of widowed persons. Levirate is a custom whereby a man marries his brother's widow. Sororate is the practice of a woman marrying her deceased sister's husband.
6. We think of marriage as involving just one man and one woman at a time (monogamy), but most societies allow a man to be married to more than one woman at a time (polygyny). Polyandry—the marriage of one woman to several husbands—is very rare.
7. The prevailing form of family in most societies is the extended family. It consists of two or more single-parent, monogamous (nuclear), polygynous, or polyandrous families linked by blood ties.

---

[54] Jean Libman Block. "Help! They've *All* Moved Back Home!" *Woman's Day*, April 26, 1983, pp. 72–76.

14

Marital Residence and Kinship

In American society, and in many other industrial societies, a young man and woman usually establish a place of residence apart from their parents or other relatives when they marry, if they had not already moved away before. Our society is so oriented toward this pattern of marital residence—*neolocal* (new-place) *residence*—that it seems to be the obvious and natural one to follow. Upper-income families in the United States, perhaps because they are financially able, begin earlier than other parents to train their children to live away from home by sending them to boarding schools at age thirteen or fourteen. In the army or at an out-of-town college, young adults learn to live away from home most of the year, yet return home for vacations. In any case, when a young person marries, he or she generally lives apart from family.

So familiar is neolocal residence to us that we tend to assume all societies practice the same pattern. On the contrary, of the 565 societies in Murdock's *World Ethnographic Sample*, only about 5 percent follow this practice.[1] About 95 percent of the world's societies have some pattern of residence whereby a new couple settles within, or very close to, the household of the parents or some other close relative of either the groom or the bride. When married couples live near kin, it stands to reason that kinship relationships will figure promi-

[1] Allan D. Coult and Robert W. Habenstein. *Cross Tabulations of Murdock's World Ethnographic Sample*. Columbia: University of Missouri Press, 1965.

nently in the social life of the society. Marital residence largely predicts the types of kin groups found in a society, as well as how people refer to and classify their various relatives.

As we will see, kin groups that include several or many families and hundreds or even thousands of people are found in many societies and structure many areas of social life. Kin groups may have important economic, social, political, and religious functions.

PATTERNS OF MARITAL RESIDENCE

In societies in which newly married couples customarily live with or close to their kin, several residence patterns may be established. Since children in all societies are required to marry outside the nuclear family (because of the incest taboo), and since couples in almost all societies live together after they are married (with a few exceptions),[2] it is not possible for an entire society to practice a system in which all married offspring reside with their own parents. Some children, then, have to leave home when they marry. But which married children remain at home and which reside elsewhere? Societies vary in the way they deal with this question, but there are not that many different patterns. Actually, only four occur with any sizable frequency:

1. **Patrilocal residence:** the son stays and the daughter leaves, so that the married couple lives with or near the husband's parents (67 percent of all societies).
2. **Matrilocal residence:** the daughter stays and the son leaves, so that the married couple lives with or near the wife's parents (15 percent of all societies).
3. **Bilocal residence:** either the son or the daughter leaves, so that the married couple lives with or near either the wife's or the husband's parents (7 percent of all societies).
4. **Avunculocal residence:** both son and daughter normally leave, but the son and his wife settle with or near his mother's brother (4 percent of all societies).[3]

In these definitions, we use the phrase "the married couple lives *with or near*" a particular set of in-laws. We should point out that when couples live with or near the kin of a spouse, the couple may live in the same household with those kin, creating an *extended-family* household, or they may live separately in an *independent-family* household, but nearby.

A fifth pattern of residence, of course, is neolocal, in which the newly married couple does not live with or near kin.

5. **Neolocal residence:** both son and daughter leave; married couples live apart from the relatives of either spouse (5 percent of all societies).

[2] The very few societies in which married couples live apart, each with his or her own kin, practice a *duolocal* (two-place) pattern of residence.
[3] Percentages calculated from Coult and Habenstein, *Cross Tabulations of Murdock's World Ethnographic Sample.*

How does place of residence for the couple affect their social life? Because the pattern of residence governs with whom or near whom individuals live, it largely determines the people those individuals interact with and the people they have to depend upon. If a married couple is surrounded by the kin of the husband, for example, the chances are that those relatives will figure importantly in the couple's entire future. Whether the couple lives with or near the husband's or the wife's kin can also be expected to have important consequences for the status of the husband or wife. If married couples live patrilocally, as occurs in most societies, the wife may be far from her own kin. In any case, she will be an outsider among a group of male relatives who have grown up together. The feeling of being an outsider is particularly strong when the wife has moved into a patrilocal extended-family household.

A somewhat different situation exists if the husband comes to live with or near his wife's parents. Here, the wife and her kin take on somewhat greater importance, and the husband is the outsider. As we shall see, however, the matrilocal situation is not quite the mirror image of the patrilocal, since in matrilocal societies the husband's kin are often not far away. Moreover, even though residence is matrilocal, women often do not have as much to say in decision making as their brothers do.

If the married couple does not live with or near the parents or close kin of either spouse, the situation is again quite different. Here, we would hardly be surprised to find that relatives and kinship connections do not figure very largely in everyday life.

EXPLANATIONS OF VARIATION IN RESIDENCE

A number of questions can be raised as to why different societies have different patterns of residence. First, since in most societies married couples live with or near kin (as in patrilocal, matrilocal, bilocal, or avunculocal residence), why in some societies, such as our own, do couples typically live apart from kin? And among the societies where couples live with or near kin, why do most choose the husband's side (patrilocal residence) and some the wife's side (matrilocal residence)? Why do some nonneolocal societies allow a married couple to go to either the wife's or the husband's kin (bilocal residence), whereas most others do not generally allow a choice? (Because matrilocal, patrilocal, and avunculocal residence each specify just one pattern, they are often called nonoptional or **unilocal** patterns of residence.)

Neolocal Residence

Why in some societies do couples live separately from kin, whereas in most societies couples live near, if not with, kin? Many anthropologists have suggested that neolocal residence is somehow related to the presence of a money or commercial economy. They argue that when people can sell their labor or their products for money, they can buy what they need to live, without having to depend on kin. Since money is not perishable (unlike crops and other foods in a world largely lacking refrigeration), it can be stored for exchange at a later time. Thus, a money-earning family can resort to its own savings during periods of unemployment or disability (or it might be able to rely on monetary aid from the government, as in our own society). This is impossible in non-money economies, where people must depend on relatives for food and other necessities if for some reason they cannot provide their own.

There is some cross-cultural evidence to support this interpretation. Neolocal residence tends to occur in societies with monetary or commercial exchange, whereas societies without money tend to have patterns of residence that locate a couple near or with kin.[4] The presence of money, then, appears to be related to neolocal residence: money, seems to *allow* a couple to live on their own. But why couples, when given money, should *prefer* to live on their own is not yet completely understood.

Matrilocal versus Patrilocal Residence

Why in some societies does a married couple live with the husband's parents, and in others with the wife's parents? Traditionally, it has been assumed that in those societies where married children live near or with kin, residence will tend to be patrilocal if males contribute more to the economy and matrilocal if women contribute more. However plausible this assumption may seem, the cross-cultural evidence does not support it. Where men do most of the subsistence work, residence is no more likely to be patrilocal than matrilocal. Conversely, where women do an equal amount or more of the subsistence work, residence is no more likely to be matrilocal than patrilocal.[5]

We can predict whether residence will be matrilocal or patrilocal from the type of warfare practiced in a society. In most societies known to anthropology, neighboring communities or districts are often enemies. The type of warfare that breaks out periodically between such groups may be called internal, since the fighting occurs between groups speaking the same language. In other societies, the warfare is never within the same society, but only with other language groups. This pattern of warfare is referred to as purely external. Cross-cultural evidence suggests that in societies where warfare is at least sometimes internal, residence is almost always patrilocal rather than matrilocal. In contrast, residence is almost always matrilocal when warfare is purely external.[6]

[4] Melvin Ember. "The Emergence of Neolocal Residence." *Transactions of the New York Academy of Sciences*, 30 (1967): 291–302.

[5] Melvin Ember and Carol R. Ember. "The Conditions Favoring Matrilocal versus Patrilocal Residence." *American Anthropologist*, 73 (1971): 571–94. See also William T. Divale, "Migration, External Warfare, and Matrilocal Residence," *Behavior Science Research*, 9 (1974): 75–133.

[6] Ember and Ember. "The Conditions Favoring Matrilocal versus Patrilocal Residence," pp. 583–85; and Divale. "Migration, External Warfare, and Matrilocal Residence," p. 100.

How can we explain this relationship between type of warfare and matrilocal versus patrilocal residence? One theory is that patrilocal residence tends to occur with internal warfare because there may be concern over keeping sons close to home to help with defense. Since women do not usually constitute the fighting force in any society, having sons reside at home after marriage might be favored as a means of maintaining a loyal and quickly mobilized fighting force in case of surprise attack from nearby. However, if warfare is purely external, people may not be so concerned about keeping their sons at home because families need not fear attack from neighboring communities or districts.

With purely external warfare, then, residence may be determined by other considerations, especially economic ones. If in societies with purely external warfare the women do most of the work, families might want their daughters to remain at home after marriage; so the pattern of residence might become matrilocal. (If warfare is purely external but men still do more of the work, residence should still be patrilocal.) Thus, the need to keep sons at home after marriage when there is internal warfare may take precedence over any considerations based on division of labor. It is perhaps only when internal warfare is nonexistent that a female-dominant division of labor may give rise to matrilocal residence.[7]

Bilocal Residence

In societies that practice bilocal residence, a married couple goes to live with or near either the husband's or the wife's parents. Although this pattern seems to involve a choice for the married couple, theory and research suggest that bilocal residence may occur out of necessity. Elman Service has suggested that bilocal residence is likely to occur in societies that have recently suffered a severe and drastic loss of population because of the introduction of new infectious diseases.[8] Over the last 400 years, contact with Europeans in many parts of the world has resulted in severe population losses among non-European societies that lacked resistance to the Europeans' diseases. If couples need to live with some set of kin in order to make a living in noncommercial societies, it seems likely that couples in depopulated, noncommercial societies might have to live with whichever spouse's parents (and other relatives) are still alive. This interpretation seems to be supported by the cross-cultural evidence. Recently depopulated societies tend to have bilocal residence or frequent departures from unilocality, whereas societies that are

---

[7] Ember and Ember. "The Conditions Favoring Matrilocal versus Patrilocal Residence." For a different theory—that matrilocal residence precedes, rather than follows, the development of purely external warfare—see Divale, "Migration, External Warfare, and Matrilocal Residence."

[8] Elman R. Service. *Primitive Social Organization: An Evolutionary Perspective.* New York: Random House. 1962, p. 137.

not recently depopulated tend to have one pattern or another of unilocal residence.[9]

In hunter-gatherer societies, a few other circumstances may also favor bilocal residence. Bilocality tends to be found among those hunter-gatherers who have very small bands or unpredictable and low rainfall. Residential "choice" in these cases may be a question of adjusting marital residence to where the couple will have the best chance to survive or to find close relatives to live and work with.[10]

THE STRUCTURE OF KINSHIP

In noncommercial societies, kinship connections structure many areas of social life—from the kind of access an individual has to productive resources to the kind of political alliances formed between communities and larger territorial groups. In some societies, in fact, kinship connections have an important bearing on matters of life and death.

Recall the social system described in Shakespeare's *Romeo and Juliet*. The Capulets and the Montagues were groups of kin engaged in lethal competition with each other, and the fatal outcome of Romeo and Juliet's romance was related to that competition. Although Romeo and Juliet's society had a commercial economy (but not, of course, an industrialized one), the political system of the city they lived in was a reflection of the way kinship was structured. Sets of kin of common descent lived together, and the various kin groups competed (and sometimes fought) for a prominent, or at least secure, place in the political hierarchy of the city-state.

If a preindustrial commercial society could be so structured by kinship, we can imagine how much more important kinship connections and kin groups are in many noncommercial societies that lack political mechanisms such as princes and councils of lords to keep the peace and initiate other activities on behalf of the community. It is no wonder that anthropologists often speak of the web of kinship as providing the main structure of social action in noncommercial societies.

If kinship is important, there is still the question of which set of kin a person affiliates with and depends on. After all, if every single relative were counted as equally important, there would be an unmanageably large number of people in each person's kinship network. Consequently, in most societies where kinship connections are important, rules allocate each person to a particular and definable set of kin.

[9] Carol R. Ember and Melvin Ember. "The Conditions Favoring Multilocal Residence." *Southwestern Journal of Anthropology*, 28 (1972): 382–400.

[10] Carol R. Ember. "Residential Variation among Hunter-Gatherers." *Behavior Science Research*, 9 (1975): 135–49.

Rules of Descent

Rules that connect individuals with particular sets of kin because of known or presumed common ancestry are called **rules of descent**. By the particular rule of descent operating in their society, individuals can know more or less immediately which set of kin to turn to for support and help.

There are only a few known rules of descent that affiliate individuals with different sets of kin:

1. **Patrilineal descent** (the most frequent rule) affiliates an individual with kin of both sexes related to him or her *through men only*. As Figure 14-1 indicates, in patrilineal systems the children in each generation belong to the kin group of their father; their father, in turn, belongs to the group of his father; and so on. Although a man's sons and daughters are all members of the same descent group, affiliation with that group is transmitted only by the sons to their children.

2. **Matrilineal descent** affiliates an individual with kin of both sexes related to him or her *through women only*. In each generation, then, children belong to the kin group of their mother (see Figure 14-2). Although a woman's sons and daughters are all members of the same descent group, only her daughters can pass on their descent affiliation to their children.

3. **Ambilineal descent** affiliates an individual with kin related to him or her through men *or* women. In other words, some people in the society affiliate with a group of kin through their fathers; others, through their mothers. Consequently, the descent groups show both female and male genealogical links, as illustrated in Figure 14-3.

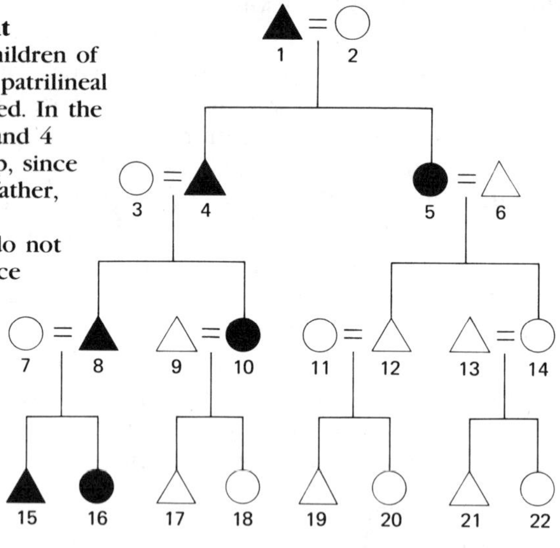

FIGURE 14-1   Patrilineal Descent

Individuals 4 and 5, who are the children of 1 and 2, affiliate with their father's patrilineal kin group, represented by the shaded. In the next generation, the children of 3 and 4 also belong to the shaded kin group, since they take their descent from their father, who is a member of that group. However, the children of 5 and 6 do not belong to this patrilineal group, since they take their descent from their father, who is a member of a different group. That is, although the mother of 12 and 14 belongs to the shaded patrilineal group, she cannot pass on her descent affiliation to her children, and since her husband (6) does not belong to her patrilineage, her children (12 and 14) belong to their father's group. In the fourth generation, only 15 and 16 belong to the shaded patrilineal group, since their father is the only male member of the preceding generation who belongs to the shaded patrilineal group. In this diagram, then, 1, 4, 5, 8, 10, 15, and 16 are affiliated by patrilineal descent; all the other individuals belong to other patrilineal groups.

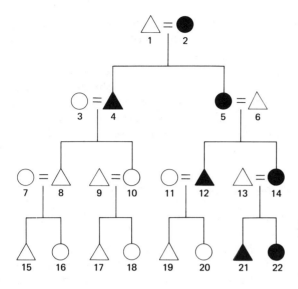

FIGURE 14-2   Matrilineal Descent

Individuals 4 and 5, who are the children 1 and 2, affiliate with their mother's kin group, represented by shading. In the next generation, the children of 5 and 6 also belong to the shaded kin group since they take their descent from their mother, who is a member of that group. However, the children of 3 and 4 do not belong to this matrilineal group since they take their descent from their mother, who is a member of a different group; their father, although a member of the shaded matrilineal group, cannot pass his affiliation on to them under the rule of matrilineal descent. In the fourth generation, only 21 and 22 belong to the shaded matrilineal group, since their mother is the only female member of the preceding generation who belongs. Thus, individuals 2, 4, 5, 12, 14, 21, and 22 belong to the same matrilineal group. This rule of descent generates a group that is almost a mirror image of the group generated by a patrilineal rule.

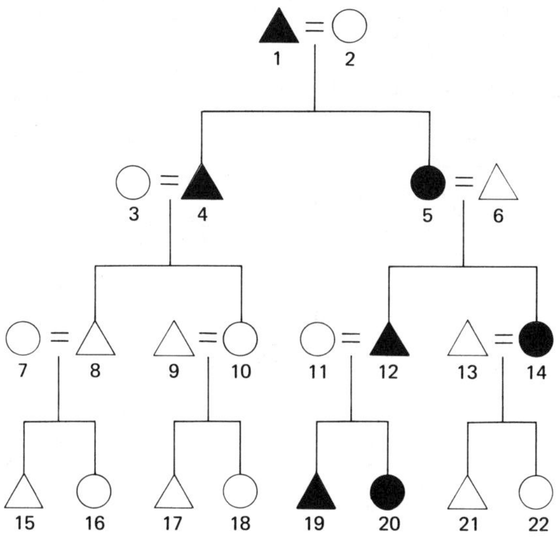

FIGURE 14-3   Ambilineal Descent

A hypothetical ambilineal group of kin is indicated by solid black. Members 4 and 5 belong to this group because of a male link, their father (1); members 12 and 14 belong because of a female link, their mother (5); and members 19 and 20 belong because of a male link, their father (12). This is a hypothetical example because any combination of lineal links is possible in an ambilineal descent group.

These three rules are usually, but not always, mutually exclusive. Most societies can be characterized as having only one rule of descent, but sometimes two principles are used to affiliate individuals with different sets of kin for different purposes. Some societies have then what is called **double descent**, or **double unilineal descent**, whereby an individual affiliates for some purposes with a group of matrilineal kin and for other purposes with a group of patrilineal kin. Thus, two rules of descent, each traced through links of one sex only, are operative at the same time. Other combinations also occur. A society may have matrilineal and ambilineal groups or patrilineal and ambilineal groups.

Bilateral Kinship

Many societies, including our own, do not have lineal (matrilineal, patrilineal, or ambilineal) descent groups—sets of kin who believe they descend from a common ancestor. They are therefore called **bilateral** societies. *Bilateral* means "two-sided," and here it refers to the fact that one's relatives on both mother's and father's sides are generally equal in importance or (more usually) in unimportance. Kinship reckoning in bilateral societies does not refer to common descent, but rather is horizontal (see Figure 14-4), moving outward from close to more distant relatives, rather than upward to common ancestors.

FIGURE 14-4 Bilateral Kinship
In a bilateral system the kindred is ego-centered; hence, it varies with different points of reference (except for brothers and sisters). In any bilateral society, the kindred minimally includes parents, grandparents, aunts, uncles, and first cousins. So, if we look at the close kindred of the brother and sister 20 and 21 (enclosed by the solid line), it would include their parents (9 and 10), their aunts and uncles (7, 8, 11, 12), their grandparents (1, 2, 3, 4) and their first cousins (16-19, 22-25). But the kindred of the brother and sister 24 and 25 (shown by the dotted line) includes only some of the same people (3, 4, 10-12, 20-23); in addition, the kindred of 24 and 25 includes people not in the kindred of 20 and 21 (5, 6, 13-15, 26-29).

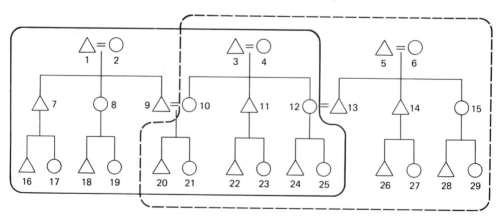

The term **kindred** describes a person's bilateral set of relatives who may be called upon for some purpose. In our society, we think of the kindred as including the people we might invite to weddings, funerals, or some other ceremonial occasion; the kindred, however, is not usually a definite group. As anyone who has been involved in the planning of a wedding-invitation list knows, a great deal of time may be spent deciding which relatives ought to be invited and which ones can legitimately be excluded. Societies with bilateral kinship differ in precisely how distant relatives have to be before they are lost track of or before they are not included in ceremonial activities. In societies such as our own, in which kinship is relatively unimportant, fewer relatives are included in the kindred. In other bilateral societies, however, where kinship connections are somewhat more important, more would be included.

The distinctiveness of bilateral kinship is that aside from brothers and sisters, no two persons belong to exactly the same kin group. Your kindred contains close relatives spreading out on both your father's and mother's sides, but the members of your kindred are affiliated only by way of their connection to you. Thus, the kindred is an *ego-centered* group of kin. Since different people (except for brothers and sisters) have different mothers and fathers, your first cousins will have different kindreds, and even your own children will have a different kindred from yours. It is the ego-centered nature of the kindred that makes it difficult for it to act as a permanent or persistent group. The only thing the people in a kindred have in common is the **ego** who brings it together. The kindred usually has no name, no common purpose, and only temporary meetings centered around ego.[11] Furthermore, since everyone belongs to many different and overlapping kindreds, the society is not divided into clear-cut groups.

Unilineal Descent

Both matrilineal and patrilineal rules of descent are **unilineal** rules, in that a person is affiliated with a group of kin though descent links of one sex only—either males or females only. Unilineal rules of descent affiliate an individual with a line of kin extending back in time and into the future. By virtue of this line of descent (whether it extends though males or females), some very close relatives are excluded. For example, in a patrilineal system, your mother and your mother's parents do not belong to your patrilineal group, but your father and his father (and their sisters) do. In your own generation in a matrilineal or patrilineal system, some cousins are excluded, and in your children's generation, some of your nieces and nephews are excluded.

However, although unilineal rules of descent exclude certain relatives from membership in one's kin group (just as practical considerations restrict the effective size of kinship networks in our own society), the excluded

[11] J. D. Freeman. "On the Concept of the Kindred." *Journal of the Royal Anthropological Institute*, 91 (1961): 192–220.

relatives are not necessarily ignored or forgotten. Indeed, in many unilineal societies they may be entrusted with important responsibilities. For example, when a person dies in a patrilineal society, some members of his or her mother's patrilineal descent group may customarily be accorded the right to perform certain rituals at the funeral.

Unlike bilateral kinship, unilineal rules of descent can form clear-cut, and hence unambiguous, groups of kin, which can act as separate units even after the death of individual members. Referring again to Figures 14-1 and 14-2, we can see that the individuals in the shaded groups belong to the same patrilineal or matrilineal descent group without ambiguity—an individual in the fourth generation belongs to the group just as much as one in the first generation. If we imagine that the patrilineal group, for instance, has a name, say the Hawks, then an individual knows immediately whether or not he or she is a Hawk. If the individual is not a Hawk, then he or she belongs to some other group—for each person belongs to only one line.

This fact is important if kin groups are to act as separate or nonoverlapping units. It is difficult for people to act together unless they know exactly who should get together. And it is easier for individuals to act together as a group if each one belongs to only one such group or line. Recall that in a bilateral system, not only is it sometimes unclear where the boundary of the kindred is, but one person belongs to many different kindreds—one's own and others' (children's, cousins', and so forth). Consequently, it is not surprising that a kindred only gets together temporarily for ceremonial occasions.

Types of Unilineal Descent Groups.   In a society with unilineal descent, people usually refer to themselves as belonging to a particular unilineal group or set of groups because they believe they share common descent in either the male line (patrilineal) or the female line (matrilineal). These people form what is called a *unilineal descent group.* Several types of unilineal descent groups are distinguished by anthropologists: lineages, clans, phratries, and moieties.

Lineages.   A **lineage** is a set of kin whose members trace descent from a common ancestor through known links. There may be **patrilineages** or **matrilineages**, depending, of course, on whether the links are traced through males only or through females only. Lineages are often designated by the name of the common ancestor or ancestress. In some societies, people belong to a hierarchy of lineages. That is, they first trace their descent back to the ancestor of a minor lineage, then to the ancestor of a larger and more inclusive major lineage, and so on.

Clans.   A **clan** (also called a **sib**) is a set of kin whose members believe themselves to be descended from a common ancestor or ancestress, but the links back to that ancestor are not specified. In fact, the common ancestor may not even be known. Clans with patrilineal descent are called **patriclans**; clans with matrilineal descent are called **matriclans**. Clans are often designated by an animal or plant name (called a **totem**), which may have some special significance for the group, and at the very least provides a means of group identification. Thus, if someone says he or she belongs to the Bear, Wolf, or Turtle group, for example, others will know whether or not that person is a clan member.

Although it may seem strange to us that an animal or plant should be a symbol of a kin group, animals as symbols of groups are familiar in our own culture. Football and baseball teams, for example, are often named for animals (Detroit Tigers, Los Angeles Rams, Philadelphia Eagles, Atlanta Falcons). Voluntary associations, such as men's clubs, are sometimes called by the name of an animal (Elks, Moose, Lions). Entire nations may be represented by an animal; we speak, for instance, of the American Eagle, the British Lion and the Russian Bear.[12]

Phratries.   A **phratry** is a unilineal descent group composed of a number of supposedly related clans or sibs. As with clans, the descent links in phratries are unspecified.

Moieties.   When a whole society is divided into two unilineal descent groups, we call each group a **moiety**. (The word *moiety* comes from a French word meaning "half.") The people in each moiety believe themselves to be descended from a common ancestor, although they cannot specify how. Societies with moiety systems usually have relatively small populations (less than 9000). Societies with phratries and clans tend to be larger.[13]

Combinations.   Although we have distinguished several different types of unilineal descent groups, we do not wish to imply that all unilineal societies have only one type of descent group. Many societies have two or more types in various combinations. For example, some societies have lineages and clans; others may have clans and phratries but no lineages; and still others may have clans and moieties but neither phratries nor lineages. Aside from the fact that a society that has phratries must also have clans (since phratries are combinations of clans), all combinations of descent groups are possible. Even if societies have more than one type of unilineal kin group—for example, lineages and clans—there is no ambiguity about membership: small groups are simply subsets of larger units. The larger units just include people who say they are unilineally related further back in time.

Patrilineal Organization.   Patrilineal organization is the most frequent type of descent system. The Kapauku Papuans, a people living in the central highlands of western New Guinea, are an example of a patrilineal society with many types of descent groups.[14] The hierarchy of groups to which Kapauku are affiliated by virtue of the patrilineal descent system plays an extremely important part in their lives. Every Kapauku belongs to a patri-

---

[12] George P. Murdock. *Social Structure*. New York: Macmillan, 1949, pp. 49–50.

[13] Carol R. Ember, Melvin Ember, and Burton Pasternak. "On the Development of Unilineal Descent." *Journal of Anthropological Research*, 30 (1974): 84–89.

[14] Leopold Pospisil. *The Kapauku Papuans of West New Guinea*. New York: Rinehart & Winston, 1963.

lineage, to a patriclan that includes his or her lineage, and to a patriphratry that includes his or her clan.

The male members of a patrilineage—all the living males who can trace their actual relationship through males to a common ancestor—constitute the male population of a single village or, more likely, a series of adjoining villages. In other words, the lineage is a *territorial* unit. The male members of the lineage live together by virtue of a patrilocal rule of residence and a fairly stable settlement pattern. A son stays near his parents and brings his wife to live in or near his father's house; the daughters leave home and go to live with their husbands. If the lineage is large, it may be divided into sublineages composed of people who trace their descent from one of the sons of the lineage ancestor. The male members of a sublineage live in a contiguous block within the larger lineage territory.

The Kapauku also belong to larger and more inclusive patrilineal descent groups—clans and phratries. All the people of the same clan believe they are related to each other in the father's line, but they are unable to say how they are related. If a member of the patriclan eats the clan's plant or animal totem, it is believed that the person will become deaf. A Kapauku is also forbidden to marry anyone from his or her clan. In other words, the clan is exogamous.

Unlike the members of the patrilineage, the male members of the patriclan do not all live together. Thus, the lineage is the largest group of patrilineal kinsmen that is localized. The lineage is also the largest group of kinsmen that acts together politically. Among clan members there is no mechanism for resolving disputes, and members of the same patriclan (who belong to different lineages) may even go to war with one another.

The most inclusive patrilineal descent group among the Kapauku is the phratry, each of which is composed of two or more clans. The Kapauku believe that the phratry was originally one clan, but that in a conflict between brothers of the founding family the younger brother was expelled and formed a new clan. The two resulting clans are, of course, viewed as patrilineally related, since their founders are said to have been brothers. The members of a phratry observe all the totemic taboos of the clans that belong to that phratry. However, although intermarriage of members of the same clan is forbidden, members of the same phratry but of different clans may marry.

The Kapauku, then, are an example of a unilineal society with many types of descent groups. They have lineages with demonstrated kinship links and two kinds of descent groups with unknown descent links (clans and phratries).

Matrilineal Organization. Although societies with matrilineal descent seem in many respects like mirror images of their patrilineal counterparts, there is one important way in which they differ. That difference has to do with who exercises authority. In patrilineal systems, descent affiliation is transmitted through males, and it is also the males who exercise authority.

Consequently, in the patrilineal system, lines of descent and of authority converge. In a matrilineal system, however, although the line of descent passes through females, females rarely exercise authority in their kin groups—usually males do. Thus, the lines of authority and descent do not converge.[15] Since males exercise authority in the kin group, an individual's mother's brother becomes an important authority figure, because he is the individual's closest male matrilineal relative in the parental generation. The individual's father does not belong to the individual's own matrilineal kin group and thus has no say in kin-group matters.

The divergence of authority and descent in a matrilineal system has some effect on community organization and marriage. Most matrilineal societies practice matrilocal residence. Daughters stay at home after marriage and bring their husbands to live with them; sons leave home to join their wives. But the sons who are required to leave will be the ones who eventually exercise authority in their kin groups. This presents a problem. The solution that seems to have been arrived at in most matrilineal societies is that although the males move away to live with their wives, they usually do not move too far away—indeed, they often marry women who live in the same village. Thus, matrilineal societies tend not to be locally exogamous—that is, members often marry people from inside the village—whereas patrilineal societies are often locally exogamous.[16]

The matrilineal organization on Truk, a group of small islands in the Pacific, illustrates the general pattern of authority in matrilineal systems.[17] The Trukese have both matrilineages and matriclans. The matrilineage is a property-owning group whose members trace descent from a known common ancestor (ancestress) in the female line. The female lineage members and their husbands occupy a cluster of houses on the matrilineage's land. The property of the lineage group is administered by the oldest brother of the group. He allocates the productive property of his matrilineage and directs the work of the members. The oldest brother of the lineage also represents the group in dealings with the district chief and all outsiders, and he must be consulted on any matter that affects the group. There is also a senior woman of the lineage who exercises some authority, but only insofar as the activities of the women are concerned. She may supervise the women's cooperative work (they usually work separately from the men) and manage the household.

Although there are some differences between patrilineal and matrilineal systems, there are many similarities. In both types of systems there may be

---

[15] David M. Schneider. "The Distinctive Features of Matrilineal Descent Groups." In David M. Schneider and Kathleen Gough, eds., *Matrilineal Kinship*. Berkeley: University of California Press, 1961, pp. 1–35.

[16] Ember and Ember. "The Conditions Favoring Matrilocal vesus Patrilocal Residence," p. 581.

[17] David M. Schneider. "Truk." In Schneider and Gough, eds., *Matrilineal Kinship*, pp. 202–33; and Ward H. Goodenough. *Property, Kin, and Community on Truk*. New Haven: Yale University Press, 1951.

lineages, clans, phratries, moieties, and any combination of these. These kin groups, in either matrilineal or patrilineal societies, may perform any number of functions. They may regulate marriage; they may come to each other's aid either economically or politically; and they may perform rituals together.

Now that we have learned something about matrilineal systems, the avunculocal pattern of residence, whereby married couples live with or near the husband's mother's brother, may become clearer. Although avunculocal residence is relatively rare, all avunculocal societies are matrilineal. As we have seen, the mother's brother plays an important role in decision making in most matrilineal societies. Aside from his brothers, who is a boy's closest male matrilineal relative? His mother's brother. Going to live with mother's brother, then, provides a way of localizing male matrilineal relatives. But why should some matrilineal societies practice that form of residence? The answer may involve the prevailing type of warfare.

Avunculocal societies, in contrast with matrilocal societies, all fight internally. Just as patrilocality may be a response to keep (patrilineally) related men home after marriage, so avunculocality may be a way of keeping related (in this case, matrilineally related) men together after marriage to provide for quick mobilization in case of surprise attack from nearby. Societies that already have strong, functioning matrilineal descent groups may, when faced with fighting close to home and high male mortality, choose to practice avunculocality rather than switch to patrilocality.[18]

Functions of Unilineal Descent Groups.   Unilineal descent groups exist in societies at all levels of cultural complexity.[19] However, they are most common, apparently, in noncommercial food-producing (as opposed to food-collecting) societies.[20] Unilineal descent groups often have important functions in the social, economic, political, and religious realms of life.

Regulating Marriage.   In unilineal societies, individuals are not usually permitted to marry within their own unilineal descent groups. For example, on Truk, which has matriclans and matrilineages, a person is forbidden by the rule of descent-group exogamy to marry anyone from his or her matriclan. Since the matrilineage is included within the matriclan, the rule of descent-group exogamy also applies to the matrilineage.

Economic Functions.   Members of a person's lineage or clan are often required to side with that person in any quarrel or lawsuit, to help him or her get established economically, to contribute to a bride price or fine, and to support the person in life crises. Mutual aid often extends to economic cooperation on a regular basis. The unilineal descent group may act as a corporate unit in land ownership. For example, house sites and farmland are owned by a lineage among the Trukese and the Kapauku. Descent-group

[18] Melvin Ember. "The Conditions That May Favor Avunculocal Residence." *Behavior Science Research,* 9 (1974): 203–9.
[19] Coult and Habenstein. *Cross Tabulations of Murdock's World Ethnographic Sample.*
[20] Data from Robert B. Textor, comp., *A Cross-Cultural Summary,* New Haven: HRAF Press, 1967.

members may also support one another in such enterprises as clearing virgin bush or forest for farmland and providing food and other things for feasts, potlatches, curing rites, and ceremonial occasions, such as births, initiations, marriages, and funerals.

Money earned—either by harvesting a cash crop or by leaving the community for a time to work for cash wages—is sometimes viewed by the descent group as belonging to all. In recent times, however, young people in some places have shown an unwillingness to part with their money, viewing it as different from other kinds of economic assistance.

Political Functions.   The world *political*, as used by members of an industrialized society, generally does not apply to the rather vague powers that may be entrusted to a headman or the elders of a lineage or clan. But these persons may have the right to assign land for use by a lineage member or a clan member. Headmen or elders may also have the right to settle disputes between two members within a lineage, although they generally lack power to force a settlement. And they may act as intermediaries in disputes between a member of their own clan and a member of an opposing kin group.

Certainly one of the most important political functions of unilineal descent groups is their role in warfare—the attempt to resolve disputes within and without the society by violent action. In societies without towns or cities, the organization of such fighting is often in the hands of descent groups. The Tiv of central Nigeria, for instance, know quite well at any given moment which lineages they will fight with, which lineages they will join as allies in case of a fight, which they will fight against using only sticks, and which must be attacked using bows and arrows.

Religious Functions.   A clan or lineage may have its own religious beliefs and practices, worshiping its own gods or goddesses and ancestral spirits.

The Tallensi of West Africa revere and try to pacify their ancestors. They view life as we know it as only a part of human existence: for them, life existed before birth and will continue after death. The Tallensi believe the ancestors of their descent groups have changed their form but have retained their interest in what goes on within their society. They can show their displeasure by bringing sudden disaster or minor mishap, and their pleasure by bringing unexpected good fortune. But people can never tell what will please them; ancestral spirits are, above all, unpredictable. Thus, the Tallensi try to account for unexplainable happenings by attributing them to the ever-watchful ancestors. The Tallensi are not concerned with other people's ancestors; they believe it is only one's own ancestors who plague one.[21]

The Hopi clans figure prominently in the Hopi religion. The religion is one in which the unity of the people is evidenced by the interdependence of the clans, for each is considered a significant part of the whole. Each clan sponsors at least one of the religious festivals each year and is the guardian of

[21] Meyer Fortes. *The Web of Kinship among the Tallensi.* New York: Oxford University Press, 1949.

that festival's paraphernalia and ritual. A festival is not exclusive to one clan, for all the Hopi clans participate. This clan responsibility for ceremonies is accepted as part of the will of the spirits or deities, and each clan is believed to have been assigned its ritual role before the emergence of the Hopi people from the underworld.[22]

Development of Unilineal Systems.   Unilineal kin groups play very important roles in the organization of many societies. But not all societies have such groups. In societies that have complex systems of political organization, officials and agencies take over many of the functions that might be performed by kin groups, such as the organization of work and warfare and the allocation of land. However, not all societies that lack complex political organization have unilineal descent systems. Why, then, do some societies have unilineal descent systems but not others?

It is generally assumed that unilocal residence (patrilocal or matrilocal) is necessary for the development of unilineal descent. Patrilocal residence, if practiced for some time in a society, will generate a set of patrilineally related males who live in the same territory. Matrilocal residence over time will similarly generate a localized set of matrilineally related females. It is no wonder, then, that matrilocal and patrilocal residence are cross-culturally associated with matrilineal and patrilineal descent, respectively.[23]

But although unilocal residence might be necessary for the formation of unilineal descent groups, it is apparently not the only condition required. For one thing, many societies with unilocal residence lack unilineal descent groups. For another, merely because related males or related females live together by virtue of a patrilocal or matrilocal rule of residence, it does not necessarily follow that the related people will actually view themselves as a descent group and function as such. Thus, it appears that other conditions are needed to supply the impetus for the formation of unilineal descent groups.

There is some evidence that unilocal societies that engage in warfare are more apt to have unilineal descent groups than unilocal societies without warfare.[24] It may be, then, that the presence of fighting in societies lacking complex systems of political organization provides an impetus to the formation of unilineal descent groups. This may be because unilineal descent groups provide individuals with unambiguous groups of persons who can fight or form alliances as discrete units.[25] As we have seen, one distinguishing feature of unilineal descent groups is that there is no ambiguity about an individual's membership. It is perfectly clear whether someone belongs to a

---

[22] Fred Eggan. *The Social Organization of the Western Pueblos.* Chicago: University of Chicago Press, 1950.

[23] Data from Textor, comp., *A Cross-Cultural Summary.*

[24] Ember, Ember, and Pasternak. "On the Development of Unilineal Descent."

[25] The importance of warfare and competition as factors in the formation of unilineal descent groups is also suggested by Service, *Primitive Social Organization*; and Marshall D. Sahlins, "The Segmentary Lineage: An Organization of Predatory Expansion," *American Anthropologist*, 63 (1961): 332–45.

particular clan, phratry, or moiety. It is this feature of unilineal descent groups that enables them to act as separate and distinct units—mostly, perhaps, in warfare.

Bilateral systems, in contrast, are ego-centered, and every person, other than siblings, has a slightly different set of kin to rely on. Consequently, in bilateral societies it is often not clear whom one can turn to and which person has responsibility for aiding another. Such ambiguity, however, might not be a liability in societies without warfare, or in societies with political systems that organize fighting in behalf of large populations.

Ambilineal Systems

Societies with ambilineal descent groups are far less numerous than unilineal or even bilateral societies. However, ambilineal societies resemble unilineal ones in many ways. For instance, the members of an ambilineal descent group believe they are descended from a common ancestor, though frequently they cannot specify all the genealogical links. The descent group is commonly named and may have an identifying emblem or even a totem; land and other productive resources may be owned by the descent group; and myths and religious practices are often associated with the group. Marriage is often regulated by group membership, just as in unilineal systems, though kin-group exogamy is not nearly as common as in unilineal systems. Moreover, ambilineal societies resemble unilineal ones in having various levels or types of descent groups. They may have lineages and higher orders of descent groups, distinguished (as in unilineal systems) by whether or not all the genealogical links to the supposed common ancestors are specified.[26]

The Samoans of the South Pacific are an example of an ambilineal society.[27] There are two types of ambilineal descent groups in Samoa, corresponding to what would be called clans and subclans in a unilineal society. Both groups are exogamous. Associated with each ambilineal clan are one or more chiefs. A group takes its name from the senior chief; subclans, of which there are always at least two, may take their names from junior chiefs.

The distinctiveness of the Samoan ambilineal system, compared with unilineal systems, is that because an individual may be affiliated with an ambilineal group through his or her father or mother (and his or her parents, in turn, could be affiliated with any of their parents' groups), there are a number of ambilineal groups to which that individual could belong. Affiliation with a Samoan descent group is optional, and a person may theoretically affiliate with any or all of the ambilineal groups to which he or she is related. In practice, however, a person is primarily associated with one group—the

[26] William Davenport. "Nonunilinear Descent and Descent Groups." *American Anthropologist*, 61 (1959): 557–72.

[27] The description of the Samoan descent system is based upon Melvin Ember's 1955–1956 fieldwork. See also his "The Nonunilinear Descent Groups of Samoa," *American Anthropologist*, 61 (1959): 573–77; and Davenport, "Nonunilinear Descent and Descent Groups."

ambilineal group whose land he or she actually lives on and cultivates—although he or she may participate in the activities (housebuilding, for example) of several groups. Since a person may belong to more than one ambilineal group, the society is not divided into separate kin groups, in contrast with unilineal societies. Consequently, the core members of each ambilineal group cannot all live together (as they could in unilineal societies), since each person belongs to more than one group and cannot live in several places at once.

Not all ambilineal societies have the multiple descent-group membership that occurs in Samoa. In some ambilineal societies, a person may belong (at any one time) to only one group. In such cases, the society can be divided into separate, nonoverlapping groups of kin.

Why do some societies have ambilineal descent groups? Although the evidence is not clear-cut on this point, it may be that societies with unilineal descent groups are transformed into ambilineal ones under special conditions—particularly in the presence of depopulation. We have already noted that depopulation may transform a previously unilocal society into a bilocal society. If that previously unilocal society also had unilineal descent groups, the descent groups may become transformed into ambilineal groups. If a society used to be patrilocal and patrilineal, for example, but some couples begin to live matrilocally, then their children may be associated with a previously patrilineal descent group (on whose land they may be living) through their mother. Once this happens regularly, the unilineal principle may become transformed into an ambilineal principle.[28] Thus, ambilineal descent systems may have developed recently as a result of depopulation caused by the introduction of European diseases.

Kinship Terminology

Our society, like all others, refers to a number of different kin by the same **classificatory term**. Most of us probably never stop to think about why we name relatives the way we do. For example, we call our mother's brother and father's brother (and often mother's sister's husband and father's sister's husband) by the same term—*uncle*. It is not that we are unable to distinguish between our mother's or father's brother or that we do not know the difference between **consanguineal kin** (blood kin) and **affinal kin** (kin by marriage, or what we call *in-laws*). Instead, it seems that in our society we do not usually find it necessary to distinguish between various types of uncles.

However natural our system of classification may seem to us, countless field studies by anthropologists have revealed that societies differ markedly in how they group or distinguish relatives. The kinship terminology used in a society may reflect its prevailing kind of family, its rule of residence and its rule of descent, and other aspects of its social organization. Kin terms may

[28] Ember and Ember. "The Conditions Favoring Multilocal Residence."

also give clues to prior features of the society's social system, if, as many anthropologists believe,[29] the kin terms of a society are very resistant to change. The major systems of kinship terminology are the Omaha system, the Crow system, the Iroquois system, the Sudanese system, the Hawaiian system, and the Eskimo system.

Omaha System

The Omaha system of kin terminology is named after the Omaha Indian tribe of North America, but the system is found in many societies around the world, usually those with patrilineal descent.[30]

Referring to Figure 14-5, we can see immediately which types of kin are lumped together in an Omaha system. First, father and father's brother (numbers 2 and 3) are both referred to by the same term. This contrasts markedly with our way of classifying relatives, in which no term that applies to a member of the nuclear family (father, mother, brother, sister) is applied to any other relative. What could account for the Omaha system of lumping? One interpretation is that father and father's brother are lumped in this system because most societies in which this system is found have patrilineal kin groups. Both father and father's brother are in the parental generation of my patrilineal kin group and may behave toward me similarly. My father's brother also probably lives near me, since patrilineal societies usually have patrilocal residence. The term for father and father's brother, then, might be translated "male member of my patrilineal kin group in my father's generation."

A second lumping (which at first glance appears similar to the lumping of father and father's brother) is that of mother and mother's sister (4 and 5), both of whom are called by the same term. But more surprisingly, mother's brother's daughter (16) is also referred to by this term. Why should this be? If we think of the term as meaning "female member of my mother's patrilineage of *any* generation," then the term makes more sense. Consistent with this view, all the male members of my mother's patrilineage of any generation (mother's brother, 6; mother's brother's son, 15) are also referred to by one term.

It is apparent, then, that relatives on the father's and mother's sides are grouped differently in this system. For members of my mother's patrilineal kin group, I lump all male members together and all female members together regardless of their generation. Yet, for members of my father's patrilineal kin group, I have different terms for the male and female members of different generations. Murdock has suggested that a society lumps kin types when there are more similarities than differences among them.[31]

Using this principle, and recognizing that societies with an Omaha system usually are patrilineal, I realize that my father's patrilineal kin group is

[29] See, for example, Murdock, *Social Structure*, pp. 199–222.
[30] The association between the Omaha system and patrilineality is reported in Textor, comp., *A Cross-Cultural Summary*.
[31] Murdock. *Social Structure*, p 125.

the one to which I belong and in which I have a great many rights and obligations. Consequently, persons of my father's generation are likely to behave quite differently toward me than are persons of my own generation. Members of my patrilineal group in my father's generation are likely to exercise authority over me, and I am required to show them respect. Members of my patrilineal group in my own generation are those I am likely to play with as a child and to be friends with. Thus, in a patrilineal system, persons on my father's side belonging to different generations are likely to be distinguished. On the other hand, my mother's patrilineage is relatively unimportant to me (since I take my descent from my father). And because my residence is probably patrilocal, my mother's relatives will probably not even live near me. Thus, inasmuch as my mother's patrilineal relatives are comparatively unimportant in such a system, they become similar enough to be lumped together.

Finally, in the Omaha system, I refer to my male parallel cousins (my father's brother's son, 9, and my mother's sister's son, 13) in the same way I refer to my brother (number 11). I refer to my female parallel cousins (my father's brother's daughter, 10, and my mother's sister's daughter, 14) in the same way I refer to my sister (12). Considering that my father's brother and mother's sister are referred to by the same terms I use for my father and mother, this lumping of parallel cousins with **siblings** (brothers and sisters) is not surprising. If I call my own mother's and father's children (other than myself) "Brother" and "Sister," then the children of anyone whom I also call "Mother" and "Father" ought to be called "Brother" and "Sister" as well.

Crow System

The Crow system, named after another North American Indian tribe, has been called the mirror image of the Omaha system. The same principles of lumping kin types are employed, except that since the Crow system is associated with matrilineal descent,[32] the individuals in my mother's matrilineal group (which is my own) are not lumped across generations, whereas the individuals in my father's matrilineal group are. By comparing Figure 14-5 with Figure 14-6, we find that the lumping and separating of kin types are much the same in both, except that the lumping across generations in the Crow system appears on the father's side rather than on the mother's side. In other words, I call both my mother and my mother's sister by the same term (since both are female members of my matrilineal descent group in my mother's generation). I call my father, my father's brother, and my father's sister's son by the same term (all male members of my father's matrilineal group in any generation). I call my father's sister and my father's sister's daughter by the same term (both female members of my father's matrilineal group). And I refer to my parallel cousins in the same way I refer to my brother and sister.

---

[32] The association between the Crow system and matrilineality is reported in Textor, comp., *A Cross-Cultural Summary*.

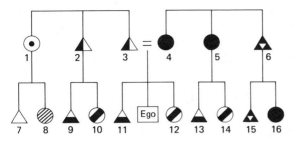

FIGURE 14-5 Omaha Kinship Terminology System

Note: Kin types referred to by the same term are marked in the same way.

Iroquois System

The Iroquois system, named after the Iroquois Indian tribe of North America, is similar to both the Omaha and Crow systems in the way in which I refer to relatives in my parents' generation (see Figure 14-7). That is, my father and my father's brother (2 and 3) are referred to by the same term, and my mother and my mother's sister (4 and 5) are referred to by the same term. However, the Iroquois system differs from the Omaha and Crow systems regarding my own generation. In the Omaha and Crow systems, one set of cross-cousins was lumped in the kinship terminology with the generation above. This is not true in the Iroquois system, where both sets of cross-cousins (mother's brother's children, 15 and 16, and father's sister's children, 7 and 8) are referred to by the same terms, distinguished by sex. That is, mother's brother's daughter and father's sister's daughter are both referred to by the same term. Also, mother's brother's son and father's sister's son are referred to by the same term. Parallel cousins always have terms different from those for cross-cousins and are sometimes, but not always, referred to by the same terms as one's brother and sister.

Like the Omaha and Crow systems, the Iroquois system has different terms for relatives on the father's and mother's sides. Such differentiation tends to be associated with unilineal descent, which is not surprising since unilineal descent involves affiliation with either mother's or father's kin. Why Iroquois, rather than Omaha or Crow, terminology occurs in a unilineal so-

FIGURE 14-6 Crow Kinship Terminology System

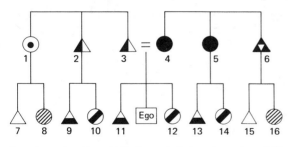

Note: Although not shown in this diagram, in the Iroquois system, parallel cousins are sometimes referred to by different terms than one's own brother and sister.

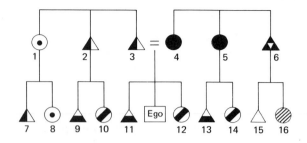

FIGURE 14-7 Iroquois Kinship Terminology System. *Note*: Although not shown in this diagram, in the Iroquois system, parallel cousins are sometimes referred to by different terms than one's own brother and sister.

ciety requires explanation. One possible explanation is that Omaha or Crow is likely to occur in a developed, as opposed to a developing or decaying, unilineal system.[33] Another possible explanation is that Iroquois terminology emerges in societies that prefer marriage with both cross-cousins,[34] who are differentiated from other relatives in an Iroquois system.

Sudanese System

One other system of kinship terminology is associated with unilineal descent—the Sudanese system. But unlike the systems we have examined so far, the Sudanese system usually does not lump any relatives in the parents' and ego's generations. That is, the Sudanese system is usually a **descriptive** system, in which a different term is used for *each* of the relatives shown in Figure 14-8. What kinds of societies are likely to have such a system? Although societies with Sudanese terminology are likely to be patrilineal, they probably are different from most patrilineal societies that have Omaha or Iroquois terms. Sudanese terminology is associated with relatively great political complexity, class stratification, and occupational specialization. It has been suggested that under such conditions, a kinship system may reflect the need to make fine distinctions among members of descent groups who have different opportunities and privileges in the occupational or class system.[35]

The Omaha, Crow, Iroquois, and Sudanese systems, although different from one another and associated with somewhat different predictors, share one important feature: the terms used for the mother's and father's side of the family are not the same. The next two systems—Hawaiian and Eskimo— are different in that the terms on the mother's and father's side of the family

[33] See Leslie A. White, "A Problem in Kinship Terminology," *American Anthropologist*, 41 (1939): 569–70.

[34] Jack Goody. "Cousin Terms." *Southwestern Journal of Anthropology*, 26 (1970): 125–42.

[35] Burton Pasternak. *Introduction to Kinship and Social Organization.* Englewood Cliffs, N.J.: Prentice-Hall, 1976, p. 142.

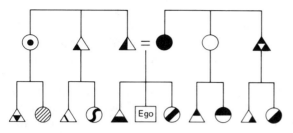

FIGURE 14-8 Sudanese Kinship Terminology System

are *exactly* the same. This suggests that both sides of the family are equally important or equally unimportant.

Hawaiian System

The Hawaiian system of kinship terminology is the least complex in that it uses the smallest number of terms. In this system, all relatives of the same sex in the same generation are referred to by the same term. Thus, all my female cousins are referred to by the same term as my sister; all male cousins are referred to by the same term as my brother. Everyone known to be related to me in my parents' generation is referred to by one term if female (including my mother) and by another term if male (including my father). (See Figure 14-9.)

Societies with Hawaiian kin terminology tend not to have unilineal descent groups,[36] which helps explain why kinship terms are the same on both sides of the family. Why are the terms for mother, father, sister, and brother used for other relatives? Perhaps because societies with Hawaiian terminology are likely to have large extended families[37] to which every type of relative in Figure 14-9 may belong because of alternative residence patterns.[38]

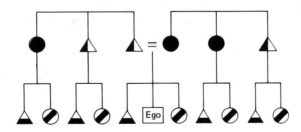

FIGURE 14-9 Hawaiian Kinship Terminology System

[36] Reported in Textor, comp., *A Cross-Cultural Summary*.
[37] Ibid.
[38] This conjecture is based on the authors' unpublished cross-cultural research.

Eskimo System

Although the Eskimo system is so named because it is found in some Eskimo societies, it is also the terminological system the United States and many other commercial societies use. (See Figure 14-10.)

The distinguishing features of the Eskimo system are that all cousins are lumped together under the same term but are distinguished from brothers and sisters, and all aunts and uncles are generally lumped under the same terms but are distinguished from mother and father. Unlike all the other systems we have discussed, in an Eskimo system no other relatives are generally referred to by the same terms used for members of the nuclear family—mother, father, brother, and sister.

Eskimo kinship terminology is not generally found where there are unilineal or ambilineal descent groups; the only kin group that appears to be present is the bilateral kindred.[39] The kindred in a bilateral kinship system is an ego-centered group. Although relatives on both my mother's and my father's sides are equally important, my most important relatives are generally those closest to me. This is particularly true in our type of society, where the nuclear family generally lives alone, separated from and not particularly involved with other relatives except on ceremonial occasions. Since the nuclear family is most important, we would expect to find that the kin types in the nuclear family are distinguished terminologically from all other relatives. And since the mother's and father's sides are equally important (or unimportant), it makes sense that we use the same terms (aunt, uncle, and cousin) for both sides of the family.

SUMMARY

1. In our society, and in many other industrial societies, a newly married couple usually establishes a place of residence apart from parents or relatives (neolocal residence). But about 95 percent of the world's societies have some pattern of residence whereby the new couple settles within, or very close to, the household of the parents or some other close relative of the groom or bride.

FIGURE 14-10 Eskimo Kinship Terminology System

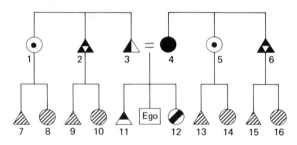

Note: In some Eskimo systems the cousin term may vary according to sex.

[39] Reported in Textor, comp., *A Cross-Cultural Summary.*

2. The four major patterns in which married couples live with or near kinsmen are these:
   a. Patrilocal residence: the couple lives with or near the husband's parents (67 percent of all societies).
   b. Matrilocal residence: the couple lives with or near the wife's parents (15 percent of all societies).
   c. Bilocal residence: the couple lives with or near either the husband's parents or the wife's parents (7 percent of all societies).
   d. Avunculocal residence: the son and his wife settle with or near his mother's brother (4 percent of all societies).
3. In most societies where kinship connections are important, a rule allocates each person to a particular and definable set of kin. The rules affiliating individuals with sets of kin are called rules of descent.
4. Only a few known rules of descent affiliate individuals with different sets of kin:
   a. Patrilineal descent affiliates an individual with kin of both sexes related to him or her through men only. In each generation, then, children belong to the kin group of their father.
   b. Matrilineal descent affiliates an individual with kin related to him or her through women only. In each generation, then, children belong to the kin group of their mother.
   c. Ambilineal descent affiliates an individual with kin related to him or her through either men or women. Consequently, the descent groups show both female and male genealogical links.
5. Societies without lineal-descent rules are bilateral societies. Relatives on both the mother's and father's sides of the family are of equal importance or (more usually) unimportance. Kindreds are ego-centered sets of kin who may be called together temporarily for some purpose.
6. With unilineal descent (patrilineal or matrilineal), people usually refer to themselves as belonging to a particular unilineal group or set of groups because they believe they share common descent in either the male or the female line. These people form what is called a unilineal descent group. There are several types:
   a. Lineages, or sets of kin whose members trace descent from a common ancestor through known links.
   b. Clans, or sets of kin who believe they are descended from a common ancestor but cannot specify the genealogical links.
   c. Phratries, or groups of supposedly related clans.
   d. Moieties, two unilineal descent groups (constituting the whole society) without specified links to the supposed common ancestor.
7. Unilineal descent groups are most common in societies in the middle range of cultural complexity—that is, in noncommercial food-producing (as opposed to food-collecting) societies. In such societies, unilineal descent groups often have important functions in the social, economic, political, and religious realms of life.
8. Societies differ markedly in how they group or distinguish relatives under the same or different kinship terms. The major systems of terminology are the Omaha, Crow, Iroquois, Sudanese, Hawaiian, and Eskimo systems.

15

Political Organization

Social Order and Disorder

For most Americans, the phrase *political life* has many connotations. It may call to mind the executive branch of government, from the president on a national level to the mayor on a local one; legislative institutions, from Congress to the city council; or administrative bureaus, from federal-government departments to local agencies. It may also evoke thoughts of political parties, interest groups, and such common political activities as lobbying, campaigning, and voting. In other words, when people living in the United States think of political life, they may think first of the complex process by which authoritative decisions (often called *public policies*) are arrived at and implemented.

But *political life* has a still wider range of meaning in America and in many other countries. It may also refer to ways of preventing or resolving troubles and disputes both within and outside our society. Internally, a complex society such as ours may employ mediation or arbitration to resolve industrial disputes; a police force to prevent crimes or track down criminals; and courts and a penal system to deal with lawbreakers as well as with social conflict in general. Externally, such a society may establish embassies in other nations and develop and utilize its armed forces both to maintain security and to support domestic and foreign interests. Complex societies have developed these mechanisms in order to establish social order and to minimize, or at least deal with, social disorder.

But many societies do not have political officials or courts or armies. Nor do they have individuals or agencies that are formally responsible for making and implementing policy or resolving disputes. Does this mean they have no political life? If we mean political life as we know it in our own society, then the answer has to be that they do not. But if we look beyond our complex formal institutions and ask what functions these institutions perform, we find that all societies have *political* activities, beliefs, and attitudes that pertain to decision making and the resolution of disputes. These activities, beliefs, and attitudes are ways and means of creating and maintaining social order and coping with social disorder.

Many kinds of groups we discussed in the two previous chapters (families, descent groups) have political functions. But when anthropologists talk about *political organization*, they are generally focusing on *territorial groups*. Territorial groups, in whose behalf political activities may be organized, range from small communities (bands, villages) to large communities (towns, cities) to multi-local groups such as districts or regions, entire nations, or even groups of nations.

As we shall see, the different types of political organization and ways of coping with conflict are strongly linked to variation in food-getting, economy, and social stratification.

VARIATIONS IN TYPES OF POLITICAL ORGANIZATION

Societies or language groups vary in *level of political integration* (the largest territorial group in whose behalf political activities are organized) and in the degree to which political authority is centralized or concentrated. In many societies known to anthropology, the small community (band or village) is the largest territorial group in whose behalf political activities are organized. The authority structure in such societies does not involve any centralization: there is no political authority whose jurisdiction includes more than one community. In other societies, political activities are sometimes organized in behalf of a multi-local group, but there is no permanent authority at the top. And in still other societies, political activities are often organized on behalf of multi-local territorial groups, and there is a centralized or supreme political authority at the top. Many anthropologists classify societies in terms of the highest level of political integration that occurs, and in terms of the nature of the political authority structure. For example, Elman Service has suggested that most societies can be classified into four principal types of political organization: bands, tribes, chiefdoms, and states.[1]

[1] Elman R. Service. *Primitive Social Organization: An Evolutionary Perspective.* New York: Random House, 1962.

Bands

Some societies are composed of a number of fairly small and usually nomadic groups of people. Each of these groups is conventionally called a **band** and is politically autonomous. That is, in band societies the local group or community is the largest group that acts as a political unit. Since most recent food collectors have had band organization, some anthropologists contend that this type of political organization characterized nearly all societies before the development of agriculture, or until about 10,000 years ago. But we have to remember that almost all of the described food-collecting societies are or were located in marginal environments; and almost all were affected by more dominant societies nearby.[2] So it is possible that what we call "band organization" may not have been typical of food collectors in the distant or prehistoric past.

Bands are typically small in size (25–50 individuals), and societies with bands have a low population density (at the most about one person per five square miles).[3] Of course, by the time they were described by anthropologists, many band societies had been severely depopulated by introduced European diseases. Band size often varies by season, the band breaking up or recombining according to the quantity of food resources available at a given time and place. Inuit (Eskimo) bands, for example, are smaller in the winter, when food is hard to find, and larger in the summer, when there is sufficient food to feed a larger group.

Political decision making within the band is generally informal. The "modest informal authority"[4] that does exist can be seen in the way decisions affecting the group are made. Since the formal, permanent office of leader generally does not exist, decisions such as when camp has to be moved or how a hunt is to be arranged are either agreed upon by the community as a whole or made by the best-qualified member. Leadership, when it is exercised by an individual, is not the consequence of bossing or throwing one's weight about. Each band may have its informal **headman**, or its most proficient hunter, or a person most accomplished in rituals. There may be one person with all these qualities, or several persons, but such a person or persons will have gained status through the community's recognition of skill, good sense, and humility. Leadership, in other words, stems not from power but from influence, not from office but from admired personal qualities, as among the Iglulik Inuit.

> Within each settlement . . . there is as a rule an older man who enjoys the respect of the others and who decides when a move is to be made to another hunting center, when a hunt is to be started, how the spoils are to be divided, when the

[2] Carmel Schrire. "Wild Surmises on Savage Thoughts." In Carmel Schrire, ed., *Past and Present in Hunter Gatherer Studies*. Orlando, Fl.: Academic Press, 1984, pp. 1–25; see also Eleanor Leacock and Richard Lee, "Introduction," in Eleanor Leacock and Richard Lee, eds., *Politics and History in Band Societies*, Cambridge: Cambridge University Press, 1982, p. 8.
[3] Julian Steward. *Theory of Culture Change*. Urbana: University of Illinois Press, 1955, p. 125.
[4] Service. *Primitive Social Organization*, p. 109.

dogs are to be fed. . . . He is called *isumaitoq*, "he who thinks." It is not always the oldest man, but as a rule an elderly man who is a clever hunter or, as head of a large family, exercises great authority. He cannot be called a chief; there is no obligation to follow his counsel; but they do so in most cases, partly because they rely on his experience, partly because it pays to be on good terms with this man.[5]

Not all known food collectors are organized at the band level, or have all the features of a band type of society. The classic exceptions are the Indians of the Northwest Coast who had enormous resources of salmon and other fish, relatively large and permanent villages, and political organization beyond the level of the typical band societies in the ethnographic record.

Tribes

What distinguishes tribal from band political organization is the presence in the former of some pan-tribal associations (such as clans and age-sets) that can potentially integrate a number of local groups into a larger whole. Such multi-local political integration, however, is *not permanent*, and it is *informal* in the sense that it is not headed by political officials. Frequently, the integration is called into play only when an external threat arises; when the threat disappears, the local groups revert to self-sufficiency.

In other words, a tribal society lacks a permanent, multi-local political authority. Situations do arise that call for intergroup cooperation of some kind, but they are transitory, and a new situation may well require the coordination of quite different groups.[6] Tribal organization may seem fragile—and of course it usually is—but the fact that there are social ways to integrate local groups into larger political entities means that societies with tribal organization are militarily a good deal more formidable than societies with band organization.

Societies with **tribal** political organization are similar to band societies in their tendency to be egalitarian. But societies with tribal organization generally are food producers. And because cultivation and animal husbandry are generally more productive than hunting and gathering, the population density of tribal societies is generally higher, local groups are generally larger, and the way of life is more sedentary than in the hunter-gatherer band.

Kinship Bonds. Frequently, pan-tribal associations are based on kinship ties. Clans are the most common pan-tribal kinship groups. In some societies, clan elders have the right to try to settle disputes between clan members or to attempt to punish wrongs committed against members by people in different clans. In addition, kinship bonds often tend to unite members of the same descent group during periods of warfare; in many societies, the organization of warfare is the responsibility of the clan.[7]

The **segmentary lineage system** is another type of pan-tribal integration

[5] Therkel Mathiassen. *Material Culture of the Iglulik Eskimos*. Copenhagen: Glydendalske, 1928.
[6] Service. *Primitive Social Organization*, pp. 114–115.
[7] Ibid., p. 126.

based on kinship. A society with such a system is composed of segments or parts, each similar to the others in structure and function. Every local segment (occupying a particular territory) belongs to a hierarchy of lineages stretching farther and farther back genealogically. The hierarchy of lineages, then, unites the segments into larger and larger genealogical groups. The closer two groups are genealogically, the greater their general closeness. In the event of a dispute between members of different segments, people related more closely to one contestant than to another take the side of their nearest kinsman.

A segmentary lineage system may generate a formidable military force, but the combinations of manpower it produces are temporary, forming and dissolving as the occasion demands.[8] Tribal political organization does not make for a political system that more or less permanently integrates a number of communities.

Age-Set Systems.   Some societies have **age-sets**, groups of persons of similar age and same sex who move through some or all of life's stages together (e.g., from warriors to elders to retired elders). Age-set systems seem to develop in societies that have frequent warfare and local groups that change in size and composition through the year.[9] Age-sets can function as the basis of a tribal type of political organization. Consider, for example, the Shavante who inhabit the Mato Grosso region of Brazil.

Although the Shavante have some agriculture, they rely primarily on food collection. Wild roots, nuts, and fruits are their staple foods, and hunting is their passion.[10] The Shavante have villages, but they rarely stay in them for more than a few weeks at a time. Instead they make frequent community treks lasting six to twenty-four weeks to hunt or collect. They spend no more than four weeks a year at their gardens, which are located at least a day's journey from the villages.

Boys emerge from the status of childhood when they are formally inducted into a named age–set and take up residence in the "bachelor hut." An induction ceremony takes place every five years, and boys from seven to twelve years of age are inducted at the same time. The five-year period of residence in the bachelor hut is relatively free of responsibility: the boys' families provide food for them, and they go out hunting and collecting when they feel like it. At the end of this period, a much more elaborate series of initiation ceremonies marks the entry by these boys into a different status— that of "young men." The day they emerge from the bachelor hut for the last time, during the final rites of initiation, the whole age-set is married, each to a small girl, usually not yet mature, chosen by the boys' parents. Marriages

[8] Marshall D. Sahlins. "The Segmentary Lineage: An Organization of Predatory Expansion." *American Anthropologist*, 63 (1961): 342–345.
[9] Madeline Lattman Ritter. "The Conditions Favoring Age-Set Organization." *Journal of Anthropological Research*, 36 (1980): 87–104.
[10] This section is based on David Maybury-Lewis, *Akwe-Shavante Society*, Oxford: Clarendon Press, 1967.

cannot be consummated at this time, since the young men must wait until their wives are more mature. When the ceremonies are over, the young men make war clubs, for they are thought of now as the warriors of the community, and they earn the privilege of sitting in the evening village council. But they have no authority at this stage and few responsibilities.

The next stage is that of the "mature men," and when an age-set is inducted into this stage the members begin to experience some authority. It is in the mature men's council that important community decisions are made. This last status position actually consists of five consecutive age-sets (because new age-sets are formed every five years and each one continues in existence until the death of its members). Among the mature men the oldest sets are considered senior to the junior ones. Members of the most junior mature men's age-set rarely talk in the council; they assert themselves more as they progress in the system.

Leadership. Tribal societies do not have formal full-time political officials whose authority extends to more than one community. At the local level, informal leadership is also characteristic. In those tribal societies where kinship provides the basic framework of social organization, the elders of the local kin groups tend to have considerable influence; where age-sets are important, a particular age-set is looked to for leadership. But why particular individuals and not others become leaders is not clear.

We now have a few studies that have investigated the personal qualities of leaders in tribal societies. One study, conducted among the Mekranoti-Kayapo of Central Brazil, finds that leaders (in contrast to followers) tend to be rated higher on intelligence, generosity, knowledgeability, ambitiousness, and aggressiveness by their peers. Leaders also tend to be older and taller. And despite the egalitarian nature of Mekranoti society (at least with respect to sharing resources), sons of leaders are more likely than others to become leaders.[11] In many respects, studies of leaders in the United States show them to be not that different from their counterparts in Brazil. But there is one major difference. Mekranoti leaders are not wealthier than others; in fact, they give their wealth away. United States leaders are wealthier than others.[12]

In some tribal societies, the quest for leadership seems quite competitive. In parts of New Guinea and South America, "big men" compete with other ambitious men to attract followers. Men who want to compete must show that they have magical powers, success in gardening, and bravery in war. But, most important, they have to collect enough goods to throw big parties where the goods are given away. "Big men" have to work very hard to attract and keep their followings; dissatisfied followers can always join other aspiring men.[13]

[11] Dennis Werner. "Chiefs and Presidents: A Comparison of Leadership Traits in the United States and among the Mekranoti-Kayapo of Central Brazil." *Ethos*, 10 (1982): 136–48.

[12] Werner. "Chiefs and Presidents."

[13] Marshall D. Sahlins. "Poor Man, Rich Man, Big-Man, Chief: Political Types in Melanesia and Polynesia." *Comparative Studies in Society and History*, 5 (1963): 285–303.

The wives of "big men" are often leaders too. For example, among the Kagwahiv, another Brazilian society, a headman's wife is usually the leader of the women in the community; she is responsible for much of the planning for feasts and often distributes the meat at them.[14]

Chiefdoms

Whereas tribes have groupings that can informally integrate more than one community, **chiefdoms** have some *formal* structure integrating multi-community political units. The formal structure could consist of a council with or without a chief, but most commonly there is a person—the **chief**—who has higher rank or authority than others. A society at the chiefdom level of political development may or may not be completely politically unified under one chief. Most societies at the chiefdom level are in fact composed of more than one multi-community political unit, each headed by a chief or a council. Compared with tribal societies, societies with chiefdoms generally are more densely populated and their communities more permanent, partly as a consequence of their generally higher economic productivity.

The position of chief, which is sometimes hereditary and generally permanent, bestows high status on its holder. Most chiefdoms have social ranking and accord the chief and his family greater access to prestige. The chief may redistribute goods, plan and direct the use of public labor, supervise religious ceremonies, and direct military activities on behalf of the chiefdom.

The Tahitians of the South Pacific had a history of large-scale warfare, and their chiefs coordinated land and naval forces in thrusts and counterthrusts. Tahitian society was clearly ranked—from the preeminence accorded the families of the paramount chiefs, who were believed to have exceptional spiritual powers, down to the lowest status of the general populace. Many of the early missionaries to Tahiti regarded the chiefs as despots because of the great deference and tribute paid to them by the common people.

In contrast to leaders in tribal societies, who generally have to earn their privileges by their personal qualities, hereditary chiefs are said to have those qualities in their "blood." A high-ranking chief in Polynesia, that huge triangular area of islands in the South Pacific, inherited special religious power called *mana*. Mana sanctified his rule and protected him.[15] Chiefs in Polynesia had so much religious power that the missionaries could convert people to Christianity only after their chiefs were converted.[16]

In most chiefdoms, the chiefs did not have the power to compel people to obey them; people would act in accordance with the chief's wishes because

[14] Waud H. Kracke. *Force and Persuasion: Leadership in an Amazonian Society.* Chicago: University of Chicago Press, 1979, p. 41.

[15] Sahlins. "Poor Man, Rich Man, Big-Man, Chief," p. 295.

[16] Marshall Sahlins. "Other Times, Other Customs: The Anthropology of History." *American Anthropologist,* 85 (1983): 519 (517–44).

the chief was respected and often had religious authority. But in the most complex chiefdoms, such as those of Hawaii and Tahiti, the chiefs seemed to have more compelling sanctions than the "power" of respect or mana. Substantial amounts of goods and services collected by the chiefs were used to support subordinates, including specialists such as high priests, political envoys, and warriors who could be sent to quell rebellious factions.[17] When redistributions do not go to everybody and a chief begins to use armed force, the political system is on the way to becoming what we call a state. Why chiefs sometimes are allowed to keep items for their own purposes is still a puzzle.

States

A **state**, according to one more or less standard definition, is "an autonomous political unit, encompassing many communities within its territory and having a centralized government with the power to collect taxes, draft men for work or war, and decree and enforce laws."[18] State societies, then, have a complex, centralized political structure, which includes a wide range of permanent institutions having legislative, executive, and judicial functions, and a large bureaucracy. Central to this definition is the concept of legitimate force used to implement policies both internally and externally. In state societies, the government tries to maintain a monopoly on the use of physical force.[19] This monopoly can be seen in the development of formal and specialized instruments of social control: a police force, a militia, a standing army.

In addition to their strictly political features, states have class stratification and hence unequal access to economic resources. State societies are generally supported by intensive agriculture. The high productivity of the agriculture presumably allows for the emergence of cities, a high degree of economic and other kinds of specialization, market or commercial exchange, and extensive foreign trade.

When states come into existence, people's access to scarce resources is radically altered. So too is their ability to *not* listen to leaders: you cannot refuse to pay taxes and go unpunished! Of course, the rules of a state do not maintain the social order by force alone. The people must believe, at least to some extent, that those in power have a legitimate right to govern. If the people think otherwise, history suggests that those in power may eventually lose their ability to control.

So force and the threat of force are not enough to explain the legitimacy of power, and the inequities that occur commonly, in state societies. But then what does? There are various theories available. The rulers of early states often claimed divine descent to buttress their legitimacy, but this claim is rare

[17] Sahlins. "Poor Man, Rich Man, Big-Man, Chief," p. 297.
[18] Robert L. Carneiro. "A Theory of the Origin of the State." *Science*, August 21, 1970, p. 733.
[19] See Max Weber, *The Theory of Social and Economic Organization*, trans. A. M. Henderson and Talcott Parsons, New York: Oxford University Press, 1947, p. 154.

nowadays. Children may be taught to accept all authority by their parents, which generalizes to the acceptance of political authority. There are those who think that people accept state authority for no good reason; the rulers are just able to fool them. Finally, some theorists think that states must provide people with real or rational advantages; otherwise people would not think the rulers deserve to exercise authority. Legitimacy is not an all or none phenomenon; it varies in degree. Why it has varied, in different times and places, remains a classic question in a number of the social sciences, including anthropology, as well as in philosophy and other humanistic disciplines.[20]

A state society can retain its legitimacy, or at least its power, for a long time. For example, the Roman Empire was a complex state society that dominated the Mediterranean and Near East for hundreds of years. It began as a city-state that waged war to acquire additional territory. At its height, the Roman Empire embraced more than 55 million people;[21] the capital city of Rome had a population of well over a million.[22] The Empire included parts of what are now Great Britain, France, Spain, Portugal, Germany, Rumania, Turkey, Greece, Armenia, Egypt, Israel, and Syria.

Another example of a state society was the kingdom of Nupe in West Africa, now part of the nation-state of Nigeria. As is characteristic of state societies generally, Nupe society was quite rigidly stratified. At the top of the social system was the king, or *etsu*. Beneath the king, members of the royal family formed the highest aristocratic class. Next in order were two other classes of nobility—the local chiefs and the military leaders. At the bottom were the commoners, who had neither prestige nor power, and no share in political authority.

The Nupe king possessed ultimate authority in many judicial matters. Minor disputes and civil cases were handled by local village councils, but serious criminal cases were the prerogative of the king. Such cases, referred to as "crimes for the king," were brought before the royal court by the king's local representatives. The king and his counselors judged the cases and determined suitable punishments.

The most powerful influence of the state over the Nupe people was in the area of taxation. The king was given the power to impose taxes and collect them from every household. Payment was made either in money (cowrie shells originally, and later British currency) or certain gifts, such as cloth, mats, and slaves. Much of the revenue collected was kept by the king, and the remainder shared with his local representatives and lords. In return for the

---

[20] For an extensive review of the various theories about legitimacy, see Ronald Cohen, "Introduction," in Ronald Cohen and Judith D. Toland, eds., *State Formation and Political Legitimacy*, Political Anthropology, Volume VI, New Brunswick, N.J.: Transaction Books, 1988, pp. 1–3.

[21] M. I. Finley. *Politics in the Ancient World.* Cambridge: Cambridge University Press, 1983.

[22] Jerome Carcopino. *Daily Life in Ancient Rome: The People and the City at the Height of the Empire.* Edited with bibliography and notes by Henry T. Rowell. Translated from the French by E. O. Lorimer. New Haven: Yale University Press, 1940, pp. 18–20.

taxes they paid, the people received security—protection against invasion and domestic disorder.[23]

Factors Associated with Political Variation

The kinds of societies we call bands, tribes, chiefdoms, and states are points on a continuum from simpler to more complex political systems, from small-scale local autonomy to large-scale regional unification. Societies of all these types are described in the ethnographic record. We see variation in political authority from a few temporary and informal political leaders to large numbers of permanent, specialized political officials, from the absence of political power to the monopoly of public force by a central authority. This continuum of political variation is associated with shifts from food collection to more intensive food production, from small to large communities, from low to high population densities, from an emphasis on reciprocity to redistribution to market exchange, and from egalitarian to rank to fully stratified class societies (see Table 15.1).[24]

Do these trends or associations provide us with an explanation for why political organization varies? Clearly, the data indicate that several factors are associated with political development, but exactly why changes in organization occur is not yet understood. Although economic development may be a necessary condition for political development,[25] that does not fully explain why political organization should become more complex just because the economy can support it. Elman Service has suggested why a society might change from a band level of political organization to a tribal level and why a tribal society might be transformed into a society with chiefdoms. Band societies are generally hunter-gatherers. With a changeover to agriculture, population density and competition between groups may increase. Service believes that such competition will foster the development of some informal organization beyond the community—namely, tribal organization—for offense and defense. Indeed, unilineal kinship groups and age-set systems both seem to be associated with warfare. With regard to chiefdoms, Service suggests they will emerge when redistribution between communities becomes important or when large-scale coordinated work groups are required. The more important these activities are, the more important (and hence more "chiefly") the organizer and his family presumably become.[26] But redistribu-

---

[23] S. F. Nadel. "Nupe State and Community." *Africa*, 8 (1935): 257–303.

[24] For the data suggesting these trends, see Melvin Ember, "The Relationship between Economic and Political Development in Nonindustrialized Societies, *Ethnology*, 2 (1963): 228–48; Robert B. Textor, comp., *A Cross-Cultural Summary*, New Haven: HRAF Press, 1967; Raoul Naroll, "Two Solutions to Galton's Problem," *Philosophy of Science*, 28 (January 1961): 15–39; and Marc H. Ross, "Socioeconomic Complexity, Socialization, and Political Differentiation: A Cross-Cultural Study," *Ethos*, 9 (1981): 217–47.

[25] Ember. "The Relationship between Economic and Political Development in Nonindustrialized Societies," pp. 244–46.

[26] Service. *Primitive Social Organization*, pp. 112, 145.

TABLE 15-1 Suggested trends in political organization and other social characteristics

Type of Organization	Highest Level of Political Integration	Specialization of Political Officials	Predominant Mode of Subsistence	Community Size and Population Density	Social Differentiation	Major Form of Distribution
Band	Local group or band	Little or none; informal leadership	Hunting and gathering	Very small communities, very low density	Egalitarian	Mostly reciprocity
Tribe	Sometimes multi-local group	Little or none; informal leadership	Extensive (shifting) agriculture and/or herding	Small communities, low density	Egalitarian	Mostly reciprocity
Chiefdom	Multi-local group	Some	Extensive or intensive agriculture and/or herding	Large communities, medium density	Rank	Reciprocity and redistribution
State	Multi-local group, often entire language group	Much	Intensive agriculture and herding	Cities and towns, high density	Class and caste	Mostly market exchange

tion is far from a universal activity of chiefs,[27] so Service's explanation of chiefdoms is probably not sufficient.

Theory and research on the anthropology of political development has focused mostly on the high end of the scale of political complexity, and particularly on the origins of the first state societies. Those earliest states apparently arose independently of one another, after about 3500 B.C., in what is now southern Iraq, Egypt, northwestern India, northern China, and central Mexico. As we discussed in Chapter 7, a number of theories have been proposed to explain the earliest states, but no one theory seems to fit all the known archaeological sequences culminating in early state formation.

The Spread of State Societies

For whatever reasons the earliest states developed, the state level of political development has come to dominate the world. Societies with states have larger communities and higher population densities, not to mention armies that are ready to fight at almost any time. State systems that have waged war against chiefdoms and tribes have almost always won, and the result has usually been the political incorporation of the losers. For example, the British and later the United States colonization of much of North America led to the defeat and incorporation of many North American Indian societies.

The defeat and incorporation of the native Americans was at least partially due to the catastrophic depopulations they suffered because of epidemic diseases (such as smallpox and measles) that European and American colonists introduced. Catastrophic depopulation was commonly the outcome of the first contacts between Euro-Americans and the natives of North and South America, as well as the natives of the far islands in the Pacific. People in the New World and the Pacific were not previously exposed (and therefore not resistant) to the diseases the Euro-Americans carried with them when they began to colonize the world. Before the expansion of Europeans, the people of the New World and the Pacific had been separated for a long time from the people and diseases on that geographically continuous land mass we separate into Europe, Africa, and Asia. Smallpox, measles, and the other former scourges of Europe had largely become childhood diseases that most individuals of European ancestry survived.[28]

Whether by depopulation, conquest, or intimidation, the number of independent political units in the world has decreased strikingly in the last 3000 years, and especially in the last 200 years. Robert Carneiro has estimated that in 1000 B.C., there may have been between 100,000 and 1 million separate political units in the world; today there are fewer than 200.[29] In the

[27] Gary Feinman and Jill Nietzel. "Too Many Types: An Overview of Sedentary Prestate Societies in the Americas." In Michael B. Schiffer, *Advances in Archaeological Method and Theory.* Orlando, Fla.: Academic Press, 1984, 7: 39–102.

[28] William H. McNeill. *Plagues and Peoples.* Garden City, N.Y.: Doubleday Anchor, 1976.

[29] Robert L. Carneiro. "Political Expansion as an Expression of the Principle of Competitive Exclusion." In Ronald Cohen and Elman Service, eds., *Origins of the State: The Anthropology of Political Evolution.* Philadelphia: Institute for the Study of Human Issues, 1978, p. 215.

ethnographic record, about 50 percent of the 2000 or so societies described within the last 150 years had only local political integration. That is, the highest level of political integration in 1 out of 2 fairly recent societies was the community.[30] Thus, most of the decrease in the number of independent political units has occurred very recently. What does this trend suggest about the future?

A number of investigators have suggested that the entire world will eventually come to be politically integrated, perhaps as soon as the twenty-third century and no later than A.D. 4850.[31] Only the future will tell if this prediction will come true. And only the future will tell if further political integration in the world will occur peacefully—with all parties agreeing—or by force or the threat of force, as has happened so often in the past.

RESOLUTION OF CONFLICT

As we noted in the beginning of the chapter, political organization implies more than the making of policy, its administration, and its enforcement. It also generally refers to the resolution of conflict, which may be accomplished peacefully by the adjudication of disputes, by the negotiation of compromises, or by the threat of social sanctions. But if such procedures fail or are not possible because of the absence of mediating procedures, then disputes may erupt into violent conflict. When violence occurs within a political unit in which disputes are usually settled peacefully, we call such violence **crime**. When the violence occurs between groups of people from separate political units—groups between which there is no procedure for settling disputes—we usually call such violence **warfare**.

Peaceful Resolution of Conflict

Most modern industrialized states have formal institutions and offices such as police, district attorneys, courts, and penal systems to deal with minor disputes and more serious conflicts that may arise in society. All these institutions generally operate according to codified laws—that is, a set of explicit (generally written) rules stipulating what is permissible and what is not. Transgression of the law by individuals gives the state the right to take action against them. The state has a monopoly on the legitimate use of force in the society, for it alone has the right to coerce subjects into agreement with regulations, customs, political edicts, and procedures.

Many societies lack such specialized offices and institutions for dealing with conflict. Yet, since all societies have peaceful, regularized ways of han-

---

[30] Data from Textor, comp., *A Cross-Cultural Summary.*

[31] Carneiro. "Political Expansion as an Expression of the Principle of Competitive Exclusion." See also Hornell Hart, "The Logistic Growth of Political Areas," *Social Forces*, 26 (1948): 396–408; Raoul Naroll, "Imperial Cycles and World Order," *Peace Research Society: Papers*, 7, Chicago Conference (1967): 83–101; and Louis A. Marano, "A Macrohistoric Trend Toward World Government," *Behavior Science Notes*, 8 (1973): 35–40.

dling at least certain disputes, some anthropologists speak of the universality of law. E. Adamson Hoebel, for example, states the principle as follows:

> Each people has its system of social control. And all but a few of the poorest of them have as a part of the control system a complex of behavior patterns and institutional mechanisms that we may properly treat as law. For, "anthropologically considered, law is merely one aspect of our culture—the aspect which employs the force of organized society to regulate individual and group conduct and to prevent redress or punish deviations from prescribed social norms."[32]

Law, then, whether informal as in simpler societies, or formal as in more complex societies, provides a means of dealing peacefully with whatever conflicts develop.

Community Action. Societies have found various ways of resolving disputes peacefully. One such way involves action on the part of the community as a whole; collective action is common in simpler societies which lack powerful authoritarian leaders.[33] Inuit societies, for example, frequently resolve disputes through community action. Within local groups, kinship ties are not particularly emphasized, and the family is regarded as autonomous in most matters.

Nevertheless, conflicts do take place and have to be resolved. Accordingly, "principles" act as guides to the community in settling trouble cases. An individual's failure to heed a taboo or to follow the suggestions of a shaman leads to expulsion from the group, since the community cannot accept a risk to its livelihood. A person who fails to share goods voluntarily will find them confiscated and distributed to the community, and he or she may be executed in the process. A single case of murder, as an act of vengeance (usually because of the abduction of a wife, or as part of a blood feud), does not concern the community, but repeated murders do. Franz Boas gives a typical example:

> There was a native of Padli by the name Padlu. He had induced the wife of a native of Cumberland Sound to desert her husband and follow him. The deserted husband, meditating revenge . . . visited his friends in Padli, but before he could accomplish his intention of killing Padlu, the latter shot him. . . . A brother of the murdered man went to Padli to avenge the death . . . but he also was killed by Padlu. A third native of Cumberland Sound, who wished to avenge the death of his relatives, was also murdered by him.
>
> On account of these outrages the natives wanted to get rid of Padlu, but yet they did not dare to attack him. When the *pimain* (headman) of the Akudmurmuit learned of these events he started southward and *asked every man in Padli whether Padlu should be killed. All agreed;* so he went with the latter deer hunting . . . and . . . shot Padlu in the back.[34]

[32] E. Adamson Hoebel. *The Law of Primitive Man.* New York: Atheneum, 1968, p. 4. Originally published in 1954. Quoting S. P. Simpson and Ruth Field, "Law and the Social Sciences," *Virginia Law Review,* 32 (1946): 858.

[33] Marc H. Ross. "Political Organization and Political Participation: Exit, Voice, and Loyalty in Preindustrial Societies," *Comparative Politics,* 20 (1988): 73–89.

[34] Franz Boas. *Central Eskimos.* Bureau of American Ethnology, Annual Report no. 6. Washington, D.C., 1888, p. 668.

The killing of an individual is the most extreme action a community can take—we call it capital punishment. The community as a whole or a political official or a court may decide to administer such punishment, but capital punishment seems to exist in nearly all societies, from the simplest to the most complex.[35] It is often assumed that capital punishment deters crime. Yet a recent cross-national study indicates that the abolition of capital punishment tends to be followed by a *decrease* in homicide rates.[36] If capital punishment really deterred crime, we would expect the abolition of capital punishment to be followed by an increase in homicide rates. But that does not seem to be true.

Informal Adjudication without Power.   Community action is not the only way societies without codified or written laws peacefully resolve disputes. Some societies have informal adjudicators who resolve cases, although these individuals do not have the formal power needed to enforce their decisions. One such society is the Nuer of East Africa.

The Nuer are a pastoral and horticultural people who live in villages grouped into districts. Each district is an informal political unit, with its own machinery for settling disputes. If, however, a district has a large population residing over a wide area, it may be a long time before certain disputes are cleared up. On the higher, interdistrict level there is little chance of bringing feuding districts to a quick settlement, and there are few means of apportioning blame or of assessing damages other than by war.

Within a single community, however, disputes are more easily settled by the use of an informal adjudicator called the "leopard-skin chief." This man is not a political chief but a mediator. His position is hereditary, has religious overtones, and makes its holder responsible for the social well-being of the district.

Matters such as cattle stealing rarely come to the attention of the leopard-skin chief; the parties involved usually prefer to settle in their own private way. But if, for example a murder has been committed, the culprit will go at once to the house of the leopard-skin chief. Immediately the chief cuts the culprit's arm so that blood flows; until the cut has been made the murderer may not eat or drink. If the murderer is afraid of vengeance by the slain man's family, he will remain at the house of the leopard-skin chief, which is considered sanctuary. Then, within the next few months, the chief attempts to mediate between the parties to the crime.

The chief acts throughout as a go-between. He has no authority to force either of the parties to negotiate, and he has no power to enforce a solution once it has been arrived at. However, he is able to take advantage of the fact that because both parties to the dispute belong to the same community and

[35] Keith F. Otterbein. *The Ultimate Coercive Sanction: A Cross-Cultural Study of Capital Punishment.* New Haven: HRAF Press, 1986, p. 107.

[36] Dane Archer and Rosemary Gartner. *Violence and Crime in Cross-National Perspective.* New Haven: Yale University Press, 1984, pp. 118–39.

are anxious to avoid a blood feud, they are usually willing to come to terms.[37]

Ritual Reconciliation—Apology. The desire to restore a harmonious relationship may also explain ceremonial apologies. An apology is based on deference—the guilty party shows obeisance and asks for forgiveness. Such ceremonies tend to occur in recent chiefdoms.[38] Among the Fijians of the South Pacific, there is a strong ethic of harmony and mutual assistance, particularly within a village. When a person offends someone of higher status, the offended person and other villagers begin to avoid, and gossip about, the offender. If the offender is sensitive to village opinion, he or she will perform a ceremony of apology called *i soro*. One of the meanings of *soro* is "surrender." In the ceremony the offender keeps his or her head bowed and remains silent while an intermediary speaks, presents a token gift, and asks the offended person for forgiveness. The apology is rarely rejected.[39]

Oaths and Ordeals. Still another way of peacefully resolving disputes is through oaths and ordeals, both of which involve appeals to supernatural power. An **oath** is the act of calling upon a deity to bear witness to the truth of what one says. An **ordeal** is a means used to determine guilt or innocence by submitting the accused to dangerous or painful tests believed to be under supernatural control.[40]

A common kind of ordeal, found in almost every part of the world, is scalding. Among the Tanala of Madagascar, the accused person, having first had his hand carefully examined for protective covering, has to reach his hand into a cauldron of boiling water and grasp, from underneath, a rock suspended there. He then plunges his hand into cold water, has it bandaged, and is led off to spend the night under guard. In the morning his hand is unbandaged and examined. If there are blisters, he is guilty.

Oaths and ordeals have also been practiced in Western societies. Both were common in medieval Europe. Even today, in our own society, vestiges of oaths can be found: children can be heard to say "Cross my heart and hope to die," and witnesses in courts of law are obliged to swear to tell the truth.

Why do some societies use oaths and ordeals? John Roberts suggests that they tend to be found in fairly complex societies where political officials lack sufficient power to make and enforce judicial decisions, or would make themselves unnecessarily vulnerable were they to attempt to do so. So the officials may use oaths and ordeals to let the gods decide guilt or innocence. When political officials gain more power, oaths and ordeals seem to decline or

[37] E. E. Evans-Pritchard. "The Nuer of the Southern Sudan." In M. Fortes and E. E. Evans-Pritchard, eds., *African Political Systems*. New York: Oxford University Press, 1940, p. 291.
[38] Letitia Hickson. "The Social Contexts of Apology in Dispute Settlement: A Cross-Cultural Study." *Ethnology*, 25 (1986): 283–94.
[39] Ibid.; and Klaus-Friedrich Koch, Soraya Altorki, Andrew Arno, and Letitia Hickson. "Ritual Reconciliation and Obviation of Grievances: A Comparative Study in the Ethnography of Law." *Ethnology*, 16 (1977): 279 (269–84).
[40] John M. Roberts. "Oaths, Autonomic Ordeals, and Power." In Clellan S. Ford, ed., *Cross-Cultural Approaches: Readings in Comparative Research*. New Haven: HRAF Press, 1967, p. 169.

disappear.[41] In contrast, smaller and less complex societies probably have no need for elaborate mechanisms such as courts and oaths and ordeals to ascertain guilt. In such societies, everyone is aware of what crimes have been committed and who the guilty parties probably are.

Codified Law and Courts.   The use of codified laws and courts to resolve disputes peacefully exists in our own society. But codified laws and courts are not limited to Western societies. From the late seventeenth to the early twentieth century, for example, the Ashanti of West Africa had a complex political system with elaborate legal arrangements. The Ashanti state was a military-based empire possessing legal codes that resembled those of many ancient civilizations.[42]

Criminal and religious law were merged by the Ashanti: crimes—especially homicide, cursing of a chief, cowardice, and sorcery—were regarded as sins against the ancestral spirits. In Ashanti court procedure, elders examined and cross-examined witnesses as well as parties to the dispute. There were also quasi-professional advocates, and appeals against a verdict could be made directly to a chief. Particularly noteworthy was the emphasis on intent when assessing guilt. Drunkenness constituted a valid defense for all crimes except murder and cursing a chief, and a plea of insanity, if proved, was upheld for all offenses.

Ashanti punishments could be severe. Physical mutilation, such as slicing off the nose or an ear—even castration in sexual offenses—was often employed. However, fines were more frequent, and death sentences could often be commuted to banishment and confiscation of goods.

Why do some societies have codified systems of law while others do not? One explanation, advanced by E. Adamson Hoebel, A. R. Radcliffe-Brown, and others, is that in small, closely knit communities there is little need for formal legal guidelines because competing interests are minimal. Simple societies need little codified law: there are relatively few matters to quarrel about, and the general will of the group is sufficiently well known and demonstrated frequently enough to deter transgressors.

This point of view is consistent with Richard Schwartz's study of two Israeli settlements. In one communal kibbutz, a young man aroused a good deal of community resentment because he had accepted an electric teakettle as a gift. It was the general opinion that he had overstepped the code about not having personal possessions, and he was so informed. Accordingly, he gave the kettle to the communal infirmary. Schwartz observed that "no organized enforcement of the decision was threatened, but had he disregarded the expressed will of the community, his life . . . would have been made intolerable by the antagonism of public opinion."[43]

[41] Roberts. "Oaths, Autonomic Ordeals, and Power," p. 192.
[42] Hoebel. *The Law of Primitive Man*, chap. 9.
[43] Richard D. Schwartz. "Social Factors in the Development of Legal Control: A Case Study of Two Israeli Settlements." *Yale Law Journal*, 63 (February 1954): 475.

In this community, where people worked and ate together, not only did everyone know about transgressions, but a wrongdoer could not escape public censure. Thus, public opinion was an effective sanction. In another Israeli community, however, where individuals lived in widely separated houses and worked and ate separately, public opinion did not work as well. Not only were community members less aware of problems, but they had no quick way of making their feelings known. As a result, they established a judicial body to handle trouble cases.

Larger, more heterogeneous and stratified societies are likely to have more frequent disputes, which at the same time are less visible to the public. Individuals in stratified societies are generally not so dependent on community members for their well-being and hence are less likely to know of, or care about, others' opinions. It is in such societies that codified laws and formal authorities for resolving disputes develop—in order, perhaps, that disputes may be settled impersonally enough so that the parties can accept the decision and social order can be restored.

A good example of how more formal systems of law develop is the experience of towns in the American West during the gold-rush period. These communities were literally swamped by total strangers. The townsfolk, having no control (authority) over these intruders because the strangers had no local ties, looked for ways to deal with the troublesome cases that were continually flaring up. A first attempt at a solution was to hire gunslingers—who were also strangers—to act as peace officers or sheriffs, but this usually failed. Eventually, towns succeeded in having federal authorities send in marshals backed by federal power.

Is there some evidence to support the theory that codified law is necessary only in larger, more complex societies? Data from a large, worldwide sample of societies suggest that codified law is generally associated with political integration beyond the local level. Murder cases, for example, are dealt with informally in societies with only local political organization. In societies with multi-local political units, murder cases tend to be adjudicated by specialized political authorities.[44] There is also some cross-cultural evidence that violence within a society tends to be less frequent when there are formal authorities (chiefs, courts) who have the power to punish murderers.[45]

Violent Resolution of Conflict

People are likely to resort to violence when regular, effective alternative means of resolving a conflict are not available. When violence occurs between political entities such as communities, districts, or nations, we call it warfare. The type of warfare, of course, varies in scope and complexity from society to

[44] Textor, comp. *A Cross-Cultural Summary.*
[45] Wilfred T. Masumura. "Law and Violence: a Cross-Cultural Study." *Journal of Anthropological Research*, 33 (1977): 388–99.

society. Sometimes a distinction is made among **feuding**, **raiding**, and large-scale confrontations.

Feuding is a state of recurring hostilities between families or groups of kin, usually apparently motivated by a desire to avenge an offense—whether insult, injury, deprivation, or death—against a member of the group. The most characteristic feature of the feud is that responsibility to avenge is carried by all members of the kin group. The killing of any member of the offender's group is considered appropriate revenge, since the kin group as a whole is regarded as responsible. Feuds are by no means limited to small-scale societies; they occur as frequently in societies with high levels of political organization.[46]

Raiding is a short-term use of force, generally carefully planned and organized, to realize a limited objective. This objective is usually the acquisition of goods, animals, or other forms of wealth belonging to another (often a neighboring) community. Raiding is especially prevalent in pastoral societies, in which cattle, horses, camels, or other animals are prized and an individual's own herd can be augmented by theft. Raids are often organized by temporary leaders or coordinators whose authority may not endure beyond the planning and execution of the venture.

Both feuding and raiding usually involve relatively small numbers of persons and almost always an element of surprise. Because they are generally attacked without warning, the victims are often unable to muster an immediate defense. Large-scale confrontations, in contrast, involve a large number of persons and planning by both sides of strategies of attack and defense.

Large-scale warfare is usually practiced among societies with intensive agriculture or industrialization. Only these societies possess a technology sufficiently advanced to support specialized armies, military leaders, strategists, and so on. However, large-scale confrontations are not limited to state societies: they occur, for example, among the horticultural Dugum Dani of central New Guinea.

The military history of the Dani, with its shifting alliances and confederations, is reminiscent of that of Europe, although Dani battles involve far fewer fighters and less sophisticated weaponry. Among the Dani, long periods of ritual warfare are characterized by formal battles announced through a challenge sent by one side to the opposing side. If the challenge is accepted, the protagonists meet at the agreed-upon battle site to set up their lines. Fighting with spears, sticks, and bows and arrows begins at midmorning and continues either until nightfall or until rain intervenes. There may also be a rest period during the midday heat during which both sides shout insults at each other or talk and rest among themselves.

The front line of battle is composed of about a dozen active warriors and

[46] Keith F. Otterbein and Charlotte Swanson Otterbein. "An Eye for an Eye, A Tooth for a Tooth: A Cross-Cultural Study of Feuding." *American Anthropologist*, 67 (1965): 1476.

a few leaders. Behind them is a second line, still within arrow range, composed of those who have just left the forward line or are preparing to join it.
The third line, outside arrow range, is composed of noncombatants—males
too old or too young to participate and those recovering from wounds. This
third line merely watches the battle taking place on the grassy plain. On the
hillsides far back from the front line, some of the old men help to direct
ancestral ghosts to the battle by gouging a line in the ground that points in the
direction of the battlefield.[47]

Yet, as total as large-scale confrontations may be, even warfare has cultural rules. Among the Dani, for instance, no fighting occurs at night, and
weapons are limited to simple spears and bows and arrows. Similarly, in state
societies, governments will sign "self-denying" pacts restricting the use of
poison gas, germ warfare, and so forth. Unofficially, private arrangements
are common. One has only to glance through the memoirs of national leaders
of the two world wars to become aware of locally arranged truces, visits to one
another's front positions, exchanges of prisoners of war, and so on.

Explaining Warfare

Most societies anthropology knows about have had warfare between communities or larger territorial groups. (Nearly 75 percent of the societies in a
recent cross-cultural study had warfare at least once every two years before
they were pacified or incorporated by more dominant societies.[48] Yet relatively
little research has been done on the possible causes of war and why it varies in
type and frequency. Why have some people fought a great deal, and others
only infrequently? Why in some societies does warfare occur within the society
or language group?

We have tentative and perhaps only partial answers to some of these
questions. There is evidence that people in preindustrial societies may mostly
go to war out of fear—particularly a fear of expectable but unpredictable
natural disasters (e.g., droughts, floods, locust infestations) that will destroy
food resources. People may think they can protect themselves against such
disasters ahead of time by taking things from defeated enemies. In any case,
preindustrial societies with higher frequencies of war are very likely to have
had a history of expectable but unpredictable disasters. Since chronic (annually recurring) food shortages do not predict higher frequencies of war, it
would appear that people may go to war in an attempt to cushion the impact
of the disasters they expect to occur in the future but cannot predict (or
control or prevent). Consistent with this tentative conclusion is the fact that
the victors in war almost always take land or other resources from the de-

---

[47] Karl Heider. *The Dugum Dani*. Chicago: Aldine, 1970, pp. 105–11. See also Karl Heider, *Grand
    Valley Dani: Peaceful Warriors*, New York: Holt, Rinehart & Winston, 1979, pp. 88–99.
[48] Melvin Ember and Carol R. Ember. "Fear of Disasters as an Engine of History: Resource Crises,
    Warfare, and Interpersonal Aggression." Paper presented at a conference on "What Is the
    Engine of History?" Texas A & M University, October 1988.

feated. And this is true for simpler as well as more complex preindustrial societies.[49] Might similar motives affect decisions about war and peace in the modern world?

We know that complex or politically centralized societies are more likely to have professional armies, hierarchies of military authority, and sophisticated weapons.[50] But surprisingly, the frequency of warfare seems to be not much greater in complex societies than in simple band or tribal societies.[51]

We have some evidence that warfare is unlikely to occur within a society if it is small in population (21,000 people or less) or territory; in a larger society there is a high likelihood of warfare within the society, between communities or larger territorial divisions.[52] In fact, complex societies even if they are politically unified are not less likely than simpler societies to have internal warfare (warfare within the society).[53]

What, if anything, do we know about recent warfare between nation-states? Here we also have some surprising findings. Although many people might think that military alliances lessen the chance of war, it turns out that nations formally allied with other nations have gone to war more often than nations lacking formal alliances. Also, trade relationships do not appear to lessen the chance of war. Rather, disputes between trading partners escalate to war more frequently than disputes between nations that do not trade much with each other. Finally, military equality between nations, particularly when preceded by a rapid military buildup, seems to increase rather than lessen the chance of war between those nations.[54] Clearly, these findings contradict some of our traditional beliefs about the effects of alliances, trade, and military preparedness on the likelihood of war.

We expect that as anthropologists and other social scientists learn more about why people go to war, we will also be learning how to avoid war. For example, if war is more likely when people fear unpredictable disasters, the risk of war could be reduced by international agreements to help countries in need.

[49] Ember and Ember. "Fear of Disasters as an Engine of History." See also Melvin Ember, "Statistical Evidence for an Ecological Explanation of Warfare," *American Anthropologist*, 84 (1982): 645–49.

[50] Keith Otterbein. *The Evolution of War*. New Haven: HRAF Press, 1970.

[51] Ember and Ember. "Fear of Disasters as an Engine of History." See also Otterbein, *The Evolution of War*; and Colin K. Loftin, "Warfare and Societal Complexity: A Cross-Cultural Study of Organized Fighting in Preindustrial Societies," Ph.D. thesis, University of North Carolina at Chapel Hill, 1971.

[52] Carol R. Ember. "An Evaluation of Alternative Theories of Matrilocal versus Patrilocal Residence." *Behavior Science Research*, 9 (1974): 135–49.

[53] Keith F. Otterbein. "Internal War: A Cross-Cultural Study." *American Anthropologist*, 70 (1968): 283 (277–89). See also Marc H. Ross, "Internal and External Conflict and Violence," *Journal of Conflict Resolution*, 29 (1985): 547–79.

[54] J. David Singer. "Accounting for International War: The State of the Discipline." *Annual Review of Sociology*, 6 (1980): 349–67.

SUMMARY

1. All societies have customs or procedures that, organized on behalf of territorial groups, result in decision making and the resolution of disputes. However, these ways of creating and maintaining social order and coping with social disorder vary from society to society.

2. Societies with a band type of political organization are composed of a number of fairly small, usually nomadic groups. Each of these bands is politically autonomous, the band being the largest group that acts as a political unit. Authority within the band is usually informal. Societies with band organization generally are egalitarian hunter-gatherers. But it is possible that band organization may not have been typical of food collectors in the distant past.

3. Societies with tribal organization are similar to those with band organization in being egalitarian. But in contrast with band societies, they generally are food producers, have a higher population density, and are more sedentary. Tribal organization is defined by the presence of groupings (such as clans and age-sets) that can integrate more than one local group into a larger whole.

4. The personal qualities of leaders in tribal societies seem to be similar to the qualities of leaders in the United States, with one major difference: United States leaders are wealthier than others in their society.

5. Chiefdoms differ from tribal organization in having formal authority structures that integrate multi-community political units. Compared with tribal societies, chiefdoms generally are more densely populated and their communities are more permanent. In contrast to "big men" in tribal societies, who generally have to earn their privileges by their personal qualities, chiefs generally hold their positions permanently. Most chiefdom societies have social ranking.

6. A state has been defined as a political unit composed of many communities and having a centralized government with the authority to make and enforce laws, collect taxes, and draft men for military service. In state societies, the government tries to maintain a monopoly on the use of physical force. In addition, states are generally characterized by class stratification, intensive agriculture (the high productivity of which presumably allows the emergence of cities), commercial exchange, a high degree of economic and other specialization, and extensive foreign trade. The rulers of a state cannot depend forever on the use or threat of force to maintain their power; the people must believe the rulers are legitimate or have the right to govern.

7. Societies have found various ways of resolving disputes peacefully. Collective action and informal adjudication are common in simpler societies. Ritual apology occurs frequently in chiefdoms. Oaths and ordeals tend to occur in complex societies where political officials lack power to enforce judicial decisions. Capital punishment seems to exist in nearly all societies, from the simplest to the most complex.

8. People are likely to resort to violence when regular, effective alternative means of resolving a conflict are not available. Violence that occurs between political entities such as communities, districts, or nations is generally referred to as warfare. The type of warfare varies in scope and complexity from society to society.

16

Religion
and Magic

As far as we know, all societies have possessed beliefs that can be grouped under the term *religion*. These beliefs vary from culture to culture and from year to year. Yet, whatever the variety of beliefs in things supernatural, we shall define **religion** as any set of attitudes, beliefs, and practices pertaining to *supernatural power*, whether that power be forces, gods, spirits, ghosts, or demons.

In our society, we divide phenomena into the natural and the supernatural, but not all languages or cultures make such a neat distinction. Moreover, what is considered **supernatural**—powers believed to be not human or not subject to the laws of nature—varies from society to society. Some of the variations are determined by what a society regards as natural law. For example, some illnesses commonly found in our society are believed to result from the natural action of germs and viruses. In other societies (and even for some people in our own society), illness is thought to result from supernatural forces, and thus forms a part of religious belief.

Beliefs about what is, or is not, a supernatural occurrence also vary within a society at a given time or over time. In Judeo-Christian traditions, for example, floods, earthquakes, volcanic eruptions, comets, and epidemics were once considered evidence of supernatural powers intervening in human affairs. It is now generally agreed that they are simply natural occurrences. Yet as recently as 1833, a particularly vivid meteor display caused thousands of intelligent Americans to climb available hills to wait for the end of the world. Thus, the line between the natural and the supernatural appears to vary in a society according to the current state of belief about the causes of things and events in the observable world.

In many cultures, what we would consider religious is embedded in other aspects of everyday life. It is often difficult to separate the religious (or economic or political) from other aspects of culture. That is, simpler cultures have little or no specialization. So the various aspects of culture we distinguish (for example, in the chapter headings of this book) are not as separate and as easily recognized in simple societies as in complex ones such as our own. However, it is sometimes difficult even for us to agree whether a particular custom of ours is religious or not. After all, the categorizing of beliefs as religious or political or social is a relatively new custom. The ancient Greeks, for instance, did not have a word for religion, but they did have many concepts concerning the behavior of their gods and their own expected duties to the gods.

VARIATION IN RELIGIOUS BELIEFS

There seems to be no general agreement among scholars as to why people need religion, or how spirits, gods, and other supernatural beings and forces come into existence. Yet there is general recognition of the enormous variation in the details of religious beliefs and practices. Societies differ in the kinds of supernatural beings or forces they believe in and the character of these beings. They also differ in the structure or hierarchy of those beings, in what the beings actually do, and in what happens to people after death. Variation exists also in the ways in which the supernatural is believed to interact with humans.

Types of Supernatural Forces and Beings

Supernatural Forces. Some peoples believe in supernatural forces that have no personlike character. For example, a supernatural, impersonal force called **mana**, after its Malayo-Polynesian name, is thought to inhabit some objects but not others, some people but not others. We can compare mana to the power a golfer may attribute to some, but unhappily not all, of his clubs. A ballplayer might think a certain shirt or pair of socks has supernatural power or force and that more runs or points will be scored when they are worn. A four-leaf clover has mana; a three-leaf clover does not. A farmer in Polynesia places stones around a field; the crops are bountiful; the stones have mana. During a subsequent year the stones may lose their mana and the crops will be poor. People may also possess mana; for example, the chiefs in Polynesia were said to. However, such power is not necessarily possessed permanently: chiefs who were unsuccessful in war or other activities were said to have lost their mana.

Objects, persons, or places can be considered **taboo**. Anthony Wallace distinguishes mana from taboo by pointing out that things containing mana are to be touched, whereas taboo things are not to be touched, for their power can cause harm.[1] Thus, those who touch them may themselves become taboo. Taboos surround food not to be eaten, places not to be entered, animals not to be killed, people not to be touched sexually, people not to be touched at all, and so on. For example, an Australian aborigine could not eat the animal that was his totem; Hebrew tribesmen were forbidden to touch a woman during menstruation or for seven days following.

Supernatural Beings. Supernatural beings fall within two broad categories: those of nonhuman origin, such as gods and spirits, and those of human origin, such as ghosts and ancestral spirits. Chief among the beings of nonhuman origin, **gods** are named personalities. They are often anthropomorphic—that is, conceived in the image of a person—although they are sometimes given the shapes of other animals or of celestial bodies such as the sun or moon. Essentially, the gods are believed to have created themselves, but some of them then created, or gave birth to, other gods. Although some are seen as creator gods, not all people include the creation of the world as one of the acts of gods.

After their efforts at creation, many creator gods retire. Having set the world in motion, they are not interested in its day-to-day operation. Other creator gods remain interested in the ordinary affairs of human beings, especially the affairs of one small, chosen segment of humanity. Whether a society has a creator god or not, the job of running creation is often left to lesser gods. The Maori of New Zealand, for example, recognize three important gods: a god of the sea, a god of the forest, and a god of agriculture. They call upon each in turn for help and try to get all three to share their knowledge of how the universe runs. The gods of the ancient Romans, on the other hand, specialized to a high degree. There were three gods of the plow, one god to help with the sowing, one for weeding, one for reaping, one for storing grain, one for manuring, and so on.

Beneath the gods in prestige, and often closer to people, are multitudes of unnamed **spirits**. Some may be guardian spirits for people. Some, who become known for particularly efficacious work, may be promoted to the rank of named gods. Some spirits who are known to the people but never invoked by them are of the hobgoblin type: they delight in mischief and can be blamed for any number of small mishaps. Other spirits take pleasure in deliberately working evil on behalf of people.

Many North American Indian groups believed in guardian spirits that had to be sought out, usually in childhood. For example, among the Sanpoil of northeastern Washington, boys and sometimes girls would be sent out on overnight vigils to acquire their guardians. Most commonly the spirits were

[1] Anthony Wallace. *Religion: An Anthropological View.* New York: Random House, 1966, pp. 60–61.

animals, but they could also be uniquely shaped rocks, lakes, mountains, whirlwinds, or clouds. The vigil was not always successful. When it was, the guardian spirit appeared in a vision or dream, and always at first in human form. Conversation with the spirit would reveal its true identity.[2]

Ghosts and **ancestor spirits** are among the supernatural beings who were once human. The belief that ghosts or their actions can be perceived by the living is apparently almost universal.[3] The near-universality of the belief in ghosts may not be difficult to explain. There are many cues in everyday experience that are associated with a loved one, and even after his or her death those cues might arouse the feeling that the dead person is still somehow present. The opening of a door, the smell of tobacco or cologne in a room may evoke the idea that the person is still present, if only for a moment. Then, too, loved ones live on in dreams. Small wonder, then, that most societies believe in ghosts. If the idea of ghosts is generated by these familiar associations, we might expect that ghosts in most societies would be close relatives and friends, not strangers—and they are.[4]

Although the belief in ghosts is nearly universal, the spirits of the dead do not play an active role in the life of the living in all societies. In his cross-cultural study of fifty societies, Guy Swanson found that people are likely to believe in active ancestral spirits where descent groups are important decision-making units. The descent group is an entity that exists over time, back into the past as well as forward into the future, despite the deaths of individual members.[5] The dead feel concern for the fortunes, the prestige, and the continuity of their descent group as strongly as the living. As a Lugbara elder (of northern Uganda in Africa) put it, "Are our ancestors not people of our lineage? They are our fathers and we are their children whom they have begotten. Those that have died stay near us in our homes and we feed and respect them. Does not a man help his father when he is old?"[6]

The Character of Supernatural Beings

Whatever types they may be, the gods or spirits venerated in a given culture tend to have certain personality or character traits. They may be unpredictable or predictable, aloof from or interested in human affairs, helpful or punishing. Why do the gods and spirits in a particular culture exhibit certain character traits rather than others?

[2] Verne F. Ray. *The Sanpoil and Nespelem: Salishan Peoples of Northeastern Washington.* New Haven: Human Relations Area Files, 1954, pp. 172–89.

[3] Paul C. Rosenblatt, R. Patricia Walsh, and Douglas A. Jackson. *Grief and Mourning in Cross-Cultural Perspective.* New Haven: HRAF Press, 1976, p. 51.

[4] Ibid., p. 55.

[5] Guy E. Swanson. *The Birth of the Gods: The Origin of Primitive Beliefs.* Ann Arbor: University of Michigan Press, 1969, pp. 97–108.

[6] John Middleton. "The Cult of the Dead: Ancestors and Ghosts." In William A. Lessa and Evon Z. Vogt, eds., *Reader in Comparative Religion: An Anthropological Approach*, 3rd ed. New York: Harper & Row, Pub., 1971, p. 488.

We have some evidence from cross-cultural studies that the character of supernatural beings may be related to the nature of child training. Melford Spiro and Roy D'Andrade suggest that the god-human relationship is a projection of the parent-child relationship, in which case child-training practices might well be relived in dealings with the supernatural.[7] For example, if a child was nurtured immediately by her parents when she cried or waved her arms about or kicked, then she might grow up expecting to be nurtured by the gods when she performed a ritual. On the other hand, if her parents often punished her, she would grow up expecting the gods to punish her if she disobeyed them. William Lambert, Leigh Triandis, and Margery Wolf, in another cross-cultural study, found that societies with hurtful or punitive child-training practices are likely to believe that their gods are aggressive and malevolent. On the other hand, societies with less punitive child training are more likely to believe that the gods are benevolent.[8] It is worth noting in this context that some people refer to the god as their father and to themselves as his children.

Structure or Hierarchy of Supernatural Beings

The range of social structures in human societies from egalitarian to highly stratified has its counterpart in the supernatural world. Some societies have a number of gods or spirits that are not ranked. One god has about as much power as another. Other societies have gods or spirits that are ranked in prestige and power. For example, on the Pacific islands of Palau, which was a rank society, gods were ranked like people were. Each clan worshiped a god and a goddess that had names or titles similar to clan titles. Although a clan god was generally important only to the members of that clan, the gods of the various clans in a village were believed to be ranked in the same order that the clans were. Thus, the god of the highest-ranking clan was respected by all the clans of the village. Its shrine was given the place of honor in the center of the village and was larger and more elaborately decorated than other shrines.[9]

Although the Palauans did not believe in a high god or supreme being who outranked all the other gods, some societies do. Consider Judaism, Christianity, and Islam, which we call **monotheistic** religions. Although *monotheism* means "one god," most monotheistic religions actually include more than one supernatural being (e.g., demons, angels, the Devil). But the supreme being or high god, as the creator of the universe or the director of

---

[7] Melford E. Spiro and Roy G. D'Andrade. "A Cross-Cultural Study of Some Supernatural Beliefs." *American Anthropologist*, 60 (1958): 456–66.

[8] William W. Lambert, Leigh Minturn Triandis, and Margery Wolf. "Some Correlates of Beliefs in the Malevolence and Benevolence of Supernatural Beings: A Cross-Societal Study." *Journal of Abnormal and Social Psychology*, 58 (1959): 162–69. See also Ronald P. Rohner, *They Love Me, They Love Me Not: A Worldwide Study of the Effects of Parental Acceptance and Rejection*, New Haven: HRAF Press, 1975, p. 108.

[9] H. G. Barnett. *Being a Palauan*. New York: Holt, Rinehart & Winston, 1960, pp. 79–85.

events (or both), is believed to be ultimately responsible for all events.[10] A **polytheistic** religion recognizes many important gods, no one of which is supreme.

Why do some societies have a belief in a high god while others do not? Swanson suggests that people invent gods that personify the important decision-making groups in their society. He therefore hypothesizes that societies with hierarchical political systems should be more likely to believe in a high god. In his cross-cultural study of fifty societies (none of which practice any of the major world religions), he found that a belief in a high god is strongly associated with three or more levels of decision-making groups (for example, family, clan, chiefdom).[11] This and other results strongly suggest that the realm of the gods may reflect the everyday social and political world.

Intervention of the Gods in Human Affairs

According to Clifford Geertz, it is when faced with ignorance, pain, and the unjustness of life that a person explains events by the intervention of the gods.[12] Thus, in Greek religion the direct intervention of Poseidon as ruler of the seas prevented Odysseus from getting home for ten years. In the Old Testament, the direct intervention of Yahweh caused the great flood that killed most of the people in the time of Noah. In other societies, a man may search his memory for a violated taboo that has brought him punishment through the spirit's intervention.

In addition to unasked-for divine interference, there are numerous examples of requests for divine intervention, either for good for oneself and friends or for evil for others. Gods are asked to intervene in the weather and make the crops grow, to send fish to the fisherman and game to the hunter, to find lost things, and to accompany travelers and prevent accidents. They are asked to stop the flow of lava down the side of a volcano, to stop a war, or to cure an illness.

The gods do not intervene in all societies. In some they intervene in human affairs; in others, they are not the slightest bit interested; and in still others they interfere only occasionally. We have little research on why gods are believed to interfere in some societies and not in others. However, we have some evidence as to the kinds of societies in which the gods take an interest in the morality of human behavior.

Swanson's study suggests that the gods are likely to intervene in the moral behavior of a people when there are varying degrees of wealth in the society. In such a society, the gods seem likely to create sanctions against behavior that threatens the status quo.[13] It may be that supernatural support

---

[10] Swanson. *The Birth of the Gods*, p. 56.

[11] Ibid., pp. 55–81.

[12] Clifford Geertz. "Religion as a Cultural System." In Michael Banton, ed., *Anthropological Approaches to the Study of Religion*. Association of Social Anthropologists of the Commonwealth, Monograph no. 3. New York: Praeger, 1966, pp. 1–46.

[13] Swanson. *The Birth of the Gods*, pp. 153–74.

of moral behavior is particularly useful when there are inequalities that tax the ability of the political system to maintain social order and minimize social disorder. Envy of others' privileges may strain moral behavior.

VARIATION IN RELIGIOUS PRACTICE

Beliefs are not the only elements of religion that vary from society to society. There is also variation in how people interact with the supernatural. The manner of approach to the supernatural varies from application (requests, prayers, and so on) to manipulation. And societies vary in the kinds of religious practitioners they have.

Ways to Interact with the Supernatural

How to get in touch with the supernatural has proved to be a universal problem. Wallace suggests a number of activities may be used, including prayer, doing things to the body or mind, simulation, feasts, and sacrifices.[14]

Prayer can be spontaneous or memorized, private or public, silent or spoken. The Lugbara do not say the words of a prayer aloud, for that would be too powerful; they simply think about the things that are bothering them. The gods know all languages.

Doing things to the body or mind may involve drugs (peyote, the magic mushroom), sensory deprivation, mortification of the flesh (self-flagellation, prolonged sleeplessness, piercing of the flesh, amputation of a finger joint, running till exhausted), and deprivation of food or water. These methods may produce an altered state of consciousness; the person is said to be possessed by a spirit or the person's soul is said to be temporarily absent. Erika Bourguignon refers to these altered states as "trances" (a "possession trance" involves the belief that a person is possessed by a spirit). Bourguignon's cross-cultural study found that trances are not at all a rare phenomenon; they are culturally patterned in 90 percent of the world's societies.[15] Possession trances are especially likely in societies that depend on agriculture and are politically complex.[16]

Voodoo employs simulation, or the imitation of things. Dolls are made in the likeness of an enemy and then are mistreated so that the enemy will experience pain and even death. Simulation is often employed during **divination**, or getting the supernatural to provide guidance. Many people in our society have their fortunes read in crystal balls, tea leaves, Ouija boards, or

[14] Anthony Wallace. *Religion: An Anthropological View*, pp. 52–67.
[15] Erika Bourguignon. "Introduction: A Framework for the Comparative Study of Altered States of Consciousness." In Erika Bourguignon, *Religion, Altered States of Consciousness, and Social Change*. Columbus: Ohio State University Press, 1973, pp. 3–35.
[16] Erika Bourguignon and Thomas L. Evascu. "Altered States of Consciousness within a General Evolutionary Perspective: A Holocultural Analysis." *Behavior Science Research*, 12 (1977): 197–216.

cards. Or they may choose a course of action by a toss of a coin or a throw of dice. All are variations of methods used in other cultures.

The ostensible purpose of divination is to learn something only the supernatural powers know. Omar Moore suggests that for the Naskapi hunters of Labrador, divination is an adaptive strategy for successful hunting. The Naskapi consult the diviner every three or four days when they have no luck in hunting. The diviner holds a caribou bone over the fire, and the burns and cracks that appear in it indicate where the group should hunt. Moore, unlike the Naskapi, does not believe that the diviner really can find out where the animals will be; the cracks in the bones merely provide a way of randomly choosing where to hunt. Since humans are likely to develop customary patterns of action, they might be likely to look for game according to some plan. But game might learn to avoid hunters who operate according to a plan. Thus, any method of ensuring against patterning or predictable plans—any random strategy—may be advantageous. Divination by "reading" the bones would seem to be a random strategy. It also relieves any individual of the responsibility of deciding where to hunt, a decision that might arouse anger if the hunt failed.[17]

The eating of a sacred meal is found in many religions. The Australian aborigines, forbidden to eat their totem animal, have one totem feast a year at which they eat the totem, presumably as a gesture of symbolic cannibalism. The feast is a part of marriage and funeral ceremonies, as well as a fringe benefit of the sacrifice of food to the gods.

Some societies make sacrifices to gods in order to divert their anger or to attract their goodwill. Characteristic of all sacrifices is that something of value is given up to the gods, whether it be food, drink, sex, household goods, money, or the life of an animal or person. Some societies feel that the god is obligated to act on their behalf if they make the appropriate sacrifice. Others use the sacrifice in an attempt to persuade the god, realizing there is no guarantee that the attempt will be successful.

Of all types of sacrifice, we probably think that the taking of human life is the ultimate. Nevertheless, human sacrifice is not rare in the ethnographic and historical record. Why have some societies practiced it? A recent cross-cultural study finds that among preindustrial societies, those with full-time craft specialists, slavery, and the corvée are most likely to practice human sacrifice. The suggested explanation is that the sacrifice mirrors what is socially important: societies that depend mainly on human labor for energy (rather than animals or machines) may think of a human life as an appropriate offering to the gods when people want something very important.[18]

---

[17] Omar Khayyám Moore. "Divination: A New Perspective." *American Anthropologist,* 59 (1957): 69–74.
[18] Dean Sheils. "A Comparative Study of Human Sacrifice." *Behavior Science Research,* 15 (1980): 245–62.

Magic

All these modes of interacting with the supernatural can be categorized in various ways. One dimension of variation is how much people in society rely on pleading or asking or trying to persuade the supernatural being (or force) to act on their behalf, as opposed to whether they believe they can compel such behavior by certain acts. For example, prayer is asking; performing voodoo is presumably compelling. When people believe their action can compel the supernatural to act in some particular and intended way, anthropologists often refer to the belief and related practice as **magic**.

Magic may involve manipulation of the supernatural for good or for evil purposes. Many societies have magical rituals designed to ensure good crops, the replenishment of game, the fertility of domestic animals, and the avoidance and cure of illness in humans. As we will see, the witch doctor and the shaman often employ magic to effect a cure. But the use of magic to bring about harm has evoked perhaps the most interest.

Sorcery and Witchcraft.   Sorcery and witchcraft are attempts to invoke the spirits to work harm against people. Although the words *sorcery* and *witchcraft* are often used interchangeably, they are also often distinguished. **Sorcery** may include the use of materials, objects, and medicines to invoke supernatural malevolence. **Witchcraft** may be said to accomplish the same ills by means of thought and emotion alone. Evidence of witchcraft can never be found. This lack of visible evidence makes an accusation of witchcraft both harder to prove and harder to disprove.

To the Azande of Zaire (central Africa) witchcraft is part of everyday living. It is not used to explain events for which the cause is known, such as carelessness or violation of a taboo, but to explain the otherwise unexplainable. A man is gored by an elephant. He must have been bewitched, because he had not been gored on other elephant hunts. A man goes to his beer hut at night, lights some straw, and holds it aloft to look at his beer. The thatch catches fire and the hut burns down. The man has been bewitched, for huts did not catch fire on hundreds of other nights when he and others did the same thing. Some people are sitting in the cool shade under a granary, and it collapses on them, injuring them. They are bewitched because, although the Azande admit that termites eating through the wooden posts caused the granary to collapse, witchcraft made it collapse at the precise moment on those particular people. Some of the pots of a skilled potter break; some of the bowls of a skilled carver crack. Witchcraft: other pots, other bowls treated exactly the same have not broken.[19]

The witch craze in Europe during the sixteenth and seventeenth centuries and the witch trials in 1692 in Salem, Massachusetts, remind us that the fear of others, which the belief in witchcraft presumably represents, has not

[19] E. E. Evans-Pritchard. "Witchcraft Explains Unfortunate Events." In William A. Lessa and Evon Z. Vogt, eds., *Reader in Comparative Religion: An Anthropological Approach*, 4th ed. New York: Harper & Row, 1979, pp. 362–66.

been lacking in Western societies. Many scholars have tried to explain these witch hunts. One factor often suggested is political turmoil, which may give rise to widespread distrust and a search for scapegoats. In the case of western Europe during the sixteenth and seventeenth centuries, small regional political units were being incorporated into national states, and political allegiances were in flux. In addition, as Swanson has noted, the commercial revolution and related changes were producing a new social class, the middle class, and "were promoting the growth of Protestantism and other heresies from Roman Catholicism."[20] In the case of Salem, the government of the colony of Massachusetts was unstable and there was much internal dissension. In 1692, the year of the witchcraft hysteria, Massachusetts was left without an English governor and judicial practices broke down. These extraordinary conditions saw the accusation of a single person for witchcraft become the accusation of hundreds and the execution of twenty. Swanson suggests that the undermining of legitimate political procedures may have generated the widespread fear of witches.[21]

It is also possible that epidemics of witchcraft accusation, as in Salem, may be the result of real epidemics—epidemics of disease. The disease implicated in Salem is the fungus disease called ergot. The rye flour that went into the bread that the Salem people ate may have been contaminated by ergot. It is now known that people who eat grain products contaminated by ergot suffer from convulsions, hallucinations, and other symptoms such as crawling sensations in the skin. We also now know that ergot contains LSD, the drug that produces hallucinations and other delusions that resemble those occurring in severe mental disorders. Some scholars have recently suggested that there may have been an epidemic of ergot disease in Salem before the witchcraft trials, because the conditions then—a severely cold winter followed by a cool, moist spring—are now known to be conducive to the growth of ergot on rye plants. The presumed victims of bewitchment in Salem had symptoms similar to victims of ergot poisoning today. They suffered from convulsions and the sensations of being pricked, pinched, or bitten. They had visions and felt as if they were flying through the air.[22] Interestingly, when witchcraft hysteria was greatest in Europe, Europeans were using an ointment containing a skin-penetrating substance that we now know produces hallucinations and a vivid sensation of flying.[23] It is perhaps no wonder that our

---

[20] Swanson. *The Birth of the Gods*, p. 150. See also H. R. Trevor-Roper, "The European Witch-Craze of the Sixteenth and Seventeenth Centuries," in Lessa and Vogt, eds., *Reader in Comparative Religion*, 3rd ed., pp. 444–49.

[21] Swanson. *The Birth of the Gods*, pp. 150–51.

[22] Linda R. Caporael. "Ergotism: The Satan Loosed in Salem?" *Science*, April 2, 1976, pp. 21–26; and Mary K. Matossian. "Ergot and the Salem Witchcraft Affair." *American Scientist*, 70 (1982): 355–57.

[23] Michael Harner. "The Role of Hallucinogenic Plants in European Witchcraft." In Michael Harner, ed., *Hallucinogens and Shamanism*. New York: Oxford University Press, 1972, pp. 127–50.

popular image of witches is one of people flying through the air on broom-sticks.

But even if epidemics of witchcraft hysteria are due to epidemics of ergot poisoning and/or episodes of political turmoil, we still have to understand why so many societies in the ethnographic record believe in witchcraft and sorcery in the first place. Why do so many societies believe that there are ways to invoke the spirits to work harm against people? One possible explanation, suggested by Beatrice Whiting, is that sorcery or witchcraft will be found in societies that lack procedures or judicial authorities to deal with crime and other offenses. Her theory is that all societies need some form of social control—some way of deterring most would-be offenders and of dealing with actual offenders. In the absence of judicial officials who (if present) might deter and deal with antisocial behavior, sorcery may be a very effective social-control mechanism. If you misbehave, the person you were bad to might cause you to become ill or even die. The cross-cultural evidence seems to support this theory: sorcery is more important in societies lacking judicial authorities.[24]

Types of Practitioner

Individuals may believe that they can directly contact the supernatural, but almost all societies also have part-time or full-time religious or magical practitioners. Recent research suggests there are four major types of practitioner: shamans; sorcerers or witches; mediums; and priests. As we shall see, the number of types of practitioner seems to vary with degree of cultural complexity.[25]

The Shaman.   The **shaman** is usually a part-time male specialist who has fairly high status in his community and is often involved in healing.[26] Westerners often call shamans "witch doctors" because they don't believe that shamans can effectively cure people. Do shamans effectively cure? Actually, Westerners are not the only skeptics. An American Indian named Quesalid from the Kwakiutl of the Northwest Coast didn't believe that shamanism was effective either. So he began to associate with the shamans in order to spy on them and was taken into their group. In his first lessons, he learned

> a curious mixture of pantomime, prestidigitation, and empirical knowledge, including the art of simulating fainting and nervous fits, . . . sacred song, the technique for inducing vomiting, rather precise notions of auscultation or listening to sounds within the body to detect disorders and obstetrics, and the use of "dreamers," that is, spies who listen to private conversations and secretly convey to the shaman bits of information concerning the origins and symptoms of the

[24] Beatrice B. Whiting, *Paiute Sorcery*. Viking Fund Publications in Anthropology, no. 15. New York: Wenner-Gren Foundation, 1950, pp. 36–37. See also Swanson, *The Birth of the Gods*, pp. 137–52, 240–41.

[25] Michael James Winkelman. "Magico-Religious Practitioner Types and Socioeconomic Conditions." *Behavior Science Research*, 20 (1986): 17–46.

[26] Ibid., pp. 28–29.

ills suffered by different people. Above all, he learned the *ars magna* . . . The shaman hides a little tuft of down in the corner of his mouth, and he throws it up, covered with blood at the proper moment—after having bitten his tongue or made his gums bleed—and solemnly presents it to his patient and the onlookers as the pathological foreign body extracted as a result of his sucking and manipulations.[27]

His suspicions were confirmed, but his first curing was a success. The patient had heard that Quesalid had joined the shamans and believed that only he would heal him. Quesalid remained with the shamans for the four-year apprenticeship, during which he could take no fee, and he became increasingly aware that his methods worked. He visited other villages, competed with other shamans in curing hopeless cases and won, and finally seemed convinced that his curing system was more valid than those of other shamans. Instead of denouncing the trickery of shamans, he continued to practice as a renowned shaman.[28]

After working with shamans in Africa, E. Fuller Torrey, a psychiatrist and anthropologist, concluded that they use the same mechanisms and techniques to cure patients as psychiatrists and achieve about the same results. He isolates four categories used by healers the world over:

1. *The naming process.* If a disease has a name—"neurasthenia" or "phobia" or "possession by an ancestral spirit" will do—then it is curable; the patient realizes that the doctor understands his case.
2. *The personality of the doctor.* Those who demonstrate some empathy, non-possessive warmth, and genuine interest in the patient get results.
3. *The patient's expectations.* One way of raising the patient's expectations of being cured is the trip to the doctor; the longer the trip—to the Mayo Clinic, Menninger Clinic, Delphi, or Lourdes—the easier the cure. An impressive setting (the medical center) and impressive paraphernalia (the stethoscope, the couch, attendants in uniform, the rattle, the whistle, the drum, the mask) also raise the patient's expectations. The healer's training is important: the Ute Indian has his dreams analyzed; the Blackfoot Indian has a seven-year training course; the American psychiatrist spends four years in medical school and three in hospital training and has diplomas on the wall. High fees also help to raise a patient's expectations. (The Paiute doctors always collect their fees before starting a cure; if they don't, it is believed that they will fall ill.)
4. *Curing techniques.* Drugs, shock treatment, conditioning techniques, and so on have long been used in many different parts of the world.[29]

Medical research suggests that psychological factors are sometimes very important in illness. Patients who believe that medicine will help them often

---

[27] Claude Lévi-Strauss. "The Sorcerer and His Magic." In Claude Lévi-Strauss, *Structural Anthropology*, trans. Claire Jacobsen and Brooke Grundfest Schoepf. New York: Basic Books, 1963, p. 169.
[28] Franz Boas. *The Religion of the Kwakiutl.* Columbia University Contributions to Anthropology, vol. 10, pt. II. New York, 1930, pp. 1–41. Reported in Lévi-Strauss, *Structural Anthropology*, pp. 169–73.
[29] E. Fuller Torrey. *The Mind Game: Witchdoctors and Psychiatrists.* New York: Emerson Hall, n.d.

recover quickly even if the medicine is only a sugar pill. Patients who "lose the will to live" may succumb to illness easily. Still, as pharmaceutical companies have discovered, many "folk medicines" collected in anthropological field-work do work.

Sorcerers and Witches. In contrast with shamans, who have fairly high status, sorcerers and witches of both sexes tend to have very low social and economic status in their societies. Whereas shamans may seek out their role and train for it, the males and females who become part-time sorcerers and witches acquire their roles because others think they are suited or fated for them.[30] Suspected sorcerers and witches are usually feared because they are thought to know how to invoke the supernatural to cause illness, injury, and death. Since sorcerers use materials for their magic, evidence of sorcery can be found, and suspected sorcerers are often killed for their malevolent activities. Because witchcraft supposedly is accomplished by thought and emotion alone, it may be harder to prove someone is a witch, as we have mentioned. However, as we have also seen, this has not prevented people from accusing and killing others for being witches.

Mediums. **Mediums** tend to be females. These part-time practitioners are asked to heal and divine while in possession trances—that is, when they are thought to be possessed by spirits. Mediums are described as having tremors, convulsions, seizures, and temporary amnesia.

Priests. **Priests** are generally full-time male specialists who officiate at public events. They generally have very high status and are thought to be able to relate to superior or high gods who are beyond the ordinary person's control. In most societies with priests, the people who get to be priests tend to obtain their offices through inheritance or political appointment.[31] Priests are sometimes distinguished from other people by special clothing or a different hair style. The training of a priest can be vigorous and long, including fasting, praying, and physical labor as well as learning the dogma and the ritual of his religion. Priests in America generally complete four years of theological school and sometimes serve first as apprentices under established priests. The priest generally does not receive a fee for each of his services but is supported by donations from parishioners or followers. Since priests often have some political power as a result of their office—the chief priest is sometimes also the head of state, or is a close advisor to the chief of state—their material well-being is a direct reflection of their position in the priestly hierarchy.

It is the dependence on memorized ritual that both marks and protects the priest. If a shaman repeatedly fails to effect a cure, he will probably lose his following, for he has obviously lost the support of the spirits. However, if a priest performs his ritual perfectly and the gods choose not to respond, the priest will usually retain his position and the ritual will preserve its assumed

---

[30] Winkelman. "Magico-Religious Practitioner Types and Socioeconomic Conditions," p. 28.
[31] Ibid., p. 27.

effectiveness. The nonresponse of the gods will be explained in terms of the people's unworthiness of supernatural favor.

Practitioners and Social Complexity.   More complex societies tend to have more types of religious or magical practitioners. If a society has only one type of practitioner, it is almost always a shaman; such societies tend to be nomadic or semi-nomadic food collectors. Societies with two types of practitioner (usually shaman/healers and priests) have agriculture. Those with three types of practitioner are agriculturists or pastoralists with political integration beyond the community (the additional practitioner type tends to be either a sorcerer/witch or a medium). Finally, societies with all four types of practitioners have agriculture, political integration beyond the community, and social classes.[32]

RELIGION AND ADAPTATION

Many anthropologists take the view that religions are generally adaptive because they reduce the anxieties and uncertainties to which all people are subject. We do not really know that religion is the only means of reducing anxiety and uncertainty, or even that individuals or societies *have* to reduce their anxiety and uncertainty. Still, it seems likely that certain religious beliefs and practices have directly adaptive consequences.

For example, the Hindu belief in the sacred cow has seemed to many to be the very opposite of a useful or adaptive custom. Their religion does not permit Hindus to slaughter cows. Why do the Hindus retain such a belief? Why do they allow all those cows to wander around freely, defecating all over the place, and not slaughter any of them? The contrast with our own use of cows could hardly be greater.

Marvin Harris has suggested, however, that the Hindu use of cows may have beneficial consequences that some other use of cows would not have. Harris points out that there may be a sound economic reason for not slaughtering cattle in India. The cows (and the males they produce) provide a number of resources that could not easily be provided otherwise. At the same time, their wandering around to forage is no strain on the food-producing economy. The resources provided by the cows are varied. First, a team of oxen and a plow are essential for the many small farms in India. The Indians could produce oxen with fewer cows, but to do so they would have to devote some of their food production to the feeding of those cows. In the present system, they do not feed the cows, and even though this makes the cows relatively infertile, males (which are castrated to make oxen) are still produced at no cost to the economy.

Second, cow dung is essential as a cooking fuel and fertilizer. The National Council of Applied Economic Research estimates that an amount of dung equivalent to 45 million tons of coal is burned annually. Moreover, it is

[32] Ibid., pp. 35–37.

delivered practically to the door each day at no cost. Alternative sources of fuel, such as wood, are scarce or costly. In addition, about 340 million tons of dung are used as manure—essential in a country obliged to derive three harvests a year from its intensively cultivated land. Third, although Hindus do not eat beef, cattle that die naturally or are butchered by non-Hindus are eaten by the lower castes, who, without the upper-caste taboo against eating beef, might not get this needed protein. Fourth, the hides and horns of the cattle that die are used in India's enormous leather industry. Therefore, since the sacred cows do not themselves consume resources needed by people, and since it would be impossible to provide traction, fuel, and fertilizer as cheaply by other means, the taboo against slaughtering cattle may be quite adaptive.[33]

Religious Change as Revitalization

The long history of religion includes periods of strong resistance to change as well as periods of radical change. Anthropologists have been especially interested in the founding of new religions or sects. The appearance of new religions is one of the things that may happen when cultures are disrupted by contact with dominant societies. Various terms have been suggested for these religious movements—cargo cults, nativistic movements, messianic movements, and millenarian cults. Wallace suggests that they are all examples of **revitalization movements**, efforts to save a culture by infusing it with a new purpose and new life.[34]

After the American Revolution, the Seneca Indians, an Iroquois tribe, lost their lands and were confined to isolated reservations amid an alien people. They were in a state of despondency when a man named Handsome Lake received a vision from God that led him to stop drinking and to preach a new religion that would revitalize the Seneca. This was not the first such movement among the Iroquois. In the fifteenth century, they were an unorganized people, warring against each other and being warred upon by other tribes. Hiawatha, living as a highwayman and a cannibal, was visited by the god Dekanawidal. He became God's spokesman in persuading the five tribes to give up their feuding and to unite as the League of the Iroquois. The Condolence Ritual was adopted, which precluded feuding and blood revenge. The radical new movement that had united and revitalized the Iroquois settled into a belief that conserved their integrity.[35]

Although many scholars believe cultural stress gives rise to new religious movements, it is still important to understand exactly what the stresses are and how strong they have to become before a new movement emerges. Do different kinds of stresses produce different types of movements? And does the nature of the movement depend on the cultural elements already present?

---

[33] Marvin Harris. "The Cultural Ecology of India's Sacred Cattle." *Current Anthropology*, 7 (1966): 51–63.
[34] Wallace. *Religion*, p. 30.
[35] Ibid., pp. 31–34.

Let us consider some theory and research on the causes of the millenarian cargo cults that began to appear in Melanesia from about 1885 on.

The cargo cults can be thought of as religious movements "in which there is an expectation of, and preparation for, the coming of a period of supernatural bliss."[36] Thus, an explicit belief of the cargo cults was the notion that some liberating power would bring all the Western goods (*cargo* in pidgin English) the people might want. For example, around 1932, on Buka in the Solomon Islands, the leaders of a cult prophesied that a tidal wave would sweep away the villages and a ship would arrive with iron, axes, food, tobacco, cars, and arms. Work in the gardens ceased, and wharves and docks were built for the expected cargo.[37]

What may explain such cults? Peter Worsley has suggested that an important factor in the rise of cargo cults and millenarian movements in general is the existence of oppression—in the case of Melanesia, colonial oppression. But he suggests the cults there have taken religious rather than political forms because they are a way of pulling together people who have had no political unity, who have lived in small, isolated social groups.[38] Other scholars, such as David Aberle, think *relative deprivation* is more important than oppression in explaining the origins of cults.[39] In a comparative study of cargo cults, Bruce Knauft found that such cults were more important in those Melanesian societies that had had *decreasing* cultural contact with the West, and presumably decreasing contact with valued goods, within the year prior to the cult's emergence.[40] Knauft's study supports Aberle's general interpretation, but it goes further in specifying the nature of the deprivation involved.

If the recent as well as distant past is any guide, religious belief and practice will continue to be revitalized periodically.

SUMMARY

1. Religion is any set of attitudes, beliefs, and practices pertaining to supernatural power. Such beliefs may vary within a culture as well as among societies, and they may change over time.
2. There are wide variations in religious beliefs and practices. Societies vary in the number and kinds of supernatural entities in which they believe. There may be disembodied supernatural forces, supernatural beings of nonhuman origin (gods or spirits), and supernatural beings of human origin (ghosts). The religious belief system of a society may include any or all such entities.

---

[36] Peter Worsley. *The Trumpet Shall Sound: A Study of "Cargo" Cults in Melanesia.* London: MacGibbon & Kee, 1957, p. 12.

[37] Ibid., pp. 11, 115.

[38] Ibid., p. 122.

[39] David Aberle. "A Note on Relative Deprivation Theory as Applied to Millenarian and Other Cult Movements." In Lessa and Vogt, eds., *Reader in Comparative Religion*, 3rd ed., pp. 528–31.

[40] Bruce M. Knauft. "Cargo Cults and Relational Separation." *Behavior Science Research*, 13 (1978): 185–240.

3. In some societies, all gods are equal in rank; in others, there is a hierarchy of prestige and power among gods and spirits, just as among humans.
4. A monotheistic religion is one in which there is one high god and all other supernatural beings are either subordinate to, or function as alternative manifestations of, this god. A high god is generally found in societies with a high level of political development.
5. Faced with ignorance, pain, and injustice, people frequently explain events by claiming intervention by the gods. Such intervention has also been sought by people who hope it will help them achieve their own ends.
6. Various methods have been used to attempt communication with the supernatural. In some societies, intermediaries such as shamans or priests communicate with the supernatural on behalf of others. Societies with religious intermediaries tend to be more complex and have greater specialization; religious specialization seems to be part of this general specialization.
7. When people believe their actions can compel the supernatural to act in a particular and intended way, anthropologists refer to the belief and related practice as magic.
8. Sorcery and witchcraft are attempts to make the spirits work harm against people.
9. Recent cross-cultural research suggests there are four major types of religious practitioner: shamans, sorcerers or witches, mediums, and priests. The number of types of practitioner seems to vary with degree of cultural complexity.
10. The history of religion includes periods of strong resistance to change and periods of radical change. One explanation for this is that religious practices always originate during periods of stress. Religious movements may also be examples of revitalization movements—efforts to save a culture by infusing it with a new purpose and new life.

Epilogue

In many respects, the world of today is a shrinking one. It is not, of course, physically shrinking, but it is shrinking in the sense that it takes a shorter time to travel around it and an even shorter time to communicate around it—witness the worldwide network of TV satellites. Today it is possible to fly halfway around the globe in the time it took preindustrial humans to visit a nearby town. Newspapers, radio, television, and movies have done much to make different cultures more familiar and accessible to one another.

The world is shrinking culturally too, in the sense that more people are drawn each year into the world market economy, buying and selling similar things and, as a consequence, altering the patterns of their lives. Perhaps the most obvious illustration of what is happening to the world culturally is the appearance of Coca-Cola, razor blades, steel tools, and even drive-in movies in places that not too long ago lacked such things. But the diffusion of these items is only a small part of the picture. More important than the spread of material goods has been the introduction of selling and buying and wage labor. The diffusion of market exchange throughout the world reflects the expansion of certain nations' spheres of influence over the last century. In some places as a result of colonization or conquest, in others as a result of economic and military-aid programs, and in still others because of a desire to emulate dominant cultures (American, British, Chinese, and so on), the hundreds of different cultures that survive in the world have become more similar over the last hundred years.

Aside from whether or not these changes are desirable, from our point of view or from the point of view of the peoples experiencing them, we might ask how the shrinking cultural world affects the field of anthropology, particularly, of course, cultural anthropology.

Some cultural anthropologists have worried about the possible demise of their discipline because of the virtual disappearance of the "primitive" or noncommercial world, which in the past "provided the discipline with most of its data as well as the major inspiration for its key concepts and theoretical ideas."[1] Some of the societies known to ethnography have disappeared because of depopulation produced by the introduction of foreign infectious diseases. Others have been so altered by contact with dominant societies that their cultures now retain few of the characteristics that made them unique. To

[1] David Kaplan and Robert A. Manners. "Anthropology: Some Old Themes and New Directions." *Southwestern Journal of Anthropology*, 27 (1971): 71.

be sure, there are still some cultures in the world (in the interior of New Guinea and a few other large Melanesian islands, and in the back areas of Brazil, Peru, and Venezuela) that have not yet drastically changed. But most of these have changed somewhat, largely under the impact of commercialization, and they will probably continue to change.

Some of those who are worried about the future of cultural anthropology foresee the disappearance of their discipline because it has traditionally focused on cultural variation, and that variation is diminishing. Cultural anthropology, for these people, is synonymous with the ethnographic study of exotic, out-of-the-way cultures not previously described. Nowadays it is difficult to find cultures that have been preserved in such an undescribed and unaltered state. Thus, it is said, we are running out of subject matter because we are running out of new cultures to describe. Some of the more pessimistic cultural anthropologists envision a time when the last ethnography has been written and the last native has been handed a bottle of Coca-Cola, and the death knell rings upon cultural anthropology as a discipline. Evidence suggests, however, that such a view may be mistaken.

There is no reason to believe that cultural variation, of at least some sort, will ever disappear. The development of commonly held ideas, beliefs, and behaviors—in other words, culture—depends on the existence of groups of people relatively separate from one another. After all, most people in their daily lives are isolated from individuals at the opposite ends of the earth, or even down the road, and inasmuch as this continues to be so, they will invariably develop some cultural differences. Although it may be that modern techniques of transportation and communication facilitate the rapid spread of cultural characteristics to all parts of the globe, thus diminishing variability, it is unlikely that all parts will become alike. Although a native of Melanesia and a native of the United States may hear the same song on the same transistor radio, this does not mean that their cultures will not retain some of their original characteristics or develop some distinctive adaptations. People in different parts of the world are confronted with different physical and social environments, and hence the chances are that some aspects of their cultures will always be different, assuming that cultures generally consist of common responses adapted to particular environmental requirements.

And although cultural variability has undoubtedly decreased recently, it may also be true that much of what we see in the way of variation depends on which groups we choose to look at and when we look at them. If we move our perspective back in time, we may find (and justifiably, it seems, on the basis of present evidence) that there was less variability in the Lower Paleolithic— when humans depended solely on hunting and gathering—than in the beginning of the Neolithic, 10,000 years ago. In some areas of the world 10,000 years ago, a relatively small number of people had begun to depend on agriculture and domesticated animals; in other areas, people depended on sedentary food collection; and in still other areas (indeed most areas of the world at that time), people still depended on nomadic food collecting. With the spread of agriculture around the world, cultural variability may again have decreased.

We might expect, then, that whenever a generally adaptive cultural pattern develops and spreads over the globe, cultural variability decreases, at least for a time. Hence, with the recent spread of commercial exchange, and, even more significant, with the ongoing diffusion of industrial culture, we may be witnessing a temporary diminution of cultural variability as humanity experiences another great cultural change. But there is no reason to believe that further and differential cultural change, stemming from varying physical and social environmental requirements, will not occur in different parts of the world.

In short, it does not seem likely that cultural anthropology, the study of cultural variation, will ever run out of variability to study. The same thing can be said for physical anthropology, archeology, and linguistics. With respect to physical anthropology, there is no reason to expect variation in biological characteristics among human populations to disappear, as long as physical and social environments continue to vary. It will be a long time before the whole of humankind lives under identical environmental conditions, in one great "greenhouse." Moreover, we will always be able to explore and study that great depository of human variability—the fossil and more recent human biological records. Similarly, archeologists will always have the remains of past cultures to study and explain. With respect to linguistics, even if all linguistic variation disappears from the earth, we will always have the descriptive data on past languages to study, with all the variability in those records still to be explained.

Yet, a larger question remains. Why should we study simpler cultures at all, either those that exist today or those that have existed in the past? What conceivable bearing could such studies have on the problems that beset us in the final decade of the twentieth century? To answer this question we must remind ourselves that humans, whatever culture they may belong to, are still human, and that as a species they share certain significant needs and characteristics. If we are to discover laws that account for the constants and variables in human behavior, all cultures past and present are equally important. As Claude Lévi-Strauss has said,

> the thousands of societies that exist today, or once existed on the surface of the earth, constitute so many experiments, the only ones we can make use of to formulate and test our hypotheses, since we can't very well construct or repeat them in the laboratory as physical and natural scientists do. These experiments, represented by societies unlike our own, described and analyzed by anthropologists, provide one of the surest ways to understand what happens in the human mind and how it operates. That's what anthropology is good for in the most general way and what we can expect from it in the long run.[2]

[2] Quoted in *The New York Times*, January 21, 1972, p. 41.

Glossary

Acheulian a toolmaking tradition, generally associated with *Homo erectus*, characterized by large cutting instruments such as hand axes and cleavers.

Aegyptopithecus a propliopithecid found in the Fayum area of Egypt.

Aerobic Work Capacity the degree to which oxygen can be taken in to fuel exercise.

Affinal Kin one's relatives by marriage.

Age-Set a group of persons of similar age and the same sex who move together through some or all of life's stages.

Allele one member of a pair of genes.

Allen's Rule the rule that protruding body parts (particularly arms and legs) are relatively shorter in the cooler areas of a species' range than in the warmer areas.

Ambilineal Descent the rule of descent that affiliates an individual with groups of kin related to him or her through men *or* women.

Ancestor Spirits supernatural beings who are the ghosts of dead relatives.

Anthropoids one of the two suborders of primates; includes monkeys, apes, and humans.

Anthropological Linguistics the anthropological study of languages.

Anthropology the study of differences and similarities, both biological and cultural, in human populations. Anthropology is concerned with typical biological and cultural characteristics of human populations in all periods and in all parts of the world.

Arboreal adapted to living in trees.

Archeology the study of prehistoric and historic cultures through the analysis of material remains.

Atlatl Aztec world for "spear-thrower."

Australopithecus genus of Pliocene and Pleistocene hominids.

Australopithecus afarensis a possible species of *Australopithecus* that lived 4 to 3 million years ago in East Africa.

Australopithecus africanus erect bipedal hominid that lived during the late Pliocene; dentally similar to modern humans, had a rounded brain case with a cranial capacity of 428–485 cc, and weighed between forty-five and ninety pounds.

Australopithecus boisei an East African species of *Australopithecus* similar to *A. robustus*.

Australopithecus robustus fossil hominid similar to *A. africanus*, but larger, with a body weight of 100 to 150 pounds.

Avunculocal Residence a pattern of residence in which a married couple settles with or near the husband's mother's brother.

Balanced Reciprocity giving with the expectation of a straightforward immediate or limited-time trade.

Band a fairly small, politically autonomous group of people, usually nomadic.

Behavioral Ecology the study of how all kinds of behavior may relate to the environment.

Bergmann's Rule the rule that smaller-sized subpopulations of a species inhibit the warmer parts of its geographical range and larger-sized subpopulations the cooler areas.

Bifacial Tool a tool worked or flaked on two sides.

Bilateral Kinship the type of kinship system in which individuals affiliate more or less equally with their mother's and father's relatives; descent groups are absent.

Bilocal Residence a pattern of residence in which a married couple lives with or near either the husband's parents or the wife's parents.

Bipedalism locomotion in which an animal walks on its two hind legs.

Blade a thin flake whose length is usually more than twice its width. In the blade technique of toolmaking, a core is prepared by shaping a piece of flint with hammerstones into a pyramidal or cylindrical form. Blades are then struck off until the core is used up.

Brachiation arboreal locomotion in which the animal swings from branch to branch, its weight suspended by its hands and arms.

Brachiators an animal that moves by brachiation is called a brachiator.

Bride Price (Bride Wealth) a substantial gift of goods or money given to the bride's kin by the groom or his kin at or before the marriage.

Bride Service work performed by the groom for his bride's family for a varying length of time either before or after the marriage.

Burin a chisellike stone tool used for carving and for making such artifacts as bone and antler needles, awls, and projectile points.

Canines the cone-shaped teeth immediately behind the incisors; used in most primates to seize food and in fighting and display.

Caste a ranked group, often associated with a certain occupation, in which membership is determined at birth; marriage is restricted to members of one's own caste.

Cerebral Cortex the "gray matter" of the brain; the center of speech and other higher mental activities.

Chayanov's Rule in households, the lower the ratio of able-bodied workers to consumers, the harder the workers must work.

Chief a person who exercises authority, usually on behalf of a multi-community political unit. This role is generally found in rank societies and is usually permanent and often hereditary.

Chiefdom a political unit, with a chief at its head, integrating more than one community but not necessarily the whole society or language group.

Chromosomes paired rod-shaped structures within a cell nucleus containing the genes that transmit traits from one generation to the next.

Civilization urban society.

Clan (Sib) a set of kin whose members believe themselves to be descended from a common ancestor or ancestress but cannot specify the links back to that founder; often designated by a totem.

Class a category of persons who have about the same opportunity to obtain economic resources, power, and prestige.

Class/Caste Society a society containing social groups that have unequal access to economic resources, power, and prestige.

Classificatory Terms kinship terms that merge or equate relatives who are genealogically distinct from one another; the same terms used for a number of different kin.

Cloning the exact reproduction of an individual from cellular tissue.

Cognates words or morphs that belong to different languages but have similar sounds and meanings.

Commercial Exchange see **Market or Commercial Exchange.**

Commercialization buying and selling of goods and services, with money usually a medium of exchange.

Complementary Opposition the occasional uniting of various segments of a segmentary lineage system in opposition to similar segments.

Consanguineal Kin one's biological relatives; relatives by birth.

Continental-Drift Theory the theory that the major continental land masses were not separated as they are today, but instead formed a single large supercontinent surrounded by seas. In recent geological times, the supercontinent is thought to have broken up and the continents drifted apart into the configuration they have today.

Core Vocabulary nonspecialist vocabulary.

Corvée a system of required labor.

Cretaceous geologic epoch 135 to 65 million years ago, during which dinosaurs and other reptiles ceased to be the dominant land vertebrates and mammals and birds began to become important.

Crime violence not considered legitimate that occurs within a political unit.

Cro-Magnons early *Homo sapiens sapiens* who lived in western Europe about 35,000 years ago; differed from Neanderthals in their higher foreheads, thinner and lighter bones, smaller faces and jaws, protuberant chins, and slight or nonexistent body ridges on the skull.

Cross-Cousins children of siblings of the opposite sex. One's cross-cousins are father's sisters' children and mother's brothers' children.

Cross-Cultural Researcher an ethnologist who uses ethnographic data on many societies to test possible explanations of cultural variation.

Crossing-Over   exchanges of sections of chromosomes from one chromosome to another.

Cultural Anthropology   the study of cultural variation and universals.

Cultural Relativism   the attitude that a society's customs and ideas should be viewed within the context of that society's problems and opportunities.

Culture   the set of learned behaviors, beliefs, attitudes, values, or ideals that are characteristic of a particular society or population.

Cuneiform   wedge-shaped writing invented by the Sumerians around 3000 B.C.

Descriptive Linguistics   see Structural Linguistics.

Descriptive Terms   kinship terms used to refer to genealogically distinct relatives; a different term is used for each relative.

Dialect   a variety of a language spoken in a particular area or by a particular social group.

Diurnal   active during the day.

Divination   getting the supernatural to provide guidance.

DNA   deoxyribonucleic acid; a long, two-stranded molecule in the genes that direct the making of an organism according to the instructions in its genetic code.

Domestication   the cultivation or raising of plants and animals that are different from wild varieties.

Dominant   the allele of a gene pair that is always phenotypically expressed in the heterozygous form.

Double Descent (Double Unilineal Descent)   a system that affiliates an individual with a group of matrilineal kin for some purposes, and with a group of patrilineal kin for other purposes.

Dowry   a substantial transfer of goods or money from the bride's family to the bride (usually), the groom, or the groom's family.

Dryopithecus   genus of Miocene fossil apes that inhabited Africa and Eurasia, and of which several species are known.

Egalitarian Society   a society in which all persons of a given age-sex category have equal access to economic resources, power, and prestige.

Ego   in the reckoning of kinship, the reference point or focal person.

Endogamy   the rule specifying marriage to a person within one's own (kin, caste, community) group.

Eocene   a geologic epoch 54 to 38 million years ago.

Epicanthic Fold   a bit of skin overlapping the eyelid.

Ethnocentrism   the attitude that other societies' customs and ideas can be judged in the context of one's own culture.

Ethnographer   a person who spends some time living with, interviewing, and observing a group of people so that he or she can describe their customs.

Ethnographic Analogy   inferring how a particular tool was used in the past by observing how the tool is used by members of contemporary societies, preferably societies with subsistence activities and environments similar to those of the ancient toolmakers.

Ethnography   a description of a society's customary behaviors, beliefs, and attitudes.

Ethnohistorian   an ethnologist who uses historical documents to study how a particular culture has changed over time.

Ethnolinguists   anthropologists who study the relationships between language and culture.

Ethnology   the study of how and why recent cultures differ and are similar.

Exogamy   the rule specifying marriage to a person from outside one's own (kin or community) group.

Extended Family   a family consisting of two or more single-parent, monogamous, polygynous, or polyandrous families linked by a blood tie.

Extensive (Shifting) Cultivation   a type of horticulture in which the land is worked for short periods and then left to regenerate some years before being used again.

Family   a social and economic unit consisting minimally of a parent and children.

Feuding   a state of recurring hostility between families or groups of kin, usually motivated by a desire to avenge an offense against a member of the group.

Food Collection   all forms of subsistence technology in which food-getting is dependent on naturally occurring resources—wild plants and animals.

Food Production   the form of subsistence technology in which food-getting is dependent on the cultivation and domestication of plants and animals.

Fossil   the hardened remains or impressions of plants and animals that lived in the past.

Founder Effect a form of genetic drift that occurs when a small population recently derived from a larger one expands in relative isolation. Because the founders of the new population carry only a small sample of the gene pool of the original population, the gene frequencies of the two populations may differ.

Fraternal Polyandry the marriage of a woman to two or more brothers at one time.

Gene chemical unit of heredity.

Gene Flow the process by which genes pass from the gene pool of one population to that of another through mating and reproduction.

Gene Pool all the genes possessed by the members of a given population.

Generalized Reciprocity gift giving without any immediate or planned return.

Genetic Drift the various random processes that affect gene frequencies in small, relatively isolated populations.

Genitor one's biological father.

Genotype the total complement of inherited traits or genes of an organism.

Genus a group of related speces; *pl.* genera.

Geographical Race a set of at least once-neighboring populations that has certain distinctive trait frequencies.

Ghosts supernatural beings who were once human; the souls of dead people.

Gloger's Rule the rule that populations of birds and mammals living in warm, humid climates have more melanin (and therefore darker skin, fur, or feathers) than populations of the same species living in cooler, drier areas.

Gods supernatural beings of nonhuman origin who are named personalities; often anthromorphic.

Group Marriage marriage in which more than one man is married to more than one woman at the same time; not customary in any known human society.

Headman a person who holds a powerless but symbolically unifying position in a community in an egalitarian society; may exercise influence but has no power to impose sanctions.

Heterosis the production of healthier and more numerous offspring as a result of matings between individuals with different genetic characteristics; also known as *hybrid vigor*.

Heterozygous possessing differing genes or alleles in corresponding locations on a pair of chromosomes.

Hieroglyphics "picture writing," as in ancient Egypt and in Mayan sites in Mesoamerica.

Historical Archeology a specialty within archeology that studies the remains of recent peoples who left written records.

Historical Linguistics the study of how languages change over time.

Holistic having many aspects; multifaceted.

Hominids the group of hominoids consisting of humans and their direct ancestors. It contains at least two genera: *Homo* and *Australopithecus*.

Hominoids the group of catarrhines that includes both apes and humans.

Homo genus to which modern humans and their ancentors belong.

Homo erectus a species of early humans that lived in Africa, Europe, and Asia after about 1.5 million years ago; cranial capacity of 1000 cc; associated with the Acheulian tool tradition and the first use of fire by humans.

Homo habilis designation for the skeletal remains of several hominids found at Olduvai Gorge (Tanzania) and dating from about 2 million years ago; cranial capacity of 600 to 800 cc; may have been a toolmaker.

Homo sapiens the species of primate to which modern and somewhat older humans belong. Early examples of *Homo sapiens* may have appeared between 500,000 and 200,000 years ago.

Homo sapiens sapiens modern humans, undisputed examples of which appeared after 40,000 years ago.

Homozygous possessing two identical genes or alleles in corresponding locations on a pair of chromosomes.

Horticulture plant cultivation carried out with relatively simple tools and methods; nature is allowed to replace nutrients in the soil, in the absence of permanently cultivated fields.

Human Paleontology the study of the emergence of humans and their later physical evolution.

Human Variation the study of how and why contemporary human populations vary biologically.

Hunter-Gatherers   peoples who subsist on the collection of naturally occurring plants and animals; also referred to as foragers.

Hybrid Vigor   see **Heterosis**.

Incest Taboo   prohibition of sexual intercourse or marriage between mother and son, father and daughter, and brother and sister.

Incisors   the front teeth; used for holding or seizing food, and preparing it for chewing by the other teeth.

Insectivore   an animal that eats insects.

Intensive Agriculture   food production characterized by the permanent cultivation of fields and made possible by the use of the plow, draft animals or machines, fertilizers, irrigation, water-storage techniques, and other complex agricultural techniques.

Kindred   a bilateral set of close relatives.

Kula **Ring**   a ceremonial exchange of valued shell ornaments in the Trobriand Islands, in which white shell armbands are traded around the islands in a counterclockwise direction and red shell necklaces are traded clockwise.

Kwashiorkor   a protein-deficiency disease common in tropical areas.

Levalloisian   a tool tradition developed during the Acheulian period whereby flake tools of a predetermined size could be produced from a shaped core with a prepared striking platform.

Levirate   a custom whereby a man is obliged to marry his brother's widow.

Lexical Content   vocabulary or lexicon.

Lexicon   the words and morphs, and their meanings, of a language; approximated by a dictionary.

Lineage   a set of kin whose members trace descent from a common ancestor through known links.

Linguistics   the study of language.

Local Race   a breeding population or local group whose members usually interbreed.

Magic   the performance of certain rituals that are believed to compel the supernatural powers to act in particular ways.

Mana   a supernatural, impersonal force that inhabits certain objects or people and is believed to confer success and/or strength.

Manumission   the granting of freedom to a slave.

Market or Commercial Exchange   exchanges or transactions in which the "prices" are subject to supply and demand, whether or not the transactions occur in a marketplace.

Marriage   a socially approved sexual and economic union between a man and a woman that is presumed, both by the couple and by others, to be more or less permanent, and that subsumes reciprocal rights and obligations between the two spouses and between spouses and their future children.

Matriclan   a clan tracing descent through the female line.

Matrifocal Family   a family consisting of a mother and her children.

Matrilineage   a kin group whose members trace descent through known links in the female line from a common ancestress.

Matrilineal Descent   the rule of descent that affiliates an individual with kin of both sexes related to him or her through *women* only.

Matrilocal Residence   a pattern of residence in which a married couple lives with or near the wife's parents.

Medium   part-time religious practitioner who is asked to heal and divine while in a trance.

Meiosis   the process by which reproductive cells are formed. In this process of division, the number of chromosomes in the newly formed cells is reduced by half, so that when fertilization occurs the resulting organism has the normal number of chromosomes appropriate to its species, rather than double that number.

Melanin   a dark-brown pigment in the outer layer of skin that protects the inner layers of skin against ultraviolent radiation.

Mendelian Population   a population that breeds mostly within itself.

Mesolithic   the archeological period in the Old World beginning about 12,000 B.C., during which preagricultural villages were founded.

Microlith   a small, razorlike blade fragment that was probably attached in a series to a wooden or bone handle to form a cutting edge.

Miocene geologic epoch 22.5 to 5 million years ago, during which the first hominids probably appeared.

Mitosis cellular reproduction or growth involving the duplication of chromosome pairs.

Moiety a unilineal descent group in a society that is divided into two such maximal groups; there may be smaller unilineal descent groups as well.

Molars the large teeth behind the premolars at the back of the jaw; used for chewing and grinding food.

Mongoloid Spot a dark patch of skin at the base of the spine; disappears as a person grows older.

Monogamy marriage between only one man and only one woman at a time.

Monotheistic believing that there is only one high god, and that all other supernatural beings are subordinate to, or are alternative manifestations of, this supreme being.

Morph the smallest unit of a language that has a meaning.

Morpheme one or more morphs with the same meaning.

Morphology the study of how sound sequences convey meaning.

Mousterian a Middle Paleolithic toolmaking tradition associated with Neanderthals; prepared-core and percussion-flaking techniques were used to produce flakes that were then retouched to make specialized tools.

Mutation a change in the molecular structure or DNA code of genes. Mutations usually occur randomly and are generally harmful or lethal to the organism and/or its descendants.

Natural Selection the process by which those members of a particular species that are more adapted to their environment survive longer and produce more offspring than the less adapted.

Negative Reciprocity giving and taking that attempts to take advantage of another for one's own interest.

Neolithic the archaeological period, characterized by plant and animal domestication, beginning in the Near East about 8000 B.C., in southeast Asia at 6800 B.C., in sub-Saharan Africa by 4000 B.C., and in the New World from 5600 to 5000 B.C.

Neolocal Residence a pattern of residence whereby a married couple lives separately, and usually at some distance, from the kin of either spouse.

Nocturnal active during the night.

Nonfraternal Polyandry marriage of a woman to two or more men who are not brothers.

Nonsororal Polygyny marriage of a man to two or more women who are not sisters.

Nuclear Family a family consisting of a married couple and their young children.

Oath the act of calling upon a deity to bear witness to the truth of what one says.

Obsidian a volcanic glass that can be used to make mirrors or sharp-edged tools.

Oldowan the term designating cultural materials found in the Bed I (lower Pleistocene) level at Olduvai Gorge, Tanzania.

Oligocene the geologic epoch 38 to 22.5 million years ago during which the ancestors of monkeys and apes began to evolve.

Omnivorous eating both meat and vegetation.

Opposable Thumb a thumb that can touch the tips of all the other fingers.

Optimal Foraging Theory the theory that individuals seek to maximize the returns (in calories and nutrients) on their labor in deciding which animals and plants they will go after.

Ordeal a means of determining guilt or innocence by submitting the accused to dangerous or painful tests believed to be under supernatural control.

Paleoanthropology see **Human Paleontology**.

Paleocene the geologic epoch 65 to 53.5 million years ago during which mammal forms (including the early primates) began to diverge extensively.

Parallel Cousins children of siblings of the same sex. One's parallel cousins are father's brothers' children and mother's sisters' children.

Parapithecids small monkeylike Oligocene primates found in the Fayum area of Egypt.

Pastoralism a form of subsistence technology in which food-getting is based directly or indirectly on the maintenance of domesticated animals.

Pater one's socially recognized father.

Patriclan a clan tracing descent through the male line.

Patrilineage a kin group whose members trace descent through known links in the male line from a common ancestor.

Patrilineal Descent   the rule of descent that affiliates an individual with kin of both sexes related to him or her through *men* only.

Patrilocal Residence   a pattern of residence in which a married couple lives with or near the husband's parents.

Percussion Flaking   a toolmaking technique in which one stone is struck with another to remove a flake.

Phenotype   the observable physical appearance of an organism, which may or may not reflect its genotype or total genetic constitution.

Phone   a speech sound in a language.

Phoneme   a set of slightly varying sounds that do not make any difference in meaning to the speakers of the language.

Phonology   the study of the sounds in a language and how they are used.

Phratry   a unilineal descent group composed of a number of supposedly related clans (sibs).

Physical Anthropology   the study of humans as physical organisms, dealing with the emergence and evolution of humans and with contemporary biological variations among human populations.

Pithecanthropus erectus   original name given to *Homo erectus* in Java.

Pleistocene   a geologic epoch that started 1.8 million years ago and, according to some, continues into the present. During this period, glaciers have often covered much of the earth's surface and humans became the dominant life form.

Plesiadapis   a Paleocene primate found in Europe and North America.

Pliocene   the geologic epoch 5 to 1.8 million years ago during which the earliest definite hominids appeared.

Polyandry   the marriage of one woman to more than one man at a time.

Polygamy   plural marriage; marriage to more than one spouse simultaneously.

Polygyny   the marriage of one man to more than one woman at a time.

Polytheistic   recognizing many gods, none of which is believed to be superordinate.

Postpartum Sex Taboo   prohibition of sexual intercourse between a couple after the birth of their child.

Potlatch   a feast among Northwest Coast Indians at which great quantities of food and goods are given to the guests in order to gain prestige for the host(s).

Prehistory   the time before written records.

Premolars   the teeth immediately behind the canines; used in chewing, grinding, and shearing food.

Pressure Flaking   toolmaking technique whereby small flakes are struck off by pressing against the core with a bone, antler, or wood tool.

Priest   a generally full-time male intermediary between humans and gods.

Primate   a member of the mammalian order Primates, divided into the two suborders of prosimians and anthropoids.

Propliopithecids   Oligocene apelike anthropoids, dating from about 32 million years ago, found in the Fayum area of Egypt.

Prosimians   one of the two suborders of primates; includes lemurs and lorises.

Protolanguage   a hypothesized ancestral language from which two or more languages seem to have derived.

Purdah   the seclusion and veiling of women.

Purgatorius   a fossil dating from the Late Cretaceous that is thought to be the earliest known primate.

Race   a subpopulation or variety of a single species that differs somewhat in gene frequencies from other varieties of the species but can interbreed with them and produce fertile and viable offspring.

Rachis   the seed-bearing part of the stem of a plant.

Raiding   a short-term use of force, generally planned and organized, to realize a limited objective.

Random Sample   a sample in which each case selected has had an equal chance to be included.

Rank Society   a society with no unequal access to economic resources or power, but with social groups that have unequal access to status positions and prestige.

Recessive   an allele phenotypically suppressed in the heterozygous form and expressed only in the homozygous form.

Reciprocity   giving and taking (not politically arranged) without the use of money.

Redistribution   the accumulation of goods (or labor) by a particular person, or in a particular place, and their subsequent distribution.

Religion   any set of attitudes, beliefs, and practices pertaining to supernatural power, whether that power be forces, gods, spirits, ghosts, or demons.

Revitalization Movement   a new religious movement intended to save a culture by infusing it with a new purpose and life.

RNA   ribonucleic acid; a single-stranded molecule that copies the genetic instructions from DNA and transmits them to structures in the cytoplasm of a cell.

Rules of Descent   rules that connect individuals with particular sets of kin because of known or presumed common ancestry.

Savanna   tropical grassland.

Sedentarism   settled life.

Sediment   the dust and debris and decay that accumulates over time.

Segmentary Lineage System   a hierarchy of more and more inclusive lineages; usually functions only in conflict situations.

Segregation   the random sorting of chromosomes in meiosis.

Sexual Dimorphism   the differentiation of males from females in size and appearance.

Shaman   a religious intermediary, usually part-time, whose primary function is to cure people through sacred songs, pantomime, and other means; sometimes called "witch doctor" by Westerners.

Shifting Cultivation   see **Extensive Cultivation**.

Sib   see **Clan**.

Sibling Language   one of two or more languages derived from a common ancestral language. For example, German is a sibling language to English.

Siblings   a person's brothers or sisters.

Sickle-Cell Anemia (Sicklemia)   a condition in which red blood cells assume a crescent (sickle) shape when deprived of oxygen, instead of the normal (disk) shape. Severe anemia, painful circulatory problems, enlargement of the heart, brain-cell atrophy, and early death may result.

Sivapithecus   a genus of Miocene apes.

Slash-and-Burn   a form of shifting cultivation in which the natural vegetation is cut down and burned off. The cleared ground is used for a short time and then left to regenerate.

Slaves   a class of persons who do not own their own labor or the products thereof.

Society   a territorial population speaking a language not generally understood by neighboring territorial populations.

Sociobiology   the application of biological evolutionary principles to the social behavior of animals.

Sociolinguistics   the study of cultural and subcultural patterns of speaking in different social contexts.

Sorcery   the use of certain materials to invoke supernatural powers to harm people.

Sororal Polygyny   the marriage of a man to two or more sisters at the same time.

Sororate   a custom whereby a woman is obliged to marry her deceased sister's husband.

Speciation   the development of a new species.

Species   a population that consists of organisms able to interbreed and produce fertile and viable offspring.

Spirits   unnamed supernatural beings of nonhuman origin who are beneath the gods in prestige and often closer to the people; may be helpful, mischievous, or evil.

State   a political unit with centralized decision making affecting a large population. Most states have cities with public buildings; full-time craft and religious specialists; an "official" art style; a hierarchical social structure topped by an elite class; and a governmental monopoly on the legitimate use of force to implement policies.

Status   a position of prestige in a society.

Structural (Descriptive) Linguistics   the study of how languages are constructed.

Subculture   the shared customs of a subgroup within a society.

Subsistence Technology   the methods humans use to procure food.

Supernatural   believed to be not human or not subject to the laws of nature.

Syntax   the ways in which words are arranged to form phrases and sentences.

Taboo   a prohibition that, if violated, is believed to bring supernatural punishment.

Taxonomy   the classification of extinct and living organisms.

Totem   a plant or animal associated with a clan (sib) as a mean of group identification; may have other special significance for the group.

Transformational/Generative Theory   the theory about syntax suggesting that a language has a *surface structure* and a *deep structure*.

Tribe   a type of political system characterized by kin or non-kin groupings that can informally and temporarily integrate a number of local groups into a larger whole.

Tundra   treeless plains characteristic of subarctic and Arctic regions.

Unifacial Tool   a tool worked or flaked on one side only.

Unilineal Descent   affiliation with a group of kin through descent links of one sex only.

Unilocal Residence   a pattern of residence (patrilocal, matrilocal, or a avunculocal) that specifies just one set of relatives that the married couple lives with or near.

Warfare   violence between political entities such as communities, districts, or nations.

Witchcraft   the practice of attempting to harm people by supernatural means, but through emotions and thought alone, not through the use of tangible objects.

Bibliography

'ABD ALLAH, MAHMUD M. "Siwan Customs." *Harvard African Studies,* 1 (1917): 1–28.

ABERLE, DAVID. "A Note on Relative Deprivation Theory as Applied to Millenarian and Other Cult Movements." In Lessa and Vogt, eds., *Reader in Comparative Religion,* 3rd ed.

ABERLE, DAVID F., URIE BRONFENBRENNER, ECKHARD H. HESS, DANIEL R. MILLER, DAVID M. SCHNEIDER, AND JAMES M. SPUHLER. "The Incest Taboo and the Mating Patterns of Animals." *American Anthropologist,* 65 (1963): 253–65.

ADAMS, ROBERT M. "The Origin of Cities." *Scientific American,* September 1960, pp. 153–68.

ADAMS, ROBERT McC. *Heartland of Cities: Surveys of Ancient Settlement and Land Use on the Central Floodplain of the Euphrates.* Chicago: University of Chicago Press, 1981.

AKMAJIAN, ADRIAN, RICHARD A. DEMERS, AND ROBERT M. HARNISH. *Linguistics: An Introduction to Language and Communication,* 2nd ed. Cambridge, Mass.: M.I.T. Press, 1984.

ALLISON, ANTHONY C. "Sickle Cells and Evolution." *Scientific American,* August 1956, pp. 87–96.

ARCHER, DANE, AND ROSEMARY GARTNER. *Violence and Crime in Cross-National Perspective.* New Haven: Yale University Press, 1984.

ASCH, NANCY B., AND DAVID L. ASCH. "The Economic Potential of *Iva annua* and Its Prehistoric Importance in the Lower Illinois Valley." In Richard I. Ford, ed., *The Nature and Status of Ethnobotany.* Anthropological Papers, Museum of Anthropology, no. 67. Ann Arbor: University of Michigan, 1978, pp. 301–42.

ASCH, SOLOMON. "Studies of Independence and Conformity: A Minority of One against a Unanimous Majority." *Psychological Monographs,*70 (1956): 1–70.

BALDI, PHILIP. *An Introduction to the Indo-European Languages.* Carbondale: Southern Illinois University Press, 1983.

BALIKCI, ASEN. *The Netsilik Eskimo.* Garden City, NY: Natural History Press, 1970.

BANTON, MICHAEL, ed. *Anthropological Approaches to the Study of Religion.* Association of Social Anthropologists of the Commonwealth, Monograph no. 3. New York: Praeger, 1966.

BARASH, DAVID P. *Sociobiology and Behavior.* New York: Elsevier, 1977.

BARLETT, PEGGY F., ed. *Agricultural Decision-Making: Anthropological Contributions to Rural Development.* New York: Academic Press, 1980.

BARNETT, H. G. *Being a Palauan.* New York: Holt, Rinehart & Winston, 1960.

BARTH, FREDRIK. "Nomadism in the Mountain and Plateau Areas of South West Asia." In *The Problems of the Arid Zone.* Paris: UNESCO, 1960.

BEADLE, GEORGE, AND MURIEL BEADLE. *The Language of Life.* Garden City, N.Y.: Doubleday, 1966.

BEARDER, SIMON K. "Lorises, Bushbabies, and Tarsiers: Diverse Societies in Solitary Foragers." In Smuts et al., eds., *Primate Societies,* pp. 11–33.

BERGGREN, W. A., AND J. A. VAN COUVERING. "The Late Neocene: Biostratigraphy, Geochronology and Paleoclimatology of the Last 15 Million Years in Marine and Continental Sequences." *Palaeogeography, Palaeoclimatology, Palaeoecology,* 16 (1974): 1–216.

BERLIN, BRENT, AND PAUL KAY. *Basic Color Terms: Their Universality and Evolution.* Berkeley: University of California Press, 1969.

BERREMAN, GERALD D. "Caste in India and the United States." *American Journal of Sociology,* 66 (1960): 120–27.

BERREMAN, GERALD D. "Caste in the Modern World." Morristown, N.J.: General Learning Press, 1973.

BERREMAN, GERALD D. "Race, Caste and Other Invidious Distinctions in Social Stratification." *Race,* 13 (1972): 403–14.

BERREMAN, GERALD D., ed. *Social Inequality: Comparative and Developmental Approaches.* New York: Academic Press, 1981.

BICKERTON, DEREK. "Creole Languages." *Scientific American,* July 1983, pp. 116–22.

BINFORD, LEWIS R. *Faunal Remains from Klasies River Mouth.* Orlando, Fla.: Academic Press, 1984.

BINFORD, LEWIS R. "Post-Pleistocene Adaptations." In Struever, ed., *Prehistoric Agriculture.*

BINFORD, LEWIS R. "Were There Elephant Hunters at Torralba?" In Nitecki and Nitecki, eds. *The Evolution of Human Hunting,* pp. 47–105.

BINFORD, SALLY R., AND LEWIS R. BINFORD, eds. *New Perspectives in Archaeology.* Chicago, Aldine, 1968.

BINFORD, SALLY R., AND LEWIS R. BINFORD. "Stone Tools and Human Behavior." *Scientific American,* 220 (April 1969): 70–84.

"Biology and Culture Meet in Milk." *Science,* January 2, 1981.

BLANTON, RICHARD. *Monte Albán: Settlement Patterns at the Ancient Zapotec Capital.* New York: Academic Press, 1978.

BLANTON, RICHARD. "The Origins of Monte Albán." In C. Cleland, ed., *Cultural Continuity and Change*. New York: Academic Press, 1976.

BLANTON, RICHARD E. "The Rise of Cities." In Jeremy A. Sabloff, ed., *Supplement to the Handbook of Middle American Indians*. Austin: University of Texas Press, 1981, 1: 392–400.

BLANTON, RICHARD E., STEPHEN A. KOWALEWSKI, GARY FEINMAN, AND JILL APPEL. *Ancient Mesoamerica: A Comparison of Change in Three Regions*. Cambridge: Cambridge University Press, 1981.

BLOCK, JEAN L. "Help! They're *All* Moved Back Home!" *Woman's Day*, April 26, 1983, pp. 72–76.

BLUMBERG, RAE L. *Stratification: Socioeconomic and Sexual Inequality*. Dubuque, Iowa: Wm. C. Brown, 1978.

BOAS, FRANZ. *Central Eskimos*. Bureau of American Ethnology Annual Report no. 6. Washington, D.C., 1888.

BOAS, FRANZ. *Geographical Names of the Kwakiutl Indians.* New York: Columbia University Press, 1934.

BOAS, FRANZ. "On Grammatical Categories." In Hymes, ed., *Language in Culture and Society*, pp. 121–23.

BOAS, FRANZ. *The Religion of the Kwakiutl*. Columbia University Contributions to Anthropology, vol. 10, pt. II. New York, 1930.

BOAZ, N. T. "Morphological Trends and Phylogenetic Relationships from Middle Miocene Hominoids to Late Pliocene Hominids." In Ciochon and Corruccini, eds., *New Interpretations of Ape and Human Ancestry*, pp. 705–20.

BOAZ, NOEL T. "Hominid Evolution in Eastern Africa during the Pliocene and Early Pleistocene." *Annual Review of Anthropology*, 8 (1979): 71–85.

BODMER, W. F., AND L. L. CAVALLI-SFORZA. *Genetics, Evolution, and Man*. San Francisco: W. H. Freeman & Company Publishers, 1976.

BOGORAS, WALDEMAR. "The Chukchee," pt. 3. *Memoirs of the American Museum of Natural History*, 2 (1909).

BOHANNAN, PAUL. "The Migration and Expansion of the Tiv." *Africa*, 24 (1954): 2–16.

BONNER, JOHN T. *The Evolution of Culture in Animals*. Princeton: Princeton University Press, 1980.

BORDAZ, JACQUES. *Tools of the Old and New Stone Age*. Garden City, N.Y.: Natural History Press, 1970.

BORDES, FRANÇOIS. "Mousterian Cultures in France." *Science*, September 22, 1961, pp. 803–10.

BORNSTEIN, MARC H. "The Psychophysiological Component of Cultural Difference in Color Naming and Illusion Susceptibility." *Behavior Science Notes*, 8 (1973): 41–101.

BOSERUP, ESTER. *The Conditions of Agricultural Growth: The Economics of Agrarian Change under Population Pressure*. Chicago: Aldine, 1965.

BOSERUP, ESTER. *Woman's Role in Economic Development*. New York: St. Martin's Press, 1970.

BOURGUIGNON, ERIKA. "Introduction: A Framework for the Comparative Study of Altered States of Consciousness." In Erika Bourguignon, *Religion, Altered States of Consciousness, and Social Change*. Columbus: Ohio State University Press, 1973, pp. 3–35.

BOURGUIGNON, ERIKA, AND THOMAS L. EVASCU. "Altered States of Consciousness within a General Evolutionary Perspective: A Holocultural Analysis." *Behavior Science Research*, 12 (1977): 197–216.

BRADLEY, CANDICE. "The Sexual Division of Labor and the Value of Children." *Behavior Science Research*, 19 (1984–1985): 159–85.

BRAIDWOOD, ROBERT J. "The Agricultural Revolution." *Scientific American*, September 1960, pp. 130–48.

BRAIDWOOD, ROBERT J., AND GORDON R. WILLEY. "Conclusions and Afterthoughts." In Robert J. Braidwood and Gordon R. Willey, eds., *Courses Toward Urban Life: Archaeological Considerations of Some Cultural Alternatives*. Viking Fund Publications in Anthropology, no. 32. Chicago: Aldine, 1962.

BRANDA, RICHARD F., AND JOHN W. EATON. "Skin Color and Nutrient Photolysis: An Evolutionary Hypothesis." *Science*, August 18, 1978, pp. 625–26.

BRAUER, GUNTER. "A Craniological Approach to the Origin of Anatomically Modern *Homo sapiens* in Africa and Implications for the Appearance of Modern Europeans." In Smith and Spencer, eds., *The Origins of Modern Humans*, pp. 327–410.

BRITTAIN, JOHN A. *Inheritance and the Inequality of Material Wealth*. Washington, D.C.: Brookings Institution, 1978.

BRODEY, JANE E. "Effects of Milk on Blacks Noted." *New York Times*, October 15, 1971, p. 15.

BROUDE, GWEN J. "Cross-Cultural Patterning of Some Sexual Attitudes and Practices." *Behavior Science Research*, 11 (1976): 227–62.

BROUDE, GWEN J. "Extramarital Sex Norms in Cross-Cultural Perspective." *Behavior Science Research*, 15 (1980): 181–218.

BROUDE, GWEN J., AND SARAH J. GREENE. "Cross-Cultural Codes on Twenty Sexual Attitudes and Practices." *Ethnology*, 15 (1976): 409–29.

BROWN, CECIL H. "Folk Botanical Life-Forms: Their Universality and Growth." *American Anthropologist*, 79 (1977): 317–42.

BROWN, CECIL H. "Folk Zoological Life-Forms: Their Universality and Growth." *American Anthropologist*, 81 (1979): 791–817.

BROWN, CECIL H. "World View and Lexical Uniformities." *Reviews in Anthropology*, 11 (1984): 99–112.

BROWN, CECIL H., AND STANLEY R. WITKOWSKI. "Language Universals." Appendix B in Levinson and Malone, eds., *Toward Explaining Human Culture*.

BROWN, JUDITH K. "Economic Organization and the Position of Women among the Iroquois." *Ethnohistory*, 17 (1970): 151–67.

BROWN, JUDITH K. "A Note on the Division of Labor by Sex." *American Anthropologist*, 72 (1970), 1073–78.

BROWN, ROGER. "The First Sentence of Child and Chimpanzee." In Sebeok and Umiker-Sebeok, eds., *Speaking of Apes*, pp. 85–101.

BROWN, ROGER. *Social Psychology*. New York: Free Press, 1965.

BROWN, ROGER, AND MARGUERITE FORD. "Address in American English." *Journal of Abnormal and Social Psychology*, 62 (1961): 375–85.

BRUMFIEL, ELIZABETH. "Aztec State Making: Ecology, Structure, and the Origin of the State." *American Anthropologist*, 85 (1983): pp. 261–84.

BRUMFIEL, ELIZABETH. "Regional Growth in the Eastern Valley of Mexico: A Test of the 'Population Pressure' Hypothesis." In Kent V. Flannery, ed., *The Early Mesoamerican Village*. New York: Academic Press, 1976, pp. 234–50.

BURLING, R. *Man's Many Voices: Language in Its Cultural Context*. New York: Holt, Rinehart & Winston, 1970.

BUTZER, KARL W. "Geomorphology and Sediment Stratigraphy." In Singer and Wymer, *The Middle Stone Age at Klasies River Mouth in South Africa*, pp. 33–42.

CAMPBELL, BERNARD G. *Humankind Emerging*, 4th ed. Boston: Little, Brown, 1985.

CAMPBELL, BERNARD G. *Humankind Emerging*, 5th ed. Glenview, Ill.: Scott, Foresman, 1988.

CAMPBELL, DONALD T. "Variation and Selective Retention in Socio-Cultural Evolution." In Herbert Barringer, George Blankstein, and Raymond Mack, eds., *Social Change in Developing Areas: A Re-Interpretation of Evolutionary Theory*. Cambridge, Mass.: Schenkman, 1965.

CAPLAN, A. L. *The Sociobiology Debate: Readings on Ethical and Scientific Issues*. New York. Harper & Row, Pub., 1978.

CAPORAEL, LINNDA R. "Ergotism: The Satan Loosed in Salem?" *Science*, April 2, 1976, pp. 21–26.

CARCOPINO, JEROME. *Daily Life in Ancient Rome: The People and the City at the Height of the Empire*. Edited with bibliography and notes by Henry T. Rowell. Translated from the French by E. O. Lorimer. New Haven: Yale University Press, 1940.

CARLISLE, RONALD C., AND MICHAEL I. SIEGEL. "Additional Comments on Problems in the Interpretation of Neanderthal Speech Capabilities." *American Anthropologist*, 80 (1978): 367–72.

CARNEIRO, ROBERT L. "Political Expansion as an Expression of the Principle of Competitive Exclusion." In Cohen and Service, eds., *Origins of the State*.

CARNEIRO, ROBERT L. "Slash-and-Burn Cultivation among the Kuikuru and Its Implications for Settlement Patterns." In Yehudi Cohen, ed., *Man in Adaptation: The Cultural Present*. Chicago: Aldine, 1968.

CARNEIRO, ROBERT L. "A Theory of the Origin of the State." *Science*, August 21, 1970, pp. 733–38.

CARRASCO, PEDRO. "The Civil-Religious Hierarchy in Mesoamerican Communities: Pre-Spanish Background and Colonial Development." *American Anthropologist*, 63 (1961): 483–97.

CARROLL, JOHN B., ed. *Language, Thought, and Reality: Selecting Writings of Benjamin Lee Whorf*. New York: John Wiley, 1956.

CARTMILL, MATT. "Rethinking Primate Origins." *Science*, April 26, 1974, pp. 436–43.

CASAGRANDE, JOSEPH B., ed. *In the Company of Man: Twenty Portraits by Anthropologists*. New York: Harper & Row, Pub., 1960.

CASHDAN, ELIZABETH A. "Egalitarianism among Hunters and Gatherers." *American Anthropologist*, 82 (1980): 116–20.

CHANG, K. C. "In Search of China's Beginnings: New Light on an Old Civilization." *American Scientist*, 69 (1981): 148–60.

CHANG, KWANG-CHIH. *The Archaeology of Ancient China*. New Haven: Yale University Press, 1968.

CHANG, KWANG-CHIH. "The Beginnings of Agriculture in the Far East." *Antiquity*, 44, no. 175 (September 1970): 175–85.

CHARD, CHESTER S. *Man in Prehistory*. New York: McGraw-Hill, 1969.

CHAUCER, GEOFFREY. *The Prologue to the Canterbury Tales, the Knightes Tale, the Nonnes Prestes Tale*, ed. Mark H. Liddell. New York: The Macmillan Company, 1926.

CHAYANOV, ALEXANDER V. *The Theory of Peasant Economy*, ed. Daniel Thorner, Basile Kerblay, and R. E. F. Smith. Homewood, Ill.: Richard D. Irwin, 1966.

CHIBNIK, MICHAEL. "The Economic Effects of Household Demography: A Cross-Cultural Assessment of Chayanov's Theory." In Maclachlan, ed., *Household Economies and Their Transformations*, pp. 74–106.

CHIBNIK, MICHAEL. "The Evolution of Cultural Rules." *Journal of Anthropological Research*, 37 (1981): 256–68.

CHIBNIK, MICHAEL. "The Statistical Behavior Approach: The Choice between Wage Labor and Cash Cropping in Rural Belize." In Barlett, ed., *Agricultural Decision-Making*, pp. 87–114.

CHOMSKY, NOAM. *Reflections on Language*. New York: Pantheon, 1975.

CIOCHON, R. L., AND J. G. FLEAGLE, eds. *Primate Evolution and Human Origins*. Hawthorne, N.Y.: Aldine de Gruyter, 1987.

CIOCHON, RUSSELL L., AND ROBERT S. CORRUCCINI, eds. *New Interpretations of Ape and Human Ancestry*. New York: Plenum, 1983.

CLARK, J. DESMOND. "Interpretations of Prehistoric Technology from Ancient Egyptian and Other Sources. Part II: Prehistoric Arrow Forms in Africa as Shown by Surviving Examples of the Traditional Arrows of the San Bushmen." *Paleorient*, 3 (1977): 127–150.

CLARK, J. DESMOND. "Prehistoric Populations and Pressures Favoring Plant Domestication in Africa." In Harlan, De Wet, and Stemler, eds., *Origins of African Plant Domestication*, pp. 67–105.

CLARK, J. DESMOND. *The Prehistory of Africa*. New York: Praeger, 1970.

COE, MICHAEL D. *The Maya*. New York: Praeger, 1966.

COHEN, MARK N. *The Food Crisis in Prehistory: Overpopulation and the Origins of Agriculture*. New Haven: Yale University Press, 1977.

COHEN, MARK N. "Population Pressure and the Origins of Agriculture." In Reed, ed., *Origins of Agriculture*, pp. 138–41.

COHEN, MARK N. "The Significance of Long-Term Changes in Human Diet and Food Economy." In Harris and Ross, eds. *Food and Evolution: Toward a Theory of Human Food Habits*, pp. 259–83.

COHEN, MARK NATHAN, AND GEORGE J. ARMELAGOS, eds. *Paleopathology at the Origins of Agriculture*. Orlando, Fla.: Academic Press, 1984.

COHEN, MYRON. "Developmental Process in the Chinese Domestic Group." In Maurice Freedman, ed., *Family and Kinship in Chinese Society*. Stanford, Calif.: Stanford University Press, 1970.

COHEN, MYRON. "Variations in Complexity among Chinese Family Groups: The Impact of Modernization." *Transactions of the New York Academy of Sciences*, 29 (1967): 638–44.

COHEN, RONALD. "Introduction." In Ronald Cohen and Judith D. Toland, eds., *State Formation and Political Legitimacy*. Political Anthropology, Volume VI. New Brunswick, N.J.: Transaction Books, 1988.

COHEN, RONALD, AND ELMAN R. SERVICE, eds. *Origins of the State: The Anthropology of Political Evolution*. Philadelphia: Institute for the Study of Human Issues, 1978.

COLLIER, STEPHEN, AND J. PETER WHITE. "Get Them Young? Age and Sex Inferences on Animal Domestication in Archaeology." *American Antiquity*, 41 (1976): 96–102.

COLLINS, DESMOND. "Later Hunters in Europe." In D. Collins, ed., *The Origins of Europe*. New York: Thomas Y. Crowell, 1976.

COULT, ALLAN D., AND ROBERT W. HABENSTEIN. *Cross Tabulations of Murdock's World Ethnographic Sample*. Columbia: University of Missouri Press, 1965.

CRONIN, J. E. "Apes, Humans, and Molecular Clocks: A Reappraisal." In Ciochon and Corruccini, eds., *New Interpretations of Ape and Human Ancestry*, pp. 115–36.

CURTIS, G. H., et al. "Age of the KBS Tuff in Koobi Fora Formation, East Rudolf, Kenya." *Nature*, 258 (1975): 395–98.

CUTRIGHT, PHILLIPS. "Inequality: A Cross-National Analysis." *American Sociological Review*, 32 (1967): 562–78.

DAHLBERG, FRANCES, ed. *Woman the Gatherer*. New Haven: Yale University Press, 1981.

DALTON, GEORGE, ed. *Tribal and Peasant Economies: Readings in Economic Anthropology*. Garden City, N.Y.: Natural History Press, 1967.

DAMON, ALBERT. "Stature Increase among Italian-Americans: Environmental, Genetic, or Both?" *American Journal of Physical Anthropology*, 23 (1965): 401–8.

DARWIN, CHARLES. "*The Origin of Species*." In Young, ed., *Evolution of Man*.

DAVENPORT, WILLIAM. "Nonunilinear Descent and Descent Groups." *American Anthropologist*, 61 (1959): 557–72.

DE VILLIERS, PETER A., AND JILL G. DE VILLIERS. *Early Language*. Cambridge, Mass.: Harvard University Press, 1979.

DELSON, ERIC, ed. *Ancestors: The Hard Evidence*. New York: Alan R. Liss, 1985.

DENNY, J. PETER. "The 'Extendedness' Variable in Classifier Semantics: Universal Features and Cultural Variation." In Madeleine Mathiot, ed., *Ethnolinguistics: Boas, Sapir and Whorf Revisited*. The Hague: Mouton, 1979, pp. 97–119.

DEVORE, IRVEN, AND MELVIN J. KONNER. "Infancy in Hunter-Gatherer Life: An Ethological Perspective." In N. F. White, ed., *Ethology and Psychiatry*. Toronto: Ontario Mental Health Foundation and University of Toronto Press, 1974, pp. 113–41.

DINCAUZE, DENA F. "An Archaeo-Logical Evaluation of the Case for Pre-Clovis Occupations." In Fred Wendorf and Angela E. Close, eds., *Advances in World Archaeology*. Orlando, Fla.: Academic Press, 1984, 3:275–323.

DIVALE, WILLIAM T. "Migration, External Warfare, and Matrilocal Residence." *Behavior Science Research*, 9 (1974): 75–133.

DIVALE, WILLIAM T., AND MARVIN HARRIS. "Population, Warfare, and the Male Supremacist Complex." *American Anthropologist*, 78 (1976): 521–38.

DOBZHANSKY, THEODOSIUS. *Genetic Diversity and Human Equality*. New York: Basic Books, 1973.

DOBZHANSKY, THEODOSIUS. *Mankind Evolving: The Evolution of the Human Species*. New Haven: Yale University Press, 1962.

DOWLING, JOHN H. "Property Relations and Productive Strategies in Pastoral Societies." *American Ethnologist*, 2 (1975): 419–26.

DRAPER, PATRICIA. "!Kung Women: Contrasts in Sexual Egalitarianism in Foraging and Sedentary Contexts." In Rayna R. Reiter, ed., *Toward an Anthropology of Women*. New York: Monthly Review Press, 1975, pp. 77–109.

DRAPER, PATRICIA, AND ELIZABETH CASHDAN. "Technological Change and Child Behavior among the !Kung." *Ethology*, 27 (1988): 339–65.

DRUCKER, PHILIP. *Cultures of the North Pacific Coast*. San Francisco: Chandler, 1965.

DRUCKER, PHILIP. "The Potlatch." In Dalton, ed., *Tribal and Peasant Economies*.

DURHAM, WILLIAM H. *Coevolution: Genes, Culture, and Human Diversity.* Stanford, Calif.: Stanford University Press, 1991.

DURKHEIM, EMILE. *The Rules of Sociological Method.* 8th ed. trans., Sarah A. Soloway and John H. Mueller, ed. George E. Catlin. New York: Free Press, 1938 (originally published 1895).

"Dwindling Numbers on the Farm." *Nation's Business,* April 1988, p. 16.

DYSON-HUDSON, RADA, AND ERIC ALDEN SMITH. "Human Territoriality: An Ecological Reassessment." *American Anthropologist,* 80 (1978): 21–41.

EDGERTON, ROBERT B., AND L. L. LANGNESS. *Methods and Styles in the Study of Culture.* San Francisco: Chandler & Sharp, 1974.

EGGAN, FRED. *The Social Organization of the Western Pueblos.* Chicago: University of Chicago Press, 1950.

ELDREDGE, NILES, AND IAN TATTERSALL. *The Myths of Human Evolution.* New York: Columbia University Press, 1982.

ELIOT, T. S. "The Love Song of J. Alfred Prufrock." In *Collected Poems, 1909–1962.* New York: Harcourt Brace, & World, 1963.

ELLIS, LEE. "Evidence of Neuroandrogenic Etiology of Sex Roles from a Combined Analysis of Human, Nonhuman Primate and Nonprimate Mammalian Studies." *Personality and Individual Differences,* 7 (1986): 519–52.

EMBER, CAROL R. "A Cross-Cultural Perspective on Sex Differences." In Munroe, Munroe, and Whiting, eds., *Handbook of Cross-Cultural Human Development.*

EMBER, CAROL R. "An Evaluation of Alternative Theories of Matrilocal versus Patrilocal Residence." *Behavior Science Research,* 9 (1974): 135–49.

EMBER, CAROL R. "Feminine Task Assignment and the Social Behavior of Boys." *Ethos,* 1 (1973): 424–39.

EMBER, CAROL R. "Myths about Hunter-Gatherers." *Ethnology,* 17 (1978): 439–48.

EMBER, CAROL R. "The Relative Decline in Women's Contribution to Agriculture with Intensification." *American Anthropologist,* 85 (1983): 285–304.

EMBER, CAROL R. "Residential Variation among Hunter-Gatherers." *Behavior Science Research,* 9 (1975): 135–49.

EMBER, CAROL R., AND MELVIN EMBER. "The Conditions Favoring Multilocal Residence." *Southwestern Journal of Anthropology,* 28 (1972): 382–400.

EMBER, CAROL R., AND MELVIN EMBER. "The Evolution of Human Female Sexuality: A Cross-Species Perspective." *Journal of Anthropological Research,* 40 (1984): 202–10.

EMBER, CAROL R., MELVIN EMBER, AND BURTON PASTERNAK. "On the Development of Unilineal Descent." *Journal of Anthropological Research,* 30 (1974): 69–94.

EMBER, MELVIN. "Alternative Predictors of Polygyny." *Behavior Science Research,* 19 (1985): 1–23.

EMBER, MELVIN. "The Conditions That May Favor Avunculocal Residence." *Behavior Science Research,* 9 (1974): 203–9.

EMBER, MELVIN. "The Emergence of Neolocal Residence." *Transactions of the New York Academy of Sciences,* 30 (1967) 291–302.

EMBER, MELVIN. "The Nonunilinear Descent Groups of Samoa." *American Anthropologist,* 61 (1959): 573–77.

EMBER, MELVIN. "On the Origin and Extension of the Incest Taboo." *Behavior Science Research,* 10 (1975): 249–81.

EMBER, MELVIN. "The Relationship between Economic and Political Development in Nonindustrialized Societies." *Ethnology,* 2 (1963): 228–48.

EMBER, MELVIN. "Size of Color Lexicon: Interaction of Cultural and Biological Factors." *American Anthropologist,* 80 (1978): 364–67.

EMBER, MELVIN. "Statistical Evidence for an Ecological Explanation of Warfare." *American Anthropologist,* 84 (1982): 645–49.

EMBER, MELVIN. "Warfare, Sex Ratio, and Polygyny." *Ethnology,* 13 (1974): 197–206

EMBER, MELVIN, AND CAROL R. EMBER. "The Conditions Favoring Matrilocal versus Patrilocal Residence." *American Anthropologist,* 73 (1971): 571–94.

EMBER, MELVIN, AND CAROL R. EMBER. "Fear of Disasters as an Engine of History: Resource Crises, Warfare, and Interpersonal Aggression." Paper presented at a conference on "What Is the Engine of History?" Texas A & M University, October 1988.

EMBER, MELVIN, AND CAROL R. EMBER. "Male-Female Bonding: A Cross-Species Study of Mammals and Birds." *Behavior Science Research,* 14 (1979): 37–56.

EMBER, MELVIN, AND CAROL R. EMBER. *Marriage, Family and Kinship: Comparative Studies of Social Organization.* New Haven: HRAF Press, 1983.

ETIENNE, MONA, AND ELEANOR LEACOCK, eds. *Women and Colonization: Anthropological Perspectives.* New York: Praeger, 1980.

EURIPIDES. *The Trojan Women.*

EVANS-PRITCHARD, E. E. "The Nuer of the Southern Sudan." In M. Fortes and E. E. Evans-Pritchard, eds., *African Political Systems.* New York: Oxford University Press, 1940.

EVANS-PRITCHARD, E. E. "Witchcraft Explains Unfortunate Events." In Lessa and Vogt, eds., *Reader in Comparative Religion,* 4th ed.

FAGAN, BRIAN M. *People of the Earth: An Introduction to World Prehistory,* 6th ed. Glenview, Ill.: Scott, Foresman and Company, 1989.

FEATHERMAN, DAVID L., AND ROBERT M. HAUSER. *Opportunity and Change.* New York: Academic Press, 1978.

FEINMAN, GARY M., STEPHEN A. KOWALEWSKI, LAURA FINSTEN, RICHARD E. BLANTON, AND LINDA NICHOLAS. "Long-term Demographic Change: A Perspective from the Valley of Oaxaca, Mexico." *Journal of Field Archaeology,* 12 (1985): 333–62.

FEINMAN, GARY, AND JILL NEITZEL. "Too Many Types: An Overview of Sedentary Prestate Societies in the Americas." In Michael B. Schiffer, *Advances in Archaeological Methods and Theory.* Orlando, Fla.: Academic Press, 1984, 7: 39–102.

FERGUSON, R. BRIAN., ed. *Warfare, Culture, and Environment.* Orlando, Fla.: Academic Press, 1984.

FINLEY, M. I. *Politics in the Ancient World.* Cambridge: Cambridge University Press, 1983.

"The First Dentist." *Newsweek,* March 5, 1973, p. 73.

FISH, PAUL R. "Beyond Tools: Middle Paleolithic Debitage Analysis and Cultural Inference." *Journal of Anthropological Research,* 37 (1981): 374–86.

FLANNERY, KENT V. "The Cultural Evolution of Civilizations." *Annual Review of Ecology and Systematics,* 3 (1972): 399–426.

FLANNERY, KENT V. "The Ecology of Early Food Production in Mesopotamia." *Science,* March 12, 1965, pp. 1247–56.

FLANNERY, KENT V. "The Origins and Ecological Effects of Early Domestication in Iran and the Near East." In Struever, ed., *Prehistoric Agriculture* (originally published in Ucko and Dimbleby, eds., *The Domestication and Exploitation of Plants and Animals*).

FLANNERY, KENT V. "The Origins of Agriculture." *Annual Review of Anthropology,* 2 (1973): 271–310.

FLANNERY, KENT V. "The Origins of the Village as a Settlement Type in Mesoamerica and the Near East: A Comparative Study." In Ruth Tringham, ed., *Territoriality and Proxemics.* Andover, Mass.: Warner Modular Publications, 1973.

FLANNERY, KENT V. "The Research Problem." In Kent V. Flannery, ed., *Guila Naquitz: Archaic Foraging and Early Agriculture in Oaxaca, Mexico.* Orlando, Fla: Academic Press, 1986, pp. 3–18.

FLEAGLE, J. G., AND R. F. KAY . "New Interpretations of the Phyletic Position of Oligocene Hominoids." In Ciochon and Corruccini, eds., *New Interpretations of Ape and Human Ancestry,* pp. 181–210.

FLEAGLE, JOHN G. *Primate Adaptation & Evolution.* San Diego: Academic Press, 1988.

FLEAGLE, JOHN G., AND RICHARD F. KAY. "The Paleobiology of Catarrhines." In Delson, ed., *Ancestors,* pp. 23–36.

FORD, CLELLAN S., AND FRANK A. BEACH. *Patterns of Sexual Behavior.* New York: Harper 1951.

FORTES, M. *The Web of Kinship among the Tallensi.* New York: Oxford University Press, 1949.

FOSTER, BRIAN L. "Ethnicity and Commerce." *American Ethnologist,* 1 (1974): 437–47.

FOWLER, MELVIN L. "A Pre-Columbian Urban Center on the Mississippi." *Scientific American,* August 1975, pp. 92–101.

FOX, ROBIN. *Kinship and Marriage: An Anthropological Perspective.* Cambridge: Cambridge University Press, 1983.

FRANCISCUS, ROBERT G., AND ERIK TRINKAUS. "Nasal Morphology and the Emergence of *Homo erectus.*" *American Journal of Physical Anthropology,* 75 (1988): 517–27.

FREEMAN, J. D. "On the Concept of the Kindred." *Journal of the Royal Anthropological Institute,* 91 (1961): 192–220.

FREILICH, MORRIS, ed. *The Meaning of Culture.* Lexington, Mass.: Xerox, 1972.

FREUD, SIGMUND. *A General Introduction to Psychoanalysis.* Garden City, N.Y.: Garden City Publishing Co., 1943 (originally published in German, 1917).

FRIED, MORTON H. *The Evolution of Political Society: An Essay in Political Anthropology.* New York: Random House, 1967.

FRIEDRICH, PAUL. *The Language of Parallax.* Austin: University of Texas Press, 1986.

FRIEDRICH, PAUL. *Proto-Indo-European Trees: The Arboreal System of a Prehistoric People.* Chicago: University of Chicago Press. 1970.

FRISANCHO, A. R., J. SANCHEZ, D. PALLARDEL, AND L. YANEZ. "Adaptive Significance of Small Body Size under Poor Socioeconomic Conditions in Southern Peru." *American Journal of Physical Anthropology,* 39 (1973): 255–62.

FRISANCHO, A. ROBERTO. *Human Adaptation: A Functional Interpretation.* Ann Arbor: University of Michigan Press, 1981.

FRISCH, ROSE E. "Fatness, Puberty, and Fertility." *Natural History,* October 1980, pp. 16–27.

GARDNER, BEATRICE T., AND R. ALLEN GARDNER. "Two Comparative Psychologists Look at Language Acquisition." In K. E. Nelson, ed., *Children's Language.* New York: Halsted Press, 1980, 2: 331–69.

GARDNER, R. ALLEN, AND BEATRICE T. GARDNER. "Comparative Psychology and Language Acquisition." In Sebeok and Umiker-Sebeok, eds., *Speaking of Apes,* pp. 287–330.

GARDNER, R. ALLEN, AND BEATRICE T. GARDNER. "Teaching Sign Language to a Chimpanzee." *Science,* August 15, 1969, pp. 664–72.

GARN, STANLEY M. *Human Races,* 3rd ed. Springfield, Ill.: Charles C. Thomas, 1971.

GARN, STANLEY M., MEINHARD ROBINOW, AND STEPHEN M. BAILEY. "Genetic and Nutritional Interactions." In Jelliffe and Jelliffe, eds., *Nutrition and Growth,* pp. 31–64.

GEERTZ, CLIFFORD. "Religion as a Cultural System." In Banton, ed., *Anthropological Approaches to the Study of Religion.*

GIBBS, JAMES L., JR., ed. *Peoples of Africa.* New York: Holt, Rinehart & Winston, 1965.

GIMBUTAS, MARIJA. "An Archaeologist's View of PIE* in 1975." *Journal of Indo European Studies,* 2 (1974): 289–307.

GINGERICH, P. D. *Cranial Anatomy and Evolution of Early Tertiary Plesiadapidae (Mammalia, Primates).* Papers on Paleontology, no. 15. Ann Arbor: Museum of Paleontology, University of Michigan, 1976.

GLADWIN, CHRISTINA H. "A Theory of Real-Life Choice: Applications to Agricultural Decisions." In Barlett, ed., *Agricultural Decision-Making,* pp. 45–85.

GLASS, H. BENTLEY. "The Genetics of the Dunkers." *Scientific American,* August 1953, pp. 76–81.

GOLDE, PEGGY, ed. *Women in the Field: Anthropological Experiences,* 2nd ed. Berkeley: University of California Press, 1986.

GOLDSTEIN, MELVYN C. "Stratification, Polyandry, and Family Structure in Central Tibet." *Southwestern Journal of Anthropology,* 27 (1971): 65–74.

GOODE, WILLIAM J. *The Family.* Englewood Cliffs, N.J.: Prentice-Hall, 1964.

GOODE, WILLIAM J. *World Revolution and Family Patterns.* New York: Free Press, 1970.

GOODENOUGH, WARD H. *Property, Kin, and Community on Truk.* New Haven: Yale University Press, 1951.

GOODMAN, ALAN H., AND GEORGE J. ARMELAGOS. "Disease and Death at Dr. Dickson's Mounds." *Natural History,* September 1985, pp. 12–19.

GOODMAN, ALAN H., JOHN LALLO, GEORGE J. ARMELAGOS, AND JEROME C. ROSE. "Health Changes at Dickson Mounds, Illinois (A.D. 950–1300)." In Cohen and Armelagos, eds., *Paleopathology at the Origins of Agriculture,* pp. 271–301.

GOODMAN, MADELEINE J., P. BION GRIFFIN, AGNES A. ESTIOKO-GRIFFIN, AND JOHN S. GROVE. "The Compatibility of Hunting and Mothering among the Agta Hunter-Gatherers of the Philippines." *Sex Roles,* 12 (1985): 1199–209.

GOODRICH, L. CARRINGTON. *A Short History of the Chinese People,* 3rd ed. New York: Harper & Row, 1959.

GOODY, JACK. "Cousin Terms." *Southwestern Journal of Anthropology,* 26 (1970): 125–42.

GOODY, JACK, AND S. J. TAMBIAH. *Bridewealth and Dowry.* Cambridge: Cambridge University Press, 1973.

GORMAN, CHESTER. "The Hoabinhian and After: Subsistence Patterns in Southeast Asia during the late Pleistocene and Early Recent Periods." *World Archaeology,* 2 (1970): 315–19.

GOULD, RICHARD A. *Yiwara: Foragers of the Australian Desert.* New York: Scribner's, 1969.

GRABURN, NELSON H. *Eskimos Without Igloos.* Boston: Little, Brown, 1969.

GRAHAM, SUSAN BRANDT. "Biology and Human Social Behavior: A Response to van den Berghe and Barash." *American Anthropologist,* 81 (1979): 357–60.

GRAY, J. PATRICK, AND LINDA D. WOLFE. "Height and Sexual Dimorphism of Stature among Human Societies." *American Journal of Physical Anthropology,* 53 (1980): 446–52.

GRAYSON, DONALD K. "Explaining Pleistocene Extinctions: Thoughts on the Structure of a Debate." In Paul S. Martin and Richard G. Klein, eds., *Quaternary Extinctions: A Prehistoric Revolution.* Tucson: University of Arizona Press, 1984, pp. 807–23.

GRAYSON, DONALD K. "Pleistocene Avifaunas and the Overkill Hypothesis." *Science,* February 18, 1977, pp. 691–92.

GREENBERG, JOSEPH H. *Anthropological Linguistics: An Introduction.* New York: Random House, 1968.

GREENBERG, JOSEPH H. "Linguistic Evidence Regarding Bantu Origins." *Journal of African History,* 13 (1972): 189–216.

GRÖGER, B. LISA. "Of Men and Machines: Co-operation among French Family Farmers." *Ethnology,* 20 (1981): 163–75.

GUIORA, ALEXANDER A., BENJAMIN BEIT-HALLAHMI, RISTO FRIED, AND CECELIA YODER. "Language Environment and Gender Identity Attainment." *Language Learning,* 32 (1982): 289–304.

GUMPERZ, JOHN J. "Dialect Differences and Social Stratification in a North Indian Village." In *Language in Social Groups: Essays by John L. Gumperz,* selected and introduced by Anwar S. Dil. Stanford, Calif.: Stanford University Press, 1971, pp. 25–47.

GUMPERZ, JOHN J. "Speech Variation and the Study of Indian Civilization." *American Anthropologist,* 63 (1961): 976–88.

GUNDERS, S., AND J. W. M. WHITING. "Mother-Infant Separation and Physical Growth." *Ethnology,* 7 (1968): 196–206.

GUTHRIE, R. DALE. "Mosaics, Allelochemics, and Nutrients: An Ecological Theory of Late Pleistocene Megafaunal Extinctions." In Paul S. Martin and Richard G. Klein, eds., *Quarternary Extinctions: A Prehistoric Revolution.* Tucson: University of Arizona Press, 1984, pp. 259–98.

HAAS, MARY R. "Men's and Women's Speech in Koasati." *Language,* 20 (1944): 142–49.

HAHN, EMILY. "Chimpanzees and Language." *New Yorker,* April 24, 1971, pp. 54ff.

HALDANE, J. B. S. "Human Evolution: Past and Future." In Glenn L. Jepsen, Ernst Mayr, and George Gaylord Simpson, eds., *Genetics, Paleontology, and Evolution.* New York: Atheneum, 1963.

HALL, EDWARD T. *The Hidden Dimension.* Garden City, N.Y.: Doubleday, 1966.

HALLAM, A. "Alfred Wegener and the Hypothesis of Continental Drift." *Scientific American,* February 1975, pp. 88–97.

HANDWERKER, W. PENN, AND PAUL V. CROSBIE. "Sex and Dominance." *American Anthropologist,* 84 (1982): 97–104.

HARLAN, JACK R. "A Wild Wheat Harvest in Turkey." *Archaeology,* 20, no. 3 (June 1967): 197–201.

HARLAN, JACK R., J. M. J. DE WET, AND ANN STEMLER, eds. *Origins of African Plant Domestication.* The Hague: Mouton, 1976, pp. 3–19.

HARLAN, JACK R., J. M. J. DE WET, AND ANN STEMLER. "Plant Domestication and Indigenous African Agriculture." In Harlan, De Wet, and Stemler, eds., *Origins of African Plant Domestication,* pp. 3–19.

HARLAN, JACK R., AND ANN STEMLER. "The Races of Sorghum in Africa." In Harlan, De Wet, and Stemler, eds., *Origins of African Plant Domestication,* pp. 465–78.

HARNER, MICHAEL. "The Role of Hallucinogenic Plants in European Witchcraft." In Michael Harner, ed., *Hallucinogens and Shamanism.* New York: Oxford University Press, 1972, pp. 127–50.

HARNER, MICHAEL J. "Scarcity, the Factors of Production, and Social Evolution." In Steven Polgar, ed., *Population, Ecology, and Social Evolution.* The Hague: Mouton, 1975.

HARRIS, DAVID R. "Settling Down: An Evolutionary Model for the Transformation of Mobile Bands into Sedentary Communities." In J. Friedman and M. J. Rowlands, eds., *The Evolution of Social Systems.* London: Duckworth, 1977.

HARRIS, MARVIN. *Cows, Pigs, Wars and Witches: The Riddles of Culture.* New York: Random House, Vintage, 1975.

HARRIS, MARVIN. "The Cultural Ecology of India's Sacred Cattle." *Current Anthropology,* 7 (1966): 51–63.

HARRIS, MARVIN. *Cultural Materialism: The Struggle for a Science of Culture.* New York: Random House, 1979.

HARRIS, MARVIN. *Patterns of Race in the Americas.* New York: Walker, 1964.

HARRIS, MARVIN, AND ERIC B. ROSS. *Food and Evolution: Toward a Theory of Human Food Habits.* Philadelphia: Temple University Press, 1987.

HARRISON, G. A., J. M. TANNER, D. R. PILBEAM, AND P. T. BAKER. *Human Biology: An Introduction to Human Evolution, Variation, Growth, and Adaptability,* 3rd ed. Oxford: Oxford University Press, 1988.

HARRISON, GAIL G. "Primary Adult Lactase Deficiency: A Problem in Anthropological Genetics." *American Anthropologist,* 77 (1975): 812–35.

HARRISON, PETER D., AND B. L. TURNER II, eds. *Pre-Hispanic Maya Agriculture.* Albuquerque: University of New Mexico Press, 1978.

HART, HORNELL. "The Logistic Growth of Political Areas." *Social Forces,* 26 (1948): 396–408.

HASSAN, FEKRI A. *Demographic Archaeology.* New York: Academic Press, 1981.

HAYES, KEITH J., AND CATHERINE H. HAYES. "The Intellectual Development of a Home-Raised Chimpanzee." *Proceedings of the American Philosophical Society,* 95 (1951): 105–9.

HEALD, FELIX P. "The Adolescent." In Jelliffe and Jelliffe, eds., *Nutrition and Growth,* pp. 239–52.

HEIDER, KARL. *The Dugum Dani.* Chicago: Aldine, 1970.

HEIDER, KARL. *Grand Valley Dani: Peaceful Warriors.* New York: Holt, Rinehart & Winston, 1979.

HEISE, DAVID R. "Cultural Patterning of Sexual Socialization." *American Sociological Review,* 32 (1967): 726–39.

HEISER, CHARLES B., JR. *Of Plants and People.* Norman: University of Oklahoma Press, 1985.

HELMS, MARY W. *Middle America.* Englewood Cliffs, N.J.: Prentice-Hall, 1975.

HEWES, GORDON W. "Food Transport and the Origin of Hominid Bipedalism." *American Anthropologist,* 63 (1961): 687–710.

HIATT, L. R. "Polyandry in Sri Lanka: A Test Case for Parental Investment Theory." *Man,* 15 (1980): 583–98.

HICKEY, GERALD CANNON. *Village in Vietnam.* New Haven: Yale University Press, 1964.

HICKSON, LETITIA. "The Social Contexts of Apology in Dispute Settlement: A Cross-Cultural Study." *Ethnology,* 25 (1986): 283–94.

HILL, JANE H. "Apes and Language." *Annual Review of Anthropology,* 7 (1978): 89–112.

HILL, KIM, HILLARD KAPLAN, KRISTEN HAWKES AND A. MAGDALENA HURTADO. "Foraging Decisions among Aché Hunter-Gatherers: New Data and Implications for Optimal Foraging Models." *Ethology and Sociobiology,* 8 (1987): 1–36.

HOCKETT, C. F., AND R. ASCHER. "The Human Revolution." *Current Anthropology,* 5 (1964): 135–68.

HOEBEL, E. ADAMSON. *The Law of Primitive Man.* New York: Atheneum, 1968 (originally published 1954).

HOIJER, HARRY. "Cultural Implications of Some Navaho Linguistic Categories." In Hymes, ed., *Language in Culture and Society.* Originally published in *Language,* 27 (1951): 111–20.

HOLE, FRANK, KENT V. FLANNERY, AND JAMES A. NEELY. *Prehistory and Human Ecology of the Deh Luran Plain.* Memoirs of the Museum of Anthropology, no. 1. Ann Arbor: University of Michigan, 1969.

HOLLOWAY, RALPH L. "The Casts of Fossil Hominid Brains." *Scientific American,* July 1974, pp. 106–15.

HOUSTON, STEPHEN D. "The Phonetic Decipherment of Mayan Glyphs." *Antiquity,* 62 (1988): 126–35.

HOWELL, F. CLARK. "Observations on the Earlier Phases of the European Lower Paleolithic." In *Recent Studies in Paleoanthropology. American Anthropologist,* special publication, April 1966, pp. 88–200.

HOWELL, NANCY. *Demography of the Dobe !Kung.* New York: Academic Press, 1979.

HUNT, MORTON. *Sexual Behavior in the 1970s.* Chicago: Playboy Press, 1974.

HURTADO, ANA M., KRISTEN HAWKES, KIM HILL, AND HILLARD KAPLAN. "Female Subsistence Strategies among the Aché Hunter-Gatherers of Eastern Paraguay." *Human Ecology,* 13 (1985): 1–28.

HUXLEY, JULIAN. *Evolution in Action.* New York: Mentor Books, 1957.

HYMES, DELL. *Foundations in Sociolinguistics: An Ethnographic Approach.* Philadelphia: University of Pennsylvania Press, 1974.

HYMES, DELL, ed. *Language in Culture and Society: A Reader in Linguistics and Anthropology.* New York: Harper & Row, Pub., 1964.

ISAAC, GLYNN. "The Diet of Early Man: Aspects of Archaeological Evidence from Lower and Middle Pleistocene Sites in Africa." *World Archaeology,* 2 (1971): 277–99.

ISAAC, GLYNN LL. "The Archaeology of Human Origins: Studies of the Lower Pleistocene in East Africa, 1971–1981." In Fred Wendorf and Angela E. Close, eds., *Advances in World Archaeology.* Orlando, Fla.: Academic Press, 1984, 3: 1–87.

ITANI, JUN'ICHIRO. "The Society of Japanese Monkeys." *Japan Quarterly,* 8 (1961): 421–30.

JANZEN, DANIEL H. "Tropical Agroecosystems." *Science,* December 21, 1973, pp. 1212–19.

JELLIFFE, DERRICK B., AND E. F. PATRICE JELLIFFE, eds. *Nutrition and Growth.* New York: Plenum, 1979.

JENNINGS, J. D. *Prehistory of North America.* New York: McGraw-Hill, 1968.

JENSEN, ARTHUR. "How Much Can We Boost IQ and Scholastic Achievement?" *Harvard Educational Review,* 29 (1969): 1–123.

JOHANSON, DONALD C., AND MAITLAND EDEY. *Lucy: The Beginnings of Humankind.* New York: Simon & Schuster, 1981.

JOHANSON, DONALD C., AND TIM D. WHITE. "A Systematic Assessment of Early African Hominids." *Science,* January 26, 1979, pp. 321–30.

JOLLY, ALISON. *The Evolution of Primate Behavior,* 2nd ed. New York: Macmillan, 1985.

JUDGE, W. JAMES, AND JERRY DAWSON. "Paleo-Indian Settlement Technology in New Mexico." *Science,* June 16, 1972, pp. 1210–16.

JUNGERS, WILLIAM L. "Relative Joint Size and Hominoid Locomotor Adaptations with Implications for the Evolution of Hominid Bipedalism." *Journal of Human Evolution,* 17 (1988): 247–65.

KAPLAN, DAVID, AND ROBERT A. MANNERS. "Anthropology: Some Old Themes and New Directions." *Southwestern Journal of Anthropology,* 27 (1971).

KAPLAN, HILLARD, AND KIM HILL. "Food Sharing among Aché Foragers: Tests of Explanatory Hypotheses." *Current Anthropology,* 26 (1985): 223–46.

KASARDA, JOHN D. "Economic Structure and Fertility: A Comparative Analysis." *Demography,* 8, no. 3 (August 1971): 307–18.

KEELEY, LAWRENCE H. *Experimental Determination of Stone Tool Uses: A Microwear Analysis.* Chicago: University of Chicago Press, 1980.

KELLER, HELEN. *The Story of My Life.* New York: Dell, 1974 (originally published 1902).

KELLY, RAYMOND C. "Witchcraft and Sexual Relations: An Exploration in the Social and Semantic Implications of the Structure of Belief." Paper presented at the annual meeting of the American Anthropological Association, Mexico City, 1974.

KING, SETH S. "Some Farm Machinery Seems Less Than Human." *New York Times,* April 8, 1979, p. E9.

KLEIN, RICHARD G. "The Ecology of Early Man in Southern Africa." *Science,* July 8, 1977, pp. 115–126.

KLEIN, RICHARD G. "Ice-Age Hunters of the Ukraine." *Scientific American,* June 1974, pp. 96–105.

KLEIN, RICHARD G. "Reconstructing How Early People Exploited Animals: Problems and Prospects." In Nitecki and Nitecki, eds., *The Evolution of Human Hunting,* pp. 11–45.

KLEIN, RICHARD G. "The Stone Age Prehistory of Southern Africa." *Annual Review of Anthropology,* 12 (1983): 25–48.

KLIMA, BOHUSLAV. "The First Ground-Plan of an Upper Paleolithic Loess Settlement in Middle Europe and Its Meaning." In Robert J. Braidwood and Gordon R. Willey, eds., *Courses Toward Urban Life: Archaeological Consideration of Some Cultural Alternatives.* Viking Fund Publications in Anthropology, no. 32. Chicago: Aldine, 1962.

KLINEBERG, OTTO, ed. *Characteristics of the American Negro.* New York: Harper & Brothers, 1944.

KLINEBERG, OTTO. *Negro Intelligence and Selective Migration.* New York: Columbia University Press, 1935.

KLUCKHOHN, CLYDE. "As an Anthropologist Views It." In A. Deutsch, ed., *Sex Habits of American Men.* Englewood Cliffs, N.J.: Prentice-Hall, 1948.

KLUCKHOHN, CLYDE. "Recurrent Themes in Myths and Mythmaking." In Dundes, ed., *The Study of Folklore.*

KNAUFT, BRUCE M. "Cargo Cults and Relational Separation." *Behavior Science Research,* 13 (1978): 185–240.

KOCH, KLAUS-FRIEDRICH, SORAYA ALTORKI, ANDREW ARNO, AND LETITIA HICKSON. "Ritual Reconciliation and the Obviation of Grievances: A Comparative Study in the Ethnography of Law." *Ethnology,* 16 (1977): 269–84.

KONNER, MELVIN. *The Tangled Wing: Biological Constraints on the Human Spirit.* New York: Harper & Row, Pub., 1982.

KONNER, MELVIN, AND CAROL WORTHMAN. "Nursing Frequency, Gonadal Function, and Birth Spacing among !Kung Hunter-Gatherers." *Science,* February 15, 1980, pp. 788–91.

KRACKE, WAUD H. *Force and Persuasion: Leadership in an Amazonian Society.* Chicago: University of Chicago Press, 1979.

KRAMER, SAMUEL NOEL. *The Sumerians: Their History, Culture, and Character.* Chicago: University of Chicago Press, 1963.

KREBS, J. R., AND N. B. DAVIES, eds. *Behavioural Ecology: An Evolutionary Approach,* 2nd ed. Sunderland, Mass.: Sinauer Associates, 1984.

KROEBER, ALFRED L. *The Nature of Culture.* Chicago: University of Chicago Press, 1952.

KUMMER, HANS. *Primate Societies: Group Techniques of Ecological Adaptation.* Chicago: Aldine-Atherton, 1971.

LAITMAN, JEFFREY. "The Anatomy of Human Speech." *Natural History,* August 1984, pp. 20–27.

LAMBERT, WILLIAM W., LEIGH MINTURN TRIANDIS, AND MARGERY WOLF. "Some Correlates of Beliefs in the Malevolence and Benevolence of Supernatural Beings: A Cross-Societal Study." *Journal of Abnormal and Social Psychology,* 58 (1959): 162-69.

LANDAUER, THOMAS K. "Infantile Vaccination and the Secular Trend in Stature." *Ethos,* 1 (1973): 499–503.

LANDAUER, THOMAS K., AND JOHN W. M. WHITING. "Correlates and Consequences of Stress in Infancy." In Munroe, Munroe, and Whiting, eds., *Handbook of Cross-Cultural Human Development,* pp. 355–75.

LANDAUER, THOMAS K., AND JOHN W. M. WHITING. "Infantile Stimulation and Adult Stature of Human Males." *American Anthropologist,* 66 (1964): 1007–28.

LEACH, JERRY W. "Introduction." In Jerry W. Leach and Edmund Leach, eds., *The Kula: New Perspectives on Massim Exchange.* Cambridge: Cambridge University Press, 1983, pp. 1–26.

LEACOCK, ELEANOR AND RICHARD LEE. "Introduction." In Eleanor Leacock and Richard Lee, eds., *Politics and History in Band Societies.* Cambridge: Cambridge University Press, 1982, pp. 1–20.

LEAKEY, L. S. B. "Finding the World's Earliest Man." *National Geographic,* September 1960, pp. 420–35.

LEAKEY, R. E. F. "An Overview of the East Rudolf Hominidae." In Yves Coppens, F. Clark Howell, Glynn Ll. Isaac, and Richard E. F. Leakey, eds., *Earliest Man and Environments in the Lake Rudolf Basin.* Chicago: University of Chicago Press, 1976.

LEAKEY, RICHARD E. *The Making of Mankind.* New York: Dutton, 1981.

LEE, RICHARD B. *The !Kung San: Men, Women, and Work in a Foraging Society.* Cambridge: Cambridge University Press, 1979.

LEE, RICHARD B. "Population Growth and the Beginnings of Sedentary Life among the !Kung Bushmen." In Brian Spooner, ed., *Population Growth: Anthropological Implications.* Cambridge, Mass.: M.I.T. Press, 1972.

LEE, RICHARD B. "What Hunters Do for a Living, or, How to Make Out on Scarce Resources." In Lee and DeVore, eds., *Man the Hunter.*

LEE, RICHARD B., AND IRVEN DEVORE, eds. *Man the Hunter.* Chicago: Aldine, 1968.

LEES, SUSAN H., AND DANIEL G. BATES. "The Origins of Specialized Nomadic Pastoralism: A Systemic Model." *American Antiquity,* 39 (1974): 187–93.

LEHMANN, ARTHUR C., AND JAMES E. MYERS. *Magic, Witchcraft, and Religion: An Anthropological Study of the Supernatural.* Palo Alto, Calif.: Mayfield, 1985.

LEIBOWITZ, LILA. *Females, Males, Families: A Biosocial Approach.* North Scituate, Mass.: Duxbury, 1978.

LENSKI, GERHARD. *Power and Privilege: A Theory of Social Stratification.* Chapel Hill, N.C.: University of North Carolina Press, 1984.

LEROI-GOURHAN, ANDRÉ. "The Evolution of Paleolithic Art." *Scientific American,* February 1968, pp. 58–70.

LESSA, WILLIAM A., AND EVON Z. VOGT, eds. *Reader in Comparative Religion: An Anthropological Approach,* 3rd ed. New York: Harper & Row, Pub., 1971.

LESSA, WILLIAM A., AND EVON Z. VOGT, eds. *Reader in Comparative Religion: An Anthropological Approach,* 4th ed. New York: Harper & Row, Pub., 1979.

LEVINE, NANCY E. "Women's Work and Infant Feeding: A Case from Rural Nepal." *Ethnology,* 27 (1988): 231–51.

LEVINE, ROBERT A., AND BARBARA B. LEVINE. "Nyansongo: A Gusii Community in Kenya." In Beatrice B. Whiting, ed., *Six Cultures.* New York: John Wiley, 1963.

LEVINSON, DAVID, AND MARTIN J. MALONE, eds. *Toward Explaining Human Culture: A Critical Review of the Findings of Worldwide Cross-Cultural Research.* New Haven: HRAF Press, 1980.

LÉVI-STRAUSS, CLAUDE. "The Sorcerer and His Magic." In Lévi-Strauss, *Structural Anthropology.*

LÉVI-STRAUSS, CLAUDE. *Structural Anthropology,* trans. Claire Jacobson and Brooke Grundfest Schoepf. New York: Basic Books, 1963.

LÉVI-STRAUSS, CLAUDE. *New York Times,* January 21, 1972, p. 41; reprinted from *Diacritics,* Cornell University.

LEWIN, ROGER. "Ethiopian Stone Tools Are World's Oldest." *Science,* February 20, 1981, pp. 806–7.

LEWIN, ROGER. "Is the Orangutan a Living Fossil?" *Science,* December 16, 1983, pp. 1222–23.

LEWIS, OSCAR. *Life in a Mexican Village: Tepoztlan Revisited.* Urbana: University of Illinois Press, 1951.

LEWONTIN, R. C. "The Apportionment of Human Diversity." In Theodosius Dobzhansky, ed., *Evolutionary Biology.* New York: Plenum, 1972, pp. 381–98.

LIEBERMAN, PHILIP. *The Biology and Evolution of Language.* Cambridge, Mass.: Harvard University Press, 1984.

LINTON, RALPH. *The Cultural Background of Personality.* New York: Appleton-Century-Crofts, 1945.

LINTON, RALPH. *The Study of Man.* New York: Appleton-Century-Crofts, 1936.

LIVINGSTON, FRANK B. "Malaria and Human Polymorphisms." *Annual Review of Genetics* 5 (1971): 33–64.

LOEHLIN, JOHN C., GARDNER LINDZEY, AND J. N. SPUHLER. *Race Differences in Intelligence.* San Francisco: W. H. Freeman & Company Publishers, 1975.

LOFTIN, COLIN K. "Warfare and Societal Complexity: A Cross-Cultural Study of Organized Fighting in Preindustrial Societies." Ph.D. thesis, University of North Carolina at Chapel Hill, 1971.

LOOMIS, W. FARNSWORTH. "Skin-Pigment Regulation of Vitamin-D Biosynthesis in Man." *Science,* August 4, 1967, pp. 501–6.

LOVEJOY, C. OWEN. "Evolution of Human Walking." *Scientific American,* November 1988, pp. 118–25.

LOVEJOY, C. OWEN. "The Origin of Man." *Science,* January 23, 1981, pp. 341–50.
LOVEJOY, OWEN, KINGSBURY HEIPLE, AND ALBERT BERNSTEIN. "The Gait of *Australopithecus.*" *American Journal of Physical Anthropology,* 38 (1973): 757–79.
LYND, ROBERT S., AND HELEN MERRELL LYND. *Middletown.* New York: Harcourt, Brace, 1929.
LYND, ROBERT S., AND HELEN MERRELL LYND. *Middletown in Transition.* New York: Harcourt, Brace, 1937.
McCARTHY, FREDERICK D., AND MARGARET McARTHUR. "The Food Quest and the Time Factor in Aboriginal Economic Life." In C. P. Mountford, ed., *Records of the Australian-American Scientific Expedition to Arnhem Land, Volume 2: Anthropology and Nutrition.* Melbourne: Melbourne University Press, 1960.
McCLELLAND, DAVID C. *The Achieving Society.* New York: Van Nostrand, 1961.
MACCOBY, ELEANOR E., AND CAROL N. JACKLIN. *The Psychology of Sex Differences.* Stanford, Calif.: Stanford University Press, 1974.
McCRACKEN, ROBERT D. "Lactase Deficiency: An Example of Dietary Evolution." *Current Anthropology,* 12 (1971): 479–500.
McHENRY, HENRY M. "The Pattern of Human Evolution: Studies on Bipedalism, Mastication, and Encephalization." *Annual Review of Anthropology,* 11 (1982): 151–73.
McKENNA, MALCOLM C. "Was Europe Connected Directly to North America Prior to the Middle Eocene?" In T. Dobzhansky, M. K. Hecht, and W. C. Steere, eds., *Evolutionary Biology,* vol 6. New York: Appleton-Century-Crofts, 1972.
MACLACHLAN, M. D., ed. *Household Economies and Their Transformations.* Monographs in Economic Anthropology, No. 3. Lanham, Md.: University Press of America, 1987.
McNEILL, WILLIAM H. *Plagues and Peoples.* Garden City, N.Y.: Doubleday Anchor, 1976.
MacNEISH, RICHARD S. "The Evaluation of Community Patterns in the Tehuacán Valley of Mexico and Speculations about the Cultural Processes." In Ruth Tringham, ed., *Ecology and Agricultural Settlements.* Andover, Mass.: Warner Modular Publications, 1973.
MALEFIJT, ANNEMARIE DE WAAL. *Religion and Culture: An Introduction to Anthropology of Religion.* New York: Macmillan, 1968.
MALINOWSKI, BRONISLAW. *Magic, Science and Religion and Other Essays.* Garden City, N.Y.: Doubleday, 1954.
MALINOWSKI, BRONISLAW. *Sex and Repression in Savage Society.* London: Kegan Paul, Trench, Trubner Co., 1927.
MALINOWSKI, BRONISLAW. *The Sexual Life of Savages in Northwestern Melanesia.* New York: Halcyon House, 1932.
MARANO, LOUIS A. "A Macrohistoric Trend toward World Government." *Behavior Science Notes,* 8 (1973): 35–40.
MARCUS, JOYCE. "On the Nature of the Mesoamerican City." In Evon Z. Vogt and Richard M. Leventhal, eds., *Prehistoric Settlement Patterns: Essays in Honor of Gordon R. Willey.* Albuquerque: University of New Mexico Press, 1983, pp. 195–242.
MARLER, PETER. "Primate Vocalization: Affective or Symbolic?" In Sebeok and Umiker-Sebeok, eds., *Speaking of Apes,* pp. 221–29.
MARSHACK, ALEXANDER. *The Roots of Civilization.* New York: McGraw-Hill, 1972.
MARSHALL, LARRY G. "Who Killed Cock Robin?: An Investigation of the Extinction Controversy." In Paul S. Martin and Richard G. Klein, eds., *Quaternary Extinctions: A Prehistoric Revolution.* Tucson: University of Arizona Press, 1984, pp. 785–806.
MARSHALL, LORNA. "The !Kung Bushmen of the Kalahari Desert." In Gibbs, Jr., ed., *Peoples of Africa,* pp. 241–78.
MARSHALL, LORNA. "Sharing, Talking and Giving: Relief of Social Tensions among !Kung Bushmen." *Africa,* 31 (1961): 239–42.
MARTIN, M. KAY, AND BARBARA VOORHIES. *Female of the Species.* New York: Columbia University Press, 1975.
MARTIN, PAUL S. "The Discovery of America." *Science,* March 9, 1973, pp. 969–74.
MARTIN, ROBERT D. "Strategies of Reproduction." *Natural History,* November 1975, pp. 48–57.
MASUMURA, WILFRED T. "Law and Violence: A Cross-Cultural Study." *Journal of Anthropological Research,* 33 (1977): 388–99.
MATHIASSEN, THERKEL. *Material Culture of Iglulik Eskimos.* Copenhagen: Glydendalske, 1928.
MATOSSIAN, MARY K. "Ergot and the Salem Witchcraft Affair." *American Scientist* 70 (1982): 355–57.
MAYBURY-LEWIS, DAVID. *Akwe-Shavante Society.* Oxford: Clarendon Press, 1967.
MEAD, MARGARET. *Coming of Age in Samoa,* 3rd ed. New York: Morrow, 1961 (originally published 1928).
MEAD, MARGARET. *Sex and Temperament in Three Primitive Societies.* New York: Mentor, 1950 (originally published 1935).
MEEK, C. K. *Land Law and Custom in the Colonies.* London: Oxford University Press, 1940.
MIDDLETON, JOHN. "The Cult of the Dead: Ancestors and Ghosts." In Lessa and Vogt, eds., *Reader in Comparative Religion,* 3rd ed.
MIDDLETON, RUSSELL. "Brother-Sister and Father-Daughter Marriage in Ancient Egypt." *American Sociological Review,* 27 (1962): 603–11.
MILLON, RENÉ. "Social Relations in Ancient Teotihuacán." In Eric R. Wolf, ed., *The Valley of Mexico: Studies in Pre-Hispanic Ecology and Society.* Albuquerque: University of New Mexico Press, 1976, pp. 205–49.
MILLON, RENÉ. "Teotihuacán." *Scientific American,* June 1967, pp. 38–48.
MINER, HORACE. "Body Rituals among the Nacirema." *American Anthropologist,* 58 (1956): 504–5.

MONTAGU, ASHLEY. Introduction to Thomas H. Huxley, "Man's Place in Nature." In Young, ed., *Evolution of Man.*

MOONEY, KATHLEEN A. "The Effects of Rank and Wealth on Exchange among the Coast Salish." *Ethnology,* 17 (1978): 391–406.

MOORE, OMAR KHAYYÁM. "Divination: A New Perspective." *American Anthropologist,* 59 (1957): 69–74.

MORRIS, JOHN. *Living with Lepchas: A Book about the Sikkim Himalayas.* London: Heinemann, 1938.

MORRIS, LAURA NEWELL. "Gene Flow." In Morris, ed., *Human Populations, Genetic Variation, and Evolution.*

MORRIS, LAURA NEWELL. "The Small Population." In Morris, ed., *Human Populations, Genetic Variation, and Evolution.*

MORRIS, LAURA NEWELL, ed. *Human Populations, Genetic Variation, and Evolution.* San Francisco: Chandler, 1971.

MOTULSKY, ARNO. "Metabolic Polymorphisms and the Role of Infectious Diseases in Human Evolution." In Morris, ed., *Human Populations, Genetic Variation, and Evolution.*

MUKHOPADHYAY, CAROL C., AND PATRICIA J. HIGGINS. "Anthropological Studies of Women's Status Revisited: 1977–1987." *Annual Review of Anthropology,* 17 (1988): 461–95.

MUNROE, ROBERT L., RUTH H. MUNROE, AND JOHN W. M. WHITING. "Male Sex-Role Resolutions." In Munroe, Munroe, and Whiting, eds., *Handbook of Cross-Cultural Human Development,* pp. 611–32.

MUNROE, RUTH H., ROBERT L. MUNROE, AND BEATRICE B. WHITING, eds. *Handbook of Cross-Cultural Human Development.* New York: Garland Press, 1981.

MURDOCK, GEORGE P. *Social Structure.* New York: Macmillan, 1949.

MURDOCK, GEORGE P., AND CATERINA PROVOST. "Factors in the Division of Labor by Sex: A Cross-Cultural Analysis." *Ethnology,* 12 (1973): 203–25.

MYERS, FRED R. "Critical Trends in the Study of Hunter-Gatherers." *Annual Review of Anthropology,* 17 (1988): 261–82.

NADEL, S. F. *A Black Byzantium: The Kingdom of Nupe in Nigeria.* London: Oxford University Press, 1942.

NADEL, S. F. "Nupe State and Community." *Africa,* 8 (1935): 257–303.

NAG, MONI, BENJAMIN N. F. WHITE, AND R. CREIGHTON PEET. "An Anthropological Approach to the Study of the Economic Value of Children in Java and Nepal." *Current Anthropology,* 19 (1978): 293–301.

NAPIER, J. "The Antiquity of Human Walking." *Scientific American,* April 1967, pp. 56–66.

NAPIER, J. R., AND P. H. NAPIER. *A Handbook of Living Primates.* New York: Academic Press, 1967.

NAROLL, RAOUL. "Imperial Cycles and World Order." *Peace Research Society: Papers,* 7, Chicago Conference (1967): 83–101.

NAROLL, RAOUL. "Two Solutions to Galton's Problem." *Philosophy of Science,* 28 (January 1961): 15–39.

NEEL, JAMES V., WILLARD R. CENTERWALL, NAPOLEON A. CHAGNON, AND HELEN L. CASEY. "Notes on the Effect of Measles and Measles Vaccine in a Virgin-Soil Population of South American Indians." *American Journal of Epidemiology,* 91 (1970): 418–29.

NERLOVE, SARA B. "Women's Workload and Infant Feeding Practices: A Relationship with Demographic Implications." *Ethnology,* 13 (1974): 207–14.

NEVINS, ALLAN. *The American States During and After the Revolution.* New York: Macmillan, 1972.

NEWMAN, MARSHALL T. "The Application of Ecological Rules to the Racial Anthropology of the Aboriginal New World." *American Anthropologist,* 55 (1953): 311–27.

NIEDERBERGER, CHRISTINE. "Early Sedentary Economy in the Basin of Mexico." *Science.* January 12, 1979, pp. 131–42.

NIMKOFF, M. F., AND RUSSELL MIDDLETON. "Types of Family and Types of Economy." *American Journal of Sociology,* 66 (1960): 215–25.

NISSEN, HENRY W. "Axes of Behavioral Comparison." In Anne Roe and George Gaylord Simpson, eds., *Behavior and Evolution.* New Haven: Yale University Press, 1958.

NITECKI, MATTHEW H., AND DORIS V. NITECKI, eds. *The Evolution of Human Hunting.* New York: Plenum, 1987.

NORBECK, EDWARD. "Continuities in Japanese Social Stratification." In Leonard Plotnicov and Arthur Tuden, eds., *Essays in Comparative Social Stratification.* Pittsburgh: University of Pittsburgh Press, 1970.

OAKLEY, KENNETH. "On Man's Use of Fire, With Comments on Tool-Making and Hunting." In S. L. Washburn, ed., *Social Life of Early Man.* Chicago: Aldine, 1964.

OLIVER, DOUGLAS L. *Ancient Tahitian Society, Volume 1: Ethnography.* Honolulu: University of Hawaii Press, 1974.

ORTIZ, SUTTI, ed. *Economic Anthropology: Topics and Theories.* Monographs in Economic Anthropology, no. 1. Lanham, Md.: University Press of America, 1983.

OTTERBEIN, KEITH. *The Evolution of War.* New Haven: HRAF Press, 1970.

OTTERBEIN, KEITH. "Internal War: A Cross-Cultural Study." *American Anthropologist,* 70 (1968): 277–89.

OTTERBEIN, KEITH. *The Ultimate Coercive Sanction: A Cross-Cultural Study of Capital Punishment.* New Haven: HRAF Press, 1986.

OTTERBEIN, KEITH F. "Warfare: A Hitherto Unrecognized Critical Variable." *American Behavioral Scientist,* 20 (1977): 693–710.

OTTERBEIN, KEITH, AND CHARLOTTE S. OTTERBEIN. "An Eye for an Eye, A Tooth for a Tooth: A Cross-Cultural Study of Feuding." *American Anthropologist,* 67 (1965): 1470–82.

OVERFIELD, THERESA. *Biologic Variation in Health and Illness: Race, Age, and Sex Differences.* Menlo Park, Calif.: Addison-Wesley, 1985.

OWEN, ROGER C. "The Americas: The Case against an Ice-Age Human Population." In Smith and Spencer, eds., *The Origins of Modern Humans,* pp. 517–63.

PARKER, HILDA, AND SEYMOUR PARKER. "Father-Daughter Sexual Abuse: An Emerging Perspective." *American Journal of Orthopsychiatry,* 56 (1986): 531–49.

PARKER, SEYMOUR. "Cultural Rules, Rituals, and Behavior Regulation." *American Anthropologist,* 86 (1984): 584–600.

PARKER, SEYMOUR. "The Precultural Basis of the Incest Taboo: Toward a Biosocial Theory." *American Anthropologist,* 78 (1976): 285–305.

PASTERNAK, BURTON. *Introduction to Kinship and Social Organization.* Englewood Cliffs, N.J.: Prentice-Hall, 1976.

PASTERNAK, BURTON, CAROL R. EMBER, AND MELVIN EMBER. "On the Conditions Favoring Extended Family Households." *Journal of Anthropological Research,* 32 (1976): 109–23.

PATTERSON, COLIN. *Evolution.* London: British Museum; Ithaca, N.Y.: Cornell University Press, 1978.

PATTERSON, THOMAS C. *America's Past: A New World Archaeology.* Glenview, Ill.: Scott, Foresman, 1973.

PATTERSON, THOMAS C. *The Evolution of Ancient Societies: A World Archaeology.* Englewood Cliffs, N.J.: Prentice-Hall, 1981.

PELTO, PETRI J., AND GRETEL H. PELTO. "Intra-Cultural Diversity: Some Theoretical Issues." *American Ethnologist,* 2 (1975): 1–18.

PHILLIPSON, D. W. "Archaeology and Bantu Linguistics." *World Archaeology,* 8 (1976): 65–82.

PHILLIPSON, DAVID W. *African Archaeology.* Cambridge: Cambridge University Press, 1985.

PICKERSGILL, BARBARA, AND CHARLES B. HEISER, JR. "Origins and Distribution of Plants Domesticated in the New World Tropics." In Reed, ed., *Origins of Agriculture,* pp. 803–36.

PICKFORD, M. "Sequence and Environments of the Lower and Middle Miocene Hominoids of Western Kenya." In Ciochon and Corruccini, eds., *New Interpretations of Ape and Human Ancestry,* pp. 421–40.

PILBEAM, DAVID. *The Ascent of Man.* New York: Macmillan, 1972.

PILBEAM, DAVID. "The Descent of Hominoids and Hominids." *Scientific American,* March 1984, pp. 84–96.

PILBEAM, DAVID. "Recent Finds and Interpretations of Miocene Hominoids." *Annual Review of Anthropology,* 8 (1979): 333–52.

PILBEAM, DAVID, AND STEPHEN JAY GOULD. "Size and Scaling in Human Evolution." *Science,* December 6, 1974, pp. 892–900.

PLATTNER, STUART. "Introduction." In Plattner, ed., *Markets and Marketing,* pp. vii–xx.

PLATTNER, STUART, ed. *Markets and Marketing.* Monographs in Economic Anthropology, No. 4. Lanham, Md.: University Press of America, 1985.

POLANYI, KARL. "The Economy of Instituted Process." In Polanyi, Arensberg, and Pearson, eds., *Trade and Market in the Early Empires.*

POLANYI, KARL, CONRAD M. ARENSBERG, AND HARRY W. PEARSON, eds. *Trade and Market in the Early Empires.* New York: Free Press, 1957.

POLEDNAK, ANTHONY P. "Connective Tissue Responses in Negroes in Relation to Disease." *American Journal of Physical Anthropology,* 41 (1974): 49–57.

POSPISIL, LEOPOLD. *The Kapauku Papuans of West New Guinea.* New York: Holt, Rinehart & Winston, 1963.

POST, PETER W., FARRINGTON DANIELS, JR., AND ROBERT T. BINFORD, JR. "Cold Injury and the Evolution of 'White' Skin." *Human Biology,* 47 (1975): 65–80.

PREMACK, ANN JAMES, AND DAVID PREMACK. "Teaching Language to an Ape." *Scientific American,* October 1972, pp. 92–99.

PRICE, T. DOUGLAS, AND JAMES A. BROWN. *Prehistoric Hunter-Gatherers: The Emergence of Cultural Complexity.* Orlando, Fla.: Academic Press, 1985.

PRYOR, FREDERIC L. *The Origins of the Economy: A Comparative Study of Distribution in Primitive and Peasant Economies.* New York: Academic Press, 1977.

PURSEGLOVE, J. W. "The Origins and Migrations of Crops in Tropical Africa." In Harlan, De Wet, and Stemler, eds., *Origins of African Plant Domestication,* pp. 291–309.

QUINN, NAOMI. "Anthropological Studies on Women's Status." *Annual Review of Anthropology,* 6 (1977): 181–225.

RATHJE, WILLIAM L. "The Origin and Development of Lowland Classic Maya Civilization." *American Antiquity,* 36 (1971): 275–85.

RAY, VERNE, F. *The Sanpoil and Nespelem: Salishan Peoples of Northeastern Washington.* New Haven: Human Relations Area Files, 1954, pp. 172–89.

REDMAN, CHARLES L. *The Rise of Civilization: From Early Farmers to Urban Society in the Ancient Near East.* San Francisco: W. H. Freeman & Company Publishers, 1978.

REED, CHARLES A., ed. *Origins of Agriculture.* The Hague: Mouton, 1977.

RICE, PATRICIA C., AND ANN L. PATERSON. "Cave Art and Bones: Exploring the Interrelationships." *American Anthropologist,* 87 (1985): 94–100.

RICE, PATRICIA C., AND ANN L. PATERSON. "Validating the Cave Art—Archeofaunal Relationship in Cantabrian Spain." *American Anthropologist,* 88 (1986): 658–67.

RICHARD, ALISON F. *Primates in Nature.* New York: W. H. Freeman & Company Publishers, 1985.

RIESENFELD, ALPHONSE. "The Effect of Extreme Temperatures and Starvation on the Body Proportions of the Rat." *American Journal of Physical Anthropology*, 39 (1973): 427–59.

RIGHTMIRE, G. P. "The Tempo of Change in the Evolution of Mid-Pleistocene *Homo*." In Delson, ed., *Ancestors*, pp. 255–64.

RIGHTMIRE, G. PHILIP. "*Homo sapiens* in Sub-Saharan Africa." In Smith and Spencer, eds., *The Origins of Modern Humans*, pp. 295–326.

RITTER, MADELINE LATTMAN. "The Conditions Favoring Age-Set Organization." *Journal of Anthropological Research*, 36 (1980): 87–104.

RIVERS, W. H. R. *The Todas*. Oosterhout, N. B., The Netherlands: Anthropological Publications, 1967 (originally published 1906).

ROBERTS, D. F. "Body Weight, Race, and Climate." *American Journal of Physical Anthropology*, 2 (1953): 533–58.

ROBERTS, D. F. *Climate and Human Variability*, 2nd ed. Menlo Park, Calif.: Cummings, 1978.

ROBERTS, JOHN M. "Oaths, Autonomic Ordeals, and Power." In Clellan S. Ford, ed., *Cross-Cultural Approaches: Readings in Comparative Research*. New Haven: HRAF Press, 1967.

ROHNER, RONALD P. "Sex Differences in Aggression: Phylogenetic and Enculturation Perspectives." *Ethos*, 4 (1976): 57–72.

ROHNER, RONALD P. *They Love Me, They Love Me Not: A Worldwide Study of the Effects of Parental Acceptance and Rejection*. New Haven: HRAF Press, 1975.

ROOSEVELT, ANNA CURTENIUS. "Population, Health, and the Evolution of Subsistence: Conclusions from the Conference." In Cohen and Armelagos, eds., *Paleopathology at the Origins of Agriculture*, pp. 559–84.

ROSALDO, MICHELLE Z., AND LOUISE LAMPHERE, eds. *Woman, Culture, and Society*. Stanford, Calif.: Stanford University Press, 1974.

ROSE, M. D. "Food Acquisition and the Evolution of Positional Behaviour: The Case of Bipedalism." In David J. Chivers, Bernard A. Wood, and Alan Bilsborough, eds., *Food Acquisition and Processing in Primates*. New York: Plenum, 1984, pp. 509–24.

ROSENBLATT, PAUL C., R. PATRICIA WALSH, AND DOUGLAS A. JACKSON. *Grief and Mourning in Cross-Cultural Perspective*. New Haven: HRAF Press, 1976.

ROSS, MARC H. "Female Political Participation: A Cross-Cultural Explanation." *American Anthropologist*, 88 (1986): 843–58.

ROSS, MARC H. "Internal and External Conflict and Violence." *Journal of Conflict Resolution*, 29 (1985): 547–79.

ROSS, MARC H. "Political Organization and Political Participation: Exit, Voice, and Loyalty in Preindustrial Societies." *Comparative Politics*, 20 (1988): 73–89.

ROSS, MARC H. "Socioeconomic Complexity, Socialization, and Political Differentiation: A Cross-Cultural Study." *Ethos*, 9 (1981): 217–47.

RUBIN, J. Z., F. J. PROVENZANO, AND R. F. HASKETT. "The Eye of the Beholder: Parents' Views on the Sex of Newborns." *American Journal of Orthopsychiatry*, 44 (1974): 512–19.

RUDMIN, FLOYD W. "Dominance, Social Control, and Ownership: A History and a Cross-Cultural Study of Motivations for Private Property." *Behavior Science Research*, 22 (1988): 130–60.

RUMBAUGH, DUANE M. "Learning Skills of Anthropoids." In L. A. Rosenblum, ed., *Primate Behavior*, vol. 1. New York: Academic Press, 1970.

RUMBAUGH, DUANE M., TIMOTHY V. GILL, AND E. C. VON GLASERSFELD. "Reading and Sentence Completion by a Chimpanzee (Pan)." *Science*, November 16, 1973, pp. 731–33.

RUSSELL, D. E. "Les Mammifères Paléocènes." *Mémoires du Muséum d'Histoire Naturelle*, 13 (1964): 1–324. Cited in Elwyn L. Simons, *Primate Evolution: An Introduction to Man's Place in Nature*, New York: Macmillan, 1972, pp. 110–12.

SAGAN, CARL. "A Cosmic Calendar." *Natural History*, December 1975, pp. 70–73.

SAHLINS, MARSHALL. "Other Times, Other Customs: The Anthropology of History." *American Anthropologist*, 85 (1983): 517–44.

SAHLINS, MARSHALL D. "Poor Man, Rich Man, Big-Man, Chief: Political Types in Melanesia and Polynesia." *Comparative Studies in Society and History*, 5 (1963): 285–303.

SAHLINS, MARSHALL D. "The Segmentary Lineage: An Organization of Predatory Expansion." *American Anthropologist*, 63 (1961): 332–45.

SAHLINS, MARSHALL D. *Social Stratification in Polynesia*. Seattle: University of Washington Press, 1958.

SAHLINS, MARSHALL D. *Stone Age Economics*. Chicago: Aldine, 1972.

SANDAY, PEGGY R. "Female Status in the Public Domain." In Rosaldo and Lamphere, eds., *Woman, Culture, and Society*.

SANDAY, PEGGY R. "Toward a Theory of the Status of Women." *American Anthropologist*, 75 (1973): 1682–1700.

SANDERS, WILLIAM T. "Hydraulic Agriculture, Economic Symbiosis, and the Evolution of States in Central Mexico." In Betty J. Meggers, ed., *Anthropological Archaeology in the Americas*. Washington, D.C.: Anthropological Society of Washington, 1968.

SANDERS, WILLIAM T., JEFFREY R. PARSONS, AND ROBERT S. SANTLEY. *The Basin of Mexico: Ecological Processes in the Evolution of a Civilization*. New York: Academic Press, 1979.

SANDERS, WILLIAM T., AND BARBARA J. PRICE. *Mesoamerica*. New York: Random House, 1968.

SAPIR, E. *Language: An Introduction to the Study of Speech*. New York: Harcourt Brace Jovanovich, 1949 (originally published 1921).

SAPIR, E., AND M. SWADESH. "American Indian Grammatical Categories." In Hymes, ed., *Language in Culture and Society*, pp. 100–11.

SAPIR, EDWARD. "Conceptual Categories in Primitive Languages." Paper presented at the autumn meeting of the National Academy of Sciences, New Haven, 1931. Published in *Science*, 74 (1931).

SAPIR, EDWARD. "Why Cultural Anthropology Needs the Psychiatrist." *Psychiatry*, 1 (1938): 7–12. Cited by Pelto and Pelto, "Intra-Cultural Diversity," p. 1.

SARICH, VINCENT M. "The Origin of Hominids: An Immunological Approach." In S. L. Washburn and Phyllis C. Jay, eds., *Perspectives on Human Evolution*, vol. 1. New York: Holt, Rinehart & Winston, 1968.

SARICH, VINCENT M., AND ALLAN C. WILSON. "Quantitative Immunochemistry and the Evolution of Primate Albumins: Micro-Component Fixations." *Science*, December 23, 1966, pp. 1563–66.

SCHALLER, GEORGE B. *The Serengeti Lion: A Study of Predator-Prey Relations*. Chicago: University of Chicago Press, 1972.

SCHALLER, GEORGE. *The Year of the Gorilla*. Chicago: University of Chicago Press, 1964.

SCHLEGEL, ALICE, ed. *Sexual Stratification: A Cross-Cultural View*. New York: Columbia University Press, 1977.

SCHLEGEL, ALICE, AND HERBERT BARRY III. "The Cultural Consequences of Female Contribution to Subsistence." *American Anthropologist*, 88 (1986): 142–50.

SCHNEIDER, DAVID M. "The Distinctive Features of Matrilineal Descent Groups." In Schneider and Gough, eds., *Matrilineal Kinship*.

SCHNEIDER, DAVID M. "Truk." In Schneider and Gough, eds., *Matrilineal Kinship*.

SCHNEIDER, DAVID M., AND KATHLEEN GOUGH, eds. *Matrilineal Kinship*. Berkeley: University of California Press, 1961.

SCHRIRE, CARMEL. "An Inquiry Into the Evolutionary Status and Apparent Identity of San Hunter-Gatherers." *Human Ecology*, 8 (1980): 9–32.

SCHRIRE, CARMEL, ed. *Past and Present in Hunter Gatherer Studies*. Orlando, Fla.: Academic Press, 1984.

SCHRIRE, CARMEL, ed. "Wild Surmises on Savage Thoughts." In Schrire, ed., *Past and Present in Hunter Gatherer Studies*.

SCHWARTZ, RICHARD D. "Social Factors in the Development of Legal Control: A Case Study of Two Israeli Settlements." *Yale Law Journal*, 63 (February 1954): 471–91.

SCOLLON, RON, AND SUZANNE B. K. SCOLLON. *Narrative, Literacy and Face in Interethnic Communication*. Norwood, N.J.: ABLEX Publishing Corporation, 1981.

SEBEOK, THOMAS A., AND JEAN UMIKER-SEBEOCK, eds. *Speaking of Apes: A Critical Anthology of Two-Way Communication with Man*. New York: Plenum: 1980.

SEMENOV, S. A. *Prehistoric Technology*, trans. M. W. Thompson. Bath, England: Adams & Dart, 1970.

SERVICE, ELMAN R. *The Hunters*, 2nd ed. Englewood Cliffs, N.J.: Prentice-Hall, 1979.

SERVICE, ELMAN R. *Origins of the State and Civilization: The Process of Cultural Evolution*. New York: W. W. Norton & Co., Inc. 1975.

SERVICE, ELMAN R. *Primitive Social Organization: An Evolutionary Perspective*. New York: Random House, 1962.

SERVICE, ELMAN R. *Profiles in Ethnology*, 3rd ed. New York: Harper & Row, Pub., 1978.

SEYFARTH, ROBERT M., AND DOROTHY L. CHENEY. "How Monkeys See the World: A Review of Recent Research on East African Vervet Monkeys." In Snowdon, Brown, and Petersen, eds., *Primate Communication*, pp. 239–52.

SEYFARTH, ROBERT M., DOROTHY L. CHENEY, AND PETER MARLER. "Monkey Response to Three Different Alarm Calls: Evidence of Predator Classification and Semantic Communication." *Science*, November 14, 1980, pp. 801–3.

SHIELS, DEAN. "A Comparative Study of Human Sacrifice." *Behavior Science Research*, 15 (1980): 245–62.

SHIPMAN, PAT. "Scavenging or Hunting in Early Hominids: Theoretical Framework and Tests." *American Anthropologist*, 88 (1986): 27–43.

SIMMONS, ALAN H., ILSE KOHLER-ROLLEFSON, GARY O. ROLLEFSON, ROLFE MANDEL, AND ZEIDAN KAFAFI. " 'Ain Ghazal: A Major Neolithic Settlement in Central Jordan." *Science*, April 1, 1988, pp. 35–39.

SIMMONS, LEO W. *Sun Chief*. New Haven: Yale University Press, 1942.

SIMONS, ELWYN L. *Primate Evolution: An Introduction to Man's place in Nature*. New York: Macmillan, 1972.

SIMPSON, GEORGE GAYLORD. *The Meaning of Evolution*. New York: Bantam, 1971.

SIMPSON, S. P., AND RUTH FIELD. "Law and the Social Sciences." *Virginia Law Review*, 32 (1946): 858.

SINGER, J. DAVID. "Accounting for International War: The State of the Discipline." *Annual Review of Sociology*, 6 (1980): 349–67.

SINGER, RONALD, AND JOHN WYMER. *The Middle Stone Age at Klasies River Mouth in South Africa*. Chicago: University of Chicago Press, 1982.

SKOMAL, SUSAN N., AND EDGAR C. POLOMÉ, eds. *Proto-Indo-European: The Archaeology of a Linguistic Problem*. Washington, D.C.: Washington Institute for the Study of Man, 1987.

SMITH, ERIC A. "Anthropological Applications of Optimal Foraging Theory: A Critical Review." *Current Anthropology*, 24 (1983): 625–40.

SMITH, FRED H. "Fossil Hominids from the Upper Pleistocene of Central Europe and the Origin of Modern Humans." In Smith and Spencer, eds., *The Origins of Modern Humans*, pp. 137–210.

SMITH, FRED H., AND FRANK SPENCER, eds. *The Origins of Modern Humans: A World Survey of the Fossil Evidence*. New York: Alan R. Liss, 1984.

SMITH, JOHN M., ed. *Evolution Now: A Century after Darwin.* San Francisco: W. H. Freeman & Company Publishers, 1982.

SMITH, M. W. "Alfred Binet's Remarkable Questions: A Cross-National and Cross-Temporal Analysis of the Cultural Biases Built Into the Stanford-Binet Intelligence Scale and Other Binet Tests." *Genetic Psychology Monographs,* 89 (1974): 307–34.

SMITH, MICHAEL G. "Pre-Industrial Stratification Systems." In Neil J. Smelser and Seymour Martin Lipset, eds., *Social Structure and Mobility in Economic Development.* Chicago: Aldine, 1966.

SMITH, WALDEMAR R. *The Fiesta System and Economic Change.* New York: Columbia University Press, 1977.

SMUTS, BARBARA B., DOROTHY L. CHENEY, ROBERT M. SEYFARTH, RICHARD W. WRANGHAM, AND THOMAS T. STRUHSAKER, eds. *Primate Societies.* Chicago: University of Chicago Press, 1987.

SNOWDON, CHARLES T., CHARLES H. BROWN, AND MICHAEL R. PETERSEN, eds. *Primate Communication.* New York: Cambridge University Press, 1982.

SOUTHWORTH, FRANKLIN C., AND CHANDLER J. DASWANI. *Foundations of Linguistics.* New York: Free Press, 1974.

SPENCER, FRANK. "The Neandertals and Their Evolutionary Significance: A Brief Historical Survey." In Smith and Spencer, eds., *The Origins of Modern Humans,* pp. 1–50.

SPETH, JOHN D., AND DAVE D. DAVIS. "Seasonal Variability in Early Hominid Predation." *Science,* April 30, 1976, pp. 441–45.

SPETH, JOHN D., AND KATHERINE A. SPIELMANN. "Energy Source, Protein Metabolism, and Hunter-Gatherer Subsistence Strategies." *Journal of Anthropological Archaeology,* 2 (1983): 1–31.

SPINDLER, GEORGE D., ed. *Being an Anthropologist: Fieldwork in Eleven Cultures.* New York: Holt, Rinehart, & Winston, 1970.

SPIRO, MELFORD E., AND ROY G. D'ANDRADE. "A Cross-Cultural Study of Some Supernatural Beliefs." *American Anthropologist,* 60 (1958): 456–66.

STEBBINS, G. LEDYARD. *Processes of Organic Evolution,* 3rd ed. Englewood Cliffs, N.J.: Prentice-Hall, 1977.

STEEGMAN, A. T., JR. "Human Adaptation to Cold." In Albert Damon, ed., *Physiological Anthropology.* New York: Oxford University Press, 1975.

STEPHENS, WILLIAM N. "A Cross-Cultural Study of Modesty." *Behavior Science Notes,* 7 (1972): 1–28.

STEPHENS, WILLIAM N. *The Family in Cross-Cultural Perspective.* New York: Holt, Rinehart & Winston, 1963.

STERN, CURT. *Principles of Human Genetics,* 3rd ed. San Francisco: W. H. Freeman & Company Publishers, 1973.

STEWARD, JULIAN H. *Theory of Culture Change.* Urbana: University of Illinois Press, 1955.

STEWARD, JULIAN H., AND LOUIS C. FARON. *Native Peoples of South America.* New York: McGraw-Hill, 1959.

STINI, WILLIAM A. *Ecology and Human Adaptation.* Dubuque, Iowa: Wm. C. Brown, 1975.

STOGDILL, RALPH M. *Handbook of Leadership: A Survey of Theory and Research.* New York: Macmillan, 1974.

STRAUS, LAWRENCE GUY. "Comment on White." *Current Anthropology,* 23 (1982): 185–86.

STRINGER, C. "Evolution of a Species." *Geographical Magazine,* 57 (1985): 601–7.

STRINGER, C. B., J. J. HUBLIN, AND B. VANDERMEERSCH. "The Origin of Anatomically Modern Humans in Western Europe." In Smith and Spencer, eds., *The Origins of Modern Humans,* p. 107.

STRUEVER, STUART, ed. *Prehistoric Agriculture.* Garden City, N.Y.: Natural History Press, 1971.

SUSMAN, RANDALL L., JACK T. STERN, JR., AND WILLIAM L. JUNGERS. "Locomotor Adaptations in the Hadar Hominids." In Delson, ed., *Ancestors,* pp. 184–92.

SUSSMAN, ROBERT. "Child Transport, Family Size, and the Increase in Human Population Size during the Neolithic." *Current Anthropology,* 13 (April 1972): 258–67.

SUSSMAN, ROBERT W. *The Ecology and Behavior of Free-ranging Primates.* New York: Macmillan, forthcoming.

SUSSMAN, ROBERT W., AND PETER H. RAVEN. "Pollination by Lemurs and Marsupials: An Archaic Coevolutionary System." *Science,* May 19, 1978, pp. 734–35.

SWANSON, GUY E. *The Birth of the Gods: The Origin of Primitive Beliefs.* Ann Arbor: University of Michigan Press, 1969.

SZALAY, FREDERICK S. "The Beginnings of Primates." *Evolution,* 22 (1968): 19–36.

SZALAY, FREDERICK S. "Hunting-Scavenging Protohominids: A Model for Hominid Origins." *Man,* 10 (1975): 420–29.

SZALAY, F. S., AND E. DELSON. *Evolutionary History of the Primates.* New York: Academic Press, 1979.

TALMON, YONINA. "Mate Selection in Collective Settlements." *American Sociological Review,* 29 (1964): 491–508.

TATTERSALL, IAN. *Man's Ancestors.* London: John Murray, 1970.

TEXTOR, ROBERT B., comp. *A Cross-Cultural Summary.* New Haven: HRAF Press, 1967.

THOMPSON, ELIZABETH BARTLETT. *Africa, Past and Present.* Boston: Houghton Mifflin, 1966.

THOMPSON, STITH. "Star Husband Tale." In Dundes, ed., *The Study of Folklore.*

THOMPSON-HANDLER, NANCY, RICHARD K. MALENKY AND NOEL BADRIAN. "Sexual Behavior of *Pan paniscus* under Natural Conditions in the Lomako Forest, Equateur, Zaire." In Randall L. Susman, ed., *The Pygmy Chimpanzee: Evolutionary Biology and Behavior.* New York: Plenum, 1984, pp. 347–66.

THURNWALD, R. C. "Pigs and Currency in Buin: Observations about Primitive Standards of Value and Economics." *Oceania,* 5 (1934): 119–41.

TORREY, E. FULLER. *The Mind Game: Witchdoctors and Psychiatrists.* New York: Emerson Hall, n.d.

TREVOR-ROPER, H.R. "The European Witch-Craze of the Sixteenth and Seventeenth Centuries." In Lessa and Vogt, eds. *Reader in Comparative Religion,* 3rd ed.

TRINKAUS, ERIK. "Bodies, Brawn, Brains and Noses: Human Ancestors and Human Predation." In Nitecki and Nitecki, eds., *The Evolution of Human Hunting*, pp. 107–45.

TRINKAUS, ERIK. "The Neandertals and Modern Human Origins." *Annual Review of Anthropology*, 15 (1986): 193–218.

TRINKAUS, ERIK. "Pathology and the Posture of the La Chapelle-aux-Saints Neandertal." *American Journal of Physical Anthropology*, 67 (1985): 19–41.

TRINKAUS, ERIK. "Western Asia." In Smith and Spencer, eds., *The Origins of Modern Humans*, pp. 251–95.

TINKAUS, ERIK, AND WILLIAM W. HOWELLS. "The Neanderthals." *Scientific American*, December 1979, pp. 118–33.

TRUDGILL, PETER. *Sociolinguistics: An Introduction to Language and Society*, rev. ed. New York: Penguin, 1983.

TURNER, B. L. "Population Density in the Classic Maya Lowlands: New Evidence for Old Approaches." *Geographical Review*, 66, no. 1 (January 1970): 72–82.

UBEROI, J. P. SINGH. *The Politics of the Kula Ring: An Analysis of the Findings of Bronislaw Malinowski*. Manchester, England: University of Manchester Press, 1962.

UCKO, PETER J., AND G. W. DIMBLEBY, eds. *The Domestication and Exploitation of Plants and Animals*. Chicago: Aldine, 1969.

UCKO, PETER J., AND ANDRÉE ROSENFELD. *Paleolithic Cave Art*. New York: McGraw-Hill, 1967.

UCKO, PETER J., RUTH TRINGHAM, AND G. W. DIMBLEBY, eds. *Man, Settlement, and Urbanism*. London: Duckworth, Cambridge, Mass.: Schenkman, 1972.

UNDERHILL, RUTH M. *Social Organization of the Papago Indians*. New York: Columbia University Press, 1938.

VAN LAWICK-GOODALL, JANE. *In the Shadow of Man*. Boston: Houghton-Mifflin, 1971.

VAN VALEN, L., AND R. E. SLOAN. "The Earliest Primates." *Science*, November 5, 1965, pp. 743–45.

VANNEMAN, REEVE, AND LYNN WEBER CANNON. *The American Perception of Class*. Philadelphia: Temple University Press, 1987.

VAYDA, ANDREW P., ANTHONY LEEDS, AND DAVID B. SMITH. "The Place of Pigs in Melanesian Subsistence." In Viola E. Garfield, ed., *Symposium: Patterns of Land Utilization, and Other Papers*. Proceedings of the Annual Spring Meeting of the American Ethnological Society, 1961. Seattle: University of Washington Press, 1962.

VON FRISCH, K. "Dialects in the Language of the Bees." *Scientific American*, August 1962, pp. 78–87.

WAGLEY, CHARLES. "Cultural Influences on Population: A Comparison of Two Tupi Tribes." In Patricia J. Lyon, ed., *Native South Americans: Ethnology of the Least Known Continent*. Boston: Little, Brown, 1974.

WALLACE, ALFRED RUSSELL. "On the Tendency of Varieties to Depart Indefinitely from the Original Type." *Journal of the Proceedings of the Linnaean Society*, August 1858. Reprinted in Young, ed., *Evolution of Man*.

WALLACE, ANTHONY. *Religion: An Anthropological View*. New York: Random House, 1966.

WANNER, ERIC, AND LILA R. GLEITMAN, EDS. *Language Acquisition: The State of the Art*. Cambridge: Cambridge University Press, 1982.

WARNER, W. LLOYD, AND PAUL S. LUNT. *The Social Life of a Modern Community*. New Haven: Yale University Press, 1941.

WASHBURN, SHERWOOD. "Tools and Human Evolution." *Scientific American*, September 1960, pp. 62–75.

WEBB, KAREN E. "An Evolutionary Aspect of Social Structure and a Verb 'Have.'" *American Anthropologist*, 79 (1977): 42–49.

WEBER, MAX. *The Theory of Social and Economic Organization*, trans. A. M. Henderson and Talcott Parsons. New York: Oxford University Press, 1947.

WEINER, J. S. "Nose Shape and Climate." *Journal of Physical Anthropology*, 4 (1954): 615–18.

WEINREICH, URIEL. *Languages in Contact*. The Hague: Mouton, 1968.

WENKE, ROBERT J. *Patterns in Prehistory: Humankind's First Three Million Years*, 2nd ed. New York: Oxford University Press, 1984.

WENKE, ROBERT J. *Patterns in Prehistory: Humankind's First Three Million Years*, 3rd ed. New York: Oxford University Press, 1990.

WERNER, DENNIS. "Chiefs and Presidents: A Comparison of Leadership Traits in the United States and among the Mekranoti-Kayapo of Central Brazil." *Ethos*, 10 (1982): 136–48.

WERNER, DENNIS. "Child Care and Influence among the Mekranoti of Central Brazil." *Sex Roles*, 10 (1984): 395–404.

WERNER, DENNIS. "A Cross-Cultural Perspective on Theory and Research on Male Homosexuality." *Journal of Homosexuality*, 4 (1979): 345–62.

WERNER, DENNIS. "On the Societal Acceptance or Rejection of Male Homosexuality." M.A. thesis, Hunter College of the City University of New York, 1975.

WERNER, DENNIS. "Trekking in the Amazon Forest." *Natural History*, November 1978, pp. 42–54.

WESTERMARCK, EDWARD. *The History of Human Marriage*. London: Macmillan, 1894.

WHEAT, JOE B. "A Paleo-Indian Bison Kill." *Scientific American*, January 1967, pp. 44–52.

WHEATLEY, PAUL. *The Pivot of the Four Quarters*. Chicago: Aldine, 1971.

WHITE, BENJAMIN. "Demand for Labor and Population Growth in Colonial Java." *Human Ecology*, 1, no. 3 (March 1973): 217–36.

WHITE, DOUGLAS R., AND MICHAEL L. BURTON. "Causes of Polygyny: Ecology, Economy, Kinship, and Warfare." *American Anthropologist*, 90 (1988): 871–87.

WHITE, DOUGLAS R., MICHAEL L. BURTON, AND LILYAN A. BRUDNER. "Entailment Theory and Method: A Cross-Cultural Analysis of the Sexual Division of Labor." *Behavior Science Research,* 12 (1977): 1–24.
WHITE, LESLIE A. "The Expansion of the Scope of Science." In Morton H. Fried, ed., *Readings in Anthropology,* 2nd ed., vol. 1., New York: Thomas Y. Crowell, 1968.
WHITE, LESLIE A. "A Problem in Kinship Terminology." *American Anthropologist,* 41 (1939): 569–70.
WHITE, LESLIE A. *The Science of Culture: A Study of Man and Civilization.* New York: Farrar, Straus & Cudahy, 1949.
WHITE, RANDALL. "Rethinking the Middle/Upper Paleolithic Transition." *Current Anthropology,* 23 (1982): 169–75.
WHITE, TIM D. "Les Australopithèques." *La Recherche,* November 1982, pp. 1258–70.
WHITE, TIM D., DONALD C. JOHANSON, AND WILLIAM H. KIMBEL. "*Australopithecus africanus:* Its Phyletic Position Reconsidered." *South African Journal of Science,* 77 (1981): 445–70.
WHITING, BEATRICE B. *Paiute Sorcery.* Viking Fund Publications in Anthropology, no. 15. New York: Wenner-Gren Foundation, 1950.
WHITING, BEATRICE, B., AND CAROLYN P. EDWARDS (in collaboration with Carol R. Ember, Gerald M. Erchak, Sara Harkness, Robert L. Munroe, Ruth H. Munroe, Sara B. Nerlove, Susan Seymour, Charles M. Super, Thomas S. Weisner, and Martha Wenger). *Children of Different Worlds: The Formation of Social Behavior.* Cambridge, Mass.: Harvard University Press, 1988.
WHITING, BEATRICE B., AND CAROLYN P. EDWARDS. "A Cross-Cultural Analysis of Sex Differences in the Behavior of Children Aged Three through Eleven." *Journal of Social Psychology,* 91 (1973): 171–88.
WHITING, BEATRICE B., AND JOHN W. M. WHITING (in collaboration with Richard Longabaugh). *Children of Six Cultures: A Psycho-Cultural Analysis.* Cambridge, Mass.: Harvard University Press, 1975.
WHITING, JOHN W. M. "Effects of Climate on Certain Cultural Practices." In Ward H. Goodenough, ed., *Explorations in Cultural Anthropology.* New York: McGraw-Hill, 1964.
WHYTE, MARTIN K. "Cross-Cultural Codes Dealing with the Relative Status of Women." *Ethnology,* 17 (1978): 211–37.
WHYTE, MARTIN K. *The Status of Women in Preindustrial Societies.* Princeton, N.J.: Princeton University Press, 1978.
WILSON, EDWARD O. *Sociobiology.* Cambridge, Mass.: Harvard University Press, Belknap Press, 1975.
WILSON, MONICA. *Good Company: A Study of Nyakyusa Age Villages.* Boston: Beacon Press, 1963 (originally published 1951).
WINKELMAN, MICHAEL JAMES. "Magico-Religious Practitioner Types and Socioeconomic Conditions." *Behavior Science Research,* 20 (1986): 17–46.
WITKOWSKI, STANLEY R. "Polygyny, Age of Marriage, and Female Status." Paper presented at the annual meeting of the American Anthropological Association, San Francisco, 1975.
WITKOWSKI, STANLEY R., AND CECIL H. BROWN. "Lexical Universals." *Annual Review of Anthropology,* 7 (1978): 427–51.
WITKOWSKI, STANLEY R., AND HAROLD W. BURRIS. "Societal Complexity and Lexical Growth." *Behavior Science Research,* 16 (1981): 143–59.
WITTFOGEL, KARL. *Oriental Despotism: A Comparative Study of Total Power.* New Haven: Yale University Press, 1957.
WOLANSKI, NAPOLEON. "The Adult." In Jelliffe and Jelliffe, eds., *Nutrition and Growth,* pp. 253–69.
WOLF, ARTHUR. "Adopt a Daughter-in-Law, Marry a Sister: A Chinese Solution to the Problem of the Incest Taboo." *American Anthropologist,* 70 (1968): 864–74.
WOLF, ARTHUR P., AND CHIEH-SHAN HUANG. *Marriage and Adoption in China, 1845–1945.* Stanford, Calif.: Stanford University Press, 1980.
WOLF, ERIC. "Types of Latin American Peasantry: A Preliminary Discussion." *American Anthropologist,* 57 (1955): 452–71.
WOLPOFF, M. H. "*Ramapithecus* and Human Origins: An Anthropologist's Perspective of Changing Interpretations." In Ciochon and Corruccini, eds., *New Interpretations of Ape and Human Ancestry,* pp. 651–76.
WOLPOFF, MILFORD H. "Competitive Exclusion among Lower Pleistocene Hominids: The Single Species Hypothesis." *Man,* 6 (1971): 601–13.
WOLPOFF, MILFORD H., AND ABEL NKINI. "Early and Early Middle Pleistocene Hominids from Asia and Africa." In Delson, ed., *Ancestors,* pp. 202–5.
WOODBURN, JAMES. "An Introduction to Hadza Ecology." In Lee and DeVore, eds., *Man the Hunter.*
WORSLEY, PETER. *The Trumpet Shall Sound: A Study of "Cargo" Cults in Melanesia.* London: MacGibbon & Kee, 1957.
WRIGHT, GARY A. "Origins of Food Production in Southwestern Asia: A Survey of Ideas." *Current Anthropology,* 12 (1971): 447–78.
WRIGHT, HENRY T., AND GREGORY A. JOHNSON. "Population, Exchange, and Early State Formation in Southwestern Iran." *American Anthropologist,* 77 (1975): 267–77.
WU RUKANG AND LIN SHENGLONG. "Peking Man." *Scientific American,* June 1983, pp. 86–94.
WU XINZHI AND WU MAOLIN. "Early *Homo sapiens* in China." In Wu Rukang and John W. Olsen, eds., *Paleoanthropology and Paleolithic Archaeology in the People's Republic of China.* Orlando, Fla.: Academic Press, 1985, pp. 91–106.
YARNELL, RICHARD A. "Domestication of Sunflower and Sumpweed in Eastern North America." In Richard I.

Ford, ed., *The Nature and Status of Ethnobotany.* Anthropological Papers, Museum of Anthropology, no. 67. Ann Arbor: University of Michigan, 1978, pp. 289–300.

YOUNG, LOUISE, B., ed. *Evolution of Man.* New York: Oxford University Press, 1970.

YOUNG, T. CUYLER, JR. "Population Densities and Early Mesopotamian Urbanism." In Ucko, Tringham, and Dimbleby, eds., *Man, Settlement and Urbanism.*

ZOHARY, DANIEL. "The Progenitors of Wheat and Barley in Relation to Domestication and Agricultural Dispersal in the Old World." In Ucko and Dimbleby, eds., *The Domestication and Exploitation of Plants and Animals.*

Index

Cutright, Philips, 228

Dali site, 67
D'Andrade, Roy, 328
Dani, 320–21
Darrow, Clarence, 17
Darwin, Charles, 16–17, 18, 26, 67
Dentition, 36
Descent
    ambilineal, 282, 283
    double, 284
    double unilineal, 284
    matrilineal, 282, 283
    patrilineal, 282
    unilineal, 285–93
Descriptive linguistics, 7
Descriptive system, 298
Dialects, 173
Dickson's Mounds, 125
Divination, 330–31
DNA, 20, 44
    and mutation, 22
Dobzhansky, Theodosius, 22n, 23,
    37n, 53, 99n, 103
Dolni Vestonice site, 75
Domestication, 113–20
Dominant trait, 19
Double descent, 284
Double unilineal descent, 284
Dowry, 261
Draper, Patricia, 207, 241
Dryopithecus, 42–43
Dubois, Eugene, 61–62
Durham, William, 97
Durkheim, Emile, 147

Eaton, John W., 93n
Ecology, behavioral, 24
Economic aspects, of marriage,
    260–61
Economy of effort, 235
Egalitarian societies, 126, 220, 221–22
Ego, 285
Egypt, Ancient, 133
Elandsfontein site, 67
Eliot, T. S., 162
Ember, Carol R., 31n, 32n, 123n,
    185n, 187n, 192n, 207n, 238n,
    239n, 245n, 246n, 247n, 258n,
    267n, 268n, 274n, 279n, 280n,
    281n, 287n, 289n, 292n, 294n,
    321n, 322n
Ember, Melvin, 31n, 32n, 177n, 188n,
    238n, 258n, 266n, 271n, 274n,
    279n, 280n, 281n, 287n, 290n,
    293n, 311n, 321n, 322n
Eocene epoch, 41
Epicanthic fold, 99
Epidemiology, 6
Ergot, 333
Eskimo system of kinship terminology,
    299–300
Estioko-Griffin, Agnes A., 237n
Eta, 226
Ethnocentrism, 141
Ethnographic analogy, 79
Ethnography, 8, 181–82
Ethnohistorian, 9
Ethnolinguists, 179
Ethnology, 4, 6, 8–9
Etoro, 251
Euripides, 226n
Europe, preagricultural developments
    in, 107–8
Evolution, 14–26
    of culture, 25–26
    genes in, 19–20
    hominid, 47–64

and natural selection, 16–18, 24
and origin of species, 23–24
primate, 27–44
sources of variability, 21–23
Exogamy, 266–67
Expendability theory, on division
    of labor, 236
Extended family, 273, 277
    possible reasons for, 273–75
Extensive cultivation, 188
Extramarital sex, 249–50

Face, reduction of, in
    australopithecines, 52
Facial construction, 88–90
Family. See also marriage
    definition of, 272
    extended, 273–75, 277
    variations in form of, 273–75
Family disruption theory on incest,
    264
Fayum, 41
Feuding, 320
Fiesta complex, 219
Fire
    and Acheulian tool tradition, 63–64
    and big-game eating, 64
    use of, 63
Fish, Paul, 69–70
Flannery, Kent V., 108n, 109n, 113n,
    117n, 118n, 119n, 120n, 122,
    126n, 136n
Fleagle, John G., 41n, 42n, 43n, 44n
Fluorine analysis, 61–62
Focal areas, in language, 178
Folsom point, 83
Folsom toolmakers, 83
Food collection, 185
    by Australian Aborigines, 185–87
    causes of diversity in, 193–95
    by early Homo sapiens, 71–72
    by early New World humans, 83–84
    and evidence of big-game eating, 64
    hunting, 53–54
    and inventions for killing, 79
    and land allocation, 199
    and technology, 201–2
Food production, 187–88
    commercialization of, 192
    consequences of the rise of, 123–25
    and extended-family households,
        274
    horticulture, 188–90, 200, 202, 239
    intensive agriculture, 190–92,
        200–3, 238–39
    pastoralism, 192–93, 200, 202
    plant and animal domestication,
        113–20
    preagricultural developments,
        107–12
    reasons for development of, 120–23
    spread of, 195–96
Ford, Marguerite, 181–82, 182n
Fossil, 5, 35
Fossil record, interpreting, 35–36
Founder effect, 87–88
Fouts, Roger, 161
Fraternal polyandry, 271
Free morpheme, 168
Frequency distribution, 149
Freud, Sigmund, 264
Frisch, Karl von, 157

Galactosemia, 22
Gana, 211
Gardner, Beatrice T., 33–34, 160
Gardner, R. Allen, 33–34, 160
Garfield, Viola E., 214n

Garn, Stanley M., 89n, 90n, 99
Gartner, Rosemary, 316n
Gene flow, 88
Gene pool, 88
Generalized reciprocity, 210–11, 213
Generative theory, 169
Genes, 19
    and mutation, 265
Genetic drift, 87–88
Genetic recombination, 21–22
Genotype, 19
Geographical race, 99
Ghana, 133
Ghosts, 327
Gift exchange, 261
Gimbutas, Marija, 172
Gladwin, Christina, 209
Glasersfeld, E. C. von, 160
Gloger's rule, 93
Goodall, Jane, 30
Goode, William J., 266n
Goods, distribution of, 209–10
Gould, Richard, 185–86
Grammar, 165, 178–79
Grimm, Jacob, 172
Group marriage, 268
Guiora, Alexander, 180
Gumperz, John, 174
Gusii, 260

Habenstein, Robert, 260, 273n, 276n,
    277n, 290n
Hadar, Ethiopia, 54, 55, 56, 58
Hadza, 199
Hahn, Emily, 159n
Haldane, J. B. S., 104n
Hall, Edward T., 11n, 148, 149n
Harappan civilization, 133
Harris, Marvin, 124n, 135, 204n,
    214n, 215–16, 219n, 240n, 337,
    338n
Hausa, 270
Hawaiian system of kinship
    terminology, 299
Hayes, Catherine H., 159
Hayes, Keith, 159
Headman, 304
Health, declining and food
    production, 124–25
Heidelberg site, 67
Height, 90–92
Heredity, 18–20
Heterosis, 92
Heterozygous geneotype, 19
Hewes, Gordon, 48–49
Hieroglyphics, 130
High Plains, 83
Hinduism, 140, 337–38
Historical archeology, 6–7
Historical linguistics, 7, 169–71,
    171–72
Hockett, C. F., 161n
Hoebel, E. Adamson, 198n, 315, 318
Holistic approach to anthropology, 3
Hominid cultures
    life styles, 59–61
    tool traditions, 58–59
Hominid evolution, trends in, 47–54
Homo, 43
Homo erectus, 58, 61
    cultures of, 62–64
    discovery in Java and later finds,
        61–62
    physical characteristics of, 62
    transition from, to Homo sapiens,
        66–67
Homo habilis, 58
Homo sapiens, 5
    transition from Homo erectus to,
        66–67

373